Contemporary
SOCIAL &
SOCIOLOGICAL
THEORY

THIRD EDITION

Contemporary SOCIAL& SOCIOLOGICAL THEORY

VISUALIZING SOCIAL WORLDS

THIRD EDITION

KENNETH ALLAN

University of North Carolina at Greensboro

Los Angeles | London | New Delhi
Singapore | Washington DC

Los Angeles | London | New Delhi
Singapore | Washington DC

FOR INFORMATION:

SAGE Publications, Inc.
2455 Teller Road
Thousand Oaks, California 91320
E-mail: order@sagepub.com

SAGE Publications Ltd.
1 Oliver's Yard
55 City Road
London EC1Y 1SP
United Kingdom

SAGE Publications India Pvt. Ltd.
B 1/I 1 Mohan Cooperative Industrial Area
Mathura Road, New Delhi 110 044
India

SAGE Publications Asia-Pacific Pte. Ltd.
3 Church Street
#10-04 Samsung Hub
Singapore 049483

Printed in the United States of America

Library of Congress Cataloging-in-Publication Data

Allan, Kenneth, 1951-

Contemporary social and sociological theory : visualizing social worlds / Kenneth Allan.—3rd ed.

p. cm.
Includes bibliographical references and index.

ISBN 978-1-4129-9277-0 (pbk.)

1. Sociology. 2. Sociology—Philosophy.
3. Sociologists. I. Title.

HM585.A52 2013
301—dc23   2012038586

Acquisitions Editor: David Repetto
Editorial Assistant: Brittany Coley
Production Editor: Eric Garner
Copy Editor: Teresa Herlinger
Typesetter: C&M Digitals (P) Ltd.
Proofreader: Laura Webb
Indexer: Rick Hurd
Cover Designer: Anupama Krishnan
Marketing Manager: Erica DeLuca
Permissions Editor: Karen Ehrmann

This book is printed on acid-free paper.

SUSTAINABLE FORESTRY INITIATIVE
Certified Chain of Custody
Promoting Sustainable Forestry
www.sfiprogram.org
SFI-01268
SFI label applies to text stock

13 14 15 16 10 9 8 7 6 5 4 3 2

Contents

Introduction: The Real You

This book is about you and society. When I say it's about you, I'm not necessarily talking about the personal you. I'm primarily talking about the social, theoretical you, about you as a specific kind of person living in the beginning decades of the twenty-first century. That person has changed dramatically since the start of modernity. As Stuart Hall (1996a) explains, in the history of the modern world, we've experienced three different kinds of persons: "The Enlightenment subject was based on a conception of the human person as a fully centered, unified individual, endowed with the capacities of reason, consciousness, and action" (p. 597). The next type of person, the sociological subject, came about in the latter half of the nineteenth and beginning years of the twentieth centuries. With it came the realization that "this inner core of the subject was not autonomous and self-sufficient, but was formed in relation to 'significant others'" (p. 597). This is the self that people like Sigmund Freud and George Herbert Mead explained. This person was no longer completely autonomous, but formed in dynamic relation with society: According to Hall, "Identity thus stitches . . . the subject into the structures [of society]" (p. 598). Things changed again for the person beginning in the 1980s, and these changes continue to inform our possibilities today. Of this person Hall says, "The subject, previously experienced as having a unified and stable identity, is becoming fragmented; composed, not of a single, but of several sometimes contradictory or unresolved, identities" (p. 598).

As you'll see as we journey through this book, there are many factors that have led theorists to think this way about you and society. One reason is globalization, which "brings into question foundational concepts—'society' and the 'nation state'" (McGrew, 1996, p. 468). The reason globalization is important for understanding you and society is that modernity rendered "national just about all crucial features of society: authority, identity, territory, security, law, and market" (Sassen, 2007, p. 15). As we'll see in Chapter 1, modern society was defined in direct reference to nation-states. If globalization entails processes and creates social connections that transcend national borders, then the modern idea of society may no longer hold. And if that idea no longer holds, then all of the important identities that you hold—like race, gender, sexuality, family, class, and religion—have changed as well. Each and every one of those is/was defined with reference to modern states.

Clearly, I'm still talking about the theoretical you. But what are the implications of these changes for the *real* you, the personal you, the one you directly experience? The implications are profound precisely because what we're talking about is theory. Theory isn't opinion, nor is it the opposite of facts, as in "It's only a theory." Theory explains how things work or came into existence, and theories are constantly being held up to scrutiny by experts, researchers, and scholars. Thus, theories give us eyes to see and understand what's happening in the world. So, in a very real way, the theoretical you and the personal you are intimately connected, because these theories explain the social context wherein you experience the real you. The *theoretical you* explains the context of personhood wherein you experience the *real you*.

This book, however, isn't a social psychology text—most of the chapters aren't directly about identities, selves, or you. But the person, and the way he or she thinks, feels, and acts, is unavoidably implied in theories about society. This relationship between you and society has been important since the dawn of modernity. The political and economic philosophies of the Enlightenment were centered on a particular kind of person. One way to see this is to remember that under a premodern monarchy, the main political person available was the "subject," one who is under the dominion of another. In modernity, the main political person that's available is the "citizen," one who holds the power to govern. The experiences and self-concept of a citizen are vastly different from that of a subject.

Science, too, was founded on the idea of a specific kind of person: a reasoning individual capable of discovering the fundamental laws of the empirical universe. The theories in this book, then, are vitally important for you because they explain the social world in which you live, move, and have your being. Most significantly, they can help you understand what you experience as "freedom," and they can explain the possibilities of democracy and politics in the twenty-first century.

Plan of the Book

The book is divided into four main sections. *Part I: Introductions* sets the general parameters of the book. In Chapter 1, we'll look at how the time we call modernity began. We will see that modern times began with intentional purpose and, more importantly, that it brought with it a way of knowing that is valued above all others: science. Understanding these issues is important for grasping the critiques that feminism and others bring, for understanding theories that speak of globalization and democracy, and for comprehending why you and education are important parts of the projects of modernity. This section also explains what theory is and does. You must understand theory in order to think and write theoretically (which might be a handy thing to know for a test or paper). Chapter 2, "Defining Moments in Twentieth-Century Theory," explains the impact that Talcott Parsons and the Frankfurt School of critical theory have had on social thought. Parsons gives us the primary question of sociology (social order); he gives us a way of answering that question that is undoubtedly part of your "cultural capital" as a student of society;

and, most importantly, he crystallizes the social scientific approach to theory and canonizes the classics (Marx, Weber, and Durkheim), at least for American sociology. As we'll see, Parsons significantly established the theoretical agendas of many of the other theorists in this book. The second defining moment, the Frankfurt School and the advent of critical theory, will set the stage for us to understand the critique of positivism and culture that we'll find scattered throughout the book. It also sets the stage for the theorist who most directly addresses modern democracy, Jürgen Habermas.

Part II: Individuals and Situations introduces four theories that explain what happens when you and I are in face-to-face social encounters. This section will be the one most explicitly concerned with you—it should provide you with ideas to carry through the other chapters, ideas that will help you situate yourself in the social context. We'll also see that most of these theories are formed at least in part as responses to Parsons.

In *Part III: Social Structures and Systems,* each theorist talks about structure differently—there are different kinds of social structures that pattern our relationships and actions. The structures we'll be talking about here are the ones that have been central in sociological discourse and social life: race, gender, and class. This section also includes two systems theories. Parsons's work is probably the best-known systems approach to understanding society in the twentieth century. However, Parsons's understanding of society and systems was contained within national boundaries. The systems theories in Chapters 9 and 10 are quite different: Both are cast at the world level rather than national, and one of the theorists (Castells) gives us a completely new understanding about how social connections (i.e., society) are made.

In *Part IV: Modernity: Possibilities and Problems,* we'll consider the possibilities that we are no longer modern, or if we are, the projects of modernity are either disabled or out of control. Here we'll also talk about the possibility that culture has lost meaning. The theories in Chapters 13 and 14 are perhaps the most provocative and disturbing of the book: They question the very foundations of human reality. Finally, in *Part V: Contemporary Political Identities,* we look at how race, gender, and sexuality are formed and expressed in a society infused with capitalism, mass media, advertising, social science, and dark Freudian ideas of sex.

This edition also has a new conclusion that I hope will connect the idea of the real you with the general tenor of contemporary theory. Classical theory can be relatively straightforward because most of us are fairly certain which theorists should be included. Classical theory is also "well behaved" in the sense that the ideas of people like Marx, Weber, and Durkheim fit into what we normally think of as the core ideas of sociology (of course—that's where they came from). We can also take various elements of the classical theories and bring them together into a cohesive whole. Contemporary theory, however, isn't this neat and tidy. Whatever else contemporary social theory asks, it asks that we think outside the box. In keeping with that, I use postcolonial and postmodern theories in the conclusion to invite you to have a thought. It's easy for us to allow our thoughts to move down well-known paths, as with classical theory. We might see a new shiny thing or two on these mind tracks, but by and large our minds like to travel comfortable roads. Contemporary theory asks you to "get out of line," expand your horizons, and think something new. For me, this is when we become most real, most authentic, and most valuable in our social worlds.

Do Yourself a Favor: Use This Book!

First, don't read this book—at least, not the way you normally would. Many people approach an academic book as they would a novel, by beginning with the first line and reading every word straight through to the finish. In general, this isn't a good approach to scholastic works. Be strategic in your reading of scholarship. All academic books, chapters, and articles make arguments. An argument makes an assertion and presents reasons why the assertion should be accepted. Your chief job in these sorts of works, then, is to discover the argument. This usually isn't difficult because these authors want to convince you of their argument. The easiest place to look for a book's argument is in the introductory and concluding chapters; articles and book chapters will generally have those same sections. Good introductions will give you the entire argument in brief, and conclusions will recap and sometimes extend the argument. Use those sections to write an initial outline of the argument.

When reading academic work, you should always make notes—I know it's a pain, but it really will help you. Use the initial outline to make notes about the argument and text. I also recommend that you do not highlight or underline the text. The reason for this isn't resale value; it's that most readers highlight or underline because they like a sentence or it seems important. But I've found that many times highlighters end up missing the author's real point. At this stage in my life, I underline when I read, but initially I first had to stop doing it altogether and train myself to pay attention to the argument rather than trying to understand statements.

After you've discovered the argument, look at the headings and subheadings in the chapter or paper. What is the author doing in each section? How does it fit into the overall argument and structure of the piece? Don't ever read a section until you know what the author is doing in it or what her or his point is—and don't ever lose sight of that purpose or point. It is *so* easy to get bogged down in minutia. Readers are easily sidetracked, especially readers who are hungry for knowledge and have lots of questions and ideas. If you're at all like me, you'll read a line that sparks some idea in your head and you'll be off and running with it, even though that idea isn't the author's main point. Don't get sidetracked. In academic reading, all you have to do is figure out the author's point and then move on. Be strategic and keep on point. I've also found that if a reader doesn't understand a statement, more often than not it's because the reader is trying to understand it in isolation, apart from the point of the entire section.

So, my overall advice is this: Don't read the book—figure it out. Figure out the argument's assertion, the major points, and the important concepts and terms. Once you've figured these out, move on. If you haven't approached a book like this before, this probably won't feel like reading to you. You may even be scared that you've missed something or that you don't really know the reading.

Believe me, if you follow what I've outlined, then chances are good you will know the text far better and will retain more than if you "actually read it."

Textbooks like this one are a bit different because they aren't presenting a single argument. Now, I do have an overall point to make, and you'll find it in the Introduction: The Real You, Chapter 1, and Conclusion: Post-Thinking. However, I don't *argue for* that assertion in the book; it's more of an implication of my overall approach to understanding theory. The theorists in this book do make arguments, and those are found at the chapter level. I've included some study aids that I hope will help you understand the theorist's argument. Let's talk through a chapter so you can see how it works. I'll be using Chapter 13 (Jeffrey C. Alexander) as an example, but almost all the chapters follow this design.

First, notice that I begin the discussion of every theorist with an outline. Outlines are extremely important for keeping the big picture in mind, and the big picture is vital for understanding the individual ideas. Here's an important point to keep in mind: All theoretical ideas must be kept in context—every idea must be understood in its relation to other theoretical ideas. So, I strongly encourage you to use the outline I provide, and be sure to understand every idea or concept within its context.

There are six major elements in the outline for Alexander: The Big Picture, Theorist's Digest, Concepts and Theory, Summary, Taking the Perspective, and Building Your Theory Toolbox. The purpose of The Big Picture is to introduce you to some of the more important and abiding ideas of sociology. In Chapter 13, The Big Picture is solidarity, and that section provides an overview of how this idea is situated in sociology, beginning with Durkheim. Please notice this: While solidarity is central to Alexander's theory, The Big Picture does not give you an overview of Alexander's argument. The view from The Big Picture is always larger than the individual theorists.

Next in the outline is the Theorist's Digest. In terms of discovering the theorist's argument, the Digest does three things. First, it tells you the important questions that occupy the theorist ("Central Sociological Questions"). This is significant for understanding the theory because theories are always answers to specific, empirical questions. If you ever get lost in the chapter, it may help if you come back to the central questions. For instance, everything that Alexander talks about, including things like fictional media and the law, comes back to understanding civil society. You can also use these central questions to pique your interest. You're probably like me in that I'm not interested in everything sociologists do. There are, however, certain issues that grab my attention. Use the central questions to see if the theorist is addressing one of your particular interests.

The second thing that the Digest does to help you discover the theorist's argument is to provide a short synopsis of the theory ("Simply Stated"). The theory is all there in abstract, and it should show you how the big parts of the theory fit together. The third help the Digest provides is it gives you the key terms of the theory ("Key Ideas"). As you'll see in Chapter 1, theory is made up of concepts, definitions, and relationships. The Key Ideas section of the Digest identifies the theory's most important concepts. You'll be miles ahead if you define these terms as you go through the chapter. Start by making initial notes, and expand the notes as the concept is fleshed out in the text.

The next major heading in the chapter is Concepts and Theory. These sections identify the major divisions within the theory and can help you understand ideas within their context and to identify the basic relationships in the theory. With Alexander, there are three major divisions: The New Civil Sphere, Civil Institutions, and Civil Society Outcomes. First, keep in mind that the text under each major heading relates directly to the heading. As I've said, it's really easy to get lost in theoretical text, but if you make a habit of relating everything back to the major heading, you'll be better able to keep track of the theory and argument. You can also read the headings as questions. For example, what is the civil sphere? Why is there a "new" civil sphere? How does this civil sphere work? You should also be able to relate the headings back to the Central Sociological Questions and Simply Stated sections. One of Alexander's questions focuses on the problem of cohesion in diverse societies (hence, the new civil sphere). Simply Stated tells us that civil institutions "bound" the civil sphere. At this point, you probably don't understand fully what that statement means; nevertheless, you are able to discern some of the relationships in the theory and where they are explained in the book. This is important because, as I noted above, theory is built out of relationships. Another way to begin to see the relationships is to sketch out a rough outline of the theory. In this case, it would look something like this: Civil Sphere → Civil Institutions → Civil Society Outcomes. You'll need to modify such outlines as you learn the theory, but doing something like this will help you ask good questions and organize your thinking.

The Summary section is a summary of the theoretical argument that the chapter provides. I recommend that you read the introduction to the theory (found in the Theorist's Digest) and the Summary before reading anything else. Use them both to create your initial outline. This will tell you which sections of the chapter you need to pay attention to the most. If there's something in the Digest or Summary that is completely new to you, spend extra time with it. You can plan to spend less time on parts with which you have some familiarity.

There are two final study aids: Taking the Perspective and Building Your Theory Toolbox. The Toolbox is directly related to the chapter and its theory. It provides study questions to help you test your own knowledge, as well as some prompts to help you think about how the theory can be applied and how different theories relate to one another. Taking the Perspective is new to this edition, and it gives you an overview of the theorist's perspective, along with historical developments. All theories are written from specific perspectives, and different theories come out of different ways of seeing the world (which is why sociology and psychology usually see different things when looking at a person). You are undoubtedly familiar with three of them: structural functionalism, conflict, and symbolic interaction; they're the ones usually given in introductory texts. But as you'll find, there are many more perspectives in sociology. For me, this is one of the most exciting things about contemporary theory. It's like a multifaceted gem through which we can visualize social worlds.

I'd like to close this introduction and open the rest of the book with a quote from Angela Davis, a political activist from the 1960s and now retired professor from University of California, Santa Cruz. Speaking to the graduating class of Grinnell College, Professor Davis (2007) captures my hope for you:

I hope that you will treasure the approaches and ways of thinking that you have learned more than the facts you have accumulated. For you will never discover a scarcity of facts, and these facts will be presented in such a way as to veil the ways of thinking embedded in them. And so to reveal these hidden ways of thinking, to suggest alternate frameworks, to imagine better ways of living in evolving worlds, to imagine new human relations that are freed from persisting hierarchies, whether they be racial or sexual or geopolitical—yes, I think this is the work of educated beings. I might then ask you to think about education as the practice of freedom. Freedom, then, becomes not a state for which one yearns, but rather an incessant struggle to remake our lives, our relations, our communities, and our futures. (n.p.)

Acknowledgments

How something begins oftentimes influences the entire course. Such is the case with the books I've been privileged to write for SAGE. With each edition, I realize more fully my debt to my first editors, Jerry Westby and Ben Penner. You caught the vision and kept me excited through some rough patches. I also want to acknowledge and thank my colleague Steve Kroll-Smith. As department head, you inspired creative sociological thinking; you opened up possibilities within our department; and, most importantly, you gave me an organizational environment in which I could do this work. Without your influence at the right time, none of this would have been possible. My thanks also to Dr. Steven R. Cureton, Associate Professor, UNCG Department of Sociology, for enlightening conversations and priceless insights into the writings of black Americans for Chapter 7. All the mistakes are mine; all the pearls of wisdom are his.

My current team is outstanding. My thanks to Dave Repetto for continuing to support creative sociology. My appreciation also to Eric Garner for guiding production, to Anupama Krishnan for creating a cover that captures the text, to Erica DeLuca for getting the word out (and for being a steady presence at SAGE and in the production of my books), and to Karen Ehrmann for taking care of the details that I would otherwise forget or gloss over. And to my copy editor, Teresa Herlinger, I can't say enough. You are incredibly patient with the idiotic errors I seem determined to make. More than that, you ask questions that challenge me as a sociologist, and encourage me with inspiration that can only come from someone in love with words and writing. You are simply the best. Thank you. You will forever be a part of my writing.

Finally, my thanks to the reviewers who took time out from busy schedules to provide valuable feedback and insights:

Robert Hard, Albertus Magnus College

John Bartkowski, University of Texas

Ann Strahm, California State University–Stanislaus

L. Katherine Thomson, University of San Francisco

Frank Salamone, Iona College

Part I

Introductions

Human thought is based upon perspectives and general categories. Perspectives determine what we see and don't see, and categorical systems create order. Time is a good example of both. I'm writing this in 2012, but that year only came to exist because of the centrality of Jesus Christ in Western thought. Today is Monday, which is part of a somewhat arbitrary categorical system called "the week" that orders our time and actions. In Chapter 1, you will be introduced to a perspective of modernity that many use to order sociology, theory, and society. You'll learn about the social structures and culture that created a good part of the world in which you live. You'll learn about progress and the place theory has in both technical and social progress, and you will see how the works of classical sociological theorists focus on issues salient to this understanding of modernity. In Chapter 2, you will also be introduced to two specific perspectives—structural functionalism and critical theory—that represent the poles of contemporary theoretical discourse. This perspective of modernity will set the parameters of our discussions about contemporary social and sociological theory.

In the Beginning Was Modernity

I want to start out by telling you a story. It's a story about modernity. This is, of course, a text about contemporary social and sociological theory. However, it is extremely difficult, if not impossible, to understand contemporary theory without first understanding modernity and the conditions under which the social disciplines were founded. The words *modern* and *modernity* are used in a number of different ways. Sometimes *modern* is used to mean contemporary or up-to-date. Other times it's used as an adjective, as in modern art or modern architecture. The story I'm going to tell you is about modern society and the modern way of knowing; it is, then, a story about a historical period.

This story is an important and good one, but it is only one of many possible stories that can be told about modern society and knowledge. To tell this story, I have to ignore some things and emphasize others. Any historical story is like that; there's simply too much to tell and too many perspectives. The reason I want to tell this specific story is that it will act like an *ideal type* for us, something that can frame our theories and render them sensible. It's generally a good idea to understand things by comparison, and this is certainly true with our theorists. Some of our theorists are going to argue that we are no longer modern; that the modern subject no longer exists; or that the hope of modern knowledge is illusionary, misguided, or even oppressive. We can best understand these ideas if we first have a clear idea of the kind of modernity our contemporary theorists have in mind.

The modern era is marked by significant social changes, such as massive movements of populations from small local communities to large urban settings; a high division of labor; high commodification and use of rational markets; the widespread use of bureaucracy; and large-scale integration through national identities—such as "American"—to unite differences like gender, race, religion, and so forth. In general, the defining institutions of modernity are nation-states and mass democracy, capitalism, science, and mass media; the historical moments that set the stage for modernity are the Renaissance, the Enlightenment, the Reformation, the American and French Revolutions, and the Industrial Revolution. The sweep and depth of change that thundered across first Europe and then the United States are truly breathtaking and have been the subject of countless volumes of text. Our story will be comparatively brief.

Modern Society

The beginnings of the modern age reach back to the fifteenth and sixteenth centuries. There are several cultural factors that we can point to from this time, but among the most important for understanding modernity are the Protestant Reformation and the invention of the printing press. The Protestant Reformation began when Martin Luther posted his Ninety-Five Theses on the door of Castle Church of Wittenberg, Germany, on October 31, 1517. Christianity changed remarkably as a result. It is Luther who introduced the idea that parishioners could read and interpret the Bible; he argued that priests could marry; and he strongly influenced congregational singing, believing that worship belonged in every area of one's life. But the effects of the Protestant Reformation on culture as a whole are much more profound and widespread; we'll consider two.

First, Luther's doctrine helped form the basis of the modern individual. In traditional Catholicism, the Church mediates salvation and spiritual life. Salvation comes not through individual decision and faith but by keeping the sacraments, such as baptism, confession, and the Eucharist. In Catholicism, the Church is everything: The sacraments place one inside the Church, and it is the Church that is saved, not the individual. This isn't a doctrine of works, where one's good works must outweigh the bad, because "good works" implies an individual capable of them. Rather, this is a doctrine of mercy, one motivated by the belief that all of humankind is condemned under Adam's original sin and thus utterly incapable in spiritual matters: "By this 'unity of the human race' all men are implicated in Adam's sin, as all are implicated in Christ's justice" (Catechism of the Catholic Church, n.d.). In Adam, all of humanity is condemned; in the Church, all may be saved. In both cases, it's the unity or collective that matters, not the individual. Luther, on the other hand, argued that each individual will stand or fall on his or her own faith—the implication here is that individuals are capable of making such a choice. The Protestant Reformation is one of the birthplaces of modern *individualism: "Individualism is a belief system that privileges the individual over the group . . . it is an ideology based on self-determination, where free actors are assumed to make choices that have direct consequences for their own unique destiny"* (Callero, 2009, p. 17). This belief in the individual formed the basis of democracy, capitalism, and—as we will soon see—the modern way of knowing.

The second impact that the Protestant Reformation had was to give secularization a boost. *Secularization* is the "process by which sectors of society and culture are removed from the domination of religious institutions and symbols" (Berger, 1967, p. 107). Looking back at religious history, we can see that early systems of belief didn't make a separation between the physical and spiritual. The gods were the vital force within every physical element and event, such as storms, seasons, plant growth, death, and so on. Over time and for a variety of reasons, humans began to think of the gods as dwelling in the heavens amongst the stars. We evolved from magic, to polytheism, to pantheism, and finally to monotheism. In magic, the physical and spiritual forces are inextricably intertwined; in polytheism and pantheism, physical things begin to be divested of the spirits that were seen to energize them; and in monotheism, God exists outside of time and space and thus not in the material world at all. This progressive divestment is what is meant by secularization.

Catholicism still teaches that spiritual entities can inhabit material things, as in the Eucharist (Holy Communion). In Catholicism, the bread and wine literally become the body and blood of Christ—in the Eucharist there is an amalgamation of spirit and matter. That's why it can impart salvation: The spirit of Christ imbues the bread and wine. In Protestantism communion only *symbolizes* the body and blood of Christ and does not have the power to impart salvation. The bread and wine are only emblems of faith. Further, in Catholicism, angels and saints also have access to this world, and there are various levels of intercession. There is also still union between government and religion—the government and religion of the Vatican are synonymous, and the Church has a living disciple in the Pope, directly descended from Peter. Thus, even though the Catholic Church is monotheistic and God is viewed as eternal, the physical and spiritual still meet. It was Protestantism that finally and completely divested the universe of spiritual presence: "The Protestant believer no longer lives in a world ongoingly penetrated by sacred beings and forces" (Berger, 1967, p. 111). This emptying out of spiritual essence was a major factor in allowing science to explain the empirical universe.

The advent of the printing press also had significant effects on Western culture and society. Invented by Johannes Gutenberg in 1440, the printing press of course led to the mass production of books, and that in itself had profound effects. Mass-produced books meant that the knowledge contained in the books became available to the public for the first time, rather than being restricted to the elite few. This first mass medium also facilitated the rise and spread of the Protestant Reformation, the Renaissance, and the Scientific Revolution. Because the first commercially viable printed book was the Bible and there was no comparable text in Asian countries, mechanized printing did not take hold as rapidly in Asia, which in turn facilitated the European advantage over the East in the Industrial

Revolution and technological domination. Printing also fueled all the political revolutions and reformations of the eighteenth and nineteenth centuries. We can see the importance of printing for politics in the U.S. Constitutional right to freedom of the press. The printing press also influenced the way in which people think. The transmission of information changed from artistic expression (with hand printing) to chiefly textual. This shift facilitated the conversion from metaphorical to linear thinking, and linear thinking is the foundation of the causal explanations found in science.

Individualism, secularization, and the first form of mass media paved the way for later developments in the march toward modernity, such as *industrialization*. The Industrial Age began in England toward the end of the eighteenth century. We can point to a number of beginning points, but among the most important was the invention of the steam engine, perfected by James Watt around 1775. This invention provided the pivotal shift in energy from wind and waterpower to fossil fuels (refined coal) that was needed for sustained industrial growth. Watt's work, along with improvements in the quality and production of iron, also paved the way for one of the most important developments in transportation technology since the wheel: railroads. The first intercity railroad—the Liverpool and Manchester Railway (L&MR)—was completed in 1830. The L&MR system was built to supply raw material and finished products from port to city. National markets, a necessary factor in the growth of capitalism, began to emerge as such railways expanded across England and Europe.

The use of machines in the production of textiles also fueled the English Industrial Revolution. Several inventions spanning at least 70 years moved the industrialization of British textiles along, including John Kay's invention of the flying shuttle for weaving cloth, James Hargreaves' spinning jenny, and Edmund Cartwright's power loom. Prior to such inventions, textiles were by and large produced in homes with all family members participating. The mechanization of textiles irresistibly moved people from small, kin-based rural communities to large cities—a process called *urbanization*. During the nineteenth century, the population of London grew by almost 700% to become the world's largest city at that time. London was also the site where British industrial power was given center stage at the 1851 "Great Exhibition of the Works of Industry of All Nations." The massive Crystal Palace of the exhibition held some 13,000 to 14,000 exhibits and entertained over 6 million guests. The real income of people in England grew remarkably as well, about doubling from 1760–1860.

This same pattern was duplicated first in France and then later in Germany and the United States as they entered the Industrial Era. Improvements in transportation opened new markets, which, in turn, pushed for industrialization and increases in the division of labor. These pressures opened up new jobs in the cities where factories were located, and people moved from the country to the city; urbanization then impacted the family structure as people left extended families and the nuclear family took form. New markets along with increases in discretionary money created demands for new products, and the endless commodification of the lifeworld began. This cycle of industrialization, commodification, and market expansion is obviously the bedrock of capitalism, a system that moves through ever-expanding cycles of capital investment → profit → capital investment. Capitalism created an entirely new set of social relationships: class. Previously, social status and relations were oriented around kinship, territory, and religion; and each of these was generally determined by birth. Capitalism radically lessened these influences and in their stead, connected people primarily through economic relationships. Further, the development of capitalism is also linked with democracy and the nation-state.

The culture undergirding modern democracy grew out of the Reformation and Enlightenment. As we've seen, Luther was instrumental in creating a culture in which individualism could exist. Individual faith also had implications for secular government. In explaining the relationship between the individual and state, Luther (1523/1991) said,

> Each must decide at his own peril what he is to believe, and must see to it that he believes rightly. . . . [Governments] ought therefore to content themselves with attending to their own business, and allow people to believe what they can, and what they want, and they must use no coercion in this matter against anyone. (p. 25)

Luther's freedom of faith thus formed a cornerstone of democratic relations. To this the Enlightenment added the idea of natural rights, the belief that every human being by birth has "certain unalienable rights, that among these are life, liberty and the pursuit of happiness. That to secure these rights, governments are instituted among men, deriving their just powers from the consent of the governed." This sentiment, first embodied in the U.S. Declaration of Independence, is also found in the Universal Declaration of Human Rights, ratified by the United Nations in response to the atrocities of World War II:

> Whereas recognition of the inherent dignity and of the equal and inalienable rights of all members of the human family is the foundation of freedom, justice and peace in the world. . . . All human beings are born free and equal in dignity and rights. They are endowed with reason and conscience and should act towards one another in a spirit of brotherhood.

Capitalism's link to democracy was that the structure could assure that social standing was a result of one's own efforts rather than birth, thus ensuring equality of opportunity. Adam Smith (1776/1937), considered the father of modern economics, referred to capitalism as the system of *natural liberty:* "the obvious and simple system of natural liberty establishes itself of its own accord. Every man . . . is left perfectly free to pursue his own interest his own way" (p. 651). Specifically, Smith argued that humans have a natural inclination to barter, to realize profit from the exchange of goods and services. This motivation is based on the "natural effort of every individual to better his own condition, when suffered to exert itself with freedom and security" (p. 508).

In early modernity, then, capitalism was seen as an important facet of civil society. *Civil society* is an institutional sphere that exists between the state and private citizen—it is the sphere where the practices of democracy emerge. In the most general sense, civil society occurs when any group of people voluntarily meet for any specific purpose. In civil association, "people learn through practice such essential democratic habits as trust, collaboration, and compromise" (Eberly, 2000, p. 4). Civil society brings together individuals with self-interests and weaves them into joint projects. In working together voluntarily, democratic "[s]entiments and ideas renew themselves, the heart is enlarged, and the human mind is developed only by the reciprocal action of men upon one another" (Tocqueville, 1835–1840/2002, p. 491). Capitalism was assumed to be an ideal mechanism for this because it would function almost automatically. According to Adam Smith (1776/1937), in capitalism the individual

> neither intends to promote the public interest, nor knows how much he is promoting it. . . . [H]e intends only his own gain, and he is in this . . . led by an invisible hand to promote an end which was no part of his intention. (p. 421)

Bound up with capitalism and civil society is, of course, the modern nation-state. What is perhaps not as apparent is that the very idea we have of *society* is likewise intertwined with the existence of the nation-state: "To the extent there is something called 'society,' then this should be seen as a sovereign social entity with a nation-state at its centre that organises the rights and duties of each citizen" (Urry, 2006, p. 168). The modern state organizes more than citizenship; it regulates the internal relationships among the different social structures that make up society and it manages the external relationships among different societies. One of the implications here is that modern society is a system of interdependent yet separate institutions. Modern society is thus structurally and socially differentiated.

While such things as industrialization and capitalism more or less simply emerged out of social activities, the creation of the modern, democratic nation-state was intentional. Speaking of the Europeans who first colonized America, Tocqueville (1835–1840/2002) noted, "they tore themselves away from the sweetness of their native country to obey a purely intellectual need; in exposing themselves to the inevitable miseries of exile, the way to make *an idea* triumph" (p. 32). President Barack Obama echoed this observation in his 2011 State of the Union Address: "What's more, we are the first nation to be founded for the sake of an idea—the idea that each of us deserves the chance to shape our own destiny." The various national constitutions stand as testimony to this intentionality. Specific institutional arrangements, such as the separation of church and state, were logically thought through and set up. The same is true for the relationships between the nation and its people, as evidenced in the U.S. Bill of Rights. Thus, above all else, modernity is noted as the Age of Reason, a time when humankind would make decisions rationally and thus decide its own fate. These decisions were to be based on a specific way of knowing—knowledge that is unique to modernity.

Modern Knowledge

The modern way of knowing is rooted in the Enlightenment and positivist philosophy. The Enlightenment was a European intellectual movement that began around the time Sir Isaac Newton published *Principia Mathematica* in 1686, though the beginnings go back to Bacon, Hobbes, and Descartes. The natural sciences grew out of this intellectual movement and are, of course, extremely important for our lives today. However, as Roy Porter (2001) points out, "Central to the aspirations of enlightened minds was the search for a true 'science of man'" (p. 11). While conceiving of the physical world as subject to natural laws rather than God's direction was significant, the idea that human beings are best understood through science rather than religion was earth shattering.

This search for scientific understanding of humankind was dependent upon three pillars: the reasoning individual, a clear object of study, and a specific epistemological method. As we've already seen, the idea of the modern individual arose in Protestantism and was elaborated through the Enlightenment. The Enlightenment's idea of the individual wasn't just that the person is seen as autonomous, separate from the group. It was also assumed that the individual, barring any naturally occurring limitation, is capable of reason and self-development. One of the most important contributors to this idea of the reasoning individual was Antoine-Nicolas de Condorcet, a French philosopher and mathematician. His book *Sketch for a Historical Picture of the Progress of the Human Mind* (1795/1955) is considered a foundation for the idea of human progress. Condorcet wrote, the aim of the work that I have undertaken . . . will be to show . . . that nature has set no term to the perfection of human faculties; that the perfectibility of man is truly indefinite; and that the progress of this perfectibility, from now onwards is independent of any power that might wish to halt it, has no other limits than the duration of the globe upon which nature has cast us. (p. 4)

German philosopher Immanuel Kant (1798/1999) also saw this idea of the reasoning, indefinitely perfectible individual as the defining feature of the Enlightenment:

> *Enlightenment is the human being's emergence from his self-incurred minority.* Minority is the inability to make use of one's own understanding without direction from another. . . . Have courage to make use of your *own* understanding! is thus the motto of enlightenment. (p. 17)

The idea of *progress* is central to modernity. In fact, I would hazard a guess and say that the success or failure of modernity is wrapped up with our belief in progress. Yet, prior to the Enlightenment, the idea of progress wasn't important—the dominant worldviews were based in tradition and religion. Traditional knowledge is by definition embedded in long periods of time and thus resists change and progress. Religion is based upon revelation, which, again by definition, makes change dependent upon God's disclosure and not upon us developing or advancing. The idea of progress, on the other hand, brings to the center human agency and human-defined goals. Generally speaking, these goals are orientated toward explaining, predicting, and controlling our environments, specifically nature and society. This idea of secular progress, along with belief in individualism, formed the basis of Enlightenment humanism.

The institution of the reasoning person and hope in progress go hand in hand with another institutional change specific to modernity: the shift from education for the elite to education for the masses, from religious to scientific education. Condorcet saw the progress of the individual mind as linked to education and became one of the architects of the new French education system. He created the base that ultimately led to the secularization of education (previously education had been the domain of the Catholic Church), mandatory primary education for both boys and girls (Condorcet supported full citizenship for women, arguing that gender differences are mostly based on differences in education not biology), and the standardization of the French language (to combat class differences). Condorcet also proposed the merging of the moral and physical sciences in studying human behavior; this amalgamation eventually became the discipline of sociology.

The second pillar of "the science of man" is a clear object of study. Every knowledge system is based on assumptions. One of the assumptions of science is that the world is empirical or objective. Merriam-Webster (2002) defines *objective* as relating to an object, and an object as "something that is put or may be regarded as put in the way of some of the senses . . . by which the mind or any of its activities is directed." Thus, objective things don't exist in the mind; rather, they exist outside the individual and are there for anyone to observe through the natural senses of sight, hearing, and so forth. This is fairly easy for us to see when it comes to the physical sciences—geologists study rock formations that exist apart from humans— but we really need to think about this issue when it comes to society. Society as we know and understand it today is a relatively new thing. The word *society* came into the English language from French and has a Latin base. The Latin root for society means "companion" or "fellowship," and up until the middle of the eighteenth century, it kept this basic meaning (Williams, 1983, pp. 291–292). Society thus initially referred to a group of friends or associates, like a legal or religious society. Toward the end of the seventeenth and through the middle of the eighteenth century, the idea of society began to be used in more abstract ways to refer to something larger.

Society not only became seen as something bigger than face-to-face social interactions, but it also came to be understood as a separate entity, an entity unto itself with its own nature and laws of existence separate from the people who make it up. In other words, society became objective. Significantly, this larger, objective entity began to be perceived as something that could exert independent influence over people. As Émile Durkheim (1895/1938) argued, society is a set of social facts that are "external to the individual, and endowed with a power of coercion, by reason of which they control him" (p. 3). This quote captures what sociologists mean when they talk about social structures. Like Durkheim, many sociologists argue that the existence of society as a fact, comparable to any other scientific fact, is established by its objective nature and felt influence. Society exists apart from individuals; it was present before any specific individual was born and will exist after that person's death. Further, society appears to unavoidably influence the individual from the outside—people conform to its demands even if they don't want to. Modern society thus operates according to its own laws, which may be discovered by reasoning individuals through scientific inquiry.

Positivism and Sociology

Epistemology is the study of knowledge and is specifically concerned with the methods through which knowledge is created. The idea of epistemology is fascinating because it sensitizes us to the fact that knowledge isn't simply there to be found. Knowledge doesn't exist separately from the methods we use to construct it. Auguste Comte (1798–1857), generally considered the founder of sociology, argued that the methods we used changed as we tried to gain greater control over the natural environment. In the beginning stages of human society and knowledge, we had little control over the sources of basic essentials. Hunter-gatherer groups had to continually move from one place to another so as not to deplete the food sources. As humanity figured out how to plant seeds and then to irrigate fields, we became less dependent upon nature in its pure form—we began to change nature to fit our needs. Civilization marches forward, then, as we increase this span of control. According to Comte, this control becomes greater as our mental powers increase. Comte argued that both mind and knowledge have moved through three distinct stages—each phase defined by the relative weights of imagination and observation. Comte saw these stages as necessary and building on the previous.

The first stage is *theological* and "is the necessary point of departure of the human understanding" (Comte, 1830–1842/1975a, pp. 71–72). In this stage, people sought after absolute knowledge: the essential nature and ultimate cause of everything. These emphases meant that people wanted to know *why* things happen—their focus was behind the scenes, not on the thing itself. If a farmer's crop was wiped out during this stage of knowledge, his first and dominant reaction was, "Why? Why me?" These sorts of questions makes the farmer more concerned with the unseen forces behind the blight rather than how the blight actually works. Thus, in this phase, imagination ruled over observation: "the facts observed are explained . . . by means of invented facts" (p. 29). And these "invented facts" were seen as existing before (*a priori*) the observed ones—people made empirical observations fit in with already established beliefs. In addition to the relative weights of imagination and observation, societies, and thus the purpose or outcome of knowledge, vary on a continuum from military to industry, conquest to production. In the theological phase of the mind, "Society makes conquest its one permanent aim" (p. 52). Because knowledge is certain in the theological phase, it is certain that everyone must believe the same.

The second stage of knowledge is *metaphysical* and is a transitory phase. Comte (1822/1975b) argued that the mind couldn't make the leap straightaway from theology to the positive stage. The metaphysical stage had "a mongrel nature, connecting facts by ideas that are no longer entirely supernatural and have not yet become completely natural" (p. 29). The third phase is *positive* and is ultimately where all knowledge systems will end up in Comte's scheme. Generally speaking, then, the ideal modern epistemological method is positivism, or what we usually call the scientific method. The most important tenet of this method is that the universe is *empirical*. Something is empirical if it is based on direct sense experience or observation. In its time, this assumption was radically critical and formulated in opposition to religion. Religion assumes that the true reality of the universe is spiritual. The physical world is perceived as temporary or illusionary, something that will fade away and has no real substance. Positivism assumes just the opposite: The only reality that we can know with any certainty is physical, and knowledge about that universe is acquired through observation.

Further, positivism assumes that this empirical world operates according to natural *invariant laws*. For science, there are no hidden forces in back of the world; rather, there are universal or general laws that produce all observed regularities. The most famous example of such a law, and one that Comte noted, is Newton's law of gravity. It's pretty clear that Newton wasn't the first to notice that apples fall to the ground; this is an empirical regularity that's been around for quite some time. Newton went past that observation and explained *how it works* (his explanation had to do with the masses of and distance between two objects). Because his explanation got to the underlying dynamics, we are able to predict with great regularity how gravity will work. Newton's law also has the quality of being universal: It reaches beyond the immediate situation (objects falling on Earth) to explain how bodies in space interact. The purpose of the positive method is to discover these laws and use them to improve the human condition. For example, because we understand the law of gravity and the principles of aerodynamics, we have been able to create technologies that allow us to travel from New York to London in seven hours and put people on the Moon. Comte (1830–1842/1975a) saw society working in this same way, "as subjected to invariable natural *laws*" (p. 75), and sociology's purpose as improving the social world in which we live: "The positive philosophy offers the only solid basis for . . . social reorganization" (p. 83).

Theory: The Key to Modern Knowledge

For Comte, positivistic theory expresses the invariant laws of society. Knowing these laws allows us to explain, predict, and control our environments and thus progress. As such, the first and most important function of theory is that it explains how something works or comes into existence—*theory is a logically formed argument that explains an empirical phenomenon in general terms*. Knowing how something works is fundamental to knowing how to exercise control for the benefit of humankind. This function of theory is key, yet it is something that is difficult for most to grasp. I came across two statements that may help illustrate this idea. A recent issue of *Discover* magazine contained the following statement: "Iron deficiency, in particular, can induce strange tastes, though it's not known why" (Kagan, 2008, p. 16). There are many of these empirical observations in science and medicine. For example, it's not known why some people get motion sickness and others don't, nor is it known why more women than men get Raynaud's disease (a disorder of the blood vessels that causes cold hands and feet). Observations like these that simply link two empirical variables together are not theoretical. The second statement, which follows, appeared in an article about how exercise improves memory and may delay the onset of Alzheimer's. In linking these variables, the article says, "It works like this: aerobic exercise increases blood flow to the brain, which nourishes brain cells and allows them to function more effectively" (Redford & Kinosian, 2008, p. 26). Unlike the first statement, this one offers an explanation of how things work. This, then, is a theoretical statement. It describes how the empirical association between exercise and improved memory works.

Theory is built out of concepts, definitions, and relationships. *Theoretical concepts* are usually fairly abstract because the more abstract a theory is, the more it can explain. The problem with abstract concepts is that they are indefinite, which is why definitions are so important. *Theoretical definitions* specify two things: stipulative conditions and dynamic qualities. Stipulative conditions explain how a concept is specifically unique. Let's use religion as an illustration. Merriam-Webster (2002) gives us the following dictionary definition of religion: "the personal commitment to and serving of God . . . one of the systems of faith and worship." That's how most of us think of it and would use it in a sentence, but it has little if any theoretical value.

Karl Marx (1932/1978b) defined religion as "the sigh of the oppressed creature, the sentiment of a heartless world, and the soul of soulless conditions. It is the *opium* of the people" (p. 54). Émile Durkheim (1912/1995) defined religion as "a unified system of beliefs and practices relative to sacred things, that is to say, things set apart and forbidden—beliefs and practices which unite into one single moral community called a Church, all those who adhere to them" (p. 44). The first thing you probably noticed is that these two definitions are different; they are different from the dictionary definition and they are different from one another. That's precisely what we mean when we say that theoretical definitions are stipulative: *They stipulate the necessary characteristics to be such a thing in a specific case.* Another way to put this is that theoretical definitions are contextual; they are always understood within the broader context in which they appear. Marx's specific take on religion fits within the broader context of his theory of species-being and false consciousness, and Durkheim's within his theory of social solidarity and collective consciousness. One of the important implications of theoretical definitions is that they identify precisely what the theory needs to explain. Durkheim's theory, for example, would have to explain how religion creates the collective consciousness and solidarity—it would not have to explain how religion functions as the opium of the people.

The second thing a theoretical definition has to do is explain the dynamic qualities of a factor. Theoretical concepts are always active; they create effects. Borrowing from John W. Carroll, physicists Stephen Hawking and Leonard Mlodinow (2010, p. 28) give us an example using gold and uranium-235 that might help to clarify this concept. It is empirically true that all spheres of gold and uranium-235 are less than a mile in diameter—no human has ever seen one that big. In terms of simple observation, we could make a general statement and say that we will never see a ball of gold or uranium-235 larger than a mile in diameter—it's a fact. However, that's not quite true, at least not in terms of *scientific* facts. You see, there's nothing about the intrinsic properties of gold that make a mile-wide ball of gold impossible; we've just never seen one. However, a sphere of uranium-235 a mile in diameter is theoretically impossible because a ball of uranium-235 wider than 6 inches will create a nuclear explosion.

That knowledge—that fact—is based on a theoretical explanation of how the substance works. Because physicists understand how uranium-235 works, they can *make predictions about its behavior.* No such prediction can be made about the sphere of gold.

Full theories also need to explain the relationships among the concepts. There are at least two concerns in spelling out *theoretical relationships.* The first is the direction of the relationship. There are two basic possibilities, positive and negative. A relationship is positive if the concepts vary in the same direction (either both increase or both decrease); relationships are negative if they vary in opposite directions (if one increases, the other decreases). Let's use a simple example—education and occupation. The relationship between these two concepts is generally positive (at least, that's your working hypothesis for being in school): Increasing years of education will produce higher-rated jobs for the individual. Notice that because the relationship is positive, it works the same in reverse: Lower years of education produce lower-rated jobs.

The second concern with relationships is more difficult: We need to explain how the relationship works. More years of education might equate to a better job, but how does that work? If you think about this a moment, you'll see that the theoretical task just grew tremendously. What is it about education that would affect jobs in that way? How does this relationship work? Historically, it wasn't always true that formal education and occupation were related. Why are they now? Many people in our society know that higher levels of education lead to better jobs, but most can't explain how it works because most don't have a theoretical understanding of the process.

The Classical Theorists

The people we now consider classical social and sociological theorists were directly concerned with issues of modernity. Besides systemizing the positivistic approach, Comte was also the forerunner of *functionalism.* This perspective was probably the first to see society as an objective whole that could be analyzed scientifically. The basic premise of functional analysis is that society works as an interdependent system of separate structures, just like a biological organism. Society thus evolves over time, becoming more complex and therefore adaptable. Herbert Spencer (1820–1903) elaborated this notion and argued that evolutionary progress occurs around three axes or functional needs: the *regulative function,* which regulates or governs the overall system and its boundaries; the *operative function,* which supplies everything the system needs; and the *distributive system,* which moves needed supplies among the various parts. Modern society is characterized by the differentiation and specialization of these functions into different social institutions. Rather than these functions overlapping, they become separate. A good example of this is the relationship between religion and government. Prior to modernity, religion and government coincided: Governments were legitimated as God-ordained, and individual behaviors were subject to God's laws. In modernity, there is separation between religion and the state; there is also separation (or differentiation) between religion and the economy, the economy and education, and so on. The bulk of Spencer's theory is concerned with how a structurally complex (modern) rather than structurally simple society can function. His answer is that the social system pushes for increased state regulation to guide complex structural relations. Too much regulation, however, can stagnate the system. Thus, in the long run, modern society is characterized by cycles of growth (deregulation) and stagnation (regulation).

Émile Durkheim (1858–1917) was likewise concerned with the complexity of modern societies—his famous typology of mechanical and organic solidarity is a way of understanding this issue. Where Spencer was concerned about structural differentiation, Durkheim was more troubled by the cultural diversity that modern, complex societies generated. Durkheim argued that social connections among people are held together by culture, or the collective consciousness. Common culture—a set of shared symbols, feelings, norms, values, and beliefs—is naturally developed in simpler, religiously or traditionally based societies. However, modern conditions, specifically structural differentiation and high division of labor, tend to generate cultures specific to smaller groups rather than society at large. Thus, Durkheim's question is, how can a culturally diverse (modern) society be integrated? The main solution to this problem is an evolving, more general moral culture—able to embrace greater levels of social diversity through the formation of intermediary groups, restitutive law, the cult of the individual (individualism), and social and structural interdependency. Durkheim was, however, worried that society wouldn't be able to create this more universal collective consciousness. There are, thus, real dangers of society pathologies in modernity, like egoism, anomie, suicide, and economic inequality.

Karl Marx (1818–1883) was specifically concerned with the class inequality that capitalism generated. Marx argued that rather than creating natural liberty through the invisible hand of the market, capitalism creates a new system of inequality based on class. To understand the insidious nature of class inequality, Marx argued that like all other animal species, human nature is defined by the way we adapt to the physical environment. Our evolutionary advantage or species adaptation is economic production. Thus, when economic production is driven by endless capital accumulation (greed) as well as never-ending commodification and market expansion (egoism rather than individualism), the result can only be alienation and false consciousness. Rather than progress, Marx saw capitalism as the darkest point in human history. Yet Marx also believed that humanity would eventually triumph. Marx argued that capitalism is based on certain structural factors that create tensions in capitalism—most notably exploitation and overproduction. These tensions invariably create the recurring cycles of economic recession to which capitalism is susceptible. These cycles generate a small class of wealthy capitalists and a large class of dependent and deprived workers. Each economic crisis is deeper than the previous, which in turn concentrates wealth and power in fewer and fewer hands, with the working class experiencing greater levels of economic, physical, and psychological suffering, which eventually creates class consciousness. In the long run, these cycles will cause capitalism to implode, which, in turn, brings economic and social change—first to socialism and then to communism.

Marx was also doubtful about the possibilities of the modern state. Marx was born scant decades after the French and American Revolutions and the founding of modern democracy. This modern state is based on a set of social structures and laws that guarantee an active civil society and the right to self-determination through equal voting. Marx, however, recognizing the dependency of capitalism on state government, argued that capitalism "colonized" the state. Capitalism thus "conquered for itself, in the modern representative State, exclusive political sway. The executive of the modern State is but a committee for managing the common affairs of the whole bourgeoisie" (Marx & Engels, 1848/1978, p. 475).

Like Marx, Max Weber (1864–1920) was focused on the inequality that modern society produced. Yet he saw more than Marx and argued that there are at least three stratification systems intrinsic to modernity: class, status, and power. Social change in modernity is thus more complex than Marx thought. These three systems create a multitude of possible configurations of inequality, which generally prevents anything like class consciousness. But Weber's chief concern about modern society was the relentless expansion of rational control. As we've seen, control of every aspect of human existence is central to modernity. It's the purpose of positivistic knowledge in the natural, social, and behavioral sciences; and it's the central purpose of constitutional state government. Rational control, however, can have irrational results. These unintended consequences are easy to see in such things as environmental disasters and modern warfare. In modernity, oil spills and nuclear plant meltdowns are "normal accidents" (Perrow, 1999), and the atomic weaponry that was meant to preserve democracy holds us under a constant threat of obliteration. Weber's concern, however, went deeper: The extension of reason and rational control utterly changes the social and personal worlds in which we live. The modern world is a demystified world; it's a cold world understood in calculative, rational terms, a world denuded of ethics, values, and the emotional, traditional connections that had bound people together for millennia. Because of constant association with bureaucracy, modern individuals are noted for their bureaucratic personality, an inner self organized around a value system based upon means-ends efficiency. Thus, Enlightenment humanism—through the reduction of human activity, subjectivity, and social relations to the routinized prescriptions of bureaucratic management and expert systems—would, in fact, dehumanize people.

Weber was also doubtful of the possibilities of a modern, democratic state. The modern state is a bureaucratized state, and bureaucracies are built around expert knowledge and rational-legal management. Weber argued that once in place, bureaucracies create an iron cage that cannot be replaced. The election of leaders, then, is more or less simply replacing the top and more public positions, and the actual governing structure remains the same, primarily because it is dependent upon expert knowledge. There are two important implications of this process. First, because of the

> inescapable rule of bureaucracy, which first brought the modern concept of the "citizen of the state" into being, the ballot slip is the *only* instrument of power which is at all *capable* of giving the people who are subject to bureaucratic rule a minimal right of codetermination. (Weber, 1917/1994, pp. 105–106)

In such a system, "there is simply no place in which non-expert citizens could make a contribution" (Barbalet, 2010, p. 209). The second implication of bureaucratic government is that modern politics is a struggle for legitimacy that tends to focus on individual leaders. This implies that people in a modern democratic state vote for people based on personalities rather than actual political issues and democratic principles: "Since the time of the constitutional state, and definitely since democracy has been established, the 'demagogue' has been the typical political leader" (Weber, 1921/1948, p. 96).

Complexities of Contemporary Theory

Our story of modernity began like a bright morning star. Humankind could at last obtain control over the natural forces that had so long dominated. Science would discover the laws of nature and society and, through theory, help people to make decisions based on reason, rather than fear and misplaced faith. Democracy and enlightened education would assure each individual a part in the human enterprise. Belief in the supreme dignity of the person—belief in individualism—became the rallying point and binding agent in society. People believed that capitalism would guarantee that every person's worth was determined by his, and later her, own efforts. Further, capitalism and industry replaced scarcity with abundance, and constitutional government guaranteed the pursuit of happiness.

Our classical theorists focused their investigation on the structural changes that modernity brought: The central themes of modernity all occupied center stage for the founders of sociology: society as a system that could be regulated and controlled, the modern state and individual freedom, the place of religion in modern society, class and capitalism, rationality and bureaucratic management, and so on. Moreover, most of the classical theorists held to a modern, positivistic hope. Spencer saw little else but evolutionary progress, and Durkheim (1912/1995) believed that, "A day will come when our societies once again will know hours of creative effervescence during which new ideals will again spring forth" (p. 429). Even Marx was hopeful. Without a doubt, he contended that society was irresistibly moving toward a utopian end. Capitalism was simply a misplaced hope, the darkest hour before the dawn. Weber, however, didn't share this modern hope. He wasn't quite certain that we would be able to pull ourselves out of the iron cage of modernity we had constructed. In that, he was one of the first to question the assumptions of rationality upon which the entire modern project is based.

Contemporary society is similar to early modern society in many ways, but it is also quite distinct. The economic structure is still capitalistic, but it is now global rather than national. Economies in core nations have shifted from industrial to postindustrial production, which brings new complexities to class relations. Commodification and advertising have created a new type of product, one purchased more for its symbolic value than actual use. Communication and transportation technologies have far exceeded those of early modernity and have virtually removed the limits of time and place on human interaction and organization. As a result, social groups have lost some of their ability to protect their symbols, and people can more easily put on and take off identities at will. The organizing principles of contemporary society are different, substituting the characteristics of computer networks for those of social institutions and bureaucratic management. Our contemporary theorists are thus dealing with a different social world.

The spirit of the age is different now as well. The twentieth century was a time of immense technical progress—but the twentieth century also brought doubt and despair. The "war to end all wars" (World War I) did not do any such thing. World War II came and brought with it the Holocaust, a haunting testimony to the depths the human soul can sink. The twentieth century also initiated the atomic age and catastrophic risk—risk due not only to nuclear escalation but also to the ever-expanding potential for global ecological destruction. In addition, after World War II the last remnants of the British Empire fell, and with it came the end of colonialism: "For the peoples of most of the earth, much of the twentieth century involved the long struggle and eventual triumph against colonial rule" (Young, 2003, p. 3). In the West, we became increasingly aware that modern democracy is built on inequality—the twentieth century made it painfully obvious that not all "men" are created equal. We also awakened to the destructive side of capitalism and science— the exploitation of people and land can have long-term and initially hidden effects. The decades surrounding the sixties stand out: Politicians and equal rights leaders were assassinated, demonstrating students were killed, the underbelly of democracy was exposed through such events like Watergate—the list is almost endless.

The twentieth century also brought philosophies that cast doubt upon modernist ideals. *Existentialism* made a question out of the driving force in Enlightenment humanism. In existentialism, human existence is the problem, rather than the locus of assumed natural rights. Rather than humanness being the motive for progress, the very existence of human nature is central. Human beings are the only animals consumed with their own existence. Human nature is thus defined by the presence of questions of existence, which are themselves prompted by the knowledge of universal, impending death. Humanness, then, is characterized by angst rather than reason and progress. Other philosophies, such as *phenomenology,* set aside the assumption of objective existence upon which science is founded and in its place put the structures of consciousness that determine experience. In its pure form, phenomenology reduces everything to the individual point of view, to the study of subjective consciousness, which is only available to the subject. *Poststructuralism* takes language itself as the central problem. In the beginning of the twentieth century, scholars of semiology (the study of signs) set out to study language in the same way that modern scholars study anything, but doing so revealed an intrinsic problem. Every modern discipline takes language for granted; language is the medium through which discoveries are expressed. The same is true for the study of language: All discoveries about language have to be expressed in language. Semiotics thus revealed the reflexive nature of human language and reality. There is, then, nothing but language for human beings. As we'll see, our contemporary theorists were influenced by these different systems of philosophy as well as the changes in social structures and systems.

As I said, my story of modernity is simply our beginning; it's our touchstone, the place from which to organize our thinking. In this book, you'll find people who adhere to the modernist approach outlined above. For example, Janet Chafetz

(Chapter 7) gives us a scientific understanding of how gender inequality works. Yet, as you move through the book, you'll also find many contemporary theorists who point to social factors and processes that make it difficult to be a reasoned social actor. There are also theories that indicate that the social world may not be ordered, but rather is a kind of chaotic system—one that cannot be controlled and guided. More fundamentally, the social world may not be objective, but may simply be a subjective attribution of meaning. Further, some critical theorists argue that this idea of modern knowledge is intrinsically linked to power and is thus oppressive. To begin our exploration of contemporary theory, we're going to consider two defining "moments" in the twentieth century: those of Talcott Parsons and the Frankfurt School of Critical Theory.

Summary

- Our story of modernity focuses on the unique configurations of social struc-tures and knowledge that began to take shape in the fifteenth and sixteenth centuries. Modern social systems are characterized by structural differentia-tion and specialization: The democratic nation-state separated itself from religion and the economy; the economy became thoroughly industrialized and dominated by capitalist concerns. Capitalism was intended to be a system of equal opportunity and freedom, where one's social standing was deter-mined by individual effort and not group or family membership. In order to assure equality, bureaucracy became the chief method of social organization.

- Tied up with these social changes were cultural transformations. At the core of these transformations was the enlightened, reasoning individual. For the techni-cal and social projects of modernity to succeed, society had to be based on indi-viduals who were capable of freethinking and agency. The ideology in back of this individualism was based upon progress and the indefinite perfectibility of the human mind. Auguste Comte argued that the knowledge system best suited to these beliefs was positivism. Positivism assumes that the universe is empirical, that it operates according to invariant laws, and that humans can discover those laws and use them to better the human condition. The most significant way these laws could be expressed was theory—a logical explanation of how things work expressed in general concepts, definitions, and dynamic relations.

- Classical social theory emerged from this caldron of social and cultural change. Early theorists, such as Spencer and Comte, focused on understand-ing society as an objective, functioning system. Later theorists, like Marx, Weber, and Durkheim, saw problems in society that prevented or hampered modern progress; Marx was specifically concerned with capitalism, Weber with rationality, and Durkheim with cultural segmentation.

- Contemporary theorists work within and from this heritage. Most are con-cerned with different sources of inequality, and many envision a social system quite different from that of early modernity. Contemporary theorists are also influenced by philosophy systems dissimilar from positivism.

BUILDING YOUR THEORY TOOLBOX

At the end of every chapter, I will be giving you exercises and projects. These activities are designed to help you understand and use the theories you've learned. The intent of these first two chapters is to provide you with a background for the rest of the book. I am thus keeping these toolboxes brief. The most important things I want you to take away from these two chapters are ideas that you can use to think through and analyze the theories that follow.

- After studying this chapter, you should be able to define the following concepts (Make your definitions as theoretically robust as possible, and don't be afraid to consult other sources. You'll want these definitions to work for you throughout the book.): empiricism, society, democracy, natural liberty, progress, individualism, secularism, industrialization, urbanization, capitalism, civil society, epistemology, theological knowledge, metaphysical knowledge, positivistic knowledge, definition and purpose of theory, three building blocks of theory.

- You should also be able to write a reasoned response to the following:

  o Explain the most important cultural and structural roots of modernity. What are they and what did they accomplish?

  o Explain the importance of the three pillars of modern knowledge.

  o Explain positivism as a system of knowledge. What are its assumptions and goals?

  o Explain the association between capitalism and democracy.

CHAPTER 2

Defining Moments in Twentieth-Century Theory

Talcott Parsons and the Frankfurt School

Talcott Parsons: Defining Sociology
    Parsons's Vision for the Social Sciences
    Parsons's Theoretical Project
    The Problem of Social Order
        Voluntaristic Action
        Patterning Voluntaristic Action
The Frankfurt School: The Problem with Sociology
    Historical Roots
    The Problem with Positivism: Max Horkheimer
      and Theodor Adorno
Building Your Theory Toolbox

Source: Copyright © The Granger Collection.

I n Chapter 1, we saw that understanding modernity is vital for understanding contemporary theory and sociology. It's equally important for us to also understand a couple of the developments in the mid-twentieth century that formed contemporary theory, especially in the United States. For our purposes, the two most significant are Talcott Parsons and the **Frankfurt School.** In many ways, these two forces took the social disciplines in opposite directions: Parsons saw himself as building on the ideals of modern knowledge, whereas the Frankfurt School did just the opposite and argued that rather than leading to social justice, social science destroys the possibility of freedom and equality. Both were centrally concerned with culture: Parsons saw culture as the most important factor leading to social cohesion and harmony, while the Frankfurt School saw culture, especially popular culture, as producing false consciousness. Both have influenced contemporary theory beyond their specific ideas.

Historically, the Frankfurt School developed first. However, I'm going to start with Parsons because he extends and systematizes the things we learned about modern knowledge and society in Chapter 1. In addition, as you'll see throughout this book, Parsons's influence is more central, as many contemporary theorists continue to see themselves as arguing for or against his work. There are good reasons for giving this much influence to Parsons, but there's also a sense in which I'm making him an ideal type, similar to what I did with modernity. Both Parsons and modernity exist and are clearly important, but I'm not presenting a well-reasoned and documented case for either. I'm using them as *heuristics* for our discussion throughout the book—they represent ways for us to discover questions, ideas, and theories that come with each of our theorists.

Talcott Parsons: Defining Sociology

Talcott Parsons (1902–1979) was born in Colorado Springs, Colorado. Parsons began his university studies at Amherst (Massachusetts). He had planned on becoming a physician but later changed his major to economics. After receiving his BA in 1924, Parsons studied in Europe, completing his PhD work in sociology and economics at the University of Heidelberg, Germany. After teaching a short while at Amherst, Parsons obtained a lecturing position in 1931 at Harvard and was one of the first instructors in the new sociology department.

Parsons's Vision for the Social Sciences

Parsons was a man with a grand vision. He wanted to unite the social and behavioral disciplines into a single social science and to create a single theoretical perspective. Parsons worked at this not only theoretically but also organizationally. In 1942, Parsons became the department chair of sociology at Harvard University. One of the first things he did was to combine sociology, anthropology, and psychology into one department, the Department of Social Relations. The reason he did this was to break down the barriers between disciplines in order to create a general science of human action. His desire, then, wasn't simply to understand a portion of human action (as in sociology); he wanted, rather, to comprehend the totality of the human context and to offer a full and complete explanation of social action. The department existed from 1945 to 1972 and formed the basis of other interdisciplinary programs across the United States.

After 10 years of work, Parsons's first book was published in 1937 and reissued in 1949: *The Structure of Social Action*. This book is characterized by Lewis Coser (1977) as a

watershed in the development of American sociology in general and sociological theory in particular . . . [which] set a new course—the course of functional analysis—that was to dominate theoretical developments from the early 1940s until the middle of the 1960s. (p. 562)

More than any other single book, it introduced European thinkers to American sociologists and gave birth to structural functionalism, which Desmond Ellis described in 1971 as "the major theoretical orientation in sociology today" (p. 692). Parsons's other prominent works include *The Social System, Toward a General Theory of Action, Economy and Society, Structure and Process in Modern Societies,* and *The American University.* For much of the twentieth century, Parsons was "the major theoretical figure in English-speaking sociology, if not in world sociology" (Marshall, 1998, p. 480). As Victor Lidz (2000) notes, "Talcott Parsons . . . was, and remains, the pre-eminent American sociologist" (p. 388).

Parsons's Theoretical Project

There are at least three ways in which Parsons helped shape the center of sociological discourse in the twentieth century: the way he theorized, the problem he addressed, and the theory itself. We'll start with his theorizing. Recall that science is built upon positivism and empiricism. As such, science assumes that the universe is empirical, it operates according to law-like principles, and humans can discover those laws through rigorous investigation. Science also has very specific goals, as do most knowledge systems. Through discovery, scientists want to explain, predict, and control phenomena. In addition, there are two other important issues in positivistic theory, which we find in the following quotes from prominent contemporary theorists:

The essence of science is precisely theory . . . as a *generalized* and coherent body of ideas, which explain the range of variations in the empirical world in terms of general principles. . . . [I]t is explicitly *cumulative* and *integrating.* (R. Collins, 1986, p. 1345, emphasis added)

A true science *incorporates the ideas* of its early founders in introductory texts and moves on, giving over the analysis of its founders to history and philosophy. (J. H. Turner, 1993, p. ix, emphasis added)

The first thing I want us to glean from the above quotes is that scientific theory is *generalized.* To make an idea or concept general means to make it applicable to an entire group of similar things. As you'll see when we consider Parsons's theory, his concepts are very general (and thus fairly dry—but, then, all scientific theory is that way). Scientific knowledge also involves both theory synthesis and cumulation. Synthesis involves bringing together two or more elements in order to form a new whole. For example, water is the synthesis of hydrogen and oxygen. *Theoretical synthesis,* then, involves bringing together elements from diverse theorists so as to form a theory that robustly explains a broader range of phenomena. Cumulation refers to the gradual building up of something, such as the cumulative effects of drinking alcohol. *Theory cumulation* specifically involves the building up of explanations over time. This incremental building is captured by Isaac Newton's famous dictum, "If I have seen a little further, it is by standing on the shoulders of giants." Yet, what isn't clear in Newton's quote is that the ultimate goal of theory cumulation is to forget its predecessors.

To make this clear, let's compare the writings of two authors, Edgar Allan Poe and Albert Einstein. Here's one of Poe's famous stanzas:

> *Once upon a midnight dreary, while I pondered, weak and weary,*
>
> *over many a quaint and curious volume of forgotten lore,*
>
> *While I nodded, nearly napping, suddenly there came a tapping,*
>
> *As of someone gently rapping, rapping at my chamber door.*
>
> *"Tis some visitor," I muttered, "tapping at my chamber door;*
>
> *Only this, and nothing more."*

Here's one of Einstein's famous quotes:

$$E = mc^2$$

There are some obvious differences between these two quotes: One is poetry and the other a mathematical equation. But I want you to see a bit more. Does it matter who wrote "Once upon a midnight dreary"? Yes, it does. A large part of understanding poetry is knowing who wrote it—who the poet was, how the person lived, what his or her other works are like, what style the poet wrote in, and so on. These issues are part of what makes reading Poe different from reading Emily Dickinson. Now, does it matter who wrote $E = mc^2$? Not really. You can understand everything you need to know about $E = mc^2$ simply by understanding the equation. The author in this sense is immaterial.

One of the above quotes is from Jonathan H. Turner's book *Classical Sociological Theory: A Positivist's Perspective*. Turner's (1993) goal in that book is "to codify the wisdom of the masters so that we can move on and *make books on classical theory unnecessary*" (p. ix, emphasis added). That last highlighted section is the heart of theory cumulation: Cumulating theory implies that we do away with the individual authors and historic contexts and keep only the theoretical ideas that explain, predict, and control the social world. In that spirit, here's a theoretical statement from Turner's book:

> The degree of differentiation among a population of actors is a gradual s-function of the level of competition among these actors, with the latter variable being an additive function of:
>
> A. the size of this population of actors,
> B. the rate of growth in this population,
> C. the extent of economical concentration of this population, and
> D. the rate of mobility of actors in this population. (p. 80)

First notice how general the statement is; it can be applied to any group of people, living anywhere, at any time. Notice also that there's no mention of from whom these ideas originally came. Now, you and I might know from whom this proposition comes (Durkheim), but does it matter? No. Like Einstein's formula, it's immaterial. If we are doing social science, what matters is whether or not we can show this statement to be false through scientific testing. If we can't, then we can have a certain level of confidence that the proposition accurately reflects a general process in the social world. In science, authorship is superfluous; *it's the explanatory power of the theory that matters.* The cumulation of these general statements is one of the main goals of scientific theory.

Of his groundbreaking work, Parsons (1937/1949) says, "*The Structure of Social Action* was intended to be primarily a contribution to systematic social science and not to history" (pp. A–B). His work is actually a synthesis of three theorists. Parsons (1961) notes how he used each one:

> for the conception of the social system and the bases of its integration, the work of Durkheim; for the comparative analysis of social structure and for the analysis of the borderline between social systems and culture, that of Max Weber; and for the articulation between social systems and personality, that of Freud. (p. 31)

Yet Parsons clearly wants us to forget the historical and personal origins of the theories—for science, it's the power of the synthesized theory to illuminate and delineate social factors and processes that matters. This approach to theory is also what led to the three sociological perspectives or paradigms you were taught in your introduction to sociology courses: structural functionalism, conflict theory, and interactionism. To say that someone is a functionalist, for example, is to pay more attention to the general features of the theory than to his or her original contributions.

The Problem of Social Order

Parsons saw himself as responding to *the problem of social order* posed by the philosopher Thomas Hobbes (1588–1679). Parsons's understanding of this Hobbesian problem of social order begins with the fact that all humans are ruled by passions. Furthermore, all people are motivated to fulfill these passions, and, more importantly, they have the *right* to fulfill them because "there is 'no common rule of good and evil to be taken from the nature of the objects themselves'" (Hobbes, as quoted in Parsons, 1937/1949, p. 89). In other words, things aren't good or bad in themselves, and people have different desires for diverse things—thus, there is no basis for a rule. In the absence of any rule, people will use the most efficient means possible to acquire their goals. "These means are found in the last analysis to be force and fraud" (Parsons, 1937/1949, p. 90). Thus, the most natural state of humanity is war of all against all. The question, then, is how is social order achieved? Parsons's basic response is the normative order—social order achieved through norms. While some of the language might be new to you, most of Parsons's response will probably feel familiar. The reason that's probably the case is that Parsons's answer to the problem of social order has become for many sociologists the basic answer given in introduction to sociology classes.

Voluntaristic Action

In thinking about humans, it's sometimes convenient to make the distinction between behavior and action: All living things behave; only humans have the potential to act. Action implies choice and decision, whereas behavior occurs without thought, as when a plant's leaves reach for the sun. Of course, humans behave as well as act; there are a lot of things we do on autopilot, but we have the potential for action. Theory that focuses on this issue is referred to as *action theory,* which has been an interest of philosophy since the time of Aristotle. Parsons's work on action theory draws from Max Weber, who argued that action takes place when a person's behavior is meaningfully oriented toward other social actors, usually in terms of meaningful values or rational exchange. *Voluntaristic action,* then, is never purely individualistic: People choose to act voluntarily within a context of culture and social situations in order to meet individual goals. Moreover, because human needs are met socially, people develop shortcuts to action by creating norms and by patterning action through sets of ends and means.

Parsons calls this context of action the *unit act.* There are a variety of factors in the unit act. The first, and in some ways the most important, are the conditions of action. There are of course occasions when we have some control over the initial context—for example, you may decide to go to the movies on Saturday or study for a test. But once the choice is made, the actor has little immediate agency or choice regarding the conditions under which action takes place. Parsons has in mind such things as the presence of social institutions or organizations, as well as elements that might be specific to the situation, such as the social influence of particular people or physical constraints of the environment.

The second set of factors under which people act concerns the means and ends of action. Here we can see a fundamental difference between action and reaction: Action is goal oriented and involves choice. But for people to make choices among goals and means, the choices themselves must have different meanings. According to Parsons, the meanings of and relationships between means and ends are formed through shared value hierarchy. Cultural *values* are shared ideas and emotions regarding the worth of something, and values are always understood within a hierarchy, with some goals and means more highly valued than others; otherwise it would be difficult to choose between one thing and another because you wouldn't care. Choices among means and ends are also guided by norms. *Norms* are actions that have sanctions (rewards or punishments) attached to them. In summary, Parsons is arguing that human action is distinctly cultural and thus meaningful action.

Patterning Voluntaristic Action

While Parsons has now outlined the context wherein action takes place, the problem of social order isn't adequately answered. Two things need to be specifically addressed: First, Hobbes talked about a person's inner passions driving him or her; second, social order needs patterned behavior. Parsons argues that patterning action occurs on two levels: the structuring of patterned behaviors and individual internalization or socialization. Parsons understands internalization in Freudian terms. Freud's theory works like this: People are motivated by internal energies surrounding different need dispositions. As these different psychic motives encounter the social world, they have to conform in order to be satisfied. Conformity may be successful (well-adjusted) or unsuccessful (repressed), but the point to notice here is that the structure of the individual's personality changes as a result of this encounter between psychic energy and the social world. The superego is formed through these encounters. For Parsons, the important point is that cultural traditions become meaningful to and part of the need dispositions of individuals. The way we sense and fulfill our needs is structured internally by culture—notice how Parsons reconceptualized Hobbes's concern for passions; in Parsons's scheme they are social rather than individual. For Parsons, then, the motivation to conform comes principally from within the individual through Freudian internalization patterns of value orientation and meaning.

Action is also structured socially through modes of orientation and types of action that have become institutionalized. Modes of orientation simply refer to the way we come into a social situation with specific motives and values. These motives and values come together and form three types of action: instrumental, expressive, and moral. *Instrumental action* is composed of the need for information and evaluation by objective criteria. *Expressive action* is motivated by the need for emotional attachment and the desire to be evaluated by artistic standards. *Moral action* is motivated by the need for assessment by ultimate notions of right and wrong. People will tend to be in contact with others who are interested in the same type of action.

As we interact over time with people who are likewise oriented, we produce patterns of interaction and a corresponding system of status positions, roles, and norms. Status positions tell us where we fit in the social hierarchy of esteem or honor; roles are sets of expected behaviors that generally correspond to a given status position (for example, a professor is expected to teach); and norms are expected behaviors that have positive or negative sanctions attached to them. Generally, these cluster together in institutions. For functionalists such as Parsons, institutions are enduring sets of roles, norms, status positions, and value patterns that are recognized as collectively meeting some societal need. In this context, then, **institutionalization** refers to the process through which behaviors, cognitions, and emotions become part of the taken-for-granted way of doing things in a society ("the way things are").

These clusters of institutions meet certain needs that society has—the institutions *function* to meet those needs. The most important set of institutions for Parsons are the ones that produce *latent pattern maintenance*. If something is latent, it's hidden and not noticed. Social patterns are maintained, then, through indirect management. For this task, society uses culture and socialization. The chief socializing agents in society are the structures that meet the requirement of latent pattern maintenance—structures such as religion, education, and family.

In addition to latent pattern maintenance, Parsons gives us three other requisite functions for a system: adaptation, goal attainment, and integration. The *adaptation* function is fulfilled by those structures that help a system to adapt to its environment. Adaptation draws in resources from the environment, converts them to usable elements, and distributes them throughout the system (the economy). *Goal attainment* is the subsystem that activates and guides all the other elements toward a specific goal (government). In Parsons's scheme, *integration* refers to the subsystems and structures that work to blend together and coordinate the various actions of other structures. In society, the structure most responsible for this overt coordination is the legal system. Together, these four functions are referred to as AGIL: Adaptation, Goal attainment, Integration, and Latent pattern maintenance. All of these functions are embedded within one another and form a bounded system that tends toward equilibrium or balance; in other words, they form society.

The Frankfurt School: The Problem With Sociology

Karl Marx spawned two distinct theoretical approaches. One approach focuses on conflict and class as general features of society. The intent with this more sociological approach is to analytically describe and explain conflict. Conflict and power here are understood as fundamental to society. This approach is based on the same question as Parsons: How is social order possible? The short version of Parsons's theory is that social order is achieved through commonly held norms, values, and beliefs. A norm, as you'll recall from above, is "a cultural rule that associates people's behavior or appearance with rewards or punishments" (Johnson, 2000, p. 209). This approach to understanding social order is sometimes called the "equilibrium model" because it's based on people internalizing and believing in the collective conscious. People do have selfish motivations, but they are offset by the collective consciousness, thus creating a balance between individual desires and social needs.

Conflict theorists, however, would point out that there is an element of power underlying norms. Notice in the above definition that norms are founded upon an ability to reward or punish behavior, both of which are based on power. Conflict theorists also point out that the values and beliefs commonly held in society can be explained in terms of the interests of the elite. Thus, for conflict theorists, social order is the result of constraint rather than consensus, and power is thus an essential element of society. Conflict theorists take the same basic scientific approach as Parsons, seeking generalizable processes and building theory cumulatively.

The other theoretical approach that is inspired by and draws from Marx is critical theory. In general, *critical theory* "aims to dig beneath the surface of social life and uncover the assumptions and masks that keep us from a full and true understanding of how the world works" (Johnson, 2000, p. 67). Critical theory doesn't simply explain how society operates. Rather, it uncovers the unseen or misrecognized ways in which society operates to oppress certain groups while maintaining the interests of others. Critical theory has one more defining feature: It is decidedly anti-positivistic. Thus, critical theory has a very clear agenda that stands in opposition to scientific sociology. This perspective was brought together by the Frankfurt School.

Historical Roots

Briefly, the Frankfurt School (also known as the Institute of Social Research) began in the early 1920s at the University of Frankfurt in Germany. It was formed by a tight group of radical intellectuals and, ironically, financed by Felix Weil, the son of a wealthy German merchant. Weil's goal was to create "an institutionalization of Marxist discussion beyond the confines both of middle-class academia and the ideological narrow-mindedness of the Communist Party" (Wiggershaus, 1986/1995, p. 16). As the Nazis gained control in Germany, the Frankfurt School was forced into exile in 1933, first to Switzerland, then New York, and eventually California. In 1953, the school was able to move back to its home university in Frankfurt. The various leaders and scholars associated with the school include Theodor Adorno, Max Horkheimer, Herbert Marcuse, Eric Fromm, and Jürgen Habermas.

Although there were many reasons why the Frankfurt School and its critical theory approach came into existence, one of the early problems that these theorists dealt with was the influence of Nazism in Germany. The two decades surrounding World War II were a watershed period for many disciplines. The propaganda machine in back of Nazism and the subsequent human atrocities left a world stunned at the capacity of humanity's inhumanity. The actions of the Holocaust and the beliefs that lay at their foundation spurred a large cross-disciplinary move-ment to understand human behavior and beliefs. One of the best-known attempts at understanding these issues is Stanley Milgram's (1974) psychological experi-ments in authority.

The sociological attempt at understanding this horror demanded that culture be studied as an independent entity, something Marx didn't do. It was clear that what happened in Germany was rooted in culture that was used to intentionally control people's attitudes and actions—this use of culture was formalized in 1933 with the Reich Ministry for Popular Enlightenment and Propaganda. In addition, ideology became seen as something different, something more insidious, than perhaps Marx had first suspected. The Frankfurt School asks us to see ideology as more diffuse, as not simply a direct tool of the elite, but rather, as a part of the cultural atmosphere that we breathe.

In general, the Frankfurt School elaborates and synthesizes ideas from Karl Marx, Max Weber, and Sigmund Freud, and it focuses on the social production of knowledge and its relationship to human consciousness. This kind of Marxism focuses on Marx's indebtedness to Georg Wilhelm Hegel. Marx basically inverted Hegel's argument from an emphasis on ideas to material relations in the economy. The Frankfurt School reintroduced Hegel's concern with ideas and culture but kept Marx's critical evaluation of capitalism and the state. Thus, like Marx, the Frankfurt School focuses on ideology; however, unlike Marx, critical theorists see ideological production as linked to culture and knowledge rather than simply class and the material relations of production. Ideology, according to critical theorists, is more broadly based and insidious than Marx supposed.

The Problem With Positivism: Max Horkheimer and Theodor Adorno

The clearest expression of early critical theory is found in Max Horkheimer and Theodor Adorno's book *Dialectic of Enlightenment* (1972), first published in 1944. Adorno was born in Germany on September 11, 1903. His father was a well-to-do wine merchant and musician. Adorno himself studied music composition in Vienna for 3 years beginning in 1925, after studying sociology and philosophy at the University of Frankfurt. He finished his advanced degree in philosophy under Paul Tillich (Christian socialist) in 1931, and started an informal association with the Institute of Social Research. In 2 short years, Adorno was removed by the Nazis due to his Jewish heritage. He moved to Merton College, Oxford, in 1934 and to New York City in 1938, where he fully affiliated with the Frankfurt School in exile. When the school returned to Germany, Adorno became assistant director under Max Horkheimer, who had served as director since 1930. Horkheimer was German, also Jewish, and born into a wealthy family on February 14, 1895. After World War I, Horkheimer studied psychology and philosophy, finishing his doctorate in philosophy in 1925 at Frankfurt University, where he became a lecturer and eventually met Adorno. Horkheimer became the second director of the Institute of Social Research in 1930 and continued in that position until 1958, when Adorno took the directorship.

In the *Dialectic of Enlightenment*, Horkheimer and Adorno (1944/1972) argue that the contradictions Marx saw in capitalism are eclipsed by the ones found in the Enlightenment. The Enlightenment promises freedom through the use of reason, rationality, and the scientific method. But in the end it brings a new kind of oppression, not one that is linked to the externalities of life (such as class) but one that extinguishes the spirit and breath of human nature. As we've seen, positivism is based on reason and assumes the universe is empirical. Reason is employed to discover the laws of nature in order to predict and control it. Horkheimer and Adorno argue that the very definition of scientific knowledge devalues the human questions of ethics, aesthetics, beauty, emotion, and the good life, all of which are written off by science as concerns only for literature, which under positivism isn't valued as knowledge at all.

Science is based on the Cartesian dichotomy of subject and object, but the human sciences (sociology, psychology, psychiatry, anthropology, history, and the like) have in applying the scientific method objectified the human being through and through. In objectifying, controlling, and opposing nature, the scientific method opposes human nature—human nature is treated like physical nature, objectified and controlled. It results in such things as seeing all human sensualities and sensibilities as evil forces that must be controlled (the Freudian id), and the human psyche, emotions, sensualities, and body must all be managed and brought under the regime of science. People in positivistic social sciences become statistics in a population that must be controlled for the interests of the state (current examples include sexual practices, emotion management, bodily weight, child rearing, smoking, drinking, and so on—all of which are seen as weakness or problems within the individual).

Through the Enlightenment and science, rationality has been enthroned as the supreme human trait. Yet Horkheimer and Adorno trace this ascendency back to fear of the unknown. Rationality began in religion, as magicians, shamans, and priests began to organize and write doctrine. This impetus toward safety and control accelerated as society relieved such people from the burden of daily work; spirit guides became professional. Their work systematized and provided control over rituals and capricious spirits. Eventually, God was rendered predictable through the ideas of sin and ritualized redemption, and the idea of direct cause and effect was established. Religious issues became universal, with one version of reality, one explanation of the cosmos and humankind's place in it. The hierarchy of gods and individual responses were thus replaced by instrumental reason. The same fear of uncertainty was the motive behind science as well. The technical control of the physical world promised to relieve threats from disease, hunger, and pestilence, and to one degree or another it has done that. Yet science, like religion before it, takes on mythic form and reifies its own method. As with religion, science claims one true reality, one true form of knowledge, and only one way of validating knowledge.

This unstoppable engine of rationality also extends to the control of everyday life (and we can see how much we've "progressed" in this since the time of Horkheimer and Adorno). The modern life is an *administered life*. Every aspect is open to experts and analysis and is cut off from real social contact and dependency. People are isolated through technology, whether it's the technologies of travel (cars and planes), technologies of communication (such as phones and computers), or the technology of management (bureaucracies). People rationally manage time, space, and relationships, as well as their own self. Self-help is the prescription of the day, guided by experts of every kind. But what's lost is self-actualization—there are only remnants of a self that haven't been administered, only small portions to self-actualize, and even those are squashed in the name of the administered life.

Originally, the Enlightenment had an element of critical thought, where the process of thinking was examined. But it soon became as mechanical as the technologies that it creates, and it denies other ways of knowing and being. Horkheimer and Adorno's story of the Enlightenment is, then, "an account of how humankind, in its efforts to free itself from subjugation to nature, has created new and more all-encompassing forms of domination and repression" (Alway, 1995, p. 33).

The irony and problem is that the Enlightenment was meant to free humankind, yet it has created a new kind of *unfreedom*, a binding of the mind that prevents it from perceiving its own chains of bondage. This of course is what Marx meant when he spoke of **false consciousness,** but for Horkheimer and Adorno, the blindness is ever more insidious. The very tools of thought that were to bring enlightenment instead bring the administered life. How is it possible to get out of this conundrum? This is precisely where critical theory comes in.

First, it's important to understand that there isn't a specific goal or program. Gone are the lofty goals of the Enlightenment, and the method of reason and rationality are useless as well. In back of this negation is a caution and realization. The caution is about being derailed again by believing that we've found *the way*—unlike the capitalists in Marx's scheme, the philosophers of the Enlightenment may be seen as having the best of intentions. We should, then, be cautious of any single answer. The realization is that human beings are social beings; we reflect and express the spirit of the age and the position we hold in society. Knowledge is therefore never pure.

Knowing thus implies a second feature of critical theory: The way to freedom is through continual process and critical thinking, the goal of which is to unearth. In his introduction to Adorno's *Culture Industry,* Bernstein (1991) notes,

> In reading Adorno, especially his writings on the culture industry, it is important to keep firmly in mind the thought that he is not attempting an objective, sociological analysis of the phenomena in question. Rather, the *question* of the culture industry is raised from the perspective of its relation to the possibilities for social transformation. The culture industry is to be understood from the perspective of its potentialities for promoting or blocking "integral freedom." (p. 2)

Notice that Adorno's reading of the culture industry is not intended as a systematic, objective, sociological study. Rather, it is an act of interrogation. But it is questioning with a purpose: in Adorno's case, to assess the potential for integral freedom that pop culture provides. The image of integral freedom calls up many images, but among the most important are that freedom must be understood with reference to the whole being of human—including social relations, economic achievement, spirituality, sensuality, aesthetics, and so on—and that its chief value is the dignity of the person. "Reason can realize its reasonableness only through reflecting on the disease of the world as produced and reproduced by man" (Horkheimer, 2004, p. 120).

Summary

- Two theoretical schools epitomize sociology in the twentieth century. Parsons worked to systematize sociology into a scientific discipline through theory synthesis and cumulation. This approach finds its roots in Auguste Comte's positivism. Parsons also proposed that the theoretical paradigm that could unite sociology is structural functionalism. Parsons argued that the basic issue facing the human sciences is the problem of social order: How and why do people cooperate? The fundamental reason for cooperating is to meet social needs, understood as adaptation, goal attainment, integration, and latent pattern maintenance. As rational actors seek to meet these collective needs, they build up explicit modes of orientation and types of action, which in turn become institutionalized and internalized.

- Driven by the atrocities of World War II, critical theory takes humanity's inhumanity as the central problem of social order. Social order is always at the expense of oppressed groups and is achieved through cultural structures.

Critical theory, then, seeks to uncover the taken-for-granted ways in which people are denied and oppressed through ideology. Yet the most insidious tool of oppression isn't found in specific race- or gender-based ideologies. Rather, the Enlightenment itself intrinsically oppresses the human spirit through objectification. Science assumes objects of study; to use science to study people thus reduces the human spirit to quantifiable entities. Modernity and positivistic knowledge thus administer human life: They organize, guide, and control people rather than assuring freedom and the pursuit of happiness.

BUILDING YOUR THEORY TOOLBOX

Define the following terms (Make your definitions as theoretically robust as possible. Don't be afraid to consult other sources. You will want these definitions to work for you throughout the book.): generalized theory, theoretical synthesis, theory cumulation, the problem of social order, voluntaristic action, the unit act, values, norms, socialization, types of action, status positions, latent pattern maintenance, adaptation, goal attainment, integration, conflict theory, critical theory, administered life, unfreedom.

- Answer the following questions:
  - Explain Parsons's vision for the social sciences.
  - Describe the way in which Parsons theorized. Here I want you to write what we might think of as the ideal definition for social science.
  - Explain how Parsons solves the problem of social order. In other words, according to Parsons, how are social actions patterned across time and space?
  - Describe how and why the Frankfurt School came into existence.
  - Explain critical theory's assessment of positivistic theory.

Part II

Individuals and Situations

As I argued in Chapter 1, modernity was founded on a specific theory of the person; democracy and civil society depended upon it. In this sense, citizenship is more than a cluster of legal rights—it is a state of being, a form of consciousness. That education is key to this idea of the citizen is without a doubt. In referring to the founders of American democracy, Tocqueville (1835–1840/2002) said, "there was a greater mass of enlightenment spread among those men. . . . All, perhaps without exception, had received a quite advanced education" (p. 32). Harriet Martineau (1838/2003), who, like Tocqueville, came to study American democracy in the early decades of the nineteenth century, explained, "In countries where there is any popular Idea of Liberty, the universities are considered its stronghold" (p. 203). And Jane Addams (1902/2002), the first American woman to win the Nobel Peace Prize, exhorted, "we are impatient to use the dynamic power residing in the mass of men, and demand that the educator free that power" (p. 80).

Yet there's more than enlightenment to this idea of the person in civil society. This way of being in the world is based on ethical individualism. The idea of individualism had complex beginnings, and, truth be told, it's had a battered history. There is, however, a core set of themes around which the discourse of individualism forms. Steven Lukes (1973) gives us four: Essential to equality and liberty are

> respect for human dignity, autonomy, privacy and self-development . . . specifically, that the idea of human dignity or respect for persons lies at the heart of the idea of equality, while autonomy, privacy and self-development represent the three faces of liberty or freedom. (p. 125)

Modern individualism, then, is the "belief in the self as a bounded and integral agent, capable of conscious self-direction and self-control" (Gergen, 2000, p. 202).

While belief in individualism is still strong, our understanding of the individual has changed. The Enlightenment's idea of the person was based on the hope of incremental progress (the perfectibility of the mind) and the divine essence of the human self, which was most clearly articulated in the idea of natural or inalienable rights. The modern self, then, was present at birth, and the attributes of the self simply unfolded during the person's lifetime. But by the time we reached the early decades of the twentieth century, society and culture had changed. The abuses of capitalism had come to the fore (such as a two-decade long worldwide depression, forced labor, unsafe working conditions, robber barons, and so on); American manifest destiny and genocide had swept the North American continent; global slave trade culminated in an American Civil War; and the almost continuous war during the nineteenth century battered humanity and claimed countless lives around the globe. The incremental progress and perfectibility of the human condition weren't as easily assumed. Just as important in changing the idea of the person was the cultural impact of two scientific claims: Darwin's theory that the human species evolved from lower primates, and Freud's premise that there is within humankind an unconscious dynamic that is fueled by the primal desires of the id.

As a result of these social and cultural changes, the Enlightenment's idea of the intrinsic worth of the autonomous individual began to waver. In its stead, various versions of what Stuart Hall (1996a, p. 597) calls the "sociological subject" were proposed. The principal idea is that there is a necessary and symbiotic relationship between the person and society: Society creates the person through socialization, and people create society. It was George Herbert Mead who first and most clearly formulated this idea. The sociological subject forms a bridge between the individual and society, making the self intrinsically social rather than autonomous. However, the social nature of the self doesn't do away with reason, responsibility, and the possibilities of democracy. Quite the contrary, Mead (1932) argues that this view of the self is in fact a necessary precondition for democracy: "[D]emocracy, in the sense here relevant, is an attitude which depends upon the type of self which goes with the universal relations of brotherhood" (p. 286). This type of self recognizes that people are universally social—selves are reflections of society, and this in turn implies a "universal society" (p. 287).

According to Mead (1932), self and society are ongoing constructions that emerge out of the ideas and sentiments that people have formed as they moment by moment contend with the practical necessities of daily life. Other societies—other sets of attitudes—are simply, only, and precisely that: a group's way of meeting its members' physical, mental, and emotional needs. All societies are thus essentially the same; that is, the motivations and the way in which they are formed and continue to exist are identical, though the actual practices and meanings may be different. This pragmatic understanding of society and self opens the door for diverse groups coming together to form new wholes with new sets of attitudes, because all societies and selves are formed in precisely the same way. Thus, no social type or person has claim to natural superiority, an idea that had dominated early modernity and empowered Western imperialism and racism. The sociological subject undergirds a broadening base of acceptance. Or, as Mead (1932) puts it, "the individual maintains himself as a citizen only to the degree that he recognizes the rights of everyone else to belong to the same community" (p. 286).

In this section of the book, we are going to consider the contemporary self and its situations. We start with one of Mead's intellectual descendants, Herbert Blumer, in Chapter 3. He will explain how the sociological subject is capable of making decisions—we'll get a theoretical explanation of how it works—and he will also show us that the self is more an effect of language than anything else. In Chapter 4, Erving Goffman addresses something that has become increasingly important in contemporary society: the self-image. While Enlightenment thinkers undoubtedly had a self-image, there's no indication that they were particularly concerned with it. In contemporary society, however, self-image is one of the driving forces in our experience and expression of our self. In Chapter 5, Harold Garfinkel takes up Parsons's concern with social order, but he shows us that the situation, rather than institutions, is where social order is produced. In comparison to traditional or early modern society, much of our action is guided by what Max Weber called "instrumental rationality." This element in contemporary interactions is explained in Chapter 6: Social Exchanges.

We begin, then, by seeing how the way the self exists has changed from the Enlightenment and early modernity. These chapters, however, don't tell the entire tale. Because of the centrality of the individual to the projects of modernity, many of our other theorists play out some of the ramifications of structural and historical changes for the self. We will especially see this theme gain prominence in the last two parts of the book: Modernity—Possibilities and Problems, and Contemporary Political Identities.

CHAPTER 3

The Language of the Self

Herbert Blumer

Source: Reprinted with permission of the American Sociological Association.

One of the ideas of democracy that is often either overstated or undervalued is the ethical foundation upon which it is built. People seem to either be dogmatic about a particular form of religion that should form the base, or they seem to believe that any ethical or moral basis for democracy is dangerous. Many of the first sociologists would disagree with either extreme—a discourse of ethics was simply assumed by such researchers as Harriet Martineau and Alexis de Tocqueville, both of whom published in-depth analyses of American democracy in the beginning of the nineteenth century. Tocqueville considered religion to be one of the main ways that democracy is maintained in the United States. He referred to this influence more generally as "habits of the heart" and argued, "it is not so much that all citizens profess the true religion but that they profess a religion" (Tocqueville, 1835–1840/2002, p. 275, 278). Harriet Martineau (1837/2005, pp. 332–354) argued that there is a specific type of religion that best encourages democracy: Moderate religions emphasize the overall well-being of humanity through self-actualization and education, rather than doctrine and dogma. Martineau asserted that a society with a high level of this type of religion will have a culture that stresses freedom and true equality as well as broad-mindedness.

It's clear, then, that American democracy is founded on an ethical base—yet at the same time there is to be a separation between church and state. This separation wasn't intended to keep religion, ethics, and morals out of public life; it was intended to allow religion's contribution to public discussions to be democratic. In a democracy, power to govern flows from the people up. Religion, on the other hand, generally creates a theocracy, where power flows from the top down. Thus, if left alone or given a privileged voice, religion will tend to destroy democracy. We are left with the question, then, what is the source of democratic ethics and morals?

One answer to that question comes from **pragmatism,** the only philosophy born in the United States. After the Civil War, the nation was left bereft of a public philosophy: "The ideals that had served to buttress stable group life before 1861 became a casualty of that war" (Lyman & Vidich, 2000, p. 5). Out of a search to fill this gap, pragmatism was born. Pragmatism rejects the notion that there are any fundamental truths and instead proposes that *truth* is relative to time, place, and purpose. Pragmatism is thus "an idea about ideas" and a way of relativizing ideology (Menand, 2001, p. xi), but this relativizing doesn't result in relativism. In fact, pragmatism is founded upon clear and strong ethical beliefs. However, rather than these ethics being based in some outside, preexisting force or system, *the ethical basis of pragmatism* is the belief in human reason and consensus. Thus, truth, ethics, and morality in pragmatism are specific to community: Human action and decisions aren't determined or forced by society, ideology, or preexisting truths. Rather, decisions and ethics emerge out of a consensus that develops through interaction.

Rooted in pragmatism, "Blumer's sociology encapsulates a public philosophy that is neither shrouded in the metaphysical mysteries of historical process nor placed beyond the capacity of individuals—or their elected and appointed officials—to determine and direct" (Lyman & Vidich, 2000, p. 6). Blumer lived and worked during a time in which major shifts occurred in the fabric of American society. As a result of the Great Depression of the 1930s, the government ended laissez-faire capitalism and began a program of state intervention in the economy (Keynesian economics) and a social safety net for its citizens (the welfare state). Blumer's theoretical concerns were also informed by the newly established mass media and the crystallization of the mass society. While certainly not as drastic as the Civil War, the United States experienced a time of upheaval and reassessment. And, as you would expect, sociology responded to these massive changes with a number of theoretical explanations and intense data collection and analyses, all designed to increase our understanding of what was going on. However, in his search for answers, Blumer became an "ardent critic of all the major traditions of sociological reasoning"

(Plummer, 1998, p. 84). His critique was twofold: He argued that sociology had both reified its concepts and reduced the lived experiences of people to objective measurements. In order to formulate this critique, Blumer (1969) relied "chiefly on the thought of George Herbert Mead" (p. 1).

THEORIST'S DIGEST

Brief Biography

Herbert Blumer was born on March 7, 1900, in St. Louis, Missouri. He completed his PhD at the University of Chicago in 1928; his dissertation was titled "Methods in Social Psychology." Blumer was on the faculty at Chicago from 1927 to 1952, during which time he also played professional football, interviewed gang members, and mediated labor disputes. In 1952, Blumer moved to the University of California at Berkeley to chair its new Department of Sociology. Blumer edited one of sociology's premier journals, the *American Journal of Sociology,* from 1940 to 1952, and was president of the American Sociological Association (ASA) in 1955. He is best known for his book *Symbolic Interactionism: Perspective and Method* (1969), which systematized sociology's main school of social psychology; Blumer received the ASA's Career of Distinguished Scholarship Award in 1983. He passed away on April 13, 1987.

Central Sociological Questions

Blumer's primary concern was to ground sociology in the real, empirical world of human action. Thus, his main question is a simple yet powerful one: What is the most empirically real thing that people do? As Lyman and Vidich (2000) argue, there was a deeper concern that motivated this question: "Blumer presents us with the problem of finding the locus of civic virtue in the modern state" (p. 101). Behind his question about sociological theory and methods was this more significant issue: What is the basis of a democratic public philosophy?

Simply Stated

The human world is utterly symbolic, meaningful, and thus an emergent quality of the interaction. People interpret meaning through the mind and self in order to control behavior pragmatically. Both the mind and self are created through language acquisition and three stages of role-taking: play, game, and generalized other. Because human reality is symbolic, the most empirically available site for sociological investigation is the interaction. Society, then, is built up through joint actions, rather than existing as objective structures.

Key Ideas

Pragmatism, meaning, interaction, social objects, self, role-taking, generalized other, joint action, problem of reification

Concepts and Theory: Emergent Meanings

In systematizing symbolic interaction, Blumer (1969) gives us three premises upon which it is built:

> Humans act toward things on the basis of the meanings . . . the meaning of such things is derived from, or arises out of the social interaction that one has . . . these meanings are handled in, and modified through, an interpretative process used by the person in dealing with the things he encounters. (p. 2)

You'll notice that the central concept in these three tenets is *meaning*. In focusing on meaning, Blumer is actually basing his argument on an idea about human nature. As Snow and Anderson (1993) explain, "All animals are confronted with the challenge of material subsistence, but only humans are saddled with the vexing question of its meaning" (p. 230).

Meaning and Human Nature

But what is the meaning of *meaning?* It's an odd question, isn't it? At first glance, it looks like a play on words, kind of like, "How much wood could a woodchuck chuck?" But it isn't a play on words; it's a serious question that has an answer. Asking it in the form that I did helps to point out something significant about the answer. *Webster's* (1983) defines meaning as "1. that which exists in the mind . . . [and] 2. that which is intended to be, or in fact is, conveyed, denoted, signified, or understood by acts or language" (p. 1115). We're going to put the first definition aside for the moment and concentrate on the second. Meaning is something that is conveyed, denoted, or signified by acts, words, or objects. Notice what meaning *isn't*: Meaning isn't the act, word, experience, or object. By definition, meaning isn't the thing itself, whatever that thing might be.

Let's use a powerful example to see this: Think about one person killing another person. The important thing for our purposes isn't the actual act or the fact that a person's life has ended; it's the context in which the killing takes place. Killing can be war, or terrorism, or accidental homicide, or suicide, or religious sacrifice, or first-degree murder, or execution as a punishment for first-degree murder—killing can be legitimate or morally wrong, depending on its meaning context. Human life doesn't matter, in and of itself; it's the context that matters. You might remember the 1995 movie *Apollo 13,* staring Tom Hanks. When the actual event occurred, in April of 1970, the eyes of the entire world were on the three men trapped in that spacecraft. America watched the catastrophe in horror and had heartfelt concern for the lives of those three Americans—while at the same time hundreds if not thousands of people were being killed or maimed in Vietnam by American servicemen. Life itself doesn't matter; what matters is the meaning we give it.

But why do we place such importance on meaning? Why can't human beings get away from meaning? Why is it fundamental to our nature? The first part of the answer is that humans are utterly and completely social. Being social is how we as a species exist. Every species is defined by its method of survival or existence. Why are whales, lions, and hummingbirds all different? They are different because they have different ways of existing in the world. What makes human beings different from whales, lions, and hummingbirds? Humans have a different mode of existence.

But being social is only part of the answer. There are a number of species that exist socially, like ants and bees, so what makes humans different from them? It is the magnitude of our sociability, and, more importantly, the way in which we create our social bonds. Most other social species instinctually create social bonds through a variety of things such as scent, physical spacing, and so on. Humans use symbols to create meaningful social bonds and culture. Granted, there are some species that have a kind and degree of culture, but no other animal uses culture to the extent that humans do—and no other species uses symbols.

We are primarily built for and oriented toward using signs and symbols. Culture and language are the reasons we have the brain structure we do; culture is the reason we have our particular kind of vocal structures; culture is why we have the kind of hands we do—culture is the defining feature of humanity. Meaning lifts out the object from its rooted existence in time and space. This move of abstraction or transcendence is necessary for us to be conscious, to interact, to have a self, and to have society. We will revisit this notion of meaning throughout the book (after all, it is basic to human nature and society). So, keep this idea on the front burner so you can add to it as we go along.

Interactions and Emergent Meanings

This brings us to Blumer's second premise: If meaning isn't in the object, word, language, or event, then where is it? The quote above from *Webster's* says that meaning exists in the mind. However, as with most everything in a society infatuated with the individual, that definition is only partially correct. The individualized definition also lines up with an important philosophical school of thought: idealism. Idealism and realism are two sides in the philosophical debate about reality (ontology or metaphysics) and knowledge (epistemology). To even begin to scratch the surface of this debate would take much more time and text than we have (philosophers have been debating these issues for over 2,000 years), but we really don't need to. Symbolic interaction teaches us that in our day-to-day life, we are not at all interested in ontology or epistemology. Meaning for humans is a pragmatic issue.

In pragmatism, ideas and meanings are organizational instruments. That is, humans organize their behaviors based on ideas. Meaning, then, is a tool for action, and it has value to us only insofar as it facilitates behavior. Pragmatism argues that people hold onto what works, and what works is the only truth that endures for humans. In true pragmatic form, symbolic interactionism argues that meaning is found only in people's behaviors and that meaning emerges out of social interaction in response to adaptive concerns. Thus, the meaning of any idea, moral, word, symbol, or object is pragmatically determined, or determined by its practical use. Thus, while meaning comes to be in the mind, it is produced and exists within pragmatically emergent social interactions—that which is in the mind is only a residue of these social interactions. In fact, this move from the social to the individual is the only basis upon which we can share meanings.

Seeing meaning in pragmatic terms implies that meaning is defined and redefined in an ongoing manner as we interact with one another. As we would assume, symbolic interactionism has a very specific definition of interaction: It is the ongoing negotiation and melding together of individual actions. There are three distinct steps that must occur before we can say that there is **interaction.** First, an initial cue is given, but the cue itself doesn't carry any specific meaning. Let's say you see a person crying in the halls at school. What does it mean? It could mean lots of things. In order to determine—or, more properly, achieve—meaning, there has to be a response to the cue: "Is everything all right?" Yet we still don't have meaning. There must be a response to the response. After the three phases (cue, response, and response to the response), a meaning emerges: "Nothing's wrong. My boyfriend just asked me to marry him!"

We probably still aren't done, because the woman's response has become yet another cue. What does that cue mean? We can't tell until you respond to her cue and she responds to your response. This process is how meaning emerges from the interaction. Meaning results from the back-and-forth negotiation over a symbolic object. Thus, we cannot tell until after the interaction is completed what the different social objects meant to the people involved. And we may not even be done then. Quite often, we take the meaning of one interaction and make it a cue in another interaction.

Symbols and Social Objects

While meanings are negotiated through interaction, the negotiation takes place around known social objects that are indicated in an interaction; you probably wouldn't have noticed the person crying if "crying" wasn't a social object. These social objects and their symbolic meanings provide initial stimulus and orientation for interaction. In fact, social objects are our primary stimulus for action. Of course, it is possible for a physical object to provide motivation, like when a rock falls on your hand. But something truly amazing happens not long after the rock hits you—you turn both it and the pain into social objects.

To really understand the issue behind symbols and social objects, let's consider natural signs. A *sign* is something that stands for something else, like smoke stands for fire. So, if we see smoke coming out of a room, we will call and report a fire, even though we may never actually see the fire. It appears that many animals can use signs, but their ability to do so varies. For instance, a dog and a chicken will respond differently to the presence of a feed bowl on the other side of a fence. The chicken will simply pace back and forth in front of the fence in aggravation, but the dog will seek a break in the fence, go through the break, and run back to the bowl and eat. The chicken appears to be able to respond directly to only one stimulus, where the dog is able to hold his response to the food at bay while he seeks an alternative. This ability to hold responses at bay is important for higher-level thinking animals.

These signs that we've been talking about may be called *natural signs*. They are private and learned through the individual experience of each animal. So, if your dog gets excited at the sound of the treat box, it is because of the dog's individual experience with it—other dogs didn't tell your dog about the treat box. There also tends to be a natural relationship between the sign and its object, and these signs occur apart from the agency of the animal. In other words, your dog didn't make the association between the sound of the box and her treats; you did. Thus, in the absolute sense, the relationship between the sound and the treat isn't a true natural sign. Natural signs come out of the natural experiences of the animal, and the meaning of these signs is determined by a structured relationship between the sign and its object.

Humans, on the other hand, have the ability to use what symbolic interactionists call *significant gestures, symbols,* or *social objects.* In contrast to natural signs, social objects can be abstract and arbitrary. With natural signs, the relationship between the sign and its referent is natural (as with smoke and fire), whereas symbolic meaning can be quite abstract and completely arbitrary (in terms of naturally given relations). For example, the year 2013 doesn't exist in the physical world. What year it is depends on what calendar is used, and the different calendars are associated with political and religious issues, not nature (for examples, look up the Chinese and Muslim calendars on the Internet). Social objects are also reflexive, calling out the same response in the person speaking and listening. For example, I may call you up and say, "Tomorrow is Monday." Chances are that neither one of us will be happy about that situation. But while Monday is a social object and thus reflexive, it is also subject to interaction. Thus, Monday becomes something totally different when I add, "and all classes are cancelled." Symbols, then, are verbal and nonverbal signals that convey meaning, require interpretation, and are reciprocal.

According to symbolic interactionists, the meaning that a symbol or social object cues is its set of organized responses or possible actions. In other words, symbolic meaning is not the image of a thing seen at a distance, nor does it exactly correspond to the dictionary definition; rather, the meaning of a word is the *action* that it calls out. For example, the meaning of a chair is the different kinds of things we can do with it. Picture a wooden object with four legs, a seat, and a slatted back. If I sit down on this object, then the meaning of it is "chair." On the other hand, if I take that same object and break it into small pieces and use it to start a fire, it's no longer a chair—it's kindling. So the meaning of an object is defined in terms of its uses, or legitimated lines of behavior, which in turn arise from social interactions.

Because the meaning, legitimated actions, and objective availability (they are objects because we can point them out as foci for interaction) of symbols are produced in social interactions, they are social objects. Any idea or thing can be a social object. Natural features such as the Great Smoky Mountains, invisible things like ghosts, and ideas like freedom can all be social objects. There is nothing about the thing itself that makes it a social object; an entity becomes a social object to us through our interactions around it. Through interaction, we call attention to it, name it, and attach legitimate lines of behavior to it.

If you look around the room you are sitting in, everything you notice is a social object. In fact, there is a profound way in which people only see and relate to social objects. Human reality is constituted symbolically; it's a symbolic world, not a physical one, filled with social objects rather than physical objects. But can we notice things that aren't social objects? Yes, we can, but if we do, the object will be a problem for us to respond to because we won't know the meaning of the thing—note that the response itself becomes a social object (running from an unknown danger, investigating an unidentified entity, and so on).

Concepts and Theory: Self and Action

We now come to Blumer's (1969) third premise of symbolic interaction: "Meanings are handled in, and modified through, an interpretative process used by the person in dealing with the things he encounters" (p. 2). Chances are good that the first two premises contained some ideas that you found surprising—most people don't consider the meaning of meaning. Chances are also good that the subject of this third premise is something you feel comfortable with—most people have a commonsense understanding of what a "person" or "individual" is. However, you might be surprised at Blumer's understanding of the person. We just finished talking about how meanings are created and interpreted socially, through the ongoing, three-phase process of social interaction. According to Blumer's school of symbolic interaction, the individual does it in the exact same way. In other words, the person—or, more properly, the self—engages in an internal symbolic interaction through which meaning emerges. Now think about this: A conversation takes place between two or more people. So, who are these people in your head, and where did they come from?

Creating the Self

One of the difficulties confronting social and behavioral scientists is that our subject matter is generally something we all take for granted. It isn't like a physicist talking about atoms or quantum mechanics. We don't see such things on a daily basis. The self, on the other hand, is a normal part of our lives. We tend to take it for granted and don't feel it needs explanation. So, we have to in some way problematize the self; we have to ask you to think about the self and not take it for granted. The easiest way to do this might be to ask you to imagine talking to a friend about somebody else. In talking to your friend, you can point to the other person because he or she is a social object that exists outside of you. Blumer argues that the same is true about your self, except the conversation happens inside you. You talk to yourself about your self as if it were a social object, a thing existing outside of you in some way.

There is a way, then, in which the self doesn't live in the here and now; that is, the self is a transcendent thing that does not exist in the immediacy of experience. By definition, the self must exist outside of our direct experience. It is this ability to not be in the moment that allows us to monitor our behavior and produce society. The mind considers immediate behavior with reference to a mental object (the self) that is made up of selected images from the past and hoped-for images of the future. Thus, our conscious experience is predicated upon our being able to achieve a perspective divorced from the constraints of time. What this implies is that the self is a perspective—it is a symbolic platform on which to stand and view our own behaviors as if someone else were performing them.

The question, then, is where does this other self come from? How can part of us not be fixed in time, living in the moment? How can we get outside and watch ourselves? The self is a social achievement that comes through language, interaction, and most specifically through role-taking. **Role-taking** has a very specific definition: It is the process through which we place our self in the position (or role) of another in order to see our own self. Students often confuse role-taking with what might be called role-*making*. In every social situation, we make a role for ourselves. Erving Goffman (Chapter 4) wrote at length about this process and called it impression management. Role-taking is a precursor to effective role-making—we put ourselves in the position of the other in order to see how he or she wants us to act. But role-taking is distinct from impression management, and it is the main mechanism through which we are able to form a perspective outside of ourselves.

As children, we role-take through three successive stages: play, game, and generalized other. The first stage in the process of self-formation is the **play stage.** During this stage, the child can take the role, or assume the perspective, of certain significant others. Significant others are those upon whom we depend for emotional and often material support. These are the people with whom we have long-term relations and intimate (self-revealing) ties. This is called the play stage because children must literally play at being some significant other in order to see themselves. At this point, they haven't progressed much in terms of being able to think abstractly, so they must act out the role to get the perspective. Here is the important point: In order to play like this, a child must literally get outside of himself or herself.

Children play at being the mommy or being the teacher. The child will hold a doll or stuffed bear and talk to it as if she were the parent. Ask any parent; it can be a frightening experience because what you are faced with is an almost exact imitation of your own behaviors, words, and even tone of voice. It might be unnerving for the parent, but this is serious play. The child is learning to see him or her own self. So, as the child is playing Mommy or Daddy with a teddy bear, who is the bear? The child herself. She is seeing herself from the point of view of the parent, literally. This act is the origin of the *divorced* perspective that we call self. It is the genesis of the objective stance—being able to get outside of ourselves so that we can watch ourselves as if onstage.

The next stage in the development of self is the **game stage.** During this stage, the child can take the perspective of several others and can take into account the rules (sets of responses that different attitudes bring out) of society. But the role-taking at this stage is still not very abstract. In the play stage, the child could only take the perspective of a single significant other; in the game stage, the child can take on several others, but they all remain individuals. Take the example of a baseball game. The batter can role-take with each individual player in the field and determine how to bat based on their behaviors. The batter is also aware of all the rules of the game. Children at this stage can role-take with several people, and they are very concerned with social rules. But they still don't have a fully formed self. That doesn't happen until they can take the perspective of the generalized other.

The **generalized other** refers to sets of attitudes that an individual may take toward himself or herself—it is the general attitude or perspective of a community.

The generalized other allows the individual to have a more nonsegmented self as the perspectives of many others are generalized into a single view. It is through the generalized other that the community exercises control over the conduct of its individual members. Up until this point, the child has only been able to role-take with specific others. As the individual progresses in her ability to use abstract language and concepts, she is also able to think about general or abstract others. So, for example, a man in the privacy of his home may think, "If the guys at the gym could see what a couch potato I am at home, they'd die." Or a woman may look in the mirror and judge the reflection by the general image given to her by the media about how a woman should look. There are no specific people involved, but we are able to see our self through the eyes of some generalized other, and we talk to ourselves about it.

Part of what we mean by the self is this internalized conversation. We carry on an internal dialogue about who we are, what we are doing, where we are going, what the world means, and so on. This conversation is between the two parts of the self (the observer and the actor). Symbolic interactionism calls these two interactive facets of the self the "I" and the "Me." The Me is the self that results from the progressive stages of role-taking and is treated as a social object—it is that part of our self that observes our behaviors. The Me doesn't fully come into existence until we are able to role-take with the generalized other. The Me, then, is the perspective that we assume in order to view and analyze our own behaviors; the I is that part of the self that is unsocialized and spontaneous.

Notice what I just said: The self is an internalized conversation between the I and the Me. And what do we already know about conversations and interactions? They are emergent. You and I may have a good idea of what we are going to talk about when we get together at the bar, but there's also a good chance that we'll end up talking about things we couldn't have imagined. Conversations shift and change, and meanings emerge through this negotiated interaction. The same is true for the self. The self doesn't exist in any one place. It is a social object (something we give meaning to) that emerges through ongoing, internalized conversations and social interactions (role-taking). During the internalized interaction, it is specifically the I that makes the process emergent. The I is the actor, and it can act apart from the Me, apart from the perspective given by the generalized other.

The Language of the Self

This theory of the self not only explains how we become a social object to our self—how we become separate from our own actions—but it also tells us something about how the self exists. Notice that the self is an internal conversation: It exists in and through the use of language. To emphasize this point, Mead (1934) says that "the self is not something that exists first and then enters into relationship with others, but it is, so to speak, an eddy in the social current and so still a part of the current" (p. 26). Eddies are currents of air or water that run contrary to the stream. It isn't so much the contrariness that Mead wants us to see, but the fact that an eddy only exists in and because of its surrounding current. The same is true for selves: They only exist in and because of social interaction. The self doesn't have a continuous existence; it isn't something that we carry around inside of us. It's a mechanism that allows conversations and action to happen, whether that conversation occurs in the social situation or within the individual.

A contemporary theorist, R. S. Perinbanayagam (2000), elaborates this idea of the linguistic self. The conversational or discursive nature of the self implies that people use *rhetorical devices* in interactions to be seen and noticed. *Webster's* (1983) defines rhetoric as "the art or science of using words effectively in speaking or writing, so as to influence or persuade" (p. 1555). The use of rhetorical devices with the self, then, implies that people use particular ways of communicating in order to make the self felt, present, known, and in some ways indisputable to others. Perinbanayagam gives us three rhetorical modes the self uses: the reflexive process, addressive process, and process. The *reflexive process* is basic to the self and communication in general. Every act of the self is reflexive in that it involves an internalized conversation between the I and the Me. People are also reflexive in the sense that they track the acts of others "as *expressions* and *indices* of the other's attitudes in order to organize one's own self" (p. 55).

The addressive and answerability processes are the specific ways in which we present a self in the dialogic act. *Addressive processes* are ways of addressing someone. Easy examples are such titles as Mrs., Mr., Professor, and so forth. However, Perinbanayagam intends for us to understand addressive processes more generally and symbolically. For example, when I interact with the dean of my college, my entire demeanor, including the way I talk to him, addresses him as "dean," whether or not I actually use the term. Moreover, in addressing others, we also address our self. Each form of address denotes a different kind of self and has a dialogue or discourse that goes along with it. When I address my dean as dean, it implies a specific kind of person for me to be, one situated in the authority hierarchy of the college. We can do this with a third party as well. For example, I once gave a presentation at another university and in a particular part of that talk I referred to my wife. But I didn't refer to her, or, in Perinbanayagam's terms, address her as "wife"; I called her "my partner." My wife wasn't at the talk, but because I referred to her and addressed her in a specific manner, she became a significant other that was present in the act for the other people. After the talk, a lesbian graduate student came up and asked if I was married. I said, "Yes," and she replied, "You called your wife the right thing. I'm impressed." For the graduate student, "wife" is part of the hetero-normative discourse of gender. In using a different term, I stepped out of that discourse and was seen as a specific kind of person, at least in the eyes of that graduate student. So, in addressing my partner, I also addressed myself and created a specific image in the minds of the people listening.

Once addressed, selves may be answered or unanswered. When we put a particular kind of self or other into play, we risk not being answered as such. Using my talk example, if I had addressed my spouse as "wife" instead of "partner," I would have been seen differently, and that specific part of my self would not have been answered by that specific woman after the talk. How the self is answered or not answered is vitally important. In their study of the homeless, David Snow and Leon

Anderson (1993) quite clearly point out the power involved in answered and unanswered selves. The homeless are constantly putting a self into play that is unanswered. As a result, "to be homeless in America is not only to have fallen to the bottom of the status system; it is also to be confronted with gnawing doubts about self-worth and the meaning of existence" (p. 199).

This point concerning the answered and unanswered selves is, perhaps, even more important than it might seem. Perinbanayagam (2000) says that one of the principal reasons for conversation is it "*enables the individual to objectify himself or herself as well as enables the other to objectify himself or herself*" (p. 189). In fact, as Jonathan H. Turner (1988) claims, "The most central of these [motivations in interaction] is the need to sustain a self-concept" (p. 61). In other words, one of the most important reasons we engage in conversation is because we need to present a self that is answered and thus confirmed by others. In an interesting analysis of a conversation at a book club, Perinbanayagam notes that "it really didn't matter what novel they talked about, so long as they . . . gathered and discussed something and *gave presence to their selves*" (p. 195, emphasis added).

In addition to addressive processes, the self is involved in *answerability processes*. We've just talked about the answered and unanswered self, but Perinbanayagam (2000) has something else in mind with answerability processes, so be certain to keep them separate. While the concept of the answered and unanswered self is about the response others give to the presented self, answerability processes are part of the way an individual puts a self in play. Answerability refers to the obligation we have to the self we present. For example, if I present myself as a professor, I am answerable or obligated to the expectations that go along with such a self. Perinbanayagam's point is that we choose the way in which we present a self—in some ways of self presentation the answerability is clear, but in others it is not. A good example of the lack of clarity in answerability is when people dress androgynously and don't make a clear claim to a gender identity. This ambiguous answerability makes others uncomfortable because they don't know how to "answer" that person's gender. Because of this reciprocal link between selves that are put into play, Perinbanayagam concludes that making a self clearly answerable "confers a 'gift' on the other, making it an act of grace; the other can thereby understand what has been put forward and resolve—however tentatively—the mystery of the other, appreciate it, and answer it" (p. 67).

The linguistic and interactive nature of the self implies that "human agents bring both *artistry* (the intentional use of form and shape, order, and discipline) and *artfulness* (connecting method to purpose) to their performances" (Perinbanayagam, 2003, p. 78). As we'll see with Goffman, we manage the impressions we give to others. This is because we are principally oriented toward meaning. Because meaning isn't intrinsic, we have freedom to paint the canvas of life and reality any way we choose. Yet that absolute freedom of agency is tempered by the demands of dialogue and sensibility. Our art must make sense to those who view it; it must communicate to and enter into a dialogue with others. The way in which we do that becomes our style, our individuated self. "For one's life to become a work of art, for it to develop 'style,' an individual must be able to take control and fashion a self that conformed to the exacting demands of an artistry and an aesthetic" (Perinbanayagam, 2000, p. 33).

Yet the purpose of this expression isn't simply individualistic. Symbols, language, and dialogic acts are ways through which we persuade others to cooperate in our expression of self in the world. The art of selfhood thus inevitably asks others, both people and physical things, to bend to and support our expression in the world. Because of these intrinsic connections, a dialogic act is "capable of inducing an ethical dimension into it" (Perinbanayagam, 2000, p. 5). When we act, when we make our self present, we invariably insert our values and realities into the social and physical worlds around us. Because of the time period in which we live, this ethical dimension of action falls more squarely upon us as individuals than ever before. In traditional societies, and even early modern societies, there were fewer choices and fewer realities from which to choose. There were more and clearer guidelines, but people knew less of the consequences of choice. The politics of choice are more real today than ever before.

Social Action

So, why do you have a self? Symbolic interactionism teaches us that the self is created; it isn't something we're born with. In fact, there isn't anything within us as individuals that makes it natural or imperative that we have a self. Don't get me wrong, obviously there are internal preconditions that make the self possible and that predispose us toward having a self. But if it were possible for a human baby to grow to adulthood apart from society, that person wouldn't have, nor would he or she need, a self. In fact, in such a state the self would be a liability. Why? Because the self is not an intrinsic characteristic of the individual; it is a social entity. What we see from symbolic interactionism is that the self functions to control our behaviors—it allows us to act rather than react. A person who had lived alone for his or her entire existence would need to react instinctually to situations rather than respond to their social meaning. Thinking about the social ramifications of some action would slow the beast down and make it vulnerable. Thus, the self is mandated socially, not individually, so that we can act rather than react.

Blumer's symbolic interactionism argues that the act contains four distinct elements: impulse, perception, manipulation, and consummation (behavior). We feel an impulse to behave: We are hungry, tired, or angry. For most animals, the route from impulse to behavior is rather direct—they react to the stimulus using instincts or behavioristically imprinted patterns. But for humans, it is a circuitous route. After we feel the initial impulse to act, we perceive our environment. This perception entails the recognition of the pertinent symbolic elements (including other people, absent reference groups, and so on) as well as alternatives to satisfying the impulse. Perception is the all-important pause before action; this is where society becomes possible. After we symbolically take in our environment, we manipulate the different elements. This manipulation takes place in the mind and considers the possible ramifications of using different behaviors to satisfy the impulse. We role-take with significant present and generalized others, and we think about the elements available to complete the task. After we manipulate the situation symbolically, we are in a position to act.

Notice how much of human action takes place in the mind. In fact, we could say that all the action that is distinctly human takes place in the mind. What I mean by that is that all animals have impulses and all animals behave. Those are the first and last stages of the act. What makes action distinctly human are the middle two stages—perception and manipulation—both of which take place in the mind. And, guess what? The mind is social too. According to symbolic interactionists, the **mind** is a kind of behavior that involves at least five different abilities:

1. To use symbols to denote objects

2. To use a symbol as its own stimulus (it can talk to itself)

3. To read and interpret another's gestures and use them as further stimuli

4. To suspend response (not act out of impulse)

5. To imaginatively rehearse one's own behaviors before actually behaving

Let me give you an example that encompasses all these behaviors. A few years ago, our school paper ran a cartoon. In it was a picture of three people: a man and a woman arm-in-arm, and another man. The woman was introducing the men to one another. Both men were reaching out to shake one another's hands. But above the single man was a balloon of his thoughts. In it, he was picturing himself violently punching the other man. He wanted to hit the man, but he shook his hand instead and said, "Glad to meet you."

There are a lot of things we can pull out of this cartoon, but the issue we want to focus on is the disparity between what the man felt and what the man did. He had an impulse to hit the other man, perhaps because he was jealous. But he didn't. Why didn't he? Actually, that isn't a good theoretical question. Theoretically we would ask, how was he able to stop his initial impulse? He was able to not hit the other man because of his mind. His mind was able to block his initial impulse, to understand the situation symbolically, to point out to his self the symbols and possible meanings, to entertain alternative lines of behavior, and to choose the behavior that best fit the situation. The man used social objects to stimulate his own behavior rather than going with his impulse.

The mind is something that we acquire, or, more correctly, it is a set of behaviors that we learn. Infant dependency, language, and interactions are the preconditions for the formation of the mind. Human babies are completely dependent upon their parents for survival, more so and for longer periods of time than other species. They are thus forced to interact with others in already organized social environments. When babies are hungry or tired or wet, they send out what are called "unconventional gestures," gestures that do not mean the same to the sender and hearer. In other words, they cry. The caregivers must figure out what the baby needs. After they have discovered this, parents tend to vocalize their behaviors ("Oh, did Susie need a ba-ba?"). Babies eventually discover that if they mimic the parents and send out a significant gesture ("ba-ba"), they get their needs met sooner. This is the beginning of language acquisition; babies begin to understand that their environment is symbolic—the object that satisfies hunger is "ba-ba," and the object that brings it is "da-da." Eventually, a baby will understand that she has a symbol as well: "Susie." Thus, language acquisition allows the child to symbolize and eventually to symbolically manipulate her environment, including the self and others. Notice, the mind is social through and through.

Concepts and Theory: Society and Sociology

Generally speaking, sociologists see society as a macro-level entity that operates according to its own laws. One of the clearest explanations of this approach was given to us by Émile Durkheim. Durkheim argues that society exists *sui generis*—a Latin term meaning "of its own kind." Durkheim (1912/1995) uses the term to say that society exists in and of itself, not as a "mere epiphenomenon of its morphological base" (p. 426). When Durkheim uses the term "morphological base," he's referring to the people that live in society. In other words, society is more than simply the sum of all the individuals within it. Society exists as its own kind of entity, obeying its own rules and creating its own effects: "*The determining cause of a social fact should be sought among the social facts preceding it and not among the states of the individual consciousness*" (Durkheim, 1895/1938, p. 110). This view also argues that society is "endowed with a power of coercion, by reason of which they control [the person]" (p. 3).

Joint Actions

A good portion of sociology, then, is concerned with these macro-level structures that control or influence human action. This is precisely the kind of sociology of which Blumer is critical. Blumer gives us another way to see how society works and is formed—the **joint action:** interactions that are woven together as a whole. Let's take my graduate theory class for an example. I'm writing this paragraph in November. In about 6 weeks, I'll be standing in front of my graduate students. Between now and then, I will have written out my syllabus, sent it to the enrolled students, and given them their first reading assignment. They will perform whatever interactions necessary to obtain the books ("talk to Mom and Dad," "get financial aid," "drive to the bookstore," "buy the books," and so on). We'll have 15 class meetings, each of which is a separate joint action during which several unexpected ideas, conflicts, and relationships will emerge.

We will then link these class meetings together through the use of tests, papers, and discussions about theses, classes, ideas, and graduation. Those linkages will themselves be linked to other courses at the university (prerequisites and the like). All of these will be linked together through various kinds of interactions, like theses defenses and graduation ceremonies. All of those joint actions will be linked to the history of interactions and joint actions that have occurred at the place where one of the students will apply for a job or for further graduate work, and on and on, ad infinitum. For Blumer, most of what we mean by "society," then, exists in recurring patterns of joint action, all of which emerge and are not determined by an external social structure.

At every point of interaction or joint action, there is uncertainty. All human action has to be purposefully initiated, and we may or may not act. Once begun, actions, interactions, and joint actions can be interrupted, changed, or abandoned. Even during the course of an interaction, participants may have different definitions of what is going on. If there is a common definition, there still may be differences in the way each interaction is carried out: An individual may perform his lines of action differently; changes can impose themselves on the interaction in such a way as to make people define and lean upon one another differently. In addition, new situations may arise that call into question the ways things have been done in the past. Symbolic interactionism thus shifts the question of patterned behaviors from the structure to the interaction. It entertains the possibility that each interaction and joint action could be different, and it grants freedom of choice to the participants.

There are a few things to note about joint actions. First, joint actions are created as we link together various interactions. The nature of interactions lies in the way in which we intertwine the many actions that create the interaction (I hear my friend introduce you, you look at me and I look at you, I give my "nice to meet you" smile and extend my hand, you see my hand as it is extending and you extend your hand, our hands meet and we judge the firmness of the grip and carefully match what we are given, and so forth—or, we do something totally different so that it becomes a contest). The same is true of joint actions, except there we link together multiple interactions.

Second, joint actions may be spoken of as such. They stand as identifiable units to us, which is why I put quotation marks in my description of obtaining class books. We see them as distinct yet joined together—"driving to the bookstore" and "buying books" are separate actions and interactions, yet we link them together into the joint action of getting ready for school. And, third, each of the interactions and joint actions must be created anew each time it is produced. For example, weddings are not simply expressions of a causal social structure called marriage. The structure of norms, values, and beliefs doesn't determine the wedding; the people whose wedding it is do, which is why your elaborate ceremony and my barefoot event at the beach can both happen and qualify as weddings. A wedding is a repetitive and stable form of joint action, yet it is fresh and creative each time it is achieved.

Sociology

The question of whether or not society is empirical is an issue we will visit again and again in this book. The issue is important because the possibility of sociology being a science is determined by it. Many sociologists assume that society exists empirically in its structures and institutions. Not so for symbolic interactionism: Blumer (1969) argues that "the essence of society lies in an ongoing process of action—not in a posited structure of relations" (p. 71). In what way, then, does symbolic interactionism see sociology as empirical and scientific? To begin our discussion, Blumer lists six characteristics of empirical, scientific inquiry:

1. Scientific inquiry uses theory. Scientific theory is a formal and logically sound argument explaining some empirical phenomenon in general or abstract terms.

2. Theory is used to decide the kinds of questions that are asked.

3. Theory shapes what data are relevant, and how the data will be collected and tested.

4. Propositions are born out of theory: Theory informs the kinds of relationships among and between the variables that are to be tested.

5. The data are interpreted and brought back to change, modify, or confirm theory.

6. All theory and scientific research are based on concepts. Concepts are the basic building blocks of theory. They inform the way questions are asked, they are the source of data categories (sought and grouped), they form the relationships among and between the data, and they are the chief way in which the data are interpreted.

Blumer's main point is that each part of this procedure, particularly the concepts that are used, must be scrutinized to make certain it conforms to the empirical world that is being studied. Blumer contends that this examination doesn't usually occur in the social and psychological sciences. More often than not, what sociologists and psychologists study are reified concepts of the world rather than the social world itself. Here the word *reified* means to convert an idea into something concrete or objective. The problem of **reification** is rampant in the social and behavioral sciences, according to Blumer. The two most notable examples are "attitudes" in psychology and "structures or institutions" in sociology. Neither of these concepts has a "clear and fixed empirical reference" (Blumer, 1969, p. 91), yet both are seen as having some causal force in determining human behavior.

Obviously, the issue of most concern for us is the critique that social structures are not empirical. Many sociologists see social structures as connections among sets of positions that form a network. The interrelated sets of positions in society are generally defined in terms of status positions, roles, and norms. These social and cultural elements create and manage the connections among people, and it is the connections that form the structure. Social structures are used to explain patterned behavior. Patterned behavior in most other animals is seen as the result of instincts or naturally embedded mechanisms, like seasonal change. On the other hand, a social structure is generally seen as that which "accounts for much of the . . . patterns of human experience and behavior" (Johnson, 2000, p. 295).

Yet Blumer says there's a problem in attributing causal influence to social structures: Social structures aren't empirical. The only empirical social thing we can point to are real people interacting with one another. According to Blumer (1969), anytime we appeal to psychological or social structures as the impetus behind human behavior, "the human being becomes a mere medium through which such initiating factors operate to produce given actions" (p. 73). Based on this view, most social and behavioral scientists do not investigate empirical objects. It follows that if most of what they are looking at isn't empirical, then they aren't doing science. Thus, focusing on the interaction is the only possible way to create a social or behavioral science.

There are at least four methodological ramifications of Blumer's argument. First, to state the obvious, an empirical science needs to investigate empirical phenomena. Blumer argues that most of what passes as social or behavioral science is not empirical because most "social scientists" have not critiqued the reified concepts they are using to create theory, propose relationships, gather and analyze data, and interpret findings. As Blumer (1969) says, "Reality exists in the empirical world and not in the methods used to study that world" (p. 27).

Second, we need to understand social interaction as a moving process. Many sociological perspectives understand society in terms of one central form, such as conflict theory, structural functionalism, exchange theory, and so on. Blumer's point is that real people in real interactions will sometimes be in conflict, sometimes be functional, or sometimes be engaged in exchange. We need to see that human behavior is meaningful behavior and that humans can interpret meanings in multiple ways: Society is a moving process, not a static object.

Third, we need to understand social action in terms of the social actor. Here, Blumer is emphasizing the agency of interactants. The person and the interaction are not simply modes through which social structure is expressed; rather, they are the true acting units of society.

Fourth and finally, we need to be careful about using reified concepts to understand social life. The concepts of "institution," "structure," and "organizations" all fall short of the direct examination of the empirical world. Macro-level issues need to be understood in terms of the career or history of joint actions.

Notice the overall intent of Blumer's argument here: Be careful of using and attributing causation to reified concepts. Blumer isn't discrediting quantitative, statistical data analysis, nor is he saying that sociologists can't analyze or think about large-scale social processes. In fact, one of Blumer's (1990) last publications is an analysis of industrialization as an agent of social change. For many sociologists, industrialization is a causal factor, but for Blumer, it is neutral or indeterminate. However, saying that industrialization is neutral doesn't imply that the process doesn't exist—Blumer is simply making a question or problem out of what many sociologists take for granted. He defines industrialization in a way that most sociologists would, but he then identifies nine "points of contact with group life" (p. 42). Each of these points of contact constitutes a research site for the symbolic interactionist, because "it is the definition that determines the response" (p. 121), not industrialization. This definition is a quality that emerges from what people bring to the situation and the ongoing process of interaction.

Blumer isn't trying to do away with quantitative analysis either. His point is actually much more powerful. Quantitative data and statistical analysis can be used to great benefit in sociology, but as sociologists, we need to be careful about what we think is actually influencing or producing an effect. Let's say we find a statistical association between gender and salary. For the symbolic interactionist, that association isn't the end of the study; it's just the beginning. If you were the researcher, you would then have to look for the empirical actions, interactions, and joint actions in back of the association between variables. In this sense, symbolic interactionism doesn't have a specific methodology. Almost all methodological approaches can be used if human agency and social interaction are given their proper place. (See Ulmer & Wilson, 2003, for a more complete introduction to symbolic interactionism and quantitative analysis.)

However, Blumer does give us two methodological recommendations: exploration and inspection.

Exploration is by definition a flexible procedure in which the scholar shifts from one to another line of inquiry, adopts new points of observation as his study progresses, moves in new direction previously unthought of, and changes his recognition of what are relevant data as he acquires more information and better understanding. (Blumer, 1969, p. 40)

Exploration is grounded in the daily life of the real social group the investigator wants to study. Rarely does a researcher have firsthand knowledge of the social world she wants to study. Thus, rather than entering another's world with preconceptions, as much as is possible the researcher naively enters the other's world and searches for the social objects that the group regularly employs in producing their meanings through interactions. The records of such social objects and interactions become comprehensive and intimate accounts of what takes place in the real world. These accounts are in turn analyzed. The researcher seeks to sharpen the concepts she is using to describe the social world, to discover generic relationships (those that appear to hold true in various settings), and to form theoretical propositions.

Summary

- Blumer gives us a way of understanding the kind of public philosophy needed in a democracy. Drawing on pragmatism, Blumer argues that human action is based on meaning; meaning isn't an attribute of any object, event, or person—it is, rather, an emergent quality of interaction; and that individuals interpret meanings through an internal interactive process between the I and the Me. These tenets of symbolic interactionism are the basis for not only emergent group ethics, but also individual responsibility, as the individual makes decisions for action and is not heavily influenced by supposed social structures.

- Human beings survive because of meaning, and meaning is something other than the thing or experience itself. Meaning is always symbolic and pragmatically oriented, and it emerges out of social interaction, a three-step interface of action: sending a symbolic cue, responding to the cue, and responding to the response. Generally speaking, social interactions do not stop at this point but continue on through many, many iterations of these three phases. Because interactions are ongoing, meaning is constantly emerging.

- The human world is made up of various social objects. Social objects come to exist as they are indicated by the interactants, and as particular kinds of actions are intended toward the thing. Social objects may be actual things, symbolic meanings, selves, or others.

- The self is a social object that is constructed through three stages of role-taking: the play, game, and generalized other. By symbolically seeing the self from the role of the other, the person learns to divorce himself or herself from his or her own behaviors. A perspective is thus created—a place from which to view and attribute meaning to one's own behaviors. This perspective is referred to as the "Me," and the acting or impulsive side is called the "I." What we mean by the self only exists in the conversation between the I and the Me.

- The self is thus inherent in interaction and language. As such, we use reflexive, addressive, and answerability rhetorical devices to give presence to the self. In every situation, each interactant is reflexively monitoring his or her own and others' use of language to speak of and to the self. Fundamental to interaction is the way in which individuals are labeled, or addressed, in the interaction. Social interactions can't take place unless selves are presented and given ways in which they are to be addressed. Addressive processes cue others as to the kinds of selves available, and it is expected that the person will present a self that is answerable.

- The social object quality of the self allows people to consider and control their behavior. The self is what allows humans to act rather than react. A single act has four stages: impulse, perception, manipulation, and consumption. All animals have impulses—thus the distinctly human elements are found in the middle two phases.

- Society thus does not determine our actions; action is a choice. There are two ways in which society exists and has influence: through the generalized other (institutions) and as constructions of joint action. Generalized others are sets of attitudes with which interactants may role-take, and joint actions are various discrete interactions that are symbolically laced together.

- The only empirical and acting part of society is the interaction, and Blumer cautions us against the danger of reifying concepts such as institutions or social structures. In analyzing society, then, we need to focus on the interaction, realizing that it is an ongoing and moving process wherein individual actors exercise agency. This analysis should be done in two phases. The first is exploration: Because of the emergent nature of society and self, researchers must divest themselves as much as possible of preconceived notions of what might be happening in any given situation. Theory ought to be grounded in the actual behaviors and negotiations in real interactions. Second, as theoretical concepts suggest themselves from the experience of the researcher in the field, these should be inspected to see if they might hold in other settings as well.

TAKING THE PERSPECTIVE: SYMBOLIC INTERACTIONISM

Symbolic interactionism (SI) is a primary perspective in sociology; and there are several types. The one explained in this chapter is sometimes referred to as the Chicago School, because the University of Chicago was its first institutional home. This branch of SI gained force in the 1960s as a critique of Talcott Parsons's structural functionalism. Blumer (1969) specifically takes on Parsons's notion of the unit act as "the quaint notion that social interaction is a process of developing 'complimentary expectations'" (p. 53). Approaches like Parsons's cast theoretical concepts at a high level of abstraction and rely heavily on quantitative data, both of which may lead to the problem of reification that Blumer points out. Symbolic interactionism, then, as Blumer conceptualized it, is an

(Continued)

(Continued)

approach that points to the necessity of interpretation and building theory from the ground up (often referred to as "grounded theory"). More generally and historically, Blumer's work follows that of George Herbert Mead and pragmatism in emphasizing the political responsibility for choices and the emergent property of democratic ethics.

In brief, Blumer's school of symbolic interactionism is a theoretical perspective in sociology that assumes that human beings are fundamentally oriented toward meaning, that meaning is not a characteristic of a word or object, and that meaning emerges from the interaction. Central issues and questions for symbolic interactionism include the production and use of the self in interaction, how meaning is achieved, and how actions and interactions are woven together.

Work developed from this perspective has taken a variety of paths, such as Howard Becker's work on labeling theory, *Outsiders: Studies in the Sociology of Deviance* (1963); Norman Denzin's cultural studies, *Symbolic Interactionism and Cultural Studies: The Politics of Interpretation* (1992); and R. S. Perinbanayagam's theory of dialogic acts, *The Presence of Self* (2000). An outstanding resource containing primary works is Ken Plummer's *Symbolic Interactionism* (1991), volumes 1 and 2.

Another school of SI, which gained force in the 1970s, is often called the Iowa School, and is best exemplified by Manford Kuhn's work (see Kuhn, 1964a, 1964b; Kuhn & McPartland, 1951). Simply put, the major difference between the two approaches is that Kuhn's work emphasizes structure, whereas Blumer stresses emergence. Kuhn argues that people develop a core self, one that is stable across situations and interactions, and that social structures, which include norms and expectations, are relatively stable and heavily influence the interaction, as does one's sense of self. In contrast to Blumer's situational approach, sociological methods in this school use structured measurements. The one that Kuhn created that has had the greatest impact on the field is the Twenty Statements Test, which asks people to write twenty responses to the question, "Who am I?" Kuhn took the responses as indicators of a person's internalized objective social statuses, that is, the parts of a social structure to which a person most relates. Kuhn argues that these form personal expectations, which, in turn, structures an individual's behavior in any situation.

BUILDING YOUR THEORY TOOLBOX

- Write a 250-word synopsis of the theoretical perspective of symbolic interactionism.

- Define the following terms—your definitions must minimally stipulate the essential characteristics of each: pragmatism, meaning, interaction, social objects, self, role-taking, generalized other, reflexive processes, addressive processes, answerability processes, artistry in performances, joint action, problem of reification.

- After reading and understanding this chapter, you should be able to answer the following questions (remember to answer them theoretically):

  o What is pragmatism, and what is its unique association with America? How does pragmatism inform symbolic interactionist theory?

  o What is the importance of meaning, and how is it achieved?

  o How are social objects defined? What can be a social object? How are social objects used in interaction?

  o What are the mind and self, and why are they functionally necessary for society? What kind of behaviors do the mind and self engage in? How are the mind and self formed?

  o How is the self given presence through rhetorical devices?

  o What is the generalized other, and what role does it play in self and society? What is society, and how is it formed?

Learning More—Primary and Secondary Sources

- George Herbert Mead, *Mind, Self, and Society: From the Standpoint of a Social Behaviorist,* University of Chicago Press, 1934.

- Herbert Blumer, *Symbolic Interactionism: Perspective and Method,* University of California Press, 1969.

- Sheldon Stryker, *Symbolic Interactionism: A Social Structural Version,* Blackburn Press, 2003.

- Three important extensions of symbolic interactionism are

  o Affect control theory: David Heise, "Understanding Social Interaction With Affect Control Theory," in *New Directions in Contemporary Sociological Theory* (J. Berger and M. Zelditch Jr., Eds.), Rowman & Littlefield, 2002.

  o Expectation states theory: David. G. Wagner and Joseph Berger, "Expectation States Theory: An Evolving Research Program," in *New Directions in Contemporary Sociological Theory* (J. Berger and M. Zelditch Jr., Eds.), Rowman & Littlefield, 2002.

  o Cultural studies: Norman K. Denzin, *Symbolic Interactionism and Cultural Studies: The Politics of Interpretation,* Blackwell, 1992.

- For a synthesized and general theory of interaction, see J. H. Turner, *A theory of Social Interaction,* Stanford University Press, 1988.

- For further reading on the self, I would suggest that you read a standard approach: Morris Rosenberg, *Conceiving the Self,* Basic Books, 1979; and a more postmodern work: James A. Holstein and Jaber F. Gubrium, *The Self We Live By: Narrative Identity in a Postmodern World,* Oxford, 2000.

(Continued)

(Continued)

Engaging the World

- How would symbolic interactionists talk about and understand racial and gender inequality?

- Knowing what you know now about how the self is constructed, how do you think sociological counseling would look? Using your favorite Internet search engine, enter "clinical sociology." What is clinical sociology? What is the current state of this field?

- SI very clearly claims that our self is dependent upon the social groups with which we affiliate. Using SI theory, explain how the self of a person in a disenfranchised group might be different than one associated with a majority position.

Weaving the Threads

- Begin thinking about the ideas of structure, symbols, language, meaning, self, and identity as we work our way through the book.

CHAPTER 4

Imaging the Self

Erving Goffman

Source: Collections of the University of Pennsylvania Archives.

The Big Picture: Self-Image

The significance of Goffman's work for us lies in his emphasis on the presentation of self, or what we would today call image. Goffman's work was published from the 1950s through the early 1980s. This period of time is culturally marked by the emergence and then dominance of television. Prior to this period, words, whether written (books and newspapers) or spoken (radio), defined mass media. Words give importance to story, and story emphasizes coherence and meaning. Television, however, shifted the power of mass media from word to image. What became important in news, for example, was not whether the story was complete and meaningful, but, rather, whether or not there was film or video. This emphasis on image that television conveyed was bolstered by technical advances in movie and magazine production. Movies became spectacles, and magazines became filled with

59

glossy pictures. These shifts in the cultural context impacted the way people understood themselves. Self-image grew increasingly important and at the same time became less tied to real social groups and more informed by images seen in television, commercials, movies, and advertisements. The importance of meaning and coherence gave way to the power of an image to gain attention, to be attractive.

Self-imagine also increased in importance because of changes associated with identities. For most of human history, identities and selves had been embedded in actual social groups, face-to-face communities that could monitor members' activities and symbolic expressions. A cowboy, for example, was someone who worked on a ranch and herded cattle. Cowboys hung out together; and if one of their group showed up in a suit jacket, vest, shirt with a frilly bib, top hat, and trousers, the man would be ridiculed. The same of course would hold true for a nineteenth-century banker showing up in cowboy clothes. Today, social networking sites, like Facebook and Google+, along with smart phones and social networking applications like Twitter, have lifted identities and selves out of socially embedded activities and groups. Thus, the images of identity and self have become free-floating and virtually available to all. The clothes you choose to wear, your hairstyle, your mannerisms, speech, and so on express your *personal style*, rather than group membership. Self-imagine has become incredibly important because of these social factors. Goffman's theory gives us a way of understanding and talking about how we manage the impression others have of us.

THEORIST'S DIGEST

Brief Biography

Goffman was born on June 11, 1922, in Alberta, Canada. He earned his PhD from the University of Chicago. For his dissertation, he studied daily life on one of the Scottish islands (Unst). The dissertation from this study became his first book, *The Presentation of Self in Everyday Life*, which is now available in 10 different languages. In 1958, Herbert Blumer invited Goffman to teach at the University of California, Berkeley. He stayed there for 10 years, moving to the University of Pennsylvania in 1968, where he taught for the remainder of his career. Goffman also served as president of the American Sociological Association in 1981 and 1982. Goffman died of cancer on November 19, 1982.

Central Sociological Questions

Goffman (1983) was inquisitive about everything people did in face-to-face interactions: "For myself I believe that human social life is ours to study naturalistically. . . . From the perspective of the physical and biological sciences, human social life is only a small irregular scab on the face of nature, not particularly amenable to deep systematic analysis. And so it is. But it's ours" (p. 17). Goffman probed this social life incessantly. He watched people continually and asked, what are people doing? What's going on just beneath the surface of what we see? What is required for a social encounter to occur? How do these requirements influence everything that people do when they meet? Specifically, how do the constraints of presenting a self create social order?

Simply Stated

Goffman argues that for any social encounter to take place, people need to present a self. This presentation, however, isn't something that people take for granted. Impression management is serious business, and people manipulate specific cues in the setting and in their appearance and manner in order to present a specific kind of self to others. These cues are prepared in the backstage and presented in a front stage wherein the audience reads the cues and in response demands a certain kind of performance from the actor. This performance may be team based, it entails deference and demeanor rituals and face-work, and it may result in stigma if not properly executed. This fundamental need to present a self for an encounter to occur results in social order, though that is not the intent of the actors.

Key Ideas

Dramaturgy, social, personal, and ego identities, impression management, front, setting, appearance, manner, ritual states, backstage, performance teams, roles, role distance, stigma, face, deference and demeanor rituals, face-work, unfocused encounters, frames, keys, interaction order, biographies, cognitive relations

Concepts and Theory: Impression Management

Goffman's perspective has become known as dramaturgy. **Dramaturgy** is a way of understanding social encounters using the analogy of the dramatic stage. In this perspective, people are seen as performers who are vitally concerned with the presentation of their character (the self) to an audience. There are three major premises to dramaturgy. First, all we can know about a person's self is what the person shows us. The self isn't something that we can literally take out and show people. The self is perceived indirectly through the cues we offer others. Because of this limitation, people are constantly and actively involved in the second premise of dramaturgy: impression management. *Impression management* refers to the manipulation of cues in order to organize and control the impression we give to others. We use staging, fronts, props, and so on to communicate to others our "self" in the situation, and they do the same for us.

Taken alone, impression management sounds at best strategic and at worst deceitful. If everybody around us is manipulating cues in order to present a specific self, then how can we believe that it is their "true self" we see? The short answer is that we can never be sure we see an authentic self; we always have to assume that the self we see is real. But notice something here: For the interaction, it does not matter if the self we see is genuine or false—whether authentic or fake, all selves are communicated in the exact same way, through signs that are specifically given or inadvertently given off.

The third premise of dramaturgy is that there are particular features of face-to-face encounters that tend to bring order to interactions. The presentation of self places moral imperatives on interactions. Selves are delicate things and are easily discredited. If you have ever felt embarrassed, you know the painful reality of this truth. Selves depend upon not only our skill in presenting and maintaining cues, but also the willingness and support of others. Thus, the simple act of presenting a self creates a cooperative order. We'll address this issue specifically in the Concepts and Theory section called "The Interaction Order."

Goffman's idea of the self is clearly different from that of symbolic interactionism. Goffman's (1959) main concern is with the self that is the subject of impression management:

> The self . . . is not an organic thing that has a specific location, whose fundamental fate is to be born, to mature, and to die; it is a dramatic effect arising diffusely from a scene that is presented. (pp. 252–253)

However, it would be incorrect to conclude that he doesn't have a concept of the core self. In his book *Stigma,* Goffman (1963b) proposes a threefold typology of self identity: the social identity, the personal identity, and the ego identity. Each of these is like a story that is built up through social encounters. The *social identity* is the story that distant others can tell about us; for example, most of my students hold a social identity of me. The social identity is composed of social categories imputed to the individual by the self and others in defined situations. Each category has a complement of attributes felt to be ordinary and natural for members of a particular category. The category and the attributes form anticipations in given social settings. People in an encounter lean on these anticipations, transforming them into normative expectations and righteously presented demands.

That last bit about demands is very important. One of the most interesting things about humans is that they are capable of anything. Our behaviors aren't predetermined by instincts, and we have freedom of choice. However, the only way we can function around other humans is by having some way to predict their behaviors. According to Goffman, we use social categories and their accompanying attitudes to accomplish this. We use the category to presume something about how the person works inside. Further, our expectations come to have a moral or righteous feel to them. Again, the reason for this comes back to the unpredictability of humans. Since all we have are cultural expectations, we must make sure that people live up to them. So, when someone doesn't live up to those expectations—like a professor dating a student or not caring about education—we become morally offended.

A *personal identity* of us is held by people we are close to. These are the people that have known us the longest, have interacted with us in multiple situations, and to whom we have cued more of our idea of who we see ourselves to be. Personal identities have more or less abiding characteristics that are a combination of life history events that are unique to the person. The personal identity plays a "structured, routine, standardized role in social organization just because of its one-of-a-kind quality" (Goffman, 1963b, p. 57). What Goffman means is that the more you know about me (the more I present a self to you in different kinds of situations over long periods of time), the less free I am to organize my presentation of self in any old way. I am held accountable to the self image that I have presented.

Thus far, the selves we've talked about are within the range of the situational self; it is in the ego identity that Goffman hints at something else. The *ego identity* is "first of all a subjective, reflexive matter that necessarily must be felt by the individual whose identity is at issue" (Goffman, 1963b, p. 106). This identity is of the individual's own construction; it is the story we tell ourselves about who we are, to which we get emotionally attached. The ego identity is thus "the subjective sense of his own situation and his own continuity and character that an individual comes to obtain as a result of his various social experiences" (p. 105). Note that according to Goffman, the ego identity is made out of the same materials that others use to construct our personal and social identities. Our ego identity isn't something that comes from inside us, from innate personality characteristics. Rather, we construct the story through which we see our self using the same cues and categorical expectations that others use.

Performing the Self

The basic concept Goffman uses to explain the presentation of self is that of a front. A **front** is the expression of a particular self or identity that is formed by the individual and read by others. The front is like a building façade. Merriam-Webster's first definition of façade (n.d.) is remarkably like Goffman's idea of a front: A façade is "a face (as a flank or rear facing on a street or court) of a building that is given emphasis by special architectural treatment." Like a façade, a front is constructed by emphasizing and de-emphasizing certain sign vehicles. In every interaction, we hold things back, things that aren't appropriate for the situation or that we don't want those in the situation to attribute to our self; we accentuate other aspects in order to present a particular kind of self with respect to the social role. A social front is constructed using three main elements: the setting, appearance, and manner.

The idea of the *setting* is taken directly from the theater: It consists of all the physical scenery and props that we use to create the stage and background within which we present our performance. The clearest example for us is probably the classroom. The chalkboard, the room layout with all the desks facing the front, the media equipment, and so on are all used by the professor to make claim to the role of teacher. All this is obvious, but notice that the way the setting is used cues different kinds of professorial performances. I may choose to "de-center" the role of teacher and instead claim the role of facilitator by simply rearranging the desks in a circle and using multiple mobile chalkboards placed all around the room.

Settings tend to ground roles by making definitions of the situations consistent. For example, it would be more difficult (but not impossible) for me to use the classroom as a setting for the definition of a "bar." This "groundedness" of settings is part of what makes us think that roles, identities, and selves are consistent across time and space. There is a taken-for-grantedness about the definition of the situation when we are in a geographic location that becomes more pronounced the more "institutionalized" the location is. When I say that a location is *institutionalized,* I mean that the use of a specific place appears restricted: The front of the classroom looks as if students are restricted, yet it is available to many professors; the office of the CEO of Microsoft, on the other hand, is even more institutionalized and restricted. However, there is still a great deal of flexibility and creativity available to those who use the space.

However, there is one specific setting wherein there is little or no flexibility: total institutions. *Total institutions* are organizations that control all of an individual's behaviors, from the time the person gets up until he or she is fast asleep (and even then, behaviors are regulated). Clear examples of these institutional settings include psychiatric hospitals and military boot camps. Goffman (1961a) uses the idea of the total institution to demonstrate the clear association between the setting and the self: "This special kind of institutional arrangement does not so much support the self as constitute it" (p. 168).

In addition to the physical setting, a front is produced by using appearance and manner. *Appearance* cues consist of clothing, hairstyle, makeup, jewelry, cologne, backpacks, attaché cases, piercings, tattoos, and so on—in short, anything that we can place upon our bodies. While appearance refers to those things that we do *to* our bodies, *manner* refers to what we do *with* our bodies. Manner consists of the way we walk, our posture, our voice inflection, how we use our eyes, what we do with our hands, what we do with our arms, our stride, the way we sit, how we physically respond to stimuli, and so on. Both appearance and manner function to signify the performer's social statuses and temporary ritual state. What we mean by social statuses should be fairly clear. Bankers and bikers have different social statuses, and they dress differently. They don't dress differently because they have dissimilar tastes; they do so because different appearance cues are associated with different status positions.

Ritual states refer to at least two things. The most apparent is the ritual state associated with different life phases. We have fewer of these than do traditional societies, but we still mark some life transitions with rituals, like birthdays (particularly when they signify a change in social standing, like the twenty-first birthday in the United States), graduations, promotions, and retirement. The second idea that the notion of ritual state conveys is our readiness to perform a particular role. Our appearance tells others how serious we are about the role we claim. For example, if you see two people riding bicycles and they are dressed differently, one in normal street clothes and the other in matching nylon/lycra jersey and shorts along with cycling shoes and helmet, then you can surmise that one is really serious about riding and the other is less so.

As in the theater, fronts are prepared backstage and presented on the front stage. Most of what is implied in these concepts is fairly intuitive. For example, every day before you go to school, you prepare your student-self in the backstage. You pick out clothes, shower, do your hair, put on makeup, or whatever it is that corresponds to the self that you want others to see and respond to. Your work in the backstage for school is different from your work in the backstage for a date. When you get to school, you then present the student-self that you've prepared in the front stages of class, the lunchroom, hallways, and so forth. But the backstage of school extends further back than your morning preparations. All students will study, read, and write to a certain degree in preparation for class. This, too, is part of the backstage for class. Even if you don't read or study, you are preparing to perform as a certain kind of student. As I said, most of this is intuitive. However, we need to realize that there are multiple front- and backstages and that they can occur at almost any time and place.

Often, it is *performance teams* that move from front- to backstage. Just as in the theater, most performances are carried off by a troupe of actors. There are, of course, such things as one-person shows, but by and large, actors cooperate with one another to present a show to the audience. The same is true in social encounters. We can think of teamwork as being either tacit or contrived. Members of like social categories generally, though not always, assume that others within the category will cooperate in preserving the group face. For example, perhaps you and a friend went to the beach for the weekend. Monday you are both talking to a professor. Your friend, who feels she didn't do well on that morning's test, tells the professor, "I don't think I did well on the test this morning. I was sick all weekend and didn't have a chance to study." You say nothing. You're a team.

Performance teams can also be much more deliberate. Let's say you are married and are having another couple over for dinner. In the middle of dinner, your spouse asks you to help her in the kitchen. In the kitchen, you find out that what she wants your help with isn't the food, but rather, the team performance. She tells you, in no uncertain terms, that you are not to talk about the fact that she, your wife, is looking for a new job. It turns out that the couple you are having over for dinner is friends with her current boss, and she hasn't told her boss that she is leaving. You both go back to the table, then, and smoothly change the topic.

The work of Arlie Russell Hochschild (1983) takes us into an area of impression management that Goffman rarely considered. As a professor, I occasionally have students come into my office crying. They may have lost a loved one or simply want to tell me about how this has been the week from hell and they can't get their paper in on time. The thing that strikes me about this experience is that I know the student didn't start out crying at his or her dorm room or classroom and walk across campus crying all the way. The student not only managed his or her impression, but the emotions as well, in a way that was suitable for public display. Then, somewhere between the elevator and my office, the student had a backstage moment in which he or she accessed those emotions and allowed crying to be part of the front. This story about crying implies something important about impression management: Part of it involves emotion. Hochschild takes impression management into the very center of the individual and invites us to consider the managed heart.

Relating to Roles

Every definition of a social situation contains roles that are normal and regularly expected. Goffman (1961b) considers *roles* as bundles of activities that are effectively laced together into a situated activity system. Some of these role-specific activities we will be pleased to perform, and others we perhaps will not. We can thus distance ourselves from a role, or we can fully embrace it. *Role distancing* is a way of enacting the role that simultaneously allows the actor to lay claim to the role and to say that he or she is so much more than the role. Let's take the role of student, for example. There are certain kinds of behavior that are expected of students: They should read the material through several times before class, they should sit in the front row and diligently take notes, they should ask questions in class and consistently make eye contact with the professor, they should systematize and rewrite their notes at least once a week, they should make it a point to introduce themselves to the professor and stop by during office hours to go over the material, and so forth. You already know the list, though you probably haven't taken the time to write it out.

But how many of you actually perform the role in its entirety? Why don't you? It isn't a matter of ignorance or ability; you know and can perform everything we've listed and more. So, why don't you? You don't perform the role to its fullest because you want to express to people, mostly your peers, that there is more to you than simply being a student. When presenting the role of student, it is difficult to simultaneously perform another role. In this situation, you are a student. Thus, in order to convey to others that you might be more than a student, you leave gaps in the presentation. These gaps leave possibilities and questions in the minds of others: "Who else is this person?" Sometimes we fill the gaps with hints of other selves (like "athletic female" or "sensitive male") that aren't necessarily part of the definition of the situation.

Contained within the idea of role distancing is role embracement. In role embracement, we adhere to all that the role demands. We effectively become one with the role; the role becomes our self. We see and judge our self mainly through this role. We tend to embrace a role when we are new to a situation or when we feel ourselves to be institutional representatives (like a parent or teacher). When we do embrace a role like this, we idealize the situation and its roles. That is, we "incorporate and exemplify the officially accredited values of the society" (Goffman, 1959, p. 35). When we manage our front in such a way, we place claims upon the audience—first, to recognize the self that we are presenting as one that embodies society, and second, to present our self in such a way as to represent society as well.

Some of the decision to distance or embrace a role is personal, but most of it is situational. For example, we expect university students to experiment and try out different things. It's a time between highly institutionalized spaces. This kind of time is sometimes referred to as "liminal space" (V. W. Turner, 1969). You are not a child, fully under the demands of your parents, nor are you working at a job that fully demands your time, effort, and impression management. However, when you do become a full member of the economy, you won't have the time or occasion to experience different situations and the selves they entail. Your daily rounds will be more restricted and managed by others, and you will be expected to more fully embrace the self that work requires. Of course, role distancing is still possible, but you will have to work harder at it, and it will be circumscribed by your situations.

Sacred and Stigmatized Selves

Charles Horton Cooley recognized as early as 1902 that society rests on felt pride and shame (see Cooley, 1902/1964, pp. 184, 230). Both are emotions that are distinctly social in origin, and both help monitor human behavior. Goffman also sees pride and shame at work in social interactions. In every interaction, we present a front, and every time we present a front, we put the self at risk. People read our cues, categorize us, attribute attitudes, and then expect us to live up to normal traits and behaviors. We are held accountable to the role.

Often, we are unaware that we are making moral demands of someone's role performance until they are violated. These demands constitute the individual's virtual self in the situation. The interactants compare the virtual self to the actual self, the actual role-related behaviors. The differences between the virtual and actual selves—and there are always differences—create the possibility of stigma. The word *stigma* comes from the Greek and originally meant a brand or tattoo. Today, stigma is used to denote a mark of shame or discredit. There are well-known and apparent stigmas, though if we are going to be politically correct, we don't usually talk about them as such today. Among the ones that Goffman (1963a) mentions are disabilities and deformities. People with such apparent stigmas are discredited by those who Goffman calls "normals." Having someone with an obvious stigma creates tension in encounters. Normals practice careful "disattention," and the discredited use various devices to manage the tension, such as joking or downplaying.

There are also well-known but not-so-apparent stigmas. People in this category are considered discreditable by "normals": They live daily and in every situation with the potential of being stigmatized. One such category that is prominent today in the United States is that of homosexuals. Being homosexual in this society is still a stigmatized identity—the homosexual is viewed as having failed to live up to the expectations associated with being a sexual person. Many homosexuals practice information management (as compared to tension management); they work to pass as a normal. *Passing* is a concerted and well-organized effort to appear normal, based on the knowledge of possible discrediting; this impression management entails a directedness that isn't usual for normals.

Goffman's insight here is that *all of us have to pass.* We all engage in information management: We know what cues to avoid in order to successfully pull off a performance. Remember when we listed the cues associated with the perfect student? Well, we could just as easily record the signals associated with being a poor student. If we think back to the issue of role distancing, we can see that it requires a delicate balance of claiming enough cues to still be considered a student without being discredited as a poor student. Since we all pass, we are constantly in danger of being stigmatized: "The issue becomes not whether a person has experience with a stigma of his own, because he has, but rather how many varieties he has had his own experience with" (Goffman, 1963b, p. 129).

The reason that stigmas can exist and are an issue is that identities are "collective representations" in the true Durkheimian sense of the word (see Durkheim, 1912/1995, pp. 436–440). Identities belong to and represent society's values and beliefs. The representational, symbolic character of identities and the way in which we interact around those identities indicate that identities and selves are sacred objects. Durkheim defines sacred things as those objects "protected and isolated by prohibitions . . . things set apart and forbidden" (pp. 38, 44). Sacred things, then, represent society, are reserved for special use, and are protected from misuse by clear symbolic boundaries. The sacred self, like all sacred objects, has boundaries that are guarded against encroachment. The sacred quality of identities and selves is the source of shame: "As sacred objects, men are subject to slights and profanation" (Goffman, 1967, p. 31). The flip side of stigma and shame is equally related to this collective feature of identities: a sense of pride in the sacred self.

Goffman (1967) uses the idea of *face* to express the dynamics of the sacred self. Face refers to the positive social value that a person claims in an interaction. As we've seen, when we present cues and lay claim to a social identity, others grant us the identity and attribute to us a host of internal characteristics. Through role distancing, we can negotiate some of these attributions, but in order to make an effective claim on the situated self, we must keep our performance within a given set of parameters—otherwise we could not be identified. Every established identity has positive social values attached to it, and over time we can become emotionally involved with those values. As individuals, we experience these emotions as our ego identity. Every time we present an identity, we expose our face, our ego identity, to risk. We risk embarrassment, but the risk is necessary in order to feel pride and a strong sense of self.

Concepts and Theory: The Encounter

This idea of putting our face at risk implies that the encounter or interaction is a ritual order. Goffman (1967) argues that interactions are ritualized insofar as they represent "a way in which the individual must guard and design the symbolic implications of his acts while in the immediate presence of an object that has a special value to him" (p. 57). Encounters are highly ritualized social interactions, particularly around the issues of self and respect. Goffman refers to the behaviors oriented around respect as deference and demeanor rituals.

Deference is the amount of respect we give others. We may defer, or submit, to another's wishes or opinions. Deference also refers to courteous, polite, or formal behavior. All of this deference is granted in different ways. For example, we can know how much or what kind of respect to give others based on known status positions. When introduced to our physician for the first time, most of us call him or her by the title that normally goes along with the position: Doctor. This seems like a function of the status structure—we're just reflecting what the structure says. However, according to Goffman's way of seeing the world, acts of deference are prompted by someone's demeanor.

Demeanor refers most directly to the way someone holds himself or herself, as in manner. But it also entails the entire spectrum of expressive equipment we use to present a front. As such, we can see it isn't so much the structure that tells us to call our physician "Doctor," as it is the way the doctor presents herself. If the physician you visit has her office in a professional building, has the usual waiting room with glass dividers between you and the staff, has examination rooms full of medical equipment and decorated with framed college diplomas on the walls, and the doctor comes into the room wearing a white uniform and other appearance cues (like a stethoscope), then the entire atmosphere surrounding the situation screams to you to grant respect, not only in title, but in all your behaviors. On the other hand, if the office is in a remodeled home with no glass dividers, and if the exam rooms have pictures and comfortable chairs, and if the physician comes in wearing jeans and a T-shirt, and if she introduces herself as "Samantha Stevens" (rather than "Doctor Stevens"), then you will feel less concerned about exhibiting such obvious signs of respect.

Much of Goffman's concern with ritual has to do with *face-work:* actions oriented toward maintaining or modifying face. We tend to preserve our face not only because we are emotionally attached to it (we can experience pride or shame), but also because our face is bound up with the face of others in the situation. For example, if I see you once and only once, then I can present any self I desire. However, if we interact on a regular basis, then we tend to become attached to faces and we maintain consistency of behaviors. You tend to rely on my face in order to consistently present your face. Roles and faces do not come individually prepackaged; they come in sets: My being a teacher would be impossible without the role of student. And my face as a good teacher would be equally impossible without your face as a good student. Once we present an identity, we and others build later responses on it so that our faces are intrinsically bound up one with another. We thus sustain a ritualized equilibrium in interactions through accommodating one another's "lines," just like in a theatrical play.

The most basic kind of face-work is *avoidance:* We avoid contacts and requests where threats are likely to occur. For example, a student might avoid encounters where the two women he is dating might meet, or where he might see the professor to whom he owes a paper. This kind of avoidance is rather obvious, but there are also other less obvious avoidance procedures. I might, for example, change the topic of conversation because it is getting too near a place where my face might be threatened. Or, when I make a claim about myself, I can do it with belittling modesty. Let's say you see me walking from my truck carrying a guitar. The guitar cues the identity of musician and creates a certain level of expectations. First you ask to see the guitar, and then you ask me to play something. But before I do, I say, "Sure, but I haven't practiced for a long time." With such an account, I am simultaneously laying claim to the identity of musician and creating space where I might fail the normal expectations. Such a move not only allows me to avoid embarrassment, but it also opens up the possibility of my meeting the normal expectations but being seen as exceptional for doing so. I set the performance expectations low so that when I play average, it will seem like I am playing well.

All of these avoidance procedures create a safe space within the interaction: We are able to make mistakes or not meet the expectations of the identity and still maintain our self, identity, and face. Sometimes, however, things happen that would disqualify us from making positive claims to identity, face, and self. When this occurs, the encounter suffers "ritual disequilibrium," and we normally engage in a corrective process that has four moves: the challenge—participants take on the responsibility of pointing out action; the offering—the offender either renders the problem understandable by redefining the action or encounter ("I thought we were teasing.") or offers compensations or penance; the acceptance—the interactants believe the offering; and the appreciation—the offender expresses gratitude, and the interaction is repaired.

All of this necessary face-work implies the possibility of aggressive face-work. In aggressive face-work, we manipulate others' reactions by intentionally introducing a threat to equilibrium: Knowing the rules of ritualized interaction, we can alter the encounter to our own benefit. If we know that others will respond to self-effacing comments by praising us, then we can "fish for compliments." If we know that they will accept our account or apology for an offense, then we can safely offend them. And if we are particularly good at face-work, then we can arrange for others to offend us so that they will be emotionally indebted to us.

All of what I've been describing is part of what Goffman calls focused encounters. *Focused encounters* occur when two or more individuals extend to one another "a special communication license and sustain a special type of mutual activity that can exclude others who are present in the situation" (Goffman, 1963a, p. 83). The last part of the definition is a clue to understanding what Goffman is talking about. Focused encounters obviously can happen when the group engaged in mutual activity is alone, but its particular qualities stand out when we consider it around others. All focused encounters have a membrane that includes some people and excludes others. It's an invisible line that marks the gathering as an encounter of social beings belonging to just those people.

The most defining feature of a focused encounter is face engagement. We engage one another's faces through a single visual and cognitive focus of attention, a sense of mutual relevance in our actions, and by granting preferential communication rights. This is easy to illustrate. Picture yourself walking down the hallway at school. You see someone you know and speak a ritualized opening—"Hi, Steve." Once Steve responds, you visually and cognitively focus on one another to the exclusion of all others in the hall. You see Steve's subsequent behaviors as mutually relevant to yours in a way those of the others in the hall are not. And you grant communication rights to Steve that you don't give to those surrounding you. Out of this comes an emergent "we" feeling (versus everybody else in the hall). The invisible wall surrounding you and Steve is also apparent in the use of ritualized openings, closings, entrances, exits, transformations, and so on.

One of the main values of Goffman's conceptualization of focused encounters is that he calls our attention to how we manage *unfocused encounters*. We encounter people all the time, but often we are required to keep the encounter unfocused. Goffman shows us that when we are walking down the hall at school, or through the mall, or in any other public place, we are working hard to maintain the unfocused nature of our encounters. While it is our job in focused interactions to call attention to the self we are presenting, there are norms in unfocused encounters that prohibit bringing attention to our self. If for some reason we do, we must repair the encounter. For example, when a person is walking in public and stumbles, it is common practice for the person to look back at the walkway where the trip occurred. Whatever this action does for us personally, socially it conveys to everyone around us that we are in control of our actions and we were tripped by some object in our path.

Another benefit from using Goffman's idea of focused encounters is the notion of *rounds*. We can think about rounds in terms of a doctor making her rounds at the hospital: She moves from one area of the hospital to the next, checking in on her patients, the lab, the nurses' stations, and so on. The important thing in this analogy is that there is a route that is habitually covered. In our everyday lives, we tend to make our rounds as well. There are given places that we habitually frequent, like home, school, work, and the gym. These rounds of focused interactions tend to give us a sense of permanence about the self.

Concepts and Theory: Frames and Keys

In one of his last works, Goffman (1974) took on the social construction of reality, but with a twist. Generally, concern has focused on human reality itself. In contrast, Goffman begins with the individual and asks the question, "Under what conditions do we think things are real?" As such, Goffman is interested in the internal organization of individual experience: "I am not addressing the structure of social life but the structure of experience individuals have at any moment of their social lives" (p. 13). Specifically, this means that Goffman is not interested in the reality or ontological status of the world itself, but rather, in the process through which an individual might experience a portion of the world as being more real than another.

To present his answer to the reality question, Goffman (1974) shifts his analytical focus and changes his analogy. Up to this point, Goffman has been focused on the encounter. However, to analyze the reality experience, Goffman focuses on the individual, not the situation. He also changes his analogy from the stage to photography. Goffman uses the notion of a film strip (this was before digital photography) to talk about the stream of human activity: Apart from the categories, or in this case, frames, that we use, our experience of the world through time is an undifferentiated stream of intimately linked events—it's like a film strip that never ends. If we look closely at a strip of film, what we see are individual frames wherein activity is stopped or freeze-framed. This notion of *frame* is Goffman's chief concept for understanding how people have real or less real experiences. Frames are principles of organization that govern social events and our subjective involvement in them. We use frames to pick out certain elements of a situation to pay attention to and others to ignore. Just like literal picture or film-strip frames, frames of organization include and exclude certain things from the picture. For example, picture frames tell us where a piece of art ends and the mundane wall begins.

One of the things that Goffman does with his notion of frames is to expand the idea of the definition of the situation. The various definitions that a situation may have are built up from the principles of organization that are found in frames. Frames thus tell us not only what to see, but also how to be involved actively and emotionally in any occasion. Notice that we are now talking about many definitions of a situation rather than "the" definition. Goffman argues that multiple frames can be used in any setting. They can be built up and layered in almost endless ways. Thus, the human experience can be complex and layered, and since roles and selves are attached to definitions of the situation, we can play multiple roles in any location.

Structuring the experience of multiple realities are two primary frames. *Primary frames* are seen by the people using them as not based upon or requiring a previous interpretation; they initially organize activity into something that is meaningful. Primary frames divide the world into two spheres: natural and social. A *natural frame* tells people that whatever is occurring is not due to some intentional act or human agency; it is simply and purely physical. The rising of the sun is generally understood as a natural event. *Social frames,* on the other hand, imply that a human agent or willful intention is involved or necessary. Economic or political activities are two clear examples.

Primary frames can be "keyed." Goffman has in mind the keying of music, where music written in one key may be transposed into a different key. For example, a song written in the key of D might be too high for a particular singer to hit all the notes. Dropping the song a full musical step to the key of C would move all the notes of the song down and bring it into the singer's range. The music is basically the same, but it sounds different, as it is based on a different musical scale, or set of notes. Keying thus refers to sets of conventions through which a strip of activity that has already been given meaning by a primary frame is experienced by the participants as something else. That definition sounds pretty academic, but I think it will become clear once we consider the various ways we key things.

Goffman lists five basic keys employed in our society: make-believe, contests, ceremonies, technical redoings, and regroupings. Make-believe is activity that looks real, but the participants don't expect any real outcomes. One of the things that Goffman finds interesting about make-believe is that it requires our full attention and we tend to become engrossed in the process, even though everyone acknowledges that what is happening isn't real. Play, fantasy, and dramatic scripting are three examples of make-believe keying. One of the most common examples of play is when we "joke around." The very label we use—joking around—is designed to bracket off some behaviors from reality and key them into a different meaning. Make-believe fantasy keys are very common today, particularly with the widespread use of computers and the Internet. Obviously, a lot of what we do with computers is seen as real, but the territory itself—virtual reality—leads us to key action strips to utter fiction. For example, a friend of mine is one of the gentlest people you would ever meet. When he plays war games online, however, he's seen as one of the most aggressive killers on the field. In a virtual reality, we can maintain multiple virtual identities associated with a variety of avatars (or incarnations) interacting with manifold groups in imaginary rooms of our choosing.

In addition to make-believe, we also use the contest key. For example, the army regularly participates in war games. These are contests that look like the real thing and that demand full attention, yet aren't really wars, though there are always winners. Sports are another example of contest keying. Sports like boxing, football and soccer, lacrosse, hockey, and other such sporting events can be seen as ritualized violence. Another interesting type of keying is ceremonial. A ceremonial key references an event, such as the opening ceremony of the Olympic Games, wherein the event and people represent some significant social meaning. Ceremonies thus take events and social positions and idealize them and link them to a symbolic meaning that transcends the activity strip itself.

We have two more kinds of keys to consider: technical redoings and regroupings. Regroupings are, as Goffman (1974) notes, "the most troublesome of the lot" (p. 74).

The idea of regrouping references the participants' motives—some motives in performing a strip of activity are in keeping with those that are normally expected, and others are outside the normal expectations. An example of regrouping is an upper-class woman working as a salesperson at a church yard sale. In technical redoings, we take ordinary activities out of their context and perform them for reasons completely different from those that are normally understood. A male might, for example, practice different pickup lines with a close female friend; a music group might rehearse the show they will perform in a week; we watch demonstrations of laying carpet at the local Home Depot; or in therapy we might be asked to act out our feelings or talk to a dead father. Goffman notes that people can conceptualize (key) almost anything as an experiment.

By now it should be clear that our experience of life can be pretty complex. That is part of Goffman's point. People are playing with and moving in and out of keys almost continually. To top things off, keys and frames can be fabricated. There is an assumption of authenticity with any of the keyings that we've looked at. Even with such things as make-believe, we assume that it is *authentically* make-believe, that there is no other hidden agenda behind the play or fantasy. But sometimes there is something else going on, and the keyed frame that we are asked to accept is a fabrication. Under a keyed frame, all the participants have the same point of view. But under a keyed frame that is fabricated, there are different perspectives. All con games work using fabricated frames. A less dramatic example might be a high school girl who joins the school production of a play in order to be close to someone she is interested in. At rehearsal, the play is keyed (note that the play itself is the result of a keying), and everybody at rehearsal understands the key, including the young woman. However, she has a different perspective from the rest: For her, the key enables her to meet and interact with her love interest.

This multi-contextual game is probably more prominent today, in technically advanced societies, than in previous ages. The reasons for this change are extensive and complicated, but they are not our concern at the moment. Our cultural life is extremely complex and will probably become more so. Goffman's point is that no matter how complex the keys and fabrications might become, they are generally built up from two primary frames, natural and social. We can think of our experience, particularly in the beginnings of the twenty-first century, as layered from the most basic to the most abstract. We might play with virtual selves and abstract ideas like hyperreality, but the scaffolding of keys and fabrications can and will fall apart like a house of cards when reality asserts itself, as it tends to do.

Concepts and Theory: The Interaction Order

Together, impression management, all the issues of the encounter, and frames create what Goffman calls the *interaction order*. In many ways, Goffman is not so much interested in the interaction per se, as he is in the order that is demanded by interaction. This is a ritualized order, an order that is produced not because of participants' accounts about what they are doing (ethnomethodology) and not as an emergent phenomenon of negotiated meanings (symbolic interactionism). It is an order that is produced out of the simple demand that a self is needed to interact. It is ritualized—patterned in unthinking ways—because what occurs is for the express purpose of presentation, the first and primary step in a social encounter.

The content of the interaction, its meanings and motivations, isn't Goffman's concern. For us to interact, there are certain rules, ways of behaving, and effects that are demanded and come about simply because a presentation is required. These have little if anything to do with our personal motives, but have significant power over the effects of the interaction. For example, when we enter an interaction, we find out what people are talking about, what kinds of roles are important, what statuses are claimed, how involved people are in the interaction, and so on. Then, once we've checked out the terrain, we gradually introduce our talk and self into the flow of interaction. The motive behind such care, Goffman (1967) tells us, is to save our self from embarrassment. The effect, however, is that the organization of the interaction is preserved: "His aim is to save face; his effect is to save the situation" (p. 39).

Goffman, however, is quick to tell us that he is not proposing a situational reductionism, where the only thing that exists is face-to-face interactions. Goffman doesn't talk in terms of structures or institutions, but he names at least three things that exist outside of the immediate interaction. First, settings strongly inform the definition of the situation. The definition of the situation is important because it tells us what kind of selves to present, what to expect from others, how to interpret meaning, and so forth. For example, the selves, meanings, and others available in a university classroom are different from those at a local bar.

Another element that exists outside the encounter is biographies. We come into interactions with *biographies*—previously established stories about our self and others. There are two kinds of biographical stories that we use, individual and categoric. If we see someone with whom we have interacted previously, then we have an *individual biography* of that person and he or she of us. As we will see, these biographies or story lines are the result of impression management. Yet, once established, you and I are both committed to maintaining that story. When a personal biography isn't available, as when you first meet someone, then *categoric biographies* are used—stories that go along with the type of person you are meeting. For example, when you first meet a professor, there's a categoric biography that you access, a story about that person, even though you've never met before. Both individual and categoric biographies structure the encounter.

The third extra-interactional element that Goffman (1983) explicitly talks about is *cognitive relations:* "At the very center of interaction life is the cognitive relation we have with those present before us" (p. 4). As members of categoric groups, each of us has identifiable knowledge bases, and these islands of knowledge are related to other specific categoric groups. For example, let's say it's Friday after work and you've just stopped by a local bar to unwind. As you sit down at the bar, the person next to you strikes up a conversation. The small talk continues as you chat about work, the poker tournament on the television, and other bits and pieces of social life. Then one of you mentions music, and you find out that one of you plays guitar and the other drums. Suddenly, an entire horizon of shared knowledge opens up. You can almost feel the expansion from a narrow sliver of shared reality to a world of cognitive relations.

Thus, Goffman isn't arguing that more macro-level entities don't exist, or that they are any less an abstraction than the interaction order (though you might notice that the way he talks about such large-scale things is distinctly different from most structural sociologists). It's Goffman's (1983) perspective that "in all these cases [of both the macro and micro phenomena] what we get is somebody's crudely edited summaries" (p. 9). Yet Goffman is also arguing that interactions are unique in that they, more than any other social site, are "worn smooth" through constant use. People interact more in face-to-face encounters than they do in other social units, such as formal organizations (for example, Wal-Mart and Target) or nations (like the United States and England). The interaction order achieved through encounters, then, is our most stable and routine social entity, and it seems "more open to systematic analysis than are the internal or external workings of many macroscopic entities" (p. 9).

Summary

- Goffman understands interactions through the analogy of the stage. Dramaturgy assumes that all we can know about a person's self is what we can pick up by reading cues. Individuals manipulate cues through impression management, in order to claim a certain kind of self in the interaction. If people use dramaturgy, then the encounter itself may be seen as an activity system, like a particular kind of stage or background that places its own demands upon the performers. Goffman's entire analysis, then, is focused on the presentation of self that organizes the interaction order.

- One way of understanding impression management is to see it through the notion of social, personal, and ego identities. Social identities are biographies held by distant others, personal identities are stories that intimate others hold, and the ego identity is the biography that the individual holds about the self. Each of these stories, even the ego identity, is created out of the way the individual manages a dramatic front using the expressive equipment of appearance, manner, and setting. The self must be seen to be known, and it is only seen through impression management cues. Typically, this impression management is prepared in the backstage and presented to an audience on the front stage. While there are undoubtedly soliloquies in life as onstage, most of the presentations of self are managed by teams or troupes of actors.

- In an interaction, participants depend upon cues to attribute an identity and its attendant attitudes to the individual. The identity and its attitudinal and behavioral roles form righteously imputed expectations. Sensing this, most people are careful in the way they manage the impression they give others. This work can be seen to vary on a continuum from role distancing to role embracement. In role distancing, one manages impression in such a way as to simultaneously lay effective claim to the role, its virtual self, and a yet-unseen self. The purpose of such work is to claim a self that is more than the role communicates. In role embracement, the individual disappears within the virtual self. Such work idealizes the situation and its roles.

- The longer we perform a particular role or the closer we come to role embracement, the greater is the possibility of embarrassment. Goffman refers to this emotional attachment to roles as face. Every interaction represents a risk to self: We can either lose or maintain face. As such, most interactions are ritualized around face-work. Most face-work is performed through avoidance procedures. For our self, we avoid settings and topics that represent threat, we initially present a front of diffidence and composure, and we make claims about self with belittling modesty. For others, we do such things as leaving unstated "facts" that may discredit them, deliberately turning a blind eye to behaviors that might discredit them, providing accounts for them when needed, and when making "belittling demands" we may use a joking manner.

- Face is closely linked to the ideas of ego identity and sacred self. The idea of the sacred self points out the facts that the self is a social entity and that the sacredness of the self as well as our emotional attachment to the self are produced through ritualized interactions. We experience a sacred self with a sense of emotional attachment to an ego identity as a result of the nature and structure of our interactions. We experience a sense of a core, unchanging self because (a) identities and selves are grounded in geographic settings; (b) we regularly frequent a daily, weekly, or monthly round of settings; and (c) focused interactions within those settings are ritually oriented toward maintaining face.

- Settings and encounters obtain meaning through the use of frames. Frames are interpretive schemes that individuals use to section off parts of the endless stream of activities and events. There are two primary frames: natural and social. The natural frame sections off elements from the stream of life and interprets them as normal and natural—rather than due to some intentional act or human agency. The social frame interprets activities and events in terms of a human agent or willful intention. The use of these two primary frames is how individuals experience things as real. The frames, however, may be keyed through make-believe, contests, ceremonies, technical redoings, and regroupings, and those keys may be authentic or fabricated. Keys and fabrications allow for the possibility of multiple and abstract levels of meaning, yet they are all tied to one of the two primary frames.

TAKING THE PERSPECTIVE: DRAMATURGY

As Fine and Manning (2003) note, "It is difficult to trace precisely the intellectual forces that influenced Goffman's distinct creativity" (p. 41). Goffman rarely, if ever, engaged in the scholastic practice of citing sources in order to substantiate his position or to build on the work of predecessors (a distinct practice of science). What he did was to describe in minute detail the social happenings he explored. "Though Goffman was surely the sociologist he professed to be, he was every bit as much, simply, a writer" (Lemert, 1997, p. xiii). While there's little in Goffman's writings to link him to any theoretical tradition, it is undoubtedly the case that his graduate student days at the University of Chicago affected his perspective. According to Fine and Manning, his cohort took a "skeptical stance toward the dominant functionalist and quantitative perspective of mid-century American sociology, postulating an alternative . . . of interpretive sociology" (p. 41). We also know that Goffman was invited to Berkeley by Herbert Blumer, an invitation he accepted, and that both *Forms of Talk* (1981) and *Frame Analysis* (1974) were written in response to ethnomethodology.

Briefly, dramaturgy is a theoretical perspective and methodology that uses the analogy of the stage to understand and illuminate social life. In this perspective, people are seen as actors who constantly manage the impression others have of self. Importantly, the need for and emphasis upon the presentation of self in every social encounter creates an underlying structuring process that produces social order. Dramaturgists are interested in the continual production of a social self, which places moral imperatives on the interaction order.

Goffman's work continues to provide inspiration for researchers who focus on image and the presence of self in social encounters—reference to his work can be found in literally thousands of books and articles. Theoretically, Goffman's biggest impact is with frame analysis and interaction ritual theory. Frames are basic cognitive structures that guide perception and attention; frames thus tell us what is real. Frame analysis extends Goffman's theory to social movements (Benford & Snow, 2000). The argument is that before a social movement can begin, certain frames must exist that call attention to specific details in society. This can be done intentionally through frame alignment, linking new frames to existing ones. Interaction ritual theory is an elaboration by Randall Collins (2004). Drawing on both Goffman and Durkheim, Collins argues that interaction rituals are chained together through emotional energy and cultural capital. These chains provide the basic fabric of society by linking together individual situations.

BUILDING YOUR THEORY TOOLBOX

- Write a 250-word synopsis of the theoretical perspective known as dramaturgy.

- After reading and understanding this chapter, you should be able to define the following terms theoretically and explain their theoretical importance to impression management: dramaturgy, social identity, personal identity, ego identity, impression management, front, setting, appearance, manner, ritual states, backstage, performance teams, roles, role distance, stigma, face, deference and demeanor rituals, face-work, unfocused encounters, frames, keys, interaction order, biographies, and cognitive relations.

- After reading and understanding this chapter, you should be able to answer the following questions (remembering to answer them theoretically):

  o What produces the interaction order?

  o What is a front, and how is it managed?

(Continued)

(Continued)

○ What are the different ways in which we can relate to social roles? What are the effects of these different ways?

○ What are the differences between focused and unfocused encounters?

○ How are frames related to social reality, and how do they work?

Learning More—Primary and Secondary Sources

- Erving Goffman, "The Interaction Order," *American Sociological Review, 48,* 1983.

- Erving Goffman, *The Presentation of Self in Everyday Life*, Anchor Books, 1959.

- Erving Goffman, *Interaction Ritual*, Pantheon, 1967.

- *The Goffman Reader*, edited by Charles Lemert and Ann Branaman, Blackwell, 1997.

- *Goffman's Legacy*, edited by A. Javier Treviño, Rowman & Littlefield, 2003.

Engaging the World

- Compare and contrast at least two of your professors using Goffman's idea of impression management. How are their offices different? How about the way they dress and talk? How do they use the setting differently? How do their demeanors communicate different levels of expected deference?

- How would flirting and video games be understood as forms of keying? What other examples of keying can you think of?

- Using Goffman's theory, explain Internet interactions. How are they both different from and similar to face-to-face interactions?

- Using a sporting event, concert, or newscast, use frame analysis to explain the different frames that have probably been used in the past and are being used currently.

- How would a dramaturgical theory explaining class, race, gender, and sexual inequality be different from a symbolic interactionist theory? How would they complement one another?

Weaving the Threads

- What are the differences between the symbolic interactionist notion of the "Me" and Goffman's theory of ego identity?

- Compare and contrast the ways Goffman and symbolic interactionists conceive of the way behaviors and selves become patterned and predictable.

- Compare and contrast the SI notion of emergent interactions and Goffman's idea of the interaction order. Bringing them together, answer the following question: How are social encounters both emergent and patterned?

CHAPTER 5

Achieving Social Order

Harold Garfinkel

Source: Reprinted with permission of Bernard Leach, Manchester Metropolitan University.

The Big Picture: Social Constructivism

One of the easiest ways to understand social constructivism is to compare it to essentialism. Essentialism assumes that the majority of the characteristics of human life are inherent: They are biologically and genetically determined. Social constructivism assumes the opposite: Human life is socially produced. There is a sense, then, in which the majority of sociological theories have always been constructivist. Durkheim, for example, argued that the reality in back of religion is society; Marx argued that human consciousness is specific to social position; and so on. Yet social constructivism as a field within sociology most clearly emerged in the 1960s through the work of Peter Berger and Thomas Luckmann.

Berger and Luckmann took inspiration for their work from *phenomenology*, a school of thought begun by German philosopher Edmund Husserl (1859–1938). Husserl formed the phenomenological approach in response to both empiricism and rationalism. *Empiricism* is the philosophy that all knowledge comes from and is tested by sense data gathered from the physical world. *Rationalism*, on the other hand, posits that reason and logic are the tools through which true knowledge is attained. In this perspective, reason can lay hold of truths that lie beyond the grasp of sense perception. Phenomenology cuts a middle road between the two by focusing on human consciousness.

Consciousness is more than sense data. Husserl (1913/1975) argued that the only things that can exist for humans exist in consciousness. That is, only those things of which we are intentionally aware can exist for us. However, while consciousness for Husserl is more than sense data, it is less than reason. In reason, humans use cultural tools such as logic and categories to understand and make sense of the world. Husserl saw those cultural tools as obstructions to investigation. He wanted to set those aside and investigate pure consciousness through epoché, or transcendental phenomenological reduction. *Epoché* is a Greek word meaning to stop or cease, or to suspend judgment. It also refers to a position in space or set point in time. As a methodological device, Husserl was asking us to suspend our belief in the reality of the human world and to direct our investigative view to our consciousness of the world alone. Husserl felt that we could get to pure consciousness by "bracketing" or setting aside the cultural tools through which the lifeworld is recognized, organized, and understood as meaningful. Phenomenology, then, emphasizes immediate experience (or the phenomenon of pure consciousness) apart from all assumptions, language, or theories.

Phenomenology came into sociology through the work of Alfred Schutz (1899–1959). However, there is a major difference between Husserl and Schutz. Husserl wanted to reduce everything to pure consciousness and direct experience. But Schutz wasn't convinced that the lifeworld as we know it is one of pure consciousness. As a philosophy, phenomenology is concerned with consciousness and seeks to discover it in its purest form, apart from language and any preconceptions. The idea is to get at the essential structures of the human experience. But, Schutz (1967) argued, the lifeworld we directly experience is uniquely human: It comes to us prepackaged in culture and language. The lifeworld for Schutz is exactly that world that Husserl wanted to bracket. The phenomenon of the lifeworld is a culturally meaningful world, and humans can't exist apart from meaning. The focus, then, is to notice how the lifeworld (the fundamental phenomenon) presents itself to us apart from any scientific or philosophical interpretation. This phenomenon is the commonsense world of everyday reality. Schutz tells us that the purest form of human experience is found in the *natural attitude* that people have in their lifeworlds. The natural attitude is characterized by being wide awake, suspending doubt, being engaged in work, and assuming intersubjectivity (a shared inner world).

Berger and Luckmann (1966) took Schutz's idea of the natural attitude in the lifeworld and asked, "How is it possible that subjective meanings *become* objective facticities?" (p. 18). To begin, they point out that humans don't fit naturally in any single environment and that humans are instinctually underdeveloped. These features of human nature mean that we must create a world to live in—it's an anthropological necessity. Berger and Luckmann term this *externalization:* "the ongoing outpouring of human being into the world, both in the physical and the mental activity of men" (Berger, 1967, p. 4). At the most basic level, this human world of culture and knowledge is created as we work together to provide the necessities of life. Yet there is a significant way in which it's completely arbitrary: We make it up. That's why there have been so many different kinds of societies (social worlds) throughout history. The problem, then, is how to make a made-up world appear as if it is real, as if it isn't arbitrary. They call this process, aptly enough, *objectification.* Again, the phenomenological issue is to see how culture presents itself in such a way as to appear real. There are a number of ways this is accomplished, most importantly through institutionalization and legitimation. Social knowledge is placed within institutional frameworks that have history, appear to exist apart from individuals, and are available to all of us. For example, the roles of professor and student existed before we were born, and they will survive our demise. We also use various forms of legitimation, narratives that explain why something is correct or right. The most powerful of these are, of course, religious. The final phase of reality construction is *internalization.* Humans are born incomplete and have the longest dependency period. As we grow biologically, we are socialized into the culture of our society. Thus, when we look inside, the self that was produced through socialization appears natural, as if it has always been there. There's an important implication here: Human experience is reflexively constructed. We create culture, objectify it, and then re-internalize what we created. While some of these ideas may be new to you, the research agendas that have come out of this sort of work will not be. Most of what you've been exposed to in sociology about race and gender, at least, assumes this perspective.

Harold Garfinkel uses a phenomenological approach to answer the question of social order. Garfinkel was a student of Parsons and, like Parsons, he is concerned with the apparent patterning of human action. However, Garfinkel has problems with the discrepancy between what Parsons's voluntaristic action proposes and what is empirically available. Following Freud, Parsons (1951) argued that the "need disposition in the actor's own personality structure" operates unconsciously so that people don't really know why they are doing what they're doing (p. 37)—and so scientific sociology has to step in and explain it. Yet, empirically, people can give an explanation of what they are doing and why they are doing it. A potential problem, then, "arises between the . . . analyses of action developed by sociologists and the accounts of action developed . . . by the participants" (Heritage, 1984, pp. 22–23). Thus, like Berger and Luckmann, Garfinkel wants to understand the phenomenon of social order apart from any philosophical or scientific preconceptions. He wants to understand and explain how our world is presented in such a way as to appear ordered. Garfinkel asserts that people know what they are doing in achieving social order. Thus, everything we need to explain is provided in the immediate experiences of our day-to-day life.

THEORIST'S DIGEST

Brief Biography

Harold Garfinkel was born on October 29, 1917, in Newark, New Jersey. He grew up during the Depression and was discouraged from attending the university. While attending business classes at a local school, Garfinkel was exposed to the idea of "accounting practices," an idea that he later used by analogy to explain a primary feature of interaction; while there he also met a group of sociology students, which was his first introduction to the discipline. Those experiences, along with a summer spent at a work camp building a dam, prompted Garfinkel to hitchhike to the University of North Carolina, Chapel Hill (UNCCH), where he was admitted to graduate school. He completed his master's at UNCCH, after which he was drafted into the army during World War II. After the war, Garfinkel went to Harvard to study for his PhD under Talcott Parsons. In 1954, Garfinkel joined the faculty at the University of California, Los Angeles, where he stayed until his retirement in 1987. Garfinkel's most important work is *Studies in Ethnomethodology*, which was published in 1967.

Central Sociological Questions

Social order and meaning are age-old questions for sociologists, but Garfinkel's gaze penetrates beneath the usual sociological answers. For one, he wasn't so much interested in whether or not social order and meaning are actually present. That kind of concern about order and meaning always implies questions of reality, which for Garfinkel are philosophic concerns. He's interested in how we achieve a sense that there is order and meaning. This phrases the question empirically because whether or not there is really such a thing as society or meaning, it is empirically true that people have a sense that social order exists. He was also disturbed by how quickly sociologists explain order and meaning by referring to outside forces, like norms and social structures. This critique is also driven by an emphasis on what empirically exists: Garfinkel wanted to know how a sense of social order and meaning are produced in just this way and at just this time.

Simply Stated

Social orders are identical to the commonsense methods fully aware actors use to render the situation accountable and sensible. Social situations are thus reflexive and ordered by the accounts offered and enacted by participants. Accounts are indexical—that is, they reference what is commonly understood by participants—and accounts proceed using a documentary method.

Key Ideas

Lifeworld, phenomenology, ethnomethodology, accounts, documentary method, reciprocity of perspectives, reflexivity, indexical expressions, incorrigible assumptions, secondary elaborations of belief, ad hocing

Concepts and Theory: Achieving Social Order

One of the reasons that ethnomethodology can seem difficult is that it relies on what we do in unremarkable interactions to explain social order. Rather than looking for big issues like norms and structures, Garfinkel calls our attention to such small things we do unthinkingly in every social situation. The taken-for-grantedness of these behaviors is both the power and problem of the ethnomethodological account. It's powerful because it helps us see what else is going on just beneath the surface—it lets us see that you and I are more responsible for social reality than we might imagine. The ethnomethodological account is problematic for us precisely because we do these things without thinking and they seem so mundane.

Understanding Sociology

My initial exposure to Garfinkel's work came in my first semester of graduate school. I was a teaching assistant in an Introduction to Sociology class. The teacher was a visiting professor by the name of Eric Livingston. As is customary, on the first day of class, the professor explained what the course was about. He told us that we were taking an ethnomethodological approach to sociology. At the time, nobody knew what that meant. He also said something that struck us all as odd: We had a textbook, and he told us we were going to read it, but not in the usual fashion. We usually read textbooks to understand the topic. That is, we approach the text as an authoritative source: Geography books teach us about the earth, and sociology texts teach us about society—pretty straightforward, right? Well, not in this case. Professor Livingston told us that we were going to use the textbook as an example of how sociology organizes itself to be sociology. We were not to read the book to learn about society; rather, we were to study the text to see how members of sociology render situations knowable as sociology.

That last part was really confusing to me when Professor Livingston said it. But think about it: There's something going on beneath the surface in the statement, "Sociology texts teach us about society." There's an assumption there that we rarely think about: In order to study society, *one must first assume that society exists.* And while that seems commonsensical to us today, as we saw in Chapter 1, our understanding of "society" as an objective entity is historically specific. Not only is the idea of society as a reality in and of itself historically specific, but it is also highly contested. As Charles Lemert (2005) tells us, "The status of these social things has ever since [Durkheim] been a topic of debate among professional sociologists" (p. 7). We saw part of that debate in Chapter 3. Blumer argues that society as a social fact doesn't exist, but rather, what we mean by society is found in the symbolic interactions and joint actions of real people in social situations. Once we call into question the empirical basis of society, what question can we ask about a sociology course and its textbook? In other words, once we put aside assumptions about things existing outside the empirically real situation, what are we left with? The answer is simple and straightforward, but it goes against what we usually think. Garfinkel explains what Professor Livingston wanted us to see. There are two points to Garfinkel's (1967) argument:

> 1. [E]very reference to the "real world," even where the reference is to physical or biological events, is a reference to the organized activities of everyday life. . . .
>
> 2. In contrast to certain versions of Durkheim that teach that the objective reality of social facts is sociology's fundamental principle . . . the objective reality of social facts as an ongoing accomplishment of the concerted activities of daily life, with the ordinary, artful ways of that accomplishment being by members known, used, and taken for granted, is, for members doing sociology, a fundamental phenomenon. (p. vii)

Let's start with the second point. Durkheim argues that the things we refer to as social structures and institutions are social facts—they have a facticity about them that is comparable to empirical facts. Durkheim (1895/1938) also argues that the "determining cause" of any social fact is other social facts, not individual people (p. 110). This kind of argument is typical of a structuralist approach and sociology in general. Garfinkel's point is that when most sociologists come into a situation, they search for variables outside the immediate situation to explain what's happening inside it; they look for the social facts that strongly influence the observed phenomenon.

Consider the following quote from John J. Macionis's (2005) introduction to sociology textbook (one of the best-selling introductory texts ever):

> Why do industrial societies keep castelike qualities (such as letting wealth pass from generation to generation) rather than become complete meritocracies? The reason is that a pure meritocracy diminishes the importance of families and other social groupings. (p. 251)

Turn the first few pages of Macionis's book, and you'll find the heading, "Who Are the Poor?" That heading is followed by a series of subheadings: Age, Race, Ethnicity, Gender and Family Patterns, and Urban and Rural Poverty. Macionis is doing two things here: He is offering an explanation of poverty in industrialized societies, and he is listing the standard variables that describe poverty. Notice that in good Durkheimian sociological fashion, the cause of structural inequality is explained in terms of other social facts or structures: In Macionis's statement above, structural inequality persists because of the family structure. Also notice that the structure is differentiated by variables that are themselves seen as social facts: The structure of inequality varies by age, race, ethnicity, gender, family, and urban versus rural settings.

Garfinkel wouldn't challenge whether family influences the continuation of structured inequality, nor would he question whether or not inequality varies by age, race, gender, and so on. And he wouldn't provide a competing theory to explain structural inequality. Garfinkel leaves the question of the theoretical explanation untouched—because to ask such questions or to provide different theoretical explanations of the same thing would require him to assume that society exists objectively outside of situations in the form of social structures that guide and pattern human action. In other words, you can give structural explanations only in response to questions posed from a structuralist point of view. In this sense, the institutional order is sociology's achievement, without question, and ethnomethodology can't claim to know better (see Garfinkel, 1996, p. 6n).

Let me give you another example of why Garfinkel would say that the institutional order is sociology's achievement and ethnomethodology can't claim to know better. Generally speaking, when a psychologist looks at an individual, he or she sees personality, and when a sociologist looks at the person, he or she sees the self. The self and personality are two different ideas and thus two different entities. However, the self and personality don't exist within the individual, waiting to be discovered; they are produced by the differing perspectives of sociology and psychology. So, in a very real way, the self is sociology's achievement and the personality is psychology's achievement. Sociology can't really claim to know better about personality because the existence of personality is wrapped up in the language, values, and ideas of psychology. It is a psychological entity; that is, it is an entity created from the point of view of psychology.

Thus, ethnomethodology can't say anything about Durkheimian social structures—social structures exist only from the perspective of structural sociology. The basis of ethnomethodology's claim is found in Garfinkel's first statement: Sociology's subject is the everyday world that "lay" people (untrained sociologists) experience. The contrasting claim that ethnomethodology makes is found in Garfinkel's second statement: *Ethnomethodology sees social facts as an accomplishment of people within social situations.* In this case, ethnomethodology is interested in discovering the methods through which sociologists make what they do appear as sociology. Let's use the Macionis example again. What does the textbook actually do? According to Garfinkel, it doesn't teach us about society; rather, it is an example of how sociologists make what they do appear as sociology.

Garfinkel's focus is more profound than it might first appear. In adhering to the so-called rules of sociological explanation, what do sociologists do? Sociologists simultaneously create an explanation that appears to be a sociological one, and they create sociology itself. This issue is why Eric Livingston (whom I later found out actually published with Harold Garfinkel) asked the intro class to take the textbook as an example of how members of the sociology field render situations knowable as sociology. But, you might say, doesn't sociology discover and explain what is really happening in society? Maybe it does, but how would you know? How can you tell if sociology is really explaining the real world? What proof is given that sociology's explanation is correct? How is that proof produced, and who produces it? The only people who ever try to substantiate sociology are sociologists using sociological methodologies. Sounds odd, doesn't it? It may sound odd, but it's a powerful insight, which we will return to in a few moments.

Common, Everyday Methods

Garfinkel's interest, then, is in the everyday procedures or methods people use to account for their behaviors. In fact, the term *ethnomethodology* means the study of folk methods. Garfinkel (1974) began using the term as a result of a study he did on jury deliberations. He noticed that there were distinct methods used to render the conversations, deliberations, decisions, and judgments "jury-like," rather than sounding like the mundane opinions of the person on the street. In the process of "becoming a juror," these people drew on multiple sources for information, but the people themselves did not change much. In fact, according to Garfinkel (1967), "A person is 95 percent juror before he comes near the court" (p. 110). The process of becoming a juror didn't change the people that Garfinkel observed. They basically acquired knowledge and made decisions in the same way they always did. What did change were the accounts that the jurors offered for the way in which they came to their decisions. Juries and jury decisions are produced by the accounts that people tell about what they did.

Accounting

Social order, then, isn't the result of institutionalized types of social action; rather, Garfinkel argues, social order is the result of members making settings "accountable." Garfinkel is using the term account in the sense of to regard or classify, such as in the sentence, "She was accounted to be a powerful senator." To make something **accountable,** then, is to make it capable of being regarded or classified as a certain kind of object or event. As we render a situation accountable, we simultaneously produce social order and reality. For example, a few years ago I was visiting my sister in San Diego and we went to Balboa Park, a gorgeous recreational area with museums, fountains, restaurants, street musicians, art exhibits, and so forth. While we were walking through some of the gardens, my sister said, "Oh, look, a wedding." How could my sister recognize what was happening as a wedding? That sounds like a simple and maybe silly question, but the implications are important for Garfinkel. We were both able to recognize the event before us as a wedding because the people who organized the setting did it in such a way that it would appear as a wedding, not only to others but specifically to themselves.

When we as a group organize ourselves to do something, whether it is forming a queue or waging war, there are "requirements of recognizability" (Rawls, 2003, p. 129) that must be met. In meeting those requirements, the situation is rendered accountable as a recognizable social achievement. This work of accounting is the primary job of the group members. For example, if we had gone up to the people at the wedding at any time during the event (while preparing, setting up, performing, or celebrating) and asked them, "What are you doing?" their response would have been something like, "We're having a wedding." This is Garfinkel's point: The members of any situation are cognitively aware of what they are doing—they are knowingly organizing their actions in just such a way as to create a sense of social order (a wedding). Because members are knowingly producing social order within a scene, and because answerability is the simplest explanation, it follows that accounting is the primary force behind social organization.

Garfinkel thus sees social order as the result of members' practical actions that are oriented toward making the setting accountable. Notice that social order is the result of members' practical actions—not the result of people conforming to external norms, values, and beliefs that guide and guard behaviors; and not the result of social structures determining people's behaviors; and not the result of self-centered actors who cooperate only to obtain gain in a battle of profit and loss. We can see accountability practices in the story of jury selection mentioned earlier. Though the way in which they actually made decisions didn't change much, the way in which the jurors *accounted for* their decision making did change—the accounting practices rendered them jurors doing the business of the jury.

Garfinkel (1967, pp. 18–24) tells a story of a research project he worked on at the UCLA Outpatient Clinic. The research was to determine the criteria by which applicants were selected for treatment. Two graduate students examined 1,582 clinic files. As is usually the case, the student coders were provided with a coding sheet and instructions for its use. And, as is usually the case, the findings were subjected to intercoder reliability tests, which are used to determine the extent to which the coders agree with one another. It's generally thought that the higher the statistic, the greater the reliability. In other words, if I'm doing a study of television commercials and I have five different coders working from the same coding sheet and their intercoder reliability is 85%, then I can be fairly certain that what they are coding actually exists in the commercials.

However, Garfinkel found that in order to code the contents of the clinic files, the coders actually assumed knowledge of the way in which the outpatient clinic was organized. This assumed knowledge base "was most deliberately consulted whenever, for whatever reasons, the coders needed to be satisfied that they had coded 'what really happened'" (Garfinkel, 1967, p. 20). Notice something important here: The coders were to find out how the clinic was organized, yet in order to fill out the coding sheet, the coders assumed knowledge about the way the clinic was organized. Thus, the coders' reliability rate wasn't due to their reliable use of the coding sheet to document what happened in the clinic; the reliability rate was due to something the coders themselves were doing, apart from the coding sheet or the files.

Most researchers in Garfinkel's position would regard such issues as problems with the measurement instrument and as threats to the research. Garfinkel (1967) likens these responses to "complaining that if the walls of a building were only gotten out of the way one could see better what was keeping the roof on" (p. 22). Garfinkel is saying that most social scientists miss the boat: They don't see what's really going on because they are preoccupied in producing "sociology" or "psychology" rather than seeing the social world as it is. For Garfinkel, the graduate students' task as they saw it was to "follow the coding instructions." What the graduate students produced, then, was just that: a setting or scene that could be understood and accountable as "following the coding instructions." Garfinkel's ethnomethodological question in this case became, "What actual activities made up those coders' practices called 'following coding instruction'?" (p. 20).

This change in Garfinkel's question implies that we must attend to the practical, planned actions right here, right now, in just this way. Members continually demonstrate their accountability to the social scene. Their practical actions are intended to be seen and reported. When Garfinkel went back to the coders, he looked for precisely how, in just this way, at just this time, the coders' practices simultaneously (reflexively) produced and made accountable the action of "following the coding instructions."

Getting back to my experience with Eric Livingston, while he didn't use the textbook to teach us about social things, he did teach us about "society." Professor Livingston used everyday occurrences—he pointed us to the simple ways we make something social. One of the students' assignments was to learn how to dance; another assignment involved standing in a line; another was going out to lunch. On one occasion, he didn't come to class until 15 minutes after the period started. He had me come in and set a boom box on a stool in the center of the stage. I had been instructed to turn the tape player on at the beginning of class. I didn't know what was on the tape, and I wasn't to give any sort of preamble—just walk over and turn it on. I expected a taped lecture; what I got was a ringing telephone. The boom box played the sound of a ringing phone to 300 students for 15 minutes.

But, you say, dancing, lining up, lunch, and a ringing phone are no way to teach sociology! They are, if what you mean by sociology is the study of the methods people use in everyday life to render situations accountably organized as specific kinds of social events. How is it that we organize our behaviors in just such a way as to make them understandable as a dance? What are the methods we use to produce a queue? How do we in just this way and at just this time organize our behaviors to make the situation appear as "lunch"? Livingston's point, and Garfinkel's too, is that this kind of methodology—the methods used by the actual people in the actual situation—is found in every setting, large or small. The powerful implication of this point is that everything we need to understand how society works is present in the observable situation.

Seen But Unnoticed

There is something unusual about the common or mundane situations that ethnomethodologists study: They are all moral affairs in a knowable and observable sense. As with Parsons, when a sociologist talks about morals or values, he or she is usually referring to something that exists outside the immediate situation. Ethnomethodologists, however, argue that the morality of social order exists in the situation itself, and you can see it. You don't have to reference some outside source. Garfinkel gives us an everyday example.

It seems true that humans can't actually experience the world from another's point of view. We all "know" this: Just ask anybody what happens at a party when you start a secret story with one person and tell him or her to pass it on; similarly, "everybody knows" that if five people witness an accident, there will be five different stories about the accident. Yet, even though we all know this, we don't act like it. In fact, in every situation we act as if everybody knows exactly (or close enough) what we are talking about and doing. In order to successfully accomplish an interaction, we have to assume *reciprocity of perspectives;* that is, we act as if our perspectives are shared, despite whatever evidence there might be to the contrary. We assume that our standpoints are interchangeable with those around us. We assume that the world that has meaning for me also has the same meaning for you; the only difference is our particular relationship to the world. Thus, while there may be differences, I believe that you would interpret the world as I do if you stood in my place and had my experiences. We also assume that whatever differences may exist in our positions in the lifeworld are irrelevant for the purposes at hand.

In order to point out this assumption, Garfinkel (1967) had his students perform breaching demonstrations so as to discover "the socially standardized and standardizing, 'seen but unnoticed,' expected, background features of everyday scenes" (p. 36). In other words, Garfinkel wanted his students to notice the always seen but never noticed scaffolding around which daily life is built. Let me quote a few of the cases so we can get a sense of what Garfinkel is talking about (In the following dialogue, S = Subject and E = Experimenter.):

CASE 2

(S)   Hi, Ray. How is your girlfriend feeling?

(E)   What do you mean, "How is your girlfriend feeling?" Do you mean physical or mental?

(S)   I mean how is she feeling? What's the matter with you? [He looked peeved.]

(E)   Nothing. Just explain a little clearer, what do you mean?

(S)   Skip it. How are your Med School applications coming?

(E)   What do you mean, "How are they?"

(S)   You know what I mean.

(E)   I really don't.

(S)   What's the matter with you? Are you sick?

CASE 3

On Friday night my husband and I were watching television. My husband remarked that he was tired. I asked, "How are you tired? Physically, mentally, or just bored?"

(S)   I don't know, I guess physically, mainly.

(E)   You mean that your muscles ache or your bones?

(S)   I guess so. Don't be so technical.

[After more watching]

(S)   All these old movies have the same kind of old iron bedstead in them.

(E)   What do you mean? Do you mean all old movies, or some of them, or just the ones you have seen?

(S)   What's the matter with you? You know what I mean.

(E)   I wish you would be more specific.

(S)   You know what I mean! Drop dead!

CASE 4

During a conversation (with E's fiancée) the E questioned the meaning of various words used by the subject. . . .

> For the first minute and a half the subject responded to the questions as if they were legitimate inquiries. Then she responded with "Why are you asking me those questions?" and repeated this two or three times after each question. She became nervous and jittery, her face and hand movements . . . uncontrolled. She appeared bewildered and complained that I was making her nervous and demanded that I "Stop it." . . . The subject picked up a magazine and covered her face. She put down the magazine and pretended to be engrossed. When asked why she was looking at the magazine she closed her mouth and refused any further remarks. (pp. 42–43)

There are a few things that we can pick up from such tests. First, there is a great deal of "seen but unnoticed" work that goes on in organizing a setting. Second, many conversations are organized around the denial of strict rational discourse. In a rational discussion, asking for clarification would be permitted and expected (though, in the end, such clarifications are also glossed-over assumptions of shared worlds). When I bought my truck, for example, the salesperson and manager expected and cooperated with my questions that were designed to extract specific information. On the other hand, conversations organized around what Georg Simmel (1971) called "sociability," the kind of conversations that we mostly have, are specifically not organized around the sharing of specific information.

In sociability, we must not push for additional information, we must wait for clarification (that may never come), we must suspend any doubt that might come to mind as the conversation takes shape, and we must understand all statements as being of the indexical kind (referencing unseen worlds or understandings that may never materialize)—all done to give us the sense that what we are having is a "normal conversation." When we see the work that goes into making a dialogue appear to everybody as a simple conversation, we can appreciate why Garfinkel sees everything we do as an "achievement." Taken-for-granted, everyday conversations don't simply happen; they are achieved.

The third thing we can glean from these stories is that there are "sanctioned properties of common discourse" (Garfinkel, 1967, p. 41). As you probably know from your other sociology courses, sanctions are positive or negative behavioral reinforcements. For example, if in a crowded elevator you face the rear instead of looking straight ahead, you will be sanctioned. People may roll their eyes, or say "excuse me" in such a way as to convey "turn around, idiot," or "get off the elevator," or they may simply get out of your field of vision. Sociologists generally link sanctions with norms, and norms are part of the moral fabric of society.

So, we can see that there are some pretty strong norms involved in mundane conversations and surmise that there is a moral order at work. However, from the point of view of ethnomethodology, the moral basis isn't part of some cultural structure that exists outside the situation. No—in fact, we can see that there are strong norms at work. What do we see? We see sanctioning behavior. This is a very important point for understanding ethnomethodology. Such things as sanctions, norms, values, and beliefs are not preexisting social facts that tell us how to behave. "They are rather constitutive of the 'sense' of the circumstances, of 'what the circumstances are' in the first place" (Heritage, 1984, p. 98).

Garfinkel wants us to see that each and every social occasion and object is accomplished. They are accomplished through the very ways members make the situation accountable as a certain kind of gathering. We use methods that we all know and that we can all see but never pay attention to. Garfinkel wants us to notice those methods by asking, "How is (fill in the blank) made to seem as organized and real as (fill in the blank)?" We could put sociology in those blanks, or gender, or even your classroom. These methods are well-known, and people are held accountable to them. We can see the accountability in the activities of the members. Garfinkel wants us to see that accountability and not attribute it to normative structures or abstract moral systems. These methods are observable in the activities of the members of the group.

Documentary Method

To understand the practices through which we claim to be competent to offer accounts, Garfinkel (1967) uses the idea of *documentary method*: "The method consists of treating an actual appearance as 'the document of,' as 'pointing to,' as 'standing on behalf of' a presupposed underlying pattern" (p. 78). Anytime we interpret something, we make a kind of identity statement: "This is that." We do this when we interpret conversations or when we recognize the person standing outside our door as the mail carrier, for example. Thus, the documentary method is the work we do when we take an object or event and set it in correspondence with a structure of meaning. We do this all the time, but *how* do we do it?

In order to put the documentary method in sharp relief, Garfinkel (1967) did an experiment. He brought in 10 undergraduates and told them that they were part of an experiment to explore a new, alternative method of psychotherapy. The students were given the opportunity to ask the "therapist" about anything they desired. The students needed to first provide the background to the problem and then phrase their questions in such a way that they could be answered yes or no. The therapist and students were in different rooms and communicated via an intercom. The students were instructed to give the background to the problem, ask their question, listen to the therapist's answer (yes or no), and then turn the intercom off and give their reactions. The procedure was repeated for as many questions as the students wanted to ask. Of course, the hitch in the experiment was that there was no new therapy and the "therapist's" answers were given randomly. Thus, there was no real "sense" to the answers; the issue, then, was exactly how (using what methods) the students made sense out of the answers—how the students understood the answers as "standing on behalf of a presupposed underlying pattern."

Garfinkel (1967) gleaned several insights from this experiment; I'll list but a few:

The students perceived the experimenter's responses as "answers-to-questions."

After the first question, the questions the students asked were motivated by the experimenter's response—in other words, the students framed their questions by looking back at "answers" and anticipated future "helpful answers."

When the meaning of the experimenter's response wasn't apparent, the student "waited for clarification" or engaged in an "active search" for the meaning.

Incongruent answers were interpreted by imputing knowledge and motivation to the therapist.

Contradictory answers prompted an "active search" for meaning in order to rid the answer of disagreement or meaninglessness.

There was a constant search for a pattern.

The subjects made specific references to normatively valued social structures that were treated as if shared by both and as setting the conditions of meaningful decisions—for example, what "everyone knows" about family (pp. 89–94).

Garfinkel's point is that the students rendered meaningful something that was not. The work of documenting—searching for and assigning a pattern—is performed by us all in every situation. A common culture or cognitive scheme isn't so much shared as the sense of commonality in documenting is achieved. The students give us a clear case where there were no cultures or cognitive schemes shared. Nonetheless, in most cases a correspondence was achieved between the event and a meaningful structure. The students' descriptions of the events were given in such a way as to assure their "rights to manage and communicate decisions of meaning" (Garfinkel, 1967, p. 77). Further, notice that even though the individual students were doing all the work, it was perceived and reported by the students as group work, as work between the student and therapist.

Concepts and Theory: Reflexivity

The notion of *reflexivity* is at the heart of Garfinkel's work and ethnomethodology in general. Something is reflexive if it can turn back on itself. For example, circles are created through reflexive movement: The beginning and end points are the same, and the line that connects them constitutes everything that is contained within the circle. The word *reflexive* is also sometimes used to describe the introspective action of the mind. Remember that symbolic interaction defines the mind as an internalized conversation. A conversation always entails at least two interactants; so, with whom is your mind speaking? Itself, of course. The mind turns its own abilities back on its self. The mind is reflexive; the self is part of the reflexive act.

Garfinkel isn't really concerned with these issues; he is concerned with how the situation, and everything within the situation, is organized. Remember, Garfinkel (1967) is interested in "the objective reality of social facts as an ongoing accomplishment of the concerted activities of daily life" (p. vii). So, how are situations and social facts organized in just such a way as to be accountable as a socially organized setting and reality? The answer is that they are organized reflexively. Ethnomethodology's

> central recommendation is that the activities whereby members produce and manage settings of organized everyday affairs are identical with members' procedures for making those settings "account-able." The "reflexive," or "incarnate" character of accounting practices and accounts makes up the crux of that recommendation. (Garfinkel, 1967, p. 1)

One of the primary ways in which scenes are reflexively organized is through **indexical expressions.** To index something is to make reference to it or to point to it. Think of your index finger: It's the finger you use to point with. This book has an index. In this case, the index points to all the important issues that may be found in the book. This last example is very important. An indexical expression is like an index entry in a book: It points to itself. The only way a book index makes any sense at all is within the context of the book. Sometime try using the index from one book to find important items in a different book; it won't work. Indexical expressions, then, are situated verbal utterances that point to and are understood within the situation.

This is a very different notion from the one that is commonly held. Most of us, including many social scientists, believe that language, including verbal language, is *representative.* If I say "tree," then I am using that word to point to the physical object. One of the difficulties associated with this idea is that language doesn't represent very well. This problem is exemplified by color (Heritage, 1984, pp. 144–145): The human eye can distinguish about 7,500,000 colors. Yet the language with the most color names (English) only has 4,500 words that denote color, and of those 4,500 words, just 8 are commonly used.

It's plain, then, that in our everyday language we are not very concerned with representation. Part of what Garfinkel is talking about with indexical expressions is similar to symbolic interaction (Chapter 3), except what Garfinkel notes isn't the emergent quality of meaning; it is the reflexive character of meaning. For Garfinkel, the meanings of such phrases as "How's it going?" "That's a nice one," "He's a novice," and "What's up?" aren't negotiated through interaction. The meanings of indexical expressions don't emerge; they are found in the context itself. In fact, as we saw in the examples of breaching demonstrations, if you try to explicitly negotiate the meanings of indexical expressions, the chances are good that you'll be sanctioned or the setting will break up. The "one among many" in "that's a nice one" is assumed to be contextually given, as is the meaning of "nice." For example, if I am showing you the new guitar I just bought and you say, "That's a nice one," we both assume the meaning is given in the context or situation. Thus, indexical expressions are reflexive because they appear in and reference the unique context in which they occur.

Situationally Constructing Reality

However, indexical expressions are reflexive for another reason. They not only appear in and reference the situation; they also bring the situation into existence.

Mehan and Wood (1975) give us the example of "hello." Let's say you see me in the hall at school. You say, "Hello." What have you done? You have initiated or created a social situation through the use of a greeting. When you said "Hello," you immediately drew a circle around the two of us, identifying us as a social group distinct from the other people around us. That social situation, which we can call an encounter, interaction, or situated activity system, didn't exist until you said "Hello." But notice something very important about "hello": It can only exist as a social greeting within social situations. Every time "hello" is used, a social situation is created. Yet "hello" is only found in social situations, either real ones or imaginary ones (like with our example). Thus, "hello" is utterly reflexive: It simultaneously creates, exists, and finds meaning within the social situation.

It isn't just "hello" that exists reflexively. Let's take the phrase "You're beautiful." Its meaning is obviously contextual. You might say "You're beautiful" to a queen, to your partner after making love, to your friend who just made a particularly ironic comment, or to your friend dressed up to go to a Halloween party. But notice also that saying "You're beautiful" creates the situation wherein beautiful is understood. The beauty of the ironic comment didn't exist until you said it; once said, it can be understood within the context that it created. Further, indexical expressions aren't limited to these sorts of catch phrases. At one point, Garfinkel asked his students to go home and record a conversation. They were to also report on the complete meaning of what was said. The following is a small snippet of one such report (Garfinkel, 1967, pp. 25–26).

	What was said:	*What was meant:*
Husband:	Dana succeeded in putting a penny in a parking meter today without being picked up.	This afternoon as I was bringing Dana, our 4-year-old son, home from the nursery school, he succeeded in reaching high enough to put a penny in a parking meter when we parked in a metered parking zone, whereas before he has always had to be picked up to reach that high.
Wife:	Did you take him to the record store?	Since he put a penny in a meter, that means that you stopped while he was with you. I know that you stopped at the record store either on the way to get him or on the way back. Was it on the way back, so that he was with you, or did you stop there on the way to get him and somewhere else on the way back?

The first thing to point out, of course, is that what was actually said is incomprehensible apart from what the members could assume the other knew. There is an entire world of experience that the husband and wife share in the first statement about Dana that gives the statement a meaning that any observer would not be able to access. So, the first point is apparent: Vocal utterances reference or index presumed shared worlds.

The second point may not be quite so obvious. The students had a difficult time filling out the far-right column. It was hard to put down in print what was actually being said and indexically understood. However, it became a whole lot tougher when Garfinkel asked them to indexically explain what was said in the far-right column. Garfinkel wanted them to explain the explanation because the explanation itself assumed indexical worlds of meaning. Garfinkel (1967) reports that "they gave up with the complaint that the task was impossible" (p. 26). The task of explaining every explanation is impossible because all our talk is indexical. Many of us come up against this issue in the course of raising a 2-year-old. All 2-year-olds are infamous for asking the same insistent question: "Why?" And every parent knows that once started, that line of questioning never ends—every answer is just another reason to ask why. It never ends because our culture is indexical and reflexive.

Mehan and Wood (1975) further point out just how fundamentally reflexive our world really is. Every social world is founded upon incorrigible assumptions and secondary elaborations of belief. *Incorrigible assumptions* are things that we believe to be true but never question. These assumptions are incorrigible because they are incapable of being changed or amended. These assumptions form the base of our social world. *Secondary elaborations* of belief are prescribed, legitimating accounts that function to protect the incorrigible assumptions. In other words, secondary elaborations of belief are ready-made stories that we use to explain why some empirical finding doesn't line up with our incorrigible assumptions. The really interesting thing about incorrigible assumptions is that the empirical world doesn't always line up with the cultural assumptions that guide and create our reality.

Mehan and Wood (1975) give us the illustration of a lost pen. Our search for the lost pen is based on the assumption of object consistency—physical objects maintain their consistency through time and space. "Say, for example, you find your missing pen in a place you know you searched before. Although the evidence indicates that the pen was first absent and then present, that conclusion is not reached" (p. 12). To do so would challenge the incorrigible assumption upon which that reality system is based—we never consider the possibility that a poltergeist took the pen or that a black hole swallowed it up. Our assumption of object consistency is protected through secondary elaborations of belief. When we find the pen where we had already looked, we say, "I must have missed it."

I want us to take one further step into this issue of reflexivity. Not only are cultures reflexively created and protected, but evidence for any reality system is always reflexively provided as well. Let us take the incident of two automobiles colliding. What would you call it? Most of us would call it an "accident," but what is implied in calling this collision an accident? Accidents can exist only if humans assume that there are no other, outside forces in back of events. But what if one of the drivers is a fundamentalist Christian? Then the episode, from the point of view of that driver, may well be defined as "God's will."

Let's ask the obvious question first: What is the incident really? According to ethnomethodology, it isn't anything; it becomes something meaningfully as we make assumptions about the world and how it works. But once we make our assumptions, what can happen to the events around us? Think about the two cars colliding. In this example, the event becomes either an accident or God's will. Then, through a neat little trick, the event becomes proof of the system that defined it in the first place. The person who has had an "accident" is confirmed in her belief that "shit happens." The person who has experienced "God's will" is confirmed in her belief in an omnipotent and merciful God. Either way, the collision is used to legitimate an existing reality system—proof of the event's definition is provided by the self-same meaning system. The same is true for science (and sociology): What counts as "proof" for the validity of science is defined by science.

Ad Hocing

Garfinkel (1967) says something that on the surface sounds incredible: "For the purposes of conducting their everyday affairs persons refuse to permit each other to understand 'what they are really talking about' in this way" (p. 41). How can people refuse to let others know what they are really talking about? At first, that doesn't make much sense, until you remember Garfinkel's breaching experiments: "How's it going?" "What do you mean? How's what going?" People tend to get very upset when we break the assumed patterns of conversation, even in what we might think of as important, strategic conversations. Most people in most situations have very little tolerance when someone wants to know exactly what is being said. In that sense, they refuse to allow someone to know what they are really saying. Of course, the main reason for this refusal is that lying beneath every conversation are endlessly indexical worlds, and our conversations depend on a sense of shared worlds.

Yet most conversations go on without a hitch. How is that done? In general, Garfinkel (1967) says that we engage in *ad hocing*. *Ad hoc* comes from New Latin and literally means "for this." We say something is ad hoc when it is made for just this occasion or with a particular end or purpose in mind. Garfinkel uses the term to talk about the minute ways in which we gloss over potential problems in conversations. We can think of ad hocing, then, as the practices or methods used by members to sustain a sense and appearance of social organization and shared worlds.

We can see some of these ad hoc measures in the story of the students and therapist. This was a situation where the students were deliberately kept in the dark about the meanings of what was being said. In the face of such ignorance and with an assumed context (psychotherapy experiment), students "ad hoced": They used methods that allowed the conversation and social order to continue in the face of contrary or ambiguous dialogue. Read this carefully: They used their retrospective-prospective sense to place what was said in an ongoing context with a biographical past and future, they waited for clarification when they first heard something that seemed senseless, and they continually performed an active search for a meaning index. Notice that all this was done without calling anything into question and for the purpose of not interrupting the flow of events.

Ad hocing occurs anytime we assume the position of "a socially competent member of the arrangement." Socially competent members are compelled to present and maintain an accountable event, whether a conversation, wedding, funeral, the construction of a building, or the teaching of a class. As such, we must refuse to permit each other to understand what we are really talking about. It isn't that we are being intentionally deceitful; it is simply that behind every social activity lie endless fields of indexical worlds. So we use ad hoc measures to preserve a sense of shared social worlds. We let things pass and wait for clarification of statements that never comes. And we say things like "you know" (known as the "et cetera principle") to indicate that we could explain if need be, but "you know" (even though what we all "know" never appears).

Summary

- Garfinkel's perspective is unique among sociologists. He sees social order and meaning as achievements that are produced *in situ* (in position). That is, Garfinkel sees social order and meaning as achieved within its natural setting—face-to-face interactions—and not through such things as institutions that exist outside the natural setting.

- The principal way this is done is through accounting. A basic requirement of every social setting is that it be recognizable or accountable as a specific kind of setting. Thus, the practical behaviors that create a setting just as it is are seen but not noticed for what they are; they are the very behaviors that achieve the setting in the first place.

- All settings and talk are therefore indexical; they index or reference themselves. The actions that create the situation of a wedding or a class are simultaneously understood as meaningful social activities within the situation. Human activity always references itself; it is thoroughly reflexive, based upon incorrigible assumptions, discovered through the documentary method, proven through indexical methods, and protected by secondary elaborations of belief.

TAKING THE PERSPECTIVE: ETHNOMETHODOLOGY

Generally speaking, ethnomethodology came into existence as Harold Garfinkel worked through Parsons's action theory and his answer to the Hobbesian problem of social order. Garfinkel was particularly bothered by the way Parsons discounted actors' knowledge of the situation (see Heritage, 1984, p. 9). Garfinkel saw that the simple empirical truth is that people are aware of what they're doing and why they are doing it, and that any

(Continued)

(Continued)

empirically based social discipline must begin there. Garfinkel drew on Alfred Schutz's (1967) understanding of phenomenology as a way to bracket preconceptions and take the social world of empirically situated actors at face value. Simply said, "Ethnomethodology ... is the study of the methods people use for producing recognizable social orders" (Rawls, 2003, p. 123). It's based on the theoretical idea that everything needed to understand social things is located in the situation and that "to be human is to know, virtually all of the time ... both what one is doing and why one is doing it" (Giddens, 1991, p. 35).

In brief, ethnomethodology is a theoretical perspective that studies the commonsense procedures people use to reflexively achieve social order and render it sensible. Ethnomethodology assumes that social orders and the methods through which they are created are identical; in every situation, people are aware of what they are doing and why they are doing it; and that social order is an ongoing endogenous achievement in which the procedures used are recognizable and commonsensical. While general sociology takes facticity (the existence of facts) for granted, ethnomethodology takes the way people develop a sense of facticity as a subject of study. The implication of this is that ethnomethodology literally opens up every aspect of human doings and situations for study. The general form of an ethnomethodological question is, What are the local methods used whereby people organize and make sensible _____?

Because the ethnomethodological question is open-ended, there are innumerable applications and extensions of Garfinkel's work. Perhaps the most explored or well-known applications are in the areas of conversation analysis and science studies. Probably more than any other, Harvey Sacks (1995) is responsible for the ethnomethodological study of conversation. Sacks basically asked what else, besides words, is being communicated when people talk with each other. He discovered that people use certain conversational devices to accomplish specific social orders. Candace West and Don Zimmerman (1987) show us an example of Sacks's approach in studying gender. West and Zimmerman ask, what conversational mechanisms are used to order gender inequality?

Ethnomethodological studies of science look at the ways scientists create a sense of doing science and producing scientific data (see Lynch, 1997). In a recent and fascinating study, Linda Derksen (2010) looks at DNA measurement. While there are some distinctions from ethnomethodology, her approach is clearly ethnomethodological. In the article, she details the moment when what were subjective decisions of the operator became invisible and were rendered objective.

However, generally speaking, Garfinkel's work has also been hotly contested because it offers such a unique approach, one that can and does take general sociology as a topic of study. Yet Garfinkel's influence extends to many prominent general theories in sociology. One example found in this book is the work of Anthony Giddens (Chapter 14), especially in his work on self-identity. Another interesting example where Garfinkel's influence may be seen is in Jonathan H. Turner's *A Theory of Social Interaction* (1988). Turner's goal in the book, like Garfinkel, is to critique Parsons's analysis of the act, yet Turner's work itself could not be classified as ethnomethodological. Turner weaves Garfinkel's theory into a more positivistic and comprehensive explanation of the motivations and actions within social interaction.

BUILDING YOUR THEORY TOOLBOX

- Write a 200-word synopsis of phenomenology. Feel free to consult additional sources.

- Write a 250-word synopsis of the theoretical perspective of ethnomethodology.

- After reading and understanding this chapter, you should be able to define the following terms theoretically and explain their importance to ethnomethodology: lifeworld, phenomenology, ethnomethodology, accounts, documentary method, reciprocity of perspectives, reflexivity, indexical expressions, incorrigible assumptions, secondary elaborations of belief, and ad hocing.

  o After reading and understanding this chapter, you should be able to answer the following questions (remembering to answer them theoretically):

  o What does it mean that Garfinkel is interested in analyzing events "in just this way and at just this time"? What does his approach imply about social order and social structures?

  o How are situations reflexively organized? Specifically, how do accountability, indexicality, and the documentary method function to reflexively organize social events?

  o What are incorrigible assumptions and secondary elaborations of belief? How do they work to produce a sense of reality? Use an example from the newspaper or an online news source to illustrate your answer.

Learning More—Primary and Secondary Sources

- Harold Garfinkel, *Studies in Ethnomethodology,* Prentice Hall, 1967.

- Harold Garfinkel, *Ethnomethodology's Program: Working Out Durkheim's Aphorism,* edited and introduced by Anne Warfield Rawls, Rowman & Littlefield, 2002.

- Harvey Sacks, "Sociological Description," *Berkeley Journal of Sociology, 8,* 1–16, 1963.

- Don H. Zimmerman and Melvin Pollner, "The Everyday World as a Phenomenon," in Jack Douglas (Ed.), *Understanding Everyday Life: Toward the Reconstruction of Sociological Knowledge,* Aldine, 1970.

- Melvin Pollner, "Mundane Reasoning," *Philosophy of the Social Sciences, 4,* 35–54, 1974.

- Hugh Mehan and Houston Wood, *The Reality of Ethnomethodology,* Wiley, 1975.

- Anne Rawls, "Harold Garfinkel," in George Ritzer (Ed.), *The Blackwell Companion to Major Contemporary Social Theorists,* Blackwell, 2003, pp. 131–136.

- John Heritage, *Garfinkel and Ethnomethodology,* Polity Press, 1984.

- Eric Livingston, *Making Sense of Ethnomethodology,* Routledge & Kegan Paul, 1987.

- Deidre Boden and Don H. Zimmerman (Eds.), *Talk and Social Structure: Studies in Ethnomethodology and Conversation Analysis,* University of California Press, 1991.

(Continued)

(Continued)

- Michael Lynch, *Scientific Practice and Ordinary Action: Ethnomethodology and Social Studies of Science,* Cambridge University Press, 1997.

Engaging the World

- Engaging your world using ethnomethodology is both easy and difficult. It's easy because almost everything in your life, from saying hello, to science, to relations between nations, is organized ethnomethodologically. The difficult part is that it is hard to observe seen but unnoticed reflexive behaviors. But once you get it, it's difficult not to see ethnomethods. Let me give you two tasks to get you started:

  o Describe how the textbook you have in your hands is an example of reflexively constructing sociology. Remember, get specific in your descriptions—"in just this way and at just this time."

  o Write an ethnomethodological description of the social organization of grocery store checkout lines.

Weaving the Threads

- How would symbolic interactionism, dramaturgy, and ethnomethodology each account for social order or patterned behaviors? Can these perspectives be brought together?

- Evaluate each of the perspectives found in Chapters 3, 4, and 5 in terms of freedom of action. In which perspective is the actor the most free? Least free?

- Ethnomethodology is the first perspective that we've come across that didn't have a specific kind of actor. What kind of self or actor is present in symbolic interactionism and dramaturgy? What is gained or lost by Garfinkel not including such an actor? Which of the types of actor would fit best in Garfinkel's theory and why?

CHAPTER 6

Social Exchanges

*George Homans, Peter Blau,
and Randall Collins*

Source: Copyright © American
Sociological Association.

The Big Picture: Agency

There is a fundamental dualism in sociology. At its core is the issue of agency: "the capacity, condition, or state of acting or of exerting power" (Merriam-Webster, 2002). The question of agency, then, has to do with the degree of freedom or power an individual has in his or her actions. The other side of this dualism is structure (see Chapter 7), where social institutions *structure* and coerce an individual's actions, thus reducing his or her agency. This dualism is in many ways like the overworn debate concerning "free will." Sociology's stake in this should be fairly easy to see: If all action is the result of agency and free will, then there isn't much for sociology to study. Sociology is based on the assumption that social factors influence people's behaviors. In sociology, then, either society is seen as taking some degree of freedom away from the individual, or, at the more extreme end, individuals are understood simply as expressions of society.

One approach to the issue of agency is found in Talcott Parsons's (Chapter 2) action theory. For Parsons, action takes place within the context of the unit act, which is bounded by the conditions of action, such as social institutions, and by the available means and ends, which are strongly influenced by cultural norms. Further, actors themselves are also institutionalized through socialization, where the positions, norms, roles, and values of society come to live inside the individual. Dennis Wrong (1999) called this the "oversocialized conception of man," as it clearly reduces individual agency.

We've seen another approach in the last few chapters. This way of thinking about it grants a great deal of agency to the individual. Probably the most important idea in the symbolic interactionist approach is the self. Here, the self is defined as an interactive process of decision making. Action is the result of this process and is thus seen as fully under the control of the individual. In dramaturgy, people are managing the impression others have of the self. A good deal of this impression management is purposeful and thus is in the actor's agency. Ethnomethodology teaches us something similar: Being able to give an account is part of how we achieve social order; action, then, is reasonable. Also, notice that each of these approaches downplays social structures. Symbolic interactionism conceptualizes society as generalized others and joint actions, and both dramaturgy and ethnomethodology argue that everything we need to explain human action is found in the immediate situation.

There are other approaches as well, ones that blur the boundary between structure and agency, between objective and subjective. Pierre Bourdieu (Chapter 8), for example, proposes a constructivist structuralism where class relations (objective) only become meaningful and thus real when they are symbolically expressed (subjective). The cultural capital (subjective) that adheres to class is then internalized in the body (objective) and expressed in symbolic markets (subjective). Rather than being separate, structure and agency are tightly stitched together in process. Anthony Giddens (Chapter 14) provides another example of this sort of approach. Giddens argues that structure and agency form a duality: The one defines the other—they are mutually dependent. This means that agency and structure are reflexively produced: They come to exist in the same moment through the same activities.

More to the point of this chapter, there's something implied in agency that may not be obvious: Agency and free will imply rational choice. This implication brings us back to the idea of the reasoning actor that the Enlightenment assumed. Most of the Enlightenment ideas of the person were based on essentialism (inherited attributes); so, rights and reason were part of the human heritage. However, this understanding denies history: If humans are reasoning creatures by nature, then we have always been. A more sociological approach sees that the idea of the reasoning person is historically specific. The Enlightenment's ideas of natural rights and native reason didn't simply acknowledge already existing facts. On the contrary, these ideas helped create the type of person they assumed.

One way to think about this historical nature is to start with Max Weber's social action typology. The typology has four categories. *Instrumental-rational* action is behavior in which the means and ends of action are rationally and efficiently related to each other. *Value-rational action* behavior is based upon one's values or morals. For example, if there is no way you could get caught paying someone to write your term paper for you, then it would be instrumentally rational for you to do so. It would be the easiest way to achieve a desired end. However, if you don't do that because you think it would be dishonest, then your behavior is being guided by values or morals and is value-rational. *Traditional action* is action that is determined or motivated by habit or time-honored beliefs and meanings, and *affective action* is determined by people's emotions in a given situation.

Weber also argued that reason and rationality aren't simply modern ideas; they have been increasing throughout human history. His theory of religion is a good example. Weber traces the historical evolution of religion from naturalist magic to ethical monotheism. One of the primary factors that moved this evolution along was increasing technological control of the environment. Magic is based on a completely mystified view of the world. The environmental forces that determine rain, success in hunting, germination, and so on are spiritual forces that inhabit the material world. In magic, then, manipulating the physical element is tantamount to beseeching the god, the active force within the element. As humans gained technological control over the environment, the world was demystified and the gods progressively moved out of the material world until the One True God—monotheism—moved out entirely and now exists outside of time and space. Demystification and progressive rationality thus go hand in hand. This gradual process was supercharged as a result of modern social factors, most notably market capitalism and science.

In terms of Weber's typology of action, the point is that all other forms of action have decreased over time, and instrumental rationality has increased. That being the case, this implication of agency—rational choice—has thus become more important in terms of understanding human action, and, in fact, important for understanding the modern inalienable right of the "pursuit of happiness." The importance of rationality for understanding agency and happiness in modern terms is nowhere more clearly seen than in utilitarianism. Jeremy Bentham (1789/1996, pp. 11–16) is considered the father of utilitarianism; he argued that happiness and unhappiness are based on the two sovereign masters of nature: pleasure and pain. The "utility" in utilitarianism refers to those things that are useful for bringing pleasure and thus happiness. Bentham developed the felicific or utility calculus, a way of calculating the amount of happiness that any specific action is likely to bring. The calculus has seven variables: intensity, duration, certainty/uncertainty, propinquity/remoteness, fecundity, purity, and extent. Thus, Bentham introduced the idea of rational calculation being used to decide human behavior and the moral status of any act.

In many ways, utilitarianism forms the basis of the theories we'll consider in this chapter. The basic idea is that people engage in rational calculations, weighing out the costs and benefits (utilities) of any action. Historically, it would seem that this kind of action—instrumental-rational—is more important today than previously. Of all the situationist theories we've considered thus far, utilitarianisms emphasizes the use of rationality in agency more than any other. It's interesting, then, that these theorists also are the ones who give us a theory concerning the translation of micro-level exchanges into macro-level factors. In other words, they consider how the use of rationality in agency actually creates social structures in the long run.

The issue of the micro to macro link is one that is obvious in contemporary theory and virtually unknown in classical theory. For some time, sociologists thought about macro-level phenomena and micro-level interactions separately. In some ways, the two different domains seemed to discount one another. Micro-level theorists like George Herbert Mead saw social institutions more in terms of symbols and ways of thinking and behaving, with their importance and influence emerging out of interactions. On the other hand, structuralists such as Émile Durkheim saw human consciousness and behaviors as being the result of institutional arrangements. Eventually, sociologists began to see a theoretical issue here. If there are two separate fields, face-to-face interactions (the place of agency) and social structures, then how are they related? In this chapter, both Peter Blau and Randall Collins use exchange theory to provide us with answers here as well. However, our first exchange theorist, George Homans, doesn't address the macro–micro link between social structures and individual agency. Rather, he begins with the psychology of the individual and views the person from the perspective of behaviorism.

Elementary Forms of Social Behavior: George Homans

George Homans very clearly sees his theory as a corrective to Parsons. In his Presidential Address to the 1964 annual meeting of the American Sociological Association, Homans asserted that the question of social order (why individuals conform to social expectations) was the central issue in Parsons's theory. More importantly, the question of social order "is the most general intellectual issue in sociology" (p. 809). In other words, the most important question sociology addresses is that of social order. Homans characterized structural functionalism as making its beginning point the study of norms, its empirical interest the interrelationships of roles and institutions, and its concern more with the consequences (functions) rather than the causes of institutions. Homans's first point is, perhaps, the most obvious and in his mind the most detrimental. It is captured in the title of his address: "Bringing Men Back In" (today we would say, "bringing *people* back in"). If you look at the characterizations of Parsons's theory above, you'll see his point—there are no people in structural functionalism. Functionalists, according to Homans, assume the existence of norms without explaining why people would create norms in the first place.

Homans's (1964) second point is that Parsons's theory isn't theoretical in the scientific sense: "If sociology is to be a science, it must take seriously [the job] of providing explanations for the empirical relations it discovers" (p. 818). You'll remember from Chapter 1 that positivistic theory is meant to explain how something works or came into existence. In order to do that, it must contain relationships between concepts. As Homans (1961) puts it, "No explanation without propositions!" (p. 10). I invite you to go back and quickly look over Parsons's theory in Chapter 2. If you do, you'll see Homans's point. Parsons gives us an analytical scheme—a set of concepts that can be used as a perspective to describe what is happening. You won't find any propositional statements of causation.

Homans's interest and intent, however, is very similar to Parsons.' He wants to explain how social behaviors are patterned over time. To do this, he starts in a similar way to Parsons. You may recall that Parsons got down to what, in his mind at least, was the most basic piece of society: action. He then proceeded to describe how action takes place within a unit of voluntaristic action. Homans wants to bring people back in, and so he looks at what happens between two people in social encounters. What Homans sees is that behaviors that are rewarded are the ones that are repeated; these repeated, patterned behaviors are what we're concerned with in the problem of social order. Then, in order to explain how rewards work to pattern behaviors, he turns to psychological behaviorism, which provides him with a set of propositions that explain the conditions under which a person is likely to repeat behaviors. Before we consider the theory, I want to point out one thing: Homans is usually categorized as an exchange theorist, but that isn't quite accurate. While there is a back-and-forth exchange-like movement between two people, the focus of the theory is more on the individual than the relationship, and on the dynamic that produces social patterns. It's important in any theory to see where the driving force is located, and for Homans it's the individual.

THEORIST'S DIGEST

Brief Biography

George Homans was born on August 11, 1910, in Boston, Massachusetts, and was a true Bostonian, as his mother was a descendant of President John Adams. Homans graduated from Harvard University in 1932 with a degree in English Literature. He never earned a doctorate, and he came to sociology by accident, having collaborated on a sociological paper. Homans taught at Harvard between 1939 and 1971, when he retired; he served

(Continued)

(Continued)

in the U.S. Navy during World War II. His two most important books are the *The Human Group* and *Social Behavior: Its Elementary Forms*. Homans served as president of the American Sociological Association in 1964. Jonathan Turner (1991) states that Homans was "one of the most prominent theorists of this century" (p. 303). Homans died on May 29, 1989.

Central Sociological Questions

Homans (1961) studied what he called elementary social behavior, which "occurs at all times and never lacks form" (p. 4). The form that he was interested in wasn't located in the formal relationships created by social structures or rules. He was interested in social order, like Parsons, yet did not look to either institutions or even normative situations for understanding how it comes about. Homans was interested in the human relations that are more basic than those created by social statuses, norms, or roles. Elementary social behavior, for Homans, is motivated and patterned by the rewards that one specific person gives to another apart from any social distinctions: "At the level of elementary social behavior there is neither Jew nor Gentile, Greek nor barbarian, but only man" (p. 6). To phrase Homans's focus as a question, "What are the most fundamental elements of social behavior?"

Simply Stated

According to Homans, the basic social relationship is one through which people learn how to socially behave toward another. The drive behind this relationship is the desire to receive rewards and avoid punishments. Social behavior will tend to be patterned when it is repeatedly reinforced with high-value rewards. The situations where the behaviors and rewards occur can themselves become valuable to people, thus allowing for long chains of patterned actions. However, if a reward is given too often, it will lose value; and if an expectation of reward isn't met in a timely manner, the person will become angry and aggressive.

Key Ideas

Elementary social behavior, respondent behaviors, respondent conditioning, law of effect, reinforcement, matching law, stimulus proposition, value, success proposition, value proposition, deprivation-satiation proposition, frustration-aggression proposition

Concepts and Theory: Basic Principles of Behavioral Psychology

The fundamental task in behavioral psychology is to find the conditions under which a given behavior (response) will be repeated. The basic distinction is between respondent and operant behaviors. *Respondent behaviors* are automatic and occur by simple application of a stimulus; we often talk about these as "knee-jerk" reactions. The source of such behaviors is genetic and the result of natural selection, yet it is possible to control such behaviors through respondent conditioning (see Figure 6.1). The classic example is Pavlov's dogs. Dogs salivate when presented with food, a natural association between stimulus (food) and response (salivation) (Figure 6.1.A). Pavlov created an unnatural association between the presenting of food and a ringing bell, paired stimuli (Figure 6.1.B). After Pavlov repeated this association enough times, the dogs would salivate in response to the bell alone (Figure 6.1.C). The dogs' response to the bell was conditioned—the process through which the connection was made is called *respondent conditioning* (or sometimes *classical conditioning*).

Operant behaviors, on the other hand, are those where a connection is made between stimulus and behavior that isn't there naturally. Rather than some part of the environment acting as a stimulus for behavior, as with the natural association between food and salivation, the behaviors first *operate on the environment,* hence the name *operant conditioning.* All animals, including people, have general drives or

Figure 6.1 Respondent Conditioning

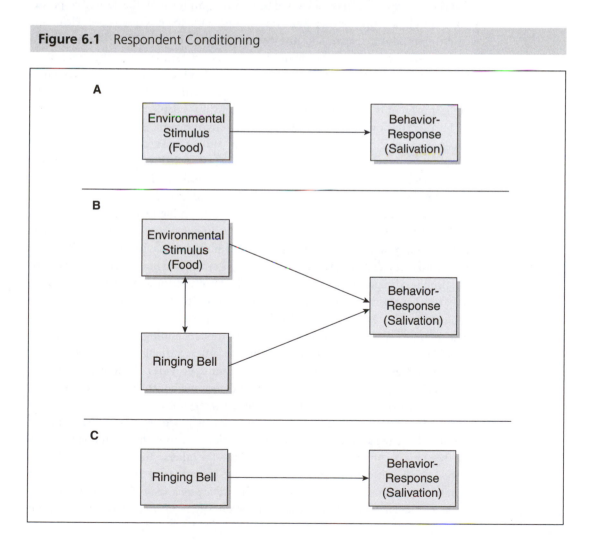

needs, such as the drive for sex or food. The strength of these drives differs by species and individuals. So, for example, one person's sex drive may be stronger than another's. When one of these drives is unfulfilled, the animal/person becomes agitated and moves about "exploring and investigating its environment" (Homans, 1987, p. 59). Eventually, this directionless activity hits upon something that satisfies a drive. The behavior has provoked a response in the environment. *Reinforcement* occurs as the link between behavior and stimulus is strengthened in such a way as to increase the probability of the behavior occurring again. Homans calls this the *stimulus proposition.*

As just described, this reinforcement of the behavior is happenstance. However, the association can also be intentional. The fundamental idea behind operant conditioning is that learning is based on consequences. Animals and people learn things that they associate with positive rewards. The goal is to either increase or decrease the frequency of the behavior. Positive responses increase the frequency, and negative responses decrease the frequency. To be effective, reinforcers must follow responsive behaviors quickly and be clearly contingent on the desired response. For example, a professor may want you to contribute to class discussion. He or she could figure out a reward (positive reinforcement) that would be given the first time you spoke up. The more frequently this association is made, the more likely you are to contribute. The trick here of course is that the reward has to offset whatever negative reinforcement you may associate with speaking up in class, like embarrassment or peer sanctions. This relationship is depicted in Figure 6.2.A.

Further, the original circumstances (the "environment" in Figure 6.2.A) may become a stimulus to behavior. This is what you see in Figure 6.2.B. Thus, in the above example, as you speak up in class and get rewarded repeatedly, simply being in class will act as a stimulus and prompt you to speak up. The next step is that the stimulus itself becomes its own reward. In our example, simply being in class becomes rewarding in and of itself. This is depicted in Figure 6.2.C.

Homans (1987) talks about this as the *matching law* and indicates it is "of the greatest importance for the understanding of human behavior" (p. 61). There are two reasons for this importance. First, humans are able to link together long chains of stimuli → response patterns. If you think about this for a moment, you'll probably see that this is yet another answer to Parsons's problem of social order. These long chains create patterns of ordered behavior, all based on operant conditioning. The second reason this law is important for understanding people, according to Homans, is that it allows the introduction of a new variable: value. *Value* here is understood as the degrees of reward a stimulus provides. Adding this variable allows Homans to describe two factors that determine how often a person will perform one action over others when confronted with choices.

The first factor is the *success proposition* and is based on relative frequency of reward. If you're faced with five different behaviors to choose from, and one of them has been more consistent in giving rewards than the others, you will be more likely to choose the consistently rewarded behavior. The second factor that determines choice is value, and Homans naturally calls this the *value proposition.* The more highly valued a particular result, the more likely a person is to perform that action. Using our

Figure 6.2   Operant Conditioning

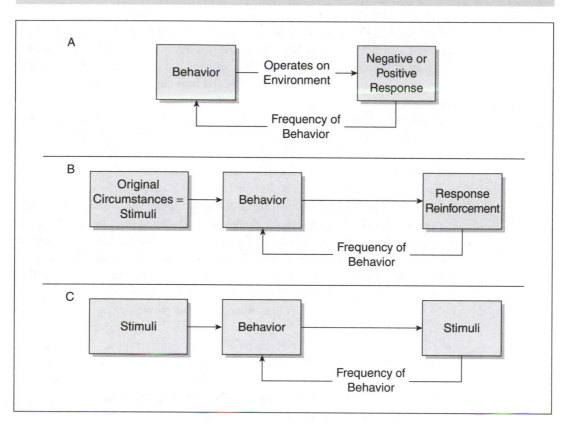

class example for both of these, if I give you a choice between working in small groups versus having a class discussion, and you have consistently received rewards in class discussion but not small-group work, you will tend to choose class discussion more consistently. If, on the other hand, you still get embarrassed in class despite my best efforts and you don't in small-group work, then avoiding embarrassment will likely have greater value for you and you will tend to choose small-group work more frequently. Note that I just introduced a new idea: *cost*. Homans (1958) calls this "adverse stimulation"—avoiding adverse stimulation is its own reward (p. 589).

Taking these together, Homans comes up with a *rationality principle*. In choosing between alternate actions, people take into account the probability of obtaining a particular reward times the value of the reward (Value x Probability = Action). Notice that the relationship is multiplicative, which basically means they reinforce one another. However—and this is a point Homans specifically wants to make—this rationality principle only holds in the moment. What this means is that you may make a decision today that in 2 years, may look really dumb. So, Homans (1987) holds this idea of rationality lightly and actually sees the *idea* of rational behavior working in a way we might not expect: "'Rational' is a normative term, used to persuade people to behave in a certain way" (p. 62).

Secondary Propositions

Homans (1987) maintains that there are two secondary propositions that "a sociologist ought to keep with the main ones in his intellectual kit if he is to understand human social behavior" (p. 62). These are derived from the above and are the deprivation-satiation proposition and the frustration-aggression proposition. The *deprivation-satiation proposition* says that people have thresholds of value. Thus, if a person's action is rewarded past this threshold, subsequent rewards become less and less valuable and the frequency of behavior goes down as a result. For example, on a whim, a man might bring his wife flowers Friday evening after work. She is so surprised and delighted that her face beams, she jumps in his arms and gives him a long kiss, she excitedly brings out the best vase, and then calls her best friend to brag about her husband. A light bulb goes off in the guy's head: Friday night flowers = happy wife (stimulus proposition). So, he of course repeats the behavior next Friday (success proposition), brings his wife flowers, and gets the same response. He figures it's a gold mine and does this weekly. Soon, he notices that his wife isn't nearly as happy, he gets a slight kiss on the cheek, the flowers are laid on the table, and no phone calls are placed to the best friend (satiation). The reverse is true as well: If deprived of a thing of value, its value goes up. Homans says this principle may not hold for generalized reinforcers like money, because these may be used to obtain other, more specific rewards.

The *frustration-aggression proposition* is based on expectations. It says that if a person doesn't receive the response he or she expects or receives punishment when expecting a reward, the person will become angry and tend to act out aggressively. This emotionally driven behavior can then function in place of the reward as a way of satisfying the initial desire: A person may learn to use aggressive action like any operant that is followed by a reward.

Summary

- The basic behavioral exchange propositions are (1) the success proposition, that people will repeat behaviors for which they are rewarded; (2) the value proposition, that the more highly a person values a reward or result, the more likely he or she is to repeat behaviors associated with it; (3) the stimulus proposition, that if a particular situation has been the occasion where a person's behaviors have been rewarded, then the more closely a situation mirrors the first, the more likely the person is to repeat those behaviors; and (4) the rationality proposition, that given alternative choices among behaviors, a person will most likely choose the behavior that is seen to be the most rational, determined by the value of the reward times the probability of receiving it.

- From these are derived two secondary propositions: (1) the satiation proposition, that the more frequently in the recent past a person has received a reward, the less valued the reward becomes and the less likely the person is to perform the behaviors associated with it; and (2) the aggression proposition, that when a person does not receive an expected reward (either less than expected or a punishment), the person is likely to be angry and act aggressively, and the responses to such repeated behavior become valued.

Social Exchanges and Power: Peter Blau

Blau and Homans have an interesting intellectual relationship. Homans, for his part, uses the empirical data from Blau's book *The Dynamics of Bureaucracy* in forming his theory of the elementary forms of social behavior. Blau singles out Homans's book *Social Behavior: Its Elementary Forms* as an important influence on his thinking, "despite some fundamental differences in approach" (Blau, 2003, p. xix). I think you'll pick up on these differences right away. The most basic one is that while Homans is more focused on the behavioral dynamics of the individual, Blau is concerned with the social exchange relation itself. As I mentioned in the Homans section, it's important and informative to clearly understand where a theorist is focused.

Source: Courtesy of Judith Blau.

Broadly speaking, Blau recognizes two main influences on human behavior: (1) the situational and personal factors that influence the preferences people have and the choices they make, and (2) the external conditions that restrict or enable those choices and preferences. Blau recognizes three factors that influence choices and preferences. There are the psychological or personality aspects (individual likes and dislikes), the social-psychological factors (how social position/ class and experience influence choice and preference), and the actual properties of exchange. Blau argues that exchange is an emergent property of interaction that cannot be reduced to the psychological attributes of individuals. And so, that's where he starts.

For Blau, exchange is an elementary process of human life and the prototype of social phenomena. By definition, exchange can take place only in social settings between two or more people. Social exchange focuses on the actions of the participants and how they are influenced by both the anticipated and past actions of others. The influence, then, is decidedly social and not based on personal achievements, such as education, or individual attitudes. However, Blau claims that not all face-to-face interactions are exchanges. This is a rather unique position among exchange theorists, many of whom see exchange or rational choice as universal to all human action. Blau (1968), on the other hand, sees that "the concept of exchange loses its distinctive meaning and becomes tautological if all behavior in interpersonal relations is subsumed under it" (p. 453). Other factors he sees as influencing people in interactions are morals in the form of internalized norms, irrationality (purely emotional responses), and coercion.

THEORIST'S DIGEST

Brief Biography

Peter M. Blau was born on February 7, 1918, in Vienna, Austria, the year the Austro-Hungarian Empire fell. The son of secular Jews, he watched the rise of fascism in postwar Austria with growing concern. Blau became a U.S. citizen in 1943, and he served in the U.S. Army during World War II, earning the Bronze Star for valor. After the war, Blau attended school and was awarded his PhD from Columbia University in 1952; Robert K. Merton was his dissertation chair. His dissertation was subsequently published as *The Dynamics of Bureaucracy* and has since become a classic in organizational literature. Peter Blau held professorships at Chicago, Columbia, the State University of New York at Albany, and the University of North Carolina at Chapel Hill. He also taught at the Academy of Social Sciences in Tianjin, China, and he was president of the American Sociological Association in 1973. Blau published hundreds of articles and eleven books, and he received numerous awards for his contributions to sociology and to society at large. Peter Blau passed away on March 12, 2002.

Central Sociological Questions

Not all relationships are equal. But what makes them equal or unequal? How is power created in social relationships? How do these sorts of relationships provide the basis for larger social structures? These are the questions that occupy Blau.

Simply Stated

Blau uses two basic factors to understand how power and structures are created: reciprocity and imbalance. All social encounters happen because each actor hopes to gain something from it. Reciprocity, then, the give and take of some elements of value, is the fundamental element of social relations and is intimately related to balance. People will always try to balance out exchanges. If they are unable to, or if they can't find alternatives, then deference and compliance will be offered to balance the relationship. In the relation between a group and a single supplier, which by definition involves power, power will be legitimated if the norms of reciprocity and fair exchange are adhered to and will be opposed if they are not.

Key Ideas

Social exchanges, rational motivation, power, alternatives, marginal utilities, norm of reciprocity, norm of fair exchange, secondary exchange relations

Concepts and Theory: Social Exchanges

Social exchanges are distinct from economic exchanges in at least four ways. First, they lack specificity. All economic exchanges take place under the contract model. In other words, almost all of the elements of the exchange are laid out and understood in advance, even the simple exchanges that occur at the grocery store. Social exchanges, on the other hand, cannot be stipulated in advance; to do so would be a breach of etiquette. Imagine receiving an invitation for dinner that also stipulated exactly how you would repay the person for such a dinner ("I'll give you one dinner for two lunches."). Social exchanges, then, cannot be bargained, and repayment must be left to the discretion of the indebted.

This first difference implies the second: Social exchanges necessarily build trust, while economic exchanges do not. Since social exchanges suffer from lack of specificity, we must of necessity trust the other to reciprocate. This implies that relationships that include social exchange—and almost all do—build up slowly over time. We begin with small exchanges, like calling people on the phone, and see if they will reciprocate. If they do, then we perceive them as worthy of trust for exchanges that require longer periods of time for reciprocation, such as friendship.

The third difference between social and economic exchanges is that social exchanges are meaningful. The way we are using it here, meaning implies signification. In other words, an object or action has meaning if it signifies something beyond itself. What we are saying about exchange is that a purely economic exchange doesn't mean anything beyond itself. It is simply what it is: the exchange of money for some good or service. Social exchanges, on the other hand, always have meaning. For an example, let's take what might appear as a simple economic exchange: prostitution. If a married man gives a woman who is not his wife money for sex, it is a social exchange because it has meaning beyond itself: In this case, the meaning is adultery.

Finally, the fourth difference between social and economic exchanges is that social benefits are less detached from the source. We use money in economic exchanges, but the value of money is completely detached from the person using it. I may use money every time I go to the music store, but the value of that money for exchange is a function of the U.S. government and has nothing to do with me—the value of money is completely detached from me. However, the value in all social exchanges is dependent upon the participants in some way. For example, the social exchange between you and your professor requires you to fulfill the requirements of the course to get a grade. Someone else can't do the work, and you can't legitimately buy the grade.

Taken together, these four unique features of social exchange create diffuse social obligations. For example, let's say you and your partner invite another couple over for dinner. You expect that the invitation will be reciprocated in some way, but exactly how the other couple is to reciprocate isn't clear—nor can it be clear; to make it clear would reduce it to an economic exchange. So you have a general, unspecified expectation that the other couple will reciprocate in some way. The reciprocation has to be in the indefinite future (the other couple can't initially respond to your invitation by scheduling their "repayment" dinner—then it would really look like a repayment in economic terms), yet it has to be repaid specifically by the couple (the other couple can't have a different couple invite you for dinner and have it count for them). The dinner is meaningful, but the meaning isn't clear as of yet (Are you all going to be friends? If so, what kind of friends?). Thus, you have to trust the other couple to provide the future unspecified meaning and reciprocation. The other couple is obligated to you, but in a very diffuse manner.

Basic Exchange Principles

There are three basic exchange principles that Blau gives us. They concern motivations, alternatives, and marginal utilities. The first principle is that people are *rationally motivated* in exchanges to weigh out costs and benefits. In this respect, the ideal type of exchange is economic, where the calculations are specific and known. As we've seen, Blau argues that social exchanges are different from economic ones, and one implication of this is that our calculations will be different. They are not as specific or concrete as economic calculations. Thus, we have to view social exchange "rationality" in limited terms. It's a general motivation in back of our actions. We don't specifically think, "If I invite Bob to the barbeque, then I can borrow his truck next Thursday." It's more of a general and diffuse motivation—a broad desire for social profits and a sense of how we stand in our exchanges.

Alternatives are extremely important in exchange relations. We'll talk more about alternatives when we get to the section on power, but for now we should simply be aware that when alternatives are present, people will gravitate toward exchanges among equals. We tend to look for someone with whom we can balance out costs and benefits in the long run. These balanced exchange relations tend to reduce uncertainty and to lessen power differences. Blau also notes that balanced relationships tend to create unbalanced relations elsewhere. In this, Blau is positing that we have limited resources, and to invest resources in one relationship is to deny it to another.

Let's use the example of dating and marriage. When we get married, one of the things we are doing is committing a large amount of our personal resources to one relationship. We do so because of the anticipation of rewards, both intrinsic and extrinsic, but when we do so we simultaneously take away the possibility of using those resources in an alternative relationship. In these circumstances, friendships can only go so far. If you are married, and if one of your friends wants to exchange more than you are able due to the commitment of resources to your marriage partner, then that friendship will become an unbalanced exchange relation. Unbalanced or unequal exchange relations tend to be less strained if the differences are known, clear, and marked. We can see this easily in our marriage example: Your unbalanced relationship with your friend who wants more will be very strained if you are unclear about what you are willing and unwilling to exchange. However, the strain is lessened as the trade boundaries become clear and marked—the other person will be less likely to entertain unreal exchange expectations.

The principle of *marginal utilities* posits that people have satiation points regarding goods and services. In other words, too much of a good thing may not be a good thing. When we first enter into an exchange relationship, the profits that we glean have high value. However, repeated profits of the same kind have declining value. Thus, the value of any good or service is higher if there is some degree of uncertainty or a sporadic quality associated with it. This principle is basically the same as Homans's deprivation-satiation proposition (recall the flower example).

Concepts and Theory: Creating Power and Social Structures

There are two norms associated with social exchange: the *norm of reciprocity* and the norm of fair exchange. Blau sees exchange as the starting mechanism for social interaction and group structure. Before group identities and boundaries, and before status positions, roles, and norms are created, interaction is initiated in the hopes of gaining something from exchange. That we are dependent upon others for reaction implies that the idea of reciprocation is central in exchange. The word *reciprocate* comes from Latin and literally means to move back and forth. Exchange, then, always entails the give and take of some elements of value, such as money, emotion, favors, and so forth. As such, one of the first behaviors to gain normative power was reciprocity. The norm of reciprocity implies another basic feature of society, that of trust. As we've seen, social exchange requires that the reciprocated good or service be unspecified and that reciprocation is delayed to some undisclosed future. This lack of specificity obviously demands trust, which forms the basis of society and our initial social contact. Exchanges are also guided by the *norm of fair exchange.* Something is fair, of course, if it is characterized by honesty and free from fraud or favoritism. The expectation of fairness increases over the length of the exchange relation.

Because of the lack of specificity in social exchange and the norm of reciprocity, exchange creates bonds of friendship and establishes power relations. The basic difference between friendship and power relationships concerns the equity of exchange and is expressed in the amount of repayment discretion. Friendship is based on an equal exchange relationship: All parties feel that they give about as much as they take in the relationship. This equal reciprocity among friends leads to a social bond built on trust and a high level of discretion in repayment. On the other hand, inequality in exchange leads to unfulfilled obligations that, in turn, grant power over repayment to the other.

According to Blau (2003), there are four conditions that affect the level of social power. I've diagrammed these conditions in Figure 6.3. In the diagram, we have a social exchange relation between A and B. In thinking through the way the model works, you can visualize yourself as either person and get a sense of the way the power flows in the relationship. *Social capital* refers to the ability to participate in an exchange with goods or services that the other desires. As you can see, there is a negative relationship between social capital and power. In other words, the less ability Actor A has to control goods and services (exchange capital) that Actor B desires, the greater will be B's power over A. Alternatives are important for power as well. If I have a large number of alternatives through which I can obtain the social good or service that I desire, then others will have little power over me. However, the fewer the number of alternatives, the greater will be the power of others who control the social good. This inverse relationship is noted by the negative sign.

There are two other important factors in establishing social power: the actor's willingness to use force and the consistency of the value hierarchy. If Actor A has the ability

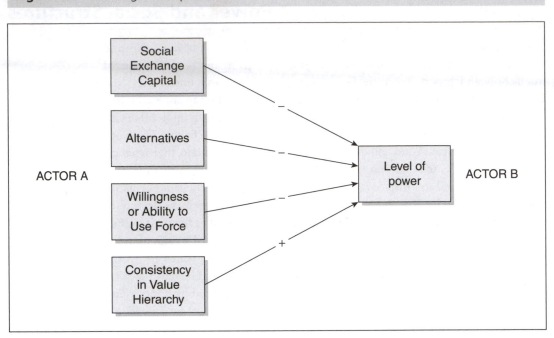

Figure 6.3 Exchange Principles of Power

and willingness to use force, then by definition there is no exchange relation and, thus, social power is impossible. This somewhat obvious condition tells us something important about social power: There is always a choice involved. With social power, "There is an element of voluntarism . . . the punishment could be chosen in preference to compliance" (Blau, 2003, p. 117). The relationship between Actor A's willingness to use force and Actor B's power is negative: The less likely Actor A is to use force to obtain social goods, the greater is the potential for social power for Actor B.

The last condition implies a consistent value hierarchy. If the value system of Actor A changes and he or she no longer values the social goods B controls, then there can be no power. If, on the other hand, Actor A consistently values the goods B has to offer, then social power will increase, if the other conditions hold as well. Try this thinking exercise: Think about the relationships that you have with various professors as exchange relations. Use each of these four variables—social capital, alternative, willingness to use force, and consistent value hierarchy—and ask the following: Who has more power and why? I believe you'll find that your professors have varying levels of power because of the different ways these factors align. At minimum, this implies that social power is not a simple function of bureaucratic position.

There are five possible responses to unequal exchanges. Four of the responses correspond to the four conditions of power and constitute attempts to change the balance of power. In other words, if you want to change the amount of power someone has over you, you could do one of the following:

- Increase your exchange capital by obtaining a good or service that the other person desires

- Find alternative sources to what you receive from the other person

- Get along without the good or service the other person controls

- Attempt to force the other person to give you what you need

The only other possible response is subordination and compliance. Compliance, unlike most features of social exchange, can be specified and functions like money: "Willingness to comply with another's demands is a generic social reward, since the power it gives him is a generalized means, parallel to money, which can be used to attain a variety of ends" (Blau, 2003, p. 22). The power to command is like a credit, an IOU in social exchange. It is what we give to others when we can't participate in an equal exchange yet we desire the goods they control.

Building Social Structures

Secondary exchange relations result from power and occur at the group level among those who are collectively indebted to someone or to another group. In order for secondary exchange relations to come into play, people who are individually indebted to a person or group must have physical proximity and be able to communicate with one another. For example, let's say you are tutoring a number of students in sociology without charging them money. Each of those individuals would be socially indebted to you, and each individual relationship would be subject to the dynamics of exchange (alternatives, marginal utilities, and norms). As long as you only met with each person individually and they were unaware of each other, the exchange relations would remain individual. On the other hand, if you decide that your time would be better spent tutoring them as a group, then secondary exchange relations could come into play. You've provided them with the ability to become a group through physical proximity and communication. When a group like this is brought together physically and able to communicate, two possibilities exist with regard to power: The group may either legitimate or oppose your power as the tutor.

Blau gives us a very basic process through which power is either legitimated or delegitimated. Both possibilities are in response to the group's perception of how those in power perform in relation to the norms of fair exchange and reciprocity. If the norms are adhered to, then social power will be legitimated. Blau posits that the path looks something like this:

> reciprocity and fair exchange with those in power → common feelings of loyalty → norm of compliance → legitimation of authority → organization → institutionalized system of exchange values

As the group communicates with one another about the level of adherence of those in power to the norms of fair exchange and reciprocity, they collectively develop feelings of loyalty and indebtedness. Out of these feelings comes the norm of compliance: The group begins to sanction itself in terms of its relationship to those in power. This process varies in the sense that the more those in power are seen as consistently generous, that is, exceeding the norms of fairness and reciprocity, the more the group will feel loyal and the stronger will be the norm of compliance and sense of legitimation. Out of legitimation come organization and an institutionalized system of values regarding authority (see Blau & Meyer, 1987, for Blau's treatment of bureaucracy).

In his theory of secondary exchange relations, Blau is giving us an explanation of the micro–macro link. We can see this move from individual exchanges to institutions in the path of secondary relations noted earlier. The "glue" that holds this path together consists of generalized trust and the norm of reciprocity. As we've already seen, all social exchanges are built on trust; the element of time and the lack of specificity in social exchanges demand trust. Organizations and institutions are, in Blau's scheme, long chains of indirect exchanges of rewards and costs. Moreover, as we've seen, exchange intrinsically entails reciprocation. Every step, then, along the chain of exchanges is held together by the norm of reciprocity.

Secondary exchange relations can thus lead to legitimated authority, but they can also lead to opposition and conflict. If those in power do not meet the norms of fair exchange and reciprocity, and if those indebted are brought together physically and are able to communicate with one another, then feelings of resentment will tend to develop. These feelings of resentment obviously lead to delegitimation of authority. This path of secondary exchange relations looks like this:

lack of reciprocity and fairness from those in power → feelings of resentment → communication (a function of physical proximity and communication technologies) → delegitimation of authority → ideology → solidarity → opposition → probability of change

Group members experiencing a lack of fairness and reciprocity that are in close physical proximity and are able to communicate with one another will tend to develop a set of beliefs and ideas that justify both their resentment and their delegitimation of authority. This ideology, in turn, enables group solidarity and overt opposition, thus increasing the probability of change. The last part of this path comes from the conflict theories of Marx and Weber. To this general theory of conflict and change, Blau adds the micro dimension of exchange: the beginning part of the path. Keep in mind that all of these factors function as variables and are therefore changeable.

Summary

- Social exchanges are different from economic exchanges because they lack specificity, they require and build trust, they are meaningful, and social benefits are detached from the source. These differences imply that social exchanges create diffuse obligations, which in turn form the basis of society—social relations must be maintained in order to guarantee repayment of these obligations. Population structures are made up from the distributions of a population along various continuums of difference or social position. These continuums of difference create or hinder opportunities for social contact, social mobility, and social conflict.

- There are three basic principles and two norms of exchange. The contours of all social exchanges are set by the principles of rational motivation, the presence of alternatives, and satiation. Because of the peculiar properties of social exchanges, rationality within them is limited, as compared to economic exchanges. People are rational in social exchanges to the extent that they tend to repeat those actions from which they received rewards in the past. People are also rational in the sense that they will gravitate toward exchanges that are equal, the equality of exchanges being determined by the presence of alternatives. In addition, all social exchanges are subject to the principle of marginal utilities—a social good loses its value in exchange as people become satiated. In other words, value in exchange is determined to some extent by scarcity and uncertainty. All social exchanges are subject to the norms of reciprocity and fair exchange.

- Social actors achieve power through unequal exchanges, with inequality in exchange determined by four factors: the level of exchange capital, the number of potential source alternatives, the willingness and ability to use force, and consistency in value hierarchy. The first three are negatively related to power. That is, in an exchange relationship between Actor A and Actor B, as Actor A's capital, alternatives, and ability to use force go down, Actor B's power over Actor A increases. Consistency is a positive or at least steady relationship—continuing to value the goods that Actor B controls places Actor A in a possible subordinate position.

Ritualized Exchanges: Randall Collins

Randall Collins brings us yet another way of seeing exchanges. Like Homans, Collins has a strong individual component to his theory. But Collins isn't interested in the psychological processes of the individual. In fact, he's doubtful about the existence of what is usually implied by "the individual." He points out that what we mean by the individual varies by the social and cultural context and is thus a poor focus for social science research. There are two ways to understand his point. The first is to understand that what we mean by "the individual" is really the social point at which various social identities meet. For example, if I were to ask you to tell me who you are, most of your answers would be in the form of social categories and would involve such things as age, gender, sexuality, friendship, marital status, and so on. The individual, from this point of view, is *a reflection of sociopolitical organization rather than essential characteristics.*

Source: Courtesy of Randall Collins.

The other way to see that the individual varies by social context is much more profound. From this perspective, the entire idea of "the individual" is the product of political, religious, and social changes that have occurred in the past few centuries. More specifically, the idea of the individual came about as Western society defined civil rights (as a result of the rise of democracy) and moral responsibilities (as a result of the Protestant Reformation). The idea of the individual also became more pronounced through capitalism (consumerism) and social diversity. About the individual, Randall Collins (2004) says,

> The human individual is a quasi-enduring, quasi-transient flux in time and space. . . . It is an ideology of how we regard it proper to think about ourselves and others . . . not the most useful analytical starting point for microsociology. (p. 4)

Like Blau, Collins is more interested in what happens *between* people than within the individual, but Collins focuses on broader elements of the situation than simply the exchange relation *per se*. Collins also has a different way of seeing how "society" comes about. In the end, Blau, like Parsons, falls back on the power of norms. For Collins, social structures and systems are *heuristics*—that is, they are aids to discovery. Collins (1987) is arguing that we can use the ideas of structure and social systems to "make generalizations about the workings of the world system, formal organizations, or the class structure by making the appropriate comparisons and analyses of its own data" (pp. 194–195). But the reality behind these heuristics is the pure number of face-to-face situations strung together through time and space. In other words, *social structures are built up by the aggregation of many interactions over long periods of time and large portions of geographic space*. The primary way in which they are linked together is through emotion.

THEORIST'S DIGEST

Brief Biography

Randall Collins was born in Knoxville, Tennessee, on July 29, 1941. His father worked in U.S. military intelligence during WWII and was later a member of the state department. Collins thus spent a good deal of his early years in Europe. As a teenager, Collins was sent to a New England prep school, afterward studying at Harvard and the University of California, Berkeley, where he encountered the work of Herbert Blumer and Erving Goffman, both professors at Berkeley at the time. Collins completed his PhD in 1969. He has spent time teaching at a number of universities, such as the University of Virginia and the Universities of California at Riverside and San Diego, and has held a number of visiting professorships at Chicago, Harvard, Cambridge, and at various universities in Europe, Japan, and China. He is currently at the University of Pennsylvania.

Central Sociological Questions

Collins's work has enormous breadth. Overall, his passion is to understand how societies are produced, held together, and destroyed through emotionally rather than rationally motivated behaviors. In terms of social exchange, then, his interest is to understand how emotion forms the basic motivation and outcome of an exchange. And, like Blau, he's interested in how each individual situated exchange is linked together to form macro-level structures of inequality.

Simply Stated

Collins argues that the most general goods that are exchanged among people are emotional energy and cultural capital, and that the basic social unit is the interaction ritual. The level of ritualized activities varies by co-presence, common emotional mood and focus of attention, and barrier to outsiders. As these variables increase, the group involved will create higher levels of emotion, which then creates group solidarity and group symbols; these, in turn, are carried within the individual and provide the motivation to recreate rituals. Collins argues that this process is how stratified power and class are reproduced.

Key Ideas

Emotional energy, rituals, co-presence, shared focus of attention, rhythmic entrainment, common emotional mood, barrier to outsiders, group symbols, group solidarity, standards of morality, generalized and particularized cultural capital, reputational capital, market opportunities, stratification, deference and demeanor, principle of order giving, principle of ritual coercion, principle of anticipatory socialization, principle of bureaucratic personality, social network, authoritarian, cosmopolitan

Concepts and Theory: Emotion—The Generalized Media of Exchange

Collins's use of emotion is based on three long-standing critiques of exchange theory. First, exchange theory has a difficult time accounting for altruistic behavior. Merriam-Webster (2002) defines *altruism* as "uncalculated consideration of, regard for, or devotion to others' interests." If most or all of our interactions are exchange-based and if all our exchanges are based on self-motivated actors making rational calculations for profit, how can altruism be possible? Collins claims that exchange theorists are left arguing that the actor is actually selfish in altruistic behavior—he or she gains some profit from being altruistic. However, just what that profit is has generally been left unspecified.

Second, some evidence suggests that people in interactions are rarely rational or calculative. In support of this, Collins cites Goffman's and Garfinkel's work, the idea of bounded rationality in organizational analysis, as well as psychological experiments indicating that when people are faced with problems that should prompt them to be rational, they use non-optimizing heuristics instead. These heuristics function like approximate or sufficient answers to problems rather than the most rational or best answer.

The third criticism of exchange theory is that there is no common metric or medium of exchange. Money, of course, is the metric and medium of trade for exchanges involving economically produced goods and services; however, money isn't general enough to embrace all exchanges, all goods, and all services.

Collins sees each of these problems solved through the idea that **emotional energy** is the common denominator of rational action. Let's note from the beginning that this approach is rather adventuresome in that it combines two things that have usually been thought of as oil and water—emotion and rationality. They just don't mix. At least, they didn't before Collins came along. Emotional energy does not refer to any specific emotion; it is, rather, a very general feeling of emotion and motivation that an individual senses. It is the "amount of emotional power that flows through one's actions" (R. Collins, 1988, p. 362). Collins (2004) conceptualizes emotional energy as running on a continuum from high levels of confidence, enthusiasm, and good self-feelings to the low end of depression, lack of ambition, and negative self-feelings (p. 108). The idea of emotional energy is like that of psychological drive, but emotional energy is based in social activity.

Collins is arguing that emotional energy is general enough to embrace all exchanges. In fact, emotional energy is the underlying resource in back of every exchanged good and service, whether it's a guitar, a pet, a conversation, a car, your attendance at a show or sporting event, and so on. *More basic than money, emotional energy is the motivation behind all exchanges.* Emotional energy can also be seen in back of social exchanges that might seem counterintuitive. Why would I exchange my free time to work at a soup kitchen on Sunday mornings? This, of course, is an example of altruistic behavior. Exchange theory, apart from the idea of emotional energy, is hard-pressed to explain such behaviors in terms of exchange. Collins gives us a more general property of exchange in the form of emotional energy: People engage in altruistic behaviors because of the emotional energy they receive in exchange.

The idea of emotional energy also solves the problem of the lack of rational calculations. As Collins notes, people aren't generally observed making rational calculations during interactions. Rather than being rationally calculative, "human behavior may be characterized as emotional tropism" (R. Collins, 1993, p. 223). A *tropism* is an involuntary movement by an organism that is a negative or positive response to a stimulus. An example is the response of a plant to sunlight. The stems and leaves react positively to the sun by reaching toward it, and the roots react negatively by moving away from it and deeper in the ground. Collins is telling us that people aren't cognitively calculative in normal encounters. Instead, people emotionally feel their way to and through most interactions, much like the way leaves of a plant reach toward the sun.

Concepts and Theory: Interaction Ritual Chains

For Collins, **rituals** are patterned sequences of behavior that bring four elements together: bodily co-presence, barrier to outsiders, mutual focus of attention, and shared emotional mood. These elements are variables—as they increase, so also will the effects of ritualized behavior. There are five main effects of interaction rituals: group solidarity, group symbols, standards and feelings of morality, individual emotional energy, and individual cultural capital. Collins's theory is diagramed in Figure 6.4.

One of the first things that the model in Figure 6.4 calls our attention to is physical *co-presence*, which describes the degree of physical closeness. Even in the same room, we can be closer or further away from one another. The closer we get, the more we can sense the other person. As Durkheim (1912/1995) says,

> The very act of congregating is an exceptionally powerful stimulant. Once the individuals are gathered together, a sort of electricity is generated from their closeness and quickly launches them to an extraordinary height of exaltation. (pp. 217–218)

Bodily presence appears theoretically necessary for rituals to take place because the closer people are, the more easily they can monitor one another's behaviors.

Part of what we monitor is the level of involvement or *shared focus of attention*, the degree to which participants are attending to the same behavior, event, object, symbol, or idea at the same time (a difficult task, as any teacher knows). We watch

Figure 6.4 The Interaction Ritual

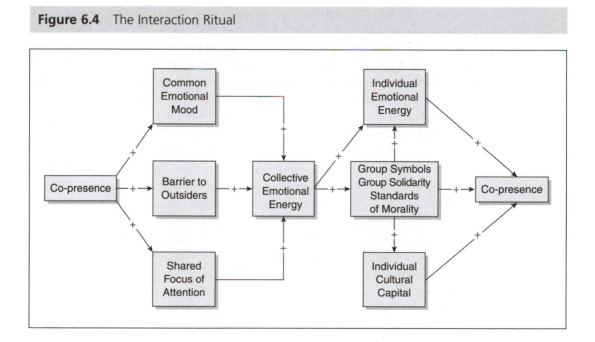

bodily cues and eye movements, and we monitor how emotions are expressed and how easily others are drawn away from an interaction. Members of similar groups have the ability to pace an interaction in terms of conversation, gestures, and cues in a like manner. Part of the success or intensity of an interaction is a function of this kind of rhythm or timing.

The key to successful rituals "is that human nervous systems become mutually attuned" (R. Collins, 2004, p. 64). Collins means that in intense interactions or ritual performance, we physically mimic one another's body rhythms; we become physically "entrained." *Rhythmic entrainment* refers to recurrent bodily patterns that become enmeshed during successful rituals. These bodily patterns may be large and noticeable as in hand or arm expressions, or they may be so quick and minute that they occur below the level of human consciousness.

It is estimated that human beings can perceive things down to about 0.2 seconds in duration (R. Collins, 2004, p. 68). Much of this entrainment occurs below that threshold, or below the level of consciousness—which indicates that people literally "feel" their way through intense ritualized interactions. Collins (2004, pp. 65–78) cites evidence from conversational analysis and audience–speaker behavior to show that humans become rhythmically coordinated with one another in interactions. Some research has shown that conversations not only become rhythmic in terms of turn-taking, but the acoustical voice frequencies become entrained as well. EEG (electroencephalogram) recordings have indicated that even the brain waves of interactants can become synchronized. In a study of body motion and speech using 16mm film, Condon and Ogston (1971) discovered that in interaction, "a hearer's body was found to 'dance' in precise harmony with the speaker" (p. 158).

A shared focus of attention and common emotional mood tend to reinforce one another through rhythmic entrainment. *Common emotional mood* refers to the degree to which participants are emotionally oriented toward the interaction in the same way. In ritual terms, it doesn't really matter what kind of emotion we're talking about. What is important is that the emotion be commonly held. Having said that, I want to point out that there is an upper and lower limit to ritual intensity. One of the things that tends to become entrained in an interaction is turn-taking. The rule for turn-taking is simple: One person speaks at a time. The speed at which turns are taken is vitally important for a ritual. The time between statements in a successful conversation will hover around 0.1 second. If the time between turns is too great, at say 1.0 seconds, the interaction will be experienced as dull and lifeless and no solidarity will be produced. If, on the other hand, conversational statements go in the other direction and overlap or interrupt one another, then the "conversation" breaks down and no feeling of solidarity results. These latter kinds of conversations are typically arguments, which can be brought about by a hostile common emotional mood. Collins (2004) points out that it is generally the case at the micro level that "solidarity processes are easier to enact than conflict processes.... The implication is that conflict is much easier to organize at a distance" (p. 74).

Being physically co-present tends to bring about the other variables, particularly, as we've seen, the shared focus of attention. Co-presence also aids in the production of ritual barriers. *Barrier to outsiders* refers to symbolic or physical obstacles we put up to other people attempting to join our interaction. The use of barriers increases the sense of belonging to the interaction that the participants experience. The more apparent and certain that boundary, the greater will be the level of ritualized interaction and production of group emotional energy. Sporting events and rock concerts are good illustrations of using physical boundaries to help create intense ritual performance.

Notice that there is a total of five effects coming out of the emotional energy that is produced in rituals. Let's first talk about the interrelated group effects: group symbols, solidarity, and standards of morality. *Group symbols* are those symbols we use to anchor social emotions. The greater the level of collective emotional energy that's created in rituals, the greater will be the level of emotion that the symbol comes to represent. It's this investment of group emotion that makes the symbol a collective one; the symbol comes to embody and represent the group. If the invested emotion is high enough, these symbols take on sacred qualities. We can think of the U.S. flag, gang insignia, and sport team emblems and colors as examples, in addition to the obvious religious ones. The symbols help to create group boundaries and identities. Group symbols have an important ritual function: They are used to facilitate ritual enactment by focusing attention and creating a common emotional mood.

Group solidarity is the sense of oneness a collective can experience. This concern originated with Durkheim (1893/1984, pp. 11–29) and meant the level of integration in a society, measured by the subjective sense of "we-ness" individuals have, the constraint of individual behaviors for the group good, and the organization of social units. Collins appears to mean it in a more general way. Group solidarity is the feeling of membership with the group that an individual experiences. It's seeing oneself as part of a larger whole. One of the important things to understand here is that the sense of membership is emotional. It is derived from creating high levels of collective effervescence. Of course, the higher the level of effervescence, the higher will be the sense of belonging to the group that an individual can have.

Standards of morality refer to group-specific behaviors that are important to group membership and are morally enforced. Feelings of group solidarity lead people to want to control the behaviors that denote or create that solidarity. That is, many of the behaviors, speech patterns, styles of dress, and so on that are associated with the group become issues of right and wrong. Groups with high moral boundaries have stringent entrance and exit rules (they are difficult to get in and out of). Today's street gangs and the Nazi Party of World War II are good examples of groups with high moral boundaries.

One of the things to notice about our example is the use of the word *moral*. Most of us probably don't agree with the ethics of street gangs. In fact, we probably think their ethics are morally wrong and reprehensible. But when sociologists use the term *moral*, we are not referring to something that we think of as being good. A group is moral if its behaviors, beliefs, feelings, speech, styles, and so forth are controlled by strong group norms and are viewed by the members in terms of right and wrong. Because the level of standards of morality any group may have is a function of their level of interaction rituals, we could safely say that, by this definition, both gangs and World War II Nazis are probably more "moral" than we are, in this sense, unless one of us is a member of a radical fringe group.

Ritualized Social Structures

Notice the arrows coming out of individual cultural capital and emotional energy in Figure 6.4. They feed into and create another co-presence—this is how interaction rituals become linked or chained together. In Collins's theory of interaction ritual chains, the individual is the carrier of the micro–macro link. There are two components to this linkage: emotional energy and cultural capital. Emotional energy is the emotional charge that people can take away with them from an interaction. As such, emotional energy predicts the likelihood of repeated interactions: If the individual comes away from an interaction with as high or higher emotional energy than he or she went in with, the person will be more likely to seek out further rituals of the same kind. Emotional energy also sets the person's initial involvement within the interaction. People entering an interaction who are charged up with emotional energy will tend to be fully involved and more readily able to experience rhythmic entrainment and collective effervescence.

Cultural capital is a shorthand way of talking about the different resources we have to culturally engage with other people. The idea of cultural capital covers a full range of cultural items: It references the way we talk; what we have to talk about; how we dress, walk, and act—in short, anything that culturally references us to others. Collins lists three different kinds of cultural capital. *Generalized cultural capital* is the individual's stock of symbols that are associated with group identity. As Figure 6.4 notes, a great deal of this comes from interaction rituals. This kind of cultural capital is group specific and can be used with strangers, somewhat the way money can. For example, the other day I was at the airport standing next to a man wearing a tie-dyed T-shirt with a dancing bear on it. Another fellow who was coming off a different flight saw him and said, "Hey, man, where ya from?" These two strangers were able to strike up a conversation because the one man recognized the group symbols of Deadheads—fans of the band The Grateful Dead. They were able to engage one another in an interaction ritual because of this generalized cultural capital.

Particularized cultural capital refers to cultural items we have in common with specific people. For example, my wife and I share a number of words, terms, songs, and so forth that are specifically meaningful to us. Hearing Louis Armstrong, for instance, instantly orients us toward one another, references shared experiences and meanings, and sets us up for an interaction ritual. But if I hear an Armstrong song around my friend Steve, it will have no social effect— there are no shared experiences (past ritual performances) that will prompt us to connect. From these two examples, you get a good sense of what cultural capital does: It orients people toward one another, gives them a shared focus or attention, and creates a common emotional mood, which are most of the ingredients of an interaction ritual.

The last kind of cultural capital that Collins talks about is *reputational capital.* If somebody knows something about you, he or she is more likely to engage you in conversation than if you are a complete stranger. That makes sense, of course, but remember that this is a variable. Jennifer Lopez, for example, has a great deal of cultural capital. If she were seen in a public space, many people would feel almost compelled to engage her in an interaction ritual, even though they are strangers to her.

Thus, every person comes into an interaction with stocks of emotional energy (EE) and cultural capital (CC) that have been gleaned from previous interactions. The likelihood of an individual seeking out an interaction ritual is based on his or her levels of emotional energy and cultural capital; the likelihood of two people interacting with one another is based on both the similarity of their stocks and the perceived probability that they might gain either emotional energy or cultural capital from the encounter. The micro–macro link for Collins, then, is created as individual carriers who are charged up with emotional energy and cultural capital seek out other interaction rituals in which to revitalize or increase their stocks.

I'd like to make one further point before we leave this idea: People have a good idea of their *market opportunities,* which is directly linked to cultural capital and indirectly to emotional energy. As we noted earlier, we exchange cultural capital in the hopes of receiving more cultural capital back. Part of our opportunity in the cultural capital market is structured: Our daily rounds keep us within our class, status, and power groups. However, our interpersonal markets are far more open in modern societies than they were in traditional ones. In these open markets, we are "rational" in the sense that we avoid those interactions where we will spend more cultural capital than we gain, and we will pursue those interactions where we have a good chance of increasing our level of cultural capital. We also tend to avoid those interactions where our lack of CC will be apparent. As a result, we tend to separate ourselves into symbolic or status groups.

Concepts and Theory: Ritualizing Stratification

Using his theory of interaction ritual chains and adding the idea of status from Weber and the notion of deference and demeanor from Goffman (Chapter 4), Collins forms a theory of stratification that has important cultural, social-psychological elements. *Stratification* is always an issue of replication: How is the unequal distribution of scarce resources perpetuated generationally by social groups? Collins's theory looks at how stratification is enacted empirically in the situation and how people subjectively experience their lives differently based on social stratification; in particular, he looks at deference and demeanor rituals. *Deference* refers to respect given and *demeanor* to the cues that indicate the level of respect anticipated. In that these are ritualized, Collins is telling us that these behaviors produce emotional energy and cultural capital and that they are generally part of our regular routine in interaction. For example, you probably don't even notice when you call your instructor "Professor" or "Doctor," but in doing so, you are performing a deference ritual that creates and perpetuates status inequalities.

The Vertical Dimension of Power

In the main, Collins argues that there are two dimensions of stratification: the vertical dimension of power and the horizontal dimension of social networks. As we make our way through Collins's ideas about power, notice that power is not so much seen as a property of social structure as it is enacted in ritual performance. On the vertical power dimension, there are four variables or principles: order giving, ritual coercion, anticipatory socialization, and bureaucratic personality. The *principle of order giving* says that the occupational position of people runs on a continuum of order giving and taking. At the high end are those who do not take orders from anyone but give orders to many, at the low end are those who only take orders and do not give them, and in the middle are those who take orders from some and give orders to others.

We can understand order giving and taking as types of Goffmanian front- and backstage rituals. Order givers dominate the front stage and give off cues through their demeanor that they are worthy of respect. They make themselves appear dominant and in control, and they internally link their organizational position with their own sense of self. We can also understand order givers as a type of sacred object in the rituals where power is at issue. They are the focus of the interaction and set the emotional mood. In some sense, "it is no longer a mere individual who speaks but a group incarnated and personified" (Durkheim, 1912/1995, p. 212). Order givers dominate the front stage and develop a front-stage personality; they idealize their jobs and see them as more than simple occupations. Order takers, on the other hand, are passive in the front stage and find their rewards in the backstage of organizational life, in such activities as being a sports fan, playing games, or watching television.

The *principle of ritual coercion* says that the more coercion and threat are used in order-giving rituals, the greater will be the level of deference demanded and given, and the greater will be the effects of the principle of order giving. Two obvious examples are medieval aristocracies and the U.S. military; both demand high levels of deference, noted by such terms as "your highness" and "sir" and "ma'am." The *principle of anticipatory socialization* explains that individuals who look forward to occupying an order-giving position sometime in the future tend to identity with that culture even if they are presently order takers. Thus, those in middle and non-management positions who expect promotion will begin to perform the deference and demeanor ritual in keeping with their anticipated position.

Finally, the *principle of bureaucratic personality* addresses the people in the middle, those who take orders from some and give orders to others. These people will have a rather unique cultural outlook and practice. Their place is in between: They stand between upper management and workers or between the organization and the public. As such, they tend to exhibit personal tendencies of both positions: They identify outwardly with the rules and regulations of the organization rather than inwardly believing in the overall mission of the group, and they tend to strictly enforce the rules and regulations on the front stage (in performance for the public or workers) because it is the only stage that they can control.

The Horizontal Dimension of Networks

The second dimension of stratification is the social network aspect of occupational cultures. Every one of us has a *social network*—a string or chain of interactions that form a pattern. The way in which that pattern is put together is vitally important. Social networks are particularly important because they form the way a person thinks and sees the world. Let's use the analogy of cloth to get a grasp on what this means.

Cloth is made out of a network of threads. Two things about this network are especially important for the kind of cloth with which we will end up: the diversity of threads and the density of the weave. The diversity of threads is a vital issue. If the threads that are used are all of one color, what will be the result? A cloth of one color. The same is true of social networks. If the diversity of a person's network is low, if she doesn't interact with different kinds of people in different kinds of situations, then her fabric will only be of one color. This kind of individual will tend to see things concretely, with very little variation. Her point of view will be very narrow and her number of lifestyle alternatives few. The inverse is true as well: If an individual's social network reveals diversity, then her ideas and perspectives will be more abstract and encompassing. She will tend to be more accepting of others and a diversity of lifestyles.

In cloth, the density of the weave helps determine how durable it is. With social networks, this function is fulfilled by network density. Network density varies by frequency and longevity of interactions. The more frequently a person interacts with the same people and the greater the length of time over which these interactions take place, the denser will be his or her network. Both network diversity and density correspond to elements in interaction rituals. The diversity of the network gets at the degree to which we share a common focus of attention. If the groups that you interact with share a common focus of attention (if there is little variety in what you are paying attention to), then the social objects that occupy your attention become reified, meaning concrete or real.

Social density brings in another ritual element—physical co-presence. Let's think about our cloth again. If the threads of a piece of cloth are tightly wound and densely packed together, what kind of cloth is the result? The cloth would be tough, inflexible, and resilient. Dense interaction networks where people spend a great deal of time in one another's presence tend to yield people who have reified ideas; that is, their ideas are seen as the only possible reality.

There's an old saying: "Birds of a feather flock together." What Collins is telling us is something a little different: "Birds *become* of a feather *because* they flock together." In other words, the most prominent characteristics of people come about because of the pattern of their interactions. People tend to be narrow-minded if their interaction pattern is not diverse; people tend to be more accepting and to hold abstract rather than particularized beliefs if their interaction pattern is diverse. Moreover, socially constructed ideas tend to be seen as objectively real when the interaction network is dense. These two variables don't necessarily have to go together, but when they do, the results are impressive. Interaction rituals that take place within homogeneous, dense networks produce high levels of social conformity. Some contemporary examples where the network is both dense and uniform include religious cults such as the People's Temple and Heaven's Gate, and the group solidarity the U.S. government fosters in military boot camps.

Reproducing Class and Power

When power and network variables come together, they form predictable patterns of personalities. Remember that for Collins, there isn't a self that people are born with, nor is the self a particularly individual entity—the self is social in both creation and function. Like Blumer, Collins sees the self as emerging from patterns of interaction. George Herbert Mead (1934), the philosopher from whom Blumer draws, explains that "the self is not something that exists first and then enters into relationship with others, but it is, so to speak, an eddy in the social current and so still a part of the current" (p. 26). Eddies are currents of air or water that run contrary to the stream. It isn't so much the contrariness that Mead wants us to see, but the fact that an eddy exists only in and because of its surrounding current. The same is true for selves: They exist only in and because of social interaction. The self doesn't have a continuous existence; it isn't something that we carry around inside of us. It's a mechanism that allows social interactions and action to happen.

With Collins, we may find the analogy of a "junction" useful. A junction is a place or point where two or more elements are joined. Here the elements are the dimensions of power and network—the person is where these two social factors meet and are expressed. Someone who is high on both network density and power will have an *authoritarian,* upper-class type personality, and he or she will display all the front-stage work that comes with it. Such people generally interact only with those with whom they share similar interests—they attend the same schools, parties, country clubs, and so forth—and they interact frequently with those people. As a result, they are quite rigid in their sense of what is right and wrong, and they attempt to impose their values on society at large.

An individual who is high on the power dimension but low on network/ritual density will have and display a cosmopolitan, upper-class personality. Merriam-Webster (2002) defines *cosmopolitan* as "marked by interest in, familiarity with, or knowledge and appreciation of many parts of the world: not provincial, local, limited, or restricted by the attitudes, interests, or loyalties of a single region, section, or sphere of activity." The cosmopolitan upper classes, then, are those that have a broad view of the world and are very accommodating in terms of accepting people. Because their ritual density is low, they associate with many, many different kinds of groups and thus give credence to a variety of viewpoints. These are the kind of upper-class people that tend to use their influence and money to help others through political and humanitarian efforts, such as Band-Aid (a music group that raises money for famine relief) and the international AIDS foundations.

The same sort of personality type is located in the working class as well, but with different practices. Someone who is low on the order giver/taker dimensions and high on the social network dimension will conform to local, working-class culture. The stereotype of a "redneck" is a good example. On the other hand, someone low on the power dimension and low on the network dimension will be part of the working-class party crowd. It isn't important for you to know these types, but it is important for you to see what Collins is arguing. Collins is showing us that class isn't simply an economic structure: It's a power structure that is modified by complex networks of ritual density. Collins takes us beyond Marx and Weber in our understanding of stratification by including Durkheim and Goffman. We'll see another interesting approach to understanding how class is reproduced with Pierre Bourdieu's theory of habitus (Chapter 8).

Summary

- Rituals are patterned sequences of behavior that entail four elements: bodily co-presence, barrier to outsiders, mutual focus of attention, and shared emotional mood. Each of these is a variable, with increasing levels of each leading to increasing ritual performance and effects. Rituals result in group solidarity, group symbols, feelings of morality, individual emotional energy, and individual cultural capital. The greater the level of ritual performance, the greater will be the levels of each of these outcomes. Emotional energy and cultural capital are particularly important because they create the links among chains of interaction rituals. As individuals move from one interaction to another, they carry differing levels of emotional energy and cultural capital. These differing levels strongly influence the likelihood and subsequent effects of further rituals.

- Drawing on Weber, Durkheim, and Goffman, Collins argues that there are two dimensions of class stratification: power and social networks. Collins conceptualizes power in terms of order taking and order giving. In their jobs, people regularly experience a given proportion of order giving and taking. These relatively stable positions result in predictable and repeated ritual performances around deference and demeanor. Order givers are the focus of attention in such rituals; thus, the greater the level of power a person has, the more he will be the ritual focus of attention, the more will his identity take on sacred qualities, and the more he will develop a front-stage personality. Social networks vary by their level of diversity and density. Network diversity and density are both associated with authoritarian or cosmopolitan orientations—higher density and lower diversity create an authoritarian outlook, and lower density and higher diversity produce the more flexible, cosmopolitan perspective. The two features of social networks tend to vary inversely, with low levels of diversity being associated with high levels of density, and high levels of diversity being associated with low levels of density. However, they don't necessarily vary in this way, and this feature adds a great deal of complexity to the class stratification system.

TAKING THE PERSPECTIVE: EXCHANGE THEORY

Georg Simmel (1858–1919) was the first sociologist to have a clearly articulated exchange theory. He saw exchange as a type of social form, a patterned mode of interaction through which people meet personal and group goals. For Simmel, exchange is the basic social form because it is based on reciprocity. His theoretical focus is on how value is set or achieved. Value is based on sacrifice and scarcity, both of which are most directly determined by the immediate exchange relationship. Even though value is felt subjectively, it is determined by the totality of elements in the exchange (how scarce the exchange object is and how much someone is willing to sacrifice for it).

Contemporary exchange theory has by and large gone in two different directions. First is an approach initially developed by Richard Emerson (1962) and his colleague Karen Cook (1978). Blau takes the exchange between two people (dyad) as the archetype of exchange. In contrast, Emerson and Cook focus more on the network of exchange rather than the exchange itself. Social networks are defined by the patterns and positions of a group's interaction. For a quick example, think about an organizational chart. A person's position on that chart determines his or her general pattern of interaction. The same is true for any social group of which you are a member. Within a group, there are specific patterns of interaction: Some members of the group interact more than others, and some members don't interact together at all, even though they are in the same group. Social networks, then, are another kind of structure that produces effects that don't originate with the individual, that don't come from social group membership or identity, and about which the individual may or may not be aware.

Rational choice theory shifts focus back to the individual and the outcomes of his or her rational choices. One of the problems posed is that what may be rational for a group may not be rational for the individual. For example, if a group of six people were to move a piano upstairs, it's rational for the group to work together but not rational for the individual. People rationally seek to avoid cost and pain; moving a piano involves one and perhaps both. From the point of view of the individual, then, it's rational to appear as if he or she is contributing but in fact allow the others to do the actual work. This is called the problem of the "free rider." Because of this tendency of rationality and because there are certain goods that can only be created by a group, people rationally develop norms that limit or require action. These norms are rights given to some individuals to control the actions of others, and members agree to these obligations in exchange for comparable limitations and obligations being place on others. (See James S. Coleman's [1990] *Foundations of Social Theory* for a systematic argument from this perspective.)

BUILDING YOUR THEORY TOOLBOX

- Write a 250-word synopsis of exchange theory.

- After reading and understanding this chapter, you should be able to define the following terms theoretically and explain their theoretical importance to Homans's theory of the elementary forms of social behavior: elementary social behavior, respondent behaviors, respondent conditioning, law of effect, reinforcement, matching law, stimulus proposition, value, success proposition, value proposition, deprivation-satiation proposition, frustration-aggression proposition.

- After reading and understanding this chapter, you should be able to define the following terms theoretically and explain their theoretical importance to Blau's exchange theory: social exchanges, rational motivation, power, alternatives, marginal utilities, norm of reciprocity, norm of fair exchange, secondary exchange relations.

- After reading and understanding this chapter, you should be able to define the following terms theoretically and explain their theoretical importance to Collins's theory of ritual exchanges: emotional energy, rituals, co-presence, shared focus of attention, rhythmic entrainment, common emotional mood, barrier to outsiders, group symbols, group solidarity, standards of morality, generalized and particularized cultural capital, reputational capital, market opportunities, stratification, deference and demeanor, principle of order giving, principle of ritual coercion, principle of anticipatory socialization, principle of bureaucratic personality, social network, authoritarian, cosmopolitan.

- After reading and understanding this chapter, you should be able to answer the following questions (remember to answer them theoretically):

  o Explain how behaviors are patterned (social order is achieved) using Homans's theory of elementary behaviors.

  o Explain how power is achieved through social exchanges.

  o What are the five possible responses to power?

  o How are social structures created through social exchange?

  o Explicate the dynamics and effects of interaction rituals.

  o How do interaction rituals produce a micro–macro link?

  o How are power and status produced and reproduced through interaction rituals?

Learning More—Primary and Secondary Sources

- Homans's two most important works are *The Human Group,* Harcourt Brace Jovanovich, 1950, and *Social Behavior: Its Elementary Forms,* Harcourt, Brace & World, 1961.

- For a very good, brief introduction to Homans's work, see "Behaviourism and After," in A. Giddens & J. H. Turner, *Social Theory Today,* Stanford University Press, 1987.

(Continued)

(Continued)

- *George C. Homans: History, Theory, and Method,* by A. Javier Trevino, Paradigm Publishers, 2007.

- Blau's most significant work in exchange theory is *Exchange and Power in Social Life,* Transaction, 2003. Blau moved on from exchange theory and became concerned with population structures. That work can be found in *Structural Contexts of Opportunities,* University of Chicago Press, 1994.

- Blau has also written two short pieces that provide an excellent overview of his ideas:

  o Social Exchange. In David L. Sills (Ed.), *International Encyclopedia of the Social Sciences,* Macmillan, 1968.

  o Macrostructural Theory. In Jonathan H. Turner (Ed.), *Handbook of Sociological Theory,* Kluwer Academic/Plenum, 2002.

- *Structures of Power and Constraint: Papers in Honor of Peter M. Blau,* edited by Craig J. Calhoun, Marshall W. Meyer, and W. Richard Scott, Cambridge University Press, 1990.

- For an introduction to Collins's central idea of interaction ritual chains, read pages 188 to 203 in his *Theoretical Sociology,* Harcourt Brace Jovanovich, 1988. For a complete exposition of this idea, read *Interaction Ritual Chains,* Princeton University Press, 2004.

- Collins integrates a number of exchange principles in his theory. For his basic ideas on this subject, read "Emotional Energy as the Common Denominator of Rational Action," *Rationality and Society,* 5, 203–230, 1993; for an interesting look at markets, see "Market Dynamics as the Engine of Historical Change," *Sociological Theory, 8,* 111–135, 1990.

- Collins is also a well-known conflict theorist. For a quick overview of his approach, read "What Does Conflict Theory Predict About America's Future?" *Sociological Perspectives, 36,* 289–313, 1993. For a complete exposition of conflict theory, see *Conflict Sociology,* Academic Press, 1975.

- Collins is one of the few contemporary theorists from whom we have a biographical statement that links his life experiences with his theorizing. See Alair Maclean and James Yocom, "Interview With Randall Collins," 2000, available at http://www.ssc .wisc.edu/theory@madison/papers/ivwCollins.pdf.

Engaging the World

- One of the enlightening aspects of exchange theory is that it helps us understand our relationships in terms of exchange. For example, what kinds of exchange dynamics are at work in your family or significant relationships? How can you understand your relationship with your professor using exchange theory? Specifically, how is power achieved and how could you reduce the level of power?

- What does Collins's theory add to understanding race, class, gender, and sexual inequalities?

- How does emotion solve the three long-standing critiques of exchange theory?

- We've now reviewed symbolic interactionism, dramaturgy, ethnomethodology, and exchange theory. Keep a diary of your daily rounds for a week. Analyze your encounters in terms of which perspective is most salient at what times and places.

- Theoretically understanding how things work ought to give us greater abilities to control and direct social processes and outcomes. Use your diary of daily rounds and examine each social encounter. How could you become a more strategic actor in those situations by using what you theoretically know about what happens in face-to-face encounters?

Weaving the Threads

- Assess Homans's and Blau's understanding of value. Which do you think is more useable and why?

- Explain how each of the theorist's assumptions—Homans, Blau, Collins—informed their approach to theorizing. What specifically did the assumptions lead them to focus on? Do you think these approaches are mutually exclusive? Justify your answer.

- Assess the strengths and weaknesses of Blau's and Collins's "social glue." Can these be synthesized to give us a more robust understanding of how microprocesses create larger macro entities? Critique this theory using Blumer's symbolic interaction.

- Garfinkel gives us a theory of how social order is achieved at the micro level. Blau gives us a theory of how power is achieved and maintained at the micro level. How can these two theories be joined? Is power a part of social order? If so, how?

- Compare and contrast Blau's and Collins's ideas of power. What is power and how does it work in these two theories?

- Compare and contrast Blau's and Collins's theories of the micro–macro link. Put them together in such a way as to begin to form a single theory. What do you think is still missing?

- We have now examined four different ways that we can conceptualize what happens when social actors get together: symbolic interaction, ethnomethodology, dramaturgy, and exchange. Come up with a one- or two-word description for what each perspective tells us is happening. Now, under each of the descriptors, list at least five points that make that perspective unique and five insights you would get using that theory (in other words, what is the theory good for?).

- Compare and contrast Blumer's theory of the self with Collins's idea of the individual. In this analysis, be certain to explore and give examples of situations where the symbolic interactionist's idea of the self is more appropriate or functional and situations where Collins's notion of the person as the carrier of ritual elements makes more sense. Which do you find more theoretically persuasive and why?

- What are the differences and similarities between Blumer's idea of joint actions and Collins's idea of chains of interaction rituals?

Part III

Social Structures and Systems

The Big Picture: Levels of Analysis

One of the stunning things about sociology is its breadth of interest. A simple definition of sociology is the study of social things. The challenging thing for us is that sociology assumes that human beings are social by nature. Everything about us is built for sociability, from our upright stance to the structure of the brain, from our vocal chords to opposable thumbs. Most of our actions are social as well, in terms of their intention or their meaning. We may brush our teeth in private, but if the reason we're brushing our teeth is to have a nice smile, it's social. Further, anytime we attach meaning or value to our behaviors, it is invariably social because we use language to create meaning, and language is utterly social. Sociology, then, has incredible breadth and complexity—we're interested in almost everything people do. One implication is that we sociologists tend to organize our thought according to levels of analysis.

Generally speaking, sociology has four levels of analysis: macro, meso, micro, and individual. The *macro* level contains social structures and systems and usually takes into account historical processes. A good portion of Chapter 1 was a macro-level analysis of various social structures that together helped create the modern era. The *meso* level is a perspective that looks at organizations and groups. Weber's analysis of bureaucracies is a good example. *Micro*-level sociology (Chapters 3–6) investigates processes that occur in face-to-face social encounters; and sociology of the *individual* analyzes how such things as the self, consciousness or mind, emotions, the body, and so on are impacted socially. You can probably guess that these levels are nested in one another. So, for example, the school where I work is a bureaucratic organization (meso) that sits within the historically specific institutional sphere of American education (macro). All the interactions I have with students, professors, and administrators (micro) take place within the organization and are informed by the institutional norms and values of education. A major part of my sense of self is orchestrated by the institutional and organizational status position of professor. Further, my consciousness of and in the world is distinctly sociological, which, as we saw in Chapter 1, is historically specific.

The issue of levels of analysis becomes important for the way a book like this one gets organized. We started at the micro and individual levels for two reasons. One, it's usually easier for students to grasp. Even sociology students have a difficult time thinking outside the box of the individual. Two, it's sociologically important to center the relationships among social structures, social history, and the person. Modernity assumed a particular type of person. *To the degree that we are no longer modern, that person no longer exists.* Starting with the person and situation places them front and center. As you'll see in the rest of the book, social structures and the historical period have changed, and these facts have profound implications for the kind of person you're likely to be and the kind of social justice and democracy that's possible. This period of time is powerful, perhaps just as significant as the early stages of modernity. Most of you came across the idea of the *sociological imagination* in your introductory class. The notion comes from C. W. Mills (1959) and is

> the idea that the individual can understand his own experience and gauge his own fate only by locating himself within this period, that he can know his own chances in life only by becoming aware of those of all individuals in his circumstances. (p. 5)

We started with you (the theoretical you) and the social phenomenon you're most familiar with, the situation. In the next three parts of the book, I am going to introduce you to some of the macro-social elements that form the context of your life.

We'll first consider structures of inequality (race, gender, class), perennial concerns for sociology because of its heritage (Chapter 1). Beginning with race and gender might appear like an odd choice. For many sociologists, race and gender are seen as recent concerns. The reason for this is that the classical race and gender theorists weren't acknowledged by our discipline until recently, though many people had written and theorized about these structures since the beginning of modernity. Race and gender might also seem odd in that these systems of inequality are based on status positions and thus aren't the most general (class and power distributions seem to impact everyone more generally). While either of these issues would be reason enough for me to begin with race and gender, I actually have another reason: Wilson and Chafetz give us important insights into the world of social structure. From Wilson, we learn to look past the obvious to the underlying structure. In answer to the question of why there is racial inequality, most people would reply "racism." According to Wilson, that's not true in contemporary society. There is another, deeper structure at work. This is the basic lesson of this kind of analysis: *Structures work below the surface in often-unseen ways.*

Chafetz teaches us two things about social structures. The basic lesson is that structures permeate every level of human existence. Chafetz's theory involves all four levels of analysis, and she's one of the very few theorists who works like this. The second lesson is hard (and more important!) for many of us to hear: *Structures limit what we can and cannot do.* In this way, social structures act like architectural structures. You may feel like you can walk anywhere you want in your home, and to a certain degree you can. But the building your home is in limits your choices as well. You can't, for instance, decide to go down to the basement if the building doesn't have a basement. Yet, even if you've made your choice in keeping with the structure, the building will limit how you enact that choice. If you decide to move from the kitchen to your bedroom, the building gives you limited ways of doing so. It's true that the building enables you to walk from the kitchen to the bedroom; it would be a rare house indeed that did not have a doorway into the bedroom. But it's also true that your actions are limited by the very structures that enable you to live in your home. This is the hard lesson in structural sociology, and Chafetz teaches it better than anyone else.

CHAPTER 7

Structures of Racial and Gender Inequality

*William Julius Wilson and
Janet Saltzman Chafetz*

Source: Reprinted with permission of the American Sociological Association.

The Big Picture: Structures

Since its beginning, modernity has been captivated by social and technical projects. The technical project is aimed at controlling the natural environment, and the social project is focused on democracy and social justice (Chapter 1). Equally apparent is that both projects have proven to have unanticipated consequences and be more difficult to master than was first believed. We've obviously had tremendous success in the technical, such as eradicating polio and smallpox, producing more food than the world has ever seen, and so on, but we've also had our share of problems, such as global warming and resistant strains of bacteria. The same is true with the social project—some resounding successes but some significant and persistent problems: In the United States, our efforts at extending social justice and equality to blacks and women have been less than successful. There has obviously been some success, but it's also true that full equality has met with resistance.

When we think of this resistance to equality, most of us think of racist or sexist individuals. While there's no doubt that such people have an effect, the theorists in this chapter view continued inequality as a result of *social structures*. Our idea of social structures as objective, obdurate entities goes back to Durkheim (Chapter 1). He argued that social structures are entities that exist connected to but independent of individual people and the micro level of social interaction. Social structures thus have their own sets of laws and dynamics. Most importantly, social structures coerce or force people to think and behave in certain ways. We saw with Parsons that social structures or institutions work to pattern human action. From this perspective, then, social structures are the underlying cause of social order. In this chapter, the order that is persisting and influencing people's thoughts and actions is stratified racial and gender inequality.

Generally speaking, the theorists in this section of the book work with different kinds of structures. So, we should begin with a general definition of structure: *Structures are composed of different substances that impose organization, boundaries, and behaviors.* From this definition, we get three questions that we can use in working with different structures. The first question we should ask is, "What is the structure made of?" For example, the organs in your body are structured. The structure is made up of cells and tissues. Socially, we can talk about linguistic structures, economic structures, organizational structures, and so on. So, our first task is to identify the structure's substance, and that may not always be as easy as you think.

Next we can ask, "What do these structures do?" For the organs of the body, the answers are fairly well known; the lungs, for example, function to extract oxygen from the air. But for a good number of the structures that matter socially, the effects aren't part of the general knowledge. For example, Jeffrey Alexander (see Chapter 13) argues that cultural structures are made up of binary oppositions of purity and impurity that prompt and guide our discussions of democracy. The next question is, "How do structures do what they do?" For Alexander (2006), binary structures define political motives, social relations, and institutions, which are then used to define in- and out-group members, civil and uncivil people. For example, the civil sphere includes people who are active and autonomous (purity) and excludes those who are passive and dependent (impurity). Keep these questions in mind as we work through a theorist's use of structure: What is it made of? What does it do? How does it work? If you do this, you'll discover how the phenomenon in question works.

In this chapter, both William Julius Wilson and Janet Saltzman Chafetz argue that the inequalities associated with race and gender continue because of certain kinds of social structures. Wilson talks about how political and economic structures pattern race relations in the United States. Chafetz actually talks about a number of different types of structures, such as the division of labor, organizational structure, and intrapsychic structures. As we move through these theories, understand and keep in mind that for these kinds of theories, *individuals aren't as important as structures*. Structures do the work of ordering society and social behaviors.

The Declining Significance of Race: William Julius Wilson

Source: Reprinted with permission of the American Sociological Association.

While gender is more universal, the use of race as a category of distinction has historically been more destructive. Though women have been seen as inferior to men, in general their essential humanity has not been denied. The modern category of race, however, is based on such a distinction. While people have obviously been aware of differences of skin tone and facial features, in premodern societies, race wasn't an important way that people marked difference. Religion, territory, and eventually civilized versus uncivilized were much more important factors for most of human history. Race, as such, became important only with the dawn of modernity and specifically capitalism. Capitalism provided the motivation (accruing profit at the least possible expense) and the means (commodification) to make race the primary marker of difference in modern nations. While slavery had always existed, it wasn't until the advent of capitalism that *chattel slavery*—people seen as property—could exist. It was also modernity that brought to the forefront the issue of human nature as a political concern. You'll recall that political rights in modernity exist for the individual simply because of his or her humanity. Thus, one's standing as a human became an issue of concern and definition.

We are without a doubt at a significant moment of change in U.S. race relations. In 2008, the United States elected its first black president. But are we now in a "post-racial" society, one in which race no longer makes a difference? Recent statistics appear to say no. The 2009 median income for white families was $62,545, while black family median income was $38,409 (U.S. Census Bureau, 2012). The U.S. Department of Justice (2008) reports that at midyear 2008 there were 4,777 black male inmates per 100,000 U.S. residents being held in state or federal prisons and local jails, compared to just 727 white male inmates per 100,000 U.S. residents. The National Urban League (2009) has an overall statistical measure of African American equality as compared to whites: The 2009 Equality Index was 71.1%. However, are these discrepancies due to racism or some other factor? William Julius Wilson gives us what is perhaps an unexpected answer.

THEORIST'S DIGEST

Brief Biography

William Julius Wilson was born on December 20, 1935, in Derry Township, Pennsylvania. Wilson attended Wilberforce and Bowling Green Universities before completing his PhD in sociology at Washington State University in 1966. His first professorship was at the University of Massachusetts at Amherst, and he joined the faculty of the University of Chicago in 1972. There he held the position of professor and was the director of the Center for the Study of Urban Inequality. He moved to Harvard in 1996, where he currently holds the Lewis P. and Linda L. Geyser University Professorship. Wilson has received many top honors in his career, including the 1998 National Medal of Science (the highest such honor given in the United States), and he was named by *Time* magazine as one of America's 25 Most Influential People in 1996. He has authored several groundbreaking and significant books including *The Declining Significance of Race, The Truly Disadvantaged,* and *When Work Disappears: The World of the New Urban Poor.*

Central Sociological Questions

Wilson is driven to discover the structural causes of poverty that exist in the United States for African Americans. His interest is fueled by the question of policy—he wants to know how racial inequality works so it can be eradicated. So, his central question is, "What social policies need to be in place to improve the lives of African Americans?"

Simply Stated

Race relations in the United States have gone through three distinct phases: the plantation economy, post–Civil War to late 1930s, and World War II to present day. Because of changes in the relationships among government, capitalists, and workers, each of these phases needs to be understood using different theories: classic Marxian analysis, split labor market theory, and class-based analysis. Wilson (1980) concludes that "economic class is now a more important factor than race in determining job placement for blacks" (p. 120).

Key Ideas

Social structure, racism, exploitation, split labor market, Jim Crow, postindustrial economy

---

Wilson gives us a unique and complex way of seeing racial inequality. Obviously, his concern is the oppression of black people in the United States, but to merely see this inequality as a product of racism is too simplistic. There are two components to *racism:* beliefs and practices. A *racist belief system* assumes that physical, mental, emotional, and behavioral characteristics are genetically inherited; attributes these characteristics to race; and believes that these characteristics are hierarchically valued, privileging one race over another. *Racist practices* are those that in fact privilege one race over another. It's important to know that these two issues don't necessarily go together. A person may believe racist ideology but never act it out. Likewise, actions that privilege one race another don't necessarily have to be based on racist beliefs. We'll see this distinction with Wilson. He argues that racism as such, entailing both beliefs and practices, requires a particular kind of structural configuration among the state, the economy, and social relations. Conceptually, this triangle of relations comes from Marx. But Wilson recognizes that the relationship between business and government changes depending on the circumstances, which Marx never saw. Wilson's approach is to first understand the state as a relatively independent actor that can limit capitalism as well as support it. He also questions whether racism is always the causal force in the oppression of blacks. In order to answer that question, Wilson analyzes black inequality in the United States from slavery to the current system.

In the end, Wilson argues that racism (entailing both beliefs and practices) as a causal factor in determining the overall condition of blacks in the United States has been declining in significance since the Civil War. To document the causal force of racism, Wilson tracks the changing relationships between the economy and the state. We'll see that to be effective, racism needs a particular kind of institutional configuration. In its absence, other factors become important for influencing the position of blacks in the United States—in particular, a split labor market and class. As we discuss Wilson's theory, keep in mind that he is not arguing that racism is no longer present or important. Racism is still a problem, but Wilson is pointing out that because of shifts in the relationship between the economy and the state, the *relative importance* of race has declined over time and has been replaced by class-based issues.

Concepts and Theory: American Racial History

Wilson divides U.S. history into three economic phases and demonstrates that different theories are best at explaining different kinds of economic race relations. There's an important insight into theory that we can glean from Wilson's approach. Most theories contain scope conditions; very few claim to be a "theory of everything." *Scope conditions* limit the applicability of any theory, and understanding this is part of critically evaluating the theory. Most students understand that scope conditions can be set by topic. So, for example, Blumer's (Chapter 3) social-psychological theory may not be the best bet for explaining globalization (Chapter 10). But scope conditions can also include issues of time or historical change. In Wilson's case, he uses three different theories—Marx's state-capitalist collusion, split labor market theory, and Wilson's own class–state theory—to explain race relations for the three different time periods: pre–Civil War, post–Civil War through the 1930s, and post–World War II to present.

The Plantation Economy

Marx's theory argues that capitalists as the dominant class use their power to exploit workers and to enlist the state's active support. Modern capitalism is defined by the endless pursuit of capital for its own sake. People have always produced and sold goods, but the purpose of such selling was to earn money to live on. The goal of modern capitalism, however, isn't to have enough money to live on, nor is it really making enough money to be rich. Both of those goals can be achieved: It's possible to acquire enough money to live on and not need any more, and it's possible to have enough money to be categorized as wealthy and not need any more. Modern capitalism is insidious in the sense that its goal or motivation is open-ended. The goal is to acquire capital in order to invest; profit from the investment is then reinvested in order to acquire more capital. Modern capitalism, then, is a never-ending project. This is why modern capitalism is restless; it is always creating new products and markets.

The fundamental source of profit and capital is exploitation. **Exploitation** is the difference between the value of what a worker produces and what a worker is paid. Capitalists must pay workers less than they earn, and they will always gravitate to the lowest possible wage. The key here is for you to see that the very nature of modern capitalism drives exploitation, and because the drive for capital has no natural limit, the drive for exploitation is just as limitless. Using race as a focus in exploitation gave capitalists a group of workers they could exploit without limit, a group that had no power: "There is a chance for exploitation on an immense scale for inordinate profit.... This chance lies in the exploitation of darker peoples" (Du Bois, 1920/1996a, pp. 504–505). With the invention of chattel slavery, capitalism changed blacks into commodities, and commodities have no power over their owners whatsoever. But notice that this type of exploitation is based on cooperation with the state. The state must support the capitalists' claim that certain racial groups have no civil rights.

In this model, the state and economy are in collusion to exploit the worker. Wilson argues that Marx's theory is best for explaining the racial-caste system that worked under the American plantation economy, at least in the South. This type of nonmanufacturing, agrarian society is characterized by a simple division of labor and a small aristocracy. In such a society, there is very little if any job market competition. During this period in the southern United States, working whites were either craftsmen or sharecroppers, and blacks were generally held as slaves. In addition, in a plantation economy there is a vast distance between the upper and lower classes. Because of this distance, there is little contact between classes, and what contact does happen is highly ritualized and subject to strong social norms of manners and etiquette. These conditions result in little to no class conflict, with the white workers having "little opportunity to challenge the control of the aristocracy" (Wilson, 1980, p. 13).

In such systems of production, the aristocracy dominates both economic and political life. In the United States, the white, landed elite were able to secure laws and policies extremely favorable to their economic interests, and they were able to propagate a ruling ideology concerning the differences between the races. As in classic Marxian thought, the system of production and the state formed a mutually reinforcing cycle. As a result, "the system of slavery severely restricted black vertical and horizontal mobility" (Wilson, 1980, p. 24), and race relations with elite whites took the form of paternalism (the care and control of subordinates as a father). An important issue to notice is *who benefits from the system:* In this case, it's the capitalist class.

Post–Civil War to New Deal Politics

After the U.S. Civil War, the industrialization of the economy grew quickly and the southern economy in particular expanded rapidly. In addition, the Thirteenth and Fourteenth Amendments to the Constitution abolished slavery and granted civil rights to the black population. As a result, from the latter part of the nineteenth century through the 1930s, there were massive changes in the system of production and race relations. This period marks a shift from race relations based on a paternal, racial-caste system to a more class-based labor market. In the South, economic expansion greatly increased the political power of the white working class. Blacks were freed but had very little economic or political power. White workers, then, attempted to control the newly available skilled and unskilled positions. The outcome was an elaborate system of *Jim Crow* segregation that was reinforced with a strong ideology of biological racism. The name "Jim Crow" doesn't refer to an actual person but to the stereotypical characterization of blacks in minstrel shows at the time. The idea of Jim Crow segregation references the laws that many states enacted after the Civil War in order to control blacks and preserve white privilege. Jim Crow segregation generally benefited the higher-paid white working class by keeping blacks out of the competition for jobs, especially in the South.

The North experienced a different configuration. Due to high levels of migration of blacks from the South and high immigration rates of European whites, blacks most often entered the job market as strikebreakers. White workers would strike for better wages or working conditions, and management would bring in black workers to keep production going. In some cases, management would preempt a strike by hiring black workers on permanently. This move obviously created high tension between black and white workers, which culminated in a number of race riots in 1917 and 1919. The Great Depression of the 1930s shifted things considerably for both black and white workers in the North. During the Depression, there was a strong movement toward unionizing. The unions themselves began to recruit black workers. As a result, black antagonism toward the unions was reduced, black and white workers saw themselves as united in their stand for economic reforms, and the practice of employers using blacks as strikebreakers was eliminated.

Wilson argues that race relations in this time period are best explained using *split labor market theory.* This theory assumes that after slavery, business would support a free and open market where all laborers compete against one another, regardless of race. This kind of competition would result in an overall higher level of exploitation because capitalists could pit blacks against whites. In addition, split labor theory proposes three key classes, rather than the two of orthodox Marxian theory: the capital business class, higher-paid labor, and cheaper labor. Understanding that there is another interest in the labor market besides capitalists, and knowing that capitalists would benefit from an open rather than restricted job market, we see that segregation benefited the white working class rather than capitalists.

The emphasis in this theory is on how the market for labor splits and who benefits. The *labor market* refers to any collective of workers vying for the same or similar positions within a capitalistic economy. A labor market splits when there are two or more social groups whose pay for the same work is different, one being lower than the other. The pay difference is primarily based on dissimilar resource levels, determined by economic and political resources and the availability of information. That is, if there is an ethnic or racial group within a labor market whose standard of living is significantly lower, who lacks the ability to politically organize, and who is less informed about labor market conditions, then the labor market will split. The important thing to see here is that when a market splits, it is more beneficial to higher-paid workers than to business owners. According to this theory, free and open competition would displace the higher-paid workforce and result in lower wages and higher exploitation generally.

Race, then, became a tool of the higher-paid working class to preserve its own economic interests. The white higher-paid working class promoted racist ideologies and discriminatory practices in order to monopolize skilled labor and management positions. It did so in part by preventing blacks from obtaining necessary skills and education and by denying blacks political resources. Thus, while race was still an issue, it originated with white workers rather than collusion between capitalists and the state. Also notice that class became increasingly important during this time. Labor markets are primarily split over class, not race. Race thus became a marker for class antagonisms rather than for racism itself.

World War II and Beyond

Before describing this time period, I want us to be clear about Wilson's theoretical argument. It's a structural argument, which means that structural arrangements determine social relations. For Marx, the driving structure is the economy: The means of production determine the relations of production. As we've seen, Wilson adds an independent state to this theory. This counters Marx's notion of the means and relations of production, asserting that it isn't just the economy that structures social relationships: The interrelations between the state and economy do so, in this case race relations and black inequality. Wilson argues that the role of the state is continuing to change from the classic Marxian model. World War II brought a ban on discrimination in defense and government agencies. This move also provided on-the-job training for blacks. Black workforce participation continued to expand under the equal employment legislation of the 1950s and 1960s and growing affirmative action programs. These changes obviously didn't come as a result of the government's desire for equality, but in response to the civil rights movement, which also boasted black political involvement. But regardless of the source or cause, the state took successive steps to address black inequality.

In addition, the trend toward industrialization that began in the North prior to the Civil War expanded geographically and exponentially from the 1940s onward. This facilitated a shift in the black population, away from rural, agricultural settings and low-paying farm jobs and toward the cities and industries with better-paying jobs. A large black population thus began to develop in urban centers, which, in turn, prompted the growth of black business owners and black professionals oriented toward serving the needs of the growing black community. As a result of affirmative action and these economic and population shifts, more and more businesses were seeking black employees. For example, during the 10-year period between 1960 and 1970, the average number of corporate recruitment visits to traditionally black colleges jumped from 4 to 297; in some southern colleges, the number rose from zero to 600 corporate visits. During this time, there was also a jump in the percentage of blacks working in government jobs, rising from 13% to almost 22%, and the overall percentage of black males in white-collar positions rose from 16% to 24% (Wilson, 1980, pp. 88–109).

However, the United States began to noticeably shift toward a **postindustrial** economy beginning in the 1970s. This move away from manufacturing and toward service- and knowledge-based commodities brought the decentralization of U.S. businesses, further expansion in government and corporate sectors, and demographic shifts from urban to suburban settings (sometimes referred to as "white flight"). These economic and population changes created a situation in which city tax resources either declined, or increased at slower-than-necessary rates. At the same time, and due to the same social factors, cities experienced a sharp increase in expenditures. This situation obviously created problems for municipal services, such as public assistance and urban schools.

The picture that Wilson gives us of the time following World War II involves two push–pull forces. On the one hand, political and economic opportunities for blacks increased dramatically. Through the 1930s, 1940s, and 1950s, the black working class experienced growing opportunities and urbanization, which at the time was a positive move. On the other hand, from the 1970s on, there was the decentralization of American business, decreases in manufacturing and increases in government and corporate jobs, and white flight from urban to suburban settings. These overlapping yet opposing forces fragmented the black labor force and resulted in "vastly different mobility opportunities for different groups in the black population" (Wilson, 1980, p. 121).

Those African Americans who were already moving toward the middle class were poised to take advantage of the economic and political shifts. They continued to experience upward mobility and "unprecedented job opportunities in the corporate and government sectors" (Wilson, 1980, p. 121). These middle-class blacks, like their white counterparts, have been able to move to more affluent neighborhoods. The other segment of the black labor force, however, has become stuck in the cycle of inner-city problems: declining city revenues in the face of increasing social needs. These are "the relatively poorly trained blacks of the inner city, including the growing number of younger blacks emerging from inferior ghetto schools" (Wilson, 1980, p. 121) who are locked into low-paying jobs with high turnover rates and little hope of advancement.

Wilson wants us to see that race, as it was used in previous times, is a declining factor in predicting the economic and political success of blacks in the United States. Again, this is a proportional evaluation. Race still matters, but class distinctions within the black population have greater impact on black opportunities than does race itself. Prior to the mid-1960s, studies indicated that "race was so much of a dominant factor that very little of black economic achievement was determined by class background" (Wilson, 1980, p. 167). Since that time, those blacks already "in the system" have continued to experience occupational and salary gains. "For those blacks who are not in the system, however, who have not entered the mainstream of the American labor market, the severe problems of low income, unemployment, underemployment, and the decline in labor-force participation remain" (Wilson, 1980, p. 171). It is thus the class positions prior to the sixties and seventies that currently oppress poor and working-class blacks rather than race itself.

In addition, Wilson (1980) argues that the character of racial strife has changed. Previous to this time period, racial tensions focused on the economy. From the Civil War through the civil rights era, racial tensions revolved around unequal access to economic opportunities for blacks. Since the segmentation of the black labor pool, racial tensions have shifted to the sociopolitical order. The actors are the same— blacks and the white working class—"but the issues now have more to do with racial control of residential areas, schools, municipal political systems, and recreational areas than with the control of jobs" (p. 121).

Concepts and Theory: Policy Implications

Wilson's basic conclusion is that concern for racial equality needs to move from a focus on race to a focus on class. In other words, policies pointed at creating a tight labor market will go further toward improving the overall condition of blacks in the United States today than will laws aimed at ending racial discrimination. The differences between a tight and a slack labor market basically revolve around the level of employment. In a *tight labor market,* there are a high number of job openings relative to the labor pool. In other words, those who want to work can work. High employment/low unemployment rates mean that it is a worker's market: Workers have choices of positions; wages are high; and unemployment, when it does occur, is relatively short. On the other hand, a *slack labor market* means that there are more workers than positions (unemployment is high). This is a capitalist's market: Business owners have their choice of workers, wages are low, and unemployment is chronic.

Unfortunately, in recent times the United States has moved away from "using public policy as a means to fight social inequality" and instead has placed emphasis "on personal responsibility, not inequalities in the larger society" (Wilson, 1996–1997, pp. 569–570). For example, in the year 2000, low-income programs made up 21% of the federal budget but constituted 67% of the spending cuts. In order to combat this trend, Wilson is acting to galvanize both private and public support for creating national performance standards for schools. Wilson specifically cites other capitalist democracies that have national policies that emphasize critical and higher-order thinking skills. Along with this emphasis on national standards, Wilson argues that national policy should provide the kind of support needed by inner-city and disadvantaged neighborhood schools to meet such standards. Currently, the unequal funding of schools produces what Jonathon Kozol (1991) refers to as "savage inequalities."

Wilson also advocates improving the family support system in the United States. Today, the United States is the only modernized country that does not provide universal preschool, child support, and parental leave programs—much-needed support structures in the face of changes in the family and the social structures surrounding it. Along with this support for the changing family structure, Wilson argues that the United States needs to do a better job of linking families, schools, and work. Currently, U.S. firms take 5 years longer than other developed nations to hire high school graduates. Whereas in Germany and Japan, students are hired directly out of high school, typically the larger firms in the United States don't hire high school graduates until they have reached their mid-twenties (Wilson, 1997).

Unfortunately, we don't have the space to review all of Wilson's proposals. Wilson has fully documented his policy concerns in *When Work Disappears: The World of the New Urban Poor* (1997), and I encourage you to read it. But from what was just discussed, you can see that Wilson has shifted the discourse concerning the plight of black Americans from one that focuses specifically on race to one that emphasizes class. I want to point out that Wilson's conclusions are based on his ability to use different theories in diverse contexts. Explanations of social injustice aren't as simple as most of us think, and this is becoming truer the more our society and economy become globalized. Having a number of theories at our disposal and possessing the flexibility of mind to use them creatively will go a long way in enabling us to see, explain, and impact the social world around us.

Wilson shows us that our very best efforts at ending racial inequality should be vitally concerned with and aimed at improving the class opportunities of Americans as a whole, especially as we keep moving into a postindustrial, globalized economy. While these efforts would alleviate the economic suffering of many people,

> Their most important contribution would be their effect on the children of the ghetto, who would be able to anticipate a future of economic mobility and share the hopes and aspirations that so many of their fellow citizens experience as part of the American way of life. (Wilson, 1997, p. 238)

Summary

- Wilson considers three different theories in explaining race relations in the United States: Marxist elite theory, which sees complicity between elite capitalists and the state; split labor market theory, which calls attention to the different resource levels of diverse class positions; and Wilson's own class–state theory. Wilson's theory argues that economic and race relations are based on changing configurations among the state, economy, and class relations. Further, Wilson argues that racism requires a specific kind of relationship between economic elite and polity (government) that was most purely found in the plantation South.

- Using these three different theories, Wilson examines three periods of American race relations: pre–and early post–Civil War, the latter 1800s to the

1930s, and the period from World War II on. The race relations within each of these periods are best explained by different theories: Marxist elite theory best explains the racism prevalent in pre–and post–Civil War America, split labor market theory explains the class growth period up until the Great Depression of the 1930s, and Wilson's class–state theory describes current race relations. Wilson's conclusion is that over time there has been a declining significance of race in explaining the position of African Americans.

- Based on his analysis, Wilson proposes a number of policy changes aimed at improving the overall welfare of the American worker, which in turn will improve the conditions of African Americans.

TAKING THE PERSPECTIVE: AMERICAN RACE THEORY

I've found that the writings of people who study and think about race tend to be distinct and different from people writing about other sociological issues. Probably the best known of "classic" race theorists in the United States is W. E. B. Du Bois, who wrote from the 1890s through the early 1960s. Du Bois gave us a number of significant theoretical ideas, such as double consciousness, and produced some of the first social scientific studies of black Americans. Yet, reading Du Bois is more than reading theory and data; it is an experience. In his writing, Du Bois moves back and forth among intellectual argumentation, song, prayer, poetry, irony, parable, data, riddles, analogy, and declaration. He weaves a tapestry for the reader, one that touches every part of the reader's being. He wants us to be able to understand the objective state of blackness as well as experience its soul.

This dual approach of blending theory and experience seems fairly common among African American writers. A colleague of mine who teaches African American Social Thought in our department said it this way: "When [black writers] write . . . they are presenting a lens of dual reality, blackness in America, America on blackness: 'How do I feel about my country and how does my country feel about me?'" (S. Cureton, personal communication, October 9, 2009). However, this issue isn't limited to sociologists—it runs deeper. Quite a few African American authors writing about race in fiction, essay, poetry, and the like tend to include what we see as social and sociological theory, because "challenging race legacy touches on everything we know to be sociological!" (S. Cureton, personal communication, October 9, 2009).

I think that part of the reason for this twofold nature of black writing is due to the fact that to write about blackness is to write about humanness. Frantz Fanon (1961/2004), writing about colonialism and race, said, "The ruling *species* is first and foremost the outsider from elsewhere, different from the indigenous population, 'the others'" (p. 5, emphasis added). He wrote this in comparison to Marx's idea of the "ruling class." For Fanon, "ruling class" does not adequately capture how this type of ruling takes place. It's not a class issue; it is a species issue. Racial oppression squarely stands on denying or limiting the humanness of blacks. Thus, centering race in writing, either creative or scientific, can

(Continued)

(Continued)

always evoke the existential cry, "How does it feel to be a problem?" in response to "measuring one's soul by the tape of a world that looks on in amused contempt and pity" (Du Bois, 1903/1996b, pp. 101–102).

In addition, this approach to doing sociology and writing chronicles and puts in the public record the very human experiences of blacks living under inhuman circumstances. This record serves two purposes. It first preserves a truer history of black experience for the African American community. The writings, both academic and otherwise, contain generational knowledge that provides the building stones for a black identity that "speaks to the existential issues of what it means to be a degraded African" . . . and "involves self-respect and self-regard, realms inseparable from, yet not identical to, political power and economic status" (West, 1993/2001, p. 97). The second purpose is that these writings offer for "public consumption the 'soul of blackness' . . . in a society that addresses blackness as deviant" (S. Cureton, personal communication, November 20, 2009). They proclaim the strength of a people proven in a cauldron of suffering. This was undoubtedly the intent that Du Bois had when he penned the above words for the beginning lines of *The Souls of Black Folk.*

The Structures of Gender Inequality: Janet Saltzman Chafetz

Source: Courtesy of Henry Chafetz.

Throughout history, the social category of gender has been and continues to be the most fundamental way in which distinctions are made among people. As such, gender as a social category influences almost every form of discrimination. Take the obvious example of class. According to a U.S. Congressional Report (Joint Economic Committee, 2010), women now comprise half of the U.S. workforce, as compared to 35.6% in 1970. Women's workforce participation is high in some key economic areas of growth. For example, women hold 77.4% of the jobs in the fastest growing job market: education and health services. Women also now earn more bachelor's degrees than men. In 1970, women earned 40% of bachelor's degrees; today, they earn 60%.

While encouraging, the report also tells us that "virtually no progress has been made in closing the [wage] gap since 2001" (Joint Economic Committee, 2010, p. 9). In 2009, women earned, on average, 77 cents for every dollar men earned. The gender wage gap holds across most education levels: Women high school graduates earn almost 70% of men; and female college graduates earn about 71% of what a male graduate earns. The gap becomes more severe at the professional degree level: "[P]rofessional women earn 57.9 cents for every dollar earned by professional men, or $67,245 as compared to men's $116,136" (p. 19). Those figures are averages—there are data that indicate the gap worsens over time. A study of University of Chicago's MBA graduates shows that the gap immediately after graduation is 11%; the gap increased to 31% after 5 years and to 60% 10 years or more after graduation (p. 10).

Women also experience what is referred to as "the glass ceiling," an invisible wall that stops women from advancing up corporate and political ladders past a certain point. Thus, men hold most of the top company positions in the United States. The Joint Economic Committee's (2010) report also indicates that while about 46% of all employees at Fortune 500 companies are women, "they make up just 15.7% of board seats, 14.4% of executive officers, 7.6% of top earning executive offices, and 2.4% of chief executive officers (CEOs)" (p. 11). More recent data from a *Huffington Post* report indicate that in 2012 there were 18 CEOs of Fortune 500 companies, which comes to 3.6% (Bosker, 2012). Men also hold most of the political positions in the United States: As of 2011, women held 16.8% of the seats in both the U.S. Senate and the House of Representatives.

The list of the social consequences of gender is almost endless: Women are more likely to have been sexually molested than men; women suffer far more domestic violence than men; women have less decision-making power in organizations and relationships; women typically receive less education than men; women control fewer conversations than men; women are more supportive in conversations than men; the sexual expectations for women are oppressive when compared to men; women are more likely to be hassled in public than are men; and on and on.

THEORIST'S DIGEST

Brief Biography

Janet Saltzman Chafetz was born in Montclair, New Jersey, in 1942. She received her BA in history from Cornell University and her MA in history from the University of Connecticut. While at the University of Connecticut, she began graduate studies in sociology and completed her PhD at the University of Texas at Austin. Chafetz served as president of Sociologists for Women in Society (SWS), 1984–1986, and as chairperson of the American Sociological Society (ASA) Theory Section, 1998–1999. Chafetz was also honored as the first invited lecturer for the Cheryl Allyn Miller Endowed Lectureship Series, sponsored by SWS; her book *Gender Equity* won the American Educational Studies Association Critic's Choice Panel Award (1990) and was selected by *Choice* magazine for their list, Outstanding Academic Books (1990–1991). Professor Chafetz passed away on July 6, 2006, after a 7-year struggle with cancer.

Central Sociological Questions

Chafetz is a positivist seeking to understand and facilitate change in the system of gender inequality. She approaches gender inequality like a scientist would approach disease. In order to eradicate a disease, the laboratory researcher must first understand how it

(Continued)

(Continued)

works. Understanding how it works can lead to targeted methods of cure rather than trial-and-error shots in the dark. As Chafetz (1990) says, "In practical terms, a better understanding of how change occurs . . . could contribute to the development by activists of better strategies to produce change" (p. 100).

Simply Stated

Gender inequality is replicated by four different levels of structure: macro, meso, micro, and individual. The chief structuring agent is the gendered division of labor in the economy—proportionately, there are fewer women than men in the economy, and women who do work have significantly less power, prestige, and pay associated with their jobs than men who do the same work. This pattern of workforce participation creates organizational structures that reduce women's opportunities for advancement and their relative numbers, as well as ghettoizing women in positions with little power. These three issues work collectively to create a sense of learned helplessness, which in turn produce practices that affirm gender stereotypes. Because women have fewer economic resources, when they marry they are in an unequal exchange relation. In order to balance the exchange, women offer compliance and deference to men; men use this power to control women's access to work and to gender the household division of labor. Boys and girls raised in such a home learn that they are rewarded when they perform according to gender stereotypes and punished when they do not. In addition, the fact that the man is little involved in the home and parenting sets up dynamics that form gendered intrapsychic structures, which then provide the basis for women continuing to "choose" to be oppressed by believing in and replicating the very actions that produce gender inequality, most notably the choices associated with workforce participation.

Key Ideas

Feminism, social structure, levels of analysis, women's workforce participation, organizational variables (career path, organizational power, relative numbers), social exchange, micro power, gender definitions, legitimation, intrapsychic structures, social learning, gendered impression management, unintentional and intentional forces of change

Concepts and Theory: Coercive Structures of Gender Inequality

Chafetz is one of very few sociologists whose work encompasses all four levels of analysis I mentioned earlier. Her work is Marxian in the sense that the macro-level economic structure is most powerful and sets the stage for the organizational, interactional, and personal levels. The macro-level structure is created out of the capitalist division of labor; this, in turn, creates structures at the organizational level that involve career paths, the distribution of power, and relative numbers of people within the organization—which obviously all reinforce the unequal division of labor at the macro level. Relationships between men and women are determined by the structure of social exchange, women generally having fewer resources due to the gendered division of labor and structured gendered positions in economic organizations. Unequal exchange relations create different patterns of role performance and impression management at the micro level, all of which are internalized by individuals through intrapsychic structures.

Macro-Level Coercive Structures

Chafetz draws from specific theories to explain how the coercive and voluntaristic features work. The coercive theories tend to correspond to the three levels of analysis, so that there is a particular theory that is used at each level. Her primary orientation for the macro-level structural features of gender stratification comes from Marxian feminist theory. The basic orientation here is that patriarchy and capitalism work together to maintain the oppression of women, and the central dynamic in the theory is *women's workforce participation*. Marx argued that social structure sets the conditions of social intercourse. In this sense, society itself has an objective existence, and it thus strongly influences human behavior. More than that, social change occurs *because* of structural change. In Marx's theory, the economic structure itself contains dynamics that push history along. In general, Chafetz draws from Marx's emphasis on the economy as the most important site for social stability and change. She also explores his ideas about the way capitalism works.

Capitalism requires a group that controls the means of production as well as a group that is exploited. This basic social relationship is what allows capitalists to create profit. Patriarchy provides both: men who control the means of production and profit and women who provide cheap and often free labor. That latter part is particularly important. Much of what women do in our society is done for free. No wages are paid for the wife's domestic labor—this work constitutes the unpaid labor force of capitalism. Without this labor, capitalism would crumble. Paying women for caring for children and domestic work would significantly reduce profit margins and the capitalists' ability to accumulate capital. In addition, the man's ability to fully work is dependent upon the woman's exploitation as well. When women are allowed in the workforce, they are often kept in menial positions or given lower wages for the same work as men.

Because of the importance of women's cheap and free labor to the capitalist system, elite males formulate and preach a patriarchic ideology that gives society a basis for believing in the rightness of women's primary call to child rearing and domestic labor. Elite men also use their structural power to disadvantage women's workforce participation. For example, in the United States, elite males have been able to systematically block most attempts at passing national comparable worth amendments or laws that would guarantee equal pay for equal work.

In brief, Chafetz argues that the greater the workforce participation of women, particularly in high-paying jobs, the less the structure of inequality is able to be maintained. The inverse is true as well: The less workforce involvement on the part of women, the greater the inequality on all levels. Thus, the type and level of their involvement in the workforce (macro) play out at both the meso and micro levels. Though we've framed our discussion in terms of capitalism, Chafetz notes that since humans first began to farm and herd animals, men have disproportionately controlled the means of production and its surplus. Throughout time, men have been slow to give up their economic positions.

Meso-Level Coercive Structures

To explicate the dynamics that sustain gender inequality at the meso level, Chafetz cites Rosabeth Kanter's (1977) work on organizations. Kanter gives us a social-psychological argument where the structural position of the person influences his or her psychological states and behaviors. Kanter points to three factors related to occupational position that influence work and gender in this way: the possibility of advancement, the power to achieve goals, and the relative number of a specific type of person within the position. Each of these factors in turn influences the individual's attitudes and work performance—or what we could call his or her organizational personality.

The possibility of advancement. Most positions in an organization fall within a specific career path for advancement. The path for a professor, for example, goes from assistant, to associate, to full professor. The position of dean doesn't fall within that path. A professor could aspire to become dean, but she would have to change her career trajectory. Kanter (1977) argues that women typically occupy positions within an organization that have limited paths for advancement. We can think of the occupational path for women as constricted in two ways: (1) The opportunities for advancement in feminized occupations, such as administrative assistant or secretary, are limited by the nature of the position; and (2) women who are on a professional career path more often than not run into a glass ceiling that hinders their progress.

The power to achieve goals. Positions also have different levels of power associated with them. Again, this is a feature of the location within the organization, not of the individual. For example, if you were in my theory class, I would have you write theory journals. Most of my students do the journals because I tell them to. But my authority to assign work doesn't have anything to do with me; it's a quality of the position. If there were another person in my position, the students would do what he or she told them. Please note that this power is different from the power that comes out of exchanges between men and women in long-term relations (see next page). Again, women typically hold positions with less power attached to them than do men. Clearly, there are some women who transcend this situation. But women who are in positions of power are typically seen as "tokens," because there are no similar others in those positions within the company (Kanter's third organizational variable).

Relative numbers. One of the things within organizations that facilitates upward mobility is the relative number of a social type within a position. Imagine being a white male and reporting to work on your first day. You're given a tour of the facilities. As you are introduced to different people in the company, you notice that almost all the positions of power are held by black men. Most of the offices are occupied by black men, and most of the important decisions are made by black men. There are whites at this place of employment, but they almost all hold menial jobs. By and large, they are the secretaries and assistants and frontline workers. Being white, how would you gauge your chances for advancement at such a firm? Further, imagine that after the end of your first week, you notice that there are two or three whites who seem to hold important positions. Would the presence of a few whites in management change your perception? It isn't likely. Though we like to talk as if individuals are the only things that matter, in fact, humans respond more readily to social types than to individual figures. That's why the few minorities that do make it up the corporate ladder are seen as tokens—exceptions to the rule—rather than as any real hope that things are changing.

One of the important insights of sociology is that context matters. As Durkheim pointed out, increasing the division of labor in a society increases the level of social diversity. In Kanter's theory, this is specifically important because different organizational positions hold dissimilar levels of power and opportunity. These contexts influence the way the incumbents—the people that occupy the position—think and act. In situations where power is available and the gates in the organizational flow lines are open, people develop a sense of efficacy. They feel empowered to control their destiny within the organization, and they behave in a "take charge" manner. The reverse is true as well: People in positions where there are few opportunities and where power is limited are much less certain about showing positively aggressive behaviors. They feel ineffectual and limited in what they can achieve within the organization.

These issues are true for any who occupy these different positions. Humans are intimately connected to their context. Our social environment always influences who we are and how we act. The problem in organizations is that women are systematically excluded from positions of power and opportunity. As a result, they experience and manifest a self that corresponds to the position, one that feels and behaves ineffectually and limited. Though these differences in behavior and attitude are linked to organizational position, people generally attribute them to the person. Thus, women who occupy positions that have little power or hope of advancement demonstrate powerlessness and passivity. These attitudes and behaviors are then used to reinforce negative stereotypes of gender and work, which in turn are used to reinforce gender inequality within the organization.

I've modeled the relationships we've talked about so far in Figure 7.1. Follow the arrows and think through the relationships—remember, these are theoretical relationships and speak of the direction of the relationships. So, signs on the arrows (paths of effects) may not mean what you think at first. The negative sign (–) means that the relationship is inverse. That is, if one variable goes up, the other will go down (and the opposite is true as well). The positive sign (+) means that the relationship is positive and both variables move in the same direction, either up or down. To get you started, let's look at part of one of the paths. The path from the level of capitalist exploitation to women's workforce participation is marked with a

Figure 7.1 Macro–Meso Dynamics of Gender Inequality

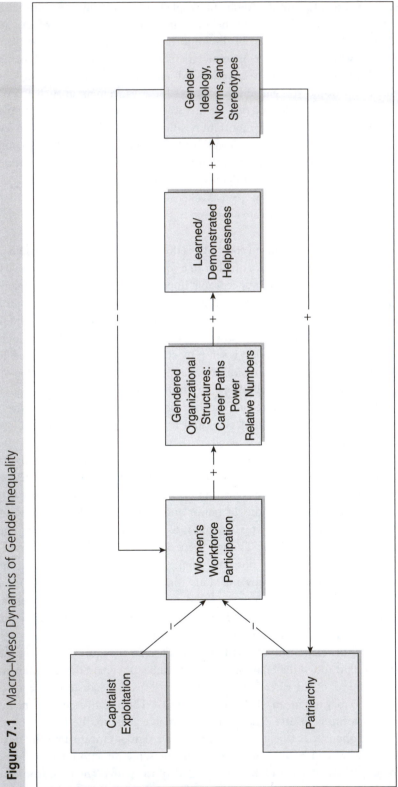

negative sign. This means as exploitation goes up, women's presence in the job market goes down. As women's workforce participation goes down, the three organizational variables (career path, power, relative numbers) all go down as well. Keep working through the model until you understand the relationships.

Concepts and Theory: Micro-Level Coercive Structures

Before we begin this section, I want to point out that even though we are talking about the micro level, Chafetz is talking about structures that have the power of coercion. This is important to keep in mind because many micro-level theories are oriented toward choice and agency. Chafetz talks about those issues in the section on voluntaristic gender inequality, but for now we are considering how gender inequality is a structural force at the micro level. Chafetz uses exchange theory to begin to explicate coercive processes at the micro level.

Gendered Social Exchanges

Exchange theory argues that people gravitate toward equal exchanges. Both partners in an exchange need to feel they are getting as much as they are giving. If an exchange isn't balanced, if one of the participants has more resources than the other, the person who has less will balance the exchange by offering compliance and deference. Because everyone has access to his or her own behaviors and abilities, compliance and deference are generalized goods. What that means is that they can be offered in exchange for almost anything else (because they are the one thing that everyone has). According to exchange theory, this is the source of power in social relationships.

Exchange theory also makes a distinction between economic and social exchanges. Economic exchanges are governed by explicit agreements, often in the form of contracts. The particulars of the exchange are well known in advance, and there is a discernable end to the exchange. For example, if you are buying a car on credit, you know exactly how much you have to pay every month and when the payments will stop. You know when your debt is paid off. However, in social exchanges, the terms of the exchange cannot be clearly stated or given in advance. Thus, social exchange is implicit rather than explicit and it is never clear when a debt has been paid in full (see Chapter 6).

Chafetz argues that these two issues together create a coercive micro structure that perpetuates gender inequality for women. Because of their systematic exclusion from specific workforce participation, women typically come into intimate relationships with fewer resources than men in terms of power, status, and class. The imbalance is offset by the woman offering deference and compliance to the man. This arrangement gives the man *micro power* within the relationship. The man's power in this exchange relationship is insidious precisely because it is based on social exchange. As we've seen, social exchanges are characterized by implicit agreements rather than explicit ones, with no clear payoff date or marker. While insidious, this micro power is variable. Generally speaking, the more the economic structure favors men in the division of labor, the greater will be a man's material resources relative to the woman's, and the greater will be his micro-level power. The inverse is also true: "The higher the ratio of women's material resource contribution to men's, the less the deference/compliance of wives to their husbands" (Chafetz, 1990, p. 48).

The greater power that men typically have is used in a variety of ways. One common way is in relation to household work. Much of the work around the home, especially in caring for the young, is dull, repetitive, and dirty. Men typically choose the kinds of tasks that they will do around the home, as well as the level of work they contribute. Thus, men usually do more of the occasional work rather than repetitive work, such as mowing the lawn or fixing the car rather than the daily tasks of doing dishes or changing diapers. Men can also use their power to decide whether or not women work out of the home and to influence what kinds of occupations their wives take. Because women in unbalanced resource relations bear the greater workload responsibility for the children and home, they are restricted to jobs that can provide flexible hours and close proximity to home and school.

I've modeled the micro-level variables in Figure 7.2. Notice that I've also taken the liberty of placing the different issues in voluntaristic gender inequality in the model as well. As you can see from the model, the micro-level variables are all driven by the level of women's workforce participation and their subsequent ability to participate in equal exchanges with their life partner. This is precisely what you would expect from a theory that begins with Marx's idea that economic relations are the things that ultimately drive everything else in society. Again, follow the direction of the relationships. The relationship between equality in exchange and men's micro power is negative, which means the more the exchange is equal, the less

Figure 7.2   Micro-Level Dynamics of Gender Inequality

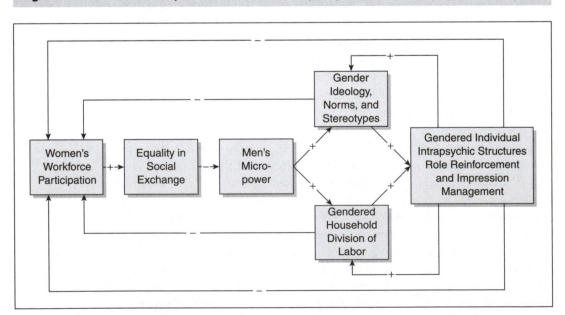

micro power men will have. And, obviously, the reverse is true. In an unequal exchange relation, women offer deference and compliance and men use their micro power to control gender ideologies, norms, and stereotypes, as well as the gendered household division of labor. Controlling those factors decreases women's workforce participation (shown by the feedback arrows), and it increases the level that individuals are socialized into gender-specific practices and tend to see and experience themselves as gendered individuals.

Voluntaristic Gender Inequality

As we noted before, gender inequality usually functions without coercion. This implies that women cooperate in their own oppression. More exactly, "people of both genders tend to make choices that conform to the dictates of the gender system status quo" (Chafetz, 1990, p. 64). Chafetz refers to this as voluntaristic action; but, as we'll see, some of these behaviors and attitudes are unthinkingly expressed and so aren't "voluntary" in the sense of chosen. The patterns that support gender inequality are latently maintained; they are quiet and hidden. The reason for this kind of maintenance is simple, and it is how society works in general (see Chapter 2): We simply believe in the culture that supports our social structures. Max Weber pointed this out many years ago. Every structural system is sustained through legitimation, whether it is a system of inequality or the most egalitarian organization imaginable, and legitimation provides the moral basis for power—it gives us reasons to believe in the right to rule. Part of the way legitimation works has to do with the place culture has in human existence: Culture works for humans as instinct does for animals. Another important reason for the significance of legitimation is that coercive power is simply too expensive, in terms of costs of surveillance and enforcement, to use on anything but an occasional basis.

Thus, Chafetz argues that much of what sustains the system of gender inequality is voluntarism. Both men and women continue to freely make choices and display behaviors that are stereotypically gendered. There are three types of *gender definitions* that go into creating gendered voluntaristic action: gender ideology, norms, and stereotypes. These three types vary by the level of social consensus and the extent to which gender differences are assumed. Chafetz draws on three theoretical traditions to explain these issues: Freudian psychodynamic theory; social learning theory; and theories of everyday life, including symbolic interactionism, ethnomethodology, and dramaturgy.

Intrapsychic structure. Nancy Chodorow's (1978) work forms the basis of Chafetz's psychodynamic theory. Chodorow argues that men's and women's psyches are structured differently due to dissimilar childhood experiences. The principal difference is that the majority of parenting is done by the mother with an absent father. Before we talk too much about Chodorow's theory, we need to make sure we understand the idea of psychic structure, or, more specifically, *intrapsychic structure.* The idea comes from Freud, who argues that the psychic energy of an individual gets divided up into three parts: the id, the ego, and the superego. These three areas exist as structures in the obdurate sense. They are hard and inflexible and produce boundaries between the different internal elements of the person. Thus, when we are talking about intrapsychic structures, we mean the parts of the inner person that are fixed and divided off from one another. It's almost like we're talking about the structure of the brain. The "intra" part of intrapsychic structures refers to how these three parts are internally related to each other. Thus, Chodorow's, and Chafetz's, argument is that the internal workings of boys and girls are structurally different—their intrapsychic structures are gendered.

Both boys and girls grow up with their chief emotional attachment being to their mother. Girls are able to learn their gender identity from their mothers, but boys have to sever their emotional attachment to their mother in order to learn their gender identity. The problem, of course, is that the father has historically been absent. His principal orientation is to work, a situation that was exacerbated through industrialization and the shift of work from the agricultural home to the factory. Girls' intrapsychic structure, then, is one that is built around consistency and relatedness—they don't have to break away to learn gender, and their social network is organically based in their mother. Women, then, value relationships and are intrapsychically oriented toward feelings, caring, and nurturing. Boys have to separate from their mother in order to learn gender, but there isn't a clear model for them to attach to and emulate. More exactly, the model they have is "absence."

The male psyche, then, is one that is disconnected from others, values and understands individuality, is more comfortable with objective things than relational emotions, and has and values strong ego boundaries. According to Freud, this male psyche also develops a fear and hatred of women (misogyny)—as the boy tries to break away from his mother, she continues to parent because of the absent father. The boy unconsciously perceives her continued efforts to "mother" as attempts to smother his masculinity under an avalanche of femininity. He thus feels threatened and fights back against all that is feminine.

Remember, these differences between males and females are dissimilarities in the structure of their psyches. This is a much stronger statement than saying that boys and girls are socialized differently. Intrapsychic structures are at the core of each person, according to Freudian theory, and much of what happens at this level is unconscious. Chafetz isn't necessarily saying that men consciously fear or hate women—it's much deeper than that. It is at the core of their being. But also keep in mind that these structures vary according to the kind of parenting configuration a child has. It's very possible today for a boy to be raised principally by the father while the mother works (though our economic structure makes this unlikely), or for a single father to raise a child. The intrapsychic structure of such a boy would be dramatically different from that of boys raised in a situation where maleness is defined by absence and separation.

These intrapsychic differences play themselves out not only in male–female relationships, but also in the kinds of jobs men and women are drawn to. Generally, men are drawn to the kinds of positions that demand individualism, objectification, and control. Women, on the other hand, are drawn to helping occupations where they can nurture and support. While there have certainly been changes in occupational distribution over the past 30 years, most of the stereotypically gendered fields continue to have disproportionate representation. Thus, for example, while there are more male primary school teachers and nurses today than 30 years ago, the majority continue to be women; and while there are more women who are CEOs, construction workers, and politicians today, those fields continue to be dominated by men. The important point that Chafetz is bringing out here is that the "personal preference" individuals feel to be in one kind of occupation rather than another is strongly informed by gendered intrapsychic structures. These personal choices, then, "voluntarily" perpetuate gender structures of inequality.

Gendered social learning. Chafetz also draws on socialization theories such as social learning to explain the voluntaristic choices men and women make. The important components of social learning theory come to us from Albert Bandura (1977). Bandura argues that learning through experimentation is costly, and therefore people tend to learn through modeling. For example, it's much easier to learn that fire is hot by the way others act around it than by sticking your hand in it. Social learning occurs through four stages: attention, retention, motor reproduction, and motivation.

Children pay attention to those models of behavior that seem to be the most distinctive, prevalent, or emotionally invested or have functional value. They retain those models through symbolic encoding and cognitive organization, as well as rehearsing the behaviors symbolically and physically. Motor reproduction refers to acting out the behaviors in front of others. Further motivation to repeat behaviors comes through rewards and positive reinforcement. Children are discouraged from repeating inappropriate behaviors through punishment and negative reinforcement. Eventually, children negatively or positively reinforce their own behaviors— as adults we thus self-sanction most of our gendered behaviors.

Gendered impression management. Theories of everyday life look at how people produce social order at the level of the interaction and manage their self-identities. Chafetz specifically draws on Erving Goffman's (1977) work on gender. Goffman argues that selves are hidden, and the only way others know the kind of self we are claiming is by the cues we send out. Others read these cues, attribute the kind of self that is claimed, and then form righteously imputed expectations. People expect us to live up to the social self we claim. If we don't, that part of our self will be discredited and stigmatized.

Because gender is arguably the very first categorization that we make of people— one of the first things we "see" about someone is whether the person claims to be male or female—gender is thus an extremely important part of impression management and self-validation. As such, Goffman (1959) would see gender as a form of idealized performance in that we "incorporate and exemplify the officially accredited values of the society" (p. 35). In other words, social norms, ideologies, and stereotypes are used more strongly in gendered performances than in most others. Goffman also sees idealization as referencing a part of the "sacred center of the common values of the society" (p. 36) and this kind of performance as a ritual.

Because gender is seen as a sacred center of social values, gender is an especially meaningful and risky performance that is produced in almost every situation. We tend to pay particular attention to the cues we give out about our gender and the cues others present. Goffman further points out that we look to the opposite gender to affirm our managed impression. Our gendered performances, then, are specifically targeted to the opposite sex and tend to be highly stereotypical. According to Chafetz (1990), "For men, this quest [for affirmation] entails demonstrations of strength and competence. However, for women it entails demonstrations of weakness, vulnerability, and ineptitude" (p. 26).

The Structure of Gender Inequality

In Figure 7.3, I've placed our two models together to give us a complete picture of how gender inequality is structured. It's extremely important that you think through each of the relationships keeping in mind two things. First, notice the direction of the relationship. The reason this is important is that Chafetz is going to tell us how to change gender inequality. Good theories explain how something works and in doing so, they also explain how to change something. If this model depicts a good theory of gender stratification, then changing it involves working within the theoretical relationships that it gives us. The second thing I want you to think through is why or how each of the variables influences the others. Knowing that the gendered division of labor in the household has a positive relationship to gendered individuals is good, but it isn't enough. What is it about gendered household chores that impacts intrapsychic structures, role reinforcement, and impression management? So, a good theorist will know both the direction and the reasons for the relationship.

Concepts and Theory: Changing Gender Inequality

To begin this section, we should note that Chafetz argues that structural rather than cultural changes are necessary to bring about gender equality. As we will see throughout this book, sociologists give different weights to culture and structure. Some argue that culture is an extremely important and independent variable within society; others claim that culture simply reinforces structure and that structure is the most important feature of society. Chafetz falls into the latter camp. While voluntaristic processes, which are associated in one way or another with culture, are the key way gender inequality is sustained, "substantial and lasting change must flow 'downward' from the macro to the micro levels" (Chafetz, 1990, p. 108).

Unintentional Change

As with her understanding of gender stability, Chafetz divides her theory of gender change into unintentional and intentional processes. Quite a bit of the change regarding the roles of women in society has been the result of unintended consequences. Another way to put this is that the bulk of changes in the gender system of inequality happen for structural reasons, not because people willingly and intentionally want to change things. For example, the moves from hunter-gatherer to horticulture to agrarian economies were motivated by advances in knowledge and technology. But these moves also produced the first forms of gender

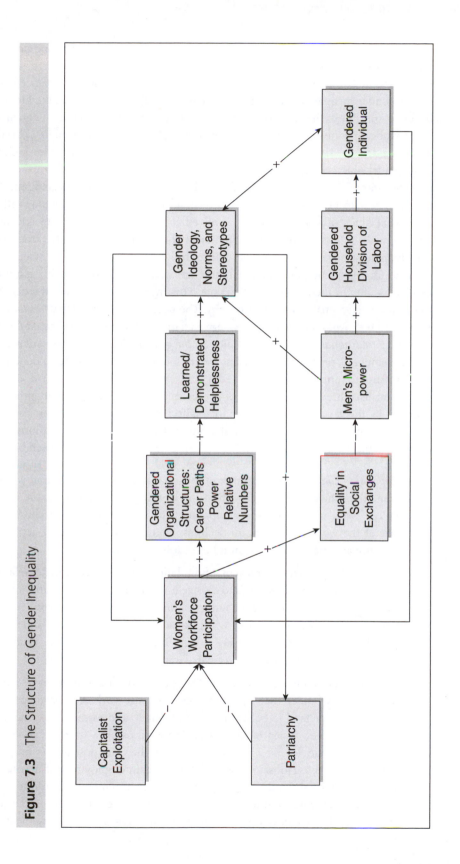

Figure 7.3 The Structure of Gender Inequality

inequality, as men came to protect the land (which gave them weapons and power) and to control economic surplus through inheritance and the control of sexual reproduction (women's bodies). The intent behind technological advancement wasn't gender inequality; the intent was first survival and then to make life less burdensome. But in the end, economic developments produced gender inequality.

In explicating the unintended change processes, Chafetz is interested in what she terms the demand side. She argues that quite a bit of work on gender focuses on the supply side, which concentrates on the general attributes of women. For example, contemporary women tend to have fewer children, to be better educated, and to marry later than in previous generations. These supply-side attributes may influence what kinds of women become involved in the economy, but they "do not determine the rate of women's participation" (Chafetz, 1990, p. 122). For example, a woman may have a master's-level education, but unless there is a structural demand for this quality, she will remain unemployed. In addition, Chafetz assumes gender stability in theorizing about change. This means that males are the default to occupy a given position in the economy. The bottom line here is that "*as long as there are a sufficient number of working-age men available to meet the demand for the work they traditionally perform, no change in the gender division of labor will occur*" (p. 125, emphasis original). Thus, what we are looking for are structural demands that outrun the supply of male labor.

Chafetz lists three different kinds of processes that can unintentionally produce changes in the structure of gender inequality: population growth or decline, changes in the sex ratio of the population, and technological innovations and changes in the economic structure. The processes and their effects are listed below:

- *Population changes:* If the number of jobs that need to be filled remains constant, then the greater the growth in the working-age population, the lower will be women's workforce participation. The inverse is true as well: As the size of the working population declines, women will gain greater access to traditionally male jobs, if the number of jobs remains constant.

- *Sex ratio changes:* The sex ratio of a population, the number of males relative to the number of females, tends to change under conditions of war and migration. If in the long run there is a reduction in the sex ratio (more women than men) of a population, women will gain access to higher-paying and more prestigious work roles. Conversely, if there is an increase in the sex ratio, the restrictions on women's workforce participation will tend to increase.

- *Economic and technological changes:* There are two general features of men's and women's bodies that can influence women's workforce participation: Men on average tend to be stronger than women, and women carry, deliver, and nurse babies. When technological innovations alter strength, mobility, and length of employment requirements, then there are possibilities for gender change in those jobs. Women will tend to gain employment if new technologies reduce strength, mobility, and time requirements. In addition to work requirements, technology can also change the structure of the job market. As the economy expands due to technological innovations, women will tend to achieve greater workforce participation (holding population growth constant). On the other hand, if the economy contracts for whatever reason, women will tend to lose resource-generating work roles.

Intentional Change

In addition to unintentional change processes, Chafetz argues that there are specific ways in which people can act that help to address gender inequality. But before we get into those processes, we need to note that Chafetz maintains that gender change is particularly difficult for two reasons. First, women have more cross-cutting influences than any other group (see Patricia Hill Collins's work in Chapter 15). Think about it this way: Almost every social group is gendered. This means that women are black, white, Latino, Baptist, Buddhist, Jewish, pagan, homosexual, bisexual, heterosexual, homeless, professional, and so on. Women thus "differ extensively on all social variables except gender" (Chafetz, 1990, p. 170). These cross-cutting group affiliations make it extremely difficult to form a woman's ideology that doesn't cut across or offend some of the women the ideology is trying to embrace. The second issue is that women, unlike many disenfranchised groups, do not live in segregated neighborhoods. Chafetz argues that this reduces women's political clout because they are "dispersed throughout all electoral districts" (p. 171). Because of these difficulties, gender change may occur more slowly or diffusely than other types of change.

I've placed Chafetz's additional intentional change factors into the model we've developed thus far (see Figure 7.4). Again, I want you to think through the relationships both in terms of direction and influence (What specifically does this factor accomplish?). You'll notice that the initial variables (capitalism and patriarchy) have been replaced with macro-level variables. Chafetz's approach to gender is similar to the way Karl Marx saw the production of class consciousness. According to Marxian theory, structure leads to social change. Class consciousness is necessary for social change, but it is produced as dialectical elements of the economic structure, such as increasingly disruptive business cycles and overproduction, play themselves out. For Marx, it is the structure that pushes people together and gives them the ability to see their oppression, communicate with one another, and mount the resistance that will lead to the demise of capitalism.

The macro-structural changes that Chafetz focuses on are *industrialization, urbanization, and the size of the middle class.* Chafetz claims that historically almost all women's movements have been led by middle-class women. These women are among the first to experience gender consciousness due to the effects of industrialization and urbanization. Industrialization initiates a large number of social changes such as increases in urbanization, commodification, the use of money and markets, worker education, transportation and communication technologies, and so forth. These all work together to expand the size of the middle class. The importance of this expansion isn't simply that there are more middle-class people; it also means that there are more middle-class jobs available. Many of these are nondomestic jobs that may be filled by women.

Figure 7.4 Reducing Gender Inequality

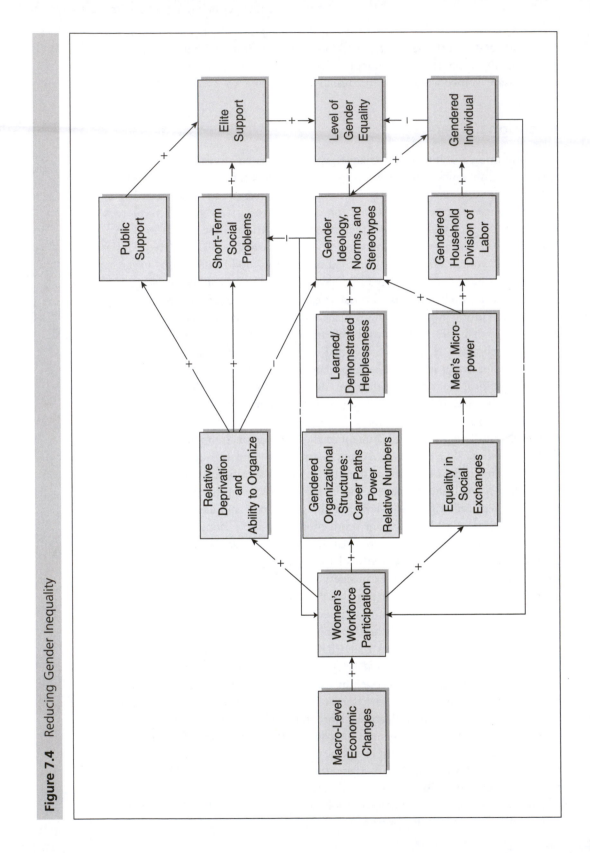

Industrialization thus structurally creates workforce demands that women can fill. Women are more likely to be called upon to fill these roles when the number of males is kept fairly constant, or at least the number doesn't increase at the same rate as the demand for labor. The more rapid the growth of industrialization and urbanization, the more likely the demand for labor will outpace the supply of men. As women increase their workforce participation, they increase their level of material and political resources as well, thus decreasing males' relative micro power and the level of gender differentiation, as well as weakening gender stereotypes, ideologies, and normative expectations (gender social definitions). In addition, as women's resources and thus their micro power increase, they are more able to influence the household division of labor and men's contribution to familial and domestic work. Moreover, as men contribute more to domestic and familial work, women are more able to gain resources through workforce participation. So far what we've talked about all fits with the model in Figure 7.4. It's the structural changes that put into motion the possibility of successful social movements.

In addition to influencing these micro-level issues, industrialization, urbanization, and women's increased workforce participation do two other things: They increase women's experience of relative deprivation and the number of women's social contacts. While absolute deprivation implies uncertain survival, relative deprivation is a subjective, comparative sense of being disadvantaged. Social movements are extremely unlikely with groups that experience absolute deprivation. They have neither the will nor the resources to organize political movements. *Relative deprivation,* on the other hand, implies a group that has resources and experiences rising expectations. Thus, women who are newly moving into the workforce will tend to experience relative deprivation. They will begin to see that their salaries are not comparable to men's, and they will begin to accumulate resources that can potentially be used to become politically active.

Urbanization and industrialization also increase a group's ability to organize. Ralf Dahrendorf (1957/1959) talked about this ability to organize as the principal difference between quasi-groups and interest groups. *Quasi-groups* are those collectives that have latent identical role interests; they are people that hold the same structural position and thus have similar interests but do not experience a sense of "belongingness." *Interest groups,* on the other hand, "have a structure, a form of organization, a program or goal, and a personnel of members" (p. 180).

The interest group's identity and sense of belonging are produced when people have the ability to communicate, recruit members, form leadership, and create a unifying ideology. Urbanization and industrialization structurally increase the probability that these conditions of interest group membership will be met. Women living and working in technologically advanced urban settings are more likely to come into contact with like others who are experiencing relative deprivation and the status and role dilemmas that come from women working a *double workday.*

As women begin to organize and as traditional gender definitions become weakened, public support for change is likely to arise. Chafetz argues that a significant portion of what women's movements have been able to achieve is related to articulated critical gender ideologies and radical feminist goals. While the public may not buy into a radical ideology or its set of goals, the ideologies and goals of women's movements will tend to justify gender change more broadly. This support, along with pressure from short-term social problems and a direct effect from women's workforce participation, places pressure upon elites to create laws, policies, and programs to help alleviate the unequal distribution of scarce resources by gender.

Let's pause a moment and talk about *short-term social problems*. Chafetz argues that as a result of women having and using greater levels of resources, short-term social problems are likely to arise. Chafetz uses the term "social problem" in a general sense to indicate the challenges that society at large have to overcome anytime significant change occurs. In other words, change to the social system brings a kind of disequilibrium that has to be solved so that actions and interactions can once again be patterned. Such social problems tend to accompany any type of social change as a society adjusts culturally and socially. In the case of gender, the short-term problems are related to women having greater levels of resources and thus higher levels of independence and power. Examples of these kinds of problems include increases in the divorce rate and women's demands for control over their own bodies. Social disruptions such as these tend to motivate elite support of women's rights in order to restore social order.

Sociologists have learned that every social movement eventually requires support from the elite. *The elite* not only pass laws and oversee their enforcement, but they can also lend other material or political support, such as money and social capital (networks of people in powerful positions). The first way elites show up is in the way we have been talking about so far. Elites create new legislation or support already established laws that help bring social order. In this case, the support comes mostly because elites perceive some form of social disorder. In other words, "they may perceive that basic problems faced by their society, which negatively affect large numbers of people and may possibly jeopardize their incumbency in elite roles, are exacerbated by a gender system that devalues and disadvantages women" (Chafetz, 1990, p. 152). This kind of change may be incremental and not specifically associated with women's movements. Elites may also support women's movements as women are perceived as a political resource.

I'm going to restate Chafetz's theory of gender change in brief propositions, since this is the discourse in which Chafetz works. Be sure to follow the elements of the propositions through the model. This way you'll be able to get a textual and visual rendering of the ideas:

- Taken together, the level of reduction in gender stratification due to intentional efforts is a positive function of the level of male domestic labor, elite support, and women's control of material resource and is a negative effect of the level of male micro power.

- Women's level of control over material resources is a positive function of industrialization, urbanization, and the size of the middle class. Elite support in general is a positive function of the level of women's control over material resources, the level of short-term social problems, the level of public support for changes advanced by women's movements, and elite competition.

Summary

- In general, Chafetz argues that workforce participation and control over material resources both stabilize and change a system of gender inequality. Gender inequality is perpetuated when women's participation in the workforce is restricted, and reduced when women are allowed to work and control material resources.

- Chafetz argues that gender is stabilized more through voluntaristic actions rather than the use of coercive power. When men control the division of labor in society, they are able to exercise authority at the meso level through assuring male incumbency in elite positions and at the micro level through women's enacting of deference and compliance for material resources. Men thus control gender social definitions that set up engenderment processes: psychodynamic structuring, gender socialization, and the idealized expression of gender through impression management and interaction. Engenderment and wifely compliance work in turn to solidify women's exclusion from the workforce, to impose double duty upon those women who do work, to stabilize the unequal distribution of opportunities and resources, and to define negative worker attributes for women but positive ones for men.

- Gender inequality is reduced as women are allowed greater participation in the workforce and increased control over material resources. These factors decrease women's reliance upon men and men's authority over women. Men then contribute more to domestic and familial work, which further frees women to participate in the workforce and weakens gender stereotypes, norms, and ideologies. In addition, women's access to resource-generating work roles increases the probability of women's political movements, which along with weakened gender definitions positively impacts public opinion and elite support for women. Short-term social issues that come about because of women's increased workforce participation also impact elite support, as well as the elite's desire to consolidate or gain political power. Gender stratification is reduced as women move into the workforce and control more material resources, as elites support women's rights and legislation, and as men's micro resource power is reduced and their domestic contribution increased.

TAKING THE PERSPECTIVE: FEMINISM

One of the delights of working with Chafetz's theory is that she brings together a number of really interesting theoretical issues. The first is the way in which she theorizes. She is one of the best examples of the positivist approach to theory cumulation. The number and diversity of theories and ideas she draws upon is astounding. In explaining gender inequality, Chafetz brings together the work of Karl Marx, Rosabeth Kanter, Nancy

(Continued)

(Continued)

Chodorow, Albert Bandura, Erving Goffman, and Ralf Dahrendorf, as well as elements from exchange theory and social movements theory.

Chafetz also focuses our attention on gender and feminism. Though the issue itself was decentered for much of sociology's history, the study of gender for the discipline goes back to the work of Harriet Martineau (1802–1876). Martineau (1838/2003) argued that the test of any democratic nation is the "condition of that half of society over which the other half has power" (p. 291). Her assessment of the condition of gender in the United States in the beginning of the nineteenth century is that "tried by this test, the American civilization appears to be of a lower order than might have been expected" (p. 291). Karl Marx saw gender as a central social issue. Marx and Engels (Engels, 1884/1978) argued that the communist household "Implies the supremacy of women" and that the oppression of women in the home "contains within itself in miniature all the antagonisms which later develop on a wide scale within society and its state" (pp. 735, 737).

The term *feminism* was first used to refer to feminine traits. It wasn't until the First International Women's Conference of 1892 that the term took on its critical, political bent. Since then, it has been associated with two principal ideas. The first is a set of ideas and beliefs about knowledge and ways of governing that are defined as distinctly feminist and are set against the masculinist ways of exercising power and knowing about the world. Because of the way knowledge is challenged, this approach is usually seen as a type of critical theory. The second refers to a variety of theories that are used to understand how gender inequality works. While this is an overgeneralization, this approach can be typed as positivistic or scientific. These two main approaches can blend together in various ways for different theorists, but Chafetz clearly falls into the latter.

In Western European societies, inequalities of gender have been addressed through three waves of feminism. Inklings of the first wave began when ideas about the equal rights of women emerged during the Enlightenment. The first significant expression of these concerns was Mary Wollstonecraft's book *A Vindication of the Rights of Woman* (1792/1993). But the first wave of feminism didn't become organized until the 1848 Seneca Falls Convention, which called for equal rights to vote and own property, full access to educational opportunities, and equal compensation for equal work.

The second wave of feminism grew out of the civil rights movements of the 1960s. Publication of Simone de Beauvoir's *The Second Sex* (1949/1989) and Betty Friedan's *The Feminine Mystique* (1963/1997) were particularly important for this second wave of feminists, as was the founding in 1966 of the National Organization for Women (NOW). Central issues for this movement were pay equity; equal access to jobs and higher education; and women's control over their own bodies, including but not limited to sexuality, reproduction, and the eradication of physical abuse and rape.

In the early 1970s, two clear divisions began to appear among second-wave feminists. One camp emphasized the more traditional concerns of women's rights groups and generally focused on the similarities between men and women. Their primary concern was structural inequality. The other group moved to more radical issues. Rather than emphasizing similarities, they focused on fundamental differences between men and women. This more critical group is often described as a "third wave" of feminism.

The idea of third-wave feminism began to take hold around the intersection between race and gender—there are marked distinctions between the experiences of black and white women. But more recently, it has gained currency with reference to age. It appears that the experiences of young, contemporary feminists are different from those of second-wave feminists. Young feminists today grew up in a social world where feminism was part of common culture. These young women are also playing out some of the postmodern ideas of fluid identities. The result is that many young feminists can best be described through contradiction and ambiguity. As Jennifer Drake (1997) says in a review essay, "What unites the Third Wave is our negotiation of contradiction, our rejection of dogma, our need to say 'both/and'" (p. 104). For example, third wavers might claim their right to dress sexy for fun while simultaneously criticizing patriarchy for objectifying women.

In this book, there are three theorists that specifically address gender. Two of them, Dorothy Smith and Judith Butler, are among those that take the more radical view of feminism. For them, the life experiences and perspectives of men and women are different, and gender equality is more fundamental than structural equality. Dorothy Smith (Chapter 16) focuses on the unique consciousness and lived experience of women. Smith argues that women have a bifurcated awareness of the world, split between the objective world of men and their own lived experiences. Judith Butler (Chapter 17) focuses first on the body and secondarily on consciousness, or more accurately, subjectivity. She argues that gender inequality presumes a more basic construction: the normative sexing of the body.

Both Smith and Butler present critical understandings that show how women are controlled through systems of knowledge and embodiment. This type of control is deeply embedded in the mind and body, and it generally functions below the level of awareness. The key to achieving sex or gender equality for Smith and Butler seems to lie in subversion—practices that critically expose the assumptions upon which the control of women is based.

BUILDING YOUR THEORY TOOLBOX

- Drawing on at least two additional sources, write a theoretical definition for levels of analysis and structures.

- Write a 250-word synopsis of the theoretical perspective of race.

- Write a 250-word synopsis of the theoretical perspective of feminism.

- After reading and understanding this chapter, you should be able to define the following terms theoretically and explain their importance to structural theories of race and

(Continued)

(Continued)

gender inequality: from Wilson—social structure, racism, exploitation, split labor market, Jim Crow, postindustrial economy; from Chafetz—feminism, social structure, levels of analysis, women's workforce participation, organizational variables (career path, organizational power, relative numbers), social exchange, micro power, gender definitions, legitimation, intrapsychic structures, social learning, gendered impression management, unintentional and intentional forces of change.

- After reading and understanding this chapter, you should be able to

  o Compare and contrast Marxian elite theory, split labor market theory, and Wilson's class–state theory.

  o Explain Wilson's three periods of American race relations and use Marxian elite theory, split labor market theory, and Wilson's class–state theory to analyze the different periods. In other words, you should be able to demonstrate, using Wilson's theory, that class is becoming more important in race relations than race itself.

  o Explain why the workforce of women is so important to Chafetz's theory.

  o Explain how exchange processes work to produce gender inequalities. How do men use their micro power to their gendered advantage?

  o Explain the differences between the intrapsychic structures of boys and girls. Explain how they are created and how they influence gender inequality.

  o Explain how social learning theory and dramaturgy contribute to our understanding of how gender inequality is voluntaristically reproduced.

  o Explain how gender inequality unintentionally changes.

  o Tell which two characteristics of gender, according to Chafetz, make change difficult. (Be sure to explain them fully.)

  o Explain how women's movements form and how they influence changes in gender inequality. What does this tell us about social movements in general?

Learning More: Primary and Secondary Sources

Janet Saltzman Chafetz:

- *Gender Equity: An Integrated Theory of Stability and Change,* Sage, 1990.

- Chafetz is also the editor of the excellent *Handbook of the Sociology of Gender,* Kluwer/Plenum, 1999.

- In 1993, Chafetz joined Rae Lesser Blumberg, Scott Coltrane, Randall Collins, and Jonathan Turner to produce a synthesized theory of gender stratification. This is their rare and powerful effort: "Toward an Integrated Theory of Gender Stratification," *Sociological Perspectives, 36,* 185–216.

William Julius Wilson:

- *The Declining Significance of Race* (2nd ed.), University of Chicago Press, 1980.

- *The Truly Disadvantaged,* University of Chicago Press, 1987.

- *When Work Disappears,* Vintage, 1997.

Engaging the World

- Using your favorite Internet search engine, type in "African American policy." Thoroughly review at least three sites. Would you say that the information and thrust of the sites are in keeping with Wilson's analysis and policy implications? In not, why do you think that is? If so, which policies do you think will have the greatest impact on structural inequality? How can you get involved in promoting this or other policy changes?

- Consult at least four reliable Internet sources to learn about the "separation of spheres." What is it, and how does it figure into Chafetz's theory? How is it historically specific? List at least six ways that the separation of spheres influences your life.

- Using your favorite search engine, type in "global gender inequality." Based on information from at least three different societies, prepare a report on the state of gender inequality in these diverse countries. Also, compare and contrast these societies with the one you live in. How applicable do you think Chafetz's theory would be in those other three societies?

- Volunteer at a local women's shelter or resource center.

CHAPTER 8

Structuring Class

Pierre Bourdieu

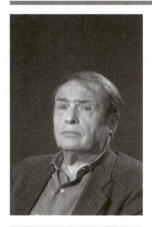

Source: © Alain Nogues/ Sygma/Corbis.

The Big Picture: Class

As I mentioned in Chapter 1, modernity may be the most self-aware era in human history. The social modernists wanted to make an idea triumph, and they set about designing a society that would fulfill the hopes of Enlightenment. Capitalism was part of the plan. The foundational ideology of capitalism claimed that it had evolved to be the system in which each person could achieve any social standing through hard work and determination. The plan backfired. Ever since Marx, we've known that capitalism created its own structure of inequality, one that was virtually unique to modernity: class. Prior to modernity, class had reference mainly to education; our use of *classic* and *classical* to refer to authoritative works of study came from this application. The true modern use of the term *class* came into existence between 1770 and 1840—a time period that corresponds to the Industrial Revolution as well as the French and American political revolutions. Modernity, then, brought with it a "new sense of a SOCIETY . . . or a particular *social system* which actually created social divisions, including new kinds of divisions" (Williams, 1985, p. 62).

For Marx, the structure of class was built around the means of production and the division of labor. While there were several classes at the beginning of capitalism, Marx argued that the dialectics inherent within the system would in the long run create two classes: owners and workers. Capitalists exploit the workers in order to feed the mill of endless capital accumulation and thus alienate workers from species-being (authentic humanity). The class structure is replicated through false consciousness and ideology, which prevent the workers from changing the system, as well as overlapping economic and political structures. In Marx's scheme, the state passes and enforces laws favorable to capitalism. In addition, the class structure tends to be replicated due to consumerism—in more Marxian terms, egoistic actors get caught up in commodity fetish.

Weber gave us a different way to understand class inequality. First, in Weber's theory, class isn't sharply divided in two; the class structure is much more complex. Weber argued that class has two main axes: property ownership and market position. Property ownership includes Marx's means of production, but it also entails other relationships to property, such as with stockholders and landlords. Market position is defined simply as control over a good or service. This axis includes different professionals and experts, such as medical doctors and professors. Weber undoubtedly included this dimension due to the increased use of bureaucratic control in economic and political management since Marx's time; in doing so, he gave us a way to conceptualize the middle class. This is important because the components this class structure is built from include differing levels of education and credentials; Marx didn't include these building materials. In addition, Weber saw inequality in these two dimensions as varying along a continuum, thus creating a complex set of class relations. Marx was right: Class conflict is more likely to occur when there are only two positions; thus, Weber's complex structure of class relations means that it is far more difficult for people to feel "class-conscious" than Marx thought. Notice that this is a *structural effect*, not something individuals directly control. In Weber's scheme, the complexity of the class structure means it's less likely people will question its legitimacy. Moreover, Weber adds two other structures of inequality—power and status—that do not simply mirror the class structure.

The issue I want you to see here is the importance of understanding the composition and effects of structure. For Marx, class structure is made up of positions relative to the ownership of the means of production. This kind of structure works to create exploitation, alienation, false consciousness, and commodity fetishism. Weber's theory of class structure includes the same material as Marx's—ownership of the means of production—but it is also built out of other social things, such as education and credentials. Thus, the quality of class structure is different and so are the effects, such as the bureaucratic personality rather than alienation. Equally important is the insight that social change is dependent upon different processes due to the distinct structures. Social change is much more complex in Weber's scheme, and it isn't simply an effect of the dialectic pressures in capitalism, as it is in Marx. The complexity that Weber introduced through class, status, and power is put to good use in Chapter 15 by Patricia Hill Collins in her theory of intersectionality. In the present chapter, we'll be looking at Pierre Bourdieu's theory of class stratification, which, as you'll see, has different characteristics from either Marx or Weber and is built out of utterly different materials.

THEORIST'S DIGEST

Brief Biography

Pierre Bourdieu was born on August 1, 1930, in Denguin, France. Bourdieu studied philosophy under Louis Althusser at the École Normale Supérieure in Paris. After his studies, he taught for 3 years, 1955–1958, at the Lycée Banville (advanced high school) in Moulins, France. From 1958 to 1960, Bourdieu did empirical research in Algeria that laid the groundwork for his sociology. In his career, he published over 25 books, one of which, *Distinction: A Social Critique of the Judgment of Taste* (1979/1984), was named one of the twentieth century's 10 most important works of sociology by the International Sociological Association. He was the founder and director of the Centre for European Sociology, and he held the French senior chair in sociology at Collège de France (the same chair held previously by Marcel Mauss, Émile Durkheim's nephew). Craig Calhoun (2003) writes that Bourdieu was "the most influential and original French sociologist since Durkheim" (p. 274). Bourdieu died in Paris on January 23, 2002.

Central Sociological Questions

Bourdieu's passion was intellectual honesty and rigor. He of course was concerned with class, and particularly the way class is created and recreated in subtle, nonconscious ways. But above and beyond these empirical concerns was a driving intellect bent on refining critical thinking and never settling on an answer: "An invitation to think with Bourdieu is of necessity an invitation to think beyond Bourdieu, and against him whenever required" (Wacquant, 1992, p. xiv).

Simply Stated

Bourdieu tells us that class is structured in the body through cultural capital, which is made up of tastes, habits, social and linguistic skills, and so on. People thus display their class position in an unthinking, ongoing manner, simply in the way they walk, sit, talk, and so forth. Every social encounter thus becomes a market. In interactions where class positions are comparable, people will feel comfortable because everybody's tastes are similar. The disadvantage of such encounters is that no one can gain higher levels of cultural capital. In encounters where the class positions are different, people with lower cultural capital will tend to feel uncomfortable and will likely not participate or gain very little from the exchange. For this reason, when in a position to increase cultural capital, and thus class position, most people withdraw and are unable to gain profit. Class is thus structured in the body where it insidiously restricts and replicates a person's class position in all social interactions.

Key Ideas

Economic capital, social capital, symbolic capital, cultural capital, taste, habitus, distance from necessity, education, field, linguistic market, symbolic violence, constructivist structuralism, dialectic

Concepts and Theory: Structuring Class

The basic fact of capitalism is capital. Capital is different from either wealth or income. Income is generally measured by annual salary, and wealth by the relationship between one's assets and debt. Both income and wealth are in a sense static: They are measurable facts about a person or group. Capital, on the other hand, is active: It's defined as accumulated goods devoted to the production of other goods. The entire purpose of capital is to produce more capital.

Four Kinds of Capital

Bourdieu actually talks about four forms of capital—economic, social, symbolic, and cultural—all of which are invested and used in the production of class. Bourdieu uses *economic capital* in its usual sense. Economic capital is generally determined by one's wealth and income. As with Marx, Bourdieu sees economic capital as fundamental. However, unlike Marx, Bourdieu argues that the importance of economic capital is that it strongly influences an individual's level of the other capitals, which in turn have their own independent effects. In other words, economic capital starts the ball rolling, but once things are in motion, other issues may have stronger influences on the perpetuation of class inequalities.

Social capital refers to the kind of social network an individual is set within. It refers to the people you know and how they are situated in society. The idea of social capital can be captured in the saying, "It isn't what you know but who you know that counts." The distribution of social capital is clearly associated with class. For example, if you are a member of an elite class, you will attend elite schools such as Phillips Academy, Yale, and Harvard. At those schools, you would be afforded the opportunity to make social connections with powerful people—for example, in elections over the past 30 years, there has been at least one Yale graduate running for the office of President of the United States. But economic capital doesn't exclusively determine social capital. We can build our social networks intentionally, or sometimes through happenstance. For example, if you attended Hot Springs High School in Arkansas during the early 1960s, you would have had a chance to become friends with Bill Clinton.

Symbolic capital is the capacity to use symbols to create or solidify physical and social realities. With this idea, Bourdieu begins to open our eyes to the symbolic nature of class divisions. Social groups don't exist simply because people decide to gather together. Max Weber recognized that there are technical conditions that must be met for a loose collection of people to form a social group: People must be able to communicate and meet with one another; there must be recognized leadership; and a group needs clearly articulated goals to organize. Yet, even meeting those conditions doesn't alone create a social group. Groups must be symbolically recognized as well.

With the idea of symbolic capital, Bourdieu pushes us past analyzing the use of symbols in interaction (Chapter 3). Symbolic interactionism argues that human beings are oriented toward meaning, and meaning is the emergent result of ongoing symbolic interactions. We're symbolic creatures, but meaning doesn't reside within the symbol itself; it must be pragmatically negotiated in face-to-face situations. We've learned a great deal about how people create meaning in different situations because of symbolic interactionism's insights. But Bourdieu's use of symbolic capital is quite different.

Bourdieu recognizes that all human relationships are created symbolically and not all people have equal symbolic power. For example, I write a good number of letters of recommendation for students each year. Every form I fill out asks the same question: "Relationship to applicant?" And I always put "professor." Now, the *meaning* of the professor–student relationship emerges out of my interactions with my students, and my student–professor relationships are probably somewhat different from some of my colleagues as a result. However, neither my students nor I *created* the student–professor relationship. Bourdieu (1991) tells us that objective categories and structures, such as class, race, and gender, are generated through the use of symbolic capital: "Symbolic power is a power of constructing reality" (p. 166).

Bourdieu (1989) characterizes the use of symbolic capital as both the power of constitution and the power of revelation—it is the power of

> world-making . . . the power to make groups. . . . The power to impose and to inculcate a vision of divisions, that is, the power to make visible and explicit social divisions that are implicit, is political power par excellence. (p. 23)

This power of world-making is based on two elements. First, the person using symbolic capital must have sufficient status to impose recognition. The group must be symbolically labeled by a person or group that is officially recognized as having the ability to symbolically impart identity, such as scientists, legislators, or sociologists in our society. Institutional accreditation, particularly in the form of an educational credential (school in this sense operates as a representative of the state), "frees its holder from the symbolic struggle of all against all by imposing the universally approved perspective" (p. 22).

The second element needed to world-make is some relation to a reality: "Symbolic efficacy depends on the degree to which the vision proposed is founded in reality"

(Bourdieu, 1989, p. 23). I think it's best to see this as a variable. The more social or physical reality is already present, the greater will be the effectiveness of symbolic capital. This is the sense in which symbolic capital is the power to consecrate or reveal. Symbolic power is the power to reveal the substance of an already occupied social space. But note that granting a group symbolic life "brings into existence in an instituted, constituted form . . . what existed up until then only as . . . a collection of varied persons, a purely additive series of merely juxtaposed individuals" (p. 23). Thus, because legitimated existence is dependent upon symbolic capacity, an extremely important conflict in society is the struggle over symbols and classifications.

There is a clear relationship between symbolic and *cultural capital*. The use of symbolic capital creates the symbolic field wherein cultural capital exists. In general, **cultural capital** refers to the informal social skills, habits, linguistic styles, and tastes that a person garners as a result of his or her economic resources. It is the different ways we talk, act, and make distinctions that are the result of our class. Bourdieu identifies three different kinds of cultural capital: objectified, institutionalized, and embodied. *Objectified cultural capital* refers to the material goods (such as books, computers, and paintings) that are associated with cultural capital. *Institutionalized cultural capital* alludes to the certifications (like degrees and diplomas) that give official acknowledgment to the possession of knowledge and abilities. *Embodied cultural capital* is the most important in Bourdieu's scheme. It is part of what makes up an individual's habitus (discussed below), and it refers to the cultural capital that lives in and is expressed through the body. This function of cultural capital manifests itself as taste.

Taste refers to an individual preference or fondness for something, such as "he has developed a taste for expensive wine." What Bourdieu is telling us is that our tastes aren't really individual; they are strongly influenced by our social class—our tastes are embodied cultural capital. Here, a particular taste is legitimated, exhibited, and recognized only by those who have the proper cultural code, which is class specific. To hear a piece of music and classify it as baroque rather than elevator music implies an entire world of understandings. Thus, when individuals express a preference for something or classify an object in a particular way, they are simultaneously classifying themselves. Taste may appear as an innocent and natural phenomenon, but it is an insidious revealer of position. As Bourdieu (1979/1984) says, "Taste classifies, and it classifies the classifier" (p. 6). The issue of taste is "one of the most vital stakes in the struggles fought in the field of the dominant class and the field of cultural production" (p. 11).

Habitus

Taste is part of habitus, and habitus is embodied cultural capital. Class isn't simply an economic classification (one that exists because of symbolic capital), nor is it merely a set of life circumstances of which people may become aware (class consciousness)—class is inscribed in our bodies. **Habitus** is the durable organization of one's body and its deployment in the world. It is found in our posture and our way of walking, speaking, eating, and laughing; it is found in every way we use our body. Habitus is both a system whereby people organize their own behavior and a system through which people perceive and appreciate the behavior of others.

Pay close attention: This system of organization and appreciation is *felt* in our bodies. We physically feel how we should act; we physically sense what the actions of others mean, and we approve of or censure them physically (we are comfortable or uncomfortable); we physically respond to different foods (we can become voracious or disgusted); we physically respond to certain sexual prompts and not others—the list can go on almost indefinitely. Our humanity, including our class position, is not found in just our cognitions and mental capacity; it is in our very bodies.

One way to see what Bourdieu is talking about is to use a sports analogy. I love to play sand volleyball, and I only get to play it about once every 5 years, which means I'm not very good at it. I have to constantly think about where the ball and other players are situated. I have to watch to see if the player next to me is going for the ball or if I can do so. All this watching and mental activity means that my timing is way off. I typically dive for the ball 1.5 seconds too late, and I end up with a mouthful of sand rather than the ball (but the other bunglers on my team are usually impressed with my effort). Professional volleyball players compete in a different world. They rarely have to think. They sense the ball and their teammates and they make their moves faster than they could cognitively work through all the particulars. Volleyball is inscribed in their bodies.

Explicating what he calls the Dreyfus model, Bent Flyvbjerg (2001) gives us a detailed way of seeing what is going on here. The Dreyfus model indicates that there are five levels to learning: novice, advanced beginner, competent performer, proficient performer, and expert. Novices know the rules and the objective facts of a situation, advanced beginners still have concrete knowledge but see it contextually, and the competent performer employs hierarchical decision-making skills and feels responsible for outcomes. With proficient performers and experts, we enter another level of knowledge. The first three levels are all based on cognitions, but in the final two levels, knowledge becomes embodied. Here, situations and problems are understood "intuitively" and require skills that go beyond analytical rationality. With experts, "their skills have become so much a part of themselves that they are not more aware of them than they are of their own bodies" (p. 19).

Habitus thus works below the level of conscious thought and outside the control of the will. It is the embodied, nonconscious enactment of cultural capital that gives habitus its specific power:

> Beyond the reach of introspective scrutiny or control by the will . . . in the most automatic gestures or the apparently most insignificant techniques of the body . . . [it engages] the most fundamental principles of construction and evaluation of the social world, those which most directly express the division of labour . . . or the division of the work of domination. (Bourdieu, 1979/1984, p. 466)

Bourdieu's point is that we are all, each one, experts in our class position. Our mannerisms, speech, tastes, and so on are written on our bodies beginning the day we are born.

There are two factors important in the production of habitus: distance from necessity and education. In *distance from necessity,* necessity speaks of sustenance, the things necessary for biological existence. Distance from the necessities of life enables the upper classes to experience a world that is free from urgency. In contrast, the poor must always worry about their daily existence. As humans move away from that essential existence, they are freed from that constant worry, and they are free to practice activities that constitute an end in themselves. For example, you probably have hobbies. Perhaps you like to paint, act, or play guitar as I do. There is a sense of intrinsic enjoyment that comes with those kinds of activities; they are ends in themselves. The poorer classes don't have that luxury. Daily life for them is a grind, a struggle just to make ends meet. This struggle for survival and the emotional toll it brings are paramount in their lives, leaving no time or resources for pursuing hobbies and "getting the most out of life."

We should think of distance from necessity as a continuum. You and I probably fall somewhere in the middle. We have to be somewhat concerned about our livelihood, but we also have time and energy to enjoy leisure activities. The elite are on the uppermost part of the continuum, and it shows in their every activity. For example, why do homeless people eat? They eat to survive. And if they are hungry enough, they might eat anything, as long as it isn't poisonous. Why do working classes or nearly poor people eat? For the same basic reason: The working classes are much better off than the homeless, but they still by and large live hand to mouth. However, because they are further removed from necessity, they can be more particular about what they eat, though the focus will still be on the basics of life, a "meat and potatoes" menu. Now, why do the elite eat? You could say they eat to survive, but they are never aware of that motivation. Food doesn't translate into the basics of survival. Eating for the elite classes is an aesthetic experience. For them, plate presentation is more important than getting enough calories.

Thus, the further removed we are from necessity, the more we can be concerned with abstract rather than essential issues. This ability to conceive of form rather than function—aesthetics—is dependent upon "a generalized capacity to neutralize ordinary urgencies and to bracket off practical ends, a durable inclination and aptitude for practice without a practical function" (Bourdieu, 1979/1984, p. 54). This aesthetic works itself out in every area. In art, for example, the upper-class aesthetic of luxury, or what Bourdieu calls the "pure gaze," prefers art that is abstract, while the popular taste wants art to represent reality. In addition, distance from economic necessity implies that all natural and physical desires and responses are to be sublimated and dematerialized. The working class, because it is immersed in physical reality and economic necessity, interacts in more physical ways through touching, yelling, embracing, and so forth than do the distanced elite. A lifetime of exposure to worlds so constructed confers cultural pedigrees, manners of applying aesthetic competences that differ by class position.

This embodied tendency to see the world in abstract or concrete terms is reinforced and elaborated through *education.* One obvious difference between the education of the elite and that of the working classes is the kind of social position in which education places us. The education system channels individuals toward either prestigious or devalued positions. In doing so, education manipulates subjective aspirations (self-image) and demands (self-esteem). Another essential difference in educational experience has to do with the amount of rudimentary scholastics required—the simple knowing and recognizing of facts versus more sophisticated knowledge. This factor varies by number of years of education, which in turn varies by class position. At the lower levels, the simple recitation of facts is required. At the higher levels of education, emphasis is placed on critical and creative thought. At the highest levels of education, even the idea of "fact" is understood critically and held in doubt.

Education also influences the kind of language we use to think and through which we see the world. We can conceive of language as varying from complex to simple. More complex language forms have more extensive and intricate syntactical elements. Language is made up of more than words; it also has structure. Think about the sentences that you read in a romance novel and then compare them to those in an advanced textbook. In the textbook, they are longer and more complex, and that complexity increases as you move into more scholarly books. These more complex syntactical elements allow us to construct sentences that correspond to multileveled thinking—this is true because both writing and thinking are functions of language. The more formal an education we receive, the more complex are the words and syntactical elements of our language. Because we don't just think *with* language, we think *in* language, the complexity of our language affects the complexity of our thinking. And our thinking influences the way in which we see the world.

Here's a simple example: Let's say you go to the zoo, first with my dog and then with three different people. You'd have to blindfold and muzzle my dog, but if you could get her to one of the cages and then remove the blinders, she would start barking hysterically. She would be responding to the content of the beasts in front of her. All she would know is that those things in front of her smell funny, look dangerous, and are undoubtedly capable of killing her, but she's going to go down fighting. Now picture yourself going with three different people, each from a different social class and thus education level. The first person has a high school education. As you stand in front of the same cage that you showed to my dog, he says, "Man, look at all those apes." The second person you go with has had some college education. She stands in front of the cage and says, "Gorillas are so amazing." The third person has a master's-level education and says, "Wow, I've never seen *gorilla gorilla, gorilla graueri,* and *gorilla berengei* all in the same cage."

Part of our class habitus, then, is determined by education and its relationship to language. Individuals with a complex language system will tend to see objects in terms of multiple levels of meaning and to classify them abstractly. This type of linguistic system brings sensitivity to the structure of an object; it is the learned ability to respond to an object in terms of its matrix of relationships. Conversely, the less complex an individual's classification system, the more likely are the organizing syntactical elements to be of limited range. The simple classification system is characterized by a low order of abstractedness and creates more sensitivity to the content of an object, rather than its structure.

Bourdieu uses the idea of habitus to talk about the replication of class. Class, as I mentioned earlier, isn't simply a part of the social structure; it is part of our body. We are not only categorized as middle class (or working class or elite); we *act* middle class. Differing experiences in distance from necessity and education deter-mine one's tastes, ways of seeing and experiencing the world, and "the most auto-matic gestures or apparently most insignificant techniques of the body—ways of walking or blowing one's nose, ways of eating or talking" (Bourdieu, 1979/1984, p. 466). We don't choose to act or not act according to class; it's the result of lifelong socialization. Moreover, as we act in accordance with our class, we replicate our class. Thus, Bourdieu's notion of how class is replicated is much more fundamental and insidious than Marx's and more complex than Weber's.

However, we would fall short of the mark if we simply saw habitus as a structur-ing agent. Bourdieu intentionally uses the concept (the idea originated with Aristotle) in order to talk about the creative, active, and inventive powers of the agent. He uses the concept to get out of the structuralist paradigm without falling back into issues of consciousness and unconsciousness. In habitus, class is structured, but it isn't completely objective—it doesn't merely exist outside of the individual because it's a significant part of his or her subjective experience. In habitus, class is *structured but not structuring*—because as with high-caliber athletes and experts, habitus is intuitive. The idea of habitus, then, shows us how class is replicated subjectively and in daily life, and it introduces the potential for inspired behaviors above and beyond one's class position. Indeed, the potential for exceeding one's class is much more powerful with Bourdieu's habitus than with conscious decisions—most athletes, musicians, and other experts will tell you that their highest achievements come under the inspiration of visceral intuition rather than rational processes. It is through habitus that the practices of the dialectic are performed.

Fields

Bourdieu uses the analogy of the field to explain how empirical and symbolic worlds work (see Calhoun, 2003). Bourdieu was a rugby player, which is a European game somewhat like American football, but it is considered by most to be much more grueling than football. In rugby, the play is continuous with no substitutions or time-outs (even for injury). The game can take anywhere from 60 to 90 minutes, with two halves separated by a 5-minute halftime. An important part of the game is the *scrum*. In a scrum, eight players from each side form a kind of inverted tri-angle by wrapping their arms around each other. The ball is placed in the middle, and the two bound groups of men (or women) struggle head-to-head against each other until the ball is freed from the scrum. To see the struggle of the scrum gives a whole new perspective on Bourdieu's idea of social struggle.

Rugby matches take place on a field, involve strategic plays and intense struggles, and are played by individuals who have a clear physical sense of the game. Matches are of course structured by the rules of the game and the field. The field not only delineates the parameters of the game, but each field is different and thus knowl-edge of each field of play is important for success. The rules are there and, like in all games, come into play when they are broken, but a good player embodies the rules and the methods of the game. The best plays are those that come when the player is "in the zone," or playing without thinking. Trained musicians can also experience this zone by jamming with other musicians. Often when in such a state, the musician can play things that he or she normally would not be able to, and might have a difficult time explaining after the fact. The same is true for athletes. There is more to a good game than the rules and the field; the game is embodied in the performer. Finally, there is the struggle against not only the other team, but also the limitations of the field, rules, and one's own abilities.

What I just gave you is actually an explanation of Bourdieu's theory through analogy. Keep your eyes open for how it fits. Just like in rugby, fields are delineated spaces wherein "the game" is played. Obviously, in Bourdieu's theoretical use of **field,** the parameters are not laid out using fences or lines on the ground. The parameters of the theoretical field are delineated by networks or sets of connections among objective positions. The positions within a field may be filled by individuals, groups, or organizations. However, Bourdieu is adamant that we focus on the relationships among the actors and not the agents themselves. It's not the people, groups, or even interactions that are important; it's the relationships among and between the positions that set the parameters of a field. For example, while the different culture groups (like theater groups, reading clubs, and choirs) within a region may have a lot in common, they probably do not form a field because there are no explicit objective relationships among them. On the other hand, most all the universities in the United States do form a field. They are objectively linked through accreditation, professional associations, federal guidelines, and so forth. These relationships are sites of active practices; thus, the parameters of a field are always at stake within the field itself. In other words, because fields are defined mostly through relationships, and relationships are active, which positions and relationships go into making up the field is constantly changing. Therefore, what constitutes a field is always an empirical question.

Fields are directly related to capitals. The people, groups, and organizations that fill the different objective positions are hierarchically distributed in the field, initially through the overall volume of all four capitals they possess and secondly by the relative weight of the two particular kinds of capital: symbolic and cultural. More than that, each field is different because the various capitals can have dissimilar weights. For example, cultural capital is much more important in academic rather than economic fields; conversely, economic capital is more important in economic fields than in academic ones. All four capitals or powers are present in each, but they aren't all given the same weight. It is the different weightings of the capitals that define the field, and it is the field that gives validity and function to the capitals.

While the parameters of any field cannot be determined prior to empirical investigation, the important consideration for Bourdieu is the correspondence between the empirical field and its symbolic representation. The objective field corresponds to a symbolic field, which is given legitimation and reality by those with symbolic capital. Here, symbolic capital works to both construct and recognize—it creates and legitimates the relations between and among positions within the field. In this sense, the empirical and symbolic fields are constitutive both of class and of social affairs in general. It is the symbolic field that people use to view, understand, and reproduce the objective.

Thus, for Bourdieu, the objective field isn't enough to account for class reality and replication, and that is where many sociologists stop. Bourdieu takes it further in that the objective field becomes real and potentially replicable through the use of symbolic capital, because human beings are principally oriented toward meaning. The use of symbolic capital creates the symbolic field, which in turn orders, gives meaning to, and makes real the objective field. The exercise of symbolic capital, along with the initial distribution of capitals, creates cultural capital that varies by distance from necessity and by education. In addition, cultural capital produces the internal structuring of class: habitus. But notice that the potential of habitus to replicate is held in question—it is habitus exercised in linguistic markets and symbolic struggles that decides the question.

Concepts and Theory: Replicating Class

Linguistic Markets

Bourdieu (1991) says that "every speech act and, more generally, every action" is an encounter between two independent forces (p. 37). One of those forces is habitus, particularly in our tendency to speak and say things that reveal our level of cultural capital. The other force comes from the structures of the linguistic market. A *linguistic market* is "a system of relations of force which impose themselves as a system of specific sanctions and specific censorship, and thereby help fashion linguistic production by determining the 'price' of linguistic products" (Bourdieu & Wacquant, 1992, p. 145).

The linguistic market is like any other market: It's a place of exchange and a place to seek profit. Here, exchange and profit are sought through linguistic elements such as symbols and discourses. The notion of a free market is like an ideal type: It's an idea against which empirical instances can be measured. All markets are structured to one degree or another, and linguistic markets have a fairly high degree of structuring. One of the principal ways they are structured is through formal language.

Every society has formalized its language. Even in the case where the nation might be bilingual, such as Canada, the languages are still formalized. Standard language comes as a result of the unification of the state, economy, and culture. The education system is used to impose restrictions on popular modes of speech and to propagate the standard language. We all remember times in grammar school when teachers would correct our speech. In the university, this still happens, but mostly through the application of stringent criteria for writing.

Linguistic markets are also structured through various configurations of the capitals and the empirical field. As we've seen, empirical fields are defined by the relative weights of the capitals—so, for example, religious fields give more weight to symbolic capital and artistic fields give more import to cultural capital, but they both need and use economic capital. The same is true with linguistic markets. Linguistic markets are defined through the relative weights of the capitals and by the different discourses that are valued. For example, the linguistic market of sociology is heavily based on cultural capital. In order to do well in that market, you would have to know a fair amount about Karl Marx, Émile Durkheim, Michel Foucault, Pierre Bourdieu, Dorothy Smith, and so forth. Linguistic markets are also structured by the empirical field, in particular by the gaps and asymmetries that exist between positions in the field (By their placement and position of capitals, some positions in a field are more powerful than others.). These empirical inequalities help structure the exchanges that take place within a linguistic market.

When people interact with one another, they perform speech acts—meaningful kinds of behaviors that are related to language. In a speech act, habitus and linguistic markets come together. In other words, the person's embodied class position and cultural capital are given a certain standing or evaluation within the linguistic market. The linguistic market contains the requirements of formal language; the salient contour of capitals; and the objective, unequal distribution of power within the empirical field.

Let me give you three examples from my own life. When I go to a professional conference, I present papers to and meet with other academics. My habitus has a number of different sources, among them are training in etiquette by a British mother and many years spent studying scholarly texts and engaging in academic discourse. The linguistic market in academia is formed by the emphasis on cultural and symbolic capital, and by the positions in the empirical field held by everyone at the conference; some people have more powerful positions and others less so. Each encounter, each speech act, is informed by these issues. In such circumstances, I tend to "feel at home" (habitus), and I interact freely, bantering and arguing with other academics in a kind of "one-upmanship" tournament.

This weekend, I will be going to the annual Christmas party at my wife's work. Here, the linguistic market is different. Economic capital and the cultural capital that goes along with it are much more highly prized. In addition, the empirical field is made up of differing positions and relationships achieved in the struggle of American business. Because of these differences, my market position is quite different here from what it was at the professional conference. In fact, I have no market position. Worse, my habitus remains the same. The way I talk—the words I use and the way I phrase my sentences—is very different from the other people at this event. The tempo of my speech is different (it's much slower) as is the way I walk and hold myself. In this kind of situation, I try and avoid speech acts. When encounters are unavoidable, I say as little as possible because I know that what I have to say, the way I say it, and even the tempo of my speech won't fit in.

These two different examples illustrate an extremely important point in Bourdieu's theory: Individuals in a given market recognize their institutional position, have a sense of how their habitus relates to the present market, and anticipate differing profits of distinction. In my professional conference example, I anticipate high rewards and distinction, but in the office party example, I anticipate low distinction and few rewards. In situations like the office example, anticipation acts as a *self-sanctioning mechanism* through which individuals participate in their own domination. Perhaps "domination" sounds silly with reference to an office party, but it isn't silly when it comes to job interviews, promotions, legal confrontations, encounters with government officials, and so forth. I gave you an example that you can relate to so you could more clearly understand what happens in other, more important speech acts.

These kinds of speech acts are the arena of symbolic violence. **Symbolic violence** is the exercise of violence and oppression that is not recognized as such. More specifically, "Symbolic power is that invisible power which can be exercised only with the complicity of those who do not want to know that they are subject to it or even that they themselves exercise it" (Bourdieu, 1991, p. 164). For example, for quite some time, patriarchy had been seen as part of the natural order of things. Yet, in believing in her husband's right to rule, a woman participated in and blinded herself to her own oppression. Here's another example: In believing that schools should be locally controlled and funded and that education is the legitimate path to upward social mobility, we actively participate in the perpetuation of the class system in the United States (see Kozol, 1991).

More insidious for Bourdieu is the way language is used to inflict symbolic violence. Have you ever been around someone of higher social status that you wanted to talk to but didn't? Why didn't you? If you're like me, you didn't because you were afraid of making a fool out of yourself. I had a professor in graduate school that I so admired, but I never talked to him unless it was absolutely necessary. I just knew that I would misspeak and say something foolish. Every social group has specific languages. It is easily seen with such pop culture groups as hip-hop, skaters, and graffiti taggers. But it is also true with experts and people in high-status positions, including the elite class. They typically have specialized languages. While we don't know the language, we *know* that we don't know the language, "which condemns [us] to a more or less desperate attempt to be correct, or to *silence*" (Bourdieu, 1991, p. 97).

My third example is from a conversation I had with my wife. In most conversations among equals, formal linguistic markets have little if any power. We talk and joke around, paying no attention to the demands of proper speech. I'm certain that you can think of multitudes of such speech acts: talking with friends at a café or at the gym or in your apartment. Those kinds of speech acts will always stay that way, unless one of you has a higher education or a greater distance from necessity—that is, unless your habitus is different. Even in such cases, however, linguistic markets usually won't come into play—but they can. "Every linguistic exchange contains the *potentiality* of an act of power, and all the more so when it involves agents who occupy asymmetric positions in the distribution of the relevant capital" (Bourdieu & Wacquant, 1992, p. 145). Bourdieu tells us that in such situations, where the market position is different or the habitus is different, the potential for power and symbolic violence is only set aside for the moment.

Symbolic Struggle

Social change for Bourdieu is rooted in symbolic struggles, which makes sense given Bourdieu's emphasis on symbolic capital and power. Part of that struggle occurs within the speech act or encounter. As we've seen, encounters are structured by markets of differing distinction, and habitus expresses itself naturally within those markets. We will feel at home or foreign in an encounter; we will speak up or silence ourselves, all without thought. However, we also have to keep in mind that habitus is embodied and expresses itself through intuitive feelings. Sometimes our intuitions can lead us to brilliant moves, whether on the sports field, the game board, the music stage, or the speech act. Just so, our habitus at times can lead us to speech acts that defy our cultural, symbolic, economic, or social standings.

This kind of symbolic struggle can bring some incremental change. Bourdieu gives us hints about how more dynamic change can occur, but keep in mind that his isn't a theory of social change or revolution. Bourdieu allows that there are two methods by which a symbolic struggle may be carried out, one objective and the other subjective. In both cases, symbolic disruption is the key. Objectively, individuals or groups may act in such a way as to display certain counter-realities. His example of this method is group demonstrations held to manifest the size, strength, and cohesiveness of the disenfranchised. This type of symbolic action disrupts the taken-for-grantedness that all systems of oppression must work within—it offers an objective case that things are not what they seem.

Subjectively, individuals or groups may try and transform the categories constructed by symbolic capital through which the social world is perceived. On the individual level, this may be accomplished through insults, rumors, questions, and the like. A good example of this approach is found in bell hooks's book *Talking Back: Thinking Feminist, Thinking Black* (1989): "It is that act of speech, of 'talking back,' that is no mere gesture of empty words, that is the expression of moving from object to subject—the liberated voice" (p. 9). Groups may also operate in this way by employing more political strategies. The most typical of these strategies is the redefinition of history—that is, "retrospectively reconstructing a past fitted to the needs of the present" (Bourdieu, 1989, p. 21). But notice that with each of these kinds of struggle, a response from those with symbolic capital would be required. These disruptions could bring attention to the cause, but symbolic power would be necessary to give it life and substance within the symbolic field first and then the objective field.

Concepts and Theory: Toward a New Sociology

It would be a disservice to restrict our introduction to Bourdieu to his theory of class. Bourdieu actually gives us a different way of practicing sociology. He gives us a way of looking at social behaviors as practices that overcome a sticky issue that has faced sociology probably since the time of Max Weber. This dichotomy, and those dichotomies derived from it, sets some of the basic parameters of our discipline, such as the distinction between quantitative and qualitative methods and the divergence between structuralism and interactionism. This dichotomy also sets up one of the thorniest issues sociologists address: the link between the micro and macro levels of society. The dichotomy that I am referring to is the dilemma of structure (objective) versus agency (subjective), or, as Bourdieu talks about it, social physics versus social phenomenology. He characterizes this dichotomy between objective and subjective knowledge as one of the most harmful in the social sciences. Bourdieu (1985) sees overcoming the break between objective and subjective knowledge as the most steadfast and important factor guiding his work (p. 15).

Bourdieu brings the two sides of the dichotomy together in what he calls *constructivist structuralism,* or structuralist constructivism—Bourdieu uses the term both ways—in which both structure and agency are given equal weight. Bourdieu (1989) says that within the social world, there are "objective structures independent of the consciousness and will of agents, which are capable of guiding and constraining their practices or their representations" (p. 14). He thus keeps structures in the objective social world that Durkheim gave us (although Bourdieu thinks a little differently about how and where these structures exist).

Yet, at the same time, Bourdieu emphasizes the constructivist and subjective sides. In Bourdieu's (1989) scheme, the subjective side is also structured in terms of "schemes of perception, thought, and action" (p. 14), which is habitus. Part of what Bourdieu does is detail the ways that both kinds of structures are constructed; thus, there is a kind of double structuring in his theory and research. But Bourdieu doesn't simply give us a historical account of how structures are produced. His theory also offers an explanation of how these two structures are dialectically related and how the individual uses them strategically in linguistic markets.

Dialecticism and a Theory of Practice

In preserving both sides of the dichotomy, Bourdieu has created a unique theoretical problem. He doesn't want to conflate the two sides as Giddens (Chapter 14) does, nor does he want to link them up. He wants to preserve the integrity of both domains, and yet he characterizes the dichotomy as harmful. Bourdieu is thus left with a sticky problem: How can he keep and yet change the dichotomy between the objective and subjective moments without linking them or blending them together? Let's take this issue out of the realm of theory and state it in terms that are a bit more approachable. The problem that Bourdieu is left with is the relationship between the individual and society. Do we have free choice? Bourdieu would say yes. Does society determine what we do? Again, Bourdieu would say yes. How can something be determined and yet be the product of free choice? I've stated the issue a bit too simplistically for Bourdieu's theory, but I want you to see the problem clearly. Structure and agency, or the objective and subjective moments, create tension because they stand in opposition to one another. That tension is exactly how Bourdieu solves his theoretical problem.

Bourdieu argues that the objective and constructive moments stand in a dialectical relationship. The idea of a **dialectic** was brought into sociology by Karl Marx. A dialectic contains different elements that are naturally antagonistic toward or in tension with one another. This antagonism is what energizes and brings change; it's the engine. In the material world of capitalist production, the primary contradictions are found in exploitation and overproduction. For Marx, the dialectic continues until an economic system in keeping with species-being comes into existence. Bourdieu's dialectic occurs between the field and the habitus. Both are structures; habitus is "incorporated history," and the field is "objectified history" (Bourdieu, 1980/1990, p. 66). The tension of the dialectic is between the subjective and objective structures, and the dialectic itself is found in the individual and collective struggles or practices that transform or preserve these structures through specific practices and linguistic markets. In other words, Bourdieu is arguing that a number of different elements in our lives are structured, and among them are the habitus of the individual (schemes of thought, feeling, and action) and the social field (structured social positions and the distribution of resources). These different structures dialectically exert force upon one another through the strategic actions and practices of people in interaction. As with most dialectics, the tension can produce something new and different out of the struggle; these differences can then influence the structures of habitus and field.

Reflexive Sociology

Bourdieu wants us to engage in reflexive sociology, where we move "in a spiral between theory, empirical work and back to reformulating theory again but at a different level" (Mahar, Harker, & Wilkes, 1990, p. 3). If we were to look at one of Bourdieu's books, such as *Distinction* (1979/1984), we would see this reflexive vision of theory and the social world graphically laid out. On any given page, there may be two or three different print fonts with lines separating the different text. What Bourdieu is doing graphically is moving back and forth between dense empirical descriptions and abstract theory. In this back-and-forth movement, Bourdieu proposes a concept, considers it in light of the empirical world, and then continually reconsiders it throughout the book. In this way, his methodological stand and writing are themselves theoretical statements of structural constructivism. Theory, like social practice, is embedded in the empirical world, and theory, like social structures and practice, moves dialectically: It's never finished, it never arrives, but it is always transformed through its intrinsic tensions.

Bourdieu never published a definitive statement of his theory—the closest he came to it is in *An Invitation to Reflexive Sociology* (Bourdieu & Wacquant, 1992)—and his later works don't necessarily build upon or include his earlier work. Bourdieu doesn't like "professorial definitions" but much prefers the idea of "open concepts" (Bourdieu & Wacquant, 1992, p. 95). Reflexive sociology, then, is more concerned with insight and inspiration than creed and rigor. Bourdieu gives us an inspiring way through which to bridge the gap between objective and subjective sociology. He gives us a dynamic space from which to think about the relations between structure and agency. I hope that at this point you can see the relations between this new perspective Bourdieu is introducing and his theory of class.

Summary

- Bourdieu is specifically concerned with the reproduction of class. In contrast to Marx, Bourdieu sees class replicated through symbolic violence rather than overt oppression. He argues that there are four types of capital: economic, social, symbolic, and cultural. The latter two are his greatest concern. Symbolic capital has the power to create positions within the symbolic and objective fields. The objective field refers to social positions that are determined through the distributions of the four capitals. But these positions don't become real or meaningful for us unless and until someone with symbolic capital names them. This naming gives the position, and the individuals and groups that occupy it, social viability. The symbolic field has independent effects in that it can be manipulated by those with symbolic capital; people use the symbolic field to view, understand, and reproduce the objective field.

- Cultural capital refers to the social skills, habits, linguistic abilities, and tastes that individuals have as a result of their position in the symbolic and objective fields. Cultural capital is particularly important because it becomes embodied. This embodiment of cultural capital becomes the individual's habitus: the way the body exists and is used in society. Distance from necessity and level of education are two of the most important ways in which habitus is structured, both of which are related to economic capital. Class position, then, is replicated through the embodied, nonconscious behaviors and speech acts of individuals.

- Habitus is expressed in linguistic markets. Linguistic markets are structured by different weightings of the various capitals. One's position within the market is determined by different rankings on the capitals and the embodied ability to perform within the market. Linguistic markets are played out in speech acts where individuals sense how their habitus relates to the market and thus anticipate differing profits of distinction. This nonconscious sense provides the basis for symbolic violence: Anticipating few rewards in acts where they are "outclassed," individuals simultaneously sanction themselves and legitimate the hierarchical relations of class and power.

- There is, however, the possibility of symbolic struggle. The struggle involves symbolic disruption. First, individuals or groups can act in such a way as to objectively picture alternative possibilities. This is what we normally think of as social movements or demonstrations. But because Bourdieu sees the importance of symbolic power in the replication of class, he understands these demonstrations as pictures—they are objective images of symbolic issues that disrupt the taken-for-grantedness in which oppression must operate. Second, individuals and groups can challenge the subjective meanings intrinsic within the symbolic field. In daily speech acts, the individual can disrupt the normality of the symbolic field through insults, jokes, questions, rumors, and so on. Groups can also challenge "the way things are" by redefining history.

- Bourdieu's basic approach is constructivist structuralism. With this idea, Bourdieu is attempting to give us a point of view that gives full weight to structure and agency. There is tension between constructivism and structuralism, between agency and structure, and it is that tension that Bourdieu uses to understand how both can coexist. The tension is a dialectic and is played out in symbolic markets and social practices.

TAKING THE PERSPECTIVE: CULTURAL EMBODIMENT

There are three ways we can think of Bourdieu's theoretical perspective in terms of how it is situated in the discipline. The first way is to see his theory as neo-Marxian. I have to admit that this is a very loose categorization, and a number of our theorists would fall in this category, such as the Frankfurt School (Chapter 2), William Julius Wilson (Chapter 7), Immanuel Wallerstein (Chapter 10), Jürgen Habermas (Chapter 12), and some postmodern theorists we briefly touch on in the final chapter of the book. Generally, neo-Marxian theorists are concerned with one of Marx's central issues; they usually don't see the economy quite as dominant as did Marx; and they often add elements from other theoretical approaches. This latter characteristic is most clearly seen in the Frankfurt School's use of psychoanalysis (Chapter 2).

There is a sense in which Bourdieu's theory may be seen as the mirror image of Marx. According to Marx, the economy and class are two of the most important structures in society. However, whereas Bourdieu's theory begins with material class, he clearly moves the reproduction of class structures into the symbolic realm. In the reproduction of class, it is the symbolic field and the relations expressed by and through habitus that have the greater causal force. Like Marx, Bourdieu defines the social world as the place where the competition for scarce resources takes place. The result of this competition is an unequal distribution of economic capital. But unlike Marx, Bourdieu sees much of this competition as taking place in a symbolic realm that produces an unequal distribution of four different kinds of capital: economic, social, cultural, and symbolic. Bourdieu is particularly concerned with Marx's notion of misrecognition, the idea that people fail to see or recognize the relations of production within a commodity or means of production. Bourdieu expands Marx's idea by arguing that misrecognition is present within all social practices and forms of knowledge, as well as a necessary condition for symbolic violence and oppression.

The other perspective in which Bourdieu figures prominently is that of culture. Calhoun (2003) asserts that Bourdieu's theory is the "single most important theoretical approach to the sociology of culture," and, perhaps more significantly, "he helped to bring the study of culture into a central place in sociology" (p. 303). While in many respects culture has been central to sociology since its inception, it has appeared generally as a topic of study, the way class, race, or gender are such topics. What Bourdieu helped accomplish was to move culture to the sociological approach in general. Rather than culture being something studied on its own, this cultural sociology sees it as intrinsic to everything people do: "To believe in the possibility of a cultural sociology is to subscribe to the idea that every action . . . is embedded to some extent in a horizon of affect and meaning" (Alexander & Smith, 2001, p. 136).

Bourdieu's contribution to cultural sociology is more specific than sociology's more general approach. His is a theory of cultural embodiment. Sociology has a variety of interests in the body (Frank, 1990). One of the most obvious is the medicalization of the body. The way people have understood illness, in terms of its cause and treatment, has varied across time and culture (see Bird, Conrad, Fremont, & Timmermans, 2010). For instance, the way childbirth was perceived radically changed with modern medicine. What was at one time a social event facilitated by midwives in the home became a medical event controlled by professionals in hospitals. Less apparent is the historical shift to the objectification of the body through the medical gaze; this is a central focus of Michel Foucault's analysis of the effects of modernity (Chapter 9). The body is also understood in sociology as a sign vehicle that communicates one's self-concept. Erving Goffman's dramaturgical approach (Chapter 4) is one approach; another is Victoria Pitts's (2003) understanding of body modification.

Bourdieu's focus is more closely aligned with the perspective that sees the body as a locus of social control. For Bourdieu, the body is structured in such a way as to reveal and replicate class position. Social control, then, is exercised in nonconscious, invisible ways: The body is programmed by class. We have another way of visualizing the controlled body in Judith Butler's work (Chapter 17). Butler argues that bodies are inscribed by heterosexism.

BUILDING YOUR THEORY TOOLBOX

- Using two additional sources, please write a theoretical definition of class.

- Write a 250-word synopsis of the theoretical perspective of constructivist structuralism.

- After reading and understanding this chapter, you should be able to define the following terms theoretically and explain their importance to Bourdieu's theory: economic capital, social capital, symbolic capital, cultural capital, taste, habitus, distance from necessity, education, field, linguistic market, symbolic violence, constructivist structuralism, dialectic.

- After reading and understanding this chapter, you should be able to answer the following questions (remember to answer them theoretically):

  o Explain Bourdieu's constructivist structuralism approach.

  o How are symbolic fields produced?

  o What is habitus, and how is it produced?

  o How are class inequalities replicated, and how is class contingent? (In your answer, be certain to explain linguistic markets, symbolic violence, and the role that habitus plays.)

Learning More—Primary and Secondary Sources

- Pierre Bourdieu, *Distinction: A Social Critique of the Judgment of Taste,* Harvard University Press, 1984.

- Pierre Bourdieu, "Social Space and Symbolic Power," *Sociological Theory, 7,* 14–25, 1989.

(Continued)

(Continued)

- Pierre Bourdieu, *Language and Symbolic Power,* Harvard University Press, 1991.

- Pierre Bourdieu and Loïc J. D. Wacquant, *An Invitation to Reflexive Sociology,* University of Chicago Press, 1992.

- Pierre Bourdieu, *Acts of Resistance: Against the Tyranny of the Market* (Translated by Richard Nice), New Press, 1999.

- David Swartz, *Culture and power: The Sociology of Pierre Bourdieu,* University of Chicago Press, 1998.

- Richard Jenkins, *Pierre Bourdieu* (Key Sociologists), Routledge, 2002.

Engaging the World

- Use Bourdieu's theory to describe and explain the differences between the way you talk with your best friend versus the way you talk with your theory professor.

- Using Bourdieu's take on misrecognition, analyze the following ideas: race, gender, and sexuality. What kinds of things must we misrecognize in order for these to work as part of the symbolic violence of this society? Look up Bourdieu's notion of *doxa* (1972/1993, p. 3; 1980/1990, p. 68). How do doxa and symbolic violence work together in the oppression of race, gender, and sexuality?

- Bourdieu's theory is aimed at class inequality, but his perspective can also be used to understand any system of inequality. Choose the structure of inequality other than class that you know best, like race, gender, sexuality, or religion. What specifically would Bourdieu's theory add to our understanding of how that structure of inequality is created and maintained?

Weaving the Threads

- Can you think of ways in which you could use Bourdieu's theory to make Chafetz's theory of gender inequality more robust, especially in her ideas of what happens at the micro level?

CHAPTER 9

Structures of Power

Michel Foucault

Source: ©Bettmann/CORBIS.

The Big Picture: Power

Social power is for many people an uncomfortable idea, at least in democratic settings. We like to think that democracy is more refined, more oriented toward persuasion than control. Power seems just the opposite: **Power** is "the chance of a man or a number of men to realize their own will in a social action even against the resistance of others" (Weber, 1922/1968, p. 926). Yet many social thinkers see power as basic to society, democratic or not. One reason for this view comes back to one of the basic questions of sociology: social order. The problem of social order is based on the assumption that human beings are basically motivated by self-interest. Once you assume this about human nature, then social order and cooperation become problems. If all you care about is yourself, why would you cooperate with other people to achieve goals you don't care about?

One answer to the problem of social order is found in functionalist theory, which we saw in Chapter 2. The short version of this idea is that social order is achieved through commonly held norms, values, and beliefs. This approach to understanding social order is sometimes called the equilibrium model because it's based on people internalizing and believing in the collective consciousness. However, conflict theorists point out that there is an element of power underlying norms, since norms are defined as behaviors that have sanctions attached, either rewards or punishment. All norms, then, assume a distribution of power. Conflict theorists also point out that the values and beliefs commonly held in society can be explained in terms of the interests of the elite. For conflict theorists, social order is the result of constraint rather than consensus, and power is thus an essential element of society.

In his analysis, Weber connects power—the ability to get others to do what you want—with authority. Authority is the belief structure that legitimates social power and its use. Obviously, if I have a gun, I can get you to do what I want even if you don't want to, but such coercive situations aren't where social power is put into effect. Persuasion isn't specifically what Weber has in mind either. Both persuasion and coercion are based more or less on individual personalities. Persuasion works subtly as we are drawn in by the personal magnetism or interaction skills of the other person. Moreover, the willingness to use brute coercion is based on individual characteristics as well.

Weber identified two sources of social authority: party and social organization. Party is most directly related to power, but as with class and status, it isn't power itself. Party refers to a group that is focused on the acquisition of power and may represent interests based on class or status position. As Weber (1922/1968) puts it, a party organizes "in order to attain ideal or material advantages for its active members" (p. 284). The social groups that Weber would consider parties are those whose practices are oriented toward controlling an organization and its administrative staff. The Democratic and Republican Parties in the United States are obvious examples of what Weber intends. Other examples include student unions or special interest groups like the tobacco lobby, if they are oriented toward controlling and exercising power.

As implied in the conflict perspective, social organization itself creates differing levels of authority. Ralf Dahrendorf, a contemporary theorist, used Weber's idea to give a more detailed model of how this works. According to Dahrendorf (1957/1959), "social roles [are] endowed with expectations of domination or subjection" (p. 165). In other words, the legitimated use of power is found in everyday status positions, roles, and norms used to organize human action. Because of its organizational embeddedness, Dahrendorf refers to authoritative social relations as imperatively coordinated associations (ICAs). If something is imperative, it is binding and compulsory; you must do it. So the term simply says that social relations are managed through legitimated power (authority).

The insight that Dahrendorf derives is that society is intrinsically rife with potential conflict, because every one of us is a member of ICAs. The question then becomes, under what conditions does the potential for conflict become overt? Dahrendorf gives us three sets of conditions that must be met for a group to become active in conflict. The *technical conditions* are those things without which a group simply can't function: members, ideas or ideologies (what Dahrendorf calls a "charter"), and norms; the *political conditions* refer specifically to the ability to meet and organize; and the *social conditions* include the ability to communicate and the availability of structural patterns of recruitment.

There are of course other approaches to understanding power. Feminism sees power exercised through patriarchy; contemporary Marxists talk about hegemonic culture; and futurist Alvin Toffler (1991) argues that there are three kinds of power: violence, wealth, and knowledge. Violence and wealth were sources of power in previous "waves." But since the advent of postindustrial society, knowledge is becoming the most significant source of power. This idea of Toffler's follows the dictum "knowledge is power," but he gives it an explanatory base. Postindustrial economies are based on knowledge, either theoretical knowledge that leads to technological innovations or knowledge as the ability to create or use information and information technologies. Weber actually argued something similar, but he tied it to bureaucracy: Bureaucracies function on expert knowledge.

The reason I've spent this time reviewing various ways of understanding social power will become obvious: Foucault's work is about power. My point, however, may not be as obvious. Foucault's theory of power is unlike any of the above. He argues that power in modernity is exercised differently than during any other period of time. On the surface, he appears to agree with Toffler: Knowledge is power. However, there is a profound yet easily missed difference. Toffler argues that the more modern knowledge you have, the more power you will be able to exercise. Foucault argues just the opposite: The more knowledge you have and use to understand yourself and the world around you, the more subjugated you become.

THEORIST'S DIGEST

Brief Biography

We should begin this brief biography by noting that Foucault would balk at the idea that we need to know anything about the author in order to understand his work. Further, Foucault would say that any history of the author is something that we use in order to validate a particular reading or interpretation. Having said that, Foucault was born on October 15, 1926, in Poitiers, France. Foucault studied at the École Normale Supérieure and the Institut de Psychologie in Paris. In 1960, returning to France from teaching posts in Sweden, Warsaw, and Hamburg, Foucault published *Madness and Civilization*, for

(Continued)

(Continued)

which he received France's highest academic degree, doctorat d'État. In 1966, Foucault published *The Order of Things,* which became a best-selling book in France. In 1970, Foucault received a permanent appointment at the Collège de France (France's most prestigious school) as chair of History of Systems of Thought. In 1975, Foucault published *Discipline and Punishment* and took his first trip to California, which came to hold an important place in Foucault's life, especially San Francisco. In 1976, Foucault published the first volume of his last major work, *The History of Sexuality.* The two other volumes of this history, *The Use of Pleasure* and *The Care of the Self,* were published shortly before Foucault's death in 1984.

Central Sociological Questions

In Foucault's (1984/1990a) own words,

> As for what motivated me.... It was curiosity—the only kind of curiosity, in any case, that is worth acting upon with a degree of obstinacy: not the curiosity that seeks to assimilate what it is proper for one to know, but that which enables one to get free of oneself. After all, what would be the value of the passion for knowledge if it resulted only in a certain amount of knowledgeableness and not, in one way or another and to the extent possible, in the knower's straying afield of himself? (p. 8).

In brief, Foucault was interested in how ideas and subjectivities come into existence and how they limit what is possible. But Foucault's search was not simply academic, though it was that. As the above quote tells us, Foucault sought to understand his own practices "in relationship of self with self and the forming of oneself as a subject" (p. 6).

Simply Stated

Foucault's basic premise is that human reality is language. There's an old adage that says, "There are three sides to every story: yours, mine, and the truth." Because language is human reality, Foucault would say that there are only two sides; the truth of any event or thing isn't available to humans because of our deep dependence on and use of language. This implies that any claim to represent the truth (such as my trying to convince you that my story is the right one) is an expression of power. Social power is expressed and imposed through what passes as legitimated knowledge, which orders the world around us, and through discourse, which orders our subjective positions. Modernity brought with it a specific kind of power in that the individual disciplines himself or herself—modern power is practiced from within. Modern power is also distinct in that the person is objectified by these internal practices.

Key Ideas

Truth games, counter-histories, archaeology, genealogy, episteme, discourse, governmentality, objectification, panopticon, microphysics of power, medical gaze

Concepts and Theory: The Truth About Truth

The truth about truth is that it is used to exercise power. Thus, Foucault's interest in truth isn't abstract or philosophical. Rather, Foucault is interested in analyzing what he calls *truth games*. His use of "games" isn't meant to imply that what passes as truth in any historical time is somehow false or simply a construction of language. Foucault feels that these kinds of questions can only be answered, let alone asked, after historically specific assumptions are made. In other words, something can only be "false" once a specific truth is assumed; Foucault is involved in uncovering *how* truth is assumed. Specifically, Foucault's interest in truth concerns the game of truth: the rules, resources, and practices that go into making something true for humans.

The idea of practice is fairly broad and includes such things as institutional and organizational practices as well as those of academic disciplines—in these practices, truth is formed. The idea also refers to specific practices of the body and self—these are where power is exercised. Most of us use the word *practice* to talk about the behaviors we engage in to prepare for an event, like band practice for a show. But practice has another meaning as well. This meaning is clear when we talk about a medical practice. When you go to your physician, you see someone who is "practicing" medicine. In this sense, practice refers to choreographed acts that interact with bodies—sets of behaviors that together define a way of doing something. This is the kind of practice in which Foucault is interested.

Uncovering Truth

Foucault uncovered truth games by constructing what he called *counter-histories*. When most of us think of history, we think of a factual telling of events from the past. We are aware, of course, that sometimes that telling can be politicized, which is one reason we have "Black History Month" here in the United States—we are trying to make up for having left people of color out of our telling of history. But most of us also think that the memory model is still intact; it's just getting a few tweaks. Foucault wants us to free history from the model of memory. He really doesn't say anything directly about whether any particular history is more or less true; that's not an issue for him. History in all its forms is part of and generated by discourse. Thus, Foucault's concern is how the idea of true history is used. What Foucault wants to produce for us is a counter-history—a history told from a different point of view from the progressive, linear, memory model.

The important questions then become, why is one path taken rather than another? Why is the present filled with one kind of discourse rather than others? And what has been the cost of taking this path rather than all the other potentialities? Thus, a counter-history identifies the following:

the accidents, the minute deviations—or conversely, the complete reversals—the errors, the false appraisals, and the faulty calculations that gave birth to those things that continue to exist and have value for us; it is to discover that truth or being does not lie at the root of what we know and what we are, but the exteriority of accidents. (Foucault, 1984, p. 81)

Foucault uses two terms to talk about his counter-history, archaeology and geneal-ogy. Though the distinctions are sometimes unclear, *archaeology* seems to be oriented toward uncovering the relationships among social institutions, practices, and knowl-edge that come to produce a particular kind of discourse or structure of thought. *Genealogy* may be better suited to describe Foucault's (1984[??]) work that is con-cerned with the actual inscription of discourse and power on the mind and body: "Genealogy, as an analysis of descent, is thus situated within the articulation of the body and history. Its task is to expose a body totally imprinted by history and the pro-cess of history's destruction of the body" (p. 83). We could say that archaeology is to text what genealogy is to the body. In both cases, there is an analogy to digging; search-ing; and uncovering the hidden history of order, thought, madness, sexuality, and so on. The hidden history isn't necessarily more accurate—it's simply a counter-story that is constructed more in an archaeological mode than a historical one.

Why So Critical?

What is Foucault's point in constructing counter-histories? Part of what he wants to do is expose the contingencies of what we consider reality, but to what end? Many critical perspectives are based on assumptions of what would make a better society. In other words, there must be something to which the current situa-tion is compared to demonstrate what it is lacking. But Foucault sees it otherwise. For him, *the critical perspective in itself is sufficient because it opens up possibilities.* In fact, Foucault would argue that a utopian scheme only attempts to replace one system of impoverishment with another. The point is to keep possibilities always open, to keep people critically examining their life and knowledge system so that they can perpetually be open to the possibility of something else.

According to Foucault's scheme, an important part of what creates knowledge, order, and discourse is the presence of "blank spaces." Foucault (1966/1994b) pictures knowledge as a kind of grid. The boxes in the grid are the actual linguistic categories, like mammal, flora, mineral, human, black, white, male, and female. We are familiar with those parts of the grid; they form part of our everyday language. However, there is actually a more important part of the grid: the part that creates the order—the blank spaces between the categories. "It is only in the blank spaces of this grid that order manifests itself in depth as though already there, waiting in silence for the moment of its expression" (p. xx). The true power of a discourse or knowledge system is in the spaces between the categories. As Eviatar Zerubavel (1991) notes,

> Separating one island of meaning from another entails the introduction of some mental void between them. . . . It is our perception of the void among these islands of meaning that makes them separate in our mind, and its magnitude reflects the degree of separateness we perceive among them. (pp. 21–22)

These spaces are revealed most clearly in transgression. As an illustration, let's think about a little boy of about 3 or 4 years of age. He is playful, playing with the toys he's been given and emulating the role models he sees on TV and among the neighborhood children. But one day his father comes home and finds him playing with dolls. His father grabs the doll away and tells his son firmly that boys do not play with dolls. In this instance, the category of gender was almost invisible until the young boy unwittingly attempted to cross over the boundary or space between the categories. The meaning and power of gender waited "in silence for the moment of its expression."

This idea of space is provocative. A more Durkheimian way of thinking about categories would conceptualize the space between them as a boundary or wall. Using the idea of boundary to think about the division between categories is fruitful: Walls separate and prevent passing. The young boy in our example certainly came up against a wall, and many of us have felt the walls of gender, race, or sexism. But the idea of walls makes the use of categories and knowledge seem objective, as if they somehow exist apart from us, and this is not what Foucault has in mind.

Notice that the boy in our example was unaware of the "wall" until his father showed it to him. From Foucault's position, the wall of gender was erected in the father's gendered practices. Foucault's idea of space helps us think about the practices of power. Space, in this sense, is empty until it is filled—seeing space between categories rather than a wall makes us wait to see what will go there and how it goes there. Space is undetermined. Something can be built in space, but the space itself calls our attention to potential. Foucault's research, his critical archaeology, fills in that potential—he tells us how that space became historically constructed in one way rather than any of the other potential ways.

Foucault's counter-history actually creates a space of its own. On one side, Foucault's archaeology of modernity uncovers the fundamental codes of thought that establish for all of us the order that we will use in our world. On the other side, Foucault sets the sciences and philosophical interpretations that explain why such an order exists. Between these two domains is a space of possibilities, a space wherein a critical culture can develop that sufficiently frees itself "to discover that these orders are perhaps not the only possible ones or the best ones" (Foucault, 1966/1994b, p. xx).

In other words, through the archaeology of knowledge, Foucault wants to not only expose the codes of knowledge that undergird everything we do, feel, and think; he also wants to set loose the idea that things might not be as they appear. He wants to free the possibility of thinking something different. That possibility of thought exists in the critical space between—but in this case the space isn't specified, as it is in already existing orders. Foucault doesn't necessarily have a place he is taking us; he doesn't really have a utopian vision of what knowledge and practice ought to be. His critique is aimed at freeing knowledge and creating possibility; it's aimed at creating an empty space that is undetermined.

Concepts and Theory: The Practices of Power

According to Foucault, power isn't something that a person possesses, but it is something that is part of every relationship. Foucault tells us that there are three types of domains or practices within relationships: communicative, objective, and power. Communication is directed toward producing meaning; objective practices are directed toward controlling and transforming things—science and economy are two good examples; and practices of power, which Foucault (1982) defines as "a set of actions upon other actions" (p. 220), are directed toward controlling the actions and subjectivities of people. Notice where Foucault locates power—*it's within the actions themselves,* not within the powerful person or the social structure. Foucault uses the double meaning of "conduct" to get at this insight: Conduct is a way of leading others (to conduct an orchestra, for example) and also a way of behaving (as in "Tommy conducted himself in a manner worthy of his position"). Thus, we conduct others through our conduct.

However, Foucault's intent is not to reduce power to the mundane, the simple organization of human behavior across time and place. Rather, Foucault's point is that power is exercised in a variety of ways, many of which we are unaware. Power, then, becomes insidious. Power acts in the normalcy of everyday life. It acts by imperceptible degrees, exerting gradual and hidden effects. In this way, the exercise of power entices us into a snare that feels of our own doing. But how is power exercised? Where does it exist, and how are we enticed? Foucault argues that power is exercised through the epistemes (underlying order) and discourses found in what passes as knowledge. The potential and practice of power exists in these epistemes and discourses that set the limits of what is possible and impossible, which in turn are felt and expressed through a person's relationship with himself or herself, in subjectivities—the way we feel about and relate to our inner self—and the disposition of the body.

The Power of Order

Order is an interesting idea. We order our days and lives; we order our homes and offices; we order our files and our bank accounts; we order our yards and shopping centers; we order land and sea—in short, humans order everything. *How* do we order things? One of the ways is linguistically: "Indeed, things become meaningful only when placed in some category" (Zerubavel, 1991, p. 5). But a deeper and more fundamental question can be asked: How do we order the order of things? In other words, what scheme or system underlies and creates our categorical schemes? We may use categories to order the world around us, but where do the categories get their order?

To introduce us to this question, Foucault (1966/1994a) tells a delightful story of reading a book that contains a Chinese categorical system that divides animals into those

> (a) belonging to the Emperor, (b) embalmed, (c) tame, (d) sucking pigs, (e) sirens, (f) fabulous, (g) stray dogs, (h) included in the present classification, (i) frenzied, (j) innumerable, (k) drawn with a very fine camelhair brush, (l) et cetera, (m) having just broken the water pitcher, (n) that from a long way off look like flies. (p. xv)

The thing that struck Foucault about this system of categories was the limitation of his own thinking—"the stark impossibility of thinking *that*" (p. xv). In response, Foucault asks an important set of questions: What determines the boundaries of what is possible and impossible to think? Where do these boundaries originate? What is the price of these impossibilities—what is gained and what is lost?

Foucault argues that there is a fundamental code to culture, a code that orders language, perception, values, practices, and all that gives order to the world around us. He calls these fundamental codes epistemological fields or the episteme of knowledge in any age. **Episteme** refers to the mode of thought's existence, or the way in which thought organizes itself in any historical moment. An episteme is the necessary precondition of thought. It is what exists before thought and that which makes thought possible. This foundation of thought is not held consciously. It is undoubtedly this preconscious character of the episteme that makes thought believable and ideas seem true.

Further, rather than seeing thought and knowledge as results of historical, linear processes, Foucault argues that discontinuity marks changes in knowledge. Most of us think that the knowledge we hold accumulated over time, that we have thrown out the false knowledge and replaced it with true knowledge as we progressively learned how things work. This evolutionary view of knowledge actually comes from the culture of science. It is the way we want to see our knowledge, but not necessarily the way it is. Foucault argues that knowledge doesn't progress linearly. Rather, what we know and how we know it are linked to historically specific patterns of behavior, institutional arrangements, and economic and social practices that set the rules and conditions of discourse and the limits of our possibilities. That historical path is marked by rupture: discontinuities and sudden, radical changes.

Foucault is saying that this idea of rupture implies that knowledge and truth are purely functions of institutional arrangements and practices and not the result of any real quest for truth. Thus, what counts as truth in any age—our own included—comes about through historically unique practices and institutional configurations. This implies not only that knowledge is socially constructed, but also, and more importantly, that *knowledge is nothing more and nothing less than the exercise of power*. This pure power is put into effect through discourse and the taken-for-granted ordering of human life.

The Power of Discourse

Discourse is perhaps the most powerful analytical concept to come out of Foucault's work and poststructuralism. The word itself comes from a Latin word meaning "argument" or "running about," specially running a course. Both definitions imply a specified path and set of practices or ways of doing something. Making arguments and running races don't take place haphazardly. Arguments and races are planned in advance, occur according to known sets of rules, and limit what the people involved can do. If you're running a marathon, for example, you can't just decide to take a short cut and win the race. You'd be disqualified. Arguments are like that as well. In fact, the rules of writing an argument are specific to academic disciplines. As an undergraduate, I turned in a paper for a sociology class that was returned with the comment, "This is more a philosophy of education paper rather than sociology of education." Ironically, after I'd completed my PhD in sociology, I took a philosophy class just because I was interested. In that class, the professor told me my papers weren't written according to the rules of philosophical argumentation. After training my mind to think like a sociologist, I had trouble thinking philosophically.

To understand Foucault's use of discourse, it's helpful to contrast his general approach to culture with two others: structuralist and hermeneutic (the leading approaches before Foucault's work). A *hermeneutic approach* to culture looks to understand the diverse meanings culture can have for people in different contexts. Sometimes the differences are obvious, such as the diverse meanings that the American flag can have. But it's in the more subtle differences that the hermeneutic approach becomes clear. Clifford Geertz (1973), an anthropologist, gives us a good example through the use of *thick descriptions,* accounts of social phenomena that are microscopic in detail. Geertz gives us the problem of the eye twitch versus the wink. The difference between the two cannot be photographed, but the differences in meaning are vast—a twitch can by virtually meaningless while the wink can be flirtatious. But there's more: The twitch or the wink may be parodied, in which the physical action is neither a wink nor a twitch. Further still, the parody may be practiced—it is then not a wink or twitch or parody. In order to understand the differences between the wink and the twitch and all of the ways that they may be framed, thick descriptions must be used to get at the meaning of the behavior to the actors in the situation. Geertz refers to the thick descriptions and their layers of meaning as "piled-up structures of inference and implication" (p. 7).

A *structuralist approach,* on the other hand, looks at the underlying foundations of culture and argues that structure causes or strongly influences meanings and practices. In other words, the cultural meanings that matter aren't left to individual interpretation. Meanings are set or shaped, usually through binary opposition. The clearest example is the binary good and evil; one cannot exist without the other, and thus they mutually constitute one another. Further, because they are set in opposition, they are mutually exclusive. If something is evil, it is by definition not good. Émile Durkheim's work in the area of religion is based on this sort of binary structure: the sacred and profane. Durkheim is generally seen as a founding thinker in the structuralist paradigm. In Chapter 13, we'll take a look at Jeffrey Alexander's understanding of civil society; it is a moderate Durkheimian version of structuralism. He argues that the binary categories of democracy create the discourses and practices found in any empirical civil society. Binary oppositions concerning motivations, relationships, and institutions are used to categorize civil and anti-civil, and thus determine or strongly inform the production of democratic meanings.

In Foucault's hands, culture isn't something that should simply be understood, nor is it deterministically guided by an underlying structure. Rather, cultural meanings, specifically knowledge, are *created and regulated* by historical conditions and rules of discourse. Discourses have rules that limit cultural practices and the kinds of things we can think and know. Recall the above quote: What struck Foucault about the Chinese encyclopedia is that it was impossible for him to conceive of a world divided by those categories. All discourses seem logical from the inside point of view, but are often seen as bizarre by an outsider. I once had a person describe to me a religion with Middle Eastern roots that had cannibalistic practices. The idea was appalling to my Westernized mind—that is, until he told me he was describing Christian Communion, when believers partake of the blood and body of Jesus. For believers, Communion makes sense within the discourse of Christianity, but it can look rather strange from the outside.

In addition to circumscribing what we know, discourses set up subjective positions. In the example I just gave, the discourse of Christianity creates a position wherein the subject "Christian" exists. To be a Christian, then, it is necessary to feel, think, and act in specific ways. In using this example, it's important to note that there are particular discourses within the broader category of Christianity. These more specific discourses often run along denominational lines that include some "Christians" and exclude others. Some Christian discourses, for example, categorize Jehovah's Witnesses as a cult and thus deny the subjective position of "Christian" to its members. The more fundamental a given discourse, the more specific (and closely guarded) are its qualifications for inclusion.

Let's use the more general example of gender. The discourse of gender determines the position a person must occupy in order to become the subject of a statement such as "I'm a man." For me to be a man, I must meet the conditions of existence that are set down in the discourse of gender. I not only have to meet those conditions for you; I must meet them for me as well, because the discourse sets out the conditions of subjectivity, how we think and feel about our self. Subjects, and the accompanying inner thoughts and feelings, are specific conditions within the discourse. As we locate ourselves within a discourse, we become subject to the discourse and thus subjectively answer ourselves through the discourse.

Discourse delineates what is possible and impossible for us to think, and it sets up subjective positions—symbolic spaces wherein a subject can exist. As such, discourse is an expression of power. We can look at Foucault's notion of power in two ways, one fairly obvious and the other less so. The more obvious instances are in such social categories of race and gender, which we touched on in Chapter 7. In the conclusion of this book, we'll talk about another obvious example: colonization. The colonizing efforts of Europe were legitimated by a discourse that Stuart Hall (1996a) characterizes as "the West and the Rest."

Of course, most modern nations are built upon various nationalisms, which are the same sort of discourse in that they create absolute meaning with strict inclusion and exclusion rules that determine subjective positions. In answer to the question, what is a nation, French writer Ernest Renan wrote, "a nation is . . . a large-scale solidarity, constituted by the feeling of sacrifices that one has made in the past and of those one is prepared to make in the future" (quoted in McCrone, 2006, p. 117). Note the power of these subjective positions. They provide meaning that transcends an individual's life: "The enduring attraction of war is this: Even with its destruction and carnage it can give us what we long for in life. It can give us purpose, meaning, a reason for living" (Hedges, 2002, p. 3).

These instances of power in discourse are obvious because they clearly are about one group exercising power over another. Foucault is actually more interested in the other, less obvious exercise of power. It's the power that is exercised in the taken-for-granted knowledge of our day. Even here, there are more and less obvious examples. Dorothy E. Smith gives us an example that is fairly easy to see in Chapter 16. Smith details how scientific knowledge in sociology denies the subjective experiences of women. Here the discourse of "sociology as science" determines legitimate forms of knowledge and denies all others. Legitimated knowledge in sociology is objective, determined by data and statistical analysis. This sort of knowledge subjugates and denies women's lived experiences. Patricia Hill Collins will make this same sort of argument in Chapter 15 about the intersection of race and gender.

Again, this isn't Foucault's main concern with discourse, though it is closer to the heart of it. The power of discourse that concerns Foucault the most is the power that we exercise over ourselves by using legitimated knowledge to bring our lives under its dominion. Let me give you a brief example. When I was growing up, my parents smoked cigarettes. In fact, almost everybody smoked cigarettes. When I came to my present university in 1995, cigarette smoking had just a few years prior been forbidden within the buildings. Previously, professors would commonly sit at their desks smoking. About 5 years ago, the university decided that it would become a smoke-free campus. This is happening in stages. The university first drew lines around the building doors that kept smokers 25 feet away from the entrances. Three years ago, the university implemented a change in employee health insurance benefits. In order to get the best plan, an employee was required to sign a form stating that he or she did not use tobacco products of any kind. Otherwise, the employee was forced to take an inferior plan, with a higher deductible and lower percentages and lifetime limits paid. This practice is becoming increasingly common and is being extended to such issues as bodyweight. Employers are also putting greater emphasis on overall preventative health care, providing greater benefits for those who are proactive in establishing a healthy lifestyle. In response to such measures, people are smoking less, monitoring their diet and drinking habits, participating in some form of exercise, and so on.

I've used this example many times in class and I usually get a common response: "But smoking is bad for you, and people should take care of themselves!" This is why understanding Foucault is tricky: We believe in the knowledge we hold. Remember the truth about truth we talked about previously. For Foucault, truth is a game that is played by specific rules. Foucault is interested in the rules because absolute truth is either an abstract philosophical concept or a matter of faith. Foucault has demonstrated empirically, through his counter-histories, that knowledge doesn't progress in a linear manner. In other words, it isn't the case that humanity is on the path of progressive knowledge and people were wrong in the past only because they didn't know enough—and, obviously, we're right today because we do. That's a belief of the Enlightenment, which we looked at in Chapter 1. Changes in knowledge happen in ruptures, relatively sudden breaks from the past. The breaks can't be attributed to discoveries, but rather, to changing social practices. This understanding of knowledge isn't unique to Foucault. In fact, many philosophers of science would agree (see Paul Feyerabend, 1988; Thomas Kuhn, 1970).

In Foucault's theory, then, discourse "constructs, defines and produces the objectives of knowledge in an intelligible way while excluding other forms of reasoning as unintelligible" (Barker, 2008, p. 90). Further, discourse creates subjective positions that people occupy and are thus a way in which individuals exercise control over themselves and others.

The Power of Objectification

For Foucault, then, power is not so much a quality of social structures as it is the practices or techniques that become power as individuals are turned into subjects through discourse. Foucault intends us to see both meanings of the noun *subject:* as someone to control, and as one's self-knowledge. Here, Foucault's unique interest is quite clear: Perhaps the most insidious form of power is that which is exercised by our self over how we think and feel; it is the power we exercise in the name of others over our self.

In an interesting analysis, Foucault uses the state to illustrate both meanings of subject. State rule is usually understood in terms of power over the masses. While this is a true characteristic of the state, Foucault argues that the modern state also exercises individualization techniques that exert power over the subjectivity of the person. Foucault talks about this form of ruling as *governmentality:* "The government of the self by the self in its articulation with relations to others" (Foucault, 1989, as quoted in Davidson, 1994, p. 119). Governmentality was needed because of the shift from the power of the monarch to the power of the state.

Under a monarchy, the power of the queen or king was absolute, and he or she required absolute obedience, but the scope of that control was fairly narrow. The nation-state "freed" people from the coercive control of the monarchy but at the same time broadened its scope of control. The nation-state is far more interested in controlling our behaviors today than monarchies were 300 years ago. In governmentality, the individual is enlisted by the state to exercise control over himself or herself. This is partly achieved through expert, professional knowledge that comes from medicine and the social and behavioral sciences. The state supports such scientific research, and the findings are employed to extend control, particularly as the individual uses and consults medicine, psychology, and other sciences.

A fundamental part of Foucault's argument about the practices of power is the historical shift to *objectification.* Obviously, if power is intrinsic to human affairs of all kinds, then people have always exercised power. However, the practice of power became something different and more insidious due to historical changes that objectified the subject of power. We are all probably familiar with the transitive verb *to objectify.* It means to make something an object that isn't an object, and it also means to exist apart from any internal relationship. Interestingly, most of us are probably not familiar with the transitive verb *to subjectify.* As a case in point, my word processor just highlighted "subjectify" as a misspelled word, yet it is a real word that appears in exhaustive dictionaries. We just rarely use the word, nor do we think about things becoming subjectified—we assume that we subjectively relate to everything about ourselves. But, according to Foucault, that is not the case in modernity. Today, we relate to our self, our body, and our sexuality as objects.

Foucault produced a series of books that provide a counter-history to some of the objectifying power practices found in Western societies. These books detail madness and rationality, abnormality and normality, medicine and the clinic, penal discipline and punishment, psychiatry and criminal justice, and the history of sexuality. In general, these works document how you and I exercise power over our bodies and subjectivities. While I don't have the luxury of introducing you to all of Foucault's archaeology and genealogy, it is important for us to talk about a few of his concepts so that you can get a sense of how Foucault's theoretical ideas get played out. We'll first be looking at how power is exercised over our body and then over our inner, subjective life.

Concepts and Theory: Disciplining the Body

Foucault's intent in his book *Discipline and Punish* (1975/1995) was to map a major shift in the way in which Western society handles crime and criminals. The shift is from punishment and torture to discipline. Foucault paints a graphic comparative picture in the first seven pages of this book. The first part of the picture is an account of the public torture and killing of a man named Damiens on March 2, 1757. Damiens had been convicted of murder and sentenced to having his flesh torn from his body with red-hot pincers, followed by various molten elements (such as lead, wax, and oil) poured into the open wounds. The hand that held the knife with which he had committed the murder was burnt with sulfur. Finally, he was drawn and quartered by four horses, his body burnt to ashes, and the ashes scattered to the winds.

The second image in Foucault's picture is a set of 12 rules for the daily activities of prisoners in Paris. The rules covered the prisoners' entire day and included such things as prayer, Bible reading, education, bathing, recreation, and work. These rules were in use a mere 80 years after the public torture of Damiens. The shortness of the time period indicates that the change wasn't due to gradual adjustment and progress, but rather to abrupt shifts in knowledge, perception, and power.

Foucault uses this graphic comparison to point out a fundamental change that occurred in Europe and the United States. Most of us would look at these differences and attribute the change to a dawning of compassion and a desire to treat people more humanely. Foucault, on the other hand, looks deeper and more holistically at the shift. This change not only affected the penal system; it was a fundamental social change as well. During this period of time, from the eighteenth to nineteenth centuries (also known as the Enlightenment), science gained its foothold in society. Society as a whole began to embrace what we call *scientism*—the adaptation of the methods, mental attitudes, and modes of expression typical of scientists. Scientism values control, and control is achieved by objectifying the world and reducing it to its constituent parts. The gaze of the scientist is thus penetrating, particularizing, and objectifying. This kind of gaze results in universal technologies that allow humans to regularize and routinize their control of the world.

The shift, then, was not due to society becoming more compassionate and humane; the shift from punishment to discipline was a function of scientism and the desire to more uniformly control the social environment. As Foucault (1975/1995) says, the primary objective of this shift was

> to make of the punishment and repression of illegalities a regular function, coextensive with society; not to punish less, but to punish better; to punish with an attenuated severity perhaps, but in order to punish with more universality and necessity; to insert the *power to punish more deeply into the social body.* (p. 82, emphasis added)

This new way of discipline and control is best characterized by Jeremy Bentham's panopticon. The word **panopticon** is a combination of two Greek words. The first part, "pan," comes from the word *pantos,* meaning "all." The second part comes from the word *optikos,* meaning "to see." Together, panopticon literally means "all-seeing." There is actually an optical instrument called the panopticon that combines features of both the microscope and telescope, allowing the viewer to see things both up close and far away, thus seeing all.

Jeremy Bentham developed a different kind of panopticon—a building for prisons. Bentham's panopticon was a round building with an observation tower or core that optimized surveillance. The building was divided into individual prison cells that extended from the inner core to the outer wall. Thus, each cell had inner and outer windows; each prisoner was backlit by the outer window, allowing for easy viewing. "They are like so many cages, so many small theatres, in which each actor is alone, perfectly individualized and constantly visible" (Foucault, 1975/1995, p. 200). The tower itself was fitted with venetian blinds, zigzag hallways, and partitioned intersections among the observation rooms in the tower. These made the tower guards invisible to the prisoners who were being observed. The purpose of the panopticon was to allow seeing without being seen. Here "inspection functions ceaselessly. The gaze is alert everywhere" (p. 195).

Foucault isn't really interested in the panopticon as such. He sees the idea of the panopticon as illustrative of a shift in the fundamental way people thought and the way in which power is practiced. In terms of crime and punishment, it involved a shift from the spectacle of torture (which fit well with monarchical power) to regulation in prison (which fits well with the nation-state); from seeing crime as an act against authority to an act against society; from being focused on guilt (did he or she do it?) to looking at cause (what social or psychological factors influenced the person?); and, most importantly, from punishment to discipline—more specifically, to the self-discipline imposed by the ever-present but unseen surveillance of the panopticon.

Foucault (1975/1995) refers to this kind of control as the *microphysics of power* and sees this as the explicit link between knowledge and power: "There is no power relation without the correlative constitution of a field of knowledge, nor any knowledge that does not presuppose and constitute at the same time power relations" (p. 27). The microphysics of power is exercised or practiced as knowledge is produced, appropriated by groups for use, distributed to the population through education and mass media (such as books, magazines, and the Internet), and then retained internally by those that others want to control.

The Disciplines of the Human Sciences

Obviously, all of society was not put into a physical panopticon, but society was placed within a symbolic or institutional system of surveillance. In another word play, Foucault argues that the discipline associated with panopticon surveillance of the entire population comes from the disciplines, in particular the human sciences. The modern episteme created the possibility of the human sciences, such as psychiatry, psychology, and sociology. The human has been the subject of thought and modes of control for quite some time, but in every case the human was seen holistically or as part of the universal scheme of things. In the modern episteme, however, mankind becomes the object of study, not as part of an aesthetic whole, but as a thing in its own right.

This discourse of science serves to objectify and control the individual. Psychiatry and psychology used the mechanical model of the universe to gaze inside the psyche of the person; sociology and political science looked at the external circumstances of humanity. Thus, both the internal motivations and reasons behind action as well as the external factors became the objects of science in order to fulfill its chief goal, which is control. Statistics are used to quantify and categorize; psychotherapy and psychological testing are used to probe and catalog. All of the disciplines and their methodologies are brought into "discipline" in order to fulfill this primary goal of control.

Foucault (1982) finds the human sciences particularly interesting because they are "modes of inquiry which try to give themselves the status of sciences" (p. 208). The human sciences are thus not true science; they only take on the guise of science. The human sciences did not grow out of scientific questions; they grew out of the modern episteme. Simply put, during the time that people began to talk about society and psychology, the kind of knowledge that was seen as real and valuable was science. So, in order to be accepted, the social and behavioral disciplines had to take on the guise of science.

More specifically, Foucault argues that there are three areas of knowledge in the modern episteme: mathematical and physical sciences, life and economic sciences, and philosophy. The human sciences grew out of the space created by these three knowledge systems. Asking scientific questions about things like biology and physics, which have some basis in the objective world, set the stage for those same questions to be asked about the questioner. Further, each of these sciences pursues knowledge in a distinctive manner, each with its own logic. The human sciences, on the other hand, must borrow from each of these because they have no unique domain or methodology. The human sciences stand in

> relation to all the other forms of knowledge . . . at one level or another, [they use] mathematical formalization; they proceed in accordance with models or

concepts borrowed from biology, economics, and the sciences of language; and they address themselves to that mode of being of man which philosophy is attempting to conceive. (Foucault, 1966/1994b, p. 347)

Therefore, the precariousness or uncertainty of the human sciences isn't due to, "as is often stated, the extreme density of their object" (Foucault, 1966/1994b, p. 348); rather, their uncertainty of knowledge is due to the fact that they have no true method of their own—everything is borrowed. The validity of knowledge is in some way always related to methodology. What we know is an effect of how we know it. Because the human sciences don't have their own methodology, the knowledge generated is without any basis—in the end, it is purely an expression of power that can be explicitly used by the state to control populations, but is more generally part of the control people exercise over themselves in modernity.

As such, we generally see and understand ourselves in Western cultures from the human science model. We listen endlessly to public opinion polls and voting predictions, and they become constant topics of conversation for us. Our bookstores, magazine racks, and Internet chat rooms are filled with ever-increasing numbers of self-help books, advice, and groups, respectively. We understand the family in terms of such psychosocial models as "the functional family," and we raise our children according to the latest findings. Almost everything that we think, feel, and do is scrutinized by a human science, and we are provided with that knowledge so that we, too, can understand our own life and its circumstances.

The Discipline of Medicine

But the human sciences are not alone in their objectification of humanity; they are aided by a culture produced by the *medical gaze.* The modern medical gaze is different from that of the eighteenth century. At that time, disease was organized into hierarchical categories such as families, genera, and species. In some ways the patient was superfluous to the disease. The doctor's gaze, then, was directed not so much at the patient as at the disease. Diseases transferred to the body when their makeup combined with certain qualities of the patient, like the person's temperament. Symptoms existed within the disease itself, not the patient. This way of seeing where symptoms live implies that the patient's body could actually get in the way of the doctor seeing the symptoms. For example, if the patient was old, then the symptoms associated with being elderly could obscure the doctor's view of the symptoms associated with the disease. The medical gaze was thus directed at the disease, not the body.

However, by the nineteenth century, the modern medical gaze had come to locate disease within the patient. Disease was no longer seen to exist within its own world apart from the body; from this new clinical point of view, disease is located within the body and is constituted by its symptoms. The patient can't get in the way of the symptoms; the symptoms and disease are the same and exist within the body. This shift in discourse created the clinical gaze, an objectifying way of seeing that looks within and dissects the patient. With the clinical gaze, "Western man could constitute himself in his own eyes as an object of science" (Foucault, 1963/1994a, p. 197).

Modern medicine was thus created through a gaze that makes the body an object, a thing to be dissected, either symbolically or actually, in order to find the disease within it. The culture of the clinical gaze helped to create a general disposition in Western society to see the person as an object. This disposition, along with the human sciences, made the practices of power much more effective and treacherous—objects that can be thrown away are much easier to control than subjects who demand continuing emotional and psychic connections.

Disciplining Sex

Thus, bodily regimens of exercise and diet, self-understanding and regulation of feelings and behaviors, all stem from medicine and the human sciences, which Foucault tells us make up the panopticon of modernity. But Foucault is interested in something deeper than the control of the body—he wants to document how we as individuals exercise social power over the way we relate to our own selves. Nowhere is this more clearly seen than in Foucault's counter-history of sexuality. In order to understand Foucault's intent, we will now briefly review Greek and modern ideas of sexuality.

Greek Sexuality

Ancient Greece was the birthplace of democracy and Western philosophy. There was, in fact, a connection between democracy and philosophy. In Athens, in response to an upheaval by the masses against their tyrannical leader, a politician named Cleisthenes introduced a completely new organization of political institutions called democracy (the rule of common people). Through democratic elections, the elite incrementally lost their advantage in the assemblies and the common people ruled. Unfortunately, the masses were susceptible to impassioned speech and ended up making several decisions that conflicted with one another or entailed high costs. This series of crises created a desire in the elite for absolutes: What are the truths upon which all decisions and governance should be based? Truth obviously couldn't be found simply through rhetoric; they believed that there had to be some absolutes upon which decisions could be based.

Along with other factors, this impetus helped produce the Greek notion of the soul. For the Greek, the idea of the soul captured all that is meant by the inner person: his or her mind, emotions, ethics, beliefs, and so on. But in reading Plato, it's also clear that the soul was seen to be hierarchically constructed. Within the soul, the mind is preeminent and alone is immortal. The emotions and appetites, though part of the soul, are lesser and mortal. Thus, reason is godlike and education, especially philosophy, is important for proper discipline.

It is important that we see the emphasis here. The mind, emotions, and bodily appetites are viewed hierarchically, but they are all seen as part of the soul. In order to get a sense of the relationships within the soul, let's take a look at a conversation that Plato sets up between Socrates and a group of students in the third or fourth century BC. Socrates speaks first:

"Do you think that it's a philosopher's business to concern himself with what people call pleasures—food and drink, for instance?"

"Certainly not, Socrates," said Simmias.

"What about those of sex?"

"Not in the least." . . .

"Then it is your opinion in general that a man of this kind is not preoccupied with the body, but keeps his attention directed as much as he can away from it and towards the soul?"

"Yes, it is." . . .

"Then when is it that the soul attains to truth? When it tries to investigate anything with the help of the body, it is obviously liable to be led astray."

"Quite so."

"Is it not in the course of reasoning, if at all, that the soul gets a clear view of reality?"

"Yes." (Plato, 1993, pp. 117–118)

Notice how Socrates views sex: It isn't something set aside and special. It is simply seen as a bodily appetite, on a par with eating and drinking. These aren't a direct concern for the philosopher—they are only of indirect concern. If the bodily appetites get in the way of the search for reality or truth, then they are of concern, but only then. The point is to keep the mind free. A person shouldn't be preoccupied with the body, because too much attention on the body and its appetites will take his or her attention away from the quest for truth. This bit of dialogue sets us up well for the way Foucault talks about sex in Greek society.

In Greek society, sexuality existed as *aphrodisia.* This Greek word is obviously where we get our term *aphrodisiac,* but it had a much broader meaning for the Greeks. Foucault notes that neither the Greeks nor the Romans had an idea of "sexuality" or "the flesh" as distinct objects. When we think of sex, sexuality, or the flesh, we usually have in mind a single set of behaviors or desires. The Greeks, while they had words for different kinds of sexual acts and relations, didn't have a single word or concept under which they could all fit. The closest to that kind of umbrella term is *aphrodisia,* which might be translated as "sensual pleasures" or "pleasures of love," and more accurately the works and acts of Aphrodite, the goddess of love.

These works of Aphrodite, perhaps like the works of any god or goddess, cannot be fully categorized. To do so would limit the god. This lack of a catalog or objective specification of sexuality is exactly Foucault's point. In modern, Western society, particularly as expressed through Christianity, there is a definite way to index those things that are sexual, or the "works of the flesh." This identifiability is extremely important for the Western mind because sex is a moral issue; it, above all other things, defines immoral practices. So, what counts and doesn't count as sexual is imperative for us, but wasn't for the Greeks.

The Greeks also employed the idea of *chresis aphrodision* to sexuality: The phrase means "the use of pleasures." The Greeks' use of pleasure was guided by three strategies: need, timeliness, and status. The strategy of need once again highlights

Socrates' approach to sexual practices. As we've seen, in ancient Greece, the relationship to one's body was characterized by moderation, but every person's appetites and abilities to cope are different. Thus, the Greek strategy was for the individual to first know his need—to understand what the body wants, what its limits are, and how strong the mind is.

The second strategy is timeliness and simply refers to the idea that there are better and worse times to have sexual pleasures. There was a particularly good time in one's life, neither too young nor too old; a good time of the year; and good times during the day, usually connected with dietary habits. The issue of time "was one of the most important objectives, and one of the most delicate, in the art of making use of the pleasures" (Foucault, 1984/1990a, p. 57). The last strategy in the use of pleasures was status: The art of pleasure was adapted to the status of the person. The general rule was that the more an individual was in the public eye, the more he should "freely and deliberately" adapt rigorous standards regarding his use of pleasures.

Rather than seeing sexuality as moral, the Greeks saw it in terms of ascetics. *Ascetics* refers to one's attitude or relationship toward one's self, and for the Greek this was characterized through strength. The word *ascetics* comes from the Greek *asketikos*, which literally means "exercise." The idea here is not simply something we do, as in exercising control; it also carries with it a picture of active training. Here we see the Greek link between masculinity and virility. The virile man in Greek society was someone who moderated his own appetites. He was the man who voluntarily wrestled with his body in order to discipline his mind. The picture we see is that of an athlete in training. For example, the athlete knows that eating chocolate or ice cream can be very pleasurable. But while in training, the athlete willingly forgoes those pleasures for what he or she sees as a higher good. The result of this training is *enkrateia*, the mastery of one's self. It's a position of internal strength rather than weakness.

Training is always associated with a goal; there is an end to be achieved or a contest to be won. In this case, the aim of the Greek attitude toward sexuality is a state of being, something that becomes true of the individual in his daily life. This is the teleology, or ultimate goal, of sexuality, the fourth structuring factor that defines a person's relationship to sex. The goal for the Greek was freedom. We can again see this idea in the conversation with Socrates. Truth and reality were things to be sought after. Too much emphasis on sex, just like eating and drinking, can get in the way of this search. As Socrates (Plato, 1993) said, "surely the soul can reason best when it is free of all distractions such as hearing or sight or pain or pleasure of any kind" (p. 118).

Western Modern Sexuality

The Western modern view of sex is quite different from the Greek. It is, in fact, quite different from that which developed in the East. Where Eastern philosophy and religion developed a set of practices intended to guide sexual behavior to its highest and most spiritual expression and enjoyment (for instance, the Kama

Sutra), the West developed systems of external control and prohibitions. Of course, a great deal of the impetus toward this view of sex was provided by the Christian Church.

Part of this movement came from Protestantism with its emphasis on individual righteousness and redemption. Rather than being worthy of God because of Church membership and sacraments, Protestantism singled the individual out and made his or her moral conduct an expression of salvation and faith. But an important part was also played by the Counter-Reformation, a reform movement in the Catholic Church.

Confession and penance are sacraments in the Catholic Church. They are one of the ways through which salvation is imparted to Christians. The Counter-Reformation increased the frequency of confession and guided it to specific kinds of self-examination, designed to root out the sins of the flesh down to the minutest detail:

> [S]ex . . . [in all] its aspects, its correlations, and its effects must be pursued down to their slenderest ramification: a shadow in a daydream, an image too slowly dispelled, a badly exorcised complicity between the body's mechanics and the mind's complacency: everything had to be told. (Foucault, 1976/1990b, p. 19)

This was the beginning of the Western idea that sex is a deeply embedded power, one that is intrinsic to the "flesh" (*the* vehicle of sin par excellence, as compared to the Greek idea of bodily appetites), and one that must be eradicated through inward searching using an external moral code and through outward confession.

While these Christian doctrines would have influenced the general culture, they would have remained connected to the fate of Christianity alone had it not been for other secular changes and institutions beginning in the eighteenth century, most particularly in politics, economics, and medicine. With the rise of the nation-state and science, population became an economic and political issue. Previous societies had always been aware of the people gathered together in society's name, but conceiving of the people as the population is a significant change. *The idea of population transforms the people into an object that can be analyzed and controlled.*

In this transformation, science provided the tools and the nation-state the motivation and control mechanisms (ability to tax, standing armies, and so on). The population could be numbered and analyzed statistically, and those statistics became important for governance and economic pursuit. The population represented the labor force, one that needed to be trained and, more fundamentally, born. At the center of these economic and political issues was sexuality:

> It was necessary to analyze the birthrate, the age of marriage, the legitimate and illegitimate births, the precocity and frequency of sexual relations, the ways of making them fertile or sterile, the effects of unmarried life or of the prohibitions, the impact of contraceptive practices [and so on]. (Foucault, 1976/1990b, pp. 25–26)

In the latter half of the nineteenth century, medicine and psychiatry took up the sex banner as well. Psychiatry, especially through the work of Freud, set out to discover the makeup of the human mind and emotion, and it began to catalog mental illnesses, especially those connected with sex. It conceptualized masturbation as a perversion at the core of many psychological and physical problems, homosexuality as a mental illness, and the maturation of a child in terms of successive sexual issues that the child must resolve on the way to healthy adulthood. In short, psychiatry "annexed the whole of the sexual perversions as its own province" (Foucault, 1976/1990b, p. 30). Law and criminal justice also bolstered the cause, as society sought to regulate individual and bedroom behaviors. Social controls popped up everywhere that

> screened the sexuality of couples, parents and children, dangerous and endangered adolescents—undertaking to protect, separate, and forewarn, signaling perils everywhere, awakening people's attention, calling for diagnoses, piling up reports, organizing therapies. These sites radiated discourses aimed at sex. (pp. 30–31)

All of these factors worked to change the discourse of Western sexuality in the twentieth century. Sex went from the Greek model of a natural bodily appetite that could be satisfied in any number of ways, to the modern model of sex as the insidious power within. At the heart of this change is the confession, propagated by Catholicism and Protestantism and picked up by psychiatry, medicine, educators, and other experts. Confessional rhetoric is found everywhere in a society that uses Victorian prudishness as its backdrop for incessant talk about sex in magazines, journals, books, movies, and reality television shows. Repression is used as a source of discourse, and sex has become the topic of conversation—a central feature in Western discourse, and the defining feature of the human animal. Sex is suspected of "harboring a fundamental secret" concerning the truth of mankind (Foucault, 1976/1990b, p. 69).

In the modern discourse of sex, sexuality has become above all an object, a truth to discover and a thing to control. In this, sex has followed the use and development of science in general and the human sciences in particular: "The project of a science of the subject has gravitated, in ever narrowing circles, around the question of sex" (Foucault, 1976/1990b, p. 70). This form of objective control ("bio-control") over the intimacy of humanity came through science and is linked with the development of the nation-state and capitalism. While capitalism and the nation-state seem to be firmly established and the need for such control not as great, what we are left with is a way of constructing our self as the moral subject of our sexual behavior. We have inherited a certain kind of subjectivity from this discourse, a particular way of relating to our self and sexuality. This legacy of the modern discourse of sexuality sees sex as a central truth of the self, as an object that must be studied and understood. Further, the modern discourse of sexuality tells us that this part of us is intrinsically dangerous. It is at best an amoral creature and at worst a defiled beast that treads upon sacred and moral ground.

Summary

- Foucault takes the position that knowledge and power are wrapped up with one another; each produces and reinforces the other. Power as exercised and expressed through discourse creates the way in which we feel, act, think, and relate to our self. Likewise, the knowledge of any epoch defines what is mentally, emotionally, and physically possible. Foucault sees the practices involved in power and knowledge as games of truth—the use of specific rules and resources through which something is seen as truth in any given age. The games of truth that Foucault is particularly interested in are the ones that involve the practices through which we participate in the domination of our subjectivity.

- Much of Foucault's work is in the form of counter-history. The generally accepted model of history is that of history as memory: History is our collective memory of events. We also usually think of history as slowly progressing in a linear fashion. Foucault argues that history is far from a memory of linear events—history is power in use. It's a myth that is constructed according to specific values. Foucault proposes a counter-history, one that focuses on abrupt episodes of change and the way in which knowledge changes in response to various power regimes. Foucault uses an archaeological approach to uncover the practices that are associated with discourse and ways of thinking, and he uses a genealogical approach to uncover how discourse and power are inscribed on the body and mind.

- Foucault argues that the knowledge people hold is based upon historical epistemes. Episteme means the underlying order; Foucault uses it to refer to the way thought organizes itself in any historical period of time. Discourses are produced within historical epistemes. A discourse is a way of talking about something that is guided by specific rules and practices, that sets the conditions for our subjective awareness, and that subjugates through a will to truth and power.

- While power is found in all human practice, Foucault is particularly interested in the unique power of modernity. This expression of power is associated with changes in government, medicine, the institution of the human sciences, changes in the Western discourse of sexuality, and changes in the penal system. The change from rule by monarchy to rule by the nation-state demanded a new form of governmentality, one in which the individual watches over his or her own behaviors, one that increases control while preserving the illusion of freedom. This governmentality was aided by the human sciences through the ideas of population, an essentializing and mechanistic model of the person, and the value of expert knowledge. Governmentality was also produced through a new "medical gaze," which located symptoms and disease within the body, panoptical practices in controlling criminality, and changes in sexuality promoted by the Catholic confessional and Protestant individualism. Together, these created a discourse of governmentality that objectifies and controls through its own practices.

TAKING THE PERSPECTIVE: POSTSTRUCTURALISM

Many social theories take a critical perspective. Yet there is a fundamental difference between most critiques and the one offered by Foucault. With the others, there is a sense of some substance or presence, but with Foucault one gets a sense of absence. For example, with Foucault there isn't truth, only truth games; and there isn't history, just counter-histories. One way to understand this absence is to simply say that Foucault has other concerns, and that undoubtedly is part of it. But there's something deeper, more basic in back of Foucault's approach: Foucault approaches the social world as a poststructuralist.

In order to understand poststructuralism, we must first look to structuralism (since the "post" denotes that it comes after structuralism). Structuralism argues that there are deep structures that underlie and generate observable phenomena or events. This is a more radical statement than is usually made when we talk about structure in sociology (such as Parsons's structural-functionalism). For many sociologists, social structures are seen as influencing our lives; they help account for the patterned nature of human action and interaction. But social structures are usually seen as one of several influences. While we can talk about the poles of the debate in terms of structure versus agency, most sociologists acknowledge that interactions, culture, and structure all influence our behavior.

On the other hand, structuralism sees the power of structure as absolute. These structures work below the level of consciousness, and they don't simply influence or even determine our behaviors; they generate, create, and produce them. Everything that we see, think, feel, and do are in reality events or manifestations of the structure. While this may sound depressing to some of us, for structuralists this idea represented a ray of hope. As the linguistic structuralist Claude Lévi-Strauss (1963) put it, "Structural linguistics will certainly play the same renovating role with respect to the social sciences that nuclear physics, for example, has played for the physical sciences" (p. 33). It is the criticism of this belief and hope that forms the core of poststructuralism.

The basic premise of poststructuralism is that language signifies rather than represents. In other words, language doesn't refer to or represent any actual reality—all we have is language. Yet people have always sought a center for language—we have wanted language to be a response to the real world, to be tied down, moored, centered in reality. This center is what brings presence to language. The use of "presence" here functions as a technical term; it implies being or existence. In other words, humans have always sought a center to their linguistic schemes that would make language authentic, true, or real. Ideas such as essence, existence, substance, subject, transcendence, consciousness, God, man, and so forth have given language a reason for its existence, a firm foundation upon which to stand, and an "invariable presence" (Derrida, 1967/1978, pp. 279–280).

But there are two problems with this idea or desire. First, a center that moors language to some reality is by definition outside of the totality of language. The idea of a monotheistic God is a good example. God is seen to exist outside of time, space, and language, and because of that external existence, believers think that He gives reason for the universe in its totality (including time, space, and language). The clearest expression of this sort of centering is the "doctrine of plenary inspiration," the belief that every single word written in the Bible was directly inspired or dictated by God.

However, the external nature of the center reveals a contradiction. A center that is located outside the whole is by definition not inside and thus cannot be at the center of the totality. In other words, language is the totality of human existence—we think, feel, and see linguistically. But humans have always looked outside of language for the center of or reason for language. There's part of us that knows this, but we usually ascribe it to being "wrong." We say things like, "People used to talk about the earth being flat, but they were wrong." Poststructuralism wants us to see that there's never a chance of being "right" because those "truths" or "centers" are always and ever, by definition, outside of language. What we see in the idea of a center is a desire to master anxiety—anxiety about the human mode of existence. Since this is so, "the entire history of the concept of structure ... must be thought of as a series of substitutions of center for center" (Derrida, 1967/1978, p. 279). Thus, logically, there is no center to language, no firm foundation upon which to stand.

The second issue that poststructuralists want to bring to our attention is that a rupture has occurred in the history of language. Amongst all the other critiques of capitalism, race, gender, and so on, there came a time when language itself was critiqued. Writing is a profound process. Through writing, we inscribe the world around us. That's what happens when we use language to understand and make meaning out of the physical world and our experiences—we put the meaning on it; the meaning isn't "there" for language to represent. Writing/language is so profound that it writes its own critique. Think of it this way: If you were a linguist and wanted to critique language, what's the only thing you'd use? You would have to use language; you would write the critique of writing by writing it. Here, language inscribes upon itself. The rupture is that moment in time when language itself was critiqued, and it without question reveals the absolute reflexive nature of language. Thus, rather than language being centered in an independent reality, language is inherently self-referential, creating a world of oppressive power relations (Foucault's point). The implications of this are as follows:

- Poststructuralism rejects the belief in essentializing ideas that conceptualize the social world or a portion of it as a universal totality—rather, the social world is fragmented and historically specific (General social theories are thus impossible and oppressive.).

- Poststructuralism denies the possibility of knowing an independent or objective reality—rather, the human world and knowledge are utterly textual or discursive.

- Poststructuralism discards the idea that texts or language have any true meaning— rather, texts are built around difference and carry a surplus of meaning (Humanity is thus left with nothing but interpretation and interpretations of interpretation— this book is an interpretation of others' interpretations of a social world, and as you read, you produce yet another interpretation.).

- Poststructuralism rejects the idea of universal human nature developed out of the Enlightenment—rather, the meaning of the human subject is historically specific and is an effect of discourse, with the discourses of an age producing the possible bodies and subjectivities of the person.

(Continued)

(Continued)

Beyond that, Lemert (1990) points us to four uses of poststructuralism in sociology. He says that in the social sciences, we typically solve the problems or questions we pose with "reference to ideas like 'empirical reality'" (p. 244). Poststructuralism shatters the idea of a center; our texts therefore can't legitimately make reference to an empirical reality because every reality for humans is a written (inscribed) one. Thus, what we have isn't an empirical reality; it is a textual reality. What, then, can we conclude? Lemert gives us four propositions for poststructuralist sociology:

1. That theory is an inherently discursive activity

2. That the empirical reality in relation to which theoretical texts are discursive is without exception textual

3. That empirical texts depend on this relationship to theoretical texts for their intellectual or scientific value

4. That in certain, if not all, cases a discursive interpretation yields more, not less, adequate understanding (p. 244).

BUILDING YOUR THEORY TOOLBOX

- Using two additional sources, define the concept of class.

- Write a 250-word synopsis of the theoretical perspective of poststructuralism.

- After reading and understanding this chapter, you should be able to define the following terms theoretically and explain their importance to Foucault's theory of power: truth games, counter-histories, archaeology, genealogy, episteme, discourse, governmentality, objectification, panopticon, microphysics of power, medical gaze

- After reading and understanding this chapter, you should be able to answer the following questions (remembering to answer them theoretically):

  o Explain Foucault's connection between power and knowledge. How does he conceptualize power? How does knowledge function as power? What are the unique characteristics of modern power?

  o What does Foucault mean by "the order of things"? Explain how his "counter-histories" are used to expose this order.

  o Define discourse and explain how it provides a subjective position for the speaker.

o Explain the place of the social sciences (human disciplines) in creating governmentality and the microphysics of power.

o Describe how ideas about sex and sexuality changed between ancient Greek society and modern Western society.

Learning More—Primary and Secondary Sources

- Michel Foucault, *The History of Sexuality, Vol. I: An Introduction,* Vintage, 1990.

- Michel Foucault, *The Order of Things: An Archaeology of the Human Sciences,* Vintage, 1994.

- Michel Foucault, *Discipline and Punish: The Birth of the Prison,* Vintage, 1995.

- Michel Foucault, *The Birth of the Clinic: An Archaeology of Medical Perception,* Vintage Books, 1994.

- *The Essential Foucault,* edited by Paul Rabinow and Nikolas S. Rose, New Press, 2003.

- Sara Mills, *Michel Foucault,* Routledge, 2003.

- *The Cambridge Companion to Foucault,* edited by Gary Gutting, Cambridge, 1994.

- Gilles Deleuze, *Foucault,* University of Minnesota Press, 1988.

Engaging the World

- Find five examples of governmentality in your life. Explain how each one is an example and how it works in your life. In other words, how is modern society controlling you through your use of knowledge? Initially, finding examples can be difficult because this use of knowledge is ubiquitous. But once you begin to see governmentality, you'll see it everywhere.

- Spend an evening or two watching television shows (TV shows, not movies on DVD). Analyze the commercials in terms of discourse. If you only had the commercials upon which to base your analysis, how would you explain the discourse of gender? How do you see these discourses of masculinity and femininity impacting your life?

Weaving the Threads

- Using the index of this book, find the different ways power is defined and used theoretically. Evaluate each of these ways and create a theory of power that you think best explains it. Justify your answer.

- Power is a taken-for-granted part of what you learned about race, gender, and class in Chapters 7 and 8. What ways do you see Foucault's theory of power elaborating what you know about social inequality?

CHAPTER 10

World-Systems Theory

Immanuel Wallerstein

Source: Courtesy of Immanuel Wallerstein.

The Big Picture: Globalization

The idea of globalization isn't new. In fact, a globally connected economy is inherent in modern capitalism. As Marx (Marx & Engels, 1848/1978) said, "The bourgeoisie has at last, since the establishment of Modern Industry and of the world-market, conquered for itself, in the modern representative State, exclusive political sway" (p. 475). One of the reasons that modern capitalism created world markets is due to its intrinsic characteristic of expansion. People have always created products to sell in order to make a profit. What's distinct about modern capitalism is the *reason* for profit. In traditional capitalism, the profit was used to live, to maintain a standard of living. The motivation behind modern capitalism's drive for profit is investment.

In modern capitalism, the reason to gain profit is to be able to reinvest it; profit then becomes capital. Notice that in traditional capitalism, there is a natural limit to profit: A standard of living is a real thing and an achievable goal. But modern capitalism has no natural limit because its driving force is simply to make money in order to make more money, in order to make more money, ad infinitum—modern capitalism is defined by capital chasing capital without end. Thus, modern capitalism must continually push for expanding markets, commodification, and exploitation. We'll see that this constant expansion is an integral part of Immanuel Wallerstein's theory.

There are three related and important ideas that come with the idea of globalization. The first is that anytime we are talking about globalization, we are talking about *systems*. You remember that we spent a bit of time tending to the definition of social structure. We need to do the same here, and we also need to recognize that the concept of social structures implies the idea of systems. We've used the idea of structure to consider racial, gender, and class inequalities. But those structures are always understood as existing within a system; the economic, political, and religious systems are good examples that impact inequality. A system, then, "is any pattern of relationships between elements, and is regarded as having emergent properties of its own, over and above the properties of its elements" (Marshall, 1998, p. 621). What's important in approaching a systems analysis is to identify the elements, their relationships, and the emergent properties. The latter sounds more difficult than it is—it simply means that systems have their own laws and processes.

The second idea that comes out of the notion of systems is that systems always exist in environments. For example, animals are biological systems that exist within ecosystems. The important issue here is that systems have boundaries. Biological systems and ecosystems relate to one another, but they are clearly separate. This leads to the third important idea. Generally speaking, when modern sociologists talk about society, they are talking about a bounded system of interrelated structures. The assumption of most sociology is that society is a system with "a nation-state at its centre that organizes the rights and duties of each citizen" (Urry, 2006, p. 168). So, society is a system of interrelated structures whose boundaries are defined by a nation-state. We can thus, for example, talk about the United States as a society and Germany as a separate society.

As I said, the *idea* of globalization isn't new. However, there is something new about today's globalization: the extent of it. When Marx talked about world markets, he had in mind economies situated in different nations participating in global exchanges regulated by national-states. What we are seeing today challenges that picture: "Such challenges arise out of the fact that the global . . . simultaneously transcends the exclusive framing of national states yet partly inhabits national territories and institutions" (Sassen, 2007, p. 3). Saskia Sassen further tells us that contemporary globalization involves two dynamics, both of which call into question the modern idea of society (pp. 5–6). The first is the establishment of distinctly global structures and organizations—so there are elements of the system that do not exist within any nation; the second involves processes that link various nationally based actors and processes—so, while a company may in fact be based in Japan, the way it is connected to markets, other companies, and other economic systems involves issues that transcend national boundaries. The point I want you to take away from this discussion is simple yet profound: It's possible that the idea of society as a national system may be an antiquated way to think about social processes.

In this chapter and the next, we are going to look at two very different global systems. Wallerstein will tell us about the processes associated with global capitalism. As you'll see, Wallerstein draws heavily on some of Marx's most important ideas. Our next theorist, Manuel Castells (Chapter 11), will take us in a totally different direction. Rather than systems of institutions and social relations, Castells argues that globalization today is built on networks of communication, mostly structured through the Internet. These networks not only transcend the boundaries of nation; they completely redefine human connections. The globalized network society, then, can only be understood through the logics of computer networks; and in this network, social class, power, politics, meaning, and identities are radically redefined.

THEORIST'S DIGEST

Brief Biography

Immanuel Wallerstein was born in New York City on September 30, 1930. He attended Columbia University where he received his bachelor's (1951), master's (1954), and PhD (1959). Wallerstein has also formally studied at various universities around the globe, including the Université Paris Diderot, Université Libre de Bruxelles, and Universidad Nacional Autónoma de México. His primary teaching post was at Binghamton University (SUNY), where he taught from 1976 until his retirement in 1999. He has also held visiting professor posts in Amsterdam, British Columbia, and the Chinese University of Hong Kong, as well as several other locations. In addition to many professional posts, he has served as president of the International Sociological Association and director of the Fernand Braudel Center for the Study of Economies, Historical Systems, and Civilizations.

Central Sociological Questions

Wallerstein is driven first to critically understand (through a Marxian perspective) how the nations of the world are joined together in a global system of capitalism, and second to find ways to politically act to change that system.

Simply Stated

Because of exploitation and overproduction, the global capitalist economy goes through cycles of expansion and depression. Each cycle is deeper than the previous, and the cycles eventually reach a point where the economy can't rebound. During that last depression, the global system will go through a chaotic period out of which a new system will be born.

> ## Key Ideas
>
> Modern capitalism, globalization, systems, exploitation, dialectical materialism, division of labor, externalized costs, quasi-monopolies, overproduction, world empires, world economies, core states, periphery states, semi-periphery states, Kondratieff waves, world-systems theory

Concepts and Theory: The Dialectics of Capitalism

Wallerstein's theory is founded on Karl Marx's theory of capitalism. According to Marx, in humanity's purest economic form, people produced what they needed through collective cooperation, what Marx calls "primitive communism." It began small, but eventually we started using economic systems that were contrary to the social nature of humans. In such an economy, the structures have contradictions that will eventually destroy it because the system is out of sync with the social, collective nature of people. Marx talks about these economic antagonisms or contradictions as *dialectical materialism*. The *material* in his phrase isn't the physical universe as it is with most philosophers; it's the world of material goods that people create. The word *dialectic*, as you might guess, is related to *dialogue*. In this case, the dialogue is among the contradictions present in every economic form except communism.

Marx is saying that every economic system, other than one that is socially and collectively based, contains contradictions. These structural contradictions create tensions within the economy that push it toward change by resolving the contradictions in some way. In capitalism, for example, there are things capitalists must do (such as expanding markets) that naturally create pressures within the system (such as overproduction), and that will eventually lead to its downfall. Notice that the contradictions, while detrimental, are necessary for the economic system. These economic contradictions are what produce history—the contradictions are the energy that pushes for social change. As these contradictions resolve, new economies and social structures are born. In Wallerstein's hands, dialectical factors such as exploitation, accumulation, and overproduction in the long run bring about the collapse of global capitalism, out of which a new system will emerge.

The Division of Labor and Exploitation

The *division of labor* is one of the most important elements in the Marxian perspective. Marx starts his theory with the idea of species being, which contains two ideas: First, the way the human species exists is through creative production; second, humans become conscious of their existence (or being) through the mirror effect of the product. Humanity, then, is defined and knows itself through creative production. There is thus an intimate connection between producer and product: *The very existence of the product defines the nature of the producer.* If you think about it, we acknowledge this connection every time we meet someone new. One of the first questions we ask a new person is, "What do you do?" In doing so, we assume the connection between what people do and who they are.

For Wallerstein, the division of labor is the defining characteristic of an economic world-system. Labor, of course, is an essential form of human behavior; without it we would cease to exist. By extension, the division of labor creates some of the most basic kinds of social relationships; these relationships are, by definition, relations of dependency. In our division of labor, we depend upon each other to perform the work that we do not. I depend upon the farmer for food production, and the farmer depends upon teachers to educate his or her children. These relations of dependency connect different people and other social units into a structured whole or system. Wallerstein argues that the world-system is connected by the current capitalist division of labor: World-systems are defined "quite simply as a unit with a single division of labor and multiple cultural systems" (Wallerstein, 2000, p. 75). Multiple cultural systems are included because world-systems connect different societies and cultures.

The important feature of this division of labor is that it is based on exploitation, which is simply the measurable difference between what a worker gets paid and the worth of the product produced. For example, you get paid $150 for a day's work and you produce $500 worth of product; the difference is the level of exploitation. That difference is also the main source of profit for the capitalists; without it, capitalists couldn't exist. It's a simple thing, but it has some profound effects. First, because modern capitalism needs ever more capital, it will be driven to find the highest level of exploitation possible. Second, exploitation is a potential source of power for workers. Thus, there's a general tendency for workers to use that power to increase benefits and rights, such as the right to a 40-hour work week, overtime, minimum wage, health benefits, safety regulations, and so forth. Third, different societies can have different levels of exploitation. For example, if we compare the situation of automobile workers in the United States with those in Mexico, we will see that the level of exploitation is higher in Mexico.

What is important to see here is that profit is based on exploitation, and it gives workers power that could be used to increase worker benefits and wages, thus lowering the level of exploitation in a country. Yet the drive for exploitation doesn't let up; capitalists by definition are driven to increase profits. The search for new means of exploitation, then, eventually transcends national boundaries: *Capitalists export exploitation*. Because of the limitations on the exploitation of workers in advanced capitalist countries—due primarily to the effects of worker movements, state legislation, and the natural limitations of technological innovation—firms often seek other labor markets where the level of exploitation is higher. Marx had a vague notion of this, but Wallerstein's theory is based upon it. It is the exportation of exploitation that structures the division of labor upon which the world-economy is based.

Accumulation and Overproduction

As we've noted, "We are in a capitalist system only when the system gives priority to the *endless* accumulation of capital" (Wallerstein, 2004, p. 24), and we see the drive to make money in order to make more money all around us. But most people only think about the personal effects this kind of capitalism has (like the fact that Bill Gates is worth $61.3 billion). But what are the effects on the economy? Most Americans would probably say that the effect on the economy is a good one: continually expanding profits and higher standards of living. Perhaps, but Wallerstein wants us to see that something else is going on as well. In order to fully understand what he has in mind, we need to think about the role of government in the endless pursuit of the accumulation of capital.

It's obvious that for capitalism to work, it needs a strong state system. The state provides the centralized production and control of money; creates and enforces laws that grant private property rights; supplies the regulation of markets, national borders, interorganizational relations; and so forth. But there is something else that the state does in a capitalist system. We generally assume that the firm that pays the cost enjoys the benefits, as in the capitalist invests the money so he or she can enjoy the profit. However, the state actually decides what proportion of the costs of production will be paid by the firm. In this sense, capitalists are subsidized by the state.

There are three kinds of costs that the state subsidizes: the costs associated with transportation, toxicity, and the exhaustion of raw materials. Firms rarely if ever pay the full cost of transporting their goods; the bulk of the cost for this infrastructure is borne by the state, for such things as road systems. Almost all production produces toxicity, whether noxious gases, solid waste, or something that impacts the environment. How and when these costs are incurred and who pays for them are always issues. The least expensive methods are short-term and evasive (dumping the waste, pretending there isn't a problem), but the costs are eventually paid and usually by the state. Capitalist production also uses up raw materials, but again, firms rarely pay these costs. When resources are depleted, the state steps in to restore or recreate the materials. Economists refer to the expenses of capitalist production that are paid by the state as *externalized costs*, and we will see that in this matter, not all states are created equal.

However helpful these externalized costs are to the pursuit of accumulation, states that contain the most successful capitalist enterprises do even more: They provide a structure for *quasi-monopolies*. A monopoly is defined as the exclusive control of a market or the means of production; quasi-monopolies don't have exclusive control, but they do have considerable control.

Wallerstein argues that totally free markets would make the endless accumulation of capital impossible. Totally free markets imply that all factors influencing the means of production are free and available to all firms, that goods and services flow without restriction, that there is a very large number of sellers and a very large number of buyers, and that all participants have complete and full knowledge. "In such a perfect market, it would always be possible for the buyers to bargain down the sellers to an absolutely minuscule level of profit," which would destroy the basic underpinnings of capitalism (Wallerstein, 2004, pp. 25–26). The converse of a totally free market is a monopoly, and monopolized processes are far more lucrative than those of the free market. Thus, the perfect situation for a capitalist firm is to have monopolistic control; it would then be able to pursue the endless accumulation of capital with the greatest efficiency and success.

The most important way in which states facilitate quasi-monopolies is through patent laws that grant exclusive production rights for an invention for a certain number of years. This state guarantee allows companies to gain high levels of profit in a monopolistic market for long enough to obtain considerable accumulation of capital. The practice of granting patents also results in a cycle of leading products. The largest and most successful firms actively market a patented product as long as the profit margin is high. As soon as the product becomes less profitable through more open competition, the product is given over to less profitable companies, with the original firm creating new leading products. Producers of the unpatented product engage in freer competition but with less profit.

We're about ready to discuss the effect of all this, but we need to throw in one more ingredient. Marx (1932/1978b) argues that

> life involves before everything else eating and drinking, a habitation, clothing and many other things. . . . that the satisfaction of the first need . . . leads to new needs; and this production of new needs is the first historical act. (p. 156)

In other words, human beings have the unique ability to create additional or secondary "needs." Moreover, because people can create new needs, there is no limitation placed upon the proliferation of commodities.

Now think about what this means: Capitalists are driven to endlessly accumulate capital (it's the definition of modern capitalism). In this pursuit, they are subsidized by the state, most importantly through the support of quasi-monopolies. The state's support of quasi-monopolies means that new products are always being created, with the older ones still being produced. Further, by nature, human beings create new needs and thus produce and buy new commodities endlessly. Together, the continuous expansion of commodification and production inevitably leads to *overproduction*—too much production for the current demand. Capitalists will continue to create new and produce existing commodities until the market will no longer bear it. Therefore, overproduction is a fundamental property of capitalism that inexorably leads to production cutbacks, worker layoffs, and—in due course—economic downturns.

Interestingly, the issue of overproduction has entered the mind-set of popular culture. Commenting on a slow holiday season, *Time* magazine carried an article saying,

> Karl Marx theorized that capitalism was condemned to repeated depressions because of "cycles of overproduction." . . . if Marx had hit the shopping malls last week and seen the heavy discounting—or looked on the Internet and seen the emergence of cut-rate sites like Amazon.com's new outlet store—he would no doubt have felt vindicated. (Cohen et al., 2001, p. 21)

The cycles of overproduction and exploitation work in tandem, both of them driven by accumulation. Accumulation increases the demand for labor and product innovation. State protection through patent rights, tax incentives, and the like creates a state-sanctioned quasi-monopoly that in and of itself increases accumulation, better enabling the firm to engage in product innovation and increasing the demand for labor. Over time, the demand for labor decreases the size of the labor pool, which drives wages up and profits down, which in turn precipitates an economic slowdown, the collapse of small businesses, and the search for new methods of exploitation through technological innovation in the work process or exporting exploitation. In the medium run, exporting exploitation is the more efficient of the two because technologies become diffused throughout the business sector. Exporting exploitation implies the movement of specific goods outside the national boundaries, and product movement from most profitable to less profitable firms explicitly entails such a shift. Both processes, then, move goods and labor from advanced capitalist countries to rising capitalist countries, and both processes lead to the collapse of small businesses and the centralization of accumulation—that is, capital held in fewer and fewer hands.

Concepts and Theory: The End of the World as We Know It

World-Empires and World-Economies

Worlds end and worlds change. Of course, very few people living in any specific world think about their world ending, but they all do. The great Mesopotamian, Greek, and Roman empires are gone; the sun has set on the British Empire; and even more recently, the USSR crumbled and is no more. Of course, just like the phoenix, new worlds arise out of the ashes and history moves on. But what of our world? History tells us all worlds fail—when will our world fail? Generally, we in the United States live in a modern world, and more specifically, one that is defined by American capitalism. Wallerstein asks us to consider the possibility that our world is failing and that we are in a chaotic period between historical moments. Perhaps shockingly for some of us, Wallerstein argues that this shift in historical epochs will lead to the demise of the United States as we know it. So, let's take these questions seriously: In what historical epoch do we live, and how is it affecting our world?

Wallerstein argues that there have been two types of world-systems throughout history, one with a common political system and one without. Systems with a common political entity are called world-empires. *World-empires* exist through military dominance and mandatory economic tribute. The political influence of one government is spread and held in place through a strong military, but this sets up a cycle that eventually leads to the demise of the empire. Maintaining a standing army that is geographically extensive costs quite a bit of money. This money is raised through tribute (mandatory donations) and taxation. Heavy taxes make the system less efficient, in terms of economic production, and this increases the resistance of the populace as well. Increasing resistance means that the military presence must be increased, which in turn increases the cost, taxation, and resistance, and it further lowers economic efficiency. These cycles continue to worsen through structural time (see next page) until the empire falls. Examples of such world-empires include Rome and the ancient empires of China and India.

These world-empire cycles continued until about 1450, when a world-economy began to develop. Rather than a common political system, *world-economies* are defined through a common division of labor and through the endless accumulation of capital. As we saw earlier, in the absence of a political structure or common culture, the world-system is created through the structures intrinsic to capitalism. The worldwide division of labor created through the movement of products and labor from advanced capitalist nations to rising capitalist nations creates relationships of economic dependency and exploitation. These capitalist relationships are expressed through three basic types of economic states: core, semi-periphery, and periphery.

Briefly, *core states* are those that export exploitation; enjoy relatively light taxation; have a free, well-paid labor force; and constitute a large consumer market. The state systems within core states are the most powerful and are thus able to provide the strongest protection (such as trade restrictions) and capitalist inducements, such as externalizing costs, patent protection, tax incentives, and so on. *Periphery states* are those whose labor is forced (very little occupational choice and few worker protections) and underpaid. In terms of a capitalist economy and the world-system, these states are also the weakest—they are able to provide little in the way of tax and cost incentives, and they are the weakest players in the world-system. The periphery states are those to which capitalists in core states shift worker exploitation and more competitive, less profitable products. These shifts result in "a constant flow of surplus-value from the producers of peripheral products to the producers of core-like products" (Wallerstein, 2004, p. 28).

The relationship, then, between the core and the periphery is one of production processes and profitability. There is a continual shift of products and exploitation from core to periphery countries. Furthermore, there are cycles in both directions: Periphery countries are continually developing their own capitalist-state base. As we've seen, profitability is highest in quasi-monopolies, and these in turn are dependent upon powerful states. Thus, changing positions in the capitalist world-economy is dependent upon the power of the state.

Over time, periphery economies become more robust and periphery states more powerful: Worker protection laws are passed, wages increase, and product innovation begins to occur; the states can then begin to perform much like the states in core countries—they create tax incentives and externalize costs for firms, they grant product protection, and they become a more powerful player in the world-system economy. These nations move into the semi-periphery. *Semi-periphery states* are those that are in transition from being a land of exploitation to being a core player, and they both export exploitation and continue to exploit within their own country.

A good illustration of this process is the textile industry. In the 1800s, textiles were produced in very few countries, and it was one of the most important core industries; by the beginning of the twenty-first century, however, textiles had all but moved out of the core nations. A clear and recent example of this process is Nike. Nike is the world's largest manufacturer of athletic shoes, with about $10 billion in annual revenue. In 1976, Nike began moving its manufacturing concerns from the

United States to Korea and Taiwan, which at the time were considered periphery states. Within 4 years, 90% of Nike's production was located in Korea and Taiwan.

However, both Korea and Taiwan were on the cusp, and within a relatively short period of time they had moved into the semi-periphery. Other periphery states had opened up, most notably Bangladesh, China, Indonesia, and Vietnam. So, beginning in the early 1990s, Nike began moving its operations once again. Currently, Indonesia contains Nike's largest production centers, with 17 factories and 90,000 employees. But that status could change. In 1997, the Indonesian government announced a change in the minimum wage, from $2.26 per day to $2.47 per day. Nike refused to pay the increase and in response, 10,000 workers went on strike. In answer to the strike, a company spokesperson, Jim Small, said, "Indonesia could be reaching a point where it is pricing itself out of the market" (Global Exchange, 1998).

As a result of global protests, Nike has reevaluated the position exemplified by Small. Nike's current CEO, Mark Parker, says that global corporate responsibility is at a "tipping point" (as cited in Conner, 2010). In keeping with this statement, the company's current (NIKE, INC, 2012) sustainability report declares,

> The game has changed, forever. Sustainability used to be the exclusive domain of experts, activists and idealists. Then, it moved into a silo at the outskirts of the corporate landscape. Today, it is seen as an important, well-integrated part of any forward-thinking company—as one of the key drivers of success. (n.p.)

There are, of course, always questions about a corporation's sustainability reports; but, as *Business Ethics* author Michael Conner (2010) observes, "it's difficult to see how more reporting can't help, as long as it's done well." However, the more important theoretical question involves profitability and capitalism in the long run. While transparency, sustainability, and corporate responsibility have high social value, they also have high economic costs, which is what pushed for exporting exploitation in the first place.

The existence of the semi-periphery doesn't simply serve as a conversion point; it has a structural role in the world-system. Because the core, periphery, and semi-periphery share similar economic, political, and ideological interests, the semi-periphery acts as a buffer that lessens tension and conflict between the core and periphery nations. "The existence of the third category means precisely that the upper stratum is not faced with the *unified* opposition of all the others because the middle stratum is both exploited and exploiter" (Wallerstein, 2000, p. 91).

Kondratieff Waves

Since 1450, world-economies have moved through four distinct phases. These phases occur in what are called *Kondratieff waves* (K-waves), named after Nikolai Kondratieff, a Russian economist writing during the early twentieth century. Kondratieff noticed patterns of regular, structural change in the world-economy. These waves last 50 to 60 years and consist of two phases, a growth phase (the A-cycle) and a stagnation phase (the B-cycle).

Much of what drives these phases in modern economic world-systems comes from the cycles of exploitation and accumulation that we've already talked about. During the A-cycle, new products are created, markets are expanded, labor is employed, and the political and economic influence of core states moves into previously external areas—new geographic areas are brought into the periphery for labor and materials (imperialism). At 25 to 30 years into the A-cycle, profits begin to fall due to overproduction, decreasing commodity prices, and increasing labor costs. In this B-cycle, the economy enters a deep recession. Eventually, the recession bottoms out and small businesses collapse, which leaves fewer firms and greater centralization of capital accumulation (quasi-monopolistic conditions), which in turn sets the stage for the next upswing in the cycle (A2-cycle) and the next recession (B2-cycle). Historically, these waves reach a crisis point approximately every 150 years. Each wave has its own configuration of core and periphery states, with generally one dominant state, at least initially.

Wallerstein sees these waves as phases in the development of the world-system. Within each phase, three things occur: The dominant form of capitalism changes (agricultural → mercantile → industrial → consolidation), there is a geographic expansion as the division of labor expands into external areas, and a particular configuration of core and periphery states emerges. There have been four such phases thus far in the world-system. In Figure 10.1, I've outlined the different phases and their movement through time. I've also noted some of the major issues and the hegemonic core nations for easy comparison. Wallerstein (2004) uses the term *hegemonic* to denote nations that for a certain period of time,

> were able to establish the rules of the game in the interstate system, to dominate the world-economy (in production, commerce, and finance), to get their way politically with a minimal use of military force (which however they had in goodly strength), and to formulate the cultural language with which one discussed the world. (p. 58)

Figure 10.1 World-Systems Phases

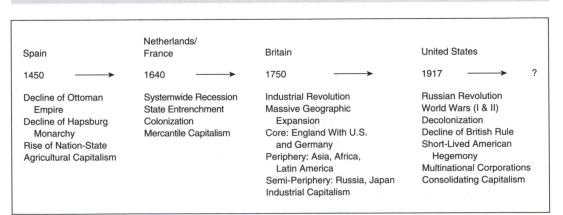

I'm not going to go into much historic detail here. You can read Wallerstein's (1974, 1980, 1989) three-volume work for the specifics. But briefly, phase 1 occurred roughly between 1450 and 1640, which marks the transition from feudalism and world-empires to the nation-state. Both the Ottoman Empire and the Hapsburg dynasty began their decline in the sixteenth century. As the world-empires weakened, Western Europe and the nation-state emerged as the core, Spain and the Mediterranean declined into the semi-periphery, and northeastern Europe and the Americas became the periphery. During this time, the major form of capitalism was agricultural, which came about as an effect of technological development and ecological conditions in Europe.

The second phase lasted from 1640 to 1750 and was precipitated by a system-wide recession that lasted approximately 80 years. During this time, nations drew in, centralized, and attempted to control all facets of the market through mercantilism, the dominant form of capitalism in this phase. Mercantilism was designed to increase the power and wealth of the emerging nations through the accumulation of gold, favorable trade balances, and foreign trading monopolies. These goals were achieved primarily through colonization (geographic expansion). As with the previous period, there was a great deal of struggle among the core nations, with a three-way conflict among the Netherlands, France, and England.

The third phase began with the Industrial Revolution. England quickly took the lead in this area. The last attempt by France to stop the spread of English power was Napoleon's continental blockade, which failed. Here, capitalism was driven by industry, and it expanded geographically to cover the entire globe. Wallerstein (2000) places the end of the third phase at the beginning of World War I and the beginning of the fourth phase at 1917 with the Russian Revolution. The Russian Revolution was driven by the lack of indigenous capital, continued resistance to industrializing from the agricultural sector, and the decay of military power and national status. Together, these meant "the Russian Revolution was essentially that of a semi-peripheral country whose internal balance of forces had been such that as of the late nineteenth century it began on a decline towards a peripheral status" (Wallerstein, 2000, p. 97). During this time, the British Empire receded due to a number of factors including decolonization, and two states in particular vied for the core position: Germany and the United States. After World War II, the United States became the leading core nation, a position it enjoyed for two decades.

Hegemonic or leading states always have a limited life span. Becoming a core nation requires a state to focus on improving the conditions of production for capitalists, but staying hegemonic requires a state to invest in political and military might. Over time, other states become economically competitive, and the leading state's economic power diminishes. In attempts to maintain its powerful position in the world-system, the hegemonic state will resort first to military threats and then to exercising its military power (note the increasing U.S. military intervention since the Korean War). The "use of military power is not only the first sign of weakness but the source of further decline," as the capricious use of force creates resentment first in the world community and then in the state's home population as the cost of war increases taxation (Wallerstein, 2004, pp. 58–59).

Thus, the cost of hegemony is always high, and it inevitably leads to the end of a state's position of power within the world-system. For the United States, the costs came from the Cold War with the USSR; competition with rising core nations such as Japan, China, and an economically united and resurgent Western Europe; and such displays of military might as the Korean, Vietnam, Gulf, and Iraq wars. The decline of U.S. hegemony since the late 1960s has meant that capitalist freedom has actually increased due to the relative size and power of global corporations. There are many multinational corporations now that are larger and more powerful than many nations. These new types of corporation "are able to maneuver against state bureaucracies whenever the national politicians become too responsive to internal worker pressures" (Wallerstein, 2000, p. 99). The overall health of world capitalism has also meant that the semi-periphery has increased in strength, facilitating growth into the core.

The Modern Crisis

There are several key points in time for the world-system, such as the Ottoman defeat in 1571, the Industrial Revolution around 1750, and the Russian Revolution in 1917. Each of these events signaled a transition from one capitalist regime to another. Wallerstein (1999) argues that one such event occurred in 1968, when revolutionary movements raced across the globe, involving China, West Germany, Poland, Italy, Japan, Vietnam, Czechoslovakia, Mexico, and the United States. So many nations were caught up in the mostly student-driven social movements that, collectively, they have been called the first world revolution. They were certainly powerful and extensive.

Wallerstein (1995) argues that these worldwide movements came out of the tension that has long existed between "two modernities—the modernity of technology and the modernity of liberation" (p. 472). Modernity grew out of the Enlightenment and positivistic philosophy. The Enlightenment refers to a period of European history from the late 1600s to the late 1700s that was characterized by the assumption that the knowledge of most worth is based on reason and observation (science) rather than faith (religion). Thinkers in the Enlightenment believed that, through reason, humans could control not only the physical universe but society as well. This was a positivist view of life as compared to fatalistic perspectives of religion. Humans could make a difference; humans could change their life course and not be subject to an impenetrable god. Part of this hope lay in technology: tools through which humanity could control the material universe and improve the physical standard of living. This hope was, of course, embodied in science and its offshoots, such as medicine.

The other pronounced hope of modernity concerned equality and was embodied in the nation-state; this is the second modernity. Many social scientists saw their place in this grand scheme of equality. For example, Harriett Martineau (1838/2003), one of the very first sociologists, argued that "every element of social life derives its importance from this great consideration . . . the relative amount of human happiness" (p. 25). For Martineau, the ultimate test of any society and its state is how well it measures up to this one great consideration. Nevertheless, modern society, especially in the United States, was founded on a contradiction: inalienable rights but only for a select group.

Wallerstein tells us that the upheavals of 1968 were directed at this contradiction and the failure of society to fulfill the hope of modernity: liberation for all. Students by and large rejected much of the benefits of technological development and proclaimed society had failed at the one thing that truly mattered: human freedom. The material benefits of technology and capitalism were seen as traps, things that had blinded people to the oppression of blacks, women, and all minorities. Further, this critique wasn't limited to technologically advanced societies:

> In country after country of the so-called Third World, the populaces turned against the movements of the Old Left and charged fraud. . . . [The people of the world] had lost faith in their states as the agents of a modernity of liberation. (Wallerstein, 1995, p. 484)

The 1968 movements in particular rejected American hegemony because of its emphasis on material wealth and hypocrisy in liberation.

In Wallerstein's (1995) scheme, the collapse of Communism was simply an extension of this revolt, one that most clearly pointed out the failure of state government to produce equality for all: "Even the most radical rhetoric was no guarantor of the modernity of liberation, and probably a poor guarantor of the modernity of technology" (p. 484). Interestingly, Wallerstein sees the collapse of Leninism as a disaster for world capitalism. Leninism had constrained the "dangerous classes," those groups oppressed through capitalist ideology and practice. Communism represented an alternative hope to the contradictions found in capitalist states. With the alternative hope gone, "The dangerous classes may now become truly dangerous once again. Politically, the world-system has become unstable" (p. 484).

Structurally, the upheavals of 1968 occurred at the beginning of a K-wave B-cycle. In other words, the world was standing at the brink of an economic downturn or stagnation, which lasted through the 1970s and 1980s. As we've seen, such B-cycles occur throughout the Kondratieff wave, but this one was particularly deep. The 20-year economic stagnation became an important political issue because of the prosperity of the preceding A-cycle. From 1945 to 1970, the world experienced more economic growth and prosperity than it ever had before. Thus, the economic downturn gave continued credence and extra political clout to worldwide social movements. Economically, the world-system responded to the downturn by attempting to roll back production costs through reducing pay scales, lowering taxes associated with the welfare state (education, medical benefits, retirement payments), and re-externalizing input costs (infrastructure, toxicity, raw materials). There was also a shift from the idea of developmentalism to globalization, which calls for the free flow of goods and capital through all nations.

Currently, while the world-system is putting effort into regaining the A-cycle, there are at least three structural problems hindering economic rebound. First, as we've noted, there are limits to exporting exploitation. Four hundred years of capitalism have depleted the world's supply of cheap labor. Every K-wave has brought continued geographic expansion, and it appears that we have reached the limit of that expansion. More and more of the world's workforce is using their political power to increase the share of surplus labor they receive. Inevitably, this will lead to a sharp increase in the costs of labor and production and a corresponding decrease in profit margins. Remember, capitalism is defined by continual accumulation. This worldwide shift, then, represents a critical point in the continuation of the current capitalist system.

Second, there is a squeeze on the middle classes. Typically, the middle classes are seen as the market base of a capitalist economy. And, as we've seen, a standard method of pulling out of a downturn is to increase the available spending money for the middle classes, either through tax breaks or through salary increases. This additional money spurs an increase in commodity purchases and subsequently in production and capital accumulation. However, this continual expanding of middle-class wages is becoming too much for firms and states to bear. One of two things must happen: Either these costs will be rolled back or they will not. If they are not reduced, "both states and enterprises will be in grave trouble and frequent bankruptcy" (Wallerstein, 1995, p. 485). If they are rolled back, "there will be significant political disaffection among precisely the strata that have provided the strongest support for the present world-system" (p. 485).

Third, as we've noted, accumulation is based on externalizing costs. Two of those costs, raw material depletion and toxicity, have natural limits and it appears that we might be reaching them. Global warming, ozone rupture, destruction of the rain forests, and land degradation from waste are themes with which we are all familiar. Nowhere does the idea of natural limits come out more clearly than in the work of Peter Vitousek, professor of biosciences at Stanford University.

Vitousek, Ehrlich, Ehrlich, and Matson (1986) argue that directly (through consumption) and indirectly (through toxic waste), human beings use up about 40% of the world's net primary production (NPP), which represents the rate of production of biomass that is available for consumption by all plants and animals. In other words, of the total amount of energy available for life on this planet, human beings use 40% of it. Predicting the earth's long-term ability to support human life is difficult to calculate, because it depends on the wealth of the population and the kinds of technologies supporting it, but we can see that humans use up a hugely disproportionate amount of the earth's resources (we are but 1 of some 5–30 million animal species on the planet) and we can see that the resources of the earth are finite.

But limits aren't the only concern; toxic waste has been accumulating for years. Typically, firms take the cheapest way of handling waste—dump it on someone else's property—until public outcry motivates governments to pass laws restricting dumping. But the laws are not retroactive, and it appears difficult to assign responsibility. The result is that government, not industry, tends to pay for the bulk of cleanup. According to an article in the *Washington Post* (Pianin, 2001), Congress was projected to spend between $14 and $16.4 billion dollars for toxic cleanup during the first decade of the twentieth century. "The number of toxic or hazardous sites requiring federal attention continues to grow, and Congress will have to spend at least $14 billion to $16.4 billion over the coming decade just to keep pace with the problem" (Pianin, 2001, p. A19).

Structural and Cultural Signs of the End

Wallerstein argues that world-systems enter a time of chaos during transition periods. How things change or into what form is not predictable. A world-system runs its cyclical courses through the Kondratieff wave, with periods of growth and stagnation, finally ending in collapse. A new configuration emerges out of this rubble, but unlike Marx, Wallerstein offers no clear predictions. However, Wallerstein (1999) does argue that the uprising of 1968 marked the beginning of the end of the current world-system. We can not only see the clear marks of the dialectical cycles near the end of a 150-year Kondratieff wave, but we can also see that the structural supports upon which capitalism has been built are limited and nearing exhaustion.

There are also cultural and structural signs that indicate that the system is in the uncertainty of transition. Wallerstein points to two cultural signs: the introduction of complexity theory in science and postmodern theory in the social sciences. In the past 20 years or so, a significant number of physical scientists and mathematicians have turned against the causal predictability of Newtonian physics. Newtonian physics postulated a universe run according to universal laws—laws that in all time and in every place could explain, predict, and control the physical features of the cosmos. According to physicists Stephen Hawking and Leonard Mlodinow (2010), while such a belief may be attractive, "what we know about modern physics makes it a difficult one to defend" (p. 44). So today we hear of quantum mechanics, complexity theory, chaos theory, strange attractors, fuzzy logic, and so on. Wallerstein's (1995) point is this: "The natural world and all its phenomena have become historicized" (p. 486). That is, the scientific view of the universe has historically changed: The old science was built on a mechanistic, linear view of the universe; the new science is not linear, nor is it mechanistic.

The idea of a historicized science is an oxymoron, at least from the initial perspective of science. Science assumed that the universe is empirical and operates according to law-like principles. These principles could be discovered and used by humans to understand, predict, and control their world. Science was in the business of producing abstract and universal truths, not truths that only hold under certain conditions. The historicity of society has always been an argument against the possibility of social science, precisely because the factors that influence human behavior and society change according to the context. The hard, laboratory sciences have now become susceptible to the same critique: According to complexity theory, all knowledge is contextual and contingent; nothing is universal and certain. "Hence the new science raises the most fundamental questions about the modernity of technology" (Wallerstein, 1995, p. 486).

The scene in the social sciences has followed suit and become even less certain than it was before. In the past 25 years, the most vocal and influential voice in the social sciences has been the proponents of postmodernism. Postmodernism in its most radical form, as it was brought into the social sciences, argues that the social world in technologically advanced societies is a virtual or hyperreal world. The cultural signs, symbols, and images that we use aren't connected to any social reality. Most of them come not from real social groups in face-to-face interaction, but are, in fact, produced by media and advertising concerns.

As a result of this cultural fragmentation and the new doubts in science, all grand narratives are held in distrust. Grand or meta-narratives are stories that attempt to embrace large populations of people. Typically, grand narratives are generated by political groups (as in nationalism and national identities). In their place, postmodernism advocates polyvocality, or many voices. Postmodernism argues that all voices are equal and should be given equal weight. These voices are of course linked to specific groups, such as men, women, blacks, Hispanics, and all the subdivisions within the groups, such as bisexual-Hispanic-Catholic males. There is thus an ethical dimension to postmodernism—"It is a mode of rejecting the modernity of technology on behalf of the modernity of liberation" (Wallerstein, 1995, p. 487).

The two structural signs that indicate we are in a time of chaotic transition are financial speculation and worldwide organization of social movements. There has been limited success in rolling back costs and reducing the press on profits, but not nearly what was needed or hoped for. As a result, capitalists have sought profit in the area of financial speculation rather than production. Many have taken great profits from this kind of speculation, but it also "renders the world-economy very volatile and subject to swings of currencies and of employment. It is in fact one of the signs of increasing chaos" (Wallerstein, 2004, p. 86).

On the political scene, since 1968 there has been a shift from movements for electoral changes to the "organization of a movement of movements" (Wallerstein, 2004, p. 86). Rather than national movements seeking change through voting within the system, radical groups are binding together internationally to seek change within the world-system. Wallerstein offers the World Social Forum (WSF) as an example. It is not itself an organization, but a virtual space for meetings among various militant groups seeking social change.

Another indicator of this political decentralization is the increase in terrorist attacks worldwide, such as the strike on the World Trade Center, September 11, 2001, and the bomb attacks on London, July 7, 2005. The terrorist groups themselves are decentralized, nonstate entities, which makes conflict between a state like the United States and these entities difficult. Nation-states are particular kinds of entities defined by a number of factors, most importantly by territory, rational law, and a standing military. These factors and the political orientation they bring mean that nation-states are most efficient at confronting other nation-states, ones that have specified territories, that legitimate rational law, and that have modern militaries. Almost everything about the terrorist groups that the United States is facing is antithetical to these qualities of the nation-state. The United States is a centralized state, and the terrorists are decentralized groups. These differences in social structure and relation to physical place make it extremely difficult for the United States to engage the terrorists—there is no interface between the two—let alone defeat or make peace with them.

But more than that, the attacks of September 11th have energized politically right-wing groups in the United States. The attacks have allowed them to cut ties with the political center and to pursue a program centered around unilateral assertions by the United States of military strength combined with an attempt to undo the cultural evolution of the world-system that occurred after the world revolution of 1968 (particularly in the fields of race and sexuality). (Wallerstein, 2004, p. 87)

This, along with attempts to do away with many of the geopolitical structures set in place after 1945 (like the United Nations), has "threatened to worsen the already-increasing instability of the world-system" (p. 87).

These issues are the reason that Wallerstein (1999) talks about the demise of world-systems theory. Remember, world-systems theory is a critical perspective of global capitalism. As global capitalism fails, the insights that world-systems thinking can give us will become less significant. Yet in the remaining years of global capitalism, world-systems theory gives us a critical perspective for social involvement.

What will follow the 400-year reign of capitalism is uncertain. World-systems theory, as Wallerstein sees it, is meant to call our attention to thinking in structural time and cyclical processes; it is meant to lift our eyes from the mundane problems of our lives so that we can perceive the world-system in all its historical power to set the stage of our lives; it is intended to give us the critical perspective to have eyes to see and ears to hear the Marxian dynamics still at work within the capitalist system; and, finally, it is intended to spur us to action. Unlike C. Wright Mills (1956), Wallerstein (1999) is not saying that "great changes are beyond [our] control"; rather, he means that "fundamental change is possible . . . and this fact makes claims on our moral responsibility to act rationally, in good faith, and with strength to seek a better historical system" (p. 3). Because the system is in a period of transition where "small inputs have large outputs" (p. 1) and "every small action during this period is likely to have significant consequences" (Wallerstein, 2004, p. 77), we must make diligent efforts to understand what is going on; we must make choices about the direction in which we want the world to move; and we must bring our convictions into action, because it is our behaviors that will affect the system. In Wallerstein's (2004) words,

> We can think of these three tasks as the intellectual, the moral, and the political tasks. They are different, but they are closely interlinked. None of us can opt out of any of these tasks. If we claim we do, we are merely making a hidden choice. (p. 90)

Summary

- Wallerstein sees his work more in terms of a type of analysis than a specific theory. His point is that it is the principles of analysis that drive the theorizing rather than the other way around. There are two main features of Wallerstein's perspective: globality and historicity. Globality conceptualizes the world in system terms, which cut across cultural and political boundaries. Historicity sees history in terms of structural time and cyclical time within the structures, rather than focusing on events, people, and linearity.

- In terms of theory, Wallerstein takes a Marxian approach. He focuses on the division of labor, exploitation, and the processes of accumulation and overproduction. In Marxian theory, exploitation is the chief source of profit. Thus, capitalists are intrinsically motivated to increase the level of exploitation. Since wages tend to go up as capitalist economies mature, reducing the level of exploitation and profit, there is therefore a constant tendency to export exploitation to nations that have a less developed capitalist economy, thus increasing the worldwide division of labor.

- Capitalist accumulation implies that capital is invested for the purpose of creating more capital, which in turn is invested in order to create more capital. In modern capitalism, this process of accumulation is augmented by the state. The state specifically bears the costs associated with transportation, toxicity, and the exhaustion of materials. More powerful states additionally provide conditions that facilitate quasi-monopolies, thus increasing capitalists' profits and the rate of accumulation.

- Overproduction is endemic to capitalism as well. Because they are driven by the capitalist need for accumulation, commodification (the process through which material and nonmaterial goods are turned into products for sale) and production are intrinsically expansive. Capitalists will continue to create new and produce existing commodities until the market will no longer bear it, thus creating more supply than demand.

- Taken together, the processes of exploitation and the division of labor and the dynamics of accumulation and overproduction create a scenario in which there is a continual movement of products and labor from more powerful to less powerful nations.

- In the world-economy, there are four types of nations: the core, semi-periphery, the periphery, and external areas, which are not actually part of the system. In general, exploitation and mass production of least-profitable goods move from the core to the external areas. However, because this is a system, there is also a move of nations as they transition from external to peripheral to core. Eventually, there will be no more areas to exploit with low-profit mass production, which will lead to system breakdown.

- The world-economy thus tends to go through cycles of expansion, depression, and breakdown. These cycles reach a crisis about every 150 years. According to Wallerstein, the world is now in its fourth phase of world-economies. The last phase began in 1917, with the United States as the world-economy's core nation. Wallerstein marks the beginning of the end of this phase with the social upheavals of 1968. In addition to the social movements, the world-economy entered a cycle of depression that was particularly deep and lasted for about 20 years. While the world-economy is actively trying to come back from this economic depression, there are three factors that are inhibiting this attempt: the system limits to exploitation, the middle-class squeeze, and the limited ability of states to pick up externalized costs. Thus, Wallerstein argues that the world-system is on the brink of collapse and is currently experiencing the chaotic period that always precedes such an end.

TAKING THE PERSPECTIVE: WORLD-SYSTEMS THEORY

I said something in the beginning of this chapter that I now need to put in context. Wallerstein prefers the word *globality* to globalization. The reason for this is that globalization is generally thought of in ahistorical, market economy terms. For example, the 2001 Nobel Prize winner in Economic Sciences, Joseph E. Stiglitz (2003), defines globalization as

> the closer integration of the countries and peoples of the world which has been brought about by the enormous reduction of costs of transportation and communication, and the breaking down of artificial barriers to the flows of goods, services, capital, knowledge, and (to a lesser extent) people across borders (p. 9).

Notice that in this definition the focus is on the market flow of goods, services, capital, and so forth; there is no mention of system (other than "closer integration"), nor is there any sense of history. The latter two are of specific concern to Wallerstein and world-systems theorists because without the ideas of history and system, the descriptions of globalization are atheoretical (without theory). World-systems analysis, on the other hand, can be theoretical precisely because it understands the phenomena, using the general dynamics of systems theory, that are able to account for historical changes and predict future outcomes.

Wallerstein intentionally uses the hyphen in world-systems theory to emphasize that he is talking about systems that constitute a world or a distinct way of existing. This approach looks at society as an interrelated whole, with every internal part systemically influencing the others. A systems approach additionally places emphasis on the relationship between the system and its environment. Thus, world-systems analysis argues that nations or collectives change in response to systemic factors that press upon it from the outside. For example, according to world-systems analysis, Peru isn't "modernizing" because it is something every nation will do; Peru is modernizing because it is caught in a global capitalist system that is pressuring it to change. Thus, world-systems analysis focuses on factors that cut across cultural and political boundaries and create an "integrated zone of activity and institutions which obey certain systemic rules" (Wallerstein, 2004, p. 17).

If social actors such as nations, institutions, and groups are related to each other through a specific system, then the history of that system is extremely important for understanding how it is working presently. Wallerstein picked up the notions of structural time and cyclical process from French historian and educator Fernand Braudel (1981–1984). Braudel criticized event-dominated history as being too idiographic and political; this is the kind of history with which we are most familiar. The prefix "idio" specifically refers to the individual or one's own. Idiographic knowledge, then, is focused on unique individuals and their events. An example of this event history approach is to understand U.S. history in terms of things like Abraham Lincoln and the Civil War, and Martin Luther King Jr. and the civil rights movement. Such an understanding doesn't see changes through history as the result of systematic social facts; rather, it perceives historical change as occurring through unique events and political figures—in other words, idiographic history is atheoretical.

(Continued)

(Continued)

Braudel felt that this kind of history is dust and tells us nothing about the true historical processes. Yet Braudel also criticized the opposite approach, nomothetic knowledge. The word *nomothetic* is related to the Greek word *nomos,* which means law. The goal in seeking nomothetic knowledge, like that of science, is to discover the abstract and universal laws that underpin the physical universe. According to Braudel, when nomothetic knowledge is sought in the social sciences, it more often than not creates mythical, grand stories that legitimate the search for universal laws instead of explaining historical social history.

Wallerstein's idea of historicity lies between the ideographic focus on events and the law-like knowledge of science. Rather than focusing on events, Wallerstein's approach concentrates on the history of structures within a world-system. For example, capitalism is a world-system that has its own particular history. There have always been people who have produced products to make a profit, but the capitalism of modernity, the kind that Weber (1904–1905/2002) termed "rational capitalism," is unique to a particular time period. An account of rational capitalism from its beginnings, from around the sixteenth century, that would include all the principal players (such as nations, firms, households, and so forth) and their systemic relations is what Wallerstein has in mind.

Historicity thus includes the unique variable of time. In taking account of world-systems rather than event history, historicity is centered upon structural time and the cyclical time within the structures. Wallerstein is telling us that structures have histories; and it is the history of structures with which we should be concerned, rather than events, because structures set the frames within which human behavior and meaning take place. Structures have life spans; they are born and they die, and within that span there are cyclical processes.

BUILDING YOUR THEORY TOOLBOX

- Drawing on at least two other sources, write a theoretical definition of globalization.

- Write a 250-word synopsis of the theoretical perspective of world-systems theory.

- After reading and understanding this chapter, you should be able to define the following terms theoretically and explain their importance to world-systems analysis: modern capitalism, globalization, systems, exploitation, dialectical materialism, division of labor, externalized costs, quasi-monopolies, overproduction, world-empires, world-economies, core states, periphery states, semi-periphery states, Kondratieff waves, world-systems theory.

- After reading and understanding this chapter, you should be able to answer the following questions (remembering to answer them theoretically):

  o What are the central features that link national economies to a global system?

  o In what ways do states externalize costs and help create quasi-monopolies?

- What are the Marxian economic dynamics in back of the relationships among the core, semi-periphery, and periphery? Explain how these dynamics work and how they are related to the demise of capitalism.
- What are Kondratieff waves, and how do they factor into global changes?
- Beginning with the events in 1968, explain Wallerstein's crisis of modernity. What are the structural and cultural signs that the system is failing?
- In the face of this crisis, what recommendations does Wallerstein have for political involvement? Be certain to explain his rationale for saying these recommendations will influence the system.

Learning More—Primary and Secondary Sources

- Wallerstein built his theory through three volumes of historical data (The *Modern World-System,* Volumes I, II, and III). The historical breadth is impressive and convincing, but I would suggest you begin your reading of Wallerstein with his later works:

  - *The End of the World as We Know It: Social Science for the Twenty-First Century,* University of Minnesota Press, 1999.
  - *World-Systems Analysis: An Introduction,* Duke University Press, 2004.

- A good chapter-length introduction to this perspective is provided by Christopher Chase-Dunn, "World-Systems Theorizing," in *Handbook of Sociological Theory,* edited by Jonathan H. Turner, Kluwer, 2002.

Engaging the World

- In reference to his work, Wallerstein (2000) has said, "My intellectual biography is one long question for an adequate explanation of contemporary reality that I and others might act upon" (p. xv). In keeping with Wallerstein, I have only one question to put to you: After reading Wallerstein, how will you engage your world?

Weaving the Threads

- Consider the approaches to inequality given us by Chafetz, Bourdieu, and now Wallerstein, and then answer the following questions: What kinds of inequalities or scarce resources are the most important in each theory? What kinds of structures perpetuate these inequalities? How is social change possible for each of these theorists? Can these three theories complement one another?

CHAPTER 11

The Network Society

Manuel Castells

Source: Photograph by
Maggie Smith (2005).

The Big Picture: Network Society

The network society is a system of connections made among people through computer technologies. That's a simple and relatively problem-free statement, yet the implications are vast. To be able to fully grasp Castells's theory, it's important to first talk about some of those implications.

There are a number of terms that are sometimes used synonymously with network society but actually emphasize different characteristics. The information society, for example, is one where the production and distribution of information is the most significant economic and cultural process. Another, more theoretically robust term is postindustrial society: "The concept 'post-industrial society' emphasizes the centrality of theoretical knowledge as the axis around which new technology, economic growth and the stratification of society will be organized" (Bell, 1999, p. 112). There are obvious overlaps, but analytically we can distinguish the concepts by their emphasis. Both information society and postindustrial society emphasize economic shifts; the idea of the network society focuses first on the network (or Internet) itself—it's the qualities of the network that matter most.

Each of these approaches is interested in understanding how social positions and relations are impacted. For example, in a postindustrial society, there's a shift in terms of ownership and scarcity. Recall Marx's theory of industrial capitalism, where ownership of the means of production and capital accumulation are the primary bases for class. In postindustrial society, knowledge—particularly theoretical— drives the economy. As such, the issue of ownership shifts from production to intellectual rights. In such a society, knowledge and time become scarce resources. Further, in a postindustrial society, capital shifts from investment in manufacturing to speculative investment driven by portfolio management and theories of the stock market. Money, then, becomes much more mobile and volatile.

The occupational structure changes as well, with significant drops in manufacturing and increases in professional and technical employment. In response, relationships among people fundamentally change. In sociology, we take terms like class and status for granted. (Blumer [Chapter 3] would say we reify these terms.) We tend to forget that class relations and status positions are functions of social structure. Remember from Chapter 8 that "class" is historically specific. Prior to the eighteenth century, people didn't relate to one another through class because capitalist classes didn't exist before then. To begin to capture the differences in relationships that a postindustrial society creates, Daniel Bell argues that the term *situses* is preferable to class or even status. The word *situs* comes from Latin and means place or site. Bell (1976a) uses the term to point to the "actual loci of occupational activities and interests" (p. 376). His point is that class denotes a stable, structured position that is determined by one's position in an economic organization. Postindustrial economies, on the other hand, create social positions that are much more complex and crosscut one another. For example, a research scientist working for a university is in a different position from that of a scientist working for Dow Chemical. The site (situs) of actual work for these two people is different, which in turn creates different interests, economic standings, and social relationships. Differences aren't created simply through status (scientist) or structure (university—corporation); there are also significant differences in *knowledge,* which is the gold standard of a postindustrial society. Situses, then, are fundamentally attached to their knowledge base, not a company, thus providing a great deal of horizontal mobility in the job market (movement from one organization to another). This has political implications as well because "the likelihood of a pure 'estate' consciousness for political purposes tends to diminish" (Bell, 1976a, p. 377). In other words, the Marxian notion of class and class consciousness is passé because class position is less important than situses. Network society theory is also interested in the effects on individuals and relationships, but as you'll see, the implications of the network society are much more profound.

The key characteristic of network theory is that *the logic of the network is imposed on the actors.* The basic idea here is one you'll be quite familiar with because social structures do the same thing. For example, you are a student and you understand your self as a student; if you were in my class, you'd relate to me as your professor. You weren't, however, born a student; you became a student as the institution of education imposed its status positions and roles on you. The same is true for all your institutionalized selves. Your sense of being masculine or feminine is a result of the structure of gender; being a mother, father, sister, or brother is a result of the institution of family; and so on. This is basic sociological knowledge: We are socialized into the positions, roles, norms, values, and beliefs of social institutions—there is thus a dependent relationship between your self and the social structures in which you live. Some part of your self comes into existence because of the configuration of social things around you.

The problem with this basic knowledge is that more often than not, we reify it. We use *the logic of social institutions* to understand almost everything about us as social beings. We understand almost every social encounter and almost every aspect of ourselves in terms of status positions, roles, norms, and so on. But status positions, roles, norms, values, and beliefs *exist only in social institutions.* What if something other than an institution manages your relationships and imprints itself upon you? Those relations and that part of yourself couldn't be understood in the same way. In other words, there wouldn't be status positions and roles; there wouldn't be norms or values, not in the way we currently understand them. You'll soon see that computer networks have very different qualities from those of social institutions. These qualities not only influence the self, but also impact what we mean by relationships, community, and political participation.

THEORIST'S DIGEST

Brief Biography

Manuel Castells (1942–) was born in La Mancha, Spain, and grew up in Valencia and Barcelona. In college, he studied law and economics and received a PhD in sociology and another in human sciences from the University of Paris–Sorbonne in 1967. While in Paris, he was a political activist, fighting against Franco's dictatorship. He taught sociology at the University of Paris from 1967 to 1979, when he took a professorship at the University of California, Berkeley. In 2003, he moved to the University of Southern California Annenberg School for Communication. Castells has written 22 books, has coauthored 21, and has published over 100 articles in academic journals. His most influential works are his trilogy, *The Information Age: Economy, Society, and Culture* (Castells, 2000a, 2000b, 2004), which has been translated into over 23 languages. Among his many awards and distinctions is the C. Wright Mills Award from the American Society for the Study of Social Problems, the Robert and Helen Lynd Award from the American Sociological Association, the National Medal of Science from Catalonia, and the Lifelong Research Award from the Committee on Computers and Information Technology of the American Sociological Association.

Central Sociological Questions

Castells's early work focuses on the issue of urban space. He uses a Marxian approach to understand how social conflicts transform the urban landscape. This initial concern with space and politics led him to consider how both are affected by information technologies. In the work we focus on here, Castells asks, how does the intrusion of computer networks impact the space in which people connect and express issues of power and identity?

Simply Stated

Castells argues that computer and information technologies have dramatically impacted human existence. These technologies have lifted out social relationships, the work of capitalism, and political activism from the boundaries of the nation-state. What we mean by society, then, is more in keeping with the dictates of computer networks than the modern ideas of national society and democracy. Importance and power in a network are determined by how much information, symbols, and imagery a position in the network can hold and process. The basis of class has changed as well, from production to managing work and flows of capital. Political activities have also shifted, from the content of a political platform to control of image and negative information.

Key Ideas

Keynesian economics, information technology, the logic of networks, annihilation of time and place, power, class, politics, identities, legitimizing identity, resistance identity, project identity, civil society, symbol mobilizers, new democracy

Concepts and Theory: Information Technology

Castells's idea is that the information revolution that began in the 1980s has restructured capitalism and created a global society that is connected via networks. Prior to World War II, the capitalist system had played out its Marxist dynamics and was in a worldwide, inexorable depression—there was no way out. Socialist movements were gaining power globally, and there was a good chance that capitalism would have collapsed had it not been for the war. During the Great Depression of the 1930s, John Maynard Keynes (1936) published a new theory of economics. The basic tenet of *Keynesian economics* is that the state can moderate the effects of free-market capitalism through controlling interest rates and by investing in the economic infrastructure, thus becoming a major consumer. But, Castells argues, Keynesian economics, just like laissez-faire capitalism before it, had built-in contradictions and limitations, which came to a head by the 1970s and resulted in rampant inflation.

From the 1970s into the 1990s, massive efforts at restructuring capitalism were underway. There were four goals: (1) Deepen the logic of profitability; (2) improve the profitability of both capital and labor; (3) globalize commodity and labor markets; and (4) use the state to maximize the profitability of the national economy, even at the cost of social programs and education. Essential to this project was flexibility, such as "just-in-time" (JIT) inventory strategies, and adaptability. Castells (2000b) argues that this attempt at restructuring would have been extremely limited without the new information technology.

By *new information technology,* Castells has in mind computer technologies, both hardware and software, which, when coupled with the Internet, have connected humanity in a way that was up to this point unthinkable. As a result of information technology, space and time have become more abstract and infinitely less meaningful in terms of patterning and organizing social connections. We can, for example, have virtual face-to-face meetings with people in China, England, the United States, and Argentina at the same "time." Further, and perhaps more importantly, information has become the focal point of economic practices and growth. As the name indicates, information technologies act on information. In industrial societies, technologies act on the production process. For example, Henry Ford's assembly-line technology, along with mass-produced, interchangeable parts, broke down the process of making a car into a series of simple tasks that unskilled workers could perform. So profound was the effect of this technology on economic production that it became known as "Fordism."

In contrast, as noted above, information technologies act upon information. As an example, let's consider something that falls a bit outside of Castells's concerns, but that most of us can relate to: music recording and playback. Before the digital age, music was recorded using analog technologies. Analog recording stores music as a continuous wave in or on the media (phonograph record or magnetic tape). It's called analog because the waves imprinted on the media are *analogous* to the sound waves of the music (the same basic idea that applies to video recordings). In digital recording, the music is translated into discrete numbers or data. The first step in this information technology was developed in 1937 by British scientist Alec Reeves—he invented pulse code modulation, one of the platforms upon which today's digital technology is based. Every step since then has involved innovations in how technology can store, transmit, and play back information. The production of these technologies for consumption is a secondary move: In a network society, technical innovation is focused primarily on producing and reproducing information— commodification comes later.

The most important information technologies have focused on computers and communication. Ever since the first digital computer was invented in the early 1940s, each new technology has been directed at storing and using information. Castells (2000b) argues that this move to information technologies is having and will continue to have pervasive effects because human activity is based on information. There have been three major technological advances that have fundamentally influenced knowledge and information: the alphabet (written language), the printing press, and the computer. We know that the effects of the first two advances were tremendous. Civilization itself is indebted to written language, and, as we saw in Chapter 1, the advent of the printing press led to the rise and spread of the Protestant Reformation, the Renaissance, the scientific revolution, and the primacy of Western Europe in the beginning stages of the modern era.

Power, Politics, and Class in the Network Society

The most significant effect of computer technology Castells sees is that *the logic of networks* will be the basis of the new social system. The idea of a *network* is rather straightforward. A network is a set of interconnected points or "nodes," which are the places where the threads or paths of the network cross. Networks can be made up of any number of things, like networks of exchange. Castells is concerned with information networks, the nodes of which are points where information is held or processed. This kind of network is possible because of computer and communication technologies, and it is defined by those technologies.

Let's think for a moment about a computer network. Because the basic properties of networks are the same, you can choose any network, such as AIM (America Online Instant Messenger), the network at your place of work, the Internet as a whole, and so on. Networks are open and extremely flexible structures. They can be of almost any size and can change without threatening the balance of the whole. Networks have no center, and they work on the binary inclusion/exclusion model: That is, a *node* is either in the network or not; if a node ceases to function, it's eliminated and the network is rearranged—for example, your computer can move into or out of a network without affecting the network as such. There is no distance between nodes and no time element. Rather than distance, such as between my computer and yours, what matters in networks are restrictions on the flow of information, and time—if used at all—is simply a marker of flow (e.g., when you sent your e-mail). A node becomes important in a network either because it can hold and process information more efficiently, or because it functions as a switch that connects different networks. Once programmed, networks function automatically and impose their logic on all the social actors using it.

Such computerized informational networks have redefined the material basis of life in our society. All animals, including humans, are fundamentally related to time and space, but computing and network technologies have changed that relationship. Rather than the biological clock of human existence, or the mechanical clock of the industrial age, new communication technologies *annihilate time and place*. Rather than the essentialness of place, new information technologies have reoriented us to a space of flows, where exists the "organizational possibility of organizing the simultaneity of social practices without geographic contiguity" (Castells, 2000a, p. 14). Thus, social organization is set free from the confines of time and space. This freedom is so profound in its implications that Castells (2000b) marks the information age as the beginning of human history, "if by history we understand the moment when . . . our species has reached the level of knowledge and social organization that will allow us to live in a predominantly social world" (pp. 508–509).

Power in any such network is dramatically reorganized from the hierarchical model of bureaucracies and social inequalities. Power in networks is a function of a node's ability to find, hold, and process information. Nodes that can act as switches between informational networks are power holders: "Since networks are multiple, the inter-operating codes and switches between networks become the fundamental sources in shaping, guiding, and misguiding societies" (Castells, 2000b, p. 502). More importantly, the informational network has provided the structure for the core activities of a global economy. Currently, the bulk of capital accumulation results from financial flows rather than production. Profit from production and consumption, from organizations and institutions, is extracted and reverted to the financial flows. Capital is then invested globally, following interests of greatest return, which are increasingly based on speculation and money markets rather than real goods and services. Financial flows are thus based on theoretical knowledge and timeliness of information. This "electronically operated global casino" decides the "fate of corporations, household savings, national currencies, and regional economies" (Castells, 2000b, p. 503).

The network society has dramatically affected *class* as well. It results first in capitalism without capitalists. The legal owners of any large business—Marx's definition of capitalists—are found in investment funds and individual portfolios, both of which are subject to networks of speculative management. The corporate managers don't make up a capitalist class either, because they do not control, nor do they know about, the movements of capital in networks of financial flows. Rather than a class that holds and uses capital, the global capital network is a network of networks that "are ultimately dependent upon the nonhuman capitalist logic of an electronically operated, random processing of information" (Castells, 2000b, p. 505).

The working class has likewise been redefined by the logics of networks. Labor has become exceedingly general. Rather than the specified labor of production, it is labor as a generic part of speculative capitalism—labor becomes a piece on the global chessboard of capital flows. Capital and labor increasingly exist in different spaces and times: capital in the space of flows and the instant/constant time of computerized communication, and labor in the space of places and the time of clocks and daily life. "At its core, capital is global. As a rule, labor is local" (Castells, 2000b, p. 506). What becomes organized through networks is work, rather than labor. The work of organizations is carried on in network fashion. Each contributing member is a node, and the network as a whole can be made up of individuals; segments of businesses; or entire companies, large or small. They can be dispersed over thousands of miles and exist in different clock-time zones. All this and more can be coordinated for a single project, thus forming an informational network. As soon as the project is finished, the nodes are disconnected and reorganized for other work. The work process is thus globally integrated but fragmented locally, resulting in the individuation of labor, increased flexibility, and instability of work.

The organizational logic of communication and informational technologies has reformed *politics* as well. In most places around the world, people now get their information about political candidates through the media, which has become the platform for politics. In a media-saturated environment, capturing attention becomes the single most important scarce resource. Politics thus becomes personalized in the cult of personality, "and image-making is power-making" (Castells, 2000b, p. 507). In the spectacle of image, with a public (an audience) dulled by a constant barrage of images and information, the most effective messages are negative: "assassination of opponents' personalities, and/or of their supporting organizations" (2000a, p. 13). Thus, the information of value in politics is anything that will spark a scandal. An entire network revolves around finding, protecting, and leaking this valued information. "Politics becomes a horse race, and a tragicomedy motivated by greed, backstage manoeuvres [sic], betrayals, and, often, sex and violence—a genre increasingly indistinguishable from TV scripts" (p. 13).

Politics cannot but influence the *state,* and the politics of spectacle and reliance on the media undermine its legitimacy and power. In response, personalities begin to build informational networks and systems of deference around themselves, further challenging the legitimacy of the state. State power is also challenged by the global flows of money and information. Part of this has to do with the pure size of capital flows and the volatility of money markets, but more basically, since the nation-state has always been defined in terms of "subordinating to orderly domination . . . a 'territory'" (Weber, 1922/1968, p. 901), the breakdown of time and space (territory) by the network society deeply undermines the power of the state. In response, states partner with other nations and build multinational and international organizational, informational networks, such as the World Trade Organization, NATO, the International Monetary Fund, and so on. The result is that "the new state is no longer a nation-state" (Castells, 2000a, p. 14); rather, it is a network state created out of negotiated decision making and power sharing.

Concepts and Theory: Networks, Identities, and Democracy

For Castells, *identities* are clusters of cultural traits that function to provide meaning for people. In order to see the implications of this, think back to the fundamental attributes of meaning from Chapter 3. Meaning isn't any *thing*—it isn't in an action or a word, it isn't inherent within an experience, nor is it located in any object. Rather, meaning is that which actions, words, and so on express or sign, and signs always point away from themselves—therefore, *meaning is never the thing-in-itself.* Moreover, meaning constitutes our reality:

> No longer can man confront reality immediately. . . . [It] seems to recede in proportion as man's symbolic activity advances. Instead of dealing with the things themselves, man is in a sense constantly conversing with himself (Cassirer, 1944, p. 42).

If meaning isn't the actual thing or event, then meaning is achieved or created, and one of the functions of identity is to provide a basis for the construction of biographical narratives of meaning. Castells (2004) defines three different types of identities. The first type, the *legitimizing identity,* is the kind found in the dominant institutions of society. Legitimations are stories or narratives that provide a moral or ethical basis for social power. Legitimizing identities, then, are those around which individuals construct meaning and a sense of self that are related to and legitimate civil society. Obvious examples include the president of the United States, corporate CEOs, male and female genders, heterosexuality, professors, and so on.

The second type in Castells's scheme is *resistance identity.* This type of identity normally comes out of a sense of exclusion from the institutions of civil society and is bound up with the formation of communities of resistance that give members a sense of solidarity and the ability to form countercultures and ideology. These communities and identities can center around such issues as religious views and other status inequities. Because they are resistance identities, they create strong boundaries of inclusion and exclusion and thus work to "exclude the excluders." It's important to note that resistance identities aren't necessarily concerned with social change; they are reactionary and seek to establish an identity where identity has been denied.

This is where the issue of meaning that we talked about above becomes important. Identities provide a meaningful ordering and framework for life. When identities are denied, or controlled to the point of redefining the person, the existential questions of life and purpose come to the forefront—conversely, when identities are unproblematic, the questions of existence are effectively silenced; legitimating identities don't tend to provoke existential questions in those claiming them. Under conditions of exclusion, resistance identities function as cultural, emotional, and psychological strongholds. Their purpose isn't to change, but to proclaim. Often these identities are born out of "the pride of self-denigration" (Castells, 2004, p. 9) and shout back at institutions with proclamations such as "black is beautiful" or "I am woman, hear me roar."

The third type of identity that concerns Castells is the *project identity*. This is an identity associated with social projects of change: "In this case, the building of identity is a project of a different life" (Castells, 2004, p. 10). Project identities produce subjects, but subjects, Castells is very clear about, are not individuals. Merriam-Webster defines *subject* (n.d.) variously as "the material from which a thing is formed," "the theme of a discourse or predication," "something that sustains or is embodied in thought or consciousness," or "something that forms a basis (as for action, study, discussion, or use)." Castells's use of the term *subject* captures all of the above. Subjects are collective actors that form the material of our sense of self and our involvement with the world. These subjects are the themes of the discourse of social change; they are the mental and emotional focus through which identity and meaning are sustained in consciousness; and, especially in the case of project identities, the subject forms the basis for action, study, and discussion.

The Network Society and the Crisis in Democracy

Castells (2004) defines *civil society* as "a set of organizations and institutions, as well as a series of structured and organized social actors, which reproduce . . . the identity that rationalizes the sources of structural domination" (p. 8). While civil society isn't identical with the state, it exists *in relation to* the state, and the state is the "object of citizenship" (p. 402). However, the state is suffering a crisis of legitimation in the network society. Its sovereignty has been undermined by "global flows and trans-organizational networks of wealth, information, and power" (p. 402); by the spectacle of politics; and by the state's increasing inability to fulfill its commitments to the safety net of minimal benefits, including unemployment benefits, retirement income, health care coverage, insuring of bank deposits, and so forth.

These effects of the network society have created a crisis of legitimation for the nation-state and, by extension, legitimizing identities and democracy.

There are two important effects growing out of this legitimation crisis. First, "a growing majority of citizens do not feel that democracy will help them very much in addressing the issues that confront them in their daily lives" (Castells, 2004, p. 413). One measure of this is what is commonly called voter apathy. In 1960, about 61% of the television sets in the United States were tuned to the October presidential debates, and voter turnout for the presidential election was almost 65% of the adult population. By the year 2000, fewer than 30% of televisions were tuned to the presidential debates, and voter turnout had dropped to 51% (Patterson, 2002).

The second outcome of the legitimation crisis is the ascent of resistance identities. Remember how Castells conceptualizes identities: They function to create meaning. In this case, *resistance identities* are created to counter the loss of meaning and direction that accompanies the legitimation crisis. To help us get a clear sense of resistance identities in the network society, let's think through the example of gender in Western nations. Prior to the women's suffrage movement of the 1800s and early 1900s, being a "woman" was by and large a legitimizing identity. The identity bound all women together and situated them in the discourse of patriarchy. The identity thus legitimated the family structure as well as the unequal power relations between men and women. The suffrage movements worked to create a project identity committed to gaining equal rights for women—in particular, the right to vote and the right to higher education. In the 1960s, a second wave of feminism emerged to address the unofficial discrimination and inequalities that still existed for women. Equal opportunities for work and political power, equal pay, cultural representations, and control over their bodies were some of the issues. Both the first and second waves of feminism had project identities.

Beginning in the early 1990s, as noted in Chapter 7, another wave of feminism arose, mostly among young women who had grown up with benefits achieved by the first two waves of feminism. These women also were most affected by the new information and communication technologies. Feminism for these women is different. Rather than having specific political, economic, or social goals, third-wave feminism challenges the definitions of woman, femininity, and feminism, which are seen as creating a sense that all women are essentially the same. All essentializing theories are rejected, including feminist theory, gender theory, conflict theory, and so on. The focus is on deconstructing such totalizing identities and discourses and insisting on diversity. Rather than either a legitimizing or project identity, third-wave feminism denies the possibility of a woman's identity: "Since no monolithic version of 'woman' exists, we can no longer speak with confidence of 'women's issues'; instead, we need to consider that such issues are as diverse as the many women who inhabit our planet" (Dicker & Piepmeier, 2006, p. 107).

While being able to trace the history of feminist identity is enlightening, most resistance identities don't have this evolving background. Today, most resistance identities are formed around such things as religious fundamentalism, geographic region, music styles, and so on. An example that has both region and music is found in Jeff Foxworthy's comments at the 2007 Country Music Television Awards ceremony, held in Nashville, Tennessee. Here are a few lines from his speech:

> I like country music because it's about the things in life that really matter. . . . It's about love, family, friends, with a few beers. . . . It doesn't take political sides even on things as ugly as war. Instead, it celebrates the men and women who go to fight 'em. . . . It's about kids and how there ain't nothing like 'em. . . . Country folks love their kids and they will jack you up if you try to mess with 'em. . . . Country music doesn't have to be politically correct. We sing about God because we believe in Him. . . . It's real music, sung by real people for real people. The people that make up the backbone of this country. . . . You can call us rednecks if you want, we're not offended, 'cause we know what we are all about. We get up and go to work, we get up and go to church, and we get up and go to war when necessary. (Foxworthy, quoted in Martin, 2007)

Foxworthy defined the country music identity by "building trenches of resistance and survival on the basis of principles different from, or opposed to, those permeating the institutions of society" (Castells, 2004, p. 8). Without specifically saying so, the statement builds strong boundaries of exclusion for anyone outside country music or the values proclaimed, and it simultaneously builds a sense of community and solidarity for country music fans. Within that solidarity, it allows little if any diversity. As Castells puts it, "In contrast to pluralistic, differentiated civil societies, cultural communes display little internal differentiation" (p. 70). That is one of the qualities of resistance identities: They provide a strong cultural center, a clear sense of right and wrong, a solid ground for meaning.

Resistance identities in the network society are acts of cultural resistance, with no real political or economic goals. Much like a third-wave feminist concerned with expressing gender, Foxworthy's country music fan is concerned with the meanings surrounding identity. They both draw a line in the sand and proclaim, this is who I am. Moreover, as you can see with both examples, resistance identities are individualized. There's a sense of cultural community that accompanies these identities, and there are clear meanings associated with them, but neither of them requires or implies that members actually group together. You can be a country music fan and believe in the boundaries that Foxworthy proclaims, and never once get together with other fans. Further, if and when you do get together, the focus will probably be on music and beer, "With a cheap woman and two-timin' man thrown in for spice" (Foxworthy, quoted in Martin, 2007). The center of discussion would probably not be political activism. If you do talk about ideas or values with which you disagree, it likely won't be with any intent of creating a project to bring about change. It will simply be a ritual that generates high levels of emotional energy that will make your identity and beliefs feel more sacred. Resistance identities thus create a strong sense of meaning in a world where meanings are becoming delegitimized and fragmented.

With the sources of legitimizing identities weakened or gone, the shared identities necessary for democracy are no longer present. Further—and this is extremely important to note—project identities in and of themselves are suffering the same fate as legitimizing identities, because both share the same social basis: the civil sphere and democratic government defined by the nation-state. Castells's theory implies is that this form of society is gone or receding, social connections now being made through the network society that is not bounded or limited by the state. The structural, systemic bases of participatory democracy as understood from the eighteenth century through the ending decades of the twentieth are gone. Further, resistance identities by themselves are nothing more than emotional constructs that give individuals and small groups a sense of meaning and purpose.

However, resistance identities can form the basis of new project identities. In fact, Castells (2004) argues that resistance identities could "be *the main potential source* of social change in the network society" (p. 70, emphasis added). These new project identities do not come out of the industrial era's "identities of civil society" (p. 422) but may emerge from the intense interactions around cultural resistance. For example, while there's an emphasis on choice in what passes as gender (expressions of femininity) in third-wave feminism, there are also a good number of third wavers who are deeply involved in political activism, not always for women's rights. So, for instance, a third-wave feminist may have a project identity built around environmental issues—specifically, feminist-as-environmentalist—yet at the same time she expresses her gender identity as resistance. However, there is nothing about resistance identities that necessarily implies project identities. Resistance identities thus represent a further danger to the idea of participatory democracy. Rather than creating new project identities, these resistance communes could simply maintain their inward gaze, occupied only with keeping the meaningfulness of their own identities. Castells (2004) ironically characterizes such narcissism as "inducing a process that might transform communal heavens into heavenly hells" (p. 70).

Among the resistance identities Castells (2004) lists as possibilities for project identities are religious communes, ethnicity, gender, territorial identities, environmentalism, and so on. Again, please notice that the content—what the identity is about—is virtually unimportant, in terms of it being the basis of a project identity. The deciding factor between resistance and project identities is the intent to bring change. In other words, project identities have projects. Project identities in the network society, however, don't generally work the same as in industrial society. As we've seen, the network society implies a new form of power. Rather than the political power of civil society, network power resides in codes of information and images of representation. Conflict over power in the network society is a battle for people's minds: "Whoever, or whatever, wins the battle of people's minds will rule, because mighty, rigid apparatuses will not be a match, in any reasonable timespan, for the minds mobilized around the power of flexible, alternative networks" (Castells, 2004, p. 425).

According to Castells (2004), there are two types of *symbol mobilizers,* those social actors able to influence information and imagery. First, there are the Prophets, symbolic personalities that can create information and imagery and mobilize the network. Recent examples include Bono of U2 (and his work on AIDS and developing nation debt forgiveness), Angelina Jolie (protesting use of landmines, helping refugees), and Sting (and his work with Amazonia, helping to save the Amazon rain forests). The second and more important avenue for mobilizing symbols and information around project identities is the decentralized activity of the network itself. The Internet can of course be used to gather people together for rallies, demonstrations, and so on, but its greatest impact is on people's awareness, thinking, and feelings about the project issue. In contrast to the Prophet motif, this "impact on society rarely stems from a concerted strategy, masterminded by a center" (Castells, 2004, p. 427). Decentralized, flexible networks of information and communication around issues of environmentalism, women's lives, sweatshop working conditions, refugees, human rights violations, and so on produce and distribute news, ideas, insights, explanations, strategies, and images around the world, thus impacting the way people see and interface with the world.

This network of social change is the breeding ground for a *new democracy*. Its form is different, without the "orderly battalions, colorful banners, and scripted proclamations" (Castells, 2004, p. 428) of civil society, and it's thus difficult to recognize. But for the same reason, there is a continuing

subtle pervasiveness of incremental changes of symbols processed through multiform networks, away from the halls of power. It is in those back alleys of society, whether in alternative electronic networks or in grassrooted networks of communal resistance, that I have sensed the embryos of a new society, labored in the fields of history by the power of identity. (p. 428)

Summary

- Castells argues that society and capitalism went through significant restructuring between the 1970s and 1990s. Essential to this restructuring were new information technologies. This new technology lifted capital and social relations from the embeddedness of time and space—they redefined the material basis of human life—and allowed for an almost infinite number of reconstructions. The accumulation of capital shifted from production to financial flows. Capital was then invested globally, following interests of greatest return, which are increasingly based on speculation and money markets rather than real goods and services.

- The basis of social connections changed and is now subject to the logic of networks. Within this logic, connections are created by nodes rather than people situated in time and place. A node is important because of the amount of information it holds and processes or the way it connects to other elements within the network. Actual people as traditionally understood in terms of a situated lifeworld become of secondary importance: A person becomes important in the network as he or she functions as a network node.

- Thus power in a network is determined by a node's ability to find, hold, and process information, and, more importantly, the node's ability to act as a switch between informational networks. Class is established more by a node's capability to organize work or direct flows of speculative capital than by production. Politics in the network society are a function of image-making and negative information, which is able to capture attention in the network. The politics of the state, then, are dependent upon network-based media personalities. The sovereignty of the state is also deconstructed by the importance of global flows of money and information, both of which fall outside the ability of the state to regulate efficiently.

- As a result of these changes in power and politics, the legitimacy of the state is questioned. And as a result of this crisis in legitimation, the majority of citizens no longer believe that traditional democracy addresses the problems faced in daily life. In addition, resistance identities become increasingly important. In the network society, there are three forms of identity: legitimating, resistance, and project. Legitimating and project identities are based on the modern ideal of state-based emancipatory politics; the former established and the latter seek to reform the distribution of civil rights. As the centrality of the state and emancipatory politics decline, so do the importance and power of legitimating and project identities. Resistance identities—which are formed around existential questions and meaning— ascend in practice and significance. In and of themselves, resistance identities are not political but are individualized, which in turn threatens the possibility of participatory democracy. However, in the network society, resistance identities represent the best possibility for the reforming of project identities. Resistance identities can be used to mobilize information and imagery, which can bring incremental changes and shifts in network power.

TAKING THE PERSPECTIVE: SOCIETY WRIT LARGE

Castells is one of those unique theorists for whom there is little antecedent and little if any subsequent related work. The focus of this theory is simply too new. However, generally speaking, his concerns are well founded in the history of social theory. From the outset, sociological theorists have been concerned with defining and then analyzing society. As noted in Chapter 1, the idea of society as a macro-level entity existing above and influencing face-to-face social situations is distinctly modern. Moreover, early sociologists spent a good deal of theoretical energy defining and explicating the dynamics of such an entity. Beginning with Comte, society has been understood as a bounded system of interrelated institutions. Marx had very clear ideas of an economic system in relation to a territorially bound state; the same was true about Weber. Durkheim's social solidarity was relative to a single culture. This approach is of course where we get our notions of social structure and institutions. However, all that work had as its background assumption the defining feature of the nation-state—society in modern terms is intrinsically linked to the democratic state defined by territory and the exclusive use of legitimated coercive power. Castells's work, even more than Wallerstein's, proposes a new base for and understanding of society, one that doesn't simply overflow national boundaries. Castells is asking us to think about society without any reference to time, place, or function.

Castells is also concerned with identity, which, again, is a central issue of modern theorists. Stuart Hall (1996b) notes that identity in the Enlightenment "was based on a conception of the human person as a fully centered, unified individual, endowed with the

(Continued)

(Continued)

capacities of reason, consciousness, and action" (p. 597). This sense of identity became the basis of the citizen and national identity—an American, for example, capable of participatory democracy. This notion of identity was also based upon the sovereignty of the state, an institution where the politics of democracy could be played out and legitimated power of the state could be directed toward equality and social justice.

As we've seen, Castells argues for a new and different basis of society and thus identity. Society—social connections—is no longer based on identities that are situated and lived in real time and place. Rather, he argues that the majority of our sociability is created through information technology networks, which transcend national borders and thus redefine power, class, and politics. So, while his concerns are clearly modern and well established, he takes us in new directions and asks that we rethink the ideas that have dominated and led the social sciences for almost 200 years.

In terms of his theoretical approach, Castells means his theory to be used as an analytic heuristic, somewhat like Bourdieu in intent. This approach implies two things. First, unlike Wallerstein, Castells's theory isn't meant to be predictive; rather, it's a way of seeing and analyzing the social world. Second, the theory is a "work in progress open to rectification by empirical research" (Castells, 2000a, p. 6). His work, then, is quite literally intended to provide ideas and concepts "to be used in the building of a sociological theory able to grasp emerging forms of social organization and conflict" (p. 6).

BUILDING YOUR THEORY TOOLBOX

- Using the information from both the chapter introduction and "Taking the Perspective," write a 250-word synopsis of network society theory.

- After reading and understanding this chapter, you should be able to define the following terms theoretically and explain their importance to Castells's theory of the network society: Keynesian economics, information technology, the logic of networks, annihilation of time and place, power, class, politics, identities, legitimizing identity, resistance identity, project identity, civil society, symbol mobilizers, new democracy.

- After reading and understanding this chapter, you should be able to answer the following questions (remembering to answer them theoretically):

  o Explain how three major technological advances have fundamentally influenced knowledge and information. Pay special attention to how the logic of networks has altered the way in which people are socially organized.

  o Explain how computer/information technologies have fundamentally altered power, politics, and class.

  o Explain how the sovereignty of the state is challenged through computer/information technologies.

- o Clarify the differences among legitimizing, resistance, and project identities.

- o Explain how civil society has changed as a result of computer and information technologies. In your explanation, be sure to explicate the new democracy.

Learning More—Primary and Secondary Sources

- The foundation of Castells's work is found in his three-volume work concerning the network society: *The Rise of the Network Society* (2000), *The Power of Identity* (2004), and *End of Millennium* (2000), Blackwell.

- Though portions of Castells's work appear in many texts, there are very few secondary sources focused exclusively on him. I can suggest the following:

  - o Felix Stalder, *Manuel Castells* (Key Contemporary Thinkers series), Polity Press, 2006.

  - o Manuel Castells and Martin Ince, *Conversations With Manuel Castells,* Polity Press, 2003.

Engaging the World

- Use Castells's notions about legitimizing, resistance, and project identities to analyze at least three identities you claim as your own.

- Using your explanation of how civil society has changed, draw out at least three implications for democracy. In other words, how has the possibility of democracy changed as a result of the process involved in the network society?

- Propose a project that would fit into Castells's notion of the new democracy. The project topic can be anything, so pick something you really care about. Using Castells's theory, explain how your project could potentially influence society.

- Speculate about possible effects of Castells's idea of the network society on sociology and other social disciplines.

Weaving the Threads

- Using Wallerstein and Castells, explain how democracy and politics have changed as a result of globalization. How has the state been decentered from the social project of modernity? How have political identities and personal practices been redefined?

- How is the modern idea of society challenged by Castells and Wallerstein? How would you now define society?

- How has capitalism changed as a result of the network society? Focus your discussion on capital and class.

- Compare and contrast Wallerstein's and Castells's theories in terms of how people can be politically involved. Which do you think is more viable and why?

- Compare and contrast Castells's theory of politics and identities with that of Wilson and Chafetz. What does the network society imply about the identities and politics of race and gender?

Part IV

Modernity

Possibilities and Problems

The Big Picture: Civil Society and Democracy

As we saw in Chapter 1, modernity is more than a period of time; it's a specific way of being in the world. It's a method of control based on a way of knowing with a vision for progress and hope. This way of being demanded a certain kind of world, one utterly objective and determined by invariant laws; such a world could be guided toward achievable ends. This way of being also demanded a particular kind of person, a reasoning actor endowed with the possibility of infinite progress. These ideas were not simply about the physical world; they touched and defined every sphere of human existence, especially society. Any progress made would otherwise be empty, if humanity could not improve the sphere in which the social animal finds its existence. Technical advances would bitterly mock a world of social oppression. Modernity was not simply about reducing the uncertainties of life, which is the providence of science and technology. More significantly, modernity was founded on the idea of the natural individual right of self-governance, which is the responsibility of democracy: Modern "nations are united by a united will, emanating from common interest created by the principles of self-government, equal rights, natural justice and social happiness" (Arieli, 1964, p. 173).

The collective good, or good society, was something to be achieved; it wasn't given: The framers of constitutional government put a *process* in place with few absolutes.

The sphere of pre-given, absolute answers—religion—was decentered so that the collective could find and enact its own good. The good society was likewise not a given; it wasn't something that would just happen on its own. This good society had to be realized through hard work, understanding, compassion, and a driving desire for freedom and equality. The founders of modern democracy envisioned a social sphere wherein this work would occur. In the United States, this sphere was guaranteed by the First Amendment: "Congress shall make no law respecting an establishment of religion, or prohibiting the free exercise thereof; or abridging the freedom of speech, or of the press; or the right of the people peaceably to assemble, and to petition the Government for a redress of grievances." This sphere came to be known as civil society.

One of the first to study American democracy, Alexis de Tocqueville (1835–1840/2002) saw civil society as one of the foundations of democracy. Civil society is made up of voluntary associations "which have an object that is in no way political" and are in addition to "commercial and industrial associations" (p. 489). Tocqueville saw Americans of all ages, conditions, and opinions coming together in a thousand different kinds of groups: "religious, moral, grave, futile, very general and very particular, immense and very small" (p. 489). He noted that in France (his home) and England, new projects were created and managed by government or the nobility. Not so in America, however: There, "you will perceive an association" (p. 489). Yet the most significant outcomes weren't found in the new hospitals or schools—the material outcomes were far less important than the democratic ones. In civil society, "Sentiments and ideas renew themselves, the heart is enlarged, and the human mind is developed only by the reciprocal action of men upon one another" (p. 491). Civil society "provides public 'space' where people learn through practice such essential democratic habits as trust, collaboration, and compromise" (Eberly, 2000, p. 4).

CHAPTER 12

Reason and Democracy

Jürgen Habermas

Source: © Ralph Orlowski/
Reuters/Corbis.

The Big Picture: Social Change

The processes through which societies change have always been a concern for sociology. The social changes that gave birth to modernity were the very first issues with which sociologists were engaged. Comte and Spencer (Chapter 1) employed the organismic analogy to understand the systemic and environmental pressures that pushed for structural differentiation and thus brought social change. Marx used the idea of dialectic tension to explain how societies change through conflict and upheaval. Weber elaborated Marx's notion of class and added cultural issues such as legitimacy to understand social change. We as sociologists have always been interested in social change, and that is certainly true for the theorists in this section.

Jürgen Habermas argues that society can change because people choose to change it. This vision of social change seems simple enough. In fact, it is the idea in back of democracy and a major reason why people vote. But we've already begun to see that this idea isn't as straightforward as it might seem. Within the boundaries of a national economic system, race, gender, and class all resist change. In Chapter 7, Wilson showed us that the lives of blacks in the United States will change only if system-wide changes are made in the mode of economic production, and Chafetz demonstrated that voluntaristic change will have little effect on gender inequality without structural changes that lay outside the ability of individuals to influence. In Chapter 8, Pierre Bourdieu revealed how the hidden structure of habitus works below the level of awareness to replicate our class position. On a global level, Immanuel Wallerstein (Chapter 10) alerted us to the possibility that the social system may be too complex for us to actually guide. And Manuel Castells in Chapter 11 is hopeful only in the tenuous possibility that resistance identities may form project identities through symbol mobilizers. Looking ahead to our next chapter, Jeffrey Alexander (2006) argues that democracy and social justice are built on binary codes that provide the energy for change, yet the outcome is never certain because "the discourse of repression is inherent in the discourse of liberty" (p. 67). In the final chapter of this section, Chapter 14, Anthony Giddens (1990) argues that modernity is like a runaway train, with no one at the helm; he asks, "Why has the generalising of 'sweet reason' not produced a world subject to our prediction and control?" (p. 151).

Yet critical theory, the perspective from which Habermas works, maintains the hope of modernity. Erich Fromm (1955)—an associate with the Frankfurt School—encapsulates this hope:

> But all these facts are not strong enough to destroy faith in man's reason, good will and sanity. As long as we can think of other alternatives, we are not lost; as long as we can consult together and plan together, we can hope. (p. 363)

In many ways, Habermas is one of the last great modernists. Can we take control of society and move it to become better, more humane, and truly free? Can reason prevail in the face of the alienating forces of modernity? Habermas thinks so, and gives us theoretical reasons for our doing the same.

THEORIST'S DIGEST

Brief Biography

Jürgen Habermas was born on June 18, 1929, in Düsseldorf, Germany. His teen years were spent under Nazi control, which undoubtedly gave Habermas his drive for freedom and democracy. His educational background is primarily in philosophy, but also includes German literature, history, and psychology. In 1956, Habermas took a position as Theodor Adorno's assistant at the Institute for Social Research in Frankfurt, which began his formal association with the Frankfurt School of critical thought. In 1961, Habermas took a professorship at the University of Heidelberg, but returned to Frankfurt in 1964 as a professor of philosophy and sociology. From 1971 to 1981, he worked as the director of the Max Planck Institute, where he began to formalize his theory of communicative action. In 1982, Habermas returned to the institute in Frankfurt, where he remained until his retirement in 1994.

Central Sociological Questions

Born out of the political oppression of Nazi Germany, Habermas is driven to produce a social theory of ethics that would not be based on political or economic power and would be universally inclusive. He is a critical theorist who sees humankind's hope of rational existence within the inherent processes of communication. Specifically, he asks, how can the civil sphere of democracy be revitalized so that participatory democracy can move forward?

Simply Stated

As a result of organized capitalism, the commodification of mass media, and the scientific study of society and human relations, democracy has been disabled through the colonization of the lifeworld and public sphere. However, the qualities inherent in critical theory and communication could form the base for the revitalization of civil society and participatory democracy as they are enacted in speech communities.

Key Ideas

Legitimacy, authority, lifeworld, liberal capitalism, depoliticized class, public sphere, pragmatic consensus, organized capitalism, legitimation crisis, colonization of the lifeworld, steering, generalized media of exchange, colonization of the public sphere, public opinion, analytic knowledge, interpretive knowledge, critical theory, speech communities, communicative action, civil society

Concepts and Theory: Capitalism and Legitimation

Drawing on Karl Marx's theory of capitalism, Max Weber's ideas of the state and legitimation, Edmund Husserl's notion of the lifeworld, and Talcott Parsons's view of social systems, Habermas gives us a model of social change and modernity. You are by now generally familiar with Marx's theory of capitalism and Parsons's argument concerning the ways in which system components are integrated, but let me take a moment to talk about Weber's and Husserl's contributions to Habermas's theory.

Legitimations are stories—narratives and myths—that a society tells to justify some portion of socially created reality. A Weberian concern with **legitimation** is specifically, though not exclusively, focused on power, authority, and the state. In order for a system of domination like the state to work, people must believe in it. Part of the reason behind this need is the cost involved in the use of power. If people don't believe in authority to some degree, they will have to be forced to comply through coercive power. The use of coercive power requires high levels of external social control mechanisms, such as monitoring (you have to be able to watch and see if people are conforming) and force (because they won't do it willingly). To maintain a system of domination not based on legitimacy costs a great deal in terms of technology and manpower. In addition, people generally respond in the long run to the use of coercion by either rebelling or giving up—the end result is thus contrary to the desired goal.

In contrast to coercive power, *authority* implies the ability to require performance that is based upon the performer's belief in the rightness of the system, which is where legitimacy comes in. Legitimacy provides people with the moral basis for believing in the system. So, for example, your professor tells you that you will be taking a test in 2 weeks, and in 2 weeks you show up to take the test. No one has to force you; you simply do it because you believe in the right of the professor to give tests. That's Weber's point: Social structures can function because of belief in a cultural system. The state, because it is almost exclusively defined in terms of power, is especially dependent upon legitimacy.

The concept of **lifeworld** originally came from Edmund Husserl. Habermas uses it to refer to the individual's everyday life—the world as it is experienced immediately by the person, a world built upon culture and social relations, and thus filled with historically and socially specific meanings. The purpose of the lifeworld is to facilitate communication: to provide a common set of goals, practices, values, languages, and so on that allow people to interact—to continually weave their meanings, practices, and goals into a shared fabric of life.

Liberal Capitalism and the Hope of Modernity

Drawing from Marx and Weber, Habermas argues that there have been two phases of capitalism: liberal capitalism and organized capitalism. Each phase is defined by the changing relationship between capitalism and the state. In *liberal capitalism,* the state has little involvement with the economy. Capitalism is thus able to function without constraint. Liberal capitalism occurred during the beginning phases of capitalism and the nation-state.

Capitalism and the nation-state came into existence as part of sweeping changes that redefined Western Europe and eventually the world. Though they began much earlier, these changes coalesced in the seventeenth and eighteenth centuries. Prior to this time, the primary form of government in Europe was feudalism, brought to Europe by the Normans in 1066. Feudalism is based on land tenure and personal relationships. These relationships, and thus the land, were organized around the monarchy with a clear social division between royalty and peasants. Thus, in the lifeworld of the everyday person in feudal Europe, one's personal obligations and relationship to the land were paramount. The everyday person was keenly aware of his or her obligations to the lord of the land (the origin of the word *landlord*). This was seen as a kind of familial relationship, and fidelity was its chief goal. Notice something important here: People under feudalism were *subjects of the monarchy,* not citizens.

Capitalism emerged out of an institutional field that included the state, Protestantism, and the Industrial Revolution. The nation-state was needed to provide the necessary uniform monetary system and strong legal codes concerning private property; the Protestant Reformation created a culture with strong values centered on individualism and the work ethic; and the Industrial Revolution gave to capitalism the level of exploitation it needed. As we've seen, capitalism created a new social category, a new way of establishing and understanding social positions. As such, Habermas argues, the nation-state and capitalism *depoliticized class* relations, proposed equality based on market competition, and thus contributed strongly to the emergence of the public sphere, or civil society.

Thus, class is no longer a political issue; it is an economic one—class relations are no longer seen in terms of personal relations and family connections, but rather as the result of free-market competition. Under capitalism and the civil liberties brought by the nation-state, all members of society are seen equally as citizens and economic competitors. Any differences among members in society are thus believed to come from economic competition and market forces, rather than birthright and personal relationships. Clearly, liberal capitalism brought momentous changes to the lifeworld: It became a world defined by democratic freedoms and responsibilities. Social relationships were no longer familial but, rather, legal and rational. The chief goal for the person in this lifeworld was full democratic participation. According to Habermas, the mechanism for this full participation was the public sphere.

The combination of the ideals of the Enlightenment, the transformation of government from feudalism to nation-state democracy, and the rise of capitalism created something that had never before existed: the public sphere. The **public sphere** is a space for democratic, public debate. Under feudalism, subjects could obviously complain about the monarchy and their way of life, and no doubt they did. But grumbling about a situation over which one has no control is vastly different from debating political issues over which one is expected to exercise control. Remember, this was the first time Europe or the Americas had citizens, with rights and civic responsibilities; there was robust belief and hope in this new person, the citizen. The ideals of the Enlightenment indicated that this citizenry would be informed and completely engaged in the democratic process, and the public sphere was the place where this strong democracy could take place.

Habermas sees the public sphere as existing between a set of cultural institutions and practices on the one hand and state power on the other. Its function is to mediate the concerns of private citizens and state interests. There are two principles of this public sphere: access to unlimited information and equal participation. The public sphere thus consists of cultural organizations such as journals and newspapers that distribute information to the people; it contains both political and commercial organizations where public discussion can take place, such as public assemblies, coffee shops, pubs, political clubs, and so forth. The goal of this public sphere is *pragmatic consensus.*

Thus, during liberal capitalism, the relationship between the state and capitalism can best be characterized as *laissez-faire*, which is French for "allow to do." The assumption undergirding this policy was that the individual will contribute most successfully to the good of the whole if left to his or her own aspirations. The place of government, then, should be as far away from capitalism as possible. In this way of thinking, capitalism represents the mechanism of equality, the place where society's elite are defined through successful competition rather than by family ties. During liberal capitalism, it was thus felt that the marketplace of capitalism had to be completely free from any interference so that the most successful could rise to the top. In this sense, faith in the "invisible hand" of market dynamics corresponded to the evolutionist belief in survival of the fittest and natural selection.

Organized Capitalism and the Legitimation Crisis

Such was the ideal world of capitalism and democracy coming out of the Enlightenment. The central orienting belief was progress; humankind was set free from the feudalistic bonds of monarchical government, and each individual would stand or fall based on his or her own efforts. In addition to economic pursuit, these efforts were to be focused on full democratic participation. Each citizen was to be fully and constantly immersed in education—education that came not only from schools but also through the public sphere. The hope of modernity was thus invested in each citizen and that person's full participation—people believed that rational discourse would lead to decisions made by reason and guided by egalitarianism.

Two economic issues changed the relationship between the economy and the state, which in turn had dramatic impacts on the lifeworld and public sphere. First, rather than producing equal competitors on an even playing field, free markets tend to create monopolies. Thus, by the end of the nineteenth and beginning of the twentieth centuries, the United States' economy was essentially run by an elite group of businessmen who came to be called "robber barons." Perhaps the attitude of these capitalists is best captured by the phrase attributed to William H. Vanderbilt, a railroad tycoon: "The public be damned." These men emphasized efficiency through a management theory called Taylorism (named after Frederick Taylor, the creator of scientific management) and economies of scale. The result was large-scale domination of markets. These monopolies weren't restricted to the market; they extended to vertical integration as well. With *vertical integration*, a company controls before-and-after manufacturing supply lines. One example is Standard Oil, who at this time dominated the market, owned wells and refineries, and controlled the railroad system that moved its product to market.

The response of the U.S. government to widespread monopolization was to enact antitrust laws. The first legislation of this type in the United States was the Sherman Antitrust Act of 1890. In part the act reads,

> Every contract, combination in the form of trust or otherwise, or conspiracy, in restraint of trade or commerce among the several States, or with foreign nations, is declared to be illegal. . . . Every person who shall monopolize, or

attempt to monopolize, or combine or conspire with any other person or persons, to monopolize any part of the trade or commerce among the several States, or with foreign nations, shall be deemed guilty of a felony.

However, capitalists fought the act on constitutional grounds, and the Supreme Court prevented the government from applying the law for a number of years. Eventually, the Court decided for the government in 1904, and the Antitrust Act was used powerfully by both presidents Theodore Roosevelt and William Taft. This regulatory power of the U.S. government was further extended under Woodrow Wilson's administration and the passing of the Clayton Antitrust Act in 1914.

The second economic issue that modified the economy's relationship with the state was economic fluctuations. As Karl Marx had indicated, capitalist economies are subject to periodic oscillations, with downturns becoming harsher as they cycle through time. By the late 1920s, the capitalist economic system went into severe decline, creating worldwide depression in the decade of the thirties. What came to be called "classic economics" fell out of favor, and myriad competitors clamored to take its place. Eventually, the ideas of John Maynard Keynes took hold and were explicated in his 1936 book, *The General Theory of Employment, Interest and Money.* His idea was simple, and reminiscent of Marx: Capitalism tends toward overproduction—the capacity of the system to produce and transport products is greater than the demand. Keynes's theory countered the then-popular belief in the invisible hand of the market and argued that active government spending and management of the economy would reduce the power and magnitude of the business cycle.

Keynes's ideas initially influenced Franklin D. Roosevelt's belief that insufficient demand produced the Depression, and after World War II, Keynes's ideas were generally accepted. Governments began to keep statistics about the economy, expanded their control of capitalism, and increased spending in order to keep demand up. This new approach continued through the 1950s and 1960s. While the economic problems of the 1970s cast doubt upon Keynesian economics, new economic policies have continued to include some level of government spending and economic manipulation.

Thus, due to the tendency of completely free markets to produce monopolies and periodic fluctuations, the state became much more involved in the control of the economy. *Organized capitalism,* then, is a kind of capitalism where economic practices are controlled, governed, or organized by the state. According to Habermas, the change from liberal to organized capitalism, along with the general dynamics of capitalism (such as commodification, market expansion, advertising, and so on), have had three major effects.

First, there has been a shift in the kind and arena of crises. As we've seen, liberal capitalism suffered from economic crises. Under organized capitalism, however, the economy is managed by the state to one degree or another. This shift means that the crisis, when it hits, is a crisis for the state rather than the economy. It is specifically a *legitimation crisis* for the state and for people's belief in rationality.

There are two things going on here in the relationship between the state and the economy: The state is attempting to organize capitalism, and the state is employing scientific knowledge to do so. Together, these issues create crises of legitimation and rationality rather than simply economic disasters. Nevertheless, Habermas argues that the economy is the core problem: Capitalism has an intrinsic set of issues that continually create economic crises. However, due to the state's attempts to govern the economy, what the population experiences are ineffectual and disjointed responses from the state rather than economic crises. More significantly, in attempting to solve economic and social problems, the state increasingly depends upon scientific knowledge and technical control. This reliance on technical control changes the character of the problems from social or economic issues to technical ones.

Concepts and Theory: The Colonization of Democracy

The other two important effects of the change from liberal to organized capitalism concern the lifeworld and the public sphere. In our discussion of legitimation and rationality crises, we can begin to see the changes in the lifeworld. The lifeworld of liberal capitalism was constructed out of a culture that believed in progress through science and reason. In this lifeworld, the person was expected to be actively involved in the democratic process. However, the general malaise that grows out of the crisis of legitimation in organized capitalism reduces people's motivation and the meaning they attach to social life.

Colonization of the Lifeworld

In addition, according to Habermas, a **colonization of the lifeworld** is taking place due to the political and economic systems. To understand what Habermas means, we have to step back a little. As I've already noted, Habermas gives us a theory that involves social evolution. In general, social evolutionists argue that society progresses by becoming more complex: Structures and systems differentiate and become more specialized. The evolutionary argument is that this specialization and complexity produce a system that is more adaptable and better able to survive in a changing environment.

One of the problems that comes up in differentiated systems concerns coordination and control, or what Habermas refers to as *steering*. In complex social systems, the institutions and structures have different values, roles, status positions, languages, and so forth (which is precisely what is meant by structural differentiation). Differentiated social structures tend to go off in their own direction. We have seen that Talcott Parsons (Chapter 2) felt this problem was solved through *generalized media of exchange*. The idea of media is important, so let's consider it again for a minute. Merriam-Webster (2002) defines *medium* (*media* is plural) as "something through or by which something is accomplished, conveyed, or carried on." For example, language is a form of media: It's the principal medium through which communication is organized and carried out. Different social institutions or structures use different media. In education, for instance, it's knowledge, and in government, it's power. These are the instruments or media through which education and government are able to perform their functions.

For Parsons, the solution to the problem of social integration and steering is for the different social subsystems to create media that are general or abstract enough that all other institutions could use them as means of exchange. We can think about this like boundary crossings. Visualize a boundary between different social structures or subsystems, such as the economy and education. How can the boundary between economy and education be crossed? Or, using a different analogy, how can the economy and education talk to each other when they have different languages and values?

Habermas is specifically concerned with the boundaries between the lifeworld and the economy and state. In Habermas's terms, Parsons basically argues that the state and economy use power and money, respectively, as media of exchange with the lifeworld. If you think about this for a moment, it makes sense: You exist in your lifeworld, so what does the economy have that you want? You might start a list of all the cars, houses, and other commodities that you want, but what do they all boil down to? Money. And how does the economy entice you to leave your lifeworld and go to work? Money. So, money is the medium of exchange between the lifeworld and the economy. The same logic holds for the boundary between the lifeworld and the state: Power is what the state has and what induces us to interact with the state.

However, Habermas (1981/1987) sees a problem:

> I want to argue against this—that in the areas of life that primarily fulfill functions of cultural reproduction, social integration, and socialization, mutual understanding cannot be replaced by media as the mechanism for coordinating action—that is, it *cannot be technicized*—though it can be expanded by technologies of communication and organizationally mediated—that is, it can be *rationalized*. (p. 267)

Habermas is arguing that there is something intrinsic about the lifeworld that cannot be reduced to media, such as money and power, "without sociopathological consequences" (p. 267). Let me give you an easy example from a different issue: having sex. Most people would agree that you cannot "technicize" this behavior using the medium of money without fundamentally changing the nature of it; there is a clear distinction between making love with your partner and having sex with a prostitute. Habermas is making the same kind of argument about humanity and communication in general. For him, the sphere of mutual understanding—the lifeworld—cannot be reduced to power and money without essentially changing it.

Yet Habermas isn't arguing that Parsons made a theoretical mistake. Parsons saw himself as an empiricist and merely sought to describe the social world. So in this sense, Parsons was right: There is something going on in modernity that tries to mediate the lifeworld. Habermas takes this idea from Parsons and argues that in imposing their media on the lifeworld, the state and economy are fundamentally changing it. The lifeworld, by definition, cannot be mediated through money or power without deeply altering it.

According to Habermas, the lifeworld is naturally achieved through *consensus*. This is basically the same thing that symbolic interactionists argue (Chapter 3): Interactions emerge and are achieved by individuals consciously and unconsciously negotiating meaning and action in face-to-face encounters. This negotiation, or consensus building, occurs chiefly through speech. Thus, using money or power fundamentally changes the lifeworld. In Habermas's (1981/1987) words, it is colonized: "The mediatization of the lifeworld assumes the form of a colonization" (p. 196).

This idea of the colonization of the lifeworld is perhaps one of Habermas's best-known and most provocative concepts. Using Merriam-Webster (2002) again, a *colony* is "a body of people settled in a new territory, foreign and often distant, retaining ties with their motherland or parent state . . . as a means of facilitating established occupation and [governance] by the parent state." Habermas is arguing that the modern state and economic system (capitalism) have imposed their media upon the lifeworld. In this sense, money and power act just like a colony—they are the means through which these distant social structures seek to occupy and dominate the local lifeworld of people.

Habermas (1981/1987, p. 356) argues that four factors in organized capitalism set the stage for the colonization of the lifeworld. First, the lifeworld is differentiated from the social systems. Historically, there was a closer association between the lifeworld and society. In fact, in the earliest societies, they were coextensive; in other words, they overlapped to the degree that they were synonymous. As society increases in differentiation and complexity, the lifeworld becomes decoupled from institutional spheres. Second, the boundaries between the lifeworld and the different social subsystems become regulated through differentiated roles. Keep in mind that social roles are scripts for behavior. In traditional societies, most social roles were related to the family. So, for example, the eldest male would be the high priest—the family and religious positions would be filled and scripted by the same role. This kind of role homogeneity made the relationship between the lifeworld and society relatively nonproblematic. More importantly, it served to connect the two spheres.

Third, the rewards for workers in organized capitalism in terms of leisure time and expendable cash offset the demands of bureaucratic domination. "Wherever bourgeois law visibly underwrites the demands of the lifeworld against bureaucratic domination, it loses the ambivalence of realizing freedom at the cost of destructive side effects" (Habermas, 1981/1987, p. 361). And fourth, the state provides comprehensive welfare. Worker protection laws, social security, and so forth reduce the impact of exploitation and create a culture of entitlement where legal subjects pursue their individual interests, and the "privatized hopes for self-actualization and self-determination are primarily located . . . in the roles of consumer and client" (p. 350).

For simplicity's sake, we can group the first two and last two items together. The first two factors are generally concerned with the effects of complex social environments. The more complex the social environment, due to structural differentiation, the greater will be the number and diversity of cultures and roles with which any individual will have to contend. This in turn dismantles the connections among the elements that comprise the lifeworld: culture, society, and personality.

The second two factors concern the effects of the state's position under organized capitalism, where the state protects the capitalist system, the capitalists, and the workers. In doing so, the state mitigates some of the issues that would otherwise produce social conflict and change. But perhaps more importantly, the state further individualizes the person. The roles of consumer and client, both associated with a climate of entitlement, overshadow the role of democratic citizen.

As a result of these factors, everything in organized capitalism that informs the lifeworld, such as culture and social positions, comes to be defined or at least influenced by money and power. Money and power have a certain logic or rationality to them. Weber talked about four distinct forms of rationality, two of which are pertinent here: instrumental and value rationality. Instrumental-rational action is behavior that is determined by pure means-and-ends calculation. For example, your action in coming to the university might be considered instrumentally rational if being here is a means to the goal of obtaining a good job or career. Value-rational behavior is action that is based upon one's values or morals. Let's take the example of filing a false income tax return in order to not pay taxes. If there is no way you could be caught, then it would be instrumentally rational for you to do so. It would be the easiest way to achieve a desired end. However, if you don't do that because you believe it is dishonest, then your behavior is being rationally guided by values or morals.

Value rationality is specifically tied to the lifeworld, and instrumental rationality to the state and economy. Thus, a good deal of what happens when the lifeworld is colonized is the ever-increasing intrusion of instrumental rationality and the emptying of value rationality from the social system. The result is that "systemic mechanisms—for example, money—steer a social intercourse that has been largely disconnected from norms and values. . . . [N]orm-conformative attitudes and identity-forming social memberships are neither necessary nor possible" (Habermas, 1981/1987, p. 154). In time, people in this kind of modern social system come to value money and power, which are seen as the principal means of success and happiness. Money is used to purchase commodities that are in turn used to construct identities and impress other people. Rather than being a humanistic value, respect becomes something demanded rather than given, a ploy of power rather than a place of honor.

To see the significance of this, recall the ideal of the lifeworld of modernity. When the lifeworld changed in the move from traditional to modern society, it took on new priorities and importance. The lifeworld was ideally to be dominated by democratic freedoms and responsibilities and occupied by citizens fully engaged in reasoning out the ways to fulfill the goals of the Enlightenment—progress and equality—through communication and consensus building. As Habermas (1981/1987) says, "The burden of social integration [shifts] more and more from religiously anchored consensus to processes of consensus formation in language" (p. 180).

As you can see, using money or power as steering media in the lifeworld is the antithesis of open communication and consensus building. One of the results of this situation is that the lifeworld decouples from, or becomes incidental to, the social system, in terms of its integrative capacities. A lifeworld colonized by money and power cannot build consensus through reasoning and communication; people in this kind of lifeworld lose their sense of responsibility to the democratic ideals of the Enlightenment.

Colonization of the Public Sphere

This process is further aggravated by developments in the public sphere. As we've seen, the public sphere and its citizens came into existence with the advent of modernity. Citizens "are endowed by their Creator with certain unalienable Rights."

This phrasing in the U.S. Declaration of Independence is interesting because it implies that these rights are moral rather than simply legal. There is a moral obligation to these rights that expresses itself in certain responsibilities:

> Whenever any Form of Government becomes destructive of these ends, it is the Right of the People to alter or to abolish it, and to institute new Government, laying its foundation on such principles and organizing its powers in such form, as to them shall seem most likely to affect their Safety and Happiness.

Thus, the most immediate place for involvement of citizens is the public sphere. In that space between power on the one hand and free information on the other, citizens are meant to engage in communication and consensus formation. It is in that space that discussion and decisions about any form of government are to be made. However, a *colonization of the public sphere* has taken place in much the same way as the lifeworld. Specifically, the public sphere, which began in the eighteenth century with the growth of independent news sources and active places of public debate, transformed into something quite different in the twentieth century. It became the place of public opinion—something that is measured through polls, used by politicians, and influenced by a mass media of entertainment.

There are two keys here. First, *public opinion* is something that is manufactured through social science. It's a statistic, not a public forum or debate that results in consensus. Recall what we saw earlier about how Habermas views the knowledge of science, even social science—its specific purpose is to control. Transforming consensus in the public sphere into a statistic makes controlling public sentiment much easier for politicians, both subjectively and objectively.

The second key issue I want us to see is the shift in news sources. Most of the venues through which we obtain our news and information today are motivated by profit. In other words, public news sources aren't primarily concerned with creating a democratic citizenry or with making available information that is socially significant. As such, information that is given out is packaged as entertainment most of the time. In a society like the United States, the consumers of mass media are more infatuated with "wicked weather" than the state of the homeless.

Concepts and Theory: Hope for Democracy

When we began our discussion, I mentioned that Habermas still holds out the promise of modernity. This hope is anchored in three areas: critical theory, speech communities, and civil society. The ideas and proposals in back of these are rather straightforward. Achieving them, however, is difficult under the conditions created by organized capitalism, where the possibility and horizon of moral discourse are stunted.

The Hope of Critical Theory

Habermas argues that there are three kinds of knowledge and interests: empirical, *analytic knowledge* that is interested in the technical control of the environment (science); hermeneutic or *interpretive knowledge* that is interested in human under-standing and cooperation; and *critical knowledge* that is interested in emancipation. Because scientific knowledge seeks to explain the dynamic processes found within a given phenomenon, social science is historically bound. That is, it sees things only as they currently exist. That being the case, scientific knowledge of human institu-tions and behaviors can only describe and thus reinforce existing political arrange-ments (since society is taken "as is").

Further, positivistic social science is blind to its own conditions of knowledge: It uncritically places itself fully within the political and economic framework of moder-nity and then proclaims to express objective truth or knowledge. Remember the first assumption of science: The universe is empirical and objective. It's out there, and we can observe it objectively and discover how it works. By definition, human beings aren't objective; they are subjectively oriented toward meaning. Nor is society "out there" in the same way the moon is. We can study the moon objectively because it truly exists apart from us; if human beings had never existed, the moon would be exactly the same. But this can't be said about society. Human beings make up society; it exists only because of us. Therefore, we can't stand outside of it to create objective knowledge—attempts to study society objectively end in denying the only questions that really matter about society: What values should guide society? What are the possibilities?

Critical knowledge, on the other hand, purposefully stands within the social world where the dramas of oppression and social justice are played out. Rather than aligning itself with the assumption of objectivity, as social science has done, critical knowledge embraces the democratic project as its foundation. The democratic values of freedom, justice, and equality are thus explicit and subject to critique, and at the center of the production of critical knowledge, rather than hidden and denied as in "objective" social science. The intent of critical knowledge is to further the democratic project and social justice by exposing the distortions, misrepresen-tations, and political values found in our knowledge and speech.

The Hope of Speech Communities

For Habermas, ideal speech communities are the basis for ethical reasoning and occur under certain guidelines of communication. Before we get to those guidelines, however, we need to consider the more basic idea of *communicative action:* action with the intent to communicate. Habermas makes the point that all social action is based on communication. That sounds commonsensical, but consider for a moment the Latin root *communicatus,* which means to share or impart. The Latin is also the root for community, and the word is used for the Christian concept of Communion. To understand Habermas's intent, it might be beneficial to consider something that looks like social communication but isn't. We can call this "strategic speech." Strate-gic speech is associated with instrumental rationality, and it is thus endemic to the lifeworld of organized capitalism as well as the social system.

In this kind of talk, the goal is not to reach consensus or understanding, but rather for the speaker to achieve his or her own personal ends. For example, the stereotypical salesperson or "closer" isn't trying to reach consensus; he or she is trying to sell something; a more immediate example is the student explaining why he or she missed the test. In strategic talk, speech isn't being practiced simply as communication; communication is being used to achieve egocentric ends, which is contrary to the function of communication: "Reaching understanding is the inherent telos [ultimate end] of human speech. Naturally, speech and understanding are not related to one another as means to end" (Habermas, 1981/1984, p. 287).

Communicative action within an ideal speech situation is based upon some important assumptions. As we are reviewing these assumptions, keep in mind that Habermas is making the argument that communication itself holds the key and power to reasoned existence and emancipatory politics. Communication has intrinsic properties that form the basis of human connection and understanding. Habermas points out that every time we simply talk with someone, in every natural speech act, we assume that communication is possible. We also assume that it is possible to share intersubjective states. These two assumptions sound similar but are a bit different. Communication simply involves your assuming that your friend can understand the words you are saying. Sharing intersubjective states is deeper than this. With intersubjectivity, we assume that others can share a significant part of our inner world—our feelings, thoughts, convictions, and experiences.

A third assumption we make in speech acts is that there is a truth that exists apart from the individual speaker. In this part of speech, we are making validity claims. We claim that what we are saying has the strength of truth or rightness. This is an extremely important point for Habermas and forms the basis of discourse ethics and universal norms. All true communication is built upon and contains claims to validity, which inherently call for reason and reflection. Further, these claims assume validity is possible; that truth or rightness can exist independent of the individual, which implies the possibility of universal norms or morals; and that validity claims can be criticized, which implies that they are in some sense active and accountable to reason. Validity claims also facilitate intersubjectivity in that they create expectations in both parties. The speaker is expected to be responsible for the reasonableness of his or her statement, and the hearer is expected to accept or reject the validity of the statement and provide a reasonable basis for either.

These assumptions are basic to speech: We assume that we can communicate, we assume we can share intersubjective worlds, and we assume that valid statements are possible. What Habermas draws out from these basic assumptions of speech is that it is feasible to reasonably decide on collective action. This is a simple but profound point: Intrinsic to the way humans communicate is the hope of decisive collective action. It is possible for humanity to use talk in order to build consensus and make reasoned decisions about social action. This is both the promise and hope of modernity and the Enlightenment.

Ethical reason and substantive rationality are thus intrinsic to speech, but it isn't enough in terms of making a difference in organized capitalism. As with all critical theorists, Habermas has a praxis component. *Praxis* in general refers to the way in which a theory or skill is realized in practice. For Habermas, praxis is centered in communication and the creation of ideal speech situations. Here, communication is a skill, one that as democratic citizens we need to cultivate in order to participate in the civil society. As we consider these points of the ideal speech community, notice how many of them have to do more with listening than with speaking. In an ideal speech situation,

- Every person who is competent to speak and act is allowed to partake in the conversation—full equality is granted, and each person is seen as an equal source of legitimate or valid statements.

- There is no sense of coercion; consensus is not forced; and there is no recourse to objective standings such as status, money, or power.

- Anyone can introduce any topic, anyone can disagree with or question any topic, and everyone is allowed to express opinions and feelings about all topics.

- Each person strives to keep his or her speech free of ideology.

Let me point out that this is an ideal against which actual speech acts can be compared and toward which all democratic communication must strive. The closer a community's speech comes to this ideal, the greater is the possibility of consensus and reasonable action.

> If we assume that the human species maintains itself through the socially coordinated activities of its members and that this coordination has to be established through communication . . . then the reproduction of the species also requires satisfying the conditions of a rationality that is inherent in communicative action. (Habermas, 1981/1984, p. 397)

The Hope of Civil Society

Ideal speech communities are based upon and give rise to civil society. Civil society for Habermas is made up of voluntary associations, organizations, and social movements that are in touch with issues that evolve out of communicative action in the public sphere. In principle, civil society is independent of any social system, such as the state, the market, capitalism in general, family, or religion. Civil society, then, functions as a midpoint between the public sphere and social interactions. The elements of civil society provide a way through which the concerns developed in a robust speech community get expressed to society at large. One of the more important things civil society does is to continually challenge political and cultural organizations in order to keep intact the freedoms of speech, assembly, and press that are constitutionally guaranteed. Examples of elements of civil society include professional organizations, unions, charities, women's organizations, advocacy groups, and so on.

Habermas gives us several conditions that must be met for a robust civil society to evolve and exist.

- It must develop within the context of liberal political culture, one that emphasizes equality for all and an active and integrated lifeworld.

- Within the boundaries of the public sphere, men and women may obtain influence based on persuasion but cannot obtain political power.

- A civil society can exist only within a social system where the state's power is limited. The state in no way occupies the position of the social actor designed to bring all society under control. The state's power must be limited, and political steering must be indirect and leave intact the internal operations of the institution or subsystem.

Overall, Habermas rekindles the social vision that was at the heart of modernity's birth. Modernity began in the fervor of the Enlightenment and held the hope that humanity could be the master of its own fate. There were two primary branches of this movement, one contained in science and the other in democratic society. In many ways, science has proven its worth through the massive technological developments that have occurred over the past 200 years or so. However, Habermas argues that the hope of democracy has run aground on the rocks of organized capitalism. Further, the use of positivistic science to understand society and human relations rationalizes us away from seeing society as we ought to and from true social discourse concerning issues of ethical and moral concern. In communicative action and civil society, he points the way to a fully involved citizenry, reasoning out and charting their own course. But what Habermas gives us is an ideal—not in the sense of fantasy, but in the sense of an exemplary vision. In his theory, it is the goal toward which societies and citizens must strive if they are to fulfill the promise of modernity. Habermas, then, lays before us a challenge, "the big question of whether we could have had, or can now have, modernity without the less attractive features of capitalism and the bureaucratic nation-state" (Outhwaite, 2003, p. 231).

Summary

- Habermas's theory of modernity is in the tradition of the Frankfurt School of critical theory. His intent is to critique the current arrangements of capitalism and the state, while at the same time reestablishing the hope of the Enlightenment, that it is possible for human beings to guide their collective life through reason.

- Habermas argues that modernity has thus far been characterized by two forms of capitalism: liberal and organized. The principal difference between these two forms is the degree of state involvement. Under liberal capitalism, the relationship between the state and capitalism was one of laissez-faire. The state practiced a hands-off policy in the belief that the invisible hand of market competition would draw out the best in people and would result in true equality based on individual effort. However, laissez-faire capitalism produced two counter-results: the tendency toward monopolization and significant economic fluctuations due to overproduction.

Both unanticipated results prompted greater state involvement and over-sight of the capitalist system.

- Organized capitalism is characterized by active government spending and management of the economy. This involvement of the state in capitalism facilitates three distinct results, all of which weaken the possibility of achiev-ing the social promise of modernity:

  1. A crisis of legitimation and rationality. Because the state is now involved in managing the economy, fluctuations, downturns, and other eco-nomic ills are perceived as problems with the state rather than the economy. When they occur, these problems threaten the legitimacy of the state in general. In addition, because the state uses social scientific methods to forecast and control economies, belief in rationality is put in jeopardy. These crises in turn reduce the levels of meaning and moti-vation felt by the citizenry.

  2. The colonization of the lifeworld. The lifeworld is colonized by the state and economy, as the media of power and money replace communication and consensus as the chief values of the lifeworld.

  3. The reduction of the public sphere to one of public opinion. This occurs principally as the media have shifted from information to entertainment value and as the state makes use of social scientific methods to measure and then control public opinion.

- However, Habermas argues that the hope of social progress and equality can be embraced once again through communicative action and a robust civil society. Communication is based upon several assumptions, the most impor-tant of which concern validity claims—these inherently call for reason and reflection. Together, such assumptions lead Habermas to conclude that the process of communication itself gives us warrant to believe it is possible to reach consensus and rationally guide our collective lives.

- Communicative action is also a practice. True communicative action occurs when full equality is granted and each person is seen as an equal source of legitimate or valid statements; objective standings such as status, money, or power are not used in any way to persuade members; all topics may be intro-duced; and each person strives to keep his or her speech free of ideology.

- Communicative action results in and is based upon a robust civil society. Civil society is made up of mid-level voluntary associations, organizations, and social movements. Such organizations grow out of educated, rational, and critical communicative actions and become the medium through which the public sphere is revitalized. A civil society is most likely to develop under the following conditions: A liberal political culture is pres-ent that emphasizes education, communication, and equality; men and women are prevented from obtaining or using power in the public sphere; the state's power is limited.

TAKING THE PERSPECTIVE: CRITICAL THEORY

As we saw in Chapter 2, critical theory took its cue and impetus from the inhumanity of Nazism and the Holocaust. These forces of destruction only became more widespread through World War II and its aftermath: the American destruction of Hiroshima and the continued threat of nuclear annihilation, and the atrocities of Stalinism and the subsequent Cold War. These were forces of destruction not just of human life but of human spirit as well. The hope with which the twentieth century began lay in ashes by the end. Even the student "revolutions" of 1968 were smothered under the weight of state-sponsored capitalism; incessant commodification and advertising; and the spread of lifeless, homogeneous popular culture through the mass media. To continue to place hope in participatory democracy and social justice seemed naive at best; more generally, the hope was swept under the rug of political apathy and the unceasing hunger for cultural stimulation with which the twenty-first century began. The face of humanity revealed during the twentieth century was as different from the one hoped for in the eighteenth century as the darkness of Hades is from the splendor of paradise.

That was critical theory's defining moment. The skepticism and critique born out of those historical moments are the weight that it bears, not as a burden (though burdensome it is), but as that which gives it presence and propels it forward. Having said that, there are questions about "whether it has any coherence as a 'school' of thought at all" (Ray, 1990, p. x). There have been at least three and maybe four phases that the Frankfurt School has gone through. There are also many works that have a sense of critical theory about them but owe little to the actual School itself. However, there are four issues around which most critical theory gathers.

First, there is an emphasis on the relationship between history and society on the one hand and social position and knowledge on the other. To understand any society, you must first understand its historical path and the structural arrangements within it. The knowledge and political interests that people hold within any society are based upon a person's social position within a historically specific social and cultural context.

Second, critical theory specifically critiques positivism and the idea that knowledge can be value-free. With humans, all knowledge is based on and reflects values. Positivistic knowledge through social science is simply blinded to its own biases and is but a reification of method. The supreme use of reason is emancipation, bringing equality and freedom to all humankind. Thus, the purpose of theory and sociology is not understanding, not control, but emancipation. Critical theory, then, is always applied to the human condition.

Third, the work of critical theory is open-ended and is simply and only dependent upon and guided by critical thinking. Overall, the work of the Frankfurt School and those who have followed indicates that it isn't possible to clearly, truthfully, and accurately plan out the right path for humanity; there is no right society, no goal toward which we strive. The idea that there is lies at the base of why "social science" is an oxymoron—control in order to bring freedom, objectification to understand the subject. Not only is the idea wrongheaded, but humans living in rationalized, commodified, mediated culture also are too entwined with the spirit of the age to see clearly. We can but see dimly at best. Critical theory and critical thinking are meant to help us examine and deconstruct our thoughts and thinking. The goal of critical theory is subversion: "The project of Critical Theory has been to develop ways of thinking so subversive of dominant legitimations, that to understand them was to resist them" (Ray, 1990, p. xviii).

This leads to the fourth quality, which is found particularly in Habermas: The vehicle for social change is participatory democracy guided by critical theory and thought. Most of what passes as "democracy" is nothing but oligarchy by the powerful elite. This rule by few produces a false totality, which in truth is antagonistic and held together by oppressive power. In contrast, the intent of social democracy is the intellectual and practical involvement of all its citizens.

BUILDING YOUR THEORY TOOLBOX

- One of the most important concepts we'll be talking about in the next chapter is civil society. It is therefore important to have a solid understanding of this idea and its relationship to democracy. Use two or three additional resources, along with the material presented in the book, and write a 250-word definition of civil society that addresses the following questions: What is civil society? What are the conditions under which it can survive? How is it important to a democratic society?

- Write a 250-word synopsis of critical theory.

- After reading and understanding this chapter, you should be able to define the following terms theoretically and explain their importance to Habermas's theory: legitimacy, authority, lifeworld, liberal capitalism, depoliticized class, public sphere, pragmatic consensus, organized capitalism, legitimation crisis, colonization of the lifeworld, steering, generalized media of exchange, colonization of the public sphere, public opinion, analytic knowledge, interpretive knowledge, critical theory, speech communities, communicative action, civil society.

- After reading and understanding this chapter, you should be able to answer the following questions (remembering to answer them theoretically):

  o Explain the differences between liberal and organized capitalism. Pay particular attention to the changing relations between the state and economy.

  o Define the lifeworld and its purpose, and explain how it became colonized.

  o Define the public sphere, and explain how it came about, its purpose, and its colonization.

(Continued)

(Continued)

- o What is communicative action, and how does it form the basis of value-rational action?

- o Define ideal speech situations (or communities), and explain how they give rise to civil society.

Learning More—Primary and Secondary Sources

- Jürgen Habermas, *The Theory of Communicative Action, Vol. 1: Reason and the Rationalization of Society,* Beacon Press, 1984; *Vol. 2: Lifeworld and System: A Critique of Functionalist Reason,* Beacon Press, 1987.

- Jürgen Habermas, *The Philosophical Discourse of Modernity: Twelve Lectures,* MIT Press, 1990.

- Jürgen Habermas, *The Structural Transformation of the Public Sphere: An Inquiry Into a Category of Bourgeois Society,* MIT Press, 1991.

- Jane Braaten, *Habermas's Critical Theory of Society,* SUNY Press, 1991.

- *Habermas and the Public Sphere,* edited by Craig Calhoun, MIT Press, 1993.

- William Outhwaite, *Habermas: A Critical Introduction,* Stanford University Press, 1995.

Engaging the World

- Using your favorite Internet search engine, look up "participatory democracy." How would Habermas's ideal speech community fit this model? Does the Internet provide greater possibilities for ideal speech situations to develop? How could Internet communities be linked to civil society?

- Racial, ethnic, gender, sexual identity, and religious groups have all been and are being disenfranchised in modern society. How does the ideal speech situation "enfranchise" these groups? In other words, how does it do away with the possibility of disenfranchised groups?

- What social group do you belong to that most nearly approximates the ideal speech community?

- How can you begin your own praxis?

Weaving the Threads

- We have now discussed several theoretically informed assessments of and guidelines for participatory democracy. Write a one-page synopsis of the assessments and principles for reinvigorating democracy for each of the following theorists: Wallerstein, Castells, and Habermas.

CHAPTER 13

Civil Society and Democracy

Jeffrey C. Alexander

The Big Picture: Solidarity

Beginning in the mid-1960s, Parsons's functionalism came under attack. Historically, the sixties was a time of social upheaval that affected a good part of the modern world. The Cold War was heating up, the civil rights movement reached its peak, the war in Vietnam was escalating along with the antiwar movement, and student uprisings and urban riots regularly made headlines. Many sociologists felt that Parsons's theory didn't offer a good explanation of conflict and social change. Parsons actually did have a theory of social change and revolution, but his clearest explanation of that theory didn't come out until 1966, perhaps too late to stem the tide of rejection.

There was a shift, then, away from understanding society as a functional system and toward conflict theory. Inspired principally by the work of Karl Marx and Max Weber, this perspective seemed more appropriate for the times. There was also a shift away from culture in mainstream, American sociology. The problems of the sixties appeared to be better understood as structural rather than cultural issues. Culture was also downplayed because of its association with Parsons and social consensus, the idea that everyone in a collective functionally needs to share a single culture.

During this same period of time, another shift occurred in social theory and philosophy. This shift is often characterized as the "linguistic turn." The term itself simply means a move to language, and it implies an approach to understanding human beings that emphasizes language above everything else. Beginning perhaps in the 1980s, this shift has had profound effects on the social disciplines: The linguistic turn brought culture back to center stage in the social disciplines, and has made it possible to think about culture structurally. We saw part of this effect in Foucault's poststructuralist theory (Chapter 9); and we'll see more issues revolving around text, language, and discourse in the remaining chapters.

Jeffrey Alexander positions his theoretical work at the junction of these two shifts. First, Alexander argues that the shift away from functionalism was ill-advised. In critiquing the idea of social equilibrium, theorists have missed the benefits that functionalist analysis brings. According to Alexander (1985), functionalism, or more accurately *neo-functionalism*, "indicates nothing so precise as a set of concepts, a method, a model, or an ideology. It indicates, rather, a tradition" (p. 9). This tradition is a distinct perspective or way of looking at society. Specifically, the parts of any system are related and influence one another; personality, culture, and social systems are distinct yet embedded; and the tension among those systems along with pressures for differentiation are major forces for social change. Alexander's early work thus set out an agenda for a new kind of functional analysis, one based on the work of Parsons that downplays the idea of system equilibrium, focuses more clearly on the structure and independent effects of culture, and maintains analytical separation among socially embedded processes.

Alexander's later work adds a critical note to his cultural, neo-functionalist approach. While blending conflict and functional theories is rare, Alexander is not the first to suggest such a move. The best known and most influential of such theorists in the United States was Lewis Coser. Coser's approach is based on the insight that since conflict is normal and universal, it must have functional effects: It must work to integrate society. Coser (1956) argued that conflict internal to the group could serve to release pent-up hostilities, create norms regulating conflict, and develop clear lines of authority and jurisdiction. Further, conflict that is directed at the group from an external source can create stronger group boundaries, higher social solidarity, and more efficient use of power and authority. Alexander's blending is somewhat different and seems to draw more from critical than conflict theories. Like many from the Durkheim–Parsons school, Alexander argues that society is held together by broad cultural ideas and values. Yet Alexander also recognizes that the collective culture in contemporary society is a sphere of conflict where the constant tension between universal and particular interests makes solidarity and democratic justice tenuous.

Alexander's main concerns are social integration and solidarity. The problem of integration has been a focus since the dawn of modernity. One of the most important defining characteristics of modern society is structural diversity. Previously, everything that a social group needed was provided through just a handful of organizational principles. For example, the way work used to be organized was usually around the home and family. In feudalism, the manor was the economic and political center as well as the family home. Craftwork in towns also revolved around the home and family, with the place of business either in the same building as the home or close to it. In comparison, modern society is structurally diversified, with various social institutions working to take care of different social needs and wants. These different institutions create a number of status positions, roles, norms, and values, and generally speaking, these don't overlap. Such differentiation creates a distinctly modern problem of integration—these differences lay in back of such typologies as Tönnies' *gemeinschaft* and *gesellschaft* and Durkheim's organic and mechanical solidarity. However, most theories of modernization simply assume that culture becomes more generalized and thus provides the basis for solidarity and integration, without explaining precisely how it happens. It is this issue that Alexander (2006) wants to open up for inquiry: "I have insisted . . . that the construction of a wider and more inclusive sphere of solidarity must be studied in itself" (p. 193). He draws on critical and functionalist approaches to show us a cultural field in process, one filled with representations of both the collective and the individual, one where beliefs in universal morals are in tension with group-specific claims, a space where solidarity and integration are constant achievements and civil society is a project. Alexander shows us the kind of solidarity and integration necessary in a diversified, democratic society.

THEORIST'S DIGEST

Brief Biography

Jeffrey C. Alexander received his PhD in 1978 from University of California, Berkeley. He was professor of sociology at the University of California, Los Angeles, from 1976–2001, where he is now professor emeritus. In 2001, Alexander took a professorship at Yale University and is currently the Lillian Chavenson Saden Professor of Sociology there, as well as codirector of Yale's Center for Cultural Sociology. Alexander has also held numerous visiting appointments, including at the University of London, the London School of Economics, Konstanz University in Germany, and the Center for Advanced Study in the Behavioral Sciences at Stanford University. Among his more important works are *Twenty Lectures: Sociological Theory Since World War Two*, *Action and Its Environments: Towards a New Synthesis*, *Structure and Meaning: Relinking Classical Sociology*, *Neofunctionalism and After*, *The Meanings of Social Life: A Cultural Sociology*, and *The Civil Sphere*.

Central Sociological Questions

Alexander is focused on two related questions. The first is purely theoretical: What effect does culture have on society? This issue is a classic one in sociology and concerns the independent

(Continued)

(Continued)

effects of culture. Many, if not most, sociologists see social structures as determining or strongly influencing human action. This structural approach usually sees culture as simply reinforcing structures and having very little impact on human action or social change. Alexander argues differently: Culture itself is a structure that is used by people to decide how to act, and that creates the power to bring about social change intentionally through such decisions. The structure of culture itself prompts and guides action. Alexander's second question is more substantial: How can complex and diverse societies hold together and act in concert? More specifically, how do civil society and power work in contemporary society?

Simply Stated

Civil society is a cultural sphere that creates the solidarity necessary for democracy. Solidarity exists in our feelings toward people—how those feelings are created, defined, and extended toward others marks the limit of society's actual democracy and the good life. Solidarity and thus civil society are created out of the tension that exists between universalism and particularism. The universal values of the civil sphere are transcendent and represent a secular faith, the ideals toward which we strive. Non-civil spheres, such as race, gender, class, and religion, generate particularistic interests that result in hierarchical differences. Civil society exists when these two segments clash, most notably through social movements.

In the sense just described, civil society itself doesn't exist in any concrete way. It's a symbolic, cultural world that emerges out of the tensions between the universals of the civil sphere and the particular interests generated by non-civil spheres. However, the civil sphere is bounded by communicative and regulative institutions that give civil society a concrete base. Communicative institutions work through influence and persuasion to impact public opinion. Regulative institutions, on the other hand, give concrete expression to the civil sphere through actual power, exercised through voting and party competition, office, and law.

Key Ideas

Civil sphere, civil society, non-civil spheres, justice solidarity, democracy, tradition of Thrasymachus, particularism–universalism, discourse, binary codes, communicative institutions, regulative institutions, social and civil power, essentialism, civil repair, time, space, function, social movements, pathways to incorporation, neo-functionalism, strong program in cultural sociology

Concepts and Theory: The New Civil Sphere

As I asserted in the beginning of this section of the book, civil society was from its inception considered a necessary ingredient for democracy, with democracy being the modern political form par excellence. Civil society was first seen as voluntary associations that were guaranteed by certain constitutional rights, such as freedom of assembly. Civil society also included a number of institutions outside the state, such as the "capitalist market and its institutions . . . voluntary religion . . . and virtually every form of cooperative social relationship that created bonds of trust" (Alexander, 2006, p. 24). Capitalism in particular was seen to be the source of self-discipline and social responsibility—attitudes important for democracy—and a decisive move away from the self-righteous elitism of aristocracy. Alexander calls this eighteenth century model *Civil Society I*. It lasted only until Marx began publishing.

Marx called attention to the underbelly of this modern economic system. As capitalism grew and became more powerful, the instrumental and exploitive aspects became clear. The robber barons ruled, and the workers were manipulated and subjected to unsafe and unhealthy working conditions that often equated to little more than indentured servitude. Further, capitalism became known for creating market egoism and commodity fetishism. Workers weren't simply exploited and alienated; the very consciousness needed for democratic participation was soiled by capitalism. As a result of the critiques of Marx and others, the fate of democracy was inextricably bound up with capitalism. For those on the political left, capitalism became the institution from which all wrong flowed. Nothing good could come out of capitalism, and only by capitalism's destruction, or at least control, could civil society again flourish. Capitalism also became the central issue for democracy by those on the political right. Defining human nature as intrinsically selfish, free market capitalism was seen as the path to the greatest social good—selfishness creates competition, which in turn supercharges humanity's progress. In addition, for those on the right, capitalism was believed to naturally lead to democracy. Introducing capitalism into a social system would invariably lead to democratic government. These discourses from the second age of civil society (*Civil Society II*) continue to inform contemporary debates, as do the ideals of the first.

In recent decades, renewed theoretical and political concerns for civil society have surfaced. Alexander argues, however, that this new thrust has so far only attempted to revive previous concepts of civil society. There is, however, a problem with these attempts at revival. The ideas of the Enlightenment that initially informed civil society can only hold for the type of social system that existed at that time, at the beginning of modernity and democracy. As Durkheim, Parsons, and others have shown us, societies in general tend to change as a result of structural differentiation, segmentation, and specialization, and these tendencies are exaggerated in the modernity of the twenty-first century. Thus, modern societies are much more complex, and the people more diverse and fragmented than during the first age of civil society. We need, then, a different understanding of civil society, one that is more dynamic and complex than the dominant ideas of early modernity.

Alexander (2006) is also clear that capitalism is no longer determinative, if it ever was: "To identify civil society with capitalism . . . is to degrade its universalizing moral implications and the capacity for criticism and repair" (p. 33). Capitalism is just one of many institutional spheres that may contribute one way or another to the workings of civil society. No social sphere, Alexander tells us, "not even the economic, should be conceived in anti-normative terms, as governed only by interest and egoism" (p. 33). The boundaries between civil and non-civil spheres aren't clear or stable enough to make such a claim. As we'll see, Alexander argues that civil society isn't an obdurate entity; it's a project, not a thing that can be destroyed as such. Further, the issues raised by Marx and others—class conflict, hierarchy, efficiency, egoism, and the rest—are occasions for civil society to express itself. They aren't random; "they are systematic to every society that opens up a civil sphere, and they make justice a possibility" (p. 34).

Defining the Civil Sphere

Alexander uses both the phrases "civil society" and "civil sphere." Although it's not quite this clear, we can think of civil society as an effect of the civil sphere. The word *society* implies social networks of people or systems of structures. While culture is part of this, it isn't given the central place that Alexander wants. As he says, "we need a theory . . . that is less myopically centered on social structure and power distribution, and more responsive to the ideas that people have in their heads and to what Tocqueville called the habits of the heart" (Alexander, 2006, p. 43). The *civil sphere,* then, is "a world of values and institutions that generates the capacity for social criticism and democratic integration at the same time" (p. 4). The civil sphere is defined by a specific type of culture that overlaps and includes some portion of those social structures, as well as organizations, networks of people, and interactions.

This cultural field of meanings and collective feelings form a "secular faith," and thus a moral or ethical sphere. The strongest feeling in the public sphere is *social solidarity.* In Durkheim's use of the concept, there are three elements: the subjective sense of individuals that they are part of the whole, the actual constraint of individual desires for the good of the collective, and the coordination of individuals and social units. These three elements can vary independently, which creates higher or lower social solidarity in a group. Alexander focuses on one specific aspect of solidarity: the feeling of connectedness to other members in a community. Yet the solidarity of the civil sphere isn't like that of particularized groups. For example, a woman may feel very connected to members of her sorority, but that isn't the solidarity of democracy. The feeling of connectedness that Alexander (2006) is referring to "transcends particular commitments, narrow loyalties, and sectional interests" (p. 43), such as sororities, teams, family, and even race and gender. The sense of connectedness in back of social solidarity is a *universal commitment to diversity,* based not so much on group identity as it is on mutual identification with a set of democratic ethics, which in turn bring democratic integration. Thus, democracy demands faith. It's a belief system that transcends individuals and particularized groups. Justice demands that there be a higher standard that pulls us upward. Without this faith, and the solidarity it brings, civil society and democracy are impossible.

Yet, look at the definition of civil sphere that Alexander gives in the quote above. Notice that Alexander not only talks about integration, but in the same breath he says that the civil sphere creates the capacity for *social criticism.* Contemporary democracy is explicitly based on tensions that were only implicit in the beginning of civil society, such as "all men are created equal." In other words, most people, back when those words were written, probably didn't experience tension; most thought they were doing a good job of treating all men equal. However, the tension existed within the structure of the statement itself, and those cultural tensions in the long run created inconsistencies in cultural values and produced a sense of alienation among those excluded. Notice that the culture itself is influencing the types of tensions we experience, the discussions we engage in, and thus the progress that democracy makes. This is the structural element of culture.

Alexander argues that the democratic culture of the civil sphere is formed through *binary structures of purity and impurity*. These structures form and pattern the ideas, values, and discourses that democracy holds dear. Binary structures are found on three levels: motives, social relations, and institutions, which are then used to define pure and impure, in- and out-group members, and civil and uncivil people. For example, the civil sphere includes people who are active and autonomous (purity) and excludes those who are passive and dependent (impurity). The kinds of relationships between people in the civil sphere are open (purity) rather than secretive (impurity), trusting and not suspicious, critical rather than deferential, and truthful instead of deceitful. Finally, civil institutions are rule regulated (purity), while anti-civil institutions are arbitrary (impurity); civil institutions are built upon law, while anti-civil upon power; and civil institutions are equal, while anti-civil are hierarchical. Notice that these pairs (binary) are the values upon which an open democracy is founded. I've listed the binary codes in Table 13.1.

Most of us today are used to hearing about binary codes in reference to computers. Computer languages are based on binary codes of on–off (1/0). These binaries then form character streams, like 11001011. However, the idea of binary codes is also found in various disciplines that study culture and language. Here, the idea is that any single idea is actually a binary. For example, the idea of "good" doesn't exist, nor can

Table 13.1   Binary Codes of the Civil Sphere

Motives		Relationships		Institutions	
Civil	*Anti-civil*	*Civil*	*Anti-civil*	*Civil*	*Anti-civil*
Active	Passive	Open	Secretive	Rule-regulated	Arbitrary
Autonomous	Dependent	Trusting	Suspicious	Law	Power
Rational	Irrational	Critical	Deferential	Equality	Hierarchy
Reasonable	Hysterical	Honorable	Self-interested	Inclusive	Exclusive
Calm	Excitable	Altruistic	Greedy	Impersonal	Personal
Self-controlled	Wild/passionate	Truthful	Deceitful	Contracts	Bonds of loyalty
Realistic	Distorted	Straightforward	Calculating	Groups	Factions
Sane	Mad	Deliberative	Conspiratorial	Office	Personality

it ever be understood, apart from bad. These binaries are set in tension with one another, to the point that they are often mutually exclusive. Durkheim's binary of sacred and profane is an example. They can't coexist; one always destroys the other. We can see an example of this in the Bible. The children of Israel were moving the Ark of the Covenant, which contained the tablets of stone upon which were written the Ten Commandments. The Ark was moved by placing two wooden poles on either side so no one would have to touch it. At one point, the people carrying the Ark lost their balance. In order to prevent the Ark from hitting the ground, one of the priests reached up and righted it. God struck him dead. The profane had to be removed so the Ark could remain sacred.

The binary codes of the civil sphere work in a similar manner: They are mutually exclusive. This implies two things. First, tension is inherent in the codes. Anytime sociologists theorize about social change, they are confronted with the problem of causal force: What pushes for or creates change? Here, the tension inherent in the code provides energy for change. In an analogous way, this is like Marx's dialecticism. Marx argued that there are structural elements in capitalism that push for change, eventually destroying the economic system. In Alexander's theory, it's the binary oppositions that give structure to the democratic discourses that push for change. For example, inclusion always brings exclusion: "The discourse of repression is inherent in the discourse of liberty" (Alexander, 2006, p. 67). Laws that grant certain civil rights, like the right to marry, simultaneously deny them to others. Laws of citizenship do the same thing: Some people are included while others are excluded. The codes of democracy are inherently conflictual, and that continually pushes for change.

The second thing the binary nature of the codes implies is *essentialism*. Because of the binary, social things that are categorized using the system seem essential. If something is deemed good, we see it as *essentially* good, in and of itself. For us to say anything is good, that it exists as good, we blind ourselves to the fact that we are constructing it as good. It appears as if it is *the essence of the thing itself* that makes it good, not our categorization of it. Acknowledging that good and bad are socially constructed "would relativize reality, creating an uncertainty that could undermine not only the cultural core but also the institutional boundaries and solidarity of civil society itself" (Alexander, 2006, p. 63).

These binary codes are used to create discourses of democracy. A **discourse** is a way of talking about something, but it is much more. Discourses set the boundaries of what is possible and impossible. Remember Foucault's (Chapter 9) example of the Chinese encyclopedia of animals. What struck him was the limitation of his own thinking: "the stark impossibility of thinking *that*" (Foucault, 1966/1994b, p. xv). Discourses also set hierarchical, subjectivizing positions. For example, the current discourse of nations tends to categorize them as developed, developing, and underdeveloped. This discourse is based on industrial capitalist standards and evaluates nations according to that value system. Being "underdeveloped" is stigmatizing in this discourse.

More specific to civil society, the American *anti-civil* discourse of race creates a hierarchy based on skin color and heritage. At its worst, the anti-civil discourse essentialized blacks as less than human: The first work of this discourse was to reduce the slave to "'chattel' in the eye of the law—placed beyond the circle of human brotherhood—cut off from his kind" (Douglass, 1850/2009a, p. 216). This denigration of human nature in the discourse of race continues to have subjective effects. According to Cornel West (2001), "black existential *angst* derives from the lived experience of ontological wounds and emotional scars inflicted by white supremacist beliefs" (p. 27). The *civil* discourse of race is also framed in universal, essentializing terms. In constructing the first civil discourse of race in the United States, Frederick Douglass (1857/2009b) proclaimed that equality is guaranteed to blacks because the Declaration of Independence is about "'We, the people'—not we, the white people—not we, the citizens . . . not we, the privileged class, and excluding all other classes . . . but we the people—the men and women, the *human* inhabitants of the United States" (p. 257, emphasis added).

There's an important implication here: Solidarity is both transcendent and particularist, connecting us to others by creating structured feelings of "being part of something larger than ourselves," while at the same time it respects "our individual personalities" (Alexander, 2006, p. 13). It is a "socially established consciousness" (p. 54) that "combines collective with individual obligations" (p. 38). The binary codes that produce solidarity create discourses that essentialize both in- and out-group members *simultaneously:* "The discourse of repression is inherent in the discourse of liberty" (p. 67). Thus, solidarity and all that comes with it—civil society, justice, democracy—isn't something that can objectively exist: It's an ongoing achievement. However, it isn't the limitations of human nature nor is it the particularistic egoism produced by non-civil spheres that prevents us from achieving full democracy and social justice. The things that we have perhaps seen as failures—the existence of groups excluded from full justice—are, in fact, the result of "processes internal to the social system itself" (p. 411). The binary codes upon which solidarity is based are irresolvable and available to civil and non-civil groups alike. The outrage we feel at injustice is the cost of democracy: "We would not be so indignant about these contradictions if we were not so fiercely committed to the ideal of a broadly solidaristic humanity, to brotherhood and sisterhood. These contradictions, in other words, are the price of civil society" (p. 9).

Concepts and Theory: Civil Institutions

As we're beginning to see, civil society does not exist *as such*. It's a project that is better understood as sets of practices and boundary relations. One of the better insights that functionalism gives us concerns system boundaries. In order for anything to exist, there must be a point at which it begins and everything else stops. A handy example is your body. The skin of the body forms a boundary that marks the place where you begin and everything else ends. The insight that functional analysis gives us is that the boundary is permeable, and it negotiates relations between internal and external systems. Your skin, for example, senses external temperature and objects, and then communicates this information to internal systems. Your body also has other boundary-negotiating structures, like your mouth and nose, which maintain a functional relationship between your biological system and everything else. There's a way in which everything that exists does so only because of its boundaries. This is particularly the case for the civil sphere.

The civil sphere is bounded by civil institutions. These institutions form boundary relations with all non-civil spheres, such as family, religion, and the economy, all of which create particularized interests. Civil institutions, then, are those that promote universalistic values and are most closely associated with promoting democracy. They create norms, goals, rewards, and sanctions; they also make exchanges, create demands, and so forth. Civil institutions express and implement the symbolic, binary codes found in the structure of democratic culture by persuasion and enforcement, specifically through communicative (persuasion) and regulative (enforcement) institutions.

Communicative Institutions

If asked, many people today would probably define *democracy* as a set of institutions and laws that guarantee people the right to vote. Wikipedia, for example, defines democracy as "an egalitarian form of government in which all the citizens of a nation together determine public policy." Merriam-Webster (2002) similarly defines democracy as "a form of government in which the supreme power is vested in the people and exercised by them directly." This way of understanding democracy doesn't just appear in popular culture. Charles Tilly (2007), a well-known contemporary sociologist, defines democracy as "a certain class of relations between states and citizens" (p. 12).

However, there is a danger in restricting our definition of democracy to specific institutions and laws. This is not to say that the structures guaranteeing voting rights and curtailing egoistic pursuits aren't important; they are vitally so. But when our understanding of democracy is focused simply on these formal arrangements, then it is "the distribution of power and force, the balance of material resources, that is important" (Alexander, 2006, p. 39). Here, Alexander argues, we are left with the tradition of Thrasymachus, a character in Plato's *Republic*. In a discussion about justice, Thrasymachus posited that "justice" is always defined by those in power and has no reference to any higher system of values. Alexander is arguing that if we only see democracy as a set of institutions and laws, then democracy is in danger because the elite class can usually gain control of those social structures. Thrasymachus's view of justice then becomes reality—might makes right. Alexander asserts that there *must be something more to democracy* than legal safeguards and institutions. Democracies need "social structures that allow egoism to be pursued but that make the aggregation of egoism impossible" (p. 42), but democracies also need more than this. Drawing on John Dewey, Alexander tells us that democracy is more than laws, institutions, and organizations. It is "primarily a mode of associated living, of conjoint communicated experience" (p. 37). It's a consciousness, a way of existing in the world that specifically seeks out social and cultural diversity, and diversity of "stimulation . . . means challenge to thought" (Dewey, 1916/2009, p. 71). Democracy is as much based on "solidarity and commonality" as it is on difference and power struggles (p. 43). It is in the communicative institutions where we find sources for solidarity.

Communicative institutions are made up of organizations and associations that create and circulate cultural meanings, as well as influence our thoughts and feelings about the civil sphere. These institutions obviously communicate, but they particularly translate the abstract ideals found in the binary codes through specific events and people. The mass media—including television, movies, books, news services, and so on—and public opinion polls are two particularly significant parts of communicative institutions. According to Alexander (2006), the mass media presents two kinds of narratives: fictional and factual. The importance of fictional mass media is that it has greater cathartic impact. Fictional media can weave stories of heroism, sacrifice, and valor using the binary codes of democratic culture, and we respond with tears, laughter, pride, heart-felt concern, and belief. We're lifted up and energized by these stories. We are also energized against stories or characters that exemplify the impure side of the binary. Fictional media in particular structure our feelings around social justice issues; they create the "intuitive criteria . . . that shape behavior in more organized and formal domains" (p. 70).

Factual media are more immediately influential, as they report such things as the news and, most importantly, public opinion. The reporting is presented as if it were factual. Every news story has an "ontology of realism" about it—the "news presents itself as homologous with the real world" (Alexander, 2006, p. 80). Factual media frequently draw on the binary codes to impute motives, define relationships, and explain the institutions of the "real world." They thus create the chronic tensions between the universal values of the civil sphere and the powers and authorities outside. What we see when we watch the morning news, read a newspaper, or listen to public radio is a collage, a constructed picture of *everything that matters* in the world we confront. It's not only the news we perceive; the news itself orders our world. Something matters precisely because it *appears as news*. The way in which something matters, or the value we give it, is also strongly informed by factual media as they draw on the binary codes. A significant part of this picture making is the reporting of public opinion polls.

The current notion of public opinion is based on a kind of imagined community. During the initial stage of civil society, it would have been more accurate to speak of a concrete, rather than imaginary, public. The existence of this real public is one of the reasons why public assembly is constitutionally guaranteed. In the early phases of modern democracy, people gathered in voluntary associations and public houses to share information and argue about ideas. These face-to-face encounters strongly informed the dominant ideas. A clear example from that time is Herbert Spencer (1820–1903), one of our first sociologists. James Collier (1904) tells us that Spencer "at no time received systematic instruction in any branch of science. What is more surprising, it may be doubted if he ever read a book on science from end to end" (p. 206). Where, then, did Spencer get his ideas and facts? According to Collier,

He *picked up* most of his facts. Spending a good part of every afternoon at the Athenaeum Club he ran through most of the periodicals . . . [and] he

habitually met with all the leading savants, many of whom were his inti-
mates. From these, by a happy mixture of suggestion and questioning, he
extracted all that they knew. (pp. 208–209)

Today, however, the "public" doesn't exist in any concrete way; it isn't based on
face-to-face communion between people: "It now assumes a symbolic rather than
concrete form" (Alexander, 2006, p. 72). Yet the significance of the public in the lives
of citizens isn't lessened because of its symbolic nature. Public opinion polls matter;
they not only matter in terms of affecting politicians' actions, but they also matter to
us personally. We see ourselves in the public: It's an imagined community in which
we exist. It's the place where the public is seen and heard, and we are part of that
public. It is this public that different conflict groups want to influence, because it is
through the public that their agendas, formed around binary cultural structures, are
given voice. Moreover, because it is an opinion, it concerns how the public feels
about a given topic. Public opinion, then, inserts itself "into social subjectivity as a
structure of feeling. . . . Public opinion is the sea within which we swim, the structure that gives us the feeling of democratic life" (Alexander, 2006, pp. 72, 75).

Many critical commentators, Habermas among them, have argued that the commodification of media has reduced them to trivialized images designed solely to
gather an audience rather than inform a public. Alexander sees this critique as
another example of the ideological rejection of all things capitalist. First, the commercialization of media actually encouraged diversity. Once the media was released
from patronage, and could thus maintain their own existence, they were freed from
ideological pressures from the elite and could respond to the diverse demands of a
pluralistic public. Second, whether or not the media produces homogeneous, commodified images devoid of any democratic content depends on some rather common
social factors, principally the differentiation of mass media organizations. This differentiation depends on the existence of impersonal markets and professionaliza-
tion. We can think of media markets varying along a continuum from impersonal,
negotiated exchanges between buyers and sellers to markets dominated by personal
and client relationships. The more the market is driven by rational exchanges rather
than patronage, the greater the diversity and ideological control. In addition, pro-
fessionalized ethics and self-regulation "allow producers, writers, directors, and
reporters more freedom to offer flexible interpretations responsive to shifting
events . . . rather than on more dogmatic interpretations that merely authenticate
loyalties to particular groups" (Alexander, 2006, p. 83).

There is one other element of communicative institutions: *civil associations.*
Alexander is quick to make the distinction between the voluntary associations that
are generally associated with civil society and these civil associations. Voluntary
associations, of the type Tocqueville is usually associated with, are groups that are
organized on a voluntary basis to achieve some collective end. A group organized
to raise money for the local library is a good example. The democratic value in
voluntary organizations is that they give people practice at working together, negotiating conflicts and interests, and coming to collective consensus. Civil associations, on the other hand, come together to influence public opinion about a specific
issue they intend to communicate. MADD (Mothers Against Drunk Driving) is a

good example. Such groups are part of the communicative institutions that border and give life to civil society because they can make their case only to the degree that they use the universals found in the binary code.

Regulative Institutions

Where communicative institutions work to persuade people toward democracy and social justice, regulative institutions guard democratic processes through power. *Regulative institutions* are made up of two broad arenas: civil power and law. Generally speaking, power in society is linked to having control over collecting taxes, creating and controlling army and police forces, and building the administrative structure of society. In times past, aristocrats controlled this state power. Aristocratic power was direct in the sense that nothing stood between individuals and governmental control. The king's word was law, pure and simple. Modern, democratic society, however, is founded on belief in natural rights, which are then constitutionally guaranteed. These rights stand between individuals and governmental control. In a very real way, it's the existence of these rights that created civil society.

The control of civil society is constantly at stake in contemporary, highly diversified societies. To talk about this issue, Alexander (2006) makes the distinction between social and civil power. *Social power* is power that is determined by particularized interests generated in non-civil spheres, such as class and religion. To the degree that the elite from any particularized group control society, "democracy doesn't exist" (p. 109). In a democracy, control of society needs to be based more in civil rather than social power. *Civil power* exists when the people "speak" through both communicative and regulative institutions. Civil power thus negatively varies by the degree of elite control and positively varies by the level of differentiated inclusion in the political process. In other words, the greater the level of elite institutional control (social power), the less will be the level of democratic civil society. On the other hand, the greater the inclusion of diverse groups (like race, gender, religion, and so forth), the greater will be the level of democratic society. The primary function of regulative institutions is thus to restrict elite control and to guarantee inclusion. There are four specific ways these institutions work: voting, political parties, office, and law.

The most basic way civil power is promoted is through the *right to vote*. The more diverse the voting population, the more democratic will be civil society and the more likely it is to promote social justice. Of course, the battles over the kinds of people who are given the right to vote have defined a good deal of the history of democracy: The fight for universal suffrage was defined by the universals found in binary codes and thus depended upon communicative institutions. But the right to vote itself only opens up the possibility of civil power. The purpose of voting is to break up the direct "translation of social into political power" (Alexander, 2006, p. 114). Elites, however, attempt to control that translation. One of the regulatory safeguards against such control is party politics.

While we each vote for an individual, a political party backs each candidate. *Political party* platforms are constructed through debate and, more importantly, must be presented to the public in terms defined by the binary codes. Political campaigns are characterized by essentialist claims of purity and impurity; thus, the other party and candidates are characterized as polluting. Many people think that this type of partisan politics is detrimental to civil society; accordingly, the ideal is to get rid of us/them political discourses. Like Habermas, such people argue that democratic discourse ought to be characterized by reason, rational deliberation, and pragmatic consensus. There are two problems with this understanding. First, the history of civil society doesn't live up to this model of consensus building: "Boundary relations with noncivil spheres have always been unsettled, civil discourse has always been deeply dichotomized" (Alexander, 2006, p. 125). Thus, when the idea of "rational deliberation" does appear, it has symbolic rather than actual value. In other words, to sway others, politicians and parties claim that their motives are reasonable and rational (see Table 13.1). Contrary to Habermas, Alexander sees these claims as *performative acts* rather than actual speech acts.

The second problem with this idea of getting rid of polarized conflict is that meaning is created through the basic process of inclusion and exclusion. That's how all categories work; one thing can only have meaning if it's not the other. A simple example is the guitar. The meaning of "guitar" requires exclusionary work: A guitar is not a violin, not a cello, not a tuba, and so on. To define something, to give it meaning, we draw boundaries or lines around it: "[I]t is their boundaries that allow us to perceive 'things' at all" (Zerubavel, 1991, p. 2). This is all the more true when we are constructing moralistic meanings, which is what democracy is based upon. Meanings that are important require the categories to be binary and the exclusions to be essentialized. Thus, "ideological polarization is normal; it emerges from the basic meaning-making structures of civil life" (Alexander, 2006, p. 129).

However, this essentialized antagonism must be balanced with common appeals to the universal elements of democratic solidarity. Each party, winners and losers both, must in the end express support of the other. Losers promise to support the winners' now democratically legitimated power, and winners give thanks and pledge to work with the other party in the democratic process. This, again, is one of those points where the balance between "social criticism and democratic integration" must be maintained. Legitimate criticism and party politics can only take place within democratic solidarity. "Antagonism at one level, in other words, can be interpreted as civility at another" (Alexander, 2006, p. 130).

Once an election is won, the politician obtains power, but even here civil society works to limit and direct that power. Party politics still has influence, as do communicative institutions. More directly, political power is circumscribed by the regulation of office. *Office* is a feature of bureaucratic management and as such carries universal understandings of how organizational authority ought to be managed and implemented. Look again at Table 13.1, and you'll see a number of elements consistent with Weber's ideal-type bureaucracy. The most obvious binary code here is "office vs. personality." Authority in a bureaucracy adheres to the office, not the person. The office of state governor (or professor), for instance, has clearly delineated authority no matter who holds the office. Other elements of the binary codes are clearly part of office as well. Actions of an officer are to be guided by written rules and not arbitrary personal likes and dislikes. All people are to be treated equally without preference to social group. Office, then, "institutionalizes a universalistic understanding of organizational authority" (Alexander, 2006, p. 133). Thus, not only are there explicit rules and regulations, but office also imposes moral or normative obligations on the incumbent to use power in specific ways. When civil society is strong, these expectations are expressed ritually, as in taking the oath of office. When the civil sphere has autonomy from the state, communicative institutions exercise surveillance of office and have at their disposal the binary codes of impurity.

The final regulative sphere is law. *Law* is multifaceted and has various functions in society, such as regulating dangerous behaviors and interorganizational relations. Law also has democratic functions. Unlike voting, party, and office, the civil sphere function of law is more clearly regulative than communicative, generally because law can impose legitimate sanctions (punishment). Yet even here there is communicative value for solidarity. In general, law translates the binary codes of the civil sphere and connects them in a real way with particularist and individual actions. The motives (why we do things) in the civil sphere are to be rational (purity), not irrational (impurity), and the relationships and institutions deliberative, not conspiratorial; rule regulated, not arbitrary; and impersonal, not personal. Thus, law isn't simply an external control that forces people to conform, but rather, it is seen as "an expression of their innate rationality, mediating between truth and mundane events" (Alexander, 2006, p. 60). Law, then, has moral qualities and effects.

Following Durkheim, Alexander (2006) argues that in "complex and differentiated societies, civil solidarity is sustained by legal rules that abstract away from particular endowments, traditions, and circumstances" (p. 172). Law is perhaps the clearest, most powerful civil space for creating social solidarity in contemporary society. Law not only expresses the moral, ethical foundation of society, but law also puts that foundation into practice in ritualized settings, such as "the arrest" and "the courtroom." The public is brought into this democratic drama through daily news reports. The news stories provide the public with continual opportunity to reaffirm their commitment to and belief in the moral code. At the same time, law is the clearest expression and guarantee of individuality. The most basic assumption of all forms of law is that the modern individual can be held responsible for his or her actions because it's assumed "that actors are in full possession of such civil faculties as rationality, sanity, and self-control" (p. 179). In no other arena is the reasoning power and free agency of the individual given such affirmation and freedom.

The basis of all democratic law is constitutional law. Constitutions are laws about laws; they determine the parameters within which law must operate in order to maintain solidarity. Constitutions are specifically concerned with restricting arbitrary actions by the state and instituting due process. As such, constitutional law is "particularly concerned with articulating the suspicions about others that mark the dark side of civil discourse" (Alexander, 2006, p. 165). Contract law is usually understood in purely instrumental-rational terms, with little if any relationship to civil society. Yet contract law, like constitutional law, enforces due process and defines such civil attributes as fairness, justice, negotiation, and reciprocity. Contracts thus are a significant mechanism for inserting the civil into the economic sphere.

Law also has an antidemocratic side that has two faces. The most blatant face is shown when the elite use money, power, and other resources to evade or bend the law to their own ends. This is a case where social power trumps civil power. The second face is less obvious and more insidious. This side evades civil society by internal attribution. As we've seen time and again, social and political systems assume a certain kind of person—these systems always make internal attributions. This antidemocratic face of the law "sees subjects of regulation as less than fully human" (p. 186), thus excluding them from civil society. Clear examples are Western colonialism, American racism, and patriarchy. Oppression of women and people of color was—and in some cases still is—legitimated by visualizing them as incapable of reason.

Underneath this oppression is something more basic, something that continues to threaten the civil sphere. Alexander argues that in back of denying full humanity to another is lack of empathy. Merriam-Webster defines *empathy* (n.d.) as the "projection of a subjective state into an object so that the object appears to be infused with it." To empathize, then, is to see another's personal experiences as the same as your own. It is to say, "You and I share the same experiences, ideas, and emotions. I see me in you." The *lack* of empathy in the absolute sense is the basis of colonialism, racism, and patriarchy. This is what Kai Erikson (1996) calls *social speciation:* "the process by which one people manages to neutralize the humanity of another" (p. 55). However, the problem of empathy for civil society doesn't end with social speciation. Both law making and law interpreting—the work of legislators and judges—are based on empathy, not only in the absolute sense, as with speciation, but also in the mundane sense of creating and interpreting civil law. If judges and legislators come from elite classes, then "their ability to apply principles of reciprocity may be undermined by their inability to experience solidarity with members of the lower class" (Alexander, 2006, p. 187). When this inability becomes typical, then for subjugated groups "there is no civil society . . . and the legal code seems to represent merely the external, coercive power of class, caste, or state" (p. 189).

Concepts and Theory: Civil Society Outcomes

One of the most important insights Alexander gives us about civil society is that it is based on contradictions and conflicts. It's actually the contradictions that open up the possibility of social justice. As we've seen, the foundation of democracy and the civil sphere is the binary codes. These codes don't simply imply conflict; they create conflict and contradiction by the manner in which they exist. Good is intrinsically and forever tied up with bad. Something can be rational only if it's possible to be irrational; equality can only be understood in terms of the leveling of hierarchy. To include is to simultaneously exclude. An identifiable group can only exist if it sets up boundaries that exclude others. To some of us, this may sound counterintuitive: Democracy accepts all people, no matter what their race, religion, gender, and so on. In thinking this way, we are right in so far as it pertains to the universal democratic principles and our belief in them. It's that belief that creates the solidarity necessary to achieve social justice. However, belief and democratic solidarity are only part of the process; they specifically belong to civil repair. Civil repair occurs after civil conflict, as we saw earlier with political parties.

Civil Repair and Social Movements

Besides the binary codes and the universal-particularist duality, there are three other sources of contradiction in civil society: space, time, and function. The discourse of modern democracy is always understood as relative to a territorial *space*. While there are imagined communities and virtual relationships, all actual societies exist in a place—it's the place that actualizes or makes concrete the idea we have of ourselves as a people, as a society. Place is fundamental to the process of inclusion and exclusion, the exercise of law, and the communication of culture. There are identifiable borders that mark where the law of France ends and the law of Spain begins. The rights that accrue to American citizens are clearly marked by territory. Nations, democratic and otherwise, exist in a place. This attachment to place creates *uncivilizing pressures.* Place becomes essentialized and the focus of ritual sacrifice: "This explains why, throughout the history of civil societies, war has been a sacred obligation; to wage war against members of other territories has been simultaneously a national and a civilizing task" (Alexander, 2006, p. 197).

Time works to essentialize civil society as well. Central to every democracy is a founding myth. We see this succinctly captured for the United States in Lincoln's Gettysburg Address: "Four score and seven years ago our fathers brought forth upon this continent, a new nation, conceived in Liberty, and dedicated to the proposition that all men are created equal." The founding myths become the focus of public ritual (like Independence Day) and convey a sense of essential differences in both the founding of a nation and its founders. Citizens tend to see something special, something transcendent, about the founders. They have come to represent pure categories of civil society—representative characters in our secular faith. The myths are employed to legitimate political stances in primordial ways, much like the practices of the early Christians in the Church. They convey a sense of "from the beginning it was thus." Because of their power to legitimate, the historical narratives are "natural" sites of civil strife.

Functional spheres within a social system also provide uncivilizing pressures. One of the defining characteristics of modern society is structural differentiation. Prior to modernity, social needs were met through a handful of institutions that overlapped with one another. Institutional overlap meant that status positions, norms, and values tended to be homogeneous and widespread in traditional society. On the other hand, modern social organization is characterized by intentional and functional differentiation. Differentiated structures mean that status positions, roles, norms, and values are institutionally distinct and not shared in common. These different arrays of social features compete with the solidarity of the civil sphere, and, as Alexander (2006) says, "These goods themselves possess a distinctive charisma" (p. 204). The values and goods of the noncivil spheres—such as money (economy), power (polity), and grace (religion)—are attractive. Further, they insert themselves into the very discourse of civil society: Money can be seen as representing moral goodness, while poverty may be viewed as the result of laziness, a decidedly anti-civil trait.

Alexander's point is that uncivilizing pressures are natural to civil society. These are, in fact, potential points of articulation, where the anti-civil inequalities provide the motivations and necessary culture and people to move democracy and social justice forward. To the degree that "the civil sphere exercises an independent force," people can be seen as having "dual memberships" (Alexander, 2006, p. 207), one foot in an anti-civil hierarchy and the other in the "universalizing solidarity that civil society implies" (p. 208). This is the only way that something like poverty becomes a "social" issue rather than an economic one. Appeals are made by or on behalf of those groups of individuals who fall on the lower end of one of these hierarchies, whether religious, economic, family, and so on. Appeals are based on the binary codes and expressed through communicative institutions; civil associations are created, and social movements are born. These social movements are movements of civil repair, times when democracy is infused with a sense of solidarity, an orientation "not only to the here and now but to the ideal, to the transcendent, to what [people] hope will be everlasting" (p. 3). Many social movements fail, but enough have succeeded that civil society has become institutionalized in varying degrees. Yet there is a danger for these groups and civil society at large. Groups will reference the binary codes and essentialize the democratic universals found there. They, like political parties, also essentialize their opponents. The danger is that in doing so, they may define the other as intrinsically poisonous to civil society. Examples include Marxian socialists who see capitalism and civil society as synonymous and some feminists who have "argued that civil societies are inherently patriarchal" (p. 209). In such cases, many have chosen to "exit [civil society] rather than to exercise voice" (p. 209).

The contradictions between the universal values of the civil sphere and the essential exclusions produced by time, space, and function are what drive social movements. Alexander's theory argues that modern social movements have always been related to the cultural structure in back of democracy. One of the main reasons the cultural component is important is that democratic states rest on and work through legitimated authority. Democratic citizens must believe their government is just and doing right. Social movements, then, attack that belief, arguing that society has failed to live up to its democratic universal ideals. In that way, social movements are translations "between the discourse of civil society and the institution-specific processes" that produce hierarchical inequities (Alexander, 2006, p. 233). Politics, especially in postindustrial societies, is a struggle over meaning and representation. The conflicts that social movements express aren't simply about the unequal distribution of scarce resources. "They are about *who will be what,* and for how long" (p. 233, emphasis added). It is always about the right to be fully human.

The success of social movements depends on a certain level of the institutionalization of civil society. The right to gather privately must be protected; the regulative institutions of voting, parties, voluntary organizations, and law must be assured; and the communicative institutions must be free of elite control and must have created symbolic values around such civil attitudes as trust, autonomy, cooperation, and so on. Social movements must use the mass media to persuade others to the universal legitimacy of their cause. In doing so, they assume and develop a wider sense of community. They must claim to represent this wider community and its universal values, and they must speak directly to this societal community on behalf of particular interests. Social movements must also work to create and enforce law, "which could enforce universalistic civil against oligarchic power" (Alexander, 2006, p. 229).

Justice and Incorporating the Other

The intent of democracy, solidarity, and social movements is justice. *Justice,* like every element in contemporary democratic society, isn't a specified object; it isn't a goal that can be achieved once and for all. Justice is a process that exists between the abstract idea of universal brotherhood and the concrete lived reality of particularized otherhood. There are dangers at either extreme. The problem of restricting justice to the high realm of morality is that it discounts or ignores the everyday world of meaningful existence, which depends on discrimination, and discussions of justice need to be based on truly democratic morals that include identity and meaning. In other words, the abstract ideals of solidarity only become meaningful and relevant in relation to particular groups and individuals in particular times and places—all of which, as we've seen, are intrinsically uncivilizing. Thus, adhering to radical universalism is a view from nowhere that in the end disables the civil sphere.

The other extreme—identifying justice with group-specific goals (dogmatic particularism)—is also crippling to civil society. The first problem is that this degree of specificity is in effect an expression of social, not civil, power. Some of these practices can be very obvious, such as a previously disenfranchised group (like women or blacks) that wants to exclude other particular groups (such as gays and lesbians) from equal civil rights. Some of what happens at this extreme is less obvious. For example, most public universities and businesses have diversity policies, and many have task forces charged with promoting diversity. These diversity issues are of course mandated by and accountable to law. Because rational-legal authority is supreme in contemporary society, accountability to the law is usually expressed in numbers. The broader the definition of diversity, the more difficult or complex will be the accounting. As a result, most diversity policies are particularistic, including only gender and racial minorities.

Real justice—democratic justice—will always include possibilities of inclusion and exclusion, emancipation and oppression. "The tension between the transcendent and the particular cannot be avoided" (Alexander, 2006, p. 22). It's imperative that we understand the restless and partial nature of justice. To believe that justice has been achieved is no more than accepting and making real the dogmatic beliefs that are actually imposed by the powerful in society, those who are already the recipients and holders of justice. To believe only in the lofty ideals of universal brotherhood is to fail to engage in the messy business of particularized interests and the creation of meaningful lives. It simply isn't realistic to "accept everybody" on general grounds, as any honest look at our world and history will reveal. There are vested interests and questions of practice that will inevitably be addressed. In addition, the binary nature of the codes themselves prevents absolute fulfillment.

This implies that the project of democracy is perpetually unfinished; yet a living democracy makes continual steps toward universal inclusion. According to Alexander, this movement toward universal inclusion has thus far gone through three phases: assimilation, hyphenation, and multiculturalism. The process of *assimilation* is what is meant when America is characterized as a melting pot. All the important differences in identity are assimilated in one general identity. *Hyphenation* is a way of creating cultural identities that brings two or more types of identity together, like Mexican-American. *Multiculturalism* is unique in that this belief system doesn't attempt to form single identities out of many; multiculturalism values different and distinct identities simply because of their diversity.

Note that all these modes can exist together, but which is most prominent is historically specific. The most important difference lies between assimilation and hyphenation on one hand and multiculturalism on the other. In both assimilation and hyphenation, differences between in- and out-groups are seen as primordial or essential. In other words, people are seen as different because it's believed that they actually *are* different. These inherent differences are hierarchical. Under assimilation and hyphenation, it is still better to be white than black, male than female, and heterosexual rather than homosexual. In both assimilation and hyphenation, inclusion into the main group occurs as the essential qualities of difference are shed and the person in one way or another becomes more like the dominant group. In these inclusion movements, the dominant group's nature is seen as more civilized, and better in some real way.

Multiculturalism is distinct because difference itself becomes valued. Rather than differences being rejected automatically, in- and out-group members struggle to "resignify and experience" the differences (Alexander, 2006, p. 451). Thus, differences aren't automatically valued hierarchically. It isn't necessarily better to be white than black, or heterosexual than homosexual, for example. There is still struggle, however. Some groups or group characteristics may be seen as too different and thus stigmatized, which, of course, sets up another binary issue of exclusion. In multiculturalism, the universal value of human nature is seen as diverse, rather than being defined by the main group's identity. In multiculturalism, incorporation and social solidarity are achievements of diversity rather than inclusion. The differences between groups of people "become reinterpreted as representing variations on the sacred quality of civility" (Alexander, 2006, p. 452). Rather than the recognition of difference leading to denigration and inhibition, as with assimilation and hyphenation, multiculturalism leads to a culture of authenticity that expands and shares cultural identities.

Summary

- Generally speaking, civil society is a sphere that was generated by the idea of natural rights and constitutional law. This sphere is the political arena that negotiates the relationship between citizens and the state in democratic societies. The way civil society works is specific to different kinds of structural arrangements and diversity. In structurally differentiated, socially diverse societies, civil society becomes an open-ended project that is energized by the contradictions between cultural universals and particularist interests. Civil society is held together by democratic solidarity, a transcendent sense of being part of something larger and more important than the group itself, while at the same time honoring the individuality that makes each person unique.

- The core of civil society is made up of binary codes delineating civil/non-civil motives, relationships, and institutions. People and groups in a democratic society are categorized as pure and impure, included and excluded, based on the codes. The binary nature of the codes creates cultural tensions and provides motivational energy for activity in the civil sphere.

- Communicative and regulative institutions bound the civil sphere. Communicative institutions in particular express the binary codes through mass media, public opinion, and civil associations. Thus, communicative institutions actualize the codes and create the structures of feeling, solidarity, that unites a diverse society. Regulative institutions also bound the civil sphere, specifically voting, political parties, office, and law. Where communicative institutions persuade, regulative institutions use power to assure and create civil, democratic processes.

- Civil society also remains a project due to the essentializing influences of time, space, and function. The universals of the civil sphere must be actualized in real, concrete situations: in a specific place, at a specific time. Yet time and space inherently produce uncivilizing pressures: nationalistic identities and narratives that demand defense at any cost. The differentiation of function also creates uncivilizing pressures. The hierarchies of class, politics, religion, family, and so on are attractive. As people are drawn to money, power, and belief, they create particularized interests that struggle with the universal beliefs undergirding modern democracy.

- The tensions created by the binary codes and time, space, and function create opportunities for social movements. Because modern states work through legitimacy, social movements must wage a cultural war. Thus, at their core, all social movements express the universal beliefs found in the binary codes.

TAKING THE PERSPECTIVE: A STRONG PROGRAM IN CULTURAL SOCIOLOGY

Alexander is a founder and director at Yale University's Center for Cultural Sociology. The Center and its work are generally guided by Alexander's *strong program in cultural sociology*. There are three elements to it. First, *culture needs to be understood meaningfully*. More than any other species on the planet, humans are oriented toward meaning. This meaning is never fixed or determined; it must be interpreted. If something is determined, interpretation isn't needed. You don't need to interpret an object falling on your head; it's determined by the law of gravity. In contrast, the "American flag" has to be interpreted because its meaning varies. Cultural sociology thus places importance on interpretation. Alexander argues that for "most of its history, sociology . . . has suffered from a numbness toward meaning" (Alexander & Smith, 2001, p. 138). While Parsons emphasized culture, his theory did not incorporate meaning, in this sense of the word. In order to give meaning its proper place, Alexander advocates the use of what's called thick descriptions. *Thick descriptions* are minute descriptions of a social phenomenon—they provide the tiniest details of human interaction.

The second element in a strong program is that the relationships that culture has to other social factors need to be *analytically bracketed*. When we bracket something analytically, we

(Continued)

(Continued)

just look at how it works all by itself. Alexander isn't saying that culture is really separate; like Parsons, he sees all subsystems as nested in one another. However, if we tried to look at all the subsystems together, we would miss how each works individually, and this is particularly important for culture. Many sociologists argue that culture is simply a by-product, something that comes out of more fundamental and real processes like social organization and power. Alexander, however, is arguing that *culture is an autonomous sphere* and can act independently because it is structured. Remember our basic definition of structure, that it is made up of explicit connections that impose themselves on other things, thus creating recognizable patterns. Alexander is arguing that culture has an intrinsic structure that operates as an independent variable with "relative autonomy in shaping actions and institutions, providing inputs every bit as vital as more material or instrumental forces" (Alexander & Smith, 2001, p. 136).

The third characteristic of a strong program in cultural sociology is the *explication of causal paths and mechanisms* that explain precisely how meaning (characteristic 1) and the structure of culture (characteristic 2) relate. As an illustration, think of the structured cultural value of education. Alexander always understands such things as coded in binary oppositions; kind of like the idea of good and bad, one can't exist without the other. For the value of education we could say that it is formed by <well-informed and reasonable> versus <ignorant and dogmatic>. That's the cultural structure for our example. Another part of this illustration is you. What does education mean to you? Meaning is subjective, so what education means to you may be something different from what it means to someone else. The third part of this example is the university you attend. That organization links you (meaning) to the cultural value of education (structure). The causal paths and mechanisms thus form bridges between the structure and meaning of culture. These causal mechanisms take the form of people, organizations, and institutions. Alexander uses this model for a strong program in cultural sociology to provide scaffolding for his theory of democracy in modern society. He argues that, by definition, modern systems are not only complex and differentiated, as Spencer and Parsons tell us, but they are also specifically democratic.

BUILDING YOUR THEORY TOOLBOX

- Using two additional sources, define democracy.

- Write a 250-word synopsis of the strong program in cultural sociology. I encourage you to think about the relationship between it and neo-functionalism.

- After reading and understanding this chapter, you should be able to define the following terms theoretically: civil sphere, civil society, non-civil spheres, justice solidarity, democracy, tradition of Thrasymachus, particularism-universalism, discourse, binary codes, communicative institutions, regulative institutions, social and civil power, essentialism, civil repair, time, space, function, social movements, pathways to incorporation, neo-functionalism, a strong program in cultural sociology.

- After reading and understanding this chapter, you should be able to answer the following questions (remembering to answer them theoretically):

  o Explain how civil society is created through communicative and regulative institutions. Be sure to explain what each factor—fictional media, public opinion, office, law, and so on—contributes to the project.

  o Explain how civil society is a project. What are dogmatic particularism and radical universalism? What does the project nature of civil society imply about radical universalism and dogmatic particularism?

  o What factors work to prevent mass media from becoming simple expressions of the elite?

  o How do time, space, and function work to essentialize universal, democratic discourse?

  o Explain the characteristics of social solidarity in contemporary society and how it works to maintain civil society.

  o Upon what features of civil society do social movements depend? In Alexander's theory, what must social movements do to succeed?

  o How do justice and inclusion work in contemporary civil society?

Learning More—Primary Sources

- Jeffrey C. Alexander, *The Civil Sphere,* Oxford, 2006.

- Jeffrey C. Alexander, *The Meanings of Social Life,* Oxford, 2003.

- Jeffrey C. Alexander, *The Performance of Politics: Obama's Victory and the Democratic Struggle for Power,* Oxford, 2010.

Engaging the World

- Given Alexander's definition of democracy, what are the implications of civil society in your life? How would you describe your relationship with solidarity and social justice?

- Explain Alexander's idea of multiculturalism, paying specific attention to its "culture of authenticity that expands and shares cultural identities." What implications does Alexander's idea of multiculturalism have for you? On a scale of 1–10, how would you rate yourself, with 10 representing the highest value of multiculturalism? Provide specific examples of *practices* in your life.

(Continued)

(Continued)

Weaving the Threads

- Compare and contrast Habermas and Alexander on capitalism. Based on their work, write an argument that explains how capitalism both influences and is influenced by civil society.

- Compare and contrast critical theory and a strong program in cultural sociology. Which do you think is the more powerful or accurate approach? Justify your answer.

- Compare and contrast Castells's and Alexander's arguments about civil society and democracy. Can these two theories be brought together to give us a fuller understanding of how these factors work in contemporary society?

CHAPTER 14

Runaway Modernity

Anthony Giddens

Source: Courtesy of Anthony Giddens.

The Big Picture: Social Ontology

Ontology, or metaphysics, is the branch of philosophy that is concerned with the nature of existence. One of the basic ideas for this philosophy is that things don't simply exist; things exist *as* something. A rock, for example, appears to exist differently from a bobcat. For non-philosophers, this question might appear silly, until you realize that one of the major ontological or metaphysical issues is the existence of God. Does God exist? If so, what does it mean to exist as God? Or, what is the ontological source for existing as God? Tied up with the God question is the problem of human existence. In fact, a well-known philosopher, Martin Heidegger (1927/1996), wrote that humans are "distinguished by the fact that in its being this being is concerned *about* its very being. . . . *Understanding of being is itself a determination of being of Da-sein*" (p. 10). *Da-sein* (pronounced "dah-zine") is Heidegger's German expression that literally means "being there." One of the things he is saying is that *understanding* existence is at the very core of being.

Sociologists aren't usually concerned with such weighty issues. In one of sociology's more famous attempts at understanding reality, Berger and Luckmann (1966) tell us that philosophers are obligated to search out the ultimate status of anything that exists; by whatever methods, the philosopher "will inquire into the ontological and epistemological status" of knowledge and reality (p. 2). "Needless to say," they continue, "the sociologist is in no position to supply answers to these questions" (pp. 2–3). In the ultimate sense, they are correct. Sociologists don't have the tools to decide whether or not God exists. Sociologists do, however, either make assumptions or arguments about the existence or ontology of society.

As I pointed out in Chapter 1, in order to study society positivistically, sociologists must assume that society has empirical, objective existence. The most important argument for the objective existence of society came from Émile Durkheim (1895/1938), who argued that society exists as a fact "external to the individual, and endowed with a power of coercion, by reason of which they control him" (p. 3). Society, Durkheim (1912/1995) claimed, "is a reality *sui generis*" (p. 15)—a reality unto itself—that "enjoys such great independence that it sometimes plays about in forms that have no aim or utility of any kind, but only for the pleasure of affirming itself" (p. 426). While the last statement is somewhat whimsical, the idea is basic scientific sociological doctrine: Society exists empirically and operates according to lawlike principles that we can discover, measure, and use to predict human action. An implication of this standard is that society acts on its own accord, which is precisely the point Durkheim was making.

But not all sociologists agree with this assumption or argument. For instance, symbolic interactionists (Chapter 3) argue that approaching society as a thing that can be measured is wrongheaded and blinds us to what is actually happening. For Blumer, society doesn't coerce us—society is better seen as an emergent phenomenon made up of social interactions and joint actions that are the direct result of people making situationally specific choices. Erving Goffman (Chapter 4) explains that the presentation of self is the main force that patterns people's behaviors, not the coercive power of structure. In Chapter 5, Harold Garfinkel asserts that the appearance of "society" is an achievement. It's the result of people using common, everyday methods to make social situations meaningful and accountable. In truth, then, the ontology of society is a significant issue for sociologists; it determines what we see, what and how we measure, and the claims we can make about society. Anthony Giddens is one of the few sociologists who make their ontology explicit—in doing so, he'll introduce us to a number of new terms.

You may have noticed a dualism in my discussion of society. There's the one side that claims that social structures exist objectively and exercise independent influence on people. The other side argues that social structures are reifications—ideas that appear real—and people are the only acting agents. For Giddens, society is more complex than either approach can capture. Giddens is going to ask us to expand our minds past the dualisms that have dominated Western thought since René Descartes. Along with his famous dictum, "I think, therefore I am," Descartes firmly divided existence into two parts: the subjective (inner) and objective (outer) worlds. Giddens is going to ask us to let go of the dualist mind-set and to think of structure and agency existing at the same moment, in the same act. While not immediately apparent, Giddens's social ontology has implications for the projects of modernity.

As we've seen, modernity began as a time when human beings believed they could control the physical and social worlds for the betterment of humankind. We've also seen, and are aware from simply living in this age, that there are problems, such as race, class, and gender. Yet Giddens takes us on another path, proposing that the idea of modernity itself contains intrinsic contradictions that make it impossible to fulfill its own reason for existence. According to Giddens (1990), modernity is a juggernaut, "a runaway engine of enormous power which, collectively as human beings, we can drive to some extent but which also threatens to rush out of our control and which could rend itself asunder" (p. 139). The word *juggernaut* comes from the Hindi word *Jagannātha,* which refers to a representation of the god Vishnu or Krishna—the lord of the universe. Every year, the god's image would be paraded down the streets amid crowds of the faithful, dancing and playing drums and cymbals. It's thought that at times believers would throw themselves under the wheels of the massive cart, to be crushed to death in a bid for early salvation. A juggernaut, then, is an irresistible force that demands blind devotion and sacrifice.

This image of an irresistible force conjures up the thrilling ride of the roller coaster, with its twin sensations of excitement and danger, but the juggernaut of modernity isn't as controllable or predictable as a roller coaster. Here we can see a chief difference between Giddens and Habermas: For Habermas, rational control is central to modernity and imminently possible, inherent in the very act of communication; however, for Giddens, modernity is almost by definition out of control. The intent of modernity is progress—but the effect of modernity is the creation of mechanisms and processes that become a runaway engine of change. And we, like the devotees of *Jagannātha,* are drawn to modernity's power and promise.

The ride is by no means wholly unpleasant or unrewarding; it can often be exhilarating and charged with hopeful anticipation. But, so long as the institutions of modernity endure, we shall never be able to control completely either the path or the pace of the journey. In turn, we shall never be able to feel entirely secure, because the terrain across which it runs is fraught with risks of high consequence. (Giddens, 1990, p. 139)

THEORIST'S DIGEST

Brief Biography

Anthony Giddens was born on January 18, 1938, in Edmonton, England. He received his undergraduate degree with honors from Hull University in 1959, studying sociology and psychology. Giddens did his master's work at the London School of Economics, finishing his thesis on the sociology of sport in 1961. From then until the early 1970s, Giddens lectured at various universities including the University of Leicester, Simon Fraser University, the University of California at Los Angeles, and Cambridge. Giddens finished his doctoral work at Cambridge in 1976. He remained there through 1996, during which time he served as dean of Social and Political Sciences. In 1997, Giddens was appointed director of the London School of Economics and Political Science. Giddens is the author of some 34 books that have been translated into over 20 languages. Giddens is also a member of the Advisory Council of the Institute for Public Policy Research (London) and has served as advisor to British Prime Minister Tony Blair.

Central Sociological Questions

Giddens is a political sociologist, driven by both political questions and political involvement. While his early work certainly contained a typical Marxian interest in class, his later work is much more concerned with the political ramifications of globalization and what he characterizes as the juggernaut of modernity or the runaway world. Given the juggernaut of modernity, he asks, how are interactions and behaviors patterned over time? How can people become politically involved? In order to answer those questions, Giddens feels one must first understand the essence of society. In this, Giddens seeks an ontology of the social world: What kinds of things go into the making of society? Precisely how does it exist?

Simply Stated

Society is not made up of objective structures that determine and pattern action across time and space. Rather, because the human world is a constructed world, people are psychologically motivated to routinize their behaviors and to see them as belonging in specific social places. In traditional society, these were assured through kinship, community, and religion. But modern society has rendered those ineffectual through radical reflexivity, the emptying of time and space, disembedding of social relationships, and globalization. The result is that the certitude of traditional society has been replaced with tenuous social relations, individualized and uncertain projects of self-actualization, and lifestyle politics rather than the politics of emancipation.

Key Ideas

Structuration theory, duality of structure, social structures, normative rules, signification codes, authoritative resources, allocative resources, time–space distanciation, modalities of structuration, domination, institutional orders, reflexive monitoring, rationalization of action, discursive consciousness, practical consciousness, routinization, regionalization, ontological security, radical reflexivity, separation of time and space, disembedding mechanisms, symbolic tokens, expert systems, reflexive project of the self, bodily regimes, organization of sensuality, pure relationships, emancipatory politics, life politics, mediated experiences

Concepts and Theory: The Reality of Society

I usually address the perspective of the theorist later in the chapter, but with Giddens, I need to put it first. In order to understand the power of what Giddens says about modernity, we have to understand his perspective first. We've seen that the social project of modernity is based on the existence of two factors: society and free agents. In order to use science to understand and guide society, society must exist as an object capable of being studied and discovered. And in order to guide society through democracy, citizens had to have the power of reason and the ability to make free choices. We have come across critiques of these issues already, but Giddens proceeds in a different direction. His grasp of modernity is based on a distinct understanding of what society is and how people can affect it. He also reformulates the problem of social order. We have to comprehend these issues before we can appreciate his theory of modernity. His understanding of society and social actors is called **structuration theory**.

The Way Society Exists

Here's the simple version: Society doesn't exist as objective structures; rather, it is continually built or structured by reflexive social actors (people). Giddens draws this idea from ethnomethodology (Chapter 5). The important thing to remember is that *actors are reflexive.* Reflexive simply means the ability to turn back on itself; related words include reflection and introspection. Humans are reflexive to a degree that no other animal reaches. Anytime you think about yourself or think about what you're doing, you're being reflexive. This simple idea has tremendous implications. First, because human beings construct their own environment, we are in many ways reflective of that environment. Most animals are connected to their natural environment in profound ways; for this reason, if you put an animal in an environment that is significantly different from the one it is suited for, it will die. The human environment is less natural and more social and cultural, and we reflect that. This is why humans from different times and cultures can be so different one from another. Second, the self you "have" and experience is a reflexive construction (Chapter 3).

A third implication, and one that is salient here, is that we are generally aware of what we are doing and we are quite purposeful in that awareness. Let's use running as an example. I run, and my dog runs. But if you ask what I'm doing, I can tell you that I'm "running a race" or "training for a marathon." Intrinsic in our actions is the reflexive component of doing things in such a way as to be recognizable as such a thing. "Running a race" is organized differently from "training for a marathon," though in both cases I'm running. Obviously, if you ask my dog what's he doing, you won't get an answer, but this inability isn't simply an issue of language. My dog is not only incapable of *saying* "I'm training for a marathon," but he is also incapable of *doing* such a thing. He can't organize his actions in just such a way that the behaviors would be seen as "training." My dog may run out of a sense of joy or fear, but in neither case does he orchestrate his running so that it would *convey the meaning* of joy or fear. Humans, on the other hand, put together specific practical actions that are intended to render a situation meaningful. This is what Harold Garfinkel (Chapter 5) means when he says situations are *accountable*. The important thing that Giddens wants us to see is that there aren't any objective social structures forcing us to act in specific ways. Society, for Giddens and Garfinkel, doesn't exist outside of accountable situations.

Step 1: Understanding Two Things at Once

Like Bourdieu, Giddens argues that the subject–object divide (or agent–structure) is a false dichotomy, created to explain away the complexity of human practice. Giddens (1986) says, "Human social activities, like some self-reproducing items in nature, are recursive" (p. 2). It's like the chicken-and-egg question, which in some ways is a silly one. When you have the egg, you have the chicken. They are one and the same, just in different phases. So, to follow the analogy, it's like this: Social actors produce social reality, but the mere fact that you have "social actors" presumes an already existing social world. The primary insight of Giddens's structuration theory is that social structures and agency are recursively and reflexively produced: They are continuously brought into existence at the same moment through the same behaviors. Rather than seeing structure and agency as a dualism, as two mutually exclusive elements, Giddens proposes a duality—two analytically distinguishable parts of the same thing. The *duality of structure* indicates that structure is both the medium and the outcome of the social activity or conduct that it reflexively organizes.

"This is a difficult concept to understand, so let me give you an example." And I just did. I put the first sentence of this paragraph in quotation marks because it is our example. Anytime we write or speak a sentence, we do a couple of things. First, and most obviously, we create the sentence. In order to put together a sentence, we have to follow the rules. If we don't, the sentence won't make any sense and it won't really be a sentence. Thus, in order to exist as a sentence, the line of words must be formed according to the rules. The second and less obvious thing we do is this: We recreate the rules through which the sentence was made in the first place.

You might say, "Wait a minute. The rules existed before the sentence." Did they? You learned the rules in school, and they are found in English grammar texts, right? In fact, we often refer to the grades before high school as "grammar school" because that's where you learn the rules of grammar. But is that really where you learned the rules? If it was, it would imply that you couldn't form a sentence before reaching that point in school. But the fact is you could form sentences well before you "learned the rules"; further, studies have shown that 5- and 6-year-olds make use of very complex grammars. In truth, the rules you learned in school are the rules you already knew. The difference is that the rules found in grammar texts are formalized interpretations of the rules that already exist in the language itself; grammars and dictionaries are produced by academics based on the study of language. Note that grammarians study the language to discover the rules—the rules are already there in the language. The rules for making the sentence are in the sentence itself—the expression and the structure are created in the same moment. According to Giddens, the same is true about social agents and structures.

Step 2: The Stuff of Social Structures

Here, Giddens simply says that social structures aren't things that exist apart from people; social structures exist in the ways that people use rules and resources. There are two kinds of rules: normative rules and codes of signification. Keep in mind that in both cases these "rules" are fluidly embedded in social practices. They don't exist abstractly or independently. Giddens (1986) also notes that rules may be consistently or rarely invoked, tacit or discursive, informal or formal, and weakly or strongly sanctioned. You should be familiar with *normative rules*—they are rules that govern behavior, such as the norm against littering. But signification codes require a bit of explanation.

Signification codes are rules through which meaning is produced. In our sentence illustration earlier, the signification code is lodged in the practices of speaking and writing. One example of the consequence of these codes or rules is the rhetoric of political spin doctors. Spin doctors want to guide us so that we interpret events in a specific manner; but in doing so they must abide by generally accepted rules of interpretation. If they don't, then chances are good that we won't buy their "spin." It's important to mention that these rules are historically and culturally specific. That's why interpretations can change over time.

In addition to the two types of rules, there are also two kinds of resources used in structuration: authoritative and allocative. *Authoritative resources* are made up of such things as techniques or technologies of management, organizational position, and expert knowledge. *Allocative resources* come from the control of material goods or the material world. Resources, then, involve the control of people and supplies.

I've pictured the duality of structure in Figure 14.1. As we've seen, Giddens argues that structure and agency are mutually formed in the same act. Just as in our sentence example, the rules and resources that are used in social encounters both create and are found in the interaction and structure. The act of social co-presence is possible only through the use of social rules and resources—and the rules and resources exist only in the act of social co-presence. Thus, structure and agency are mutually constructed through the use of the exact same rules and resources, as noted by all the two-headed arrows in the figure.

Figure 14.1 Duality of Structure

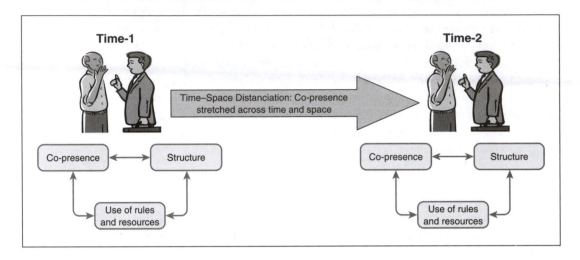

Figure 14.1 Duality of Structure

Step 3: Expressing Structure and Creating Social Order

There are two important things to see in this step. First, Giddens talks about the problem of social order, which Parsons and Garfinkel were concerned about, as really just a problem of time and space. If we're all together at once in one place, it's easy to see how we make sure everybody acts together. The problem of order comes about when different interactions are separate either as a result of geographic space or time. Notice the large arrow linking the two sets of interactions in Figure 14.1. The arrow indicates how behaviors and encounters are patterned over time. Giddens (1986) rephrases the problem of patterning action in terms of **time–space distanciation:** "The fundamental question of social theory . . . is to explicate how the limitations of individual 'presence' are transcended by the 'stretching' of social relations across time and space" (p. 35). The idea of time–space distanciation refers to the ways in which physical co-presence is stretched through time and space. This is a fairly unique and graphic way of thinking about patterning behaviors. We can think of Giddens's idea as an analogy: If you've ever played with Silly Putty or bubble gum by stretching it out, then you can see what he is talking about. What this analogy implies is that the interactions at Time-1 and Time-2 appear patterned because they are made out of the same materials that are stretched out over time and space.

The second thing Giddens wants us to see here is his answer to the question in the quote above: How are human relations stretched across time and space? His answer is found in his idea of **modalities of structuration.** The word *modality* is related to the word *mode,* which refers to a form or pattern of expression, as in someone's mode of dress or behavior. For example, in writing this book, I'm currently in my academic mode. Modalities of structuration, then, are simply ways in which rules and resources are knowingly used by people in interactions.

I've illustrated a bit of what Giddens is getting at in Figure 14.2. Notice that there are three elements in the circle: social practices, modalities, and structures. Modalities of structuration are ways in which structure and practice (or agency) are expressed. I've indicated that relationship by the use of overlapping diamonds. In a loose way, we can think of structures as the music itself; the modalities as the mode of reproduction, as in analog or digital; and the social practices as the musician. As you can see, Giddens gives us three modalities or modes of expression (interpretive schemes, facilities, and norms), corresponding on the one hand to three social practices (communication, power, and sanctions), and on the other to structures (signification, domination, and legitimation).

This isn't as complicated as it might seem. Let's use the example of you talking to your professor in class. Let's say that in this conversation, you refuse to take the test that he or she has scheduled. The professor reacts by telling you that you will fail the course if you don't take the test. What just happened? You can break it down using Giddens's modalities of structuration, following the model in Figure 14.2. First, there were actual social practices that involved communication and sanctions. Your communication was interpreted using a scheme that both you and your professor know. For convenience sake, let's call this scheme "meanings in educational settings." You know this interpretive scheme because it is part of the general signification structure of this society at the beginning of the twenty-first century. Second, the professor invoked sanctions based on norms of classroom behavior. Again, you both know these norms because they are part of the legitimation structure of this society.

Figure 14.2   Modalities of Structuration

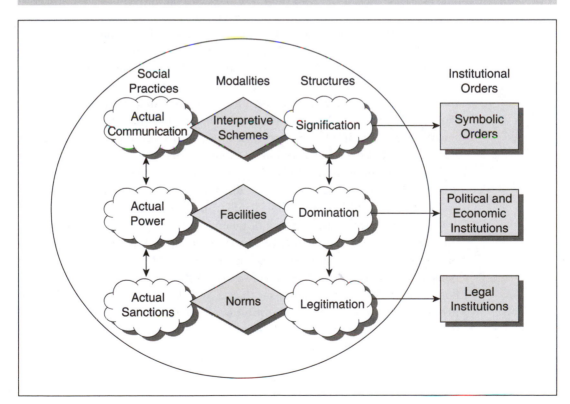

I'm sure you were able to follow this discussion through the model without any difficulty. I'm also sure that you didn't have trouble with any of the phrases I used in this explanation. Things like "society at the beginning of the twenty-first century" sound reasonable and familiar. But remember, the first principle of structuration theory is duality, not dualism. So when we use the term *society* or *structure,* we are not talking about something separate from social practices. Like our sentence illustration, the actual conversation between you and the professor, and the interpretive schemes and the structure of signification, all come into existence at the same moment. Apart from signification and interpretation, communication can't exist; likewise, without actual communication, interpretation and signification can't exist. Obviously, the same is true for the sanctions that the professor invoked.

In terms of Giddens's definition of structure as rules and resources, signification and legitimation are more closely tied to rules, and domination is more linked to resources (facilities). *Domination* is expressed as actual power through the facilities of authoritative and allocative resources. For example, part of the way the actual power of the university over me as a professor is expressed is through the facilities of classroom space, computer and Internet access, and so forth. By encircling all these elements together and by using two-headed arrows, I'm indicating that all these processes—the social practices, modalities, and structures—are reflexive and recursive. That is, they mutually and continuously influence one another.

Part of what I want you to see in Figure 14.2 is the connectedness of all social practices, modalities, and structures. They are all tied up together and expressed and produced in the same moment. Further, the recursive and interpenetrated nature of these facets of social life is what Giddens means by institutionalization, or the stretching out of co-presence across time and space. Remember, human life is ongoing. The process that I've placed a circle around in Figure 14.2 works like a ball that just keeps rolling downhill. It is this continuity of recursive practices and structures that stretches interactions across time and space. Comparing Figure 14.1 and Figure 14.2, we can think of the two men talking as moments in which we stopped the ball and looked inside. The arrow between the two sets of interactions depicts the movement of the ball between those two moments.

There's one other thing that we need to notice from Figure 14.2: All of this action of institutionalization results in different *institutional orders.* While there are some terms in there that look familiar, like "economic institutions," they aren't the same as we usually think of them. Many sociologists think of institutions as substantive and distinct (or "differentiated," in functionalist terms). In other words, most sociologists treat institutions as if they are real, separate objects with independent effects. However, Giddens is saying that institutions don't exist as substantive things or objects and they aren't truly separate and distinct. Notice that the different institutional orders are all made from the same fabric; it's just cut or put together differently in each case. They all draw from the same structures (rules and resources) of signification (S), domination (D), and legitimation (L), but emphasizing one of the elements over the others produces different kinds of institutional orders.

Making Society and Hiding It

As we've seen, the situationalists in Chapters 3, 4, and 5 all argue that we actually create society in face-to-face interactions. Giddens agrees, but goes deeper behind the scenes to see what's going on inside us as we achieve social order and reality. Some of it we're aware of, but probably not in the way you think. And some of it works below the level of our awareness. Giddens argues that there are three important things going on in interactions: reflexive monitoring of action, rationalization of action, and motivation for action. Giddens thinks of these tasks as being "stratified," or as having different levels of awareness. The behavior that we're most aware of is *reflexive monitoring*. In order to interact with one another, people must watch the behaviors of other people, monitor the flow of the conversation, and keep track of their own actions. As part of this routine accomplishment, we can also provide reasons for what we do; that is, we can provide a rationalization for our own actions.

In talking about *rationalization of action,* Giddens makes a distinction between discursive and practical consciousness. The word *discursive* is related to discourse or conversation. But it has a deeper meaning as well: It's a discourse marked by analytical reasoning. So, *discursive consciousness* refers to the ability to give a reasoned verbal account of our actions. It's what we know and can express about social practices and situations. This consciousness is clearly linked to reflexive monitoring of the encounter and the rationalization of action—discursive consciousness is our awareness of these two.

Practical consciousness refers to the knowledge that we have about how to exist and behave socially. However, people can't verbally express this knowledge. Social situations and practices are extremely complex, according to Giddens; they thus require a vast and nuanced base of knowledge, and we have to act more by intuition than by rational thought. This idea isn't as difficult as it might seem. We can think of the ability to perform an opening ritual ("Hey, how's it going?") as part of this practical consciousness. People know *how* to perform an opening ritual, but most people can't rationally explain *why* they do it.

There's an important point to note about discursive and practical consciousnesses: They aren't necessarily linked. At first glance, it might appear that discursive consciousness is our ability to explain what practical consciousness tells us to do. But notice what I said above about practical consciousness: "People can't verbally express this knowledge." So, discursive consciousness (the explanation) isn't necessarily associated in any real way with practical consciousness (the actions). We know how to act and we know how to explain our action, but both of these issues are part of the social interaction, not part of the unconscious motivations of the actor.

Unconscious Motivation

Practical consciousness is bound up with the production of routine. It's like driving a car or riding a bicycle; most of what is involved is done out of habit or practical consciousness. In the same way, most of what we do socially on a daily basis is routine.

Routinization "is a fundamental concept in structuration theory" (Giddens 1986, p. xxii) and refers to the process through which the activities of day-to-day life become habitual and taken for granted. Routinization, then, is a primary way in which face-to-face interactions are stretched across time and space (Figure 14.1). Or, put another way, routinization is one of the main ways through which the modalities of structuration are institutionalized (Figure 14.2). Part of the way we routinize activities is through *regionalization,* which is the zoning of time and space in relation to routinized social practices. In other words, because we divide physical space up, we can more easily routinize our behaviors. Thus, certain kinds of social practices occur in specific places and times. Regionalization varies by form, character, duration, and span.

The form of the region is given in terms of the kinds of barriers or boundaries that are used to section it off from other regions. The form allows greater or lesser possible levels of co-presence. When you stop and talk with someone in the hallway, there is a symbolic boundary around the two of you that is fairly permeable; it is very possible that others could join in. However, when you go into the men's or women's restroom, there is a physical and symbolic barrier that explicitly limits the possibility of co-presence.

The character of the region references the kind of social practices that can typically take place within a region. For example, people have lived in houses for centuries, but the character of the house has changed over time. In agrarian societies, the home was the center of the economy, government, and family; but in modern capitalist societies, the home is the exclusive domain of family and is thus private rather than public.

The duration and span of the region refer to the amount of geographic space and to the length or kind of time. Certain regions are usually available for social practices only during certain parts of the day or for specific lengths of time; the bedroom is an example in the sense that it is usually associated with "sleep time." Regions also span across space in varying degrees. For example, a coliseum gives unique opportunities for co-presence and social activities when compared to an airplane.

We come now to what actually patterns structuration and time–space distanciation—Giddens calls it **ontological security.** As we've seen, the word *ontology* refers to existence, so ontological security is simply being secure in the reality we've created. But even though that sounds simple, it's pretty amazing. We create reality and then we make ourselves feel secure that the created reality is actually real. The truth of the matter is that the reality of the human world is existentially moored in meaning, which is fallible, mutable, and uncertain. As the philosopher Ernst Cassirer (1944) put it,

> No longer can man confront reality immediately; he cannot see it, as it were, face to face. Physical reality seems to recede in proportion as man's symbolic activity advances. Instead of dealing with the things themselves man is in a sense constantly conversing with himself. (p. 42)

According to Giddens (1986, 1991), if people ever notice this about their reality, they will suffer deep psychological angst. We are motivated, then, as a result of this unconscious psychological insecurity about the socially created world, *to make the world routine and thus taken for granted.* Note that this anxiety is unconscious—it isn't usually experienced; but when it is, it is felt as a diffuse, general sense of unease.

Giddens (1990) states that ontological security refers to the feelings of "confidence that most humans [sic] beings have in the continuity of their self-identity and in the constancy of the surrounding social and material environments of action" (p. 92). He argues that the fundamental trust of ontological security is generally produced in early childhood and maintained through adult routines. Because most of the social practices in our lives are routine, we experience trust in the world, due to its routine character, and we can take for granted the ontological status of the world. In premodern societies, trust and routine in traditional institutions covered up the contingency of the world. Kinship and community created bonds that reliably structured actions through time and space; religion provided a cosmology that reliably ordered experience; and tradition itself structured social and natural events, because tradition by definition is routine.

Now we're about to take our final step in the journey to understand society and its people. Remember the fundamental problem of social order? It's time–space distanciation. And remember why it's a problem? Because according to Giddens, there are no such things as objective social structures that coerce us to act in certain ways. So, how and why do we do it? The how is structuration but the why is extremely important. The ultimate force behind our solving the problem of time–space distanciation is our deep-seated need for ontological security. That need drives us to routinize and regionalize behaviors.

Traditional societies provided routinization and regionalization without fail through kinship, community, and religion. However, in modern societies *none of these institutional settings produces a strong sense of trust and ontological security.* According to Giddens, those needs are met differently: Routine is integrated into abstract systems, pure relationships substitute for the connectedness of community and kin, and reflexively constructed knowledge systems replace religious cosmologies—but not with the certainty or the psychological rewards of premodern institutions. The result is that ontological insecurity—anxiety regarding the "existential anchoring of reality" (Giddens, 1991, p. 38)—is a greater possibility in modern rather than traditional societies.

Concepts and Theory: The Contours of Modernity

We have now laid the groundwork for Giddens's understanding of how society works in general: Actors are motivated to routinize social actions and interactions by the psychological need for ontological security. These routines serve to stretch out face-to-face encounters through time and space as actors use different modalities to express the social structures of signification, domination, and legitimation through their social practices. This constant structuration produces different institutional orders that, along with regionalization, work to stabilize routine. Routinization and the institutional orders that it generates stabilize time–space distanciation and thus give the individual a continual basis of trust in her or his social environment, which in turn provides the individual with ontological security.

Thus, in Giddens's scheme, society isn't structured; it doesn't exist as an obdurate object with an independent existence. The important point here is that society by its nature is continually susceptible to disruption or change. This constant possibility is, of course, what creates the diffuse and unconscious sense of insecurity that people have about the reality of society. However, this possibility is also what makes modernity an important issue, for both the process of structuration and for the person. In the next section, we will think about how living in modernity influences our experience of our self and others. But for now, simply think about how the dynamic quality of modernity radically changes structuration and time–space distanciation. There are four analytically distinct factors that produce the dynamism of modernity: radical reflexivity, the separation of time and space, disembedding mechanisms, and globalization. As we'll see, though we can separate these areas analytically, they empirically reinforce one another.

Radical Reflexivity

Giddens sees reflexivity as a variable rather than a static condition. He argues that modernity creates a level of *radical reflexivity*. Previous to this time, people didn't think much about society. In fact, the entire idea of society as an entity unto itself wasn't really conceived of until the work of people like Montesquieu and Durkheim. Today, we are quite aware of society, and we think deliberatively about our nation and the organizations and institutions in which we participate.

Progress and reflexivity are intrinsically related. It only takes a moment's reflection to see that progress demands reflexivity. It is endemic in modernity because every social unit must constantly evaluate itself in terms of its mission, goals, and practices. However, the hope of progress never materializes—the ideal of progress means that we never truly arrive. Every step in our progressive march forward is examined in the hopes of improving what we have achieved. Progress becomes a motivating value and a discursive feature of modernity, rather than a goal that is ever reached.

Here's a real-life example. Chances are good that you are attending an accredited college or university. Schools of higher education are certified by regional accrediting organizations. Being an accredited institution allows you as a student to qualify for federal financial aid and to transfer credits from one college to another, and it allows professors to apply for federal grants for research. At my university, we just finished with our reaccreditation self-study, which took 2 years to complete. Even though 2 years seems like a long time, we actually began preparing for the self-study the 2 years previous by evaluating our mission statement in light of what we knew to be the new criteria of accreditation.

Out of the first study came a new mission statement that was then used during the following study to reevaluate every aspect of the university (notice the reflexive element). The self-study produced recommendations for the next 10 years, and the study and its recommendations were scrutinized by a committee of academics and administrators sent by our regional affiliation. Changes were and will be implemented as a result of the study. The interesting thing to me is that 80 to 90% of the study deals with things that are only tangentially related to actual learning, which is what we think the university is about. Most of the study addresses symbolic or political issues that have little to do with what happens in the classroom or in your learning experience. The greater proportion of the changes, then, would not have come about except for their symbolic or political values and reflexive organization.

Modern institutions are bureaucratic in nature and are thus bound up with rational goal setting, recursive practices, and continual reflexivity. For example, the reaccreditation study I just mentioned will be repeated in 10 years and every 10 years thereafter. This year, my department is doing its self-study, and it gets repeated every 5 years. When I worked for Denny's restaurants as a manager, we had corporate plans that helped form the regional plans that helped create the unit plans, which strongly influenced my personal plans as a manager. Depending on the level, those plans were systematically evaluated every 1 to 5 years. Modern organizations, institutions, and society at large are thus defined through the continued use of reflexive evaluation.

One further point about radical reflexivity: It forms part of our basic understanding of knowledge and rational life. Modern knowledge is equivalent to scientific knowledge, and part of what makes knowledge scientific is continual scrutiny and systematic doubt. This understanding of knowledge is woven into the fabric of our culture. Every child in the United States receives training in what is called scientific literacy. According to the National Academy of Sciences (1995),

> This nation has established as a goal that all students should achieve scientific literacy. The *National Science Education Standards* are designed to enable the nation to achieve that goal. They spell out a vision of science education that will make scientific literacy for all a reality in the 21st century. (n.p.)

Thus, children in the United States are systematically trained to be reflexive about knowledge in general.

Emptying Time and Space

In this subsection, it is very important for you to keep in mind what Giddens means by *time–space distanciation*—it's his way of talking about how our behaviors and actions are patterned and are thus somewhat predictable. Therefore, whatever happens to time and space in modernity influences the patterns of interaction that make up society. With that in mind, Giddens argues that the *separation of time and space* is crucial to the dynamic quality of modernity.

In order to understand how time and space can be emptied, we have to begin by thinking about how humans have related to time and space for most of our existence. Up until the beginnings of modernity, time and space were closely linked to natural settings and cycles. People have always marked time, but it was originally associated with natural places and cycles. The cycle of the sun set the boundaries of the day, the cycle of the moon marked the month, and the year was noted by the cycles of the seasons. But the week, which is the primary tool we use to organize ourselves today, exists nowhere in nature. It's utterly abstract in terms of nature. Something similar may be said about the mechanical clock. Previous to the invention and widespread use of the mechanical clock, people regulated their behaviors around the moving of the sun (see McCready, 2001; Roy, 2001, pp. 40–45)

Thus, in modern societies, time and space have become abstract entities that have been emptied of any natural connections. Further, the concept of space itself has become stretched out and more symbolic than physical. As I mentioned, modernity is distinguished by the belief in progress. Progress implies change, and the emptying of time and space "serves to open up manifold possibilities of change by breaking free from the restraints of local habits and practices" (Giddens, 1990, p. 20). Making time and space abstract has also aided in another distinctive feature of modernity, the bureaucratic organization. Our lives are subject to rational organization precisely because time and space are emptied of their natural and face-to-face social references. My students and I can all meet at 9:45 AM in the Graham building, Room 308, for class because time and space have been emptied. And Boeing manufacturing in California can order parts from a steel plant in China to be ready for assembly beginning in January because time and space are abstract.

The emptying of time and space means that time–space distanciation can be increased almost without limit, which is one of the defining characteristics of modernity. Traditional societies are defined by close-knit social networks that create high levels of morality and an emphasis on long-established social practices and relationships. Any social form that could break with the importance of tradition would have to be built upon something other than close-knit social groups. Modernity, then, is defined as the time during which greater and greater distances are placed between people and their social relations. As we'll see, increasing time–space distanciation and escalating reflexivity mutually reinforce one another, and together they create the dynamism of modernity—the tendency for continual change.

Institutions and Disembedding Mechanisms

In discussing the transition from traditional to modern society, many sociologists talk about structural differentiation, especially functionalists. The problem that Giddens sees in institutional differentiation is that it can't give a reasoned account of a central feature of modernity: radical time–space distanciation. However, thinking about institutions in terms of disembedding mechanisms does. Thus, Giddens claims that the distinction between traditional and modern institutions isn't differentiation so much as it is embedding versus disembedding. *Disembedding mechanisms* are those practices that lift out social relations and interactions from local contexts. Again, let's picture a kind of ideal type of traditional society where most social relationships and interactions take place in encounters that are firmly entrenched in local situations. People would live in places where they knew everybody and would depend upon people they knew for help. Distant situations, along with distant others, were kept truly distant. There are two principal mechanisms that lifted life out of its local context: symbolic tokens and expert systems.

Symbolic tokens are understood in terms of media of exchange that can be passed around without any regard for a specific person or group. There are a few of these kinds of tokens around, but the example par excellence is money. Money creates a universal value system wherein every commodity can be understood according to the same value system. Of necessity, this value system is abstract; that is, it has no intrinsic worth. In order for it to stand for everything, it must have no value in itself. The universal and abstract nature of money frees it from constraint and facilitates exchanges over long distances and time periods. Thus, by its very nature, money increases time–space distanciation. Moreover, the greater the level of abstraction of money, such as through credit and soft currencies, the greater will be this effect.

The other disembedding mechanism that Giddens talks about is *expert systems.* Let's again think about a traditional community. If you were a woman who lived in a traditional community and were going to have a baby, to whom would you go? If in the same group you experienced marital problems, where would you go for advice? If you wanted to know how to grow better crops or appease the gods or construct a building or do anything that required some form of social cooperation, where would you go? The answer to all these questions, and all the rest of the details of living life, would be your social network. If you wanted to grow better crops, you might go to your friend Paul whose fields always seem full and alive. For marital advice, you would probably go to your grandparents; for childbirth help, you'd go to the neighbor's wife who had been practicing midwifery for as long as you can remember.

Where do we go for these things today? We go to experts—people we don't personally know who have been trained academically in abstract knowledge. But we don't really have to "go to" an expert to be dependent upon expert systems of knowledge. For instance, I have no idea how to construct a building that has many levels and can house myriad classrooms and offices, yet I'm dependent upon that expert knowledge every time I go to my office or teach in a classroom. Every time we turn on a computer or flick a light switch or start our car or go to buy food at the grocery store—in short, every time we do anything that is associated with living in modernity—we are dependent upon abstract, expert systems of knowledge. Systems of expert knowledge are disembedding because they shift the center of our life away from local contexts to dependence on abstract knowledge and distant others, who sometimes never appear.

Globalization

Giddens argues that four institutions in particular form the dynamic and time period of modernity: capitalism, industrialism, monopoly of violence, and surveillance. In terms of the dynamic of modernity, capitalism stands out. Capitalism is intrinsically expansive. It is driven by the perceived need for profit, which in turn drives the expansion of markets, technologies, and commodification.

Industrialization is of course linked to capitalism, but it has its own dynamics and relationships with the other institutional spheres. Industrialism, the monopoly of coercive power, and surveillance feed one another and create what is generally referred to as the industrial-military complex. A military complex is formed by a standing army and the parts of the economy that are oriented toward military production. Once a coercive force begins to use technology, it not only becomes dependent upon industrialism but also provides a constant impetus for more and better technologies of force and surveillance. A military complex by its very existence is not just available for protection; it is also in its best interests to instigate aggression whenever possible in order to expand its own base and the interests of its institutional partners.

From Chapter 10, you already know that capitalism naturally implies relationships among various nations, and if you take a moment, you'll see that the military complex also implies international relations. Thus, the institutional dimensions of modernity are explicitly tied up with globalization. Giddens (1990) defines globalization as "the intensification of worldwide social relations which link distant localities in such a way that local happenings are shaped by events occurring many miles away and vice versa" (p. 64). Globalization is thus defined in terms of a dialectic relation between the local and the distant that further stretches out co-presence through time and space. The four dimensions of globalization, according to Giddens, are the world capitalist economy, the world military order, the international division of labor, and the nation-state system.

In order to help us get a handle on what Giddens is arguing, I've drawn out the chief processes that we've been talking about in Figure 14.3. Most all of the factors on the far left of the model are interrelated in some way. For example, the use of bureaucratic, rational management increases in the presence of world capitalism

Figure 14.3 Dynamism of Modernity

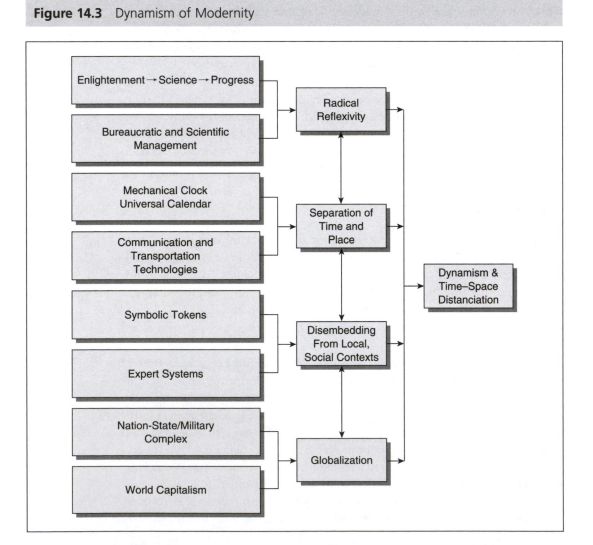

and expert systems. But to draw out all the relationships at that level would defeat the purpose of the model as a heuristic device. I have indicated the mutual effects at the next level. All of these dynamics—radical reflexivity, separation of time and space, disembedding, globalization—mutually imply and affect one another. For example, as time and space are separated from the actual, institutions can further remove the social from the local, which in turn allows more abstract connections at the global level. These all mutually reinforce one another and build the dynamism of modernity. Collectively, this figure and all that it implies answer the question, "Why are change and discontinuity endemic in modernity?" Use Figure 14.3 to think through that question and Giddens's theory of modernity.

Concepts and Theory: The Experience of Modernity

It is extremely difficult to see the effects of our own time period (modernity) in our own lives. Of course, this is true of most people in every historical era. We tend to take the world into which we are born for granted. It seems natural to us. Yet sociology teaches us that we are social beings *created for and out of social relations,* and the sociological imagination encourages us to see the intersections of biography, history, and society. Giddens paints a portrait of the modern individual and asks us to look behind (or in front of) our own subjective experiences and understand them as finding their roots in a particular social organization called modernity. Modernity is characterized by endemic reflexivity and time–space distanciation. What these factors imply for the person is that the individual and her or his subjective experiences have been lifted out of densely packed social networks. Most of the social relations we have are stretched to the point where time and space have little meaning. You and I, for instance, are connecting through this text. Yet I have no idea where you are, let alone "when" you are. As you'll see, this sort of social "disembedding" has a number of implications for the late-modern person, most specifically the reflexive project of the self, life politics, and intimate relations.

The Reflexive Project of the Self

In times previous to modernity, the self was deeply embedded in the social. People were caught up in and saw themselves only in terms of the group. The self was an extension of the group just as certainly as your arm is an extension of your body. Not only was the individual life seen as part of the group, but its trajectory was also plotted and marked socially. So, for example, a boy knew for certain when he had changed from a boy to a man—he went through a rite of passage. Such is not the case today.

In modernity, the individual stands alone. The individual is "free." You, for example, are free to express yourself in any number of ways. You have a plethora of potential identities and experiences open to you. But at the same time, you no longer have any institutional markers to guide you or to define your "progress," and there are no institutions that are directly responsible for you. In the *reflexive project of the self,* you have to reflexively define your own options and opportunities with regard to social and personal change. The self is no longer an entity embedded in known and firm social and institutional relationships and expecta-tions. This shift from the traditional, social self with clear institutional guidelines to the individual reflexive project was brought about because of the dynamics of modernity that we reviewed in the previous section.

The body is drawn into this reflexive project as well. Before radical modernity, the body was, for the most part, seen as either the medium through which work was performed or a vehicle for the soul. In either case, it was of little consequence and received little attention unless it became an obstacle to work or salvation. In radical modernity, on the other hand, the body becomes part of self-expression and helps to sustain "a coherent sense of self-identity" (Giddens, 1991, p. 99). The body becomes wrapped up with the reflexive project of the self in four possible ways: appearance, demeanor, sensuality, and through bodily regimes. We covered the first two ways in our chapter on Goffman, so we will just take time to review the last two.

The body is involved in the self project through *bodily regimes*. In radical moder-nity, "we become responsible for the design of our own bodies" (Giddens, 1991, p. 102). The body is no longer a simple reflection of one's work but can become a canvas for a self-portrait. Capitalism, mass media, advertising, fashion, and medical expert knowledge have produced an overabundance of information about how the body works and what kinds of behaviors result in what kinds of body images. We are called upon to constantly review the look and condition of our body and to make adjustments as necessary. The adjustments are carried out through various body regimes of diet, exercise, stress-reducing activities (yoga, meditation), vitamin therapies, skin cleansing and repair, hair treatments, and so forth.

With the *organization of sensuality*, Giddens has in mind the entire spectrum of sensual feeling of the body, but the idea is particularly salient for sexuality. Together, mass education, contraceptive technologies, decreasing family size, and women's political and workforce participation created the situation where "today, for the first time in human history, women claim equality with men" (Giddens, 1992, p. 1). Giddens links women's freedom with the creation of an "emotional order" that contains "an exploration of the potentialities of the 'pure relation-ship'" and "plastic sexuality" (pp. 1–2). The idea of *plastic sexuality* captures a kind of sexuality that came into existence as sex was separated from the demands of reproduction. Plastic sexuality is an explicit characteristic of modernity. For the first time in history, sexuality could become part of self-identity. We should also note that since sexuality is part of the reflexive project of the self, it is subject to reflexive scrutiny and intentional exploration.

Pure Relationships

To begin our discussion of pure relationships, let's think about friendship. Giddens points out that early Greeks didn't even have a word for friend in the way we use it today. The Greeks used the word *philos* to talk about those who were the most near and dear, but this term was used for people who were in or near to family. Moreover, the Greek *philos* network was pretty well set by the person's status position; there was little in the way of friends as we think of them, as personal choices.

In languages that did have a word for friend, these friends were seen within the context of group survival. Friends were the in-group, and others were the out-group. The distinction was between friend and enemy, or, at best, stranger. Keep in mind that groups were far more important than they are now because individual survival was closely tied to group affiliations and resources. A friend was someone you turned to in time of need; thus, the values associated with friendship were honor and sincerity. Today, however, because of disembedding mechanisms and increased time–space distanciation, not all friends are understood in terms of in-group membership and actual assistance. The individual can have distant friends and is enabled and expected to take care of himself or herself (the reflexive project).

A fundamental change has thus occurred in friendships: from friendship with honor based on group identity and survival to friendship with authenticity based on a mutual process of self-disclosure. Rather than trust being embedded in social networks and rituals, trust in modernity has to be won, and the means through which this is done is self-evident warmth and openness. By implication, this authenticity and self-regulation provide the personal, emotional component missing in trust in the abstract systems of modernity.

Intimate relations in modernity are thus characterized by *pure relationships*—friendships and intimate ties that are entered into simply for what the relationship can bring to each person. Remember that traditional relationships were first set by existing networks and institutions, and the motivation behind them was usually social, not personal. For example, most marriages were motivated by politics or economics (not by love) and were arranged for the couple by those most responsible for the social issues in question (not by the couple themselves). This is the way in which modern relationships are pure: They occur purely for the sake of the relationship. Most of our relationships are not anchored in external conditions, like the politically or economically motivated marriage. Rather, they are "free-floating." The only structural condition for a friendship or marriage is proximity: We have to be near enough to make contact. But with modern transportation and communication technologies, our physical space is almost constantly in motion and can be quite far-ranging. Furthermore, we have "virtual" space at our fingertips.

In addition to the free-floating and pure nature of these relations, they are also reflexively organized, based on commitment and mutual trust, and focus on intimacy and "self" growth. Like the reflexive project of the self, relationships are reflexively organized; that is, they are continually worked at by the individuals, who tend to consult an array of sources of information. The number of possible sources for telling us how to act and be in our friendships and sexual relations is almost endless. Daytime television is filled with programming that explores every facet of relationships; the magazine rack at the local supermarket is a cornucopia of surveys and advice on how to have the best _____ (fill in the blank with any aspect of an intimate relationship); it's estimated that over 2,000 new self-help book titles are published every year in the United States; and the Internet resources available for improving relationships are innumerable. Most of us have taken a relationship quiz with a partner at some point (if you haven't, just wait—it's coming), and all of us have no doubt asked of someone the essential question for relationships that are reflexively organized: "Is everything all right?" This kind of communication is a moral obligation in pure relationships; the gamut of communication covers everything from the mundane ("How was your day at work?") to the serious ("Do you want to break up with me?").

Choice and Life Politics

Along with the accelerating changes in modernity, there has been a shift from emancipatory politics to life politics. *Emancipatory politics* is concerned with liberating individuals and groups from the constraints that adversely affect their lives. In some ways, this type of political activity has been the theme of modernity—it was the hope that democratic nation-states could bring equality and justice for all. In some respects, this theme of modernity has failed. We are more than ever painfully aware of how many groups are disenfranchised.

Life politics, by way of contrast, is the politics of choice and lifestyle. It is not based on group membership and characteristics, as is emancipatory politics; rather, it is based on personal lifestyle choices. We have come to think of choice as a freedom we have in the United States, but it is more than that—it has become an obligation. Choice is a fundamental element in contemporary living. This principality of choice is based on disembedding mechanisms and time–space distanciation, and it results in, as we've seen, the reflexive project of the self. Part of that project comes to be centered on the politics of choice.

Mass media also plays a role in creating choice by facilitating mediated experiences. *Mediated experiences* are in contrast to social experiences that take place in face-to-face encounters and are created as people are exposed to multiple accounts of situations and others with whom they have no direct association through time and space. Every time you watch television or read a newspaper, you are exposed to lives to which you have absolutely no real connection. Like so many other features of modernity, this stretches out co-presence, but it also creates a collage effect. The pictures and stories that we receive via the media do not reflect any essential or social elements. Instead, stories and images are juxtaposed that have nothing to do with one another. The picture we get of the world, then, is a collage of diverse lifestyles and cultures, not a direct representation.

As a result of being faced with this collage, what happens to us as individuals? One implication is that the plurality of lifestyles presented to us not only allows for choice—it also necessitates choice. In other words, what becomes important is not the issue of group equality, but rather, the insistence on personal choice. What is at issue in this milieu is not so much political equality (as with emancipatory politics) as inner authenticity. In a world that is perceived as constantly changing and uprooted, it becomes important to be grounded in one's self. Life politics creates such grounding. It creates "a framework of basic trust by means of which the life-span can be understood as a unity against the backdrop of shifting social events" (Giddens, 1991, p. 215). Life politics, then, helps to diminish the possibility and effects of ontological insecurity.

A good example of life politics is veganism—the practice of not eating any meat or meat by-products. In addition, the following products are avoided: anything made with dairy, eggs, fur, leather, feathers, or any goods involving animal testing. One vegan I know summed it up nicely when she said, veganism "is an integral component of a cruelty-free lifestyle." It is a political statement against the exploitation of animals, and for some it is clearly a condemnation of capitalism—capitalism is particularly responsible for the unnatural mass production of animal flesh as well as commercial animal testing. Yet for most vegans, it is a lifestyle, one that brings harmony between the outside world and inner beliefs, and not necessarily part of a collective movement.

However, it would be wrong to conclude that life politics is powerless because it does not result in a social movement. Quite the opposite is true. Life politics springs from and focuses attention on some of the very issues that modernity represses. What life politics does is to "place a question mark against the internally referential systems of modernity" (Giddens, 1991, p. 223). Life politics asks,

> Seeing that these things are so, what manner of men and women ought we to be? In traditional society, morality was provided by the institutions, especially religion. Modernity has wiped away the social base upon which this kind of morality was based. Life politics "remoralizes" social life and demands "renewed sensitivity to questions that the institutions of modernity systematically dissolve." (p. 224)

Rather than asking for group participation, as does emancipatory politics, life politics asks for self-realization, a moral commitment to a specific way of living. Rather than being impotent in comparison to emancipatory politics, life politics "presage[s] future changes of a far-reaching sort: essentially, the development of forms of social order "on the other side" of modernity itself. (p. 214)

Summary

- According to Giddens, the central issue for social theory is to explain how actions and interactions are patterned over time and space; or, to use Giddens's terms, social theory needs to explain how the limitations inherent within physical presence are transcended through time–space distanciation. There are two primary ways through which this occurs: the dynamics of structuration and routinization.

- Structuration occurs when people use specific modalities to produce both structure (rules and resources of signification, domination, and legitimation) and practice (physical co-presence). Thus, the very method of structuration reflexively and repeatedly links structure and person and facilitates time–space distanciation.

- Routinization is psychologically motivated by a diffuse need for ontological security. The reality of society is precarious because it depends on structuration, which is reflexive and recursive. In other words, the process of structuration doesn't reference anything other than itself, and it depends on ceaseless interactional work. This precariousness is unconsciously sensed by people, which, in turn, motivates them to routinize their actions and interactions and to link their routines to physical regions and institutional orders, which further add stability.

- Routinization was unproblematically achieved in traditional societies. People rarely left their regions, and the institutional orders were slow to change. Modernity, however, is characterized by dynamism and increasing time–space distanciation. Dynamism and time–space distanciation are both directly related to radical reflexivity, extreme separation of time and place, the disembedding work of modern institutions, and globalization. These factors are related to the proliferation of science and progress, bureaucratic management, the mechanical clock and universal calendar, communication and transportation technologies, symbolic tokens and expert systems of knowledge, the military complex, and world capitalism.

- As a result of radical modernity, the individual is lifted out of the social networks and institutions that socially situated the self by acquiring certain identities, knowledge, and life course markers. The modern individual is given the reflexive project of the self that is only internally referential. As part of the reflexive project of the self, the individual involves himself or herself in strategic life planning using expert systems of knowledge and mediated experiences, all of which are permeated with pervasive doubt. The reflexive project of the self involves constant evaluation and reevaluation based on possible new information (ever revised by experts and available through mass media) and self-reflection (How am I doing? Should I be feeling this way?). The reflexive project includes lifestyle politics in which the individual must reflexively work her or his way through continuously presented and expanding arenas of social existence. Individuals, then, become hubs for social change as they reflexively order their life in response to a constantly changing political landscape.

BUILDING YOUR THEORY TOOLBOX

- Write a 250-word synopsis of the theoretical perspective of structuration theory.

- After reading and understanding this chapter, you should be able to define the following terms theoretically and explain their importance to Giddens's ontology of society and theory of modernity: structuration theory, duality of structure, social structures, normative rules, signification codes, authoritative resources, allocative resources, time–space distanciation, modalities of structuration, domination, institutional orders, reflexive monitoring, rationalization of action, discursive consciousness, practical consciousness, routinization, regionalization, ontological security, radical reflexivity, disembedding mechanisms, symbolic tokens, expert systems, reflexive project of the self, bodily regimes, organization of sensuality, pure relationships, emancipatory politics, life politics, mediated experiences.

- After reading and understanding this chapter, you should be able to answer the following questions (remembering to answer them theoretically):

  o What is time–space distanciation, and why is it the central question for Giddens? How does modernity affect time–space distanciation?

  o What are social structures in Giddens's scheme? How do they exist, and what do they do?

  o What are modalities of structuration? What are the three modalities? What is the function of modalities of structuration?

  o What are the three institutional orders, and how are they created?

  o What are practical and discursive consciousnesses, and how do they fit in with reflexive monitoring?

  o What is the unconscious motivation in human interaction? What specific processes come about due to this motivation? How does each process vary? What are their effects?

  o What are the main processes that produce the dynamic of modernity? There are at least four. Define each process and explain how it contributes to the dynamic character of modernity.

  o What is the reflexive project of the self? How did it become individualized? How is the body involved, and why do you think the body is important in this project?

  o Explain the differences between emancipatory and lifestyle politics. Why is lifestyle politics more prevalent today than emancipatory?

Learning More—Primary and Secondary Sources

- To learn more about Giddens's theory of structuration, you should read his *The Constitution of Society,* University of California Press, 1986.

- For Giddens's theory of modernity, I recommend his *Modernity and Self-Identity: Self and Society in the Late Modern Age,* Stanford University Press, 1991.

- An excellent encounter with Giddens's theory (not just a review) is Stjepan Gabriel Mestrovic's *Anthony Giddens: The Last Modernist,* Routledge, 1998.

Engaging the World

- Giddens is one of the architects and proponents of what is known as the "third way" in politics. Using your favorite Internet search engine, look up "third way." What is it, and how is Giddens involved? How can you see it related to his theory?

- Politics in late-modern societies have become diffused throughout all of our actions. Everything we do has political implications. Use Giddens's categories of emancipatory and lifestyle politics to define different areas of your life as belonging to one or the other of the categories. What ramifications do you think there are for civil society and democracy?

(Continued)

(Continued)

Weaving the Threads

- Compare and contrast Giddens's theory of structuration with Bourdieu's constructivist-structuralism approach. Specifically, how are patterns of behavior replicated in the long run? How does each one overcome the object–subject dichotomy? Do you find one approach to be more persuasive? Why or why not?

- Compare and contrast Habermas's and Giddens's views of modernity. I recommend you start with their defining characteristics of modernity and review the issues that are implied in the definitions. After you've worked your way through these comparisons, define modernity and its chief problems.

- In Chapter 11, I asked you to write a one-page synopsis of the assessments and principles for reinvigorating democracy for Wallerstein, Castells, and Habermas. Do the same now for Giddens (remembering that modernity and democracy are tied up together). Now compare, contrast, and evaluate these explanations. Based on your evaluation, synthesize these theories and create a single assessment of the democratic project of modernity. Evaluate the potential for reinvigorating democracy.

- Check the index in this book, and look up the different definitions and explanations of "social structures." Evaluate each of these approaches, and create what you feel to be a clear, robust, and correct definition-explanation of social structures. Justify your theory.

Part V

Contemporary Political Identities

The Big Picture: Politics of Identities

From the beginning, modern societies have been concerned with the person. We've seen how the idea of natural rights created a new kind of society, a civil society concerned with protecting human rights from abuses of state power. Numerous social institutions overlapped and to some degree made this civil sphere possible. Education was to provide the citizen with the training and knowledge necessary for holding the government accountable. Mass media (the press) was to provide up-to-date information about political issues, without which democratic decisions could not be reasonably made. Capitalism was to provide the path to individual achievement and happiness. Religion with its legitimating power held at bay was to provide the transcendental ideas that morally unified and guided citizens. Constitutional law was to be the law of laws, the enlightened tenets that were meant to link together all municipalities and principalities under universal democratic values. The very way in which government was structured in places like the United States was by the separation of powers, a system of checks and balances on possible abuses of power.

At the core of all this was the person, in whom all inalienable rights were invested. The American Declaration of Independence is based on the self-evident truth that

> all men are created equal, that they are endowed by their Creator with certain unalienable rights, that among these are life, liberty and the pursuit of happiness. That to secure these rights, governments are instituted among men, deriving their just powers from the consent of the governed.

The United Nations' Universal Declaration of Human Rights begins, "Whereas recognition of the inherent dignity and of the equal and inalienable rights of all members of the human family is the foundation of freedom, justice and peace in the world." The American Constitution was written on behalf of universal humanity: "We the people."

Yet it wasn't long before sociological studies revealed that in practice it isn't the person that matters as much as the person's identity. Marx showed us that class matters; Frederick Douglass and W. E. B. Du Bois told us that race matters; Mary Wollstonecraft, Harriet Martineau, and Charlotte Perkins Gilman revealed that gender matters. Identities matter—political identities matter most. "A *political identity* is an actor's experience of a shared social relation in which at least one of the parties . . . is an individual or organization controlling concentrated means of coercion" (Tilly, 2002, p. 61). Identities, then, became the fodder of social movements, political protests that critically examine "the link between civil society and the political system outside of the institutionalised patterns of political participation" (Ruzza, 2006, p. 155). These social movements took place within a nationally defined territory and were aimed at steering the state in a specific direction that would result in greater social justice. These were specifically *modern* social movements.

Yet, as we've seen, "society" isn't the same today as it was when modern democracy was founded. Globalization (Chapter 10) exceeds national boundaries and creates transnational social relationships. Rather than institutionalized social connections and identities, we are more and more being connected by and subject to the logics of computer networks (Chapter 11), and social relationships are being disembedded from time and space (Chapter 14). Even within geographic boundaries, democracy and the public sphere have been colonized (Chapter 12). We've seen how these new "societies" have impacted democratic issues. Anthony Giddens tells us that political identities have shifted from emancipatory to lifestyle politics. Manuel Castells explains how civil society, power, and democracy have changed due to the influence of computer networks and have produced new sets of identities: legitimizing, resistance, and project identities.

These changes, among others, have prompted a new theoretical perspective, commonly called "new social movements theory." Central to new social movements is the shift from industrial to postindustrial society: "[T]he novel and central feature of post-industrial society is the codification of theoretical knowledge and the new relation of science to technology" (Bell, 1999, p. xiv). This new economic system has changed the method of capitalist accumulation and created new social positions and new forms of domination; thus, "the class-oriented revolutionary movements of an earlier day [are] obsolete" (Alexander, 2006, p. 224). Because of these social changes, emancipatory politics with a focus on expanding civil rights has receded. In its place is a new political sphere: "Personal identity . . . is the property which is now being claimed and defended; this is the ground in which individual and collective resistance is taking root" (Melucci, 1980, p. 218).

A clear example of these changes is found in the three waves of feminism. The first and second waves were concerned with structured political rights: The first wave focused on voting rights and the second on equal access. Third-wave feminism, on the other hand, focuses on the personal experience of being a woman in today's society. To be third wave "is to integrate an ideology of equality and female empowerment into the very fiber of my life. It is to search for personal clarity in the midst of systematic destruction" (Walker, 2007, p. 400).

It's clear that class, race, and gender still matter for political rights. Yet in recent times, the focus of those writing in these areas has changed. In our previous theories of race and gender, Chapter 7, both Wilson and Chafetz explained how social structures are oppressive. These theories fall under the heading of emancipatory politics. They are concerned with how social structures deprive blacks and women of political and economic rights. Our next theorists aren't necessarily focused on lifestyle, but more on personal experience and how oppressive relations are the result of knowledge construction, cultural texts, and the embodied experiences of sex. Identity politics encompasses "a way of knowing that sees lived experiences as important to creating knowledge and crafting group-based political strategies. Also, [it is] a form of political resistance where an oppressed group rejects its devalued status" (P. H. Collins, 2000, p. 299).

CHAPTER 15

Being Black in America

Patricia Hill Collins and Cornel West

Source: Courtesy of
Patricia Hill Collins.

Source: © Richard Howard/
Time Life Pictures/Getty
Images.

The Big Picture: Epistemology

Epistemology is the study of knowledge and its justification. Epistemological questions ask, how is knowledge possible? What are its sources? Is knowledge justified? Generally speaking, epistemology is a concern of philosophy, and there it is often bound up with ontological issues or philosophy of the mind. Yet, epistemology was a core issue for sociology from the beginning. Comte's (Chapter 1) entire argument is based on an epistemology. He argues that knowledge has gone through three phases: theological, metaphysical, and positive. Positive philosophy argues that the universe is empirical, that it operates according to invariant laws, and that humans can discover those laws and use them for the betterment of humankind. For Comte, knowledge results from discovery. We simply need to get rid of our preconceptions, and empirical facts will yield themselves to rational investigation.

Marx, however, took us in a different direction. Consciousness, or knowledge, has a material base, but it isn't the natural world that Comte thought. The unique material of the human world is created through species being and production. Human consciousness is a reflexive function of economic production. The world we produce acts like a mirror and reflects human nature back to us. This idea implies that there could be epistemological problems if something goes awry in the production process. If production isn't linked to social life—if production, for example, is motivated and controlled by desires for personal gain (capitalism)—then the knowledge we have about ourselves and our world is based on false consciousness, and the things we think to be true are in fact ideological. For Marx, then, knowledge is based on social position and class interests. Karl Mannheim (1936) extended Marx's theory beyond economic production and argued, "there are modes of thought which cannot be adequately understood as long as their social origins are obscured" (p. 2).

Durkheim proposed a different epistemology. All knowledge is based on fundamental categories of understanding: time, space, number, cause, substance, and personality. These categories organize the information we receive from our five senses. They make our sense perceptions meaningful. Categories work by creating boundaries between one thing and another. According to Durkheim, the very first boundary humans created was between the sacred and profane. This boundary emerged because early human groups had two life cycles: One experienced in small hunter-gatherer groups that provided for biological necessities, and the other experienced when various small groups would gather for celebrations. During large group celebrations, a level of emotional energy was created that was impossible in the smaller groups. The people were caught up in this emotional effervescence, and their behaviors changed. They saw these ecstatic experiences as special, different from everyday life; they saw them as sacred. These sacred experiences led people to categorize differences in time, space, causation, and so on. Categorical concepts aren't abstract, then, "for they correspond to the way in which the special being that is society thinks about the things of its own existence" (Durkheim, 1912/1995, p. 436).

Patricia Hill Collins and Dorothy E. Smith have epistemological concerns as well. They aren't so much concerned about the ontological or material base of knowledge, as were both Marx and Durkheim; rather, they are concerned with the way certain kinds of knowledge impact specific groups. Like Foucault, they see knowledge as a method of control. This issue is obvious when we think of the goals of positivism: Scientific knowledge is used to control elements in the physical environment. You use scientific knowledge for such purpose every time you turn on the lights. Positivistic knowledge, then, is inherently controlled no matter what it is used for—the control element is always present, even if not explicit. Collins and Smith are thus concerned with the way that the "objective facts" of positivism implicitly deny the subjective experiences of women and people of color. What we know and how we know it always have ramifications that go beyond simple knowing.

Black Feminism and Intersectionality— Patricia Hill Collins

Patricia Hill Collins will ask us to see two things. First, inequality in society is a complex matter; it can't simply be reduced to considerations of race or gender. Every person stands at a crossroads that distinguishes her or him from most others. For example, being black, female, middle class, and heterosexual is quite different from being black, female, working class, and lesbian. Collins wants us to see deeper into the workings of inequality than ever before. The second thing that Collins will ask us to see is standpoint. Of course, Dorothy E. Smith asked us to do the same, but Collins wants us to see the value in the standpoint of *black* feminists. In Collins's scheme, a single system isn't enough to explain inequality. Stratification works through matrices of domination, not single systems, and one of the most powerful intersectional standpoints is that of black women. It's at that point that race and gender meet. As such, it is probably the most powerful beginning point for intersectional analysis.

THEORIST'S DIGEST

Brief Biography

Patricia Hill Collins was born on May 1, 1948, in Philadelphia, Pennsylvania. Collins received her bachelor's degree and PhD in sociology from Brandeis University and a master's degree in social science education from Harvard. Collins served as director of the African American Center at Tufts University before moving to the University of Cincinnati, where she was named the Charles Phelps Taft Distinguished Professor of Sociology in 1996. She is currently at the University of Maryland and holds a position as Wilson Elkins Professor of Sociology. Her book, *Black Feminist Thought,* received the Association for Women in Psychology's Distinguished Publication Award, the Society for the Study of Social Problems' C. Wright Mills Award, and the Association of Black Women Historians' Letitia Woods Brown Memorial Book Prize.

Central Sociological Questions

Collins, like Foucault, sees a strong connection between power and knowledge. Certain forms of knowledge can be dominating; other forms of knowledge can be liberating. Collins (2000) wants to "empower African-American women" through knowledge and changing "an individual Black woman's consciousness concerning how she understands her everyday life" (p. x).

Simply Stated

Collins critiques positivism's objective stand, emotional divestment, the idea of value-free research, and growth in knowledge based on debate. In the end, this approach denies ethical considerations and authentic involvement. A Black feminist approach to knowing and knowledge counters each of these issues. Collins's research and theory is based on intersectionality, recognizing that people sit at crossroads of multiple systems of power organized around four general domains of power: structural (the interrelationships of social structures), disciplinary (bureaucratic organization and protocol), hegemonic (cultural legitimations), and interpersonal (personal relationships).

Key Concepts

Intersectionality; Eurocentric positivism; black feminist epistemology; common challenges/ diverse responses; safe places; self-definition; rearticulation; black feminist intellectuals; matrix of domination; structural, disciplinary, hegemonic, and interpersonal domains of power

Concepts and Theory: The Standpoint of Black Women

Patricia Hill Collins is centrally concerned with the relationships among empowerment, self-definition, and knowledge, and she is particularly concerned with black women—it is the oppression with which she is most intimately familiar. But Collins is also one of the few social thinkers who are able to rise above their own experiences and to challenge us with a significant view of oppression and identity politics that not only has the possibility of changing the world, but also of opening up the prospect of continuous change.

For change to be continuous, it can't be exclusively focused on one social group. In other words, a social movement that is only concerned with racial inequality, for example, will end its influence once equality for that group is achieved. What Patricia Hill Collins gives us is a way of transcending group-specific politics that is based upon black feminist epistemology. However, it is vital to note that her intent is to place "U.S. Black women's experiences in the center of analysis without privileging those experiences" (P. H. Collins, 2000, p. 228). Collins is saying that there is something significant we can learn from black women's knowledge that can be applied to social issues generally.

Black women are located at a theoretically interesting point. Collins argues that black women are uniquely situated in that they stand at the focal point where two exceptionally powerful and prevalent systems of oppression come together: race and gender. Collins refers to this kind of social position as *intersectionality*: the crisscrossing of different systems of domination. There are obviously other systems that Collins talks about, such as class, sexuality, ethnicity, nation, and age, but it is with black women where these different influences get played out most clearly. Seeing this intersectional position of black women thus ought to compel us to see and look for other spaces where systems of inequality come together.

Just as important to this possibility of continuous change are the qualities of what Collins variously terms alternative or *black feminist epistemology*. This notion implies that one of the things that has hindered social reform is the emphasis on social, scientific knowledge. In this sense, Collins is a critical theorist who argues that all knowledge is political and can be used to serve specific group interests. Social science is particularly susceptible to this because it simultaneously objectifies its subjects and denies the validity of lived experience as a form of knowing.

Black Feminist Epistemology

Patricia Hill Collins argues that the politics of race and gender influence knowledge. In Marxian terms, race and gender are part of our "social being." In order to talk about this issue, and specifically about black feminist knowledge, Collins juxtaposes it with Eurocentric, positivistic knowledge—the kind of knowledge in back of science. As Marx tells us, there is more to knowledge than simply information. Knowledge—information and facts—can only exist within a context that is defined through specific ways of knowing and validation. For example, the "fact" that God created the heavens and earth only exists within the context of a specific religious system. The same is true for any other "facts," scientific or otherwise. Thus, what we know is dependent upon how knowledge is produced and how it is validated as true. The question here becomes, what are the ways of knowing and methods of validation that are specific to Eurocentric, positivistic knowledge? Collins gives us four points. Note that sociology is generally defined as a social science, and insofar as it is a scientific inquiry into social life, it espouses these four points.

Eurocentric Positivism

First, according to the positivistic approach, true or correct knowledge only comes when the observer separates him- or herself from that which is being studied. You undoubtedly came across this idea in your methods class: The researcher must take an objective stand in order to safeguard against bias. Second, personal emotions must be set aside in the pursuit of pure knowledge. Third, no personal ethics or values must come into the research. Social science is to be value-free, not passing judgment or trying to impose values on others. Fourth and finally, knowledge progresses through cumulation and adversarial debate.

Recall our discussion of scientific theory in the introduction to Section II. Cumulation is that process by which theories are built up through testing and rejecting elements that don't correspond to the empirical world. The ideas that pass the test are carried on, and theory cumulates in abstract statements about the general properties of whatever is being investigated. The goal is to disassociate ideas from the people who spawned them and to end up with pure theory. Thus, scientific knowledge is validated because it is tested and argued against from every angle. The belief is that only that which is left standing is truth, and it is upon those remnants that objective, scientific knowledge will be built.

Four Tenets of Black Feminist Epistemology

Collins gives us four characteristics of alternative epistemologies, ways of knowing and validating knowledge that challenge the status quo. As we discuss these, notice how each point stands in opposition to the tenets of positivistic knowledge.

The first point is that alternative epistemologies are built upon lived experience, not upon an objectified position. Social science argues that, to truly understand society and group life, one must be removed from the particulars and concerns of the subjects being studied. In this way, subjects are turned into objects of study. Patricia Hill Collins's (2000) alternative epistemology claims that it is only those men and women who experience the consequences of living under an oppressed social position who can select "topics for investigation and methodologies used" (p. 258). Black feminist epistemology, then, begins with "connected knowers," those who know from personal experience.

The second dimension of Collins's alternative epistemology is the use of dialogue rather than adversarial debate. As we've seen, knowledge claims in social science are assessed through adversarial debate. Using dialogue to evaluate implies the presence of at least two subjects—thus, knowledge isn't seen as having an objective existence apart from lived experiences; knowledge ongoingly emerges through dialogue. In alternative epistemologies, we therefore tend to see the use of personal pronouns such as "I" and "we" instead of the objectifying and distancing language of social science. Rather than disappearing, the author is central to and present in the text. In black feminist epistemology, the story is told and preserved in narrative form and not "torn apart in analysis" (P. H. Collins, 2000, p. 258).

Centering lived experiences and the use of dialogue imply that knowledge is built around ethics of caring, Collins's third characteristic of black feminist knowledge. Rather than believing that researchers can be value-free, Collins argues that all knowledge is intrinsically value-laden and should thus be tested by the presence of empathy and compassion. Collins sees this tenet as healing the binary break between the intellect and emotion that Eurocentric knowledge values. Alternative epistemology is thus holistic: It doesn't require the separation of the researcher from her or his own experiences, nor does it require separation of our thoughts from our feelings, or even assume that it is possible to do so. In addition, Patricia Hill Collins (2000) argues that the presence of emotion validates the argument: "Emotion indicates that a speaker believes in the validity of an argument" (p. 263).

Fourth, black feminist epistemology requires personal accountability. Because knowledge is built upon lived experience, the assessment of knowledge is a simultaneous assessment of an individual's character, values, and ethics. This approach puts forth that all knowledge is based upon beliefs, things assumed to be true, and belief implies personal responsibility. Think about the implications of these two different approaches to knowing, information, and truth: One approach asserts that information can be objective, and truth exists apart from any observer, while the other puts forth that all information finds its existence and "truth" within a preexisting knowledge system that must be believed in order to work. The first allows for, indeed demands, the separation of personal responsibility from knowledge—knowledge exists as an objective entity apart from the knower. The second places accountability directly on the knower. Collins would ask us, which form of knowing is more likely to lead to social justice, one that denies ethical and moral accountability or one that demands it?

Implications of Black Feminist Thought

By now we should see that, for Collins, ways of knowing and knowledge are not separable or sterile—they are not abstract entities that exist apart from the political values and beliefs of the individual. How we know and what we know have implications for who we see ourselves to be, how we live our lives, and how we treat others. Collins sees these connections as particularly important for black women in at least three ways.

First, there is a tension between common challenges and diverse experiences. Think for a moment about what it means to center the idea of lived experience. We've already touched upon several implications of this idea, but what problem might arise from this way of thinking? The notion of lived experience, if taken to an extreme, can privilege individual experience and knowledge to the exclusion of a collective standpoint. The possibility of this implication is especially probable in a society like the United States that is built around the idea of individualism. However, this isn't what Collins has in mind. One doesn't overshadow the other in intersectionality. We'll explore this idea further later, but for now it is important to see that each individual stands at a unique matrix of crosscutting interests. These interests and the diverse responses they motivate are defined through such social positions as race, class, gender, sexual identity, religion, nationality, and so on.

Thus, the lived experience of a middle-class, pagan, single, gay black woman living in Los Angeles will undoubtedly be different from that of an impoverished, Catholic, married black woman living in a small town in Mississippi. As Patricia Hill Collins (2000) says, "it is important to stress that no homogeneous Black *woman's* standpoint exists" (p. 28). However, there are core themes or issues that come from living as a black woman such that "a Black *women's* collective standpoint does exist, one characterized by the tensions that accrue to different responses to common challenges" (p. 28). In other words, a black women's epistemology recognizes this tension between common challenges and diverse responses, which in turn is producing a growing sensibility that black women, because of their gendered racial identity, "may be victimized by racism, misogyny, and poverty" (p. 26). Thus, even though individual black women may respond differently based on different crosscutting interests, there are themes or core issues that all black women can acknowledge and integrate into their self-identity.

Another implication of black feminist epistemology is informed by this growing sensibility of diversity within commonality: understanding these issues leads to the creation of safe spaces. *Safe spaces* are "social spaces where Black women speak freely" (P. H. Collins, 2000, p. 100). These safe spaces are of course common occurrences for all oppressed groups. In order for an oppressed group to continue to exist as a viable social group, the members must have spaces where they can express themselves apart from the hegemonic or ruling ideology.

Collins identifies three primary safe spaces for black women. The first is black women's relationships with one another. These relationships can form and function within informal relationships such as family and friends, or they can occur within more formal and public spaces such as black churches and black women's organizations. In this context, Patricia Hill Collins (2000) also points to the importance of mentoring within black women's circles, mentoring that empowers black women "by passing on the everyday knowledge essential to survival as African-American women" (p. 102).

The other two safe spaces are cultural and are constituted by the black women's blues tradition and the voices of black women authors. Such cultural expressions have historically given voice to the voiceless. Those who were denied political or academic power could express their ideas and experiences through story and poetry. As long as the political majority could read these as "fictions"—that is, as long as they weren't faced with the facts of oppression—blacks were allowed these cultural outlets in "race markets." However, these books, stories, and poetry allowed oppressed people to communicate with one another and to produce a sense of shared identity.

There are several reasons why the musical form known as the blues is particularly important for constructing safe spaces and identities for black women. The blues originated out of the "call and response" of slaves working in the fields. It was born out of misery but simultaneously gave birth to hope. This hope wasn't simply expressed in words; it was also more powerfully felt in the rhythm and collectivity that made slave work less arduous. The blues thus expresses to even the illiterate the experience of black America, and it wraps individual suffering in a transcendent collective consciousness that enables the oppressed to persevere in hope without bitterness.

> The music of the classic blues singers of the 1920s—almost exclusively women—marks the early written record of this dimension of U.S. Black oral culture. The songs themselves were originally sung in small communities, where boundaries distinguishing singer from audience, call from response, and thought from action were fluid and permeable. (P. H. Collins, 2000, p. 106)

The importance of these safe spaces is that they provide opportunities for self-definition, and self-definition is the first step to empowerment—if a group is not defining itself, then it is being defined by and for the use of others. These safe spaces also allow black women to escape and resist "objectification as the Other" (P. H. Collins, 2000, p. 101), the images and ideas about black women found in the larger culture.

These safe spaces, then, are spaces of diversity, not homogeneity: "[T]he resulting reality is much more complex than one of an all-powerful White majority objectifying Black women with a unified U.S. Black community staunchly challenging these external assaults" (P. H. Collins, 2000, p. 101). However, even though these spaces recognize diversity, they are nonetheless exclusionary. (Here we can clearly see the tension that Collins notes.) If these spaces did not exclude, they would not be safe: "By definition, such spaces become less 'safe' if shared with those who were not Black and female" (p. 110). Although exclusionary, the intent of these spaces is to produce "a more inclusionary, just society" (p. 110).

This idea leads us to our third implication of black feminist thought: The struggles for self-identity take place within an ongoing dialogue between group knowledge or standpoint and experiences as a heterogeneous collective. Here, Collins is reconceptualizing the tension noted earlier between common challenges and diverse responses. This is important to note because one of the central features of Collins's approach is complexity. Collins wants us to see that most social issues, factors, and processes have multiple facets. Understanding how the different facets of inequality work together is paramount for understanding any part of it. In this case, on the one hand we have a *tension* between common challenges and diverse responses, and on the other hand we have a *dialogue* between a common group standpoint and diverse experiences.

Collins is arguing that changes in thinking may alter behaviors, and altering behaviors may produce changes in thinking. Thus, for U.S. black women as a collective, "the struggle for a self-defined Black feminism occurs through an ongoing dialogue whereby action and thought inform one another" (P. H. Collins, 2000, p. 30). For example, because black Americans have been racially segregated, black feminist practice and thought have emerged within the context of black community development. Other ideas and practices, such as black nationalism, have also come about due to racial segregation. Thus, black feminism and nationalism inform one another in the context of the black community, yet they are both distinct. Moreover, the relationships are reciprocal in that black feminist and nationalist thought influences black community development.

Collins also sees this dialogue as a process of rearticulation rather than consciousness-raising. During the 1960s and 1970s, consciousness-raising was a principal method in the feminist movement. Consciousness-raising groups would generally meet weekly, consist of no more than 12 women, and would encourage women to share their *personal experiences as women.* The intent was a kind of Marxian class consciousness that would precede social change, except that it was oriented around gender rather than class.

Rearticulation, according to Collins, is a vehicle for re-expressing a consciousness that quite often already exists in the public sphere. In rearticulation, we can see the dialogic nature of Collins's perspective. Rather than a specific, limited method designed to motivate women toward social movement, Collins sees black feminism as part of an already existing national discourse. What black feminism can do is take the core themes of black gendered oppression—such as racism, misogyny, and poverty—and infuse them with the lived experience of black women's taken-for-granted, everyday knowledge. This is brought back into the national discourse where practice and ideas are in a constant dialogue: "Rather than viewing consciousness as a fixed entity, a more useful approach sees it as continually evolving and negotiated. A dynamic consciousness is vital to both individual and group agency" (P. H. Collins, 2000, p. 285).

Black Intellectuals

Within this rearticulation, black feminist intellectuals have a specific place. To set ourselves up for this consideration, we can divide social intellectuals or academics into two broad groups: pure researchers and praxis researchers. Pure researchers hold to value-free sociology, the kind we noted earlier in considering Eurocentric thought. They are interested in simply discovering and explaining the social world. Praxis or critically oriented researchers are interested in ferreting out the processes of oppression and changing the social world. Black feminist intellectuals are of the latter kind, blending the lived experiences of black women with the highly specialized knowledge of intellectualism.

This dual intellectual citizenship gives black feminist scholars critical insights into the conditions of oppression. They both experience it as a lived reality and can think about it using the tools of critical analysis. Further, in studying oppression among black women, they are less likely to walk away "when the obstacles seem overwhelming or when the rewards for staying diminish" (P. H. Collins, 2000, p. 35). Black feminist intellectuals are also more motivated in this area because they are defining themselves while studying gendered racial inequality.

Finally, Patricia Hill Collins (2000) argues that black feminist intellectuals "alone can foster the group autonomy that fosters effective coalitions with other groups" (p. 36). In thinking about this, remember that Collins recognizes that intellectuals are found within all walks of life. Intellectual status isn't simply conferred as the result of academic credentials. Black feminist intellectuals think reflexively and publicly about their own lived experiences within the context of broader social issues and ideas.

Black feminist intellectuals, then, function like intermediary groups. On the one hand, they are very much in touch with their own and their peers' experiences as a disenfranchised group; on the other hand, they are also in touch with intellectual heritages, diverse groups, and broader social justice issues.

> By advocating, refining, and disseminating Black feminist thought, individuals from other groups who are engaged in similar social justice projects—Black men, African women, White men, Latinas, White women, and members of other U.S. racial/ethnic groups, for example—can identify points of connection that further social justice projects. (P. H. Collins, 2000, p. 37)

Collins notes, however, that coalition building with other groups and intellectuals can be costly. Privileged group members often have to become traitors to the "privileges that their race, class, gender, sexuality, or citizenship status provide them" (p. 37).

Concepts and Theory: Intersectionality and Matrices of Domination

Collins is best known for her ideas of intersectionality and the matrix of domination. Intersectionality is a particular way of understanding social location in terms of crisscrossing systems of oppression. Specifically, **intersectionality** is an "analysis claiming that systems of race, social class, gender, sexuality, ethnicity, nation, and age form mutually constructing features of social organization, which shape Black women's experiences and, in turn, are shaped by Black women" (P. H. Collins, 2000, p. 299).

This idea goes back to Max Weber and Georg Simmel. To refresh our memories, Weber's concern was to understand the complications that status and power brought to Marx's idea of class stratification. According to Weber, class consciousness and social change are more difficult to achieve than Marx first thought: Status group affiliation and differences in power create concerns that may override class issues. Simmel was interested in the way the motivations for and patterns of group memberships changed as a result of living in urban rather than rural settings. Simmel noted that people living in cities tend to have greater freedom of choice and the opportunity to be members of more diverse groups than people in small towns. He was specifically concerned with the psychological and emotional effects that these different social network patterns have on people.

There is a way in which Collins blends these two approaches while at the same time going beyond them. Like Simmel, Collins is concerned with the influences of intersectionality on the individual. But the important issue for Collins is the way intersectionality creates different kinds of lived experiences and social realities. She is particularly concerned with how these interact with what passes as objective knowledge and how diverse voices of intersectionality are denied under scientism. Like Weber, she is concerned about how intersectionality creates different kinds of inequalities and how these crosscutting influences affect social change. But Collins brings Weber's notion of power into this analysis in a much more sophisticated way. Collins sees intersectionality as working within a matrix of domination.

The **matrix of domination** refers to the overall organization of power in a society. There are two features to any matrix. First, any specific matrix has a particular arrangement of intersecting systems of oppression. Just what and how these systems come together is historically and socially specific. Second, intersecting systems of oppression are specifically organized through four interrelated domains of power: structural, disciplinary, hegemonic, and interpersonal.

The *structural domain* consists of such social structures as law, polity, religion, and the economy. This domain sets the structural parameters that organize power relations. For example, prior to February 3, 1870, blacks in the United States could not legally vote. Although constitutionally enabled to vote after that date, voting didn't become a reality for many African American people until almost a century later with the passage of the Voting Rights Act of 1965, which officially ended Jim Crow laws. Collins's point is that the structural domain sets the overall organization of power within a matrix of domination and that the structural domain is slow to change, often only yielding to large-scale social movements, such as the Civil War and the upheavals of the 1950s and 1960s in the United States.

The *disciplinary domain* manages oppression. Collins borrows this idea from both Weber and Michel Foucault (Chapter 9): the disciplinary domain consists of bureaucratic organizations whose task it is to control and organize human behavior through routinization, rationalization, and surveillance. Here, the matrix of domination is expressed through organizational protocol that hides the effects of racism and sexism under the canopy of efficiency, rationality, and equal treatment. In this domain, change can come through insider resistance. Collins uses the analogy of an egg. From a distance, the surface of the egg looks smooth and seamless. But upon closer inspection, the egg is revealed to be riddled with cracks. For those interested in social justice, working in a bureaucracy is like working the cracks, finding spaces and fissures to work in and expand. Again, change is slow and incremental.

The *hegemonic domain* legitimizes oppression. Max Weber was among the first to teach us that authority functions because people believe in it. This is the cultural sphere of influence where ideology and consciousness come together. The hegemonic domain links the structural, disciplinary, and interpersonal domains. It is made up of the language we use, the images we respond to, the values we hold, and the ideas we entertain. It is produced through school curricula and textbooks, religious teachings, mass media images and contexts, community cultures, and family histories. The black feminist priorities of self-definition and critical, reflexive education are important stepping–stones to deconstructing and dissuading the hegemonic domain. As Patricia Hill Collins (2000) puts it, "Racist and sexist ideologies, if they are disbelieved, lose their impact" (p. 284).

The *interpersonal domain* influences everyday life. It is made up of the personal relationships we maintain as well as the different interactions that make up our daily life. Collins points out that change in this domain begins with the *intra*personal, that is, how an individual sees and understands her or his own self and experiences. In particular, people don't generally have a problem identifying ways in which they have been victimized. But the first step in changing the interpersonal domain of the matrix of domination is seeing how our own "thoughts and actions uphold *someone else's subordination*" (P. H. Collins, 2000, p. 287, emphasis added).

Part of this first step is seeing that people have a tendency to identify with an oppression, most likely the one they have experienced, and to consider all other oppressions as being of less importance. In the person's mind, his or her oppression has a tendency to take on a master status. This leads to a kind of contradiction where the oppressed becomes the oppressor. For example, a black heterosexual woman may discriminate against lesbians without a second thought, or a black Southern Baptist woman may believe that every school classroom ought to display the Ten Commandments. "Oppression is filled with such contradictions because these approaches fail to recognize that a matrix of domination contains few pure victims or oppressors" (P. H. Collins, 2000, p. 287).

Black Feminist Thought, Intersectionality, and Activism

There are a number of implications for activism that Collins draws out from black feminist thought and the notions of intersectionality and the matrix of domination. The first that I want to point out is the most immediate: Collins's approach to epistemology and intersectionality conceptualizes resistance as a complex interplay of a variety of forces working at several levels—that is, resistance in the four interrelated domains of power that we've just discussed.

This point of Collins's isn't an incidental issue. Remember that part of what is meant by modernity is the search for social equality. In modernity, primary paths for these social changes correspond to Collins's first domain of power. For example, the United States Declaration of Independence, Constitution, and Bill of Rights together provide for principal mechanisms of structural change: the electoral process within a civil society guaranteed by the twin freedoms of press and speech and the upheaval or revolutionary process. Though we don't usually think of the latter as a legitimated means of social change, it is how this nation began and it is how much of the more dramatic changes that surround equality have come about (for example, the social movements behind women's suffrage and civil rights).

One of the ideas that comes out of postmodernism and considerations of late modernity is the notion that guided or rational social change is no longer possible. What Collins gives us is a different take on the issues of complexity and fragmentation. While recognizing the complexity of intersectionality and the different levels of the matrix of domination, Collins also sees the four domains of power as interrelated and thus influencing one another. By themselves, the structural and disciplinary domains are most resilient to change, but the hegemonic and interpersonal domains are open to individual agency and change. Bringing these domains together creates a more dynamic system, wherein the priorities of black feminist thought and understanding the contradictions of oppression can empower social justice causes.

Collins's approach also has other important implications. Her ideas of intersectionality and the matrix of domination challenge many of our political assumptions. Black feminist epistemology, for example, challenges our assumptions concerning the separation of the private and public spheres. What it means to be a mother in a traditional black community is very different from what it means in a white community: "Black women's experiences have never fit the logic of work in the public sphere juxtaposed to family obligations in the private sphere" (P. H. Collins, 2000, p. 228). Intersectionality also challenges the assumption that gender stratification affects all women in the same way; race and class matter, as does sexual identity.

In addition, Collins's approach untangles relationships among knowledge, empowerment, and power, and opens up conceptual space to identify new connections within the matrix of domination. The idea of the matrix emphasizes connections and interdependencies rather than single structures of inequality. The idea itself prompts us to wonder about how social categories are related and mutually constituted.

For example, how do race and sexual preference work together? Asking such a question might lead us to discover that homosexuality is viewed and treated differently in different racial cultures—is the lived experience of a black gay male different from that of a white gay male? If so, we might take the next step and ask, how does class influence those differences? Or, if these lived experiences are different, we might be provoked to ask another question: Are there different masculinities in different racial or class cultures?

As you might be able to surmise from this example, Collins's approach discourages binary thinking and the labeling of one oppression or activism as more important or radical. From Collins's point of view, it would be much too simplistic to say that a white male living in poverty is enjoying white privilege. In the same way, it would be one-dimensional to say that any one group is more oppressed than another.

Collins's entire approach also shifts our understanding of social categories from bounded to fluid and highlights the processes of self-definition as constructed in conjunction with others. Intersectionality implies that social categories are not bounded or static. Your social nearness to or distance from another change as the matrix of domination shifts, depending on which scheme is salient at any given moment. You and the person next to you may both be women, but that social nearness may be severed as the indices change to include religion, race, ethnicity, sexual practices or identities, class, and so forth.

Groups are also constructed in connection to others. No group or identity stands alone. To state the obvious, the only way "white" as a social index can exist is if "black" exists. Intersectionality motivates us to look at just how our identities are constructed at the expense of others: "These examples suggest that moral positions as survivors of one expression of systemic violence become eroded in the absence of accepting responsibility of other expressions of systemic violence" (P. H. Collins, 2000, p. 247).

Here is one final implication of Collins's approach: Because groups' histories and inequalities are relational, understanding intersectionality and the matrix of domination means that some coalitions with some social groups are more difficult and less fruitful than others. Groups will more or less align on the issues of "victimization, access to positions of authority, unearned benefits, and traditions of resistance" (P. H. Collins, 2000, p. 248). The more closely aligned are these issues, the more likely and beneficial are the coalitions. These coalitions will also ebb and flow, "based on the perceived saliency of issues to group members" (p. 248). We end, then, with the insight that inequalities and dominations are complex and dynamic.

Summary

- Collins argues that black women represent a powerful place to begin theorizing about social inequality. Studies and theories on inequality generally focus on one specific issue, such as race or gender. To understand the inequality of black women, however, forces us to be concerned with at least two systems of inequality (gender and race) and their intersections.

- According to Collins, the four qualities of Eurocentric positivism hamper our understanding of how systems of inequality work. These four characteristics are (1) the objective stand, (2) emotional divestment, (3) value-free theory and research, and (4) progress through cumulation and adversarial debate. The four characteristics of black feminist knowledge counter each of these points. Black feminist knowledge (1) is built upon lived experience, (2) emphasizes emotional investment and accountability, (3) honors ethically driven research and theory, and (4) understands intellectual progress through dialogue.

- There are three primary implications of black feminist thought: first, the recognition of the tension between common challenges and diverse responses; second, the creation of safe places that honor diversity; and third, self-identity formed within a continuing dialogue between common challenges and varied experiences. This last implication has importance for rearticulating the public discourse surrounding black women.

- Black feminist intellectuals have a specific place in the construction of black women's identities and the rearticulation of the public sphere. Specifically, black feminists hold a kind of dual intellectual citizenship: They are trained in positivistic methods, yet they also have the lived experience of black women. This dual citizenship gives black feminists greater opportunities to forge coalitions with other social justice groups.

- Collins's approach to studying inequality is based on the concepts of intersectionality and a matrix of domination. Intersectionality captures the structured position of people living at the crossroads of two or more systems of inequality, such as race and gender. The different intersectionalities of a society influence the overall organization of power—what Collins refers to as the matrix of domination. These matrices are historically and socially specific, yet they are organized around four general domains of power: structural (the interrelationships of social structures), disciplinary (bureaucratic organization and protocol), hegemonic (cultural legitimations), and interpersonal (personal relationships).

- There are various implications of Collins's approach. First, activism is a complex enterprise that links together different practices in the four domains of power. In other words, activism can involve more than social movements aimed at changing the institutional arrangements of a society. Because there are four domains of power, there can be four fronts of activism. Second, her approach challenges many of the existing political assumptions and opens up new conceptual space for understanding how inequalities work. The ideas of intersectionality and a matrix of domination discourage simple, binary thinking in politics and research. Third, Collins's ideas sensitize us to the fluid nature of social categories, identities, and relations. And fourth, political coalitions can ebb and flow as different groups align to varying degrees on the issues of power, victimization, and resistance.

Commodification of Black Experience—Cornel West

There's a way in which Cornel West picks up from where William Julius Wilson left off. Wilson argued that since the civil rights movement in the 1960s, the black population in the United States has been split as never before by class. Most of the changes that have occurred with reference to race have thus benefited rising middle-class blacks and have left those African Americans at the poverty level and below as the "truly disadvantaged." West picks up Wilson's theme but moves it more into the realm of culture. Since the 1960s, the upwardly mobile black population in the United States has increasingly become the target of capitalist markets. Not only did capitalists discover a new market when African Americans entered the middle class, but they also in a sense tried to make up for lost time. Capitalists have had over two centuries of marketing to whites, but blacks have constituted a strong and viable market for only the past 40 years or so. Given the historical background of the black community in the United States, this concentrated market force has had unique effects on African Americans of all classes.

Source: © Richard Howard/ Time Life Pictures/Getty Images.

THEORIST'S DIGEST

Brief Biography

Cornel West (1953–) was born in Tulsa, Oklahoma. He began attending Harvard University at 17 and graduated 3 years later, magna cum laude. His degree was in Near Eastern languages and literature. West obtained his PhD at Princeton, where he studied with Richard Rorty, a well-known pragmatist. West has taught at Union Theological Seminary, Yale Divinity School, the University of Paris, Harvard, and is currently at Princeton. Among his most significant works are *Race Matters* and *Democracy Matters: Winning the Fight Against Imperialism.* His recent works include *Keeping Faith: Philosophy and Race in America* and a rap CD, *Never Forget: A Journey of Revelations.*

Central Sociological Questions

Cornel West's life is committed to not only the race question in America, but also to the democratic ideals of open and critical dialogue, the freedom of ideas and information, and compassion for and acceptance of diverse others. His passion, then, is to expose antidemocratic energies wherever they may be found. In this chapter, he specifically asks two questions: How has capitalist marketing affected black Americans? And how have the events of 9/11 affected democracy in America?

(Continued)

(Continued)

Simply Stated

West is concerned about race and democracy in the United States. Since the civil rights era of the 1960s, blacks have experienced greater political participation and economic upward mobility than ever before. While these changes have had obvious positive effects, they have also worked to weaken traditional black community and create a crisis in black leadership. Since the 1960s, African Americans have been subjected to intense marketing with an ever-expanding number of commodities. As a result, market moralities have replaced traditional black cultural armor and have created a sense of black nihilism. In response to these threats, West calls for a reenergizing of moral reasoning, coalition strategy, and mature black identity.

Key Ideas

False consciousness, market saturation, black cultural armor, market moralities, ontological wounds, existential angst, black nihilism, politics of conversion, crisis in black leadership, three kinds of leadership styles, racial reasoning, moral reasoning, mature black identity, coalition strategy

Concepts and Theory: Black Existence in America

West gives us two basic structural influences on blacks in the United States: the economic boom and expansion of civil rights for blacks in the 1960s, and the saturation of market forces. In terms of the economic and political well-being of blacks in the United States, West is simply saying that they both increased, particularly during the boom of the 1970s. For example, the U.S. Census Bureau (n.d.) reports that black, male, median income increased from $9,519 in 1950 to $17,055 in 1970, as measured in 2003 dollars. These changes helped define blacks as a viable market group, one with disposable income and market-specific products. In some obvious ways, these changes have benefited the black experience in America. However, the development of black economic markets has also had significant negative effects.

As a way of distributing goods and services, markets have been a part of human history for millennia. *Modern, capitalist markets,* however, have a couple of unique characteristics. Modern capitalism is defined by the endless accumulation of capital to create more capital. Because capital is its own goal, it's never achieved (capital to generate capital to generate capital and so on, endlessly). This drive implies that the need for profit is insatiable and thus continues to increase. Because markets are the mechanism through which profit and capital are gained, modern capitalist markets are intrinsically expansive: They expand vertically (through accessories for an existing product), horizontally (producing new products within a market), and geographically (extending existing markets to new social groups).

A second unique characteristic of modern capitalism is related to the factor of expanding markets: Capitalists are driven to create a never-ending stream of new or different commodities. Keep in mind that commodification is a process that converts more and more of the human lifeworld into something that can be bought and sold, and it creates new "needs" within the consumer. Human beings are not just the only animal capable of economic production; we are also the only species able to create new psychological drives and needs for the new products. There's a sense in which markets are without any morals whatsoever: They aren't restricted by any kind of ethic—they can be used to sell Bibles or guns to terrorists. This quality makes them applicable to any situation or product. However, as we will see, the absence of any ethical restrictions implies and creates a morality of its own—and these market moralities are particularly destructive for black Americans.

Black Nihilism

West characterizes this market expansion into the black community as a kind of *market saturation*. He first argues that the market saturation of the black population has stripped away community-based values and substituted market moralities. Earlier, I mentioned that markets are amoral, but this is in a restricted sense only—markets can be used for anything. Markets do, however, convey some specific cultural ideas and sensibilities. In classical theory, for example, Max Weber was extremely interested in how markets and bureaucracies create rational rather than affective culture, and Georg Simmel saw markets as contributing to cultural signs becoming frivolous.

West argues that being a focus for market activity, commodification, and advertising has changed black culture in America. Prior to market saturation, blacks had a long history of community and tradition. They were equipped with a kind of *black cultural armor* that came via black civic and religious institutions. This armor consisted of clear and strong structures of meaning and feeling that "embodied values of service and sacrifice, love and care, discipline and excellence" (West, 1993/2001, p. 24). While this is specific to black Americans, it's important to note that this general shift from community-based traditional culture to less meaningful and more pliable culture was a concern of many social theorists of modernity. We find this idea of cultural shift repeatedly in classical theory. The basic idea is that culture has dramatically changed through processes accompanying urbanization and commodification. Rather than being meaningful, normative, and cohesive, culture is trivialized, anomic, and segmented.

West is making this same kind of argument, so he follows a strong theoretical tradition. West, however, is pointing out that while the dispersion of community and the emptying of culture may have affected much of modern society during the beginning and middle stages of modernity and capitalism, the black community in America wasn't strongly influenced by these changes until after the 1960s. Until then, blacks continued to rely on community-based relations and religiously influenced culture. As a result of the twin structural influences of civil rights and upward mobility, blacks moved out of black communities and churches. The structural bases for cultural armor were weakened as a result.

In place of cultural armor, blacks have since been inundated with the *market moralities* of conspicuous consumption and material calculus. The culture of consumption orients people to the present moment and to the intensification of pleasure. This culture of pleasure uses seduction to capitalize "on every opportunity to make money" (West, 1993/2001, p. 26). It overwhelms people in a moment where the past and future are swallowed up in a never-ending "repetition of hedonistically driven pleasure" (p. 26). Further, the material calculus argues that the greatest value comes from profit-driven calculations. Every other consideration, such as love and service to others, is hidden under the bushel of profit.

As I've mentioned, most of these cultural ramifications of markets and commodification have also been present in other groups. But in West's (1993/2001) opinion, two issues make these effects particularly destructive for blacks. First, black upward mobility and the presence of the black middle class concern only a small sliver of the pie. Most of the black citizens of the United States still suffer under white oppression. The other issue that makes the black experience of market saturation distinct is the "accumulated effect of the black wounds and scars suffered in a white-dominated society" (p. 28). In other words, there is a historical and cultural heritage, no matter how much the immediacy of market saturation and pleasure tries to deny it—much of the history of the United States was built on the oppression of blacks, over the 188 years from 1776 to 1964.

Obviously, these two factors influence one another. Healing from past wounds can only take place in a present that is both nurturing and repentant, a place that does not replicate hurts from the past. According to West (1993/2001), this isn't happening for blacks in America: Cultural beliefs and media images continue to attack "black intelligence, black ability, black beauty, and black character in subtle and not-so-subtle ways" (p. 27). Moreover, as noted earlier, black upward mobility is still limited. For example, in 2002 over 30% of black children lived under the poverty line, compared to 12.3% of white children (Statistical Abstract of the United States, 2002).

In the abstract, West's argument so far looks like this: black upward mobility + increased civil rights → weakening of civic and religious community base → substitution of market moralities for cultural armor—all of which takes place within the framework of the black legacy in the United States and continued oppression. "Under these circumstances black existential *angst* derives from the lived experience of ontological wounds and emotional scars" (West, 1993/2001, p. 27). The *ontological wounds* that West is speaking of come from the ways in which black reality and existence have been denied throughout the history of the United States.

In general, *existential angst* refers to the deep and profound insecurity and dread that comes from living as a human being. This idea comes from existentialism, which starts with the problem of being or existence and argues that the very question or problem creates existence. As far as we know, human beings are the only animal that questions its existence: Why am I here? What's the meaning of life? All other animals simply exist. But human beings ask, and in asking we create human existence as a unique experience. That unique experience is existential angst, worrying over the great questions of life. But this angst can lead to the great transcendences of human life; it can lead to community as we share our existential existence.

West employs the idea of angst to describe the uniquely black experience of living under American capitalism and democracy—under slavery, blacks were denied existence as human beings and weren't allowed civil rights until the 1960s. Further, black experience is deeply historical, yet the past and the future are now buried under the market-driven pleasures of the moment. In addition, black experience is fundamentally communitarian, yet that civic and religious base is overwhelmed by market individualisms; black experience is painfully oppressive, yet it is countered only by increasing target marketing and consumerism. Thus, West argues that the result of market saturation and morality for blacks is a deeply spiritual condition of despair and insecurity. Because blacks no longer have the necessary culture, community, or leadership, this angst cannot be used productively. It is instead turned inward as anger, and this anger is played out in violence against the weak. Righteous anger, turned against the oppressor in hopes of liberation, becomes increasingly difficult to express. **Black nihilism** denies the hope in which this anger is founded. With no viable path, this anger is turned inward and found in black-against-black violence, especially against black women and children.

Crisis in Black Leadership

However, nihilism can be treated. West argues that it is a disease of the soul, one that cannot be cured, as there is always the threat of relapse. This disease must be met with love and care, not arguments and analysis. What is required is a new kind of politics, a *politics of conversion,* which reaches into the subversive memory of black people to find modes of valuation and resistance. Politics of conversion is centered on a love ethic that is energized by concern for others and the recognition of one's own worth. This kind of politics requires prophetic black leaders who will bring "hope for the future and a meaning to struggle" (West, 1993/2001, p. 28). There is, however, a *crisis in black leadership.*

For West, there is a relationship between community and leadership. Strong leaders come out of vibrant communities. With the breakdown of the black community, black leaders don't have a social base that is in touch with the real issues. There is thus no nurturing of critical consciousness in the heart of black America. Rather, much of the new black leadership in America comes out of the middle class, and black middle-class life is "principally a matter of professional conscientiousness, personal accomplishment, and cautious adjustment" (West, 1993/2001, p. 57). West maintains that what is lacking in contemporary black leadership is anger and humility; what is present in overabundance is status anxiety and concerns for personal careers.

West divides contemporary black leaders into two general types—politicians and academics—with *three kinds of leadership styles:* race-effacing managerial leaders, race-identifying protest leaders, and race-transcending prophetic leaders. There are some differences between politicians and academics, but by and large they express the same leadership styles. The managerial/elitist model is growing rapidly in the United States. This style of leadership is one that has been co-opted by bureaucratic norms. The leader navigates the political scene through political savvy and personal diplomacy. Race is downplayed in the hopes of gaining a white constituency. In academia, the elitist sees her- or himself as having a kind of monopoly over the sophisticated analysis of black America, but the analysis is flat and mediocre because of the intellectual's desire to fit into the university system. In both cases, whether under political savvy or academic abstraction, race is effaced.

The second type of leader, the protest leader, capitalizes on the race issue but in a very limited way, in what West (1993/2001) describes as "one-note racial analyses" (p. 68). Here, "Black" becomes all-powerful. West characterizes these leaders as "confining themselves to the black turf, vowing to protect their leadership status over it, and serving as power brokers with powerful nonblack elites" (p. 60). In this context, racial reasoning reigns supreme.

Racial reasoning is a way of thinking that is concerned with equality more as a group right rather than a general social issue. For West, racial reasoning begins with an assumption of the black experience. The discourse of race, then, centers on black authenticity: the notion that some black experiences and people are really black while others aren't. Racial reasoning results in blacks closing ranks, but again it is around a one-note song rather than a symphony of color. Racial reasoning results in black nationalist sentiments that "promote and encourage black cultural conservatism, especially black patriarchal (and homophobic) power" (West, 1993/2001, p. 37). Closing the ranks thus creates a hierarchy of acceptability within a black context: the black subordination of women, class divisions, and sexual orientation within black America.

Leadership for Equality

These two kinds of black leaders have promoted political cynicism among black people, and have dampened "the fire of enraged local activists who have made a difference" (West, 1993/2001, p. 68). Part of black nihilism, or nothingness, is this sense of ineffectuality, of being lost in a storm too big to change. What is needed, according to West, are black leaders founded on moral reasoning rather than racial reasoning. *Moral reasoning* is the stock and trade of race-transcending prophetic leaders. Prophetic leadership does not rest on any kind of racial supremacy, black or white. It uses a *coalition strategy*, which seeks out the antiracist traditions found in all peoples. It refuses to divide black people over other categories of distinction and rejects patriarchy and homophobia. Such an approach promotes moral rather than racial reasoning.

This framework of moral reasoning is also based on a *mature black identity* of self-love and self-respect that refuses to put "any group of people on the pedestal or in the gutter" (West, 1993/2001, p. 43). Moral reasoning also uses subversive memory, "one of the most precious heritages [black people] have" (West, 1999, p. 221). It recalls the modes of struggling and resisting that affirmed community, faith, hope, and love, rather than the contemporary market morality of individualism, conspicuous consumption, and hedonistic indulgence.

Both the coalition strategy and mature black identity are built at the local level. West (1999) sees local communities as working "from below and sometimes beneath modernity" (p. 221), as if local communities can function below the radar of markets and commodification. It is within vibrant communities and through public discourse that local leaders are accountable and earn respect and love. Such leaders merit national attention from the black community and the general public, according to West.

In this framework, the liberal focus on economic issues is rejected as simplistic. Likewise, the conservative critique of black immorality is dismissed as ignoring public responsibility for the ethical state of the union. In their places, West proposes a democratic, pragmatically driven dialogue. As I mentioned earlier, West doesn't propose absolutes. His is a prophetic call to radical democracy and faith, to finally take seriously the declaration that all people are created equal.

Together, moral reasoning, coalition strategy, and mature black identity create the black cultural armor. West's use of "armor" is a biblical reference. Christians are told in Ephesians 6:13 (New International Version) to "put on the full armor of God, so that when the day of evil comes, you may be able to stand your ground, and after you have done everything, to stand." There, the threat was the powers of darkness in heavenly places; here, the threat is black nihilism in the heart of democracy. These two battles are at least parallel if not identical for West. The fight for true democracy is a spiritual battle for the souls of humankind that have been dulled by market saturation, especially the souls of black America. West (1993/2001) exhorts black America to put on its cultural armor—a return to community life and moral reasoning along with coalition strategy and mature black identity—so as to "beat back the demons of hopelessness, meaninglessness, and lovelessness" and create anew "cultural structures of meaning and feeling" (p. 23).

Summary

- Since the 1960s, blacks in the United States have on the one hand enjoyed increased economic and political freedoms, while on the other have become the victims of market saturation. Market saturation has changed the primary orientations of blacks. Previously, blacks were strongly oriented to civic and religious institutions and the traditional ties of family and home. Market saturation has infested the black community with market moralities: fleeting hedonistic pleasure and monetary gain. The effects of markets are exaggerated for blacks because of black heritage in America. The mix of past wounds, the continuing racial prejudice, and market moralities creates black nihilism (a sense of hopelessness and meaninglessness associated with living as a black person in the United States).

- West exposes a crisis in black leadership, arguing that most black leaders either fall under the managerial/elitist model or that of protest leaders. With protest leaders, racial reasoning is paramount, which promotes ethics based on skin color alone, rather than on moral or justice issues. West calls on prophetic leaders that will transcend race and return to moral reasoning. These leaders must begin in the community, at the grassroots level, where they can participate in pragmatic community dialogue, build up trust, and maintain accountability.

BUILDING YOUR THEORY TOOLBOX

- After reading and understanding this chapter, you should be able to define the following terms theoretically and explain their importance to Collins's theory: intersectionality; Eurocentric positivism; black feminist epistemology; common challenges/diverse responses; safe places; self-definition; rearticulation; black feminist intellectuals; matrix of domination; structural, disciplinary, hegemonic, and interpersonal domains of power

- After reading and understanding this chapter, you should be able to define the following terms: false consciousness, market saturation, black cultural armor, market moralities, ontological wounds, existential angst, black nihilism, politics of conversion, crisis in black leadership, three kinds of leadership styles, racial reasoning, moral reasoning, mature black identity, coalition strategy

- After reading and understanding this chapter, you should be able to answer the following questions (remembering to answer them theoretically):

  o Compare and contrast the characteristics of Eurocentric positivism and black feminist epistemology.

  o Explicate the implications of black feminist epistemology.

  o Explain how inequality can best be understood as intersectionality and matrices of domination. In your explanation, be certain to discuss the implications of such an approach.

  o Why did market saturation affect the black community in unique ways?

  o What is black nihilism, where does it come from, and how is it affecting blacks in the United States today?

  o Why is there a black leadership crisis? What are politics of conversion?

  o What is racial reasoning? How does moral reasoning counter racial reasoning?

Learning More—Primary Sources

- Patricia Hill Collins, *Black Feminist Thought* (2nd ed.), Routledge, 2000.

- Patricia Hill Collins, *Black Sexual Politics,* Routledge, 2004

- Patricia Hill Collins, *From Black Power to Hip Hop: Racism, Nationalism, and Feminism,* Temple University Press, 2006.

- Cornel West, *Race Matters,* Vintage, 1993.

- Cornel West, *Democracy Matters: Winning the Fight Against Imperialism,* Penguin, 2004.

Engaging the Social World

- In general, what implications do you see of objectified knowledge for the way people view and experience themselves? Even though Collins's theory is directed toward black women, how would your way of seeing the social world change if you adopted Collins's feminist epistemology? What are the implications if society were to do away with objective knowledge about social things?

- List the different social categories that affect you. How do they come together to create a unique matrix of domination?

- Use Collins's theory to analyze the classes you've taken about race and gender. How would those classes be different if they took Collins's theory into account?

- Discuss the kinds of activism that Patricia Hill Collins's approach includes. In your discussion, be certain to include the four domains of power and the unique place that black feminist intellectuals have in activism.

- Become involved in campus efforts to end discrimination. Check and see if you have an office of multicultural affairs. Find out what other campus organizations are involved in ending discrimination.

- If you're African American, explore how your values and sense of self are impacted by market moralities. If you're not African American, how have market moralities affected you?

- What does West's critique of political leadership imply generally about what we should expect from leaders in a democratic society? Analyze the current national leadership using West's criteria. Think especially about Barack Obama. Where would you place him in West's scheme? Search the Internet to discover West's opinion of Obama.

Weaving the Threads

- Evaluate William Julius Wilson's class-based proposals using West's theory of black nihilism.

- Synthesize Wilson, Collins, and West into a general theory of racial inequality. How do social structures and culture work to oppress blacks?

- Compare and contrast Foucault's and West's theories of subjective experience. How can these theories be brought together to give us greater insight into how individual, subjective experiences are formed in this period of modernity?

CHAPTER 16

Text, Power, and Women

Dorothy E. Smith

G ender inequality has been studied by sociologists ever since the time of Harriet Martineau. In 1837, she published her study of America. For Martineau (1837/2005), one of the key tests of civilization and democracy in a society is the condition of women: "If a test of civilization be sought, none can be so sure as the condition of that half of society over which the other half has power" (p. 291). Granted, since that time, the topic of gender has come in and out of favor with the discipline of sociology as a whole. Nevertheless, it's safe to say that gender inequality as a topic of study has been a central concern since the 1970s, and sociologists have done countless studies and published innumerable articles, books, and essays on the subject since then.

But, what if a good many of them actually worked to suppress women rather than liberate them? Dorothy E. Smith asks us to consider this possibility. She argues that the way in which women are dominated isn't solely through the social structures that Janet Saltzman Chafetz told us about in Chapter 7. Rather, gender inequality also works through the social and behavioral sciences as they create *knowledge about women* in opposition to *women's knowledge.* This body of knowledge claims objectivity and thus authority "not on the basis of its capacity to speak truthfully, but in terms of its specific capacity to exclude the presence and experience of particular subjectivities" (D. E. Smith, 1987, p. 2). Smith wants to center social and behavioral research on the actual lived experiences of people and their encounter with texts, rather than on the texts that deny the very voices they claim to express.

THEORIST'S DIGEST

Brief Biography

Dorothy E. Smith was born in Northallerton, Yorkshire, Great Britain, in 1926. She earned her undergraduate degree in 1955 from the London School of Economics. In 1963, Smith received her PhD from the University of California at Berkeley. She has taught at Berkeley, the University of Essex, and the University of British Columbia. She is currently Adjunct Professor at the University of Victoria. In recognition of her contributions to sociology, the American Sociological Association (ASA) honored Smith with the Jessie Bernard Award in 1993 and the Career of Distinguished Scholarship Award in 1999. Her book *The Everyday World as Problematic* has received two awards from the Canadian Sociology and Anthropology Association: the Outstanding Contribution Award and the John Porter Award, both given in 1990.

Central Sociological Questions

Smith is centrally concerned with how the daily lives of men and women are quite often different. Yet, when gender is studied from a social scientific perspective, the distinct experiences and knowledge of women are written out. The relations of ruling, then, continue to be exerted even under the guise of gender inequality. "My research concern is to build an ordinary good knowledge of the text-mediated organization of power from the standpoint of women in contemporary capitalism" (D. E. Smith, 1992, p. 97).

Simply Stated

Smith argues that the social and behavioral sciences have systematically developed an objective body of knowledge about the individual, social relations, and society in general. This body of knowledge claims objectivity and thus authority "not on the basis of its capacity to speak truthfully, but in terms of its specific capacity to exclude the presence and experience of particular subjectivities" (D. E. Smith, 1987, p. 2). Because of this exclusion, social scientific texts are nothing more than an expression of the relations of ruling that continue to oppress women. Smith wants to center research on the actual lived experiences of women, and their encounters with these texts.

(Continued)

> (Continued)
>
> **Key Ideas**
>
> Practices of power, new materialism, texts, facticity, standpoint, constitutive work, relations of ruling, fault line, institutional ethnography

Concepts and Theory: The Problem With Facts

As with Giddens and West, I'm putting Smith's perspective up front rather than at the end of the chapter. The main reason for doing this is that in many ways her theory and her perspective are the same; as you'll see, it's hard to talk of one apart from the other. Plus, she gives us a different account of how gender inequality is achieved than did Chafetz (Chapter 7)—again, because she sees the world a bit differently.

Method, Not Theory

In 1992, *Sociological Theory*, the premier theoretical journal of the American Sociological Association, presented a symposium on the work of Dorothy E. Smith. Though Smith had been publishing for quite some time, her dramatic impact on sociology came with the release in 1987 of *The Everyday World as Problematic: A Feminist Sociology* and in 1990, *The Conceptual Practices of Power: A Feminist Sociology of Knowledge*. Being the subject of a special issue in *Sociological Theory* so soon after the publication of two major works attests to the impact that Smith's perspective was having on sociology. Among the commentators in that special issue were Patricia Hill Collins, Robert Connell, and Charles Lemert, each a significant theorist in her or his own right. However, Smith (1992) critiqued each of these theorists as having misinterpreted her work: "Each constructs her or his own straw Smith" (p. 88).

Of course, Collins, Connell, and Lemert had their own individual issues, but Dorothy Smith (1992) argues that they universally misconstrued her work as theory rather than method. "It is not . . . a totalizing theory. Rather it is a *method of inquiry*, always ongoing, opening things up, discovering" (p. 88). This is obviously an important point for us to note at the beginning of our discussion of Smith's work. She doesn't give us a general theory, not even a general theory of gender oppression. Smith gives us a method, but it isn't a method in the same sense as data analysis—Smith's is a theoretical method. It's grounded in a theoretical understanding of the world that results in theoretical insights. Further, for Smith these theoretical insights are themselves continually held up to evaluation and revision.

In general, Smith's work is considered "standpoint theory." As we'll see below, that's a fairly accurate description of what she does. But Smith argues that thinking about standpoint theoretically makes the idea too abstract, and it defeats the original intent. Like Pierre Bourdieu (Chapter 8), Smith is very interested in the *practices of power*. She is interested in what happens on the ground in the lived experiences of women, more so than the abstract words of sociological theory.

Let me give you an example that might help illuminate the distinction that Smith is making. Not long ago, I was talking to a friend of mine who plays and builds drums. We were talking about the special feeling that comes from building the instrument you play. He was saying that there's a kind of connection that develops between the builder and the wood, a connection that is grounded in the physical experience of the material. I agreed and told him that kind of knowledge is called *kinesthetic*. But I was painfully aware that there was a real difference between what we were each talking about. He has actually worked with the wood out of which he builds his drum kits; though I play guitar, I have never experienced that kind of connection with my instrument. I had the word for what he was talking about, but he had the actual experience.

Smith is arguing that something happens when we formalize and generalize our concepts: We can quickly move out of the realm of real experience. As such, it is possible for concepts to play a purely discursive role. Just like in my example of kinesthetic knowledge, we can talk about things of which we only have discursive or linguistic knowledge. Thus, I can talk about the intuitive connection that exists between a musician and an instrument that he or she has built, but I have no actual knowledge of it. It's purely theoretical for me.

Obviously, there are no significant consequences of my woodworking example. But in the social world, there can be important ramifications, and that's the point that Smith wants us to see. Standpoint theory isn't a theory per se; it's a method of observation that privileges the point of view of actual people over theoretical, abstract knowledge. That may sound commonsensical and you may agree with it, but Smith would contend that most of what you and I know about the social world is like my knowledge of building a musical instrument.

In thinking about Smith's approach, it is important to note that she doesn't see herself as arguing against abstractions. To one degree or another, theory is usually abstracted. When we talk about theory being abstract, we mean that it is not simply a statement or restatement of the particulars. In a fundamental way, then, most theories and theoretical terms exist outside of the actual situation as generalizations. For example, there is a significant difference between saying, "LaToya went to Food Lion to do the food shopping" and "Women generally do the grocery shopping." The first statement is particular; it refers to the behaviors of a specific person at a definite location and time. In that sense, the statement is limited and not theoretically powerful. The second statement, because it is abstract, is more theoretically powerful. Most theory is at least somewhat abstract; it's the best way for us to say something significant about what is going on. Because she focuses on the actualities of lived experience, Smith's standpoint theory can be read to mean that abstractions are themselves bad. But that isn't her intent.

Nor is she interested in simply discrediting or deconstructing the knowledge or relations of ruling. Quite a bit of critical theory is aimed at these issues. For example, chances are good that much of what you've learned in other classes about gender or race is a historical account of how patriarchy or racism came about and how it functions to oppress people. The intent in these courses is to discredit sexism or racism by deconstructing their ideological and historical bases. But discrediting isn't Smith's specific intent either.

Smith argues that in both these cases, abstractions and ideological deconstruction, the critique by itself isn't enough; it doesn't tell the actual story. Theory in both forms plays itself out in the everyday, actual world of people, and that is Smith's concern. Insofar as theory and ideology mean anything, they mean something in everyday life, whether that life is the researcher's or that of ordinary women. Smith is interested in where the rubber meets the road. In this case, the "rubber" is made up of theoretical abstractions and ideological knowledge that governs, and the "road" is the actual experiences of women. Thus, Smith isn't interested in doing away with abstractions per se, nor is she simply interested in exposing the relations of ruling. Doing so is not enough, and it runs the risk of replicating the problem, as we will soon see.

The New Materialism

As we've seen in other chapters, Marx's materialism argues that there is a relationship between one's material class interests and the knowledge one has. Smith proposes a *new materialism,* one where facts and texts rather than commodification produce alienation and objectification. With Marx, commodities and money mediate the relationships people have with themselves and others. That is, we relate and come to understand our self and others through money and products. Marx's theory was specific to industrialized capitalism—the economies of more technologically advanced societies may be different. Some of the important changes include shifts from manufacturing to "service" economies, increases in the use of credentials and in the amount and use of expert knowledge, advances in communication and transportation technologies, exponential increases in the use of advertising images and texts, and so on. In such economies, relationships and power are mediated more through texts and "facts" than commodities and money. Further, just as people misrecognized the reality in back of money and commodities, so today most people misrecognize the relations of power in back of texts and facts.

In Marx's materialism, "relations between people are mediated by (and appear as) relations between commodities and money" (Smith, 1990, p. 68), and in Smith's new materialism, "relations between individual knowers appear as facts and are mediated by relations between facts" (p. 68). Texts and the facticity that text produces are the primary medium through which power is exercised in a society such as the United States.

Texts and Facts

Though the idea of text is gaining usage and popularity, it, like culture, is one of the more difficult words to define. Winfried Nöth (1985/1995) in his *Handbook of Semiotics* says that given that textuality is defined by the researcher, "It is not surprising that semioticians of the text have been unable to agree on a definition and on criteria of their object of research" (p. 331). Smith, however, gives us a broad, clear, and useful definition of *text* that includes three elements: the actual written words or symbols, the physical medium through which words and symbols are expressed, and the materiality of the text—the actual practices of writing and reading.

Smith is specifically concerned with texts that are officially or organizationally written and read. She gives us the example of two different texts that came out of an incident in 1968 involving police and street people in Berkeley, California. One text came in the form of a letter to an underground newspaper and was written by someone who was marginally involved in the altercation. His text was "written from the standpoint of an actual experience" (D. E. Smith, 1990, p. 63) and contained specific references to people, places, times, and events. It was embedded in and expressed actual life experiences as they happened. This was a personal account of a personal experience that reflexively situated the writer in the event.

The other text was the official incident report that came from the mayor's office. The standpoint of this second text was organizational. Rather than an account of a personal experience, it was written from the point of view of anonymous police officers who are portrayed as trained professionals and organizational representatives. In addition, the official report embedded the text within "sequences of organizational action extending before and after them" (D. E. Smith, 1990, p. 64) using reports from police, courts, and probation officers. In other words, the official text brought in many elements that existed outside of the actual situation and experience. In the end, every element of the actual experience was given meaning through these extra-local concepts rather than the experience itself.

The obliteration of the historical and specific sources is part of the process of creating facts (D. E. Smith, 1990, p. 66). The facticity of a statement is thus not a property of the statement itself. A statement simply proposes a state of affairs like "the earth is flat." For a statement to become fact, there must be a corresponding set of practices that provide its plausibility base, a group of people, beliefs, and practices that give substance to the statement. *Facticity,* then, "is essentially a property of an institutional order mediated by texts" (p. 79). Facts and texts are organizational achievements, not independent truths of the world. These, then, are the texts and facts in which Smith is interested: the ones that are written and read as part of organizational method and relations of power. They create an objective reality whose existence is dependent upon specific institutionalized practices.

Concepts and Theory: Lived Experience and Knowing

Smith argues that the distinction between abstract knowledge (or text) and lived experience holds for all people, whether male, female, black, white, Hispanic, or anyone else. However, women's experience and knowledge are specifically important. Generally speaking, there are a few reasons why this would be accurate. First, knowledge of the oppressed is in some ways truer than that of the ruling. The ruling generally "believe their own press." For example, members of the ruling class generally believe the capitalist ideology that hard work results in upward social mobility.

Research indicates, however, that gender, sexuality, race, ethnicity, and religion all play into the distribution of scarce resources. Members of an oppressed group may thus have more actual knowledge of how the system works. Although it's true that black and Hispanic races are also oppressed, because it crosscuts all other social categories, the oppressive system par excellence is gender. Thus, women's knowledge is uniquely suited to help us see an oppressive structure for what it is.

Another reason for privileging women's experience is that it is more grounded in the physicality of real life than men's. We'll consider this again in the subsection on the fault line, but it bears mentioning here. While some of what Smith is saying about the difference between objective knowledge on one hand and subjective experience on the other is true about men, it is also true that women by and large take care of most of the details of life (such as cooking, cleaning, child rearing, and so on). These "details" are what specifically allow men to live a "man's life." Because women take care of the actualities, men are allowed to think that life is really about the abstract, general knowledge they construct and believe. Women thus typically provide a buffer between men and the actual demands of life. According to Smith (1987), this difference means that women's knowledge is more materially real and grounded in the physical actions of the body. A woman's body is "the place of her sensory organization of immediate experience; the place where her coordinates of here and now, before and after, are organized around herself as center" (p. 82). And that center is where the basics of life are felt, managed, and known.

In the end, this is what Smith means when she talks about standpoint. Standpoint is nothing more and nothing less than the knowledge and perspective that is produced through actual experiences. Because of her emphasis on standpoint, Smith argues that her project is not an ideological representation or movement. Often when we think of feminism, we think of a social movement with a specific agenda and ideology. While liberation from oppression is certainly part of what Smith (1987) wants to attain, she doesn't offer us "an ideological position that represents women's oppression as having a determinate character and takes up the analysis of social forms with a view to discovering in them the lineaments of what the ideologist already supposes that she knows" (pp. 106–107). Whether it comes from social science or feminism, Smith is concerned about knowledge that objectifies, that starts from a position outside the everyday world of lived experience.

Smith gives us an example of walking her dog. When walking her dog, she needs to be careful that he doesn't "do his business" in places that are inappropriate. Smith points out that her behavior in this situation would generally be understood in terms of norms. From the normative perspective, she would simply be seen as conforming to the social norms of walking a dog. However, Smith (1987) contends that the idea of norm "provides for the surface properties of my behavior, what I can be seen to be doing" (p. 155). In other words, the normative approach can only give us a surface or simplistic understanding of what is going on. What is ignored in seeing the norm is "an account of the constitutive work that is going on" (p. 155). In this case, *constitutive work* refers to the efforts Smith must put forth in conforming to the norm. Further, in the process of conforming, there are any number of contingencies that include the kind of neighborhood, the type of neighbors, the kind of leash, the breed of dog, the weather, her subjective states, and so on. All of the contingencies require practical reasoning that in turn produces a specific kind of reaction to the norm. The issue for Smith is that the normative account ignores the actual experiences of the person: how, when, and why the individual conforms to, negotiates, or ignores the demands made by the norm.

Disregarding the site of constitutive work is how "the very intellectual successes of the women's movement have created their own contradictions" (D. E. Smith, 1992, p. 88). The contradictions arise, according to Smith, as feminism becomes its own theory, a theory that is seen to exist apart from the lived experiences of the women it attempts to describe. For Smith, resistance and revolution do not—indeed, cannot—begin in theory or even sociology. Such a beginning would simply replace the ruling ideas with another set of ruling ideas. In order to create a sociology of women, or to bring about any real social change, it is imperative to begin and continue in the situated perspectives of the people in whom we are interested.

Thus, Smith's intent is to open up the space of actual experience as the site of research. This is exactly what she means by the title of her 1987 book, *The Everyday World as Problematic.* Most social research creates problems that are guided by the literature, by the researcher's career, or by the availability of funds. According to Smith, this practice results in a body of knowledge that more often than not only references itself or the relations of ruling that fund it. In Smith's work, it is the everyday world of women that is problematized. It's the actual experience of women that sets the problems and questions of research and provides the answers and theory. "Inquiry does not begin within the conceptual organization or relevances of the sociological discourse, but in actual experience as embedded in the particular historical forms of social relations that determine that experience" (D. E. Smith, 1987, p. 49).

Another way to put this issue is that most social research assumes a reciprocity of perspectives. One of the things that ethnomethodology (see Chapter 5) has taught us about the organization of social order at the micro level is that we all assume that our way of seeing things corresponds fairly closely to the way other people see things. More specifically, we assume that if another person were to walk in our shoes, they would experience the world just like we do. This is an assumption that allows us to carry on with our daily lives. It lets us act as if we share a common world, even though we may not and we can never know for sure. According to Smith, social science usually works in this way too, but she wants us to problematize that assumption in sociology. She wants us to ask, "What is it like to be that person in that body in those circumstances?"

Sociology and the Relations of Ruling

Dorothy E. Smith (1990) talks about the practices, knowledge, and social relations that are associated with power as relations of ruling. Specifically, *relations of ruling* include "what the business world calls *management*, it includes the professions, it includes government and the activities of those who are selecting, training, and indoctrinating those who will be its governors" (p. 14). In technologically advanced societies that are bureaucratically organized, ruling and governing take place specifically through abstract concepts and symbols, or text. As Michel

Foucault explained, knowledge is power; it is the currency that dominates our age. Authority and control are exercised in contemporary society through different forms of knowledge—specifically, knowledge that objectifies its subjects.

The social sciences in particular are quite good at this. They turn people into populations that can be reduced to numbers, measured, and thus controlled. Through abstract concepts and generalized theories, the social sciences empty the person of individual thoughts and feelings and reduce him or her to concepts and ideas that can be applied to all people grouped together within a specific social type. The social sciences thus create a textual reality, a reality that exists in "the literature" outside of the lived experience of people.

Much of this literature is related to data that are generated by the state, through such instruments as the U.S. Census or the FBI's Uniform Crime Reporting (UCR) Program. These data are accepted without question as the authoritative representation of reality because they are seen as *hard data*—data that correspond to the assumptions of science. These data are then used to "test" theories and hypotheses that are generated, more often than not, either from previous work or by academics seeking to establish their names in the literature. Even case histories that purport to represent the life of a specific individual are rendered as documents that substantiate established theoretical understandings.

Thus, most of the data, theory, and findings of social science are generated by a state driven by political concerns, by academics circumscribed by the discipline of their fields, by professors motivated to create a vita (résumé) of distinction, or by professionals seeking to establish their practice. All of this creates "textual surfaces of objective knowledge in public contexts" that are "to be read factually . . . as evidences of a reality 'in back of' the text" (D. E. Smith, 1990, pp. 191, 107). Therefore, a sociology that is oriented toward abstract theory and data analysis results in one that "is a systematically developed consciousness of society and social relations . . . [that] claims objectivity not on the basis of its capacity to speak truthfully, but in terms of its specific capacity to exclude the presence and experience of particular subjectivities" (D. E. Smith, 1987, p. 2).

These concepts, theories, numbers, practices, and professions become relations of ruling as they are used by the individual to understand and control her own subjectivity, as she understands herself to be a subject of the discourses of sociology, psychology, economics, and so on. We do this when we see ourselves in the sociological articles or self-help books we read, in the written histories or newspapers of society, or in business journals or reports. With or without awareness of it, we mold ourselves to the picture of reality presented in the "textual surfaces of objective knowledge."

Smith points out that this process of molding becomes explicit for those people wanting to become sociologists, psychologists, or business leaders. Disciplines socialize students into accepted theories and methods. In the end, these are specific guidelines that determine exactly what constitutes sociological knowledge. For example, most of the professors you've had are either tenured or on a tenure track. Whether an instructor has tenure or not is generally the chief distinction between assistant and associate professors. When a sociology professor comes up for tenure and promotion, one of the most important questions asked about his or her work is whether or not it qualifies as sociology. Not everything we do is necessarily sociology—it has to conform to specific methodologies, assumptions, concepts, and so on.

There is something reasonable about this work of exclusion. If I wrote an article with nothing but math concepts in it, it probably shouldn't be considered sociology. Otherwise, there wouldn't be any differences among the academic disciplines. However, Smith's point is that there is more going on than simple definitions. Definitions of methods and theory are used by the powerful to exclude the powerless. What counts as sociology and the criteria used to make the distinctions are therefore reflections of the relations of ruling. Sociology and all the social sciences have historically been masculinist enterprises, which means that what constitutes sociology is defined from the perspective of ruling men. The questions that are deemed important and the methods and theories that are used have all been established by men: "How sociology is thought—its methods, conceptual schemes, and theories—has been based on and built up within the male social universe" (D. E. Smith, 1990, p. 13).

Let me give you an example to bring this home, one that has to do with race, but the illustration still holds. In the latter part of the 1990s, two colleagues and I were untenured in our department. One of those colleagues is black. All three of us were worried about tenure and promotion—there was quite a bit of contradictory information circulating about how we could get tenure. So we had a meeting with the man who was department head at the time. Each of us had specific concerns. My black colleague's concern was race. In response to some of the things the department head said, I asked him point blank: "Will the articles that [my black colleague] has published count for tenure and promotion or not?" The head answered that he wasn't sure because the articles were published in black journals and may not therefore "count as sociology."

The Fault Line of Gender

Smith argues that since the motivations, questions, and data come out of the concerns of those that govern and not the actual experiences of those living under the relations of ruling, masculinist knowledge is by default objective and objectifying—from beginning to end, it stands outside of the actual experience of those other than the ruling. Smith's sociology is thus not specifically concerned with what usually passes as prejudice or sexism that is expressed through negative stereotypes and discrimination. Rather, "We are talking about the consequences of women's exclusion from a full share in the making of what becomes treated as our culture" (D. E. Smith, 1987, p. 20).

One of those consequences is the experience of a **fault line** for those women training as social scientists. The idea of a fault line comes from geology and in that discipline refers to the intersection between a geologic fault (a fracture in the earth's crust) and the earth's surface. Many fault lines are dramatically visible. If you've not seen one, use an Internet search engine to find an image of a fault line. Smith's analogy is quite striking. She is arguing that the fault line for women is conceptual; it occurs between the kind of knowledge that is generally produced in society, specifically through the social sciences, and the knowledge that women produce as a result of their daily experiences. There is a decisive break between the two.

We generally think there are some differences between objective culture or knowledge and the lives that people live. But because the current relations of ruling produce masculinist knowledge, men do not sense a disjuncture between what they live and what they know of the world. Part of the reason for this is that many of the activities of men match up with or correspond to abstract, objectifying knowledge. A male sociologist "works in the medium he studies" (D. E. Smith, 1990, p. 17). But even for men, there is still a clear distinction between objective knowledge, "the governing mode of our kind of society" (p. 17), and daily life. Thus, while there may be a correspondence for men, there is also a place "where things smell, where the irrelevant birds fly away in front of the window, where he has indigestion, where he dies" (p. 17). In other words, Smith is arguing that even for men there is a break between objective forms of knowledge and daily life as it is subjectively experienced. The difference is that generally men don't sense the disjunction. But why don't men sense or experience it?

The reason, Smith informs us, is that women have traditionally negotiated that break for men. Let's think about the usual distinction between boss and secretary. Generally speaking, the secretary is there to do the leg work, to take care of the mundane details through which an organization functions, and to keep the boss free from intrusions from the outside world by screening all calls and letters. Think also about the traditional division of labor in the home. Men go to work while women take care of the "small details" of running a household: grocery shopping, cooking, cleaning, and taking care of the kids. Both of these examples picture the mediation role that Smith tells us women play—women intervene between men and the actual lived world, and they take care of the actualities that make real life possible. In doing so, they shelter men from the "bifurcation of consciousness" that women experience (D. E. Smith, 1987, p. 82).

Standpoint and Text-Mediated Power

Bringing all this together, we end up with a rather new way of doing sociology, one that focuses on the experience of women as it is mediated through various texts, particularly those produced through the relations of ruling. I've diagrammed my take on Smith's ideas in Figure 16.1. As with any such model, especially one constructed to reflect a critical perspective, it is a simplification. But in some ways, I think that a simplification is exactly what Smith is after. Her argument entails elements from existentialism, phenomenology, symbolic interaction, ethnomethodology, and Marxian theory. The argument is thus not simplistic. It is quite complex and nuanced, and it can and will inspire intricate and subtle thought and research. But her point is rather straightforward—social research and theory need to be grounded in the actual lived experiences of people, particularly women.

The first thing I'd like for you to notice about Figure 16.1 is the central position of both actual lived experience and text. We've talked about the issue of lived experience, and I will come back to it in a minute, but let's start by noticing texts. As I've already noted, sociology and the social disciplines in general have experienced what has been called a linguistic turn. A good deal of this sea change can be credited

Figure 16.1   Smith's Standpoint Inquiry

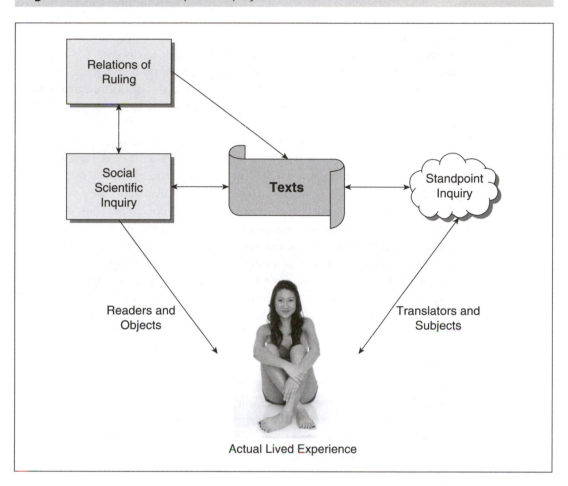

Actual Lived Experience

generally to the effects of poststructuralism and postmodernism. We can understand the linguistic turn as a shift toward the importance of text, primarily written words, though other kinds of cultural artifacts such as film are read as texts through semiotic analysis. In this perspective, culture and cultural readings are fundamentally important. The radical thread in this linguistic turn is that readings of texts are themselves seen as texts, which means that since humans are defined through meaning, all we have are texts.

In keeping with the linguistic turn, Smith (1992) acknowledges the importance of text, but she adds to it the ontology of lived experience. For her, text forms "the bridge between the actual and discursive. It is a material object that brings into actual contexts of reading a fixed form of meaning" (p. 92). The uniqueness of what Smith is arguing in light of the linguistic turn is that there is something other than text. Text isn't everything: There are embodied people who live their lives in actual situations that have real consequences.

When we become aware of the texts that surround our lived reality, they form the bridge that Smith is talking about. There are two ways through which these texts can influence us. First, we may become directly aware of them, generally through higher education but also through the media. At this point, the discursive text directly enters the everyday life of people. This kind of text is generally authoritative; it claims to be the voice of true knowledge gained through scientific or organizational inquiry. However, as Smith points out, social scientific research is based outside of actual lived experience. Its position outside is in fact what makes this knowledge appear legitimate, at least in a culture dominated by scientific discourse. It is this appearance that prompts us to privilege the objective voice above our own. But there is more to these texts, as you can see from the left side of Figure 16.1.

The relations of ruling have a reciprocal relationship with social scientific inquiry, as indicated by the double-headed arrow. We believe that legitimate research produces the only real knowledge; government finances, directs, and thus defines the kinds of research that are seen as legitimate. Social scientific inquiry, then, produces the kinds of data and knowledge that reinforce and legitimate the ruling. The single-headed arrow from relations of ruling to texts implies the top-down control of knowledge that Marx spoke of: The ruling ideas come from the ruling people, in this case men. The arrow between scientific inquiry and texts, however, is two-headed. This means that the questions and theories that social scientific research uses come from the literature rather than the real lives of people. It also implies that social science is in a dialogue with itself, between its texts and its inquiry.

The second way we can become aware of these texts is through social scientific inquiry itself. Have you ever answered the phone and found that someone wanted you to respond to a survey? Or have you ever been stopped in a mall and "asked a few questions" by someone with a clipboard? Have you ever filled out a census survey? Through all these ways and many others, we are exposed to objectifying texts by social scientific inquiry.

Notice that the arrow coming from social scientific inquiry has only one head, going toward the actual world of women, and notice that the arrow has two nouns attached: "readers" and "objects." This one-way arrow implies that social scientific research produces readers and objects. The readers are the researchers. They are trained to read or impose their text onto the actual world. They see the lived experience of women through the texts and methods of scientific research. They come to real, actual, embodied life with a preexisting script, one that has the potential to blind them to the actualities of women. Further, when the questions and methods of science are used to understand women, the women are made into objects, passive recipients of social sciences' categories and facts.

The right side of the model depicts Smith's approach. There are two important things to notice. First, there are no relations of ruling controlling standpoint inquiry. Part of this is obvious. As I've mentioned, Smith says that this way of seeing things is applicable to all types of people, but it is particularly salient for women. The reason is that the relations of ruling are masculine in a society such as ours. Men control most of the power and wealth and thus control most of the knowledge that is produced. While there is a difference between objective knowledge on the one hand and the lived experience of men on the other, women mitigate that discrepancy.

But this issue of ruling isn't quite that clear-cut for Smith. Relations of ruling are obviously associated with men. However, there is a not-so-obvious part as well. The work of women, including feminists, can fall prey to the same problem that produces social scientific inquiry. This can happen when women reify the ideas, ideology, or findings of feminist research. Anytime research begins outside of the lived experience of embodied people, it assumes an objective perspective and in the end creates abstract knowledge. This is how women's movements "have created their own contradictions" (D. E. Smith, 1992, p. 88). It's possible, then, for women's knowledge to take on the same guise as men's. In Smith's approach, there are no relations of ruling, whether coming from men or women. Standpoint inquiry must continually begin and end in the lived experiences.

The other thing I'd like to call your attention to is that all the arrows associated with standpoint inquiry are double-headed. Rather than producing readers and objects, standpoint inquiry creates space for translators and subjects. In standpoint, the lives of women aren't simply read; they aren't textually determined. A researcher using standpoint inquiry is situated in a never-ending dialogue with the actual and textual. There is a constant moving back and forth among the voice of the subject, the voice of authoritative text, and the interpretations of the researcher. Smith (1992) sees this back-and-forth interplay as a dialectic:

> The project locates itself in a dialectic between actual people located just as we are and social relations, in which we participate and to which we contribute, that have come to take on an existence and a power over [sic] against us. (pp. 94–95)

Notice that the dialectic is between actual experience and social relations. Smith is arguing that in advanced bureaucratic societies, our relationships with other people are by and large produced and understood through text. For example, you have a social relationship with the person teaching this class. What is that relationship? To state the obvious, the relationship is professor–student. Where is that relationship produced? You might be tempted to say that it is produced between you and your professor, but you would be wrong, at least from Smith's point of view. The relationship is practiced between you and your professor, but it is produced in the university documents that spell out exactly what qualifies as a professor and a student (remember, you had to apply for admittance) and how professors and students are supposed to act.

This textuality of relationships is a fact of almost every single relationship you have. Of course, the relations become individualized, but even your relationship with your parents (How many books on parenting do you think are available?) and with the person you're dating (How many articles and books have been written about dating? How many dating-related surveys have you seen in popular magazines?) are controlled and defined through text. However, as we've already seen, Smith argues that even in the midst of all this text, there is a reality of actual, lived experience. Smith is explicitly interested in the dialectic that occurs between abstract, objectifying texts on the one hand, and the lived actualities of women on the other.

We thus come to the core of Smith's project. Smith (2005) has termed this project **institutional ethnography.** The "ethnography" portion of the term is meant to convey its dependence upon lived experience. Smith's project, then, is one that emphasizes inquiry rather than abstract theory. But, again, remember that Smith isn't necessarily arguing against abstractions and generalizations. Smith herself uses abstractions. Notice this quote from Smith (1987) concerning the fault line: "This inquiry into the implications of a sociology for women begins from the discovery of a point of rupture in my/our experience as woman/women within the social forms of consciousness" (p. 49). In it she uses both abstractions and particulars: my/our, woman/women. To say anything about women—which is a universal term—is to already assume and use a theoretical abstraction. Thus, Smith uses abstract concepts, so she isn't saying that in and of themselves they are problematic—the issue is what we do with them. Her concern is for when abstractions are reduced to "a purely discursive function" (D.E. Smith, 1992, p. 89). This happens when concepts are reified or when inquiry begins in text: "To begin with the categories is to begin in discourse" (p. 90).

There are, I think, two ways that Smith uses and approaches abstractions. First, in standpoint inquiry, concepts are never taken as if they represented a static reality. Lived experience is an ongoing, interactive process in which feelings, ideas, and behaviors emerge and constantly change. Thus, the concepts that come out of standpoint inquiry are held lightly and are allowed to transform through the never-ending quest to find out "how it works."

The second and perhaps more important way that Smith approaches theoretical concepts is as part of the discursive text that constitutes the mode through which relations of ruling are established and managed. As we've seen, "The objectification of knowledge is a general feature of contemporary relations of ruling" (D. E. Smith, 1990, p. 67). A significant principle of standpoint inquiry is to reveal how texts are put together with practices at the level of lived experience. "Making these processes visible also makes visible how we participate in and incorporate them into our own practices" (D. E. Smith, 1992, p. 90) and how we involve ourselves in creating forms of consciousness "that are properties of organization or discourse rather than of individual subjects" (D. E. Smith, 1987, p. 3).

It's at this point that Smith's use of the word *institutional* is relevant. It signals that this approach is vitally concerned with exploring the influences of institutionalized power relations on the lived experiences of their subjects. Institutional ethnography is like ethnomethodology and symbolic interactionism in that it focuses on how the practical actions of people in actual situations produce a meaningful social order. But neither of these approaches gives theoretical place to society's ruling institutions, as Smith's method does. In that, her method is more like a contemporary Marxian account of power and text. Thus, institutional ethnography examines the dialectical interplay between the relations of ruling as expressed in and mediated through texts, and the actual experiences of people as they negotiate and implement those texts.

Smith uses the analogy of a map to help us see what she is getting at. Maps assist us to negotiate space. If I'm in a strange city, I can consult a map and have a fair idea of how to proceed. Maps, however, aren't the city and they aren't our experience. Smith (1992) wants sociology to function like a map—a map that gives an account of the person walking and finding her or his way (lived experience) through the objective structures of the city (text). This kind of sociology "would tie people's sites of experience and action into accounts of social organization and relations which have that ordinarily reliable kind of faithfulness to 'how it works'" (p. 94).

Specifically, Smith is interested in finding out just how the relations of ruling pervade the lives of women. These relations, as we've seen, come through texts and researchers. But in most cases, the relations of ruling are misrecognized by women. They are rendered invisible by the normalcy of their legitimacy. Part of what these maps can do, then, is make visible the relations of ruling and how they impact the lived experiences of women.

Smith is also interested in how actual women incorporate, respond to, see, and understand the texts that are written from a feminist or standpoint perspective. This is an important issue. Looking at Figure 16.1, we might get the impression that standpoint inquiry automatically and always produces translators and subjects. Another way to put this is that it appears as if standpoint inquiry is a static thing, as if, once done, the inquiry stands as the standpoint forever. This is certainly not what Smith is arguing. Notice again that double-headed arrow between standpoint and texts. Once standpoint inquiry is expressed in text, there is the danger that it will be taken as reality and become discursive. Smith's is thus an ongoing and ever-changing project that takes seriously the objectifying influence of text.

> For me, then, the standpoint of women locates a place to begin inquiry before things have shifted upwards into the transcendent subject. Once you've gone up there, settled into text-mediated discourse, irremediably stuck on the reading side of the textual surface, you can't peek around it to find the other side where you're actually *doing* your reading. You can reflect back, but you're already committed to a standpoint other than that of actual people's experience. (D. E. Smith, 1992, p. 60)

Summary

- Smith argues that in contemporary society, power is exercised through text. Smith defines text using three factors: the actual words or symbols, the physical medium, and the materiality of the text. It is the last of the three with which Smith is most concerned, the actual practices of writing and reading. Most, if not all, of the texts produced by science, social science, and organizations achieve their facticity by eliminating any reference to specific subjectivities, individuals, or experiences.

- These texts are gendered in the sense that men by and large constitute the ruling group in society. Men work and live in these texts and thus accept them as taken-for-granted expressions of the way things are. Women's experience and consciousness, on the other hand, are bifurcated: They experience themselves within the text, as the ruling discourse of the age, but they also experience a significant part of their lives outside of the text. And it is in this part of women's lives where the contingencies of actual life are met, thus giving these experiences a firmer reality base than the abstract ruling texts of men. Further, men are enabled to take objective ruling texts as true because women provide the majority of the labor that undergirds the entire order.

- The bifurcated consciousness becomes particularly problematic for those women trained in such disciplines as business, sociology, psychiatry, psychology, and political science. In these professions, women are trained to write and read ruling texts, ignoring the lived experiences of women at the fault line.

- Smith proposes a theoretical method of investigation (standpoint inquiry or institutional ethnography) that gives priority to the lived experiences of women. In this scheme, texts are not discounted or done away with, but they are put into the context of the embodied, actual experiences of women. Smith thus opens up a site of research that exists in the dialectic interplay between text and women's experience.

BUILDING YOUR THEORY TOOLBOX

- Write a 250-word synopsis of the theoretical perspective of standpoint theory.

- After reading and understanding this chapter, you should be able to define the following terms theoretically and explain their importance to standpoint theory: practices of power, new materialism, texts, facticity, standpoint, constitutive work, relations of ruling, fault line, institutional ethnography.

- After reading and understanding this chapter, you should be able to answer the following questions (remembering to answer them theoretically):

  o Explain how standpoint is more method than theory. How does some feminist work actually defeat standpoint?

  o How are the relations of ruling expressed through social science?

  o What is the new materialism? How does it affect what people accept as true or factual?

  o Explain the differences between the general sociological approach and Smith's.

  o How does the fault line perpetuate gender inequality?

  o Describe Smith's institutional ethnography. How is it dialectical? What do you think the benefits of institutional ethnography would be?

Learning More—Primary Sources

- Dorothy E. Smith, *The Everyday World as Problematic: A Feminist Sociology,* Northeastern University Press, 1987.

- Dorothy E. Smith, *The Conceptual Practices of Power: A Feminist Sociology of Knowledge,* Northeastern University Press, 1990.

- Dorothy E. Smith, *Institutional Ethnography: A Sociology for People,* AltaMira Press, 2005.

Engaging the World

- As a student, how do you see yourself being socialized to the relations of ruling? If you are a woman, do you see bifurcated consciousness in your life? As a sociologist, how will you avoid being trapped and controlled by the relations of ruling?

- In general, what implications do you see of objectified knowledge for the way people view and experience themselves? What are the implications if society were to do away with objective knowledge about social things?

- How does objectified knowledge influence your gender and relationships? Remember, "facts" and surveys are endemic in our time and continually appear on television and in various magazines. No matter where it appears, objectified knowledge will have the same sort of effects in your life. So, in answering this question, be sure to consider how often you use or refer to facts and surveys in popular media.

Weaving the Threads

- Compare and contrast Foucault's and Smith's ideas about how power is mediated.

- Compare and contrast Smith's idea of the fault line and Chafetz's theory of male micro-resource power.

- How do Patricia Hill Collins's and Smith's theories coincide? How are texts used differently or more powerfully in issues concerning race? Or, do you think that the suppression of subjective experience is the same, whether for gender or race?

- Write a brief overview of Comte's vision for positivism and sociology. Then use Collins and Smith to critique Comte's work. Overall, how would you evaluate sociology's place in the democratic project?

CHAPTER 17

Exposing Sex

Judith Butler

Source: Courtesy of Judith Butler.

Sociology is in the habit of exposing what exists beneath the surface of something. For example, when most people buy something, all they see is the thing they bought. If we ask them what it is and why they bought it, they'd probably say something like, "It's a jacket and I needed it." But a sociologist would say, no, look deeper. If you look beneath the surface of that jacket, you'll see exploitation and alienation, and the reason you "need it" is because of commodity fetish. Look further, a postmodern sociologist would say, and you'll see simulacrum and hyperreality. As sociology students, you're probably somewhat accustomed to this sociological move, and you're probably used to people looking at you a little oddly when you try to explain social things.

Judith Butler is going to ask us to do what sociologists always ask: Look beneath the surface. What she asks us to look beneath is the body. That's not new for us; Bourdieu did the same thing in Chapter 8. You thought you liked meat and potatoes just because they were good. No, Bourdieu tells us, our tastes are insidious revealers of class. Like the postmodernist, Butler is going to ask us to take the next step and look deeper. The body isn't simply classed; it's sexed: The body materializes normative heterosexuality much the same way as it materializes class.

As we go through Butler's theory, please keep in mind that there are fundamental differences between what we usually think of as socialization and Butler's idea of materialization. Gordon Marshall's (1998) *A Dictionary of Sociology* defines socialization as "the process by which we learn to become members of society, both by internalizing the norms and values of society, and also by learning to perform our social roles" (p. 624). Socialization seems to presume a preexisting person, someone to learn and then perform society's expectations. Think of it this way: For me to internalize something, an internal must already exist; it exists with reference to an external, that is, a body. Further, for me to learn anything, I must already exist. Here's a crazy thought experiment that might help us see this: It makes no sense if I say that yesterday my son who won't be born for another 5 years learned his multiplication tables. My son must already exist for me to make such a statement. The same is true here: The idea of socialization actually assumes a potential actor exists.

Butler's notion of materialization is much more profound than the idea of socialization. Butler argues that the body, that which is the exterior, is socially created. *The body materializes or brings society into physical existence.* It isn't the case, then, that we simply internalize society's norms, values, and beliefs. The very external (the body) that internalization presumes is itself a social construction. Further, the individual doesn't "learn" society; he or she comes into existence *through* society. Our subjective self is historically and socially specific. We saw a bit of this with Foucault, and Butler builds on his argument.

THEORIST'S DIGEST

Brief Biography

Judith Butler was born in Cleveland, Ohio, on February 24, 1956. She became interested in philosophy at an early age and received her PhD in it from Yale in 1984. At Yale, Butler was influenced by Maurice Natanson, a student of Alfred Schutz (see Chapter 5). Natanson was significant in exposing Butler to phenomenology. The 1990 publication of *Gender Trouble* brought Butler international acclaim. Other important works of hers include *Bodies That Matter: On the Discursive Limits of "Sex," Undoing Gender,* and *Giving an Account of Oneself.* She is currently the Maxine Elliot Professor of Rhetoric and Comparative Literature at the University of California, Berkeley.

Central Sociological Questions

In the preface to her book *Bodies That Matter: On the Discursive Limits of "Sex,"* Butler (1993) gives us the abiding curiosity that drives her thoughts:

(Continued)

(Continued)

"What are the constraints by which bodies are materialized as 'sexed,' and how are we to understand the 'matter' of sex, and of bodies more generally, as the repeated and violent circumscription and violent circumscription of cultural intelligibility? Which bodies come to matter—and why?" (pp. xi–xii).

Obviously, Butler is interested in how bodies are socially constructed, specifically how they become sexed, but there's more. Implicit in Butler's curiosity are deeper issues. Butler wants to know what the connection is between subjectivity—the way people think, feel, act, and relate toward the self—and the body (the objective part of our existence). How is it that the body forms the basis of self, subjectivity, and other? How is it that without the body, "there would be no 'I,' no 'we'"? (p. xi). Further, Butler wants to know what bodies, what possibilities, are excluded through the construction of a socially intelligible body. This question goes deeper than simple oppositions, because oppositions are part and parcel of how things are defined. Butler wants to know what kinds of bodies are denied and unidentified. How does the unknown haunt the known? What physical loss do we sense but are unable to articulate? What "specter of its own impossibility" haunts our body?

Simply Stated

The human body is usually seen as simply biological, or in sociology, it is typically seen as either a social object or something that can be used to express the self. Butler, however, shows that the body is in fact materialized, brought into existence. Humans inscribe everything with meaning, and that inscription molds, shapes, and changes the thing, including the body. The primary requirement of a social body is that it be sexed. Thus, bodies are carved by the norm of heterosexuality and called into existence through the practices of this cultural norm. In this culture, all sexualities other than heterosexuality act as subversions that overthrow the norm at its base; these acts of subversion open up possibilities.

Key Ideas

Arche-writing, hegemonic norm of heterosexuality, discursive function, iterability, performity, doer and the deed, presentist conceit, repression, melancholia, materialization, subversion, queer theory

Concepts and Theory: What's the Matter With Bodies?

For quite some time, sociology's approach to gender has been to grant a kind of independent existence to the body and sex. This approach is reflective of how social thinkers in general have thought about the body, if they thought about it at all. For example, George Herbert Mead (1934) gives us a warning about putting too much attention on the body: "It may be necessary again to utter a warning against the easy assumption . . . that the body of the individual as a perceptual object provides a center to which experiences may be attached" (p. 357). This warning from Mead is particularly important for us to see because of all the classic or original thinkers in sociology, he would be the most likely to consider the body of consequence. Yet here he warns against giving too much significance to the body. Talcott Parsons was one of the first to explicitly include the physical body in theory, but for him the body was simply a biological organism—he made a distinction between organic and psychological systems in the hierarchy of control.

When social thinkers did begin to think about the body as perhaps something more than biology, it was as a social object, a thing that can take on symbolic meanings. Thus, Chris Shilling (1993), in one of the first sociological books dedicated to the body, says, "Growing numbers of people are increasingly concerned with the health, shape, and appearance of their own bodies as expressions of individual identity" (p. 1). Notice how Shilling talks about the body: It's a thing or social object with which we are increasingly concerned. This same approach to the body is seen in Seymour Fisher's (1973) book *Body Consciousness:* "My major intent in this book is to consider the strategies that people use in learning how to make sense of their own bodies" (p. ix). Again, the body is something separate from the actual person. It's a thing that we can decorate, be concerned about, or make sense of.

Pierre Bourdieu was one of the first theorists to clearly see that the body isn't simply an organism or a social object or even a vehicle for expression. Bourdieu argued that the body is classed through habitus. In Bourdieu's scheme, our bodies become enculturated—they are socialized into class-based tastes and dispositions. Class is thus structured and replicated in our bodies. The body is where class is located. Butler takes Bourdieu's approach to the body an additional step. She tells us that the distinction between sex and gender is inaccurate. I'm sure you remember from any course on gender, even your introduction to sociology course, that your instructor said that sex and gender are different. The story goes that sex refers to the biological plumbing (the body) and gender to the socially constructed roles that are built around bodily sex differences. The reason for this division is to show that gender is a cultural entity, something that has been socially created to control and make distinctions between the sexes (the already existing body). It's a kind of ploy where sociology says, "Sure, there is biology in the form of sex, but it doesn't really matter. What matters is gender." In response, Butler says no, sex matters fundamentally.

Inscribing the Body

Butler argues that it isn't simply the *practices* associated with sex that are regulated; sex itself is controlled. It isn't just what we do; it's what we are. Butler means sex as we usually mean it when we say sex and gender—sex as the biological condition of the body. However, Butler (1993) argues that we mistakenly think that sex comes only from biology:

> The category of "sex" is, from the start, normative. . . . In this sense, then, "sex" not only functions as a norm, but is part of a regulatory practice that produces

the bodies it governs, that is, whose regulatory force is made clear as a kind of productive power, the power to produce—demarcate, circulate, differentiate—the bodies it controls. (p. 1)

Using a poststructuralist idea of writing called arche-writing, Butler is arguing that bodies are inscribed. *Arche-writing* is a form of violent etching, engraving, or carving. As an analogy, we can think of the way young lovers used to carve their initials on trees. Everything humans do is like that—we carve a significance, a meaning, a reality upon the face of an otherwise smooth and meaningless surface. Butler is arguing that sex is just such an engraving, as if the body is a formless mass of senseless cells that society sculpts into what we call sex. The etching is violent because it forcibly denies other possibilities.

Notice that from the very beginning, sex is normative. Let's be very clear about something here. When we are talking about sex, we are not talking about "having sex." It isn't the activity that interests us here. You are a sex—a principal part of your very existence as a human is sex—and that sex is normative in that sexed bodies are the result of social control. It's important to see that Butler isn't just talking about sexual behaviors or identities. Behaviors and identities are things that are about the body, but are not the body itself. It's not that things having to do with the body aren't important; they are. The way you relate to your body is crucial. You can tattoo it or not; you can condition it or not; you can abuse it through drugs and alcohol or not. In fact, the body is part of the reflexive project of the self in late modernity, according to Anthony Giddens. That's possibly one of the reasons why we are so concerned with it in our daily lives.

Butler (1993) is telling us that bodies matter intrinsically, in and of themselves—what they are and how they exist, their materiality. They matter because they are not simply biological organisms. Inside and out, the body is a social production—sex "is a regulatory ideal whose materialization is compelled, and this materialization takes place (or fails to take place) through certain highly regulated practices" (p. 1). Sex is what qualifies a body *as a body*. Try to imagine a human body without sex, and you probably come up blank. Sex is one of the essentials that qualify our bodies as specifically human—according to Butler (1993), sex is "that which qualifies a body for life within the domain of cultural intelligibility" (p. 2). We can't make sense of our bodies apart from sex.

Butler argues that the way the body is sexed is through psychodynamic processes surrounding the hegemonic norm of heterosexuality. That's a mouthful, so let's break it down, taking the easy part first: the hegemonic norm of heterosexuality. Hegemony means having superior influence or authority. Thus, what Butler is saying is that the superior authority over sex is heterosexual: two body types, male and female, that are mutually and exclusively attracted to one another. The key word in that definition is *exclusively*. Of course, it is biologically necessary for the males and females of our species to come together sexually. But it is not necessary for dimorphic (two bodies) sexual attraction to be exclusive, as Foucault demonstrated in his histories of sexuality. For example, in Greek society it was normal for men to be sexually active with boys, yet the Greeks replicated the species just fine.

The psychodynamic process is a bit more difficult to understand. Anytime we are talking about psychodynamic theory, we are alluding to or basing our ideas upon Sigmund Freud (recall his theory from Chapter 7). Freud argued that people develop an ego through psychosexual stages and the resolution of the Oedipus complex. For Freud, there are three parts to a person's inner being: the id, ego, and superego. The ego mediates the demands of the id and superego. Though there are important differences, the ego generally corresponds to what sociologists call the self.

People aren't born with either an ego or superego; at birth there is only the id, and it is the seat of our passions and desires. The important thing about the id is that it is the source of all our psychic energy, also known as the libido. It is our basic motivation in the world and corresponds to instinctual energy—the closest thing to instincts that humans have. The id pushes us to gratify our basic needs; among the most fundamental of these is sexual gratification. But the id bumps up against problems in its search for gratification. All its needs can't always be gratified immediately. This is obviously true for animals as well; the chief difference is that the basis of human gratification is other people and society. Thus, as the id meets resistance from its human environment when it cannot satisfy all of its urges, its energy kind of splits in two different directions: the ego and superego.

According to Freud, one of the most important steps in the development of the child is the Oedipus complex and its resolution. This stage occurs between the ages of 3 and 5. At the beginning of this phase, the child is fundamentally attached to the mother, most notably through breast-feeding and nurturing. This primary attachment occurs through the id and its libido energy, which means it is primarily sensual and emotional rather than intellectual. In order to successfully develop psychically, both boys and girls need to resolve this attachment issue. One of the challenges at this stage, especially for boys, is to detach from the mother and attach to the same-sex parent (for girls, this means reattaching to the mother), yet at the same time deny that sensual-emotional attachment. Resolution is achieved when the child identifies with the parent of the same sex and simultaneously represses its sexual instincts.

Remember, when babies are born they are nothing but a ball of desire. All of these desires are felt similarly and without distinction about when, why, how, or with whom the desires are met. Part of our development, then, is the channeling of these desires into their "proper" paths. A fair portion of this libido attachment that the child has to his or her mother is sexual. Freud didn't necessarily mean sexual in the way you or I might understand it. It's much more basic and primitive—part of the child's general instinctual drives. We can think of it like hunger for food. We have a fundamental instinct to eat, but what, when, and how we eat is culturally programmed. Psychodynamic theory sees sex in the same way. Sex doesn't magically appear at puberty; it's been there all along. It is a primary form of physical, sensual attachment to others. Further, as with food, the child's desires must be channeled to "appropriate" objects of sensual attachment.

Of course, sex and food are different things. Sex is far more important for the psyche. With food, there isn't a psychic perception of loss, just a sense of bodily hunger if we don't eat. But with sex there is a sense of psychic loss. Desires for the mother must be suppressed by the child in order to attach successfully to others. This idea of suppression parallels the poststructuralist notion of difference (*différance*)—significance and meaning are created by suppression. Using a mundane example, for a guitar to be a guitar, all the particular meanings of "violin" have to be suppressed, held back. In the case we're talking of here, in sex we are called upon to suppress general sensual attachment in favor of a socially defined one. Within the hegemonic norm of heterosexuality, this means that the boy needs to shift his sexual attachment to other women and the girl needs to transfer it to men. *But the suppressed desires still exist in the id or the unconscious.* It's the job of the superego and ego to keep these passions in check by denying them.

Thus, Butler draws on Freud, but she gives him a Foucauldian twist. Foucault argued that all knowledge is historically specific and is best understood in terms of discourse. What this means is that Freud's understanding of the Oedipus complex is specific to this time—it isn't an essential stage that humans universally have to work through. More importantly, it has a *discursive function.* Here, discursive has the sense of analytical reasoning or logic. According to Butler, the cultural logic behind the embodied sex of this age is heterosexism. Freud's theory occurs within a "prevailing truth-regime of 'sex'" (Butler, 1993, p. 233). *The proper or appropriate heterosexual objects of sexual desire occur only within and simply because of this truth-regime.*

Performity—Declaring a Reality

Our bodies are thus inscribed, sculpted, and brought into existence by a culturally specific sex. Sex isn't mere biology. In fact, there isn't anything that is simply biology for humans; we inscribe everything. That's how things become intelligible (and thus possible) for us. In this truth-regime of sex, our possibilities are heterosexual. Our heterosexism is inscribed upon our bodies during early childhood. Through psychodynamic processes, certain options are closed off (*différance*), the body becomes intelligible and possible, and the power of **hegemonic heterosexuality** is reflexively applied by the individual.

However, heterosexuality isn't a once-and-for-all accomplishment. The desires of the id are always present. That's why we need the superego. The superego is formed as the voice of society or the parent, most notably the father in Freud's scheme. It protects the ego from the unconscious and overwhelming demands of the id—some possibilities are held off in favor of others. Thus, our homosexual desires are continually repressed so that heterosexuality can be continuously inscribed upon our bodies.

Here, Butler uses another idea from poststructuralism: *iterability.* We are most familiar with this word in a different form. We may say something like, "To reiterate, let me state . . .". Reiterate obviously means to say again. But "iterate" doesn't mean to say the first time. If you look up both *reiterate* and *iterate* in an exhaustive dictionary, you will find that they both mean to repeat, and that's the poststructuralist's point: In order to be intelligible, all words, all text, must be in principle repeatable.

Let's imagine that you have a word that is only going to be said once in all of time. You say that word. However, if that word cannot be understood, then it isn't a word at all, just sound. But if the word is understood by others, then even if it is never said aloud again, it must in principle be possible for the word to be repeated. The word's very intelligibility demands that it be repeatable. In fact, when you say the word and others hear it and understand it, that word is already being repeated in their minds. Every iteration is thus a reiteration, every statement is a restatement, and every text is a text of a text.

To get at this idea for the sexed body, Butler uses the term *performity:* a word, phrase, or action that brings something into existence. A clear example of performity is the phrase "I now pronounce you" in a wedding ceremony; the phrase itself brings something into existence at the moment of its pronouncement. To understand performity a little better, let's talk about Erving Goffman's notion of impression management. Goffman argued that we perform or display gender for others. We construct a front through our use of appearance, manner, and setting that communicates to others the kind of gendered self we are claiming. Once effectively claimed by the self, other people impute the gendered self to the person. They act in a particular way toward the social category that has been claimed, and they expect the individual to live up to the self that has been presented. This self, then, is a dramatic enactment; it's something that we produce that allows interactions to take place. The effect of this self upon the individual comes primarily from other people: Others form righteously imputed expectations that the individual must live up to. When performances and expectations are repeated over time, the individual becomes attached to his or her "face."

Goffman's notion of performance thus gives a great deal of latitude to the performer. Butler doesn't see it like that. Individuals *must perform* or, better, iterate/reiterate sex. As I mentioned earlier, to be a body means to be sexed. Butler is talking about something that is much more fundamental than Goffman's gender display. She's talking about *existing as a body.* Other people don't simply understand us as a gender; they see us as a material being, as a person with a body. Our most important method of being embodied isn't what or how we eat, it isn't how we dress or decorate the body, and it isn't our level of health. According to Butler, we are principally embodied in and through sex. In particular, we are embodied through the performity of sex.

We need to take this one step further. Goffman claimed that others form righteous expectations, that these expectations are attributed to us, and that we then become attached to the sacred self implied in the expectations. Butler argues that performity does more than that: It constitutes the effect it names. Butler (1993) gives the illustration of a judge. When a judge makes a ruling, he or she cites the law. If the judge didn't cite the law, whatever he or she said would not be binding. The power of the judge therefore lies in the citation (iteration/reiteration) of the law. It's the citation that "gives the performative its binding or conferring power" (p. 225). Notice also that something comes into existence through citation. When the judge passes judgment citing the law, the judgment or punishment then exists. Think also of the wedding pronouncement or the act of accepting academic credentials in a graduation ceremony. These declarations are acts of performity: They simultaneously cite an authority and create a state of being. In Butler's scheme, then, heterosexual performity simultaneously cites the norm of hegemonic heterosexuality (thus giving it legitimacy) and produces heterosexual bodies (thus giving it existence). Performity in this way has ontological power—it creates the reality in which we live.

The Doer and the Deed

I must modify something I just stated. I said, "we are principally embodied in and through sex." According to Butler, that's not quite true. The problem with the statement is it makes it seem like there is a subject ("we") that exists prior to the practices of the body ("are embodied"). To critique this assumption, Butler plays off of Friedrich Nietzsche's idea of *the doer and the deed*. Most of us feel, talk, and act as if there is a doer behind every deed. In other words, a person acts and exists outside of the practice. In this way, he or she expresses agency—agents act. Nietzsche (1887/1968) turned this idea around when he said, "there is no 'being' behind doing, effecting, becoming; 'the doer' is merely a fiction added to the deed— the deed is everything" (p. 481). In other words, the idea of agency is wrongheaded. The notion that there is an independent person that preexists and is the source of action is not a reflection of the way things actually work. There isn't really a you behind your actions—the doing creates the doer.

The idea that there is a you in back of your actions is, according to Butler (1993), a

> *presentist conceit,* that is, the belief that there is a one who arrives in the world, in discourse, without a history, that this one makes oneself in and through the magic of the name, that language expresses a "will" or a "choice" rather than a complex and constitutive history of discourse and power. (p. 228, emphasis added)

Here's an illustration. Let's say you are African American. If you had been alive in 1840, it would have been impossible for there to be an African American "you" in back of your actions. African Americans couldn't and didn't exist back then. The only way there can be an American "you" in back of your actions today is that history has socially and culturally produced African Americans. The perception of an African American "you" in back of your actions is, as Nietzsche says, a fiction. It's a conceit that sees the present as somehow less historical than all other time periods that have existed up to this point.

Whatever your subjective sense of you, whether African American or heterosexual, it is historically specific. Most of "you," with all your thoughts and feelings, actually existed prior to your birth. You might be an American, black, white, male, female, a student, a short-order cook, a homeowner, a Visa card user, a licensed driver, an alcoholic, and so on, but most of the meanings and relationships that each of these elements involves existed before you were born. Each identity and subject exists apart from you. *You depend upon them for your intelligibility and viability,* not the other way around. It's thus impossible for "you" to be in back of your actions. Further, what produces a sense of you are your actions: "This repetition is not performed *by* a subject; this repetition is what enables a subject and constitutes the temporal condition for the subject" (Butler, 1993, p. 95).

I've illustrated this idea in Figure 17.1. There you will see a comparison between presentist conceit and performity. The first set of images, presentist conceit, shows how many people in contemporary societies see themselves. This view of self is powered by the idea of the individual as a free agent, an idea that gained currency as Protestantism, nation-states, and capitalism took hold. As you can see, the individual is aware of history, society, and culture, but these are bracketed off and the person is seen as independent of them. Once that is done, we are able to claim the individual as a free agent that acts. Note that this way of looking at things makes the idea of the acting individual the effect of a historically specific ideology.

Butler claims, however, that such a move gives a false sense of self. Society and culture do historically predate the individual and his or her behaviors. In fact, the only behaviors that are intelligible are those cultural practices that are historically specific. The performity of these practices reiterates society on the one hand and produces the person as a knowing and knowable subject on the other.

One of the things we may not like about the performity model is that it seems to suggest that we're simply robots carrying out the demands of society. But this isn't the case. Notice that all the arrows in this part of the figure are double-headed. This implies that all these sites mutually constitute one another. In other words, under the idea of performity, the individual can influence his or her world. Behaviors, feelings, and ideas don't directly originate with the individual; they are specific to time and place. However, the person is the site through which culture and society are enacted, and every action is in some way particular to the individual. More importantly, as we'll see, the individual may intentionally subvert the practices that cite society. Whether incidental or intentional, the person's actions influence, constitute, and change history, society, and culture.

Figure 17.1 Presentist Conceit

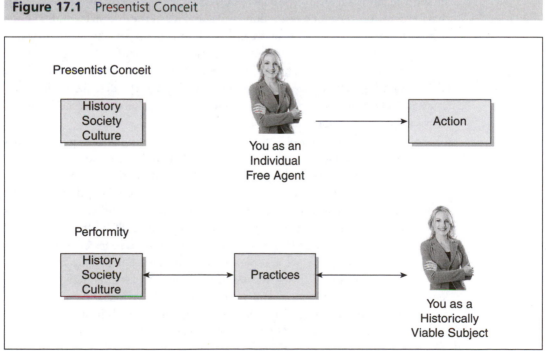

The main point here is that performity creates the subject, not the other way around. When we act in a way that can be understood by people, we are citing, iterating, and reiterating the textual scripts that have been handed to us. Our intelligibility as embodied persons begins as hegemonic heterosexuality is inscribed upon our bodies through psychodynamic processes, and it continues nonstop through our performative citation of hegemonic heterosexuality.

This citation isn't done by an independent subject that somehow transcends all history; the person's subjectivity, the ability to know and be known, is created through the naming effect of performity. "Sex is, thus, not simply what one has, or a static description of what one is: it will be one of the norms by which the 'one' becomes viable at all, that which qualifies a body for life within the domain of cultural intelligibility" (Butler, 1993, p. 4).

Concepts and Theory: Haunting, Subversion, and Queer Politics

But what about homosexuality? If sex constitutes the body as meaningful, and if sex is produced under the hegemony of heterosexuality, then how and where does homosexuality fit in? In order to begin to answer this question, we have to revisit psychodynamic theory for a moment.

As I mentioned earlier, based on Freud, humans begin with only the primitive energy of the id. The id is motivated by the libido, which is psychic power that comes from primary biological urges, particularly sexual energy. These urges come in contact with the human world and thus have to be controlled. Control happens first through the superego. The superego is the voice of society within the individual. It represents the moral restrictions and demands of the external world. The ego comes to exist as a mediator between the id and superego. The ego is oriented toward the internal world of the individual and seeks to satisfy the urges of the id within the framework given by the superego. An important way the ego mediates the relationship between the id and superego is through ego defense mechanisms, most notably repression. *Repression* serves to keep the ego unaware of the aggressive urges or painful memories associated with the libido.

According to Butler, this behavior of the ego does two important things. First, it serves to create boundaries between the individual and society and between the individual and his or her instinctual drives. These boundaries represent a crucial step in psychodynamic development—it is because of these boundaries that the individual can become self-aware, reflexive, and experience individual subjectivities. Remember that babies and infants are motivated only by their instinctual drives. At that stage of development, we are nothing but a series of never-ending desires. During this phase, we also see very little difference between ourselves and the world around us. In this sense, we feel ourselves to be a natural part of the environment, with a continuous and unbroken interplay between us and our world.

This condition is very similar to how we think most animals relate to the world, in a nonconscious flow of ongoing stimuli and experience. A prowling leopard, for example, is unaware of itself as a being separate from its natural environment. It instinctually responds to smells and sounds without having to think of itself within the situation. For the leopard, there isn't an awareness of separateness, only of continuous experience. In other words, the leopard doesn't have a self. If the leopard eats, it simply eats. If it has sex, it simply has sex. It isn't aware of itself eating—the awareness of self is a separate consciousness apart from the act of eating. The leopard cannot be "embarrassed" if it belches or makes a mess while eating. People, on the other hand, can become embarrassed, because we are aware of ourselves performing the action.

In order to be self-aware, psychodynamic theory argues that humans must first create a boundary between themselves and everything else. This happens principally through the formation of the ego. Through repression, the ego is structurally separated from the body's biological drives (the id) and from the moral demands of society (the superego). By definition, the desires of the id are not aware of themselves. The id is pure desire, just like the drives of the leopard. The demands of the superego initially come from the parent and subsequently society. Again, by definition there is no self-awareness present in the superego; it's the voice of the parent that speaks.

The person becomes self-aware when he or she individually negotiates the demands of the id and superego. A woman "finds" herself in the decision to act; her "voice" comes out of the contradictory demands of the id and superego. Interestingly, you and your subjectivity are formed as society denies your fundamental drives and desires, and since society is always politically and culturally constructed, the subjectivity that forms in response is always historically specific and fundamentally political.

In this separateness, there is a sense in which the ego becomes a substitute for the drives of the id. Let's use the eating example again. When my dog Gypsy eats, she is completely engrossed in what she is doing. She is utterly there, in the moment, caught up in her own behaviors. It's a different story when I eat. I'm generally aware of how I'm holding my fork; whether or not my mouth is closed while chewing; if I'm eating too fast, too loud, or too much. I'm not completely there in the behavior of eating; rather, a large part of me is watching the behavior and judging its appropriateness. In this sense, my ego, my self-awareness, takes the place of the object of my desire, in this case food. This is the second important effect of ego defense mechanisms, the substitution of the ego for the desire: "The turn from the object to the ego produces the ego, which substitutes for the object lost" (Butler, 1997, p. 168).

These effects are important, but the significant thing here for Butler is how this reflexive turn occurs. Notice what happens to the impulses of the id in psychodynamic theory. They don't go away; they are repressed. There is, then, a sense of loss in the formation of ego. The id, which operates according to the pleasure principle, desires something but can't have it or can't gratify the impulse immediately. The ego develops as the person tries to reasonably satisfy the desires to some degree (the reality principle). As the moral voice of authority (the superego) develops, the ego feels the demands of instinct and of society. In order to negotiate these contrary demands, the ego develops defense mechanisms. While there are several ego defense mechanisms, the most salient here is repression. The individual suppresses or pushes out of his or her consciousness the fundamental yet unsatisfied demands of the id. Therefore, the ego is principally formed and experienced through control and loss.

In Butler's scheme, this loss is experienced as melancholia. The

> substitution of ego for object does not quite work. The ego is a poor substitute for the lost object, and its failure to substitute in a way that satisfies (that is, to overcome its status as a substitution), leads to the ambivalence that distinguishes melancholia. (Butler, 1997, p. 169)

The problem with this kind of loss is that it is at once constitutive yet unspeakable. In other words, our self (ego) is created or constituted through loss; however, this loss not only occurs before it could be articulated, during early childhood, but the loss is also repressed and thus part of the unconscious—the loss creates the ego, and at the same time the ego denies the loss.

But because of the nature of loss, it haunts us. There is a sense of loss, but just what this loss is never fully appears. What we are left with is an ambivalent kind of sadness or melancholy. According to Butler (1997), this "melancholy is precisely what interiorizes the psyche" (p. 170) and permeates "the body with a pain that culminates in the projection of a surface, that is, a sexed morphology" (1993, p. 65). Both the self and the body are inscribed and circumscribed through loss. But what is this fundamental loss?

As we've seen, Butler argues that the body and ego are formed under historical conditions. For us, these conditions are set by the hegemonic norm of heterosexuality. The loss, then, is the refusal of the possibility of sexual or sensual connections between members of the same "sex." Remember that the materialization of the body, the body's ability to exist as a physical body, is normative. Biological sex is regulated socially. That's the underlying reflexive idea behind the title of Butler's 1993 book, *Bodies That Matter: On the Discursive Limits of "Sex."* Clearly, bodies matter in the sense that they are important, but more significantly, bodies *are* matter: They have material substance to them. Yet the material is socially regulated and created. The physical nature of the body is only intelligible to us under the dominion of a historically, culturally, and politically specific understanding of heterosexuality. Thus, these bodies we have are conditioned and given material through performity, the inscribing and citing of heterosexuality. This performity of the hegemonic norm, along with the Oedipal law, constitutes the modality of the materialization of the body—the method or channel through which the body becomes a body.

Further, the ego, or our subjective sense of self, is formed under these same conditions. By its very nature, the ego is denial. It is formed in order to control and refuse the impulses of the id. The single most important energy coming from the libido is sexual. In this era, our claim to a "biological" sex is the basic way we understand our body. It's more fundamental than race or weight or any other "physical" characteristic. And the single most important denial or loss that occurs under the hegemonic norm of heterosexuality is, by definition, the lost possibility of homosexuality.

Butler argues that this loss haunts us; but, more importantly, this loss is also by definition underdefined or unspecified. I don't mean that we don't know what homosexuality is; we do have some sense of it. But the idea we have can't be its full declaration. First, the definition we have is politically created to be used in the production of a specific heterosexuality. Second, and more importantly, the definition we have exists under conditions of suppression. Think about it this way: Psychotherapy usually takes years and years because ego defense mechanisms prevent the person from bringing to his or her conscious mind the desires and pains associated with the id and the effects of working out stages of development. You've probably seen psychiatrists in movies use dream analysis, hypnotherapy, or free association. These techniques are used to get at the hidden secrets of the unconscious, because the individual can't directly access them. The same thing is true with Butler's concept of homosexuality. That loss we've all experienced is hidden in the deep reaches of the psyche.

Butler isn't saying that we should all go to therapy for our loss. But she is saying that "homosexuality" has a special kind of existence for us under the hegemonic norm of heterosexuality. It haunts each of us; it is the specter of loss that we sense but can't quite reach. Because of this effect, homosexuality is a particularly easy and important site for subversion and rearticulation. In other words, Butler is arguing that homosexuality lends itself particularly well to being used as a site that facilitates social change. It's an exceptionally sensitive point in the social psyche, a point that effortlessly yields itself to pressure and rebellion.

Before moving on, we need to consider the notion of subversion. It's an important idea, especially in feminism. *Merriam-Webster's* tells us that *subversion* (n.d.) comes from the Latin *subvertere*, which is formed from *sub*, meaning down or under, and *vertere*, meaning to turn. Subversion, then, means "to overturn or overthrow from or as if from a foundation." The latter part of the definition is important because subversion implies changing or overturning something from the inside at its core. Thus, acts of subversion are those that affirm and challenge at the same time.

For example, I was watching a film for class the other day. It was a film about women's bodies as the site for political struggle. In one segment, the film showed a photo shoot with three "overweight women." The women were dressed up, playful, and acting sexy. The photographer, herself a large woman, said that the intent of the pictures was to "show the beauty of all women . . . that large women can be sexy too." Notice that the images of these women will do two things. On the one hand, they will affirm that images of women are to be objects of gaze, and on the other hand, they will subvert those same images by not conforming to the assumptions of body type that go along with women and sexiness today.

The centrality of sex to the creation of the human body, along with the domination of heterosexuality in society, means that homosexual displays are politically powerful forms of subversion. Recall the distinction I made earlier between performance and performity—acting straight isn't a performance; it's performity. Performance presumes an already existing subject; performity *creates* the subject. The practices of heterosexuals in everyday life are not a performance; heterosexual practices create, cite, and regulate the sex and subjectivity they display. It's not performance; it's production. When you act straight, you are citing the discourse that dominates and creates human bodies. You are bringing your body under dominion; you are inscribing it with the political discourse of the day; and you are creating your body, but creating it in the image of society's power—the hegemonic norm of heterosexuality.

However, there is a way in which acting "gay" is more performance than performity. It's performity in the sense that there isn't a preexisting subject, but it is performance with reference to an open field. Rather than citing a hegemonic norm, homosexual cues are like referencing a dictionary that is always being rewritten. There is no authority, there are no relations of power, and there is no social norm for homosexuality to cite. Homosexuality is repressed in us (which is why, Butler might argue, so many people react strongly to it). Since there isn't a norm of homosexuality, acting gay cannot be a citation or inscription of the ruling discourse—homosexuality is an open field wherein the practices are not foreclosed. Thus, the performance of homosexuality does not cite an authority, nor does it inscribe the body in the same way heterosexuality does. To act gay or "queer" subverts authority and leaves the body undefined and open to possibilities.

To repeat the question we began this section with, what becomes of homosexuality? In Butler's scheme, homosexual practices become acts of subversion that can facilitate change. More than most other practices, they challenge hegemonic rule, especially gender oppression and patriarchy. In this scheme, femininity and masculinity are not choices, "but the forcible citation of a norm, one whose complex historicity is indissociable from relations of discipline, regulation, punishment" (Butler, 1993, p. 232). Choice, then, lies in the undisclosed field, in the

> theatricality of gender . . . the very signification that is "queer." . . . This kind of citation will emerge as *theatrical* to the extent that it *mimes and renders hyperbolic* the discursive convention that it also *reverses*. The hyperbolic gesture is crucial to the exposure of the homophobic "law" that can no longer control the terms of its own abjecting strategies. (p. 232)

Drag in particular is a powerful political and social statement. The performance of drag—a male wearing female clothing—challenges the "truth-regime" of sex that there is correspondence between the inside and outside, that there is actually a sexed person (the doer) in back of the sexed practices (the deeds). Drag "produces a contradictory formation of gender in which no fixed 'truth' can be established" (Butler, 1993, p. 234). Keeping in mind that a "vast number of drag performers [are] straight . . . drag thus allegorizes *heterosexual melancholy*, the melancholy by which a masculine gender is formed from the refusal to grieve the masculine as a possibility of love" (p. 235).

We're now in a place to consider queer theory. Gay and lesbian studies focuses on the same kinds of issues that traditional gender studies focuses on: the unequal distribution of scarce resources by specific group identities, how those identities are claimed and managed, and how they form the basis of prejudice and discrimination. Queer theory, on the other hand, sees homosexuality and heterosexuality as mutually constructed, as part of the same process of body sexing. Thus, being gay is just as "normal" as being straight; one exists only in the presence of the other. Analysis shifts from political oppression to the ways in which the categories of homosexuality and heterosexuality are used in culture and practice. Queer politics changes from the struggle for gay rights to subversive activities aimed at challenging the hegemonic norm of heterosexuality.

Queer, then, is a specific kind of deconstruction that exposes the hidden work and inconsistencies inherent within the sexual text of our bodies. In this sense, we can define queer as subversive behaviors or theories that bring into question the assumed natural relations among the body, sex, gender, and self. Remember our discussion of subversion. Queer acts are supremely subversive, which is why drag is so powerful. Drag appears to conform to the stereotypical, even blatant cultural expectations about women and sex. However, these stereotypes are powerfully overturned because the person presenting them is male.

Further, because many drag queens are heterosexual men, the representations of sex and sexuality may be doubly subverted. Drag affirms that "the images of women = sex objects," but it subverts the first element by putting men in the place of women. So, we now have something like "images of women performed by men = sex objects." But that may not be all there is to its subversion, because there is a cultural assumption in back of men acting like women: They must be gay. So, underneath the first subversion is an assumption that makes it intelligible: A gay man may act like a female sex object in order to attract other gay men. The second subversion comes when this assumption is overturned because it is a heterosexual man in drag. Our statement then reads something like "the images of women performed by men who desire women = sex objects."

If you are having trouble making sense out of that statement, then you're experiencing the intent of queer. Every set of cultural discourses, ideas, or images is based on assumptions about exclusion. For example, in contemporary Western society, masculinity is fundamentally formed by denying femininity. Subversion, especially queer, overturns those assumptions and renders them meaningless. Specifically, the notion of queer challenges society's sex-regime by disrupting identity formation. Rather than performity, or even performance as I used the idea above, queer explicitly disturbs and dislocates both sex and gender identity formation. That's why queer isn't restricted to gay and lesbian studies. Queer theory is interested in all sites of disarticulation, such as cross-dressing, gender-corrective surgery, and hermaphroditism—anywhere the assumptions of sex, gender, and desire are challenged.

> If the term "queer" is to be a site of collective contestation, the point of departure for a set of historical reflections and futural imaginings, it will have to remain that which is, in the present, never fully owned, but always and only redeployed, twisted, queered from a prior usage and in the direction of urgent and expanding political purposes. (Butler, 1993, p. 228)

Summary

- Butler argues that both sex and gender are normative and expressions of power. The body is particularly significant in this regard because its creation sets the parameters of the person and his or her subjectivity. Like all things human, the body must conform to normative expectations in order to be intelligible. The body is primarily understood as sexed, and in this age it only becomes understandable when it conforms to the hegemonic norm of heterosexuality. This hegemonic norm is principally created through repression and performity.

- In this age, we understand and generate the body's sex nature through the eyes of Freudian theory, especially the Oedipal law. In forming the ego, certain physical impulses and options that are presented by the id and libido are repressed in order to conform to normative expectations. Initially, both boys and girls are sensually attached to their mothers. However, in order to mature psychically, both must resolve certain issues revolving around identification and desire. For boys, this is referred to as the Oedipus complex, and for girls, the Electra complex (though Freud used Oedipus for both). In both cases, the child must resolve desire toward the parent of the opposite sex and rivalry and hostility toward the parent of its own sex. Both of these elements have to be successfully resolved. The important point in Butler's theory is that both boys and girls have to attach to the parent of the same sex without doing so with sexual (libidinal) energy. This detach/reattach process is somewhat more problematic for boys than for girls, which may be one reason why heterosexual men have a more difficult time with homosexuality. Thus, the Oedipal law simultaneously leads us toward heterosexuality and leaves us haunted by the loss of homosexual possibilities.

- The ego is formed out of this dilemma of attaching to and detaching from the same sex. In order to meet the demands of the superego, the desires of the id must be repressed. Through repression, the ego forms the psychic boundaries between the id, superego, and other. More importantly, the individual becomes self-aware and produces subjectivity through the process of repression under the hegemonic norm of heterosexuality: The person becomes individually aware of the demands of the id and superego and substitutes the ego for the needs of the id and requirements of the superego. Since the superego demands are historically and culturally specific, this process points to the importance of political ideologies in the formation of individual subjectivities. In this case, our self-awareness is produced in the context of the hegemonic norm of heterosexuality. More generally, this process means that there isn't a preexisting subject in back of the body and its behaviors.

- The body and the ego are continually formed through performity. Performity refers to behaviors that cite hegemonic norms. In other words, the body becomes understandable as a body when its actions conform to the hegemonic norm of heterosexuality. Performity also implies that people bring their own bodies and subjectivities under the dominion of the existing hegemonic norm.

- But subversion is possible. Subversion occurs when hegemonic ideas or images are overturned from within. Generally, this happens as one or more of the elements that make up the image or idea are inverted while holding the rest stable. Thus, subversion simultaneously affirms and denies. The notion of queer is a particularly powerful form of subversion in that it disrupts the contemporary Western assumptions about sex and gender, about the inner person and the sexual cues he or she gives.

TAKING THE PERSPECTIVE: POSTSTRUCTURALISM AND QUEER THEORY

Judith Butler draws on a number of theorists and philosophers to form her work, most specifically poststructuralism, Sigmund Freud, and Friedrich Nietzsche. To begin our consideration of Butler's perspective, we want to focus on the ideas of possibility and intelligibility, from Foucault. The word *intelligibility* means that something is capable of being understood or grasped. For humans, for something to be possible, it must be understood; thus, intelligibility sets the parameters for possibility. Further, Foucault tells us that things are only intelligible and possible within a historic, cultural context. He argues that the limits of our language, knowledge, and discourse set the boundaries for what is possible and impossible for us to know, think, and feel. This isn't simply a matter of translation. For example, we may know that the translation of the Greek word *aphrodisiakos* is "sexual," but the translated word only calls to our minds the meanings in our language at this time, which, as Foucault demonstrated, doesn't convey the meanings that would have occurred to the minds of Greeks living before the Common Era. These limits of possible and impossible thought are themselves the implementation or practice of power. Thus, for Foucault, knowledge isn't primarily something that is used by the powerful; rather, knowledge itself is power, and it is exercised on the elite and common alike.

We need to remind ourselves of something else here as well: The knowledge, discourse, and language of any age are not an account of what actually exists. We can see this obviously in social knowledge. At one time, American society as a whole "knew" that people of color such as blacks, Indians, Chinese, and Irish are inferior. In America, we also used to "know" that homosexuality is a disease and that women are rationally inferior to men. But the historic specificity of knowledge isn't limited to social relations. Up until the time of Copernicus, we "knew" that the earth was the center of the universe. Back in the early 1800s, doctors "knew" that all disease is created by an imbalance of bodily fluids or "humors": black bile, yellow bile, phlegm, and blood. In order to heal people, doctors would try to balance out the humors, which is why they would purge or bleed their patients. But we "know better" now, right? Both science and society have progressed, right? Maybe, but how do we *know* that our knowledge has progressed?

Remember that the basic point of poststructuralism is that everything is inextricably textual. We continually write our version of the world upon the world. For example,

(Continued)

(Continued)

right now I'm looking out my home office window. I see a small forest of trees, and I see those trees as mine. They are on my property, and only I have the right to cut them, sell them, or leave them wild. However, my ownership of those trees exists only because of our cultural and legal structures of "private property." Those trees are mine only because "it is written" in legal documents that we as a society collectively accept as true and because we inscribe the meaning of private property upon the trees when we look at them. In this way, culture is utterly reflexive. The only way to ever think that we are not simply writing reality is to have a solid center—something that exists apart from our texts. But poststructuralism shows us the impossibility of that as well: Centers are by definition outside the text and thus not a center at all, and centers historically come and go.

Poststructuralism also argues that the space of possibility and meaning is opened up through difference (*différance*). If every meaning is possible, then meaningfulness is impossible. Meaning, therefore, comes through holding off some possibilities in favor of others. It's in the process of deferring that meaning is possible. Let's use an obvious example from the subject of this chapter. Masculinity has meaning only insofar as feminine possibilities are deferred. We must foreclose or deny certain possibilities (a boy can't act like a girl) in order to open other possibilities—those behaviors that are not-girl are the "boy" behaviors available or possible for a young male.

Bringing all this together, our knowledge—in Butler's case, our bodies—is a function of the historical period and culture in which we live. Thus, bodies are formed by opening up some possibilities and closing off others, and social differences are produced through specific institutional, organizational, and individual practices. Knowledge thus forms the historical condition of possibility and is the true power of any age. By definition, then, when we "know" something, we reflexively bring our thoughts, feelings, and actions under the power of that knowledge and discourse, of those possibilities.

From Freud, Butler takes the idea of psychodynamic processes and intrapsychic structures. But this really needs to be read in the context of poststructuralism. Remember Foucault's notion of truth-games? Language and discourse refer only to themselves, not some external reality. Language is its own center. When people claim to have the truth, it's a move of power, an attempt to silence all other voices. Thus, Freud didn't "discover" something universally true about people. But his theory is a truth-game, one that came out of the episteme of the time and has been used to create a discourse around heterosexuality. A note of caution here: This isn't the same as legitimation. Legitimation justifies a reality; truth-games and discourses bring it into existence. This is one of the most difficult things to understand, but also one of the most important. We tend to view the knowledge of sociology, psychology, psychiatry, medicine, history, and the like as factual; explanations about the way things are. These explanations may at times be wrong, but that's all they are—wrong, as if some other-than-linguistic reality exists. But what poststructuralism and other contemporary theories tell us is that these explanations fully create the things they discover (for an example, research repressed memories and satanic rituals). Butler's debt to Nietzsche is principally for the idea of the doer and the deed, which basically gives "body" to the ideas of discourse and truth-games.

BUILDING YOUR THEORY TOOLBOX

- Write a 250-word synopsis of the theoretical perspective that Butler uses.

- After reading and understanding this chapter, you should be able to define the following terms theoretically and explain their importance to Butler's theory of sexing the body: arche-writing, hegemonic norm of heterosexuality, discursive function, iterability, performity, doer and the deed, presentist conceit, repression, melancholia, materialization, queer theory.

- After reading and understanding this chapter, you should be able to answer the following questions (remembering to answer them theoretically):

  o How are intelligibility and possibility related to sex? How do these issues set the boundaries for the body?

  o What is the hegemonic norm of heterosexuality, and how is it inscribed upon the body through psychodynamic processes?

  o What is performity, and how is it related to the hegemonic norm of heterosexuality and the sexing of the body?

  o What is the idea of the "doer and the deed"? How is it related to one's subjective experience?

  o How are haunting, melancholia, and the ego related? How is the loss of homosexuality unspecified?

  o In what ways is "queer" a kind of deconstruction? Specifically, how does queer subvert sexuality and gender? Can you think of other issues or identities that can be "queered"?

Learning More—Primary and Secondary Sources

- Judith Butler, *Bodies That Matter: On the Discursive Limits of "Sex,"* Routledge, 1993.

- Judith Butler, *The Psychic Life of Power: Theories in Subjection,* Stanford University Press, 1997.

- Judith Butler, *Undoing Gender,* Routledge, 2004.

- *The Judith Butler Reader,* edited by Sara Salih, Blackwell, 2004.

- Sara Salih, *Judith Butler: Essential Guides for Literary Studies,* Routledge, 2002.

- *Butler Matters: Judith Butler's Impact on Feminist and Queer Studies,* edited by Margaret Sonser Breen and Warren J. Blumenfeld, Ashgate, 2005.

Weaving the Threads

- Bring Smith's and Butler's theories together to form a synthesized theory of gender construction. How are the body and consciousness involved in gender inequality? Consider Smith's and Butler's ideas of subversion with Chafetz's notion of social change. Use these three approaches to form a theory concerning gender social change. What implications do you see?

Conclusion

Post-Thinking

Formerly, one could tell simply by looking at a person that he wanted to think . . . that he now wished to become wiser and prepared himself for a thought: he set his face as for prayer and stopped walking; yes, one even stood still for hours in the middle of the road when the thought arrived— on one leg or two legs. That seemed to be required by the dignity of the matter. (Nietzsche, 1974, p. 81)

id you read the quote? If not, please do so. And let what Nietzsche says get inside of you. Have you ever had a thought? Of course, you think quite a bit. But have you ever had a thought in the way Nietzsche is describing it? This kind of thought is an event. It requires or perhaps captures the entire person. It's demanding and inspiring. Notice that Nietzsche says "formerly." He's referring to a time before the seduction of modern business. When life was slower, it was easier to have a thought, to be captured by an idea when you least expected it. Most of us today are too busy to be overtaken by an idea—but we can still quite deliberately have a thought. And that's what this book is about. Having "a thought" as a deliberate act—one that captures the thinker and opens the world to new visions and possibilities—is an effect of thinking practices that revolve around critical thinking and theory. The future is literally ours. We live in a time as eventful as the beginning of modernity, and in these times of change and shifting forces, we have the opportunity to make a difference, more so than at any other time. This book is an invitation to having a thought and making a difference.

We've come a long way from the birth of sociology and positivism. Modern societies truly were founded on the idea that we could control society and thus create happiness. Comte shared and propagated that vision, and the early sociological theorists were caught up in it. As I've pointed out, the critiques of Marx, Weber, and Durkheim were all motivated by the idea that society could be studied and guided. Perhaps above everything else, modernity is the idea that human beings can through reason make their social (freedom, equality) and physical (technology) worlds better.

Obviously, the idea of progress is intrinsically linked with every other feature of modernity. For example, the modern nation-state was specifically created to protect the inalienable rights of citizens. Capitalism is still seen by many as the great equalizer: the even playing field where neither birth nor social standing determine outcomes and life chances. This link with progress is part of what has produced the critical stands of contemporary theory. In fact, it is this critical perspective that is characteristic of contemporary theory, not modernity itself. Truly modernist theories are uncritically built upon the classics, such as Marx, Weber, Spencer, and Durkheim. Contemporary theories, on the other hand, are generally critical of the modernist project in one way or another. Even contemporary theories of modernity modify the classics and the ideas of freedom and progress. Anthony Giddens's theory provides a clear example: In "late modernity," there has been a shift from emancipatory politics to lifestyle politics and the reflexive project of the self. If you think about it, even the "self" has changed in the course of this book (compare Giddens and symbolic interaction).

If I were to single out one significant characteristic of contemporary theory, I would say it is the idea of perspectives. Perspectives determine what we see. You've known this since your introduction to sociology class: Things look different if you view them from the conflict rather than functionalist perspective. The twentieth century brought a plethora of new and different perspectives to sociology—different ways of seeing social things, such as phenomenology, existentialism, structuralism and poststructuralism, pragmatism, feminism, critical theory, social constructivism, ethnomethodology, and so on. One of the reasons for this deluge of new ways of seeing is the social changes that occurred. As I've mentioned, WWI; WWII; the Holocaust; economic crises; global warming and various ecological disasters such as Chernobyl and the *Exxon Valdez*; the civil rights movement; as well as the shifts in economic production and increases in mass media, commodification, and advertising have all combined to create more doubt than hope in progress. Things don't seem as predictable or controllable as at the beginning of modernity.

However—and that's a strong however—hope isn't dead. All of our contemporary theorists write because there is redemptive value in speaking to our social situations. One way of understanding contemporary theory, then, is as highly specialized discourse. The great thinkers wrestle with the complexities and contradictions of our becoming society. Society isn't a thing that stands still and invites discovery of timeless processes. That sort of positivistic vision is dead even in the most sophisticated of all the sciences, physics. Einstein turned Newton's utterly predictable universe on its head, and quantum mechanics took Einstein's theory further than he had imagined. The most contemporary of theoretical physics envisions our life on this planet as simply a holographic image produced by a translation point in black holes, and time as having two dimensions. Physicists Stephen Hawking and Leonard Mlodinow (2010) have abandoned the idea of strict empiricism and argue for a model-dependent realism: It no longer matters if the theory explains reality as long as the theory works for the purpose at hand.

Of what value is theory then? What do we do with theory? The value and purpose of social theory remain as they always have been: to explain the social world and make it a better place to live. We sociologists, like physicists, have had to come to terms with the fact that our object of research is more complex and more volatile than we first imagined. We can explain what's going on, and we can within given limits predict and guide it. But it's a much more difficult task than Comte, Marx, Weber, or Durkheim had thought. Class isn't the only thing that matters, and neither is race or gender. As Patricia Hill Collins points out, we each stand at a distinct locus where various relations of ruling coincide. Our identities and selves are cobbled together through social structures, popular culture, legitimated knowledge, and a variety of other inputs. Society isn't a single geographically bounded entity. States still do exist, but social relations have overflowed their boundaries and transcended the bounds of even space and time. Social groups aren't simply real; there are also neo-tribes and identities that are constructed in virtual space through commodified images.

The most important value of theory is that it helps us think better; it gives us insights that we would otherwise not have. Theory itself is about thinking and seeing. Yes, theory needs to be tested and compared to lived reality, but it is always theory that allows us to see "reality" in the first place. The best of our theories makes us see outside the box. What an amazing experience it is to actually understand Marx's idea of commodity fetishism. Once understood, you can never look at consumerism the same way again.

One of the characteristics of contemporary theory is the presence of multiple "post" theories: poststructuralism, postmodernism, postindustrialism, postcolonialism, and so on. These theories are interesting because they are by definition unsettled. Something that is "post" isn't anything in itself. It's simply something that comes after something else. The social process isn't settled, the discourse isn't mythologized, and we're not exactly sure what it is we're looking at. There is a way, then, that *to have a thought is to be post.* I don't mean this as a catchphrase or truism. If we accept the implications of discourse, then having a thought as compared to being handed a thought (or being thought) always involves moving from a position of taken-for-grantedness. To even be aware of our discourse implies some movement out of it. How far we move depends on the distance between the symbolic spaces we can think about. Though I admit the limitations of analytic dichotomies, the basic distinction is between thinking inside and thinking outside. Post-theories invite us to think outside. In that sense, they are truer versions of progress than positivism, which compresses everything into a single, objectifying discourse. As Hall (1996b) suggests that Foucault would tell us, "The knowledge which a discourse produces constitutes a kind of power, exercised over those who are 'known'" (pp. 204–205). I will leave you with two methods of post-thinking: postcolonialism and postmodernism.

Postcolonialism

In general, the word *colony* refers to a body of people settled in a new land. It also implies a continued political connection, with the original country exercising power over the colony. Interestingly, the word is also used to speak of a local population of a specific species, such as a colony of bees. In this sense, colonization refers to an invasive species that dominates or replaces the indigenous. An example of this is kudzu, a vine native to Japan brought to the southern United States as ground cover. Kudzu grows so rapidly that it kills the native shrubs and trees.

Colonization has always had an interesting relationship to modernity. In a fundamental way, especially with the United States, we can see colonization and decolonization as part of what facilitated modernization. It was the Revolutionary War that allowed the United States to move from a colonized nation to become a nation-state. As we've consistently noted, the nation-state and the accompanying ideas of citizen and individual equality are central to modernity. Many theories of modernization also argue that colonization was a necessary precursor to modernity, establishing the necessary economic and political infrastructures. These theories point to the United States as an example of the need for colonization.

Thus, both colonialism and decolonization have been prevalent in modernity. Up until about 1914, colonization continued to expand. The total geographic space occupied under colonial rule increased from 55% in 1800 to about 85% of the earth in 1914. After WWII, decolonization took hold and continued to grow through the 1960s. During that period of time, most of the colonies and protectorates in Asia and Africa won their independence. One of the most notable achievements during this period was the move for Indian independence led by Mahatma Gandhi.

Postcolonialism is an effort to understand the effects of colonization and decolonization on political systems, cultures, and individuals. Quite a bit of work in the field comes from literary criticism and is aimed at bringing the perspective of the colonized to the colonizer: "the theoretical value of *postcolonialism* inheres, in part, in its ability to elaborate the forgotten memories of this condition" (Gandhi, 1998, pp. 7–8). In 1978, postcolonialism became part of social theory with the publication of Edward Said's book *Orientalism*. Said argues that colonizing nations base much of their economic growth and stability on the markets and resources that the colonized provide. In this, Said echoed W. E. B. Du Bois' (1920/1996a) work some 60 years prior: "There is a chance for exploitation on an immense scale for inordinate profit, not simply to the very rich, but to the middle class and to the laborers. This chance lies in the exploitation of darker peoples" (p. 504–505).

Said's insight is that the structural relationship between the colonized and colonizer is based upon specific kinds of cultures, in this case, "an undeterred and unrelenting Eurocentrism" (Said, 1994, p. 222). Identities are formed through difference, and the stronger the differences, the stronger the identity and the more dramatic the effects, such as what people are willing to do in the name of their identity. The basic distinction that allows this identity and centrism to exist is the East–West divide, the social construction of the "Orient." This distinction is similar to the difference made in the United States between blacks and whites. That distinction and seeing the differences based in race are what allowed slavery, Jim Crow laws, and continued discrimination to exist. Fundamentally, "white," and all that identity entails, can only exist in reference to "black."

In the same way, the "West" became the West only in comparison to something else, something inferior. Only when the Orient is seen as inferior, underdeveloped, and deviant, and the Oriental is viewed as "the Yellow Peril" or the "Mongol hordes," can the West see itself as superior, developed, humane, rational, and so forth. The idea of the West "was central to the Enlightenment" (Hall, 1996b, p. 187). The identity of the West, its sense of itself, "was formed not only by the internal processes that gradually molded Western European countries into a distinct type of society, but also through Europe's sense of difference from other worlds" (p. 188). This superior view of Western civilization allowed and continues to allow European nations and the United States to force their brand of democracy, capitalism, and rationality upon other "uncivilized" nations. As Wallerstein points out, developing nations can only be "developing" in reference to some supposedly superior model, and this politically inspired model is invariably imposed from the outside.

An important ramification here is that while decolonized nations may no longer be directly dominated, they nonetheless continue to be colonized politically, economically, and culturally. Frantz Fanon takes this later idea and applies it at the level of individual experience. The colonized is someone who experiences his or her being or existence through others. Like Foucault's use of discourse, Fanon (1961/2004) argues that the relationship between developed and developing nations creates a subjective position for the colonized. In this vein, Robert J. C. Young (2003) asks,

> Have you ever felt that the moment you said the word 'I,' that 'I' was someone else, not you? That in some obscure way, you were not the subject of your own sentence? . . . That you live in a world of others, a world that exists *for* others? (p. 1)

Like Butler, Fanon argues that this cultural colonization is embodied. Rather than simply being able to experience the body's sensations and perceptions directly, the body and its experiences are defined by the other:

> Below the corporeal schema I had sketched a historico-racial schema. The elements that I used had been provided for me not by [sense data] . . . but by the other, the white man, who had woven me out of a thousand details, anecdotes, stories. (Fanon, 1952/1967, p. 111)

The colonized experience of the body, then, "is solely a negating activity" (p. 110): The colonized body is *not* the colonizer's, *not* white, *not* superior.

The struggle for decolonized peoples is thus not simply political and economic; it is a struggle for psychological and cultural existence. Just as the white American idea of "Manifest Destiny" implied the genocide of Native Americans, so this colonization results in the loss of a people's cultural and psychological existence. In order to avoid cultural and psychological obliteration, Fanon argues (1961/2004), the colonized must place at risk their ontological existence. In order to see what Fanon is talking about, let's continue to use the example of Native Americans. Their genocide didn't only mean physical death, though it did nearly wipe out the Native American population, from approximately 12 million prior to European contact to 250,000 by 1900. It also meant forced assimilation. If a Native American managed to physically survive the American holocaust, she or he was expected to die culturally and to become white.

We've learned that human reality is cultural. This implies that to exist as human is to exist culturally and to be recognized. Recognition implies imposition. At the most basic level, your recognition of me as a separate, viable being is dependent upon my imposing myself upon you as something different: I am not you. Part of what Fanon (1962/1967) is arguing, then, is that human existence is dependent upon cultural recognition:

> Man is human only to the extent to which he tries to impose his existence on another man in order to be recognized by him. As long as he has not been effectively recognized by the other, that other will remain the theme of his actions. (pp. 216–217)

As long as the colonized is understood only with reference to the colonizer, the colonized has no viable existence. In retrospect, this is easy to see in terms of race or the East–West divide, but it is equally true in today's discourse of "developing nations." Developing nations only exist with reference to the superior developed nations and thus have no viable existence of their own.

Thus, the task for the colonized is this: to keep, express, and demand recognition for indigenous cultures, identities, and subjectivities. To do that, the colonized must impose his or her existence upon a Westernizing world—not to dominate it, as is the intent of the colonizers, but to be recognized as fully and viably human. This move is risky—it risks ontological death—but the alternative is equally perilous: living out the themes determined by the colonizers. The themes begun in the Eurocentric East–West divide were re-expressed in the vocabulary of first, second, and third worlds, and they continue today through the distinctions made between modern developed nations and modernizing developing nations.

Postmodernism

There are numerous varieties of postmodernism. Elsewhere I've argued that they can be divided into critiques of scientific knowledge, evaluations of economic changes, and analyses of the effects of mass media and advertising (see Allan & Turner, 2000; J. H. Turner, 1998). Here I want to discuss Jean-François Lyotard's critique of knowledge. He focuses on the loss of grand narratives in postmodernity. Basically, a grand narrative is a story that encompasses and gives singular meaning to diverse narratives and cultures. The story of America as the bedrock of democracy and freedom is just such a grand narrative. The person put forth as "American" is one that transcends religion, race, and creed. It is a grand narrative that embraces all these more specific narratives. Significantly, Lyotard sees the loss of grand narratives as an effect of positivistic science.

Lyotard (1979/1984) begins by pointing out that ethnographic and anthropological studies indicate that traditionally, prior to modernity, knowledge was passed on in narrative form—that is, it was transmitted or handed down generationally. In this kind of oral tradition, histories and knowledge are passed on through the telling of stories. The characteristic of the narrative form that interests Lyotard the most is its pragmatic protocol. There is a specific protocol that sets the narrative form apart; it occurs through the positioning of different narrative posts, specifically the post of the sender and receiver of the story.

Thus, in telling the story, the speaker claims the right to be heard because of his or her position first as a hearer. Let's use a fictitious yet typical beginning line from this kind of narration: "Hear now the story of the Mugwats, which I heard from my grandmother, who heard it from her grandmother, and back to the first grandmother, who was from the beginning, which I now pass on to you." Notice first that the teller's right to speak is grounded in how she or he came to the story. Also observe that the grounding of the speaker is further established by references to contemporary hearers. Relationships among ancestors, contemporaries, and even future members are automatically established in the transmission of knowledge through narrative forms. Thus, what is given in narrative forms isn't simply knowledge; "what is transmitted through these narratives is a set of pragmatic rules that constitutes the social bond" (Lyotard, 1979/1984, p. 21).

Narrative forms, then, are a type of language game. They do what they do simply as a result of what they are. The narratives seem to belong to the past, but in truth they establish contemporary social relations in their telling. Further, like language games, narrative forms require no external legitimation. For example, there are at least as many creation myths as there are ancient societies. (For a fun excursion, type "creation myth" into your favorite search engine.) But it is only recently in modern society that any of these myths have been subjected to external legitimation. As an illustration, today we see the creation myth of Christianity as it is literally given in Genesis presented as a scientifically sound alternative to evolution. The issue in this illustration is not whether Genesis is scientifically accurate or not; the issue is that the culture in contemporary society has *created an environment in which it seems necessary for what was initially a narrative form to be legitimated externally.*

Lyotard (1979/1984) compares knowledge and narrative forms with science. When compared to narrative forms, science is unique in three important ways: falsification, exclusivism, and legitimation. One of the key pillars of science is the idea of falsification, which is based on empiricism and argumentation. Empiricism is the belief that the universe is empirically ordered and discernable. To count as theory, then, scientific explanations must be testable against empirical reality. Theories must also be open to argumentation, that is, subjected to the test of logic. The important point in falsification, for Lyotard, is that scientific knowledge must be subject to external verification. It is not like language in this sense; it has no intrinsic purpose, nor does science presuppose or create social relations, as do language games.

Science is also exclusive in its claim to knowledge. It presents itself as the knowledge system par excellence. It sees itself in a never-ending quest for the truth of reality, reality being defined in terms of the empirical universe and its law-governed organization. In comparison to science, narratives are "savage, primitive, underdeveloped, backward, alienated, composed of opinions, customs, authority, prejudice, ignorance, ideology. Narratives are gables, myths, legends, fit only for women and children" (Lyotard, 1979/1984, p. 27). Science, then, seeks to dominate and silence any other voice but its own.

According to Lyotard, this kind of behavior is a form of terrorism. It is terrorist in that science eliminates or threatens to eliminate all other languages and modes of knowing. This terrorism is exercised through access to funding and publication sources. A simple illustration from the National Science Foundation ought to suffice: The NSF has "an annual budget of about $5.5 billion. . . . In many fields such as mathematics, computer science and *the social sciences, NSF is the major source of federal backing*" (NSF at a Glance, n.d., emphasis added). Thus, funding for social research is only granted when the proposal meets the criteria of scientific research. Lyotard (1979/1984) argues that when an "institution of knowledge functions in this manner, it is acting like an ordinary power center" (p. 63).

The last unique property of science, legitimation, brings us to the postmodern condition. As we've seen, narrative forms are internally legitimated. What they do is wrapped up in what they are. Science, on the other hand, is not: It is dependent upon external legitimation. The principle of falsifiability specifically points to this issue of legitimation. Any knowledge system that is intentionally created to be falsifiable is by definition dependent upon external legitimation. Compare this idea of science with an indigenous creation myth. Creation myths are self-legitimating: They fulfill their function whether or not they correspond to empirical reality or can stand the test of argumentation.

Ironically, Lyotard (1979/1984) claims that science needs a grand narrative in order to legitimate its existence. There are two kinds of grand narratives that legitimate science, according to Lyotard: the speculative narrative and the narrative of emancipation. Both of these narratives are bound up with the Enlightenment and thus the defining features of modernity. The speculative narrative is one that extols knowledge for knowledge's sake. In this story, science releases the individual from the oppressive "priests and tyrants" and frees her or him for the pursuit of knowledge. As you can see, there is a close relationship between freedom and knowledge in this narrative, which brings us to the emancipatory narrative. The intent of the nation-state and democracy is to bring equality and freedom to all humankind. Science's role in this emancipation is to provide a means of control and rationality for the political, economic, and legal institutions.

However, Lyotard (1979/1984) defines the "postmodern as incredulity toward metanarratives" (p. xxiv). What he means is that modernity has produced a general trend toward doubt concerning grand or metanarratives. There are certainly social factors that have precipitated this trend, such as the collapse of Western colonialism, the failure of democracy to liberate humanity from oppression, wholesale training in scientific doubt, commodification, bureaucratic rationality, the endless proliferation of contradictory bits of knowledge, and so on. However, Lyotard wants us to see that these factors are almost unnecessary because "the seeds of 'delegitimation' and nihilism . . . were inherent in the grand narratives of the nineteenth century" (p. 38). In other words, the grand narratives of modernity were contradictory and unattainable from their inception.

The speculative narrative as found in science is problematic because of the way "knowledge" is produced in science. First, the way science is practiced is the direct opposite of freedom in knowledge. As we've seen, science claims exclusive rights to the truth, or, better, the production and recognition of facts. The terrorist practices of exclusion are the antithesis of scholastic freedom. Second, science as knowledge is established through a "second-level discourse." In this case, the first-level discourse of science is found between actual research and its object. For example, I have a friend who studied bees in the mountain fields of Colorado; everything immediately pertaining to that study would be first-level discourse. But because my friend's work was scientific, there was second-level discourse in his report as well.

The second-level discourse refers to methods of citation. In order to qualify as scientific work, research must be based on and cite previous works. Sir Isaac Newton embodied this scientific approach when he famously said, "If I have seen further, it is by standing on the shoulders of Giants." Thus, my friend had to not only do his field research, but he also had to cite and use other scientists in order to have his dissertation accepted as scientific. Science, then, is *reflexively legitimated;* in other words, science is legitimated by citing itself. This is radically different from the self-legitimation of traditional narrative forms. Science intentionally legitimates itself by proclaiming and using its own methods; traditional narrative is legitimated by what it intrinsically does socially: It creates social relations, which is the principal purpose of language. Lyotard (1979/1984) refers to this practice as "reduplication." Another postmodern thinker, Mark Gottdiener (1990) calls this practice "logocentrism." Lyotard claims that this self-reference legitimation means that science is continually acknowledging that in terms of the actual object of research, science "does not really know what it thinks it knows. Positive science is not a form of knowledge" (p. 38).

The second grand narrative, emancipation, is equally problematic due to the nature of scientific knowledge. But this problem is a bit easier to see. Recall that narrative knowledge intrinsically connects people with people. Science, however, stands as an abstract, isolated knowledge system. Even if science is able to make a true statement, there is nothing within science that implies that a moral or ethical statement derived from it will be just. Lyotard gives us the simple example of a closed door. In propositional logic, the language of science, there is no relationship between the statement of fact "the door is closed" and the proscriptive statement "open the door." The way science sees itself inherently produces a gap between factual and ethical statements, which is why science can be used for any ideological purpose, such as when biology was used to justify slavery or when science produced the atomic bomb.

Thus, while science is in need of legitimation, the two prime metanarratives available to it are ill-suited to science itself. Keep in mind here that Lyotard isn't criticizing or dismissing science across the board. Science has dramatically improved our living conditions; of that, there is no doubt. Lyotard's focus is on science as a system of knowledge and how the qualities of that system have produced doubt concerning grand narratives. The Enlightenment and modernity are defined by the twin narratives of intellectual freedom and political emancipation. Science draws on these narratives to legitimate itself. What is meant by "science" is so wrapped up in these aspects of the Enlightenment grand narratives that its failure precipitates disbelief in grand narratives generally and the collapse of the project of modernity.

Concluding Thoughts

I began this book with a story of modernity that focused on knowledge. In that sense, modernism is larger than a historical period or a specific set of social factors. Modernism is a perspective of the mind and an attitude of the heart, one that believes with certainty in progress, objectivity, and control. I also started with some ideas about the real you. The real you isn't purely individualistic. Neither you nor I live apart from history and society. We need to understand our time and collective existence to even begin to understand ourselves; and, of course, we need theory to comprehend the historically situated social factors that impact us. But my intent is not simply that you understand the "theoretical you"; I also hope that this book will influence the personal you, the one you experience and project into the world. This possibility is why I've chosen to end the book with post-thinking.

One of the things that post-thinking implies is that it is impossible to move backward or forward in time. To move backward implies trying to think in terms of cultures past, like trying to imagine what it was like to be a Hopi before the Europeans came. No matter how close we may think we get, whatever symbolic space we create is always and ever a "traditional-Hopi-as-imagined-by-a-twenty-first-century-person." The same is true about seemingly closer subjectivities, such as the idealized American family of the 1950s. So, we can't truly move backward in our thought, and we can't move forward either. Moving "forward" exists only as the result of an ethical standard. Currently, that standard is some form of the modern ideal of progress, and the idea of "progress" is always based on a value system. As Max Weber (1904/1949) put it, "There is no absolutely 'objective' scientific analysis of culture . . . of 'social phenomena' independent of special and 'one-sided' viewpoints according to which . . . they are selected, analyzed and organized for expository purposes" (p. 72).

To have a thought, then, is to engage in post-thinking. It isn't a call to a bygone era, nor is it valued as a step forward; it is simply a potential step outside of discourse. And since today the most profound "inside" is modernity, to have a thought is to thus in some sense be "postmodern"—to be outside the confines of modernist values and ideas. To have a thought is to be liminal; it is be outside but not yet arriving. In this way, Nietzsche misplaced his thinker in the quote that began this chapter. Rather than "in the middle of the road," perhaps we should see a person having a thought on a staircase—neither going up nor down but between, a conceptual space that is equally intentional and uncertain. Part of this uncertainty must be linked to the insight that knowledge can be an expression of power. This is true in the general sense, as Foucault argues, and more specifically as it relates to categories of distinction, such as gender, race, sexuality, nationalism, religion, and so forth.

Contemporary theory is vibrant and unruly precisely because it is post in this fashion. Theory today is also the most exciting it has been since the time of Marx, Durkheim, and Weber, where social theory was a main course in public discourse and media. The book you hold in your hands invites both you and me into this turbulent sea of ideas. Many contemporary theory books conclude with a section on "where contemporary theory is headed." I'm not sure where theory is "headed," but I can tell you that it is composed of ideas that challenge every possible boundary. I believe we are in a time of change as fundamental as modernity itself. Contemporary social theory invites you to see the world differently and become personally involved in these changes. Key to this involvement is the complexity and suppleness of mind that contemporary theory opens up in us. I leave you with one of my favorite quotes from Cornel West (2000).

> And so I want to invoke, just very briefly, jazz as a model for democratic education. Jazz of course is continuous with spirituals and blues. But reminding us of the Negro National Anthem which says what? "Lift every Voice." What a democratic sensibility. Lack of democracy: voicelessness. Democratic reality: a sense of being an agent in the world, taking control and ownership over one's sense of one's body, one's views, one's perspectives, one's arguments. Affirming that Emersonian formulation that all forms of imitation are suicide. It's a matter of finding one's own distinctive voice, one's own precious individuality that is not reduced to rugged, rapacious, ragged individualism. But rather is constituted by bouncing up against other voices within a community just like a jazz quartet, where if you haven't found your distinctive voice, it's time for you to practice more. (n.p.)

Glossary

Accountable: A theoretical idea in ethnomethodology, the term implies that the basic requirement of all social settings is that they be recognizable or accountable as whatever social setting they are supposed to be. Members visibly and knowingly work at making their scenes accountable; this work, in turn, organizes the situation and renders it meaningful and real.

AGIL: Parsons proposes four system needs and argues that every grouping of social units that acts like a system must meet these needs. These four system needs can be remembered by the acronym AGIL: adaptation, the subsystem that converts raw materials from the environment into usable stuffs; goal attainment, the subsystem that motivates and guides the system as a whole; integration, the subsystem that regulates the activities of the systems' diverse members; and latent pattern maintenance, the subsystem that indirectly preserves patterns of behavior that are needed for survival.

Black nihilism: Black nihilism is a theoretical concept from the work of Cornel West. Nihilism in general refers to the idea that human life and existence are meaningless and useless. West uses the idea to describe the African American experience as the result of market saturation.

Civil society: In its most basic form, civil society refers to the space that constitutional rights created between the individual and state. Tocqueville's definition focused on voluntary organizations that sprang to life in the United States. In the place of the aristocracy and governmental agencies so common in Europe, these voluntary groups carried the burden of work for the collective. In early modern democracy, civil society also included capitalism and religion, both due to their *voluntary nature.* Jürgen Habermas argued that religion and capitalism hampered civil society; capitalism in particular colonized the civil sphere. For Habermas, then, civil society is a social network of voluntary associations, organizations (especially mass media), and social movements; its purpose is to inform and actualize the public sphere. To function properly, the civil society must be free from control by the state, economy, and religion, and it must exist within a liberal culture that values equality and freedom. For Jeffrey Alexander, civil society itself doesn't exist in any concrete way. It's a symbolic, cultural world that emerges out of the tensions between the universals of the civil sphere and the particular interests generated by non-civil spheres. However, the civil sphere is bounded by communicative and regulative institutions that give civil society a concrete base. Communicative institutions work through influence and persuasion to impact public opinion. Regulative institutions, on the other hand, give concrete expression to the civil sphere through actual power, exercised through voting and party competition, office, and law.

Colonization of the lifeworld: A theoretical concept used by Jürgen Habermas to describe the process through which the everyday life of people is taken over by economic and political structures. By definition, the lifeworld is the primary place of intimate communication and social connections. These functions are overshadowed by the values of money and power that come from the economic and political realms, which in turn reduce true communication and sociability. Lifeworld colonization tends to increase as social structures become more complex and bureaucratized, and when the state creates a climate of entitlement.

Constructivist structuralism: Pierre Bourdieu's theoretical perspective. It's a way of seeing the social world that does away with dualisms such as object/subject and structure/agent. Bourdieu sees a dialectical tension between constructive and structuring social elements. The dialectic indicates that the elements are in tension (structuring and constructing) with one another and that the outcome includes both but is different from either.

Crosscutting stratification: Weber was the first to explore the idea of crosscutting economic, political influences. More recently, Patricia Hill Collins uses the idea of intersectionality. The basic idea is that systems of race, gender, class, nationality, sexuality, and age crisscross one another at specific social locations that form a matrix of domination. The analytical issue, then, is to empirically discover how these various systems come together for any specific person or group. Collins is specifically concerned with how these systems shape black women's experiences and are in turn influenced by black women.

Cultural capital: Cultural capital is a theoretical concept used in Randall Collins's theory of interaction ritual chains and Pierre Bourdieu's theory of class replication. For Collins, cultural capital is defined as the amount of cultural goods—such as knowledge and symbols—that a person has at his or her disposal to engage others in interaction rituals. Collins conceptualizes three types of cultural capital: generalized (group specific), particularized (specific to relationships between individuals), and reputational (what is known about the individual). For Bourdieu, there are three kinds of cultural capital: objective (material goods that vary with class), institutionalized (official recognition of knowledge and skills), and embodied (the result of class-based socialization; habitus). Generally, the concept refers to the social skills, linguistic styles, and tastes that one accrues through education and distance from necessity.

Definition of the situation: Part of symbolic interaction theory, this phrase refers to the primary meaning given to a social interaction. The definition of the situation is important because it implicitly contains identities and scripts for behavior.

Because the definition of the situation is a meaning attribution, it is flexible and negotiable—in other words, people can change it at a moment's notice and with it the available roles and selves.

Dialectic: Dialectic is a theoretical concept that describes the intrinsic dynamic relations within a phenomenon, such as the economy. The term is generally, though not exclusively, used in conflict or critical perspectives. The idea of dialecticism came to sociology through Karl Marx, and Marx, for his part, got the idea from the philosopher Georg Wilhelm Hegel. A dialectic contains different elements that are naturally antagonistic or in tension with one another—this antagonism is what energizes and brings change. Dialectics are cyclical in nature, with each new cycle bringing a different and generally unpredictable resolve. The resolve, or new set of social relations, contains its own antagonistic elements, and the cycle continues.

Discourse: Discourse is a theoretical concept that is widely used but is most specifically associated with the work of Michel Foucault. A discourse is an institutionalized way of thinking and speaking. It sets the limits of what can be spoken and, more importantly, *how* something may be spoken of. In setting these limits, discourses delineate the actors of a field, their relationships to one another, and their subjectivities. Discourses are thus an exercise of power.

Discursive consciousness: A theoretical concept used to understand the hierarchy of the agent (different levels of awareness and thus action) in Anthony Giddens's theory. Discursive consciousness refers specifically to the ability to give verbal accounts or rationalizations of action. It's what we are able to say about the social situation. Discursive consciousness is the awareness of social situations in verbal form.

Disembedding mechanisms: A theoretical concept from Anthony Giddens's theory of modernity. Disembedding speaks of processes that lift social relations and interactions out from local contexts, which has implications for time–space distanciation and ontological security. There are two types of mechanisms: symbolic tokens and expert systems.

Documentary method: A theoretical term from ethnomethodology. The documentary method is the activity through which a link is created between an event or object and an assumed meaning structure. It is more than interpretation. Documentary method refers to the actual work that people perform in a social situation that links an event to its interpretation in such a way as to authenticate the correspondence.

Dramaturgy: Dramaturgy is a theoretical perspective that is most closely associated with the work of Erving Goffman. Dramaturgy uses the analogy of the stage to analyze and understand what people do in social encounters. People are conceived of as actors, sometimes working as teams, who work to convey specific self-impressions to an audience (others present). This work is referred to as impression management. Emphasis is placed on the continual production of a social self, which places moral imperatives on the interaction order.

Emotional energy: A theoretical idea that originated with Émile Durkheim and is used by Randall Collins in his theory of interaction rituals. It is defined as the level of motivational energy an individual feels after leaving an interaction. Emotional energy is specifically linked to the level of collective emotion formed in a ritual, and it predicts the likelihood of further ritual performance and the individual's initial involvement within the ritual.

Episteme: Episteme is a theoretical concept from Michel Foucault's theory of knowledge and power. It refers to the fundamental notions of truth and validity that underlie knowledge—it's the hidden order of knowledge. Epistemes organize and are a necessary precondition for thought; they set the boundaries of what is possible and knowable. One important implication is that an episteme will maintain the order produced by a knowledge system even in the face of contradictory events or findings. Epistemes are historically specific and change through rupture rather than linear progress.

Exploitation: Exploitation is a central concept in Marx's theory of capitalism. It is the measurable difference between what a worker gets paid and the worth of the product produced—it is the source of capitalist profit. Exploitation also has the characteristic of giving workers leverage over capitalists. The dependency of capitalists upon exploitation for profit is what gives labor the power to negotiate and strike. Exploitation, then, is dialectic in nature.

Fault line: A theoretical concept specific to Dorothy E. Smith's feminist theory. Smith argues that a gap exists between official knowledge—especially knowledge generated through the social sciences—and the experience of women. This fault line is particularly important for understanding how men are unable to see the differences between objective, public knowledge and the reality of day-to-day existence: Women traditionally negotiate or obscure the disjunction for men through their caring for the daily administration of the household, including meeting the sustenance and comfort needs of both men and children.

Field: The field is a theoretical concept from Pierre Bourdieu's constructivist structuralism approach. The concept functions to orient the researcher to an arena of study. Field denotes a set of objective positions and relations that are tied together by the rules of the game and by the distribution of four fundamental powers or capitals: economic, cultural (informal social skills, habits, linguistic styles, and tastes), social (networks), and symbolic (the use of symbols to recognize and thus legitimate the other powers). People and positions are hierarchically distributed in the field through the overall volume of capital they possess. Symbolic and cultural capitals are specifically important: Cultural capital helps to form habitus and thus contributes to the replication of the field, and symbolic capital gives legitimacy and meaning to the empirical field.

Frankfurt School: The Frankfurt School is both an actual school and a school of thought (its most usual connotation today). The school began in Frankfurt, Germany, in the 1920s and has included such thinkers as Theodor Adorno, Max Horkheimer, Herbert Marcuse, Walter Benjamin, Herbert Marcuse, Eric Fromm, and—most recently—Jürgen Habermas. In general, the founding members sought to update Karl Marx's theory of material consciousness by returning to Marx's

Hegelian roots and synthesizing elements from Max Weber and Sigmund Freud. Of Marx's work, the *Economic and Philosophic Manuscripts of 1844* and *The German Ideology* were key texts. The work of the Frankfurt School is often referred to as critical theory.

Front: The theoretical idea of a front comes from Erving Goffman's dramaturgy. Front refers to the totality of identity cues offered by an individual in a social encounter. These cues come from setting, manner, and appearance.

Game stage: The second of three stages in Mead's theory of self-formation. It corresponds to the time when children are able to take the role of multiple others separately and can understand rule-based behavior.

Gender: Gender is a social category that is used to establish differences in status, power, class, roles, norms, values, and beliefs. The concept of gender is defined through its relationship with several other categories: sex, socially agreed upon biological criteria; sex category, based on sex criteria but maintained socially through specific displays; gender, the social category that uses sex to assign differences in practices, subjectivities, status, power, class, norms, values, and beliefs; and gender identity, a person's inner sense of gender.

Generalized other: A theoretical concept used in symbolic interactionism that refers to sets of perspectives and attitudes indicative of a specific group or social type with which the individual can role-take. In the formation of the self, the generalized other represents the last stage in which the child can place herself in a collective role from which to view her own behaviors. It is the time when the self is fully formed as the person takes all of society inside.

Governmentality: A theoretical term from Michel Foucault's theory of knowledge and power, governmentality refers to a specific kind of institutionalized power. In Foucault's scheme, modernity is unique because of the manner through which states control populations. Generally speaking, in previous ages power and control were exercised upon the individual from without. Governments would actively and directly control the person, when domination was necessary or desired. In contrast, modern states exercise power from within the individual. Governmentality, then, captures the process through which the person participates in her or his own domination—control is exercised within the person by the person.

Habitus: A central theoretical term from Pierre Bourdieu's theory of class replication, habitus refers to the cultural capital an individual possesses as a result of his or her class position. Habitus is embodied; that is, it works through the body at a nonconscious level. Cultural capital and thus class position are expressed unthinkingly. On the one hand, this embodied expression structures class; on the other hand, habitus works creatively, as it is possible to make intuitive leaps. Habitus varies by cultural capital and is expressed in linguistic markets.

Hegemonic heterosexuality: Hegemonic heterosexuality is an idea associated with Judith Butler's theory of materialized sexuality. The word *hegemony* means "to rule" and was originally used with reference to the political rule of one country over another. Hegemonic rule is generally indirect and distant. A clear example of a political hegemonic struggle is the Cold War between the United States and the Union of Soviet Socialist Republics (USSR)—this is the origin of the discourse of first, second, and third worlds. First-world nations were aligned with the United States, second-world nations with the USSR, and third-world nations were unaligned. The idea of *cultural hegemony* was first articulated by Antonio Gramsci (1971). Cultural hegemony is the ideological domination of one group over another, through the use of symbols, meanings, and articulating practices, which tie together various cultural elements into a belief system that becomes a "popular religion" (Thompson, 1996, p. 412). In hegemonic heterosexuality, the culture of heterosexism—the belief in only two sexes with specific natural roles—seeks to extend its rule over each person's body. It's the process through which a person's body is sexed according to heterosexual standards.

Ideal speech communities: The concept of ideal speech communities comes from the work of Jürgen Habermas. Ideal speech refers to communicative acts or interactions where every member is granted full participation and is free from any type of coercion. Each member is responsible for expressing her or his opinion, keeping her or his speech free from ideology and objective standings (such as educational credentials). The goal of ideal speech is consensus. Habermas argues that reasoned consensus—and thus emancipation—is possible because of the inherent assumptions of communication. The act of communication assumes that actual communication, intersubjectivity, and validity are all possible. The latter implies the possibility of universal norms or morals, and the fact that validity claims can be criticized implies that they are in some sense active and accountable to reason.

Ideal types: Ideal types are a part of Weber's theoretical methodology used to create systematic, objective knowledge in the face of the subjectivity of culture. Ideal types are purely conceptual constructions that are used as standards of comparison in the empirical world. There are two kinds of ideal types: historical and classificatory.

Indexical expressions: This idea comes from ethnomethodology and conceptualizes the notion that the meaning of all conversation is dependent upon a context that is assumed to be shared by all interactants. Talk, then, indexes contexts in order to be sensible and taken-for-granted.

Industrialization: In general, industrialization refers to the process through which machines replace direct human manipulation of objects in work. Industrialization is also an intrinsic part of what we mean by modernity. As such, it carries with it other factors such as high division of labor, rationalization, scientific management, urbanization, markets, and so on. Industrialization is specifically a concern for Marxian theory.

Institutional ethnography: A methodological approach developed by Dorothy E. Smith. Its focus is to understand how everyday experience is socially organized through authoritative texts. Texts, such as written documentation or research articles, are generated through professional practices and governmental policy making. These texts then come to organize local activities. The texts further provide a scheme for people within the activities to assess and experience themselves as members of the social situation. Institutional ethnography thus provides a way of mapping the social relations of power that govern daily life, particularly that of women or other minorities.

Institutionalization: The process through which institutions are created. In Parsons's theory, institutions are the result of two different paths: (1) building up of actions through identifiable modes of orientation, types of action, interactions among like-minded people, and the resulting norms, values, and status positions that constitute social structure; and (2) the internalization of society's cultures and structures.

Interaction: A central theoretical idea in symbolic interactionism, interaction is the intertwining of individual human actions. In symbolic interactionism, the interaction is the true acting unit in society. According to this view, interaction is not simply the means of expressing social structure or the individual's personality traits; rather, the interaction is the premier social domain and is thus the chief factor through which social structures and individual personalities are created and sustained. Interaction occurs via a three-part process through which meaning, society, and self emerge: the presentation of a cue, the initial response to the cue, and the response to the response. However, the end point of the process generally becomes itself an initial cue for further interaction, starting the process over again.

Intersectionality: Intersectionality is a theoretical concept in Patricia Hill Collins's theory of structured inequality. The basic idea is that systems of race, gender, class, nationality, sexuality, and age crisscross one another at specific social locations that form a matrix of domination. The analytical issue, then, is to empirically discover how these various systems come together for any specific person or group. Collins is specifically concerned with how these systems shape black women's experiences and are in turn influenced by black women.

Joint action: Joint action is a theoretical term from Blumer's symbolic interactionism that describes the process through which various individual and discrete actions and interactions are brought together to form a meaningful whole. This joining is accomplished symbolically by both individuals and groups and constitutes a significant portion of what is meant by "society." The insight of this concept is that at every point of interaction or joint action, there is uncertainty. The implication is that society is emergent.

Latent pattern maintenance: One of four subsystems in Parsons's AGIL conception of requisite needs; the subsystem that indirectly preserves patterns of behavior that are needed for survival (in the body, the autonomic nervous system; in society, education, religion, and family).

Legitimation: Legitimation is a theoretical concept that describes the effects that specific stories, histories, and myths have in granting ethical, moral, or legal status or authorization to social power and relations. Weber tells us that there are two components to any system of legitimation, subjective and objective, and he is specifically concerned with the legitimation of the three types of authorities:

charismatic, traditional, and rational-legal. The general idea of legitimation is particularly important in contemporary theories of the social construction of reality. In social constructivist theory, there are three levels of legitimation (self-evident, theoretical, and symbolic universes [i.e., religious systems]), each more powerful than the previous. Habermas also uses this idea to talk about the shift from legitimations of capitalism to the state. This change happens because of organized capitalism and results in a crisis of legitimation.

Life politics: A theoretical idea from Anthony Giddens's theory of modernity, life politics is an outgrowth of emancipatory politics. Emancipatory politics is concerned with liberating individuals and groups from the constraints that adversely affect their lives—people are thus liberated to make choices. Life politics is the politics of choice and lifestyle. It is concerned with issues that flow from the practices of self-actualization within the dialectic of the local/global, where self-realization affects global strategies. Life politics is dependent upon the individual creating and maintaining inner authenticity.

Lifeworld: The lifeworld is a theoretical concept that came into sociology through the work of Alfred Schutz. The lifeworld refers to the world as it is experienced immediately by each person. It is a cultural world filled with meaning and is made up of the sets of assumptions, beliefs, and meanings against which an individual judges and interprets everyday experiences.

Linguistic market: A theoretical concept from Pierre Bourdieu's theory of class replication, the idea emphasizes the importance of language and social skills in reproducing class. Every time a person speaks with another, there is a linguistic market within which each person has different skill levels and knowledge. These differing levels lead to distinct rewards in the market that in turn announce one's class position. The power of the market is that people tend to sanction themselves because they intuitively understand how their culture and language skills will play out in any given market.

Matrix of domination: The idea of matrices of domination comes from Patricia Hill Collins's theory of black feminist epistemology. In general, the notion of a matrix refers to a mass within which something is enclosed. This enclosure is a point of origin or growth (as in the cradle or matrix of civilization). For Collins, the issue is that current society is built of matrices of domination that form around the intersecting issues of race, gender, age, sexuality, nationality, and so on. Any matrix of domination works through four different domains: structural, disciplinary, hegemonic, and intrapersonal.

Means and relations of production: The means of production is a central concept in Marx's theory of capitalism. Simply, the means of production refers to the way in which commodities are produced. However, in Marx's hands the concept comes to connote quite a bit more. Because the basic social fabric is economic in Marxian theory, relations of production are inherent within the means of production. Thus, the means of production—such as capitalism, feudalism, and socialism—determines how people relate to the self and others (the relations of production).

Mind: According to symbolic interactionists, the mind is a social entity constituted through language and role-taking. The mind exists in certain kinds of behavior; specifically, the internalized conversation of linguistic signs and symbols, and the ability to suspend behavior and to rehearse actions. The mind is socially necessary because of its place in human behavior.

Modalities of structuration: A concept used in Anthony Giddens's structuration, modalities of structuration are the paths through which structure is expressed in social encounters. There are three modalities (interpretive schemes, facilities, and norms) that are linked on the one hand to structures (signification, domination, and legitimation) and on the other to social practices (communication, power, and sanctions). These modalities are socially and culturally specific.

Modes of orientation: The beginning element in Parsons's theory of social action and institutionalization, modes of orientation are the different values (cognitive, appreciative, and moral) and motivations (cognitive, cathectic, and evaluative) that people bring into a situation. They result in identifiable types of action (strategic, expressive, or moral) that in the long run pattern interactions across time and space and result in the taken-for-granted norms, roles, and status positions that constitute social structure and society.

Ontological security: Ontological security is a theoretical concept from Anthony Giddens's structuration theory. Ontology refers to the way things exist and specifically implies that human existence is different from all other forms of existence because of meaning. Meaning is not a necessary or intrinsic feature of any event or object, which implies that human reality is unstable. This intrinsic instability creates an unconscious need for ontological security—a sense of trust in the taken-for-grantedness of the human world. This need motivates humans to routinize and regionalize their practices.

Organismic analogy: Analogies are quite often used in sociology as ways of understanding how society works. With an analogy, there is resemblance in some particulars between things that are otherwise unlike—and analogies are used to compare something well-known to something unfamiliar. The organismic analogy is specific to functionalist theorizing and implies that society works like a biological organism in that it has survival needs and evolves to greater complexity. The analogy also implies that society, just like complex organisms, operates like a system of interrelated parts that tend toward stasis or balance, and any derivation from that life balance is seen as illness or pathology.

Panopticon: Panopticon is a theoretical concept from Michel Foucault's theory of knowledge and power. The panopticon was Jeremy Bentham's architectural design for a prison that allowed for the unobserved observation of prisoners. The idea was that if prisoners thought they were being watched, even if they weren't, the prisoners themselves would exercise control over their own behaviors. Foucault sees this physical prison as a metaphor for the way control and power are exercised in modernity. He specifically has in mind the self-administered control that comes through the knowledge produced by the social and behavioral sciences as well as medical science.

Phenomenology: A school of philosophy developed by Edmund Husserl that argues that consciousness is the only experience or phenomenon of which humans can be certain. It seeks, then, to discover the natural and primary processes of consciousness apart from the influence of culture or society. Husserl hoped to create "a descriptive account of the essential structures of the directly given," that is, the immediate experience of the world apart from preexisting values or beliefs. Social phenomenology, on the other hand, argues that nothing is directly given to humans; we experience everything through stocks of language, typifications, and so on.

Play stage: The play stage is one of the three phases in Mead's theory of self-formation. It is the initial stage wherein the child first sees herself as a social object separate from her behaviors. In the play stage, the child literally takes on the role of one significant other and acts and feels toward herself as the other does.

Power: Power is a theoretical concept found in many social and sociological theories. The short definition of power is the ability to get others to do what you want. Yet, in terms of how it works and where it resides, power is one of our most difficult and controversial terms. For Anthony Giddens (Chapter 14), power is part of every interaction and is defined in terms of autonomy and dependence; power is one result that comes from the use of allocative and authoritative resources. For exchange theorists (Chapter 6), power is the result of unequal exchange relations. Power refers to the other individual's or group's ability to recurrently impose its will on a person. Michel Foucault (Chapter 9) sees power in two ways; both are hidden rather than overt. First, power is exercised through knowledge. The knowledge that any person holds at any given time is the result of historically specific institutional arrangements and practices; accepted knowledge exercises control over people's bodies, minds, and subjectivities. The second way Foucault uses the notion of power is in daily encounters with others. In every social encounter, people's actions influence other actions; these practices enact the social discourse of knowledge and serve to guide and reinforce one another.

Practical consciousness: Practical consciousness is a concept from Anthony Giddens's theory and refers to what people know or believe about social situations and practices but can't verbally explain. It is the basis for the routinization of daily life, which in turn provides ontological security. One important ramification of practical consciousness is that it implies that behavior is often directed by nonconscious intuition and that the reasons given for action (discursive consciousness) can have a separate interactional function.

Pragmatism: A school of philosophy that argues that the only values, meanings, and truths humans hold onto are the ones that have practical benefits. These shift and change in response to different concrete experiences. Pragmatism forms the base for many American social theories, most specifically symbolic interactionism.

Public sphere: A theoretical construct from the critical work of Jürgen Habermas, the public sphere is an imaginary community or virtual space where a democratic public "gathers" for dialogue. With the idea of the public sphere, Habermas is arguing that a true democratic process demands an active, public dialogue that takes place outside the influence of government or the economy. To function properly, the public sphere demands unrestricted access to information and equal participation of all members.

Reification: Reification captures the idea that concepts and ideas may be treated as objectively real things. In social science generally, reification can be seen as a methodological problem because of the tendency to ascribe causation to ideas, as in gender causing inequality. In critical theory, reification is taken further and refers to the process through which human beings become dominated by things and become more thing-like themselves. Marx specifically argued that ideas that do not naturally spring out of species-being can only appear real through reification (making something appear real that isn't); all ideology is reified, and the furthest reach of reification is the idea of God.

Rituals: Rituals are the key to Durkheim's theory of social solidarity. In Durkheimian theory, rituals are patterned sequences of behavior that recreate high levels of co-presence, common emotional mood, and a common focus of attention. In Durkheim's scheme, rituals function to create and reinvigorate a group's moral boundaries and identity. Collins uses the same basic theory to explain a number of issues: interaction ritual chains, the macro–micro link, and social exchange.

Role-taking: Role-taking is the central mechanism in Mead's theory of the self, through which an individual is able to get outside of her or his own actions and take them as a social object. Specifically, role-taking is the process through which an individual puts herself in the position (role) of another for the express purpose of viewing herself from that other person's role.

Self: The self is a theoretical idea that describes various features of the individual. According to symbolic interactionist theory, the self is a social object, a perspective, a conversation, and a story. The self is seen as arising from diverse role-taking experiences. It is thus a social object in that it is formed through definitions given by others, especially the generalized other, and is a central meaningful feature in interactions. The idea of the self is also prominent in Goffman's dramaturgy (the presentation of self) and Giddens's understanding of modernity (the reflexive project of the self).

Setting: Setting is a theoretical concept from Goffman's dramaturgical perspective. Settings are composed of physical sign equipment that is semi-permanently attached to physical locations. The physical props of the setting cue people to a limited number of possible definitions and self-identities. Settings thus stabilize encounters. They are part of the front that people manage.

Social objects: The idea of social objects is a theoretical concept in symbolic interactionist theory. Social objects are anything in an interaction that we call attention to, attach legitimate lines of behavior to, and name. In this sense, the self and one's own feelings and thoughts can become social objects, as well as the more obvious "objects" in the environment.

Structuration theory: A theoretical perspective developed by Anthony Giddens. The perspective is more an analytical framework—or ontological scheme—than a complete theory. Structuration tells the theorist-researcher what kinds of things exist socially and what to pay attention to. It denies the existence of structure and free agency (seen as a false dualism) and argues that these generally reified concepts form an active duality: two parts of the same thing. Giddens applies this concept to the issue of time–space distanciation. Thus, in structuration, local interactions are linked with distant others through the use of known rules and resources. This way of seeing things avoids the reification of agency or structure, places the structuring (patterning) elements within the observable interaction, and encourages a historical sociology.

Symbolic capital: Symbolic capital is a theoretical concept from Pierre Bourdieu's theory of class replication and refers to socially legitimated symbolic power of definition. Bourdieu argues that social groups and status positions exist empirically and symbolically, but it is the symbolic that gives groups and positions meaning and legitimacy. This power of definition is thus an important factor in creating the social world. Symbolic capital varies by social credentials, which generally come through education and political office.

Symbolic violence: Symbolic violence is a theoretical concept from Pierre Bourdieu's theory of class replication that refers to the self-sanctioning that occurs in linguistic markets.

Time–space distanciation: Time–space distanciation is a theoretical concept from Anthony Giddens's structuration approach. This concept reformulates the problem of social order by focusing on the stretching out of time and space rather than the patterning of behaviors. Generally speaking, concentrating on how behaviors are patterned has resulted in an emphasis on either structure or agency. Giddens sees this distinction as a false dualism, and focusing on time–space distanciation avoids this issue. Specifically, time–space distanciation refers to the process through which local social interactions are linked to distant ones either through time (as in future with past interactions) or geographic space (as in an interaction in New York City with one in Los Angeles), thus ordering society.

References

Addams, J. (2002). *Democracy and social ethics.* Chicago: University of Chicago Press. (Original work published 1902)

Alexander, J. C. (1985). Introduction. In J. C. Alexander (Ed.), *Neofunctionalism.* Beverly Hills, CA: Sage.

Alexander, J. C. (2006). *The civil sphere.* Oxford, UK: Oxford University Press.

Alexander, J. C., & Smith, P. (2001). The strong program in cultural theory: Elements of a structural hermeneutics. In Jonathan H. Turner (Ed.), *Handbook of sociological theory* (pp. 135–150). New York: Kluwer Academic/Plenum.

Allan, K., & Turner, J. H. (2000). A formalization of postmodern theory. *Sociological Perspectives, 43*(3), 363–385.

Alway, J. (1995). *Critical theory and political possibilities: Conceptions of emancipatory politics in the works of Horkheimer, Adorno, Marcuse, and Habermas.* Westport, CT: Greenwood Press.

Arieli, Y. (1964). *Individualism and nationalism in American ideology.* Cambridge, MA: Harvard University Press.

Bandura, A. (1977). *Social learning theory.* New York: General Learning Press.

Barbalet, J. (2010). Citizenship in Max Weber. *Journal of Classical Sociology, 10*(3), 201–216.

Barker, C. (2008). *Cultural studies: Theory and practice* (3rd ed.). Los Angeles: Sage.

Beauvoir, S. de (1989). *The second sex* (H. M. Parshley, Ed., Trans.). New York: Vintage. (Original work published 1949)

Becker, H. S. (1963). *Outsiders: Studies in the sociology of deviance.* Glencoe, IL: The Free Press of Glencoe.

Bell, D. (1976). *The coming of post-industrial society: A venture in social forecasting.* New York: Basic Books.

Bell, D. (1999). *The coming of post-industrial society: A venture in social forecasting.* New York: Basic Books.

Bell, D. (2007). *Cyberculture theorists: Manuel Castells and Donna Haraway.* London: Routledge.

Benford, R. D., & Snow, D. A. (2000). Framing processes and social movements: An overview and assessment. *Annual Review of Sociology, 26,* 611–639.

Bentham, J. (1996). *An introduction to the principles of morals and legislation* (J. H. Burns & H. L. A. Hart, Eds.). New York: Oxford University Press. (Original work published 1789)

Berger, P. L. (1967). *The sacred canopy: Elements of a sociological theory of religion.* New York: Doubleday.

Berger, P. L., & Luckmann, T. (1966). *The social construction of reality: A treatise in the sociology of knowledge.* Garden City, NY: Doubleday.

Bernstein, J. M. (1991). Introduction. In T. Adorno, *Culture industry.* London: Routledge.

Bird, C. H., Conrad, P., Fremont, A. M., & Timmermans, S. (Eds.). (2010). *Handbook of medical sociology* (6th ed.). Nashville, TN: Vanderbilt University Press.

Blau, P. M. (1968). Social exchange. In David L. Sills (Ed.), *International encyclopedia of the social sciences.* New York: Macmillan.

Blau, P. M. (1994). *Structural contexts of opportunities.* Chicago: University of Chicago Press.

Blau, P. M. (2002). Macrostructural theory. In Jonathan H. Turner (Ed.), *Handbook of sociological theory* (pp. 343–352). New York: Kluwer Academic/Plenum.

Blau, P. M. (2003). *Exchange and power in social life.* New Brunswick, NJ: Transaction.

Blau, P. M., & Meyer, M. W. (1987). *Bureaucracy in modern society* (3rd ed.). New York: McGraw-Hill.

Blumer, H. (1969). *Symbolic interactionism: Perspective and method.* Berkeley: University of California Press.

Blumer, H. (1990). *Industrialization as an agent of social change: A critical analysis.* Chicago: Aldine.

Bosker, B. (2012). *Fortune 500 list boasts more female CEOs than ever before.* Retrieved July 10, 2012, from http://www.huffingtonpost.com/2012/05/07/fortune-500-female-ceos_n_1495734.html

Bourdieu, P. (1984). *Distinction: A social critique of the judgment of taste* (R. Nice, Trans.). Cambridge, MA: Harvard University Press. (Original work published 1979)

Bourdieu, P. (1985). The genesis of the concepts of "habitus" and of "field." *Sociocriticism, 2,* 11–29.

Bourdieu, P. (1989). Social space and symbolic power. *Sociological Theory, 7*(1), 14–25.

Bourdieu, P. (1990). *The logic of practice* (R. Nice, Trans.). Stanford, CA: Stanford University Press. (Original work published 1980)

Bourdieu, P. (1991). *Language and symbolic power* (J. B. Thompson, Ed.; G. Raymond & M. Adamson, Trans.). Cambridge, MA: Harvard University Press.

Bourdieu, P. (1993). *Outline of a theory of practice* (R. Nice, Trans.). Cambridge, UK: Cambridge University Press. (Original work published 1972)

Bourdieu, P., & Wacquant, L. J. D. (1992). *An invitation to reflexive sociology.* Chicago: University of Chicago Press.

Braudel, F. (1981–1984). *Civilization and capitalism, 15th to 18 century, 3 vols.* New York: Harper & Row.

Business and Professional Women's Foundation. (2004). *101 facts on the status of women.* Retrieved May 9, 2005, from http://www.bpwusa.org/files/public/101FactsOct07.pdf

Butler, J. (1993). *Bodies that matter: On the discursive limits of "sex."* New York: Routledge.

Butler, J. (1997). *The psychic life of power: Theories in subjection.* Stanford, CA: Stanford University Press.

Calhoun, C. (2003). Pierre Bourdieu. In G. Ritzer (Ed.), *The Blackwell companion to major contemporary social theorists* (pp. 696–730). Malden, MA: Blackwell.

Callero, P. L. (2009). *The myth of individualism: How social forces shape our lives.* Lanham, MD: Rowman & Littlefield.

Cassirer, E. (1944). *An essay on man.* New Haven, CT: Yale University Press.

Castells, M. (2000a). *End of millennium* (2nd ed.). Malden, MA: Blackwell.

Castells, M. (2000b). *The rise of the network society* (2nd ed.). Malden, MA: Blackwell.

Castells, M. (2004). *The power of identity* (2nd ed.). Malden, MA: Blackwell.

Catechism of the Catholic Church. (n.d.) Retrieved February 7, 2012, from http://www.vatican.va/archive/ENG0015/__P1C.HTM

Chafetz, J. S. (1990). *Gender equity: An integrated theory of stability and change.* Newbury Park, CA: Sage.

Chodorow, N. (1978). *The reproduction of mothering: Psychoanalysis and the sociology of gender.* Berkeley: University of California Press.

Cohen, A., Baumohl, B., Buia, C., Roston, E., Ressner, J., & Thompson, M. (2001, January 8). This time it's different. *Time, 157*(1), 18–22.

Coleman, J. S. (1990). *Foundations of social theory.* Cambridge, MA: Harvard University Press.

Collier, J. (1904). Personal reminiscences by James Collier, for nine years the secretary and for ten years the Amanuensis of Spencer. In J. Royce & J. Collier, *Herbert Spencer: An estimate and review* (pp. 187–234). New York: Fox, Duffield, & Company.

Collins, P. H. (2000). *Black feminist thought: Knowledge, consciousness, and the politics of empowerment* (2nd ed.). New York: Routledge.

Collins, R. (1975). *Conflict sociology.* New York: Academic Press.

Collins, R. (1986). Is 1980s sociology in the doldrums? *American Journal of Sociology, 91,* 1336–1355.

Collins, R. (1987). Interaction ritual chains, power and property: The micro–macro connection as an empirically based theoretical problem. In J. C. Alexander, B. Giesen, R. Münch, & N. J. Smelser (Eds.), *The micro-macro link* (pp. 193–206). Berkeley: University of California Press.

Collins, R. (1988). *Theoretical sociology.* San Diego, CA: Harcourt Brace Jovanovich.

Collins, R. (1993). Emotional energy as the common denominator of rational action. *Rationality and Society, 5,* 203–230.

Collins, R. (2004). *Interaction ritual chains.* Princeton, NJ: Princeton University Press.

Comte, A. (1975a). The positive philosophy. In G. Lenzer (Ed.), *Auguste Comte and positivism: The essential writings* (pp. 71–306). New York: Harper Torchbooks. (Original work published 1830–1842)

Comte, A. (1975b). Plan of the scientific operations necessary for reorganizing society. In G. Lenzer (Ed.), *Auguste Comte and positivism: The essential writings,* (pp. 9–67). New York: Harper Torchbooks. (Original work published 1822)

Condon, W. S., & Ogston, W. D. (1971). Speech and body motion synchrony of the speaker-hearer. In D. D. Horton & J. J. Jenkins (Eds.), *Perception of language* (pp. 150–184). Columbus, OH: Merrill.

Condorcet, A. (1955). *Sketch for a historical picture of the progress of the human mind* (J. Barraclough, Trans.). London: Weidenfeld and Nicolson. (Original work published 1795)

Conner, M. (2010). Nike: Corporate responsibility at a "tipping point." *Business Ethics: The Magazine of Corporate Responsibility.* Retrieved July 16, 2012, from http://business-ethics.com/2010/01/24/2154-nike-corporate-responsibility-at-a-tipping-point/

Cook, K. (1978). Power, equity and commitment in exchange networks. *American Journal of Sociology, 43,* 712–739.

Cooley, C. H. (1925). *Social organization: A study of the larger mind.* New York: Charles Scribner's Sons.

Cooley, C. H. (1964). *Human nature and the social order.* New York: Schocken Books. (Original work published 1902)

Coser, L. A. (1956). *The functions of social conflict.* Glencoe, IL: The Free Press.

Coser, L. A. (1977). *Masters of sociological thought: Ideas in historical and social context.* Prospect Heights, IL: Waveland Press.

Dahrendorf, R. (1959). *Class and class conflict in industrial society.* Stanford, CA: Stanford University Press. (Original work published 1957)

Davidson, A. I. (1994). Ethics as ascetics: Foucault, the history of ethics, and ancient thought. In G. Gutting (Ed.), *The Cambridge companion to Foucault* (pp. 115–140). Cambridge, UK: Cambridge University Press.

Davis, A. (2007). *Angela Y. Davis commencement address.* Retrieved July 23, 2012 from, http://www.grinnell.edu/offices/confops/commencement/archive/2007/davis

Democracy. (n.d.). In *Wikipedia*. Retrieved March 19, 2012, from http://en.wikipedia.org/wiki/Democracy

DeNavas-Walt, C., Proctor, B. D., & Smith, J. C. (2009, September). *Income, poverty, and health insurance coverage in the United States: 2008*. Retrieved July 7, 2012, from http://www.census.gov/prod/2009pubs/p60-236.pdf

Denzin, N. (1992). *Symbolic interactionism and cultural studies: The politics of interpretation*. Cambridge, UK: Blackwell.

Derksen, L. (2010). Micro/macro translations: The production of new social structures in the case of DNA profiling. *Sociological Inquiry, 80*(2).

Derrida, J. (1978). *Writing and difference* (A. Bass, Trans.). Chicago: University of Chicago Press. (Original work published 1967)

Dewey, J. (2009). *Democracy and education: An introduction to the philosophy of education*. New York: WLC Books. (Original work published 1916)

Douglass, F. (2009a). The nature of slavery. In H. Brotz (Ed.), *African-American social & political thought: 1850–1920* (pp. 215–220). New Brunswick, NJ: Transaction. (Original work published 1850)

Douglass, F. (2009b). Speech on the Dred Scott Decision. In H. Brotz (Ed.), *African-American social & political thought: 1850–1920* (pp. 247–262). New Brunswick, NJ: Transaction. (Original work published 1857)

Drake, J. (1997). Review essay: Third wave feminisms. *Feminist Studies, 23*(1), 97–108.

Du Bois, W. E. B. (1996a). Darkwater. In E. J. Sundquist (Ed.), *The Oxford W. E. B. Du Bois reader*. New York: Oxford. (Original work published 1920)

Du Bois, W. E. B. (1996b). The souls of black folk. In E. J. Sundquist (Ed.), *The Oxford W. E. B. Du Bois reader* (pp. 97–240). New York: Oxford. (Original work published 1903)

Durkheim, É. (1938). *The rules of sociological method* (G. E. G. Catlin, Ed.; S. A. Solovay & J. H. Mueller, Trans.). Glencoe, IL: The Free Press. (Original work published 1895)

Durkheim, É. (1984). *The division of labor in society* (W. D. Halls, Trans.). New York: The Free Press. (Original work published 1893)

Durkheim, É. (1995). *The elementary forms of the religious life* (K. E. Fields, Trans.). New York: The Free Press. (Original work published 1912)

Eberly, D. E. (2000). The meaning, origins, and applications of civil society. In D. E. Eberly (Ed.), *The essential civil society reader: The classic essays* (pp. 3–29). Lanham, MD: Rowman & Littlefield.

Ellis, D. P. (1971). The Hobbesian problem of order: A critical appraisal of the normative solution. *American Sociological Review, 36*, 692–703.

Emerson, R. (1962). Power–dependence relations. *American Sociological Review, 27*, 31–41.

Empathy. (n.d.). In *Merriam-Webster's third new international dictionary, unabridged*. Retrieved October 18, 2012, from http://unabridged.merriam-webster.com

Engels, F. (1978). The origin of the family, private property, and the state. In R. C. Tucker (Ed.), *The Marx–Engels reader* (pp. 734–760). New York: Norton. (Original work published 1884)

Erikson, K. (1996). On pseudospeciation and social speciation. In C. B. Strozier & M. Flynn (Eds.) *Genocide, war, and human survival* (pp. 51–57). Lanham, MA: Rowman & Littlefield.

Fanon, F. (1967). *Black skins, white masks* (C. L. Markmann, Trans.). New York: Grove Press. (Original work published 1952)

Fanon, F. (2004). *The wretched of the earth* (R. Philcox, Trans.). New York: Grove Press. (Original work published 1961)

Fausto-Sterling, A. (1993, March–April). The five sexes: Why male and female are not enough. *The Sciences, 33*(2).

Feyerabend, P. (1988). *Against method* (Rev. ed.). London: Verso.

Fine, G. A., & Manning, P. (2003). Erving Goffman. In G. Ritzer (Ed.), *The Blackwell companion to major contemporary social theorists* (pp. 34–62). Oxford, UK: Blackwell.

Fisher, S. (1973). *Body consciousness.* London: Calder & Boyars.

Flyvbjerg, B. (2001). *Making social science matter: Why social inquiry fails and how it can succeed again.* Cambridge, UK: Cambridge University Press.

Foucault, M. (1982). The subject and power. In H. L. Dreyfus & P. Rabinow (Eds.), *Michel Foucault: Beyond structuralism and hermeneutics* (pp. 208–226). Brighton, UK: Harvester Press.

Foucault, M. (1984). Nietzsche, genealogy, history. In P. Rabinow (Ed.), *The Foucault reader* (pp. 76–100). New York: Pantheon.

Foucault, M. (1988). *The history of sexuality, volume 3: The care of the self* (R. Hurley, Trans.). New York: Vintage. (Original work published 1984)

Foucault, M. (1990a). *The history of sexuality, volume 2: The use of pleasure* (R. Hurley, Trans.). New York: Vintage. (Original work published 1984)

Foucault, M. (1990b). *The history of sexuality, volume I: An introduction* (R. Hurley, Trans.). New York: Vintage. (Original work published 1976)

Foucault, M. (1994a). *The birth of the clinic: An archaeology of medical perception* (A. M. Sheridan Smith, Trans.). New York: Vintage Books. (Original work published 1963)

Foucault, M. (1994b). *The order of things: An archaeology of the human sciences.* New York: Vintage. (Original work published 1966)

Foucault, M. (1995). *Discipline and punish: The birth of the prison* (A. Sheridan, Trans.). New York: Vintage. (Original work published 1975)

Foucault, M. (1997). A preface to transgression. In D. F. Bouchard (Ed.), *Language, counter-memory, practice: Selected essays and interviews* (D. F. Bouchard & S. Simon, Trans.). New York: Cornell University Press.

Frank, A. W. (1990). Bringing bodies back in: A decade in review. *Theory, Culture & Society, 7,* 131–162.

Friedan, B. (1997). *The feminine mystique.* New York: Norton. (Original work published 1963)

Fromm, E. (1955). *The sane society.* New York: Henry Holt.

Gandhi, L. (1998). *Postcolonial theory: A critical introduction.* New York: Columbia University Press.

Garfinkel, H. (1967). *Studies in ethnomethodology.* Cambridge, UK: Polity Press.

Garfinkel, H. (1974). On the origins of the term "ethnomethodology." In R. Turner (Ed.), *Ethnomethodology: Selected readings* (pp. 15–18). Harmondsworth, UK: Penguin Education.

Garfinkel, H. (1996). Ethnomethodology's program. *Social Psychology Quarterly, 59,* 5–21.

Gergen, K. J. (2000). The self in the age of information. *The Washington Quarterly, 23,* 201–214.

Giddens, A. (1986). *The constitution of society.* Berkeley: University of California Press.

Giddens, A. (1990). *The consequences of modernity.* Stanford, CA: Stanford University Press.

Giddens, A. (1991). *Modernity and self-identity: Self and society in the late modern age.* Stanford, CA: Stanford University Press.

Giddens, A. (1992). *The transformation of intimacy: Sexuality, love and eroticism in modern societies.* Stanford, CA: Stanford University Press.

Global Exchange. (1998). *Wages and living expenses for Nike workers in Indonesia, September 1998.* Retrieved July 20, 2012, from http://www.cleanclothes.org/news/4-companies/998-wages-and-living-expenses-for-nike-workers

Goffman, E. (1959). *The presentation of self in everyday life.* Garden City, NY: Anchor.

Goffman, E. (1961a). *Asylums: Essays on the social situation of mental patients and other inmates*. Garden City, NY: Anchor Books.

Goffman, E. (1961b). *Encounters: Two studies in the sociology of interaction*. Indianapolis, IN: Bobbs-Merrill.

Goffman, E. (1963a). *Behavior in public places*. New York: The Free Press.

Goffman, E. (1963b). *Stigma*. New York: Touchstone.

Goffman, E. (1967). *Interaction ritual*. New York: Pantheon.

Goffman, E. (1974). *Frame analysis*. New York: Harper & Row.

Goffman, E. (1977). The arrangement between the sexes. *Theory and Society, 4,* 301–331.

Goffman, E. (1981). *Forms of talk*. Philadelphia: University of Pennsylvania Press.

Goffman, E. (1983). The interaction order. *American Sociological Review, 48,* 1–17.

Gottdiener, M. (1990). The logocentrism of the classics. *American Sociological Review, 55*(3), 460–463.

Gramsci, A. (1971). *Selections from the prison notebooks*. London: Lawrence & Heinemann. (Original work published 1928)

Habermas, J. (1984). *The theory of communicative action, vol. 1: Reason and the rationalization of society* (T. McCarthy, Trans.). Boston: Beacon. (Original work published 1981)

Habermas, J. (1987). *The theory of communicative action, vol. 2: Lifeworld and system: A critique of functionalist reason* (T. McCarthy, Trans.). Boston: Beacon. (Original work published 1981)

Hall, S. (1996a). The question of cultural identity. In S. Hall, D. Held, D. Hubert, & K. Thompson (Eds.), *Modernity: An introduction to modern societies* (pp. 595–634). Malden, MA: Blackwell.

Hall, S. (1996b). The West and the Rest: Discourse and power. In S. Hall, D. Held, D. Hubert, & K. Thompson (Eds.), *Modernity: An introduction to modern societies* (pp. 184–227). Malden, MA: Blackwell.

Hawking, S. & Mlodinow, L. (2010). *The grand design*. New York: Bantam Books.

Hedges, C. (2002). *War is a force that gives us meaning*. New York: Public Affairs.

Heidegger, M. (1996). *Being and time: A translation of sein und zeit* (J. Stambaugh, Trans.). Albany: State University of New York Press. (Original work published 1927)

Heritage, J. (1984). *Garfinkel and ethnomethodology*. Cambridge, UK: Polity Press.

Hochschild, A. R. (1983). *The managed heart: Commercialization of human feeling*. Berkeley: University of California Press.

Homans, G. C. (1950). *The human group*. New York: Harcourt Brace Jovanovich.

Homans, G. C. (1958). Social behavior as exchange. *The American Journal of Sociology, 63*(5), 597–606.

Homans, G. C. (1961). *Social behavior: Its elementary forms*. New York: Harcourt, Brace & World.

Homans, G. C. (1964). Bringing men back in. *American sociological review, 29*(5), 809–818.

Homans, G. C. (1987). Behaviourism and after. In A. Giddens & J. Turner (Eds.), *Social theory today* (pp. 58–81). Stanford, CA: Stanford University Press.

hooks, b. (1989). *Talking back: Thinking feminist, thinking black*. Boston: South End Press.

Horkheimer, M. (2004). *Eclipse of reason*. London: Continuum.

Horkheimer, M., & Adorno, T. W. (1972). *Dialectic of enlightenment*. New York: Herder & Herder. (Original work published 1944)

Husserl, E. (1975). *Ideas: General introduction to pure phenomenology*. London: Collier Macmillan. (Original work published 1913)

Johnson, A. G. (2000). *The Blackwell dictionary of sociology: A user's guide to sociological language* (2nd ed.). Malden, MA: Blackwell.

Joint Economic Committee. (2010). *Invest in women, invest in America: A comprehensive review of women in the U.S. economy.* Retrieved July 10, 2012, from http://www.bls.gov/cps/wlf-databook2011.htm

Kagan, H. L. (2008, March). Why did my patient develop a taste for paper? *Discover.*

Kant, I. (1999). An answer to the question: What is Enlightenment? In M. J. Gregor (Ed.), *Practical philosophy* (pp. 11–22). Cambridge: Cambridge University Press. (Original work published 1798)

Kanter, R. M. (1977). *Men and women of the corporation.* New York: Basic Books.

Keynes, J. M. (1936). *The general theory of employment, interest and money.* New York: Harcourt Brace.

Kozol, J. (1991). *Savage inequalities: Children in America's schools.* New York: Crown.

Kuhn, M. H. (1964a). Major trends in symbolic interaction theory in the past twenty-five years. *Sociological Quarterly, 5,* 61–84.

Kuhn, M. H. (1964b). The reference group reconsidered. *Sociological Quarterly, 5,* 5–24.

Kuhn, M. H., & McPartland, T. (1951). An empirical investigation of self-attitudes. *American Sociological Review, 19,* 68–76.

Kuhn, T. S. (1970). *The structure of scientific revolutions* (2nd ed.). Chicago: University of Chicago Press.

Lakatos, I. (1970). Falsification and the methodology of scientific research programmes. In I. Lakatos & A. Musgrave (Eds.), *Criticism and the growth of knowledge.* Cambridge, UK: Cambridge University Press.

Legal Information Institute. *White collar crime: An overview.* Retrieved June 30, 2005, from http://www.law.cornell.edu/topics/white_collar.html

Lemert, C. (1990). The uses of French structuralisms in sociology. In G. Ritzer (Ed.) *Frontiers of social theory: The new syntheses,* (pp. 230–254). New York: Columbia University Press.

Lemert, C. (1997). Goffman. In C. Lemert & A. Branaman (Eds.), *The Goffman reader* (pp. ix–xliii). Malden, MA: Blackwell.

Lemert, C. (2005). *Social things: An introduction to the sociological life* (3rd ed.). Lanham, MD: Rowman & Littlefield.

Lévi-Strauss, C. (1963). *Structural anthropology.* New York: Basic Books.

Lidz, V. (2000). *Talcott Parsons.* In G. Ritzer (Ed.), *The Blackwell Companion to Major Social Theorists.* Malden, MA: Blackwell

Lukes, S. (1973). *Individualism.* Oxford, UK: Basil Blackwell.

Luther, M. (1991). *On secular authority.* In *Luther and Calvin on secular authority* (H. Höpfl, Trans. & Ed.) (pp. 1–43). Cambridge, UK: Cambridge University Press. (Original work published 1523)

Lyman, S. M., & Vidich, A. J. (2000). *Selected works of Herbert Blumer: A public philosophy for mass society.* Urbana: University of Illinois Press.

Lynch, M. (1997). *Scientific practice and ordinary action: Ethnomethodology and social studies of science.* Cambridge, UK: Cambridge University Press.

Lyotard, J. (1984). *The postmodern condition: A report of knowledge* (G. Bennington & B. Massumi, Trans.). Minneapolis: University of Minnesota Press. (Original work published 1979)

Macionis, J. J. (2005). *Sociology* (10th ed.). Upper Saddle River, NJ: Prentice Hall.

Mahar, C., Harker, R., & Wilkes, C. (1990). The basic theoretical position. In R. Harker, C. Mahar, & C. Wilkes (Eds.), *An introduction to the work of Pierre Bourdieu* (pp. 1–25). London: Macmillan.

Mannheim, K. (1936). *Ideology and utopia: An introduction to the sociology of knowledge* (L. Wirth & E. Shills, Trans.). San Diego, CA: Harcourt Brace.

Marshall, G. (Ed.). (1998). *A dictionary of sociology* (2nd ed.). New York: Oxford University Press.

Martin, E. (2007). *Jeff Foxworthy's passionate, show-stopping speech at the CMT awards.* Retrieved September 3, 2009, from http://www.freerepublic.com/focus/f-news/1821089/posts

Martineau, H. (2003). *How to observe morals and manners.* New Brunswick, NJ: Transaction. (Original work published 1838)

Martineau, H. (2005). *Society in America* (S. M. Lipset, Ed.). New Brunswick, NJ: Transaction. (Original work published 1837)

Marx, K. (1978a). Economic and philosophic manuscripts of 1844. In R. C. Tucker (Ed.), *The Marx-Engels reader.* New York: Norton. (Original work published 1844)

Marx, K. (1978b). The German ideology. In R. C. Tucker (Ed.), *The Marx-Engels reader.* New York: Norton. (Original work published 1832)

Marx, K. (1978c). Manifesto of the Communist Party. In R. C. Tucker (Ed.), *The Marx-Engels reader.* New York: Norton. (Original work published 1848)

Marx, K. (1995). Economic and philosophic manuscripts of 1844. In E. Fromm (Trans.), *Marx's concept of man.* New York: Continuum. (Original work published 1932)

Marx, K., & Engels, F. (1978). Manifesto of the Communist Party. In R. C. Tucker (Ed.), *The Marx–Engels reader.* New York: Norton. (Original work published 1848)

McCready, S. (Ed.). (2001). *The discovery of time.* Naperville, IL: Sourcebooks.

McCrone, D. (2006). Nation. In J. Scott (Ed.), *Sociology: The key concepts* (pp. 117–119). London: Routledge.

McGrew, A. (1996). A global society? In S. Hall, D. Held, D. Hubert, & K. Thompson (Eds.), *Modernity: An introduction to modern societies* (pp. 466–503). Malden, MA: Blackwell.

Mead, G. H. (1932). *The philosophy of the present.* Chicago: Open Court.

Mead, G. H. (1934). *Mind, self, and society: From the standpoint of a social behaviorist* (C. W. Morris, Ed.). Chicago: University of Chicago Press.

Mehan, H., & Wood, H. (1975). *The reality of ethnomethodology.* New York: Wiley.

Melucci, A. (1980). The new social movements: A theoretical approach. *Social Science Information, 19*(2), 199–226.

Menand, L. (2001). *The metaphysical club: A story of ideas in America.* New York: Farrar, Straus & Giroux.

Milgram, S. (1974). *Obedience to authority: An experimental view.* New York: Harper & Row.

Mills, C. W. (1956). *The power elite.* New York: Oxford University Press.

Mills, C. W. (1959). *The sociological imagination.* London: Oxford University Press.

National Academy of Sciences. (1995). *National science education standards.* Retrieved August 20, 2004, from http://www.nap.edu/readingroom/books/nses/html/action.html

National Urban League. (2009). *State of black America.* Retrieved November 12, 2009, from http://www.nul.org/newsroom/publications/soba

Nietzsche, F. (1968). On the geneology of morals. In W. Kaufmann (Ed. & Trans.), *Basic writings of Nietzsche.* New York: The Modern Library. (Original work published 1887)

Nietzsche, F. (1974). *The gay science.* New York: Vintage.

NIKE, INC. (2012). *Our sustainability strategy.* Retrieved July 16, 2012, from, http://www.nikeresponsibility.com/report/content/chapter/our-sustainability-strategy

Nöth, W. (1995). *Handbook of semiotics.* Bloomington: Indiana University Press. (Original work published 1985)

NSF at a glance. (n.d.) The National Science Foundation. Retrieved June, 2005, from http://www.nsf.gov/about/

Obama, B. (2011). *Obama's second State of the Union (text).* Retrieved February 7, 2012, from http://www.nytimes.com/2011/01/26/us/politics/26obama-text.html?pagewanted=all

Outhwaite, W. (2003). Jürgen Habermas. In G. Ritzer (Ed.), *The Blackwell companion to major contemporary social theorists*. Malden, MA: Blackwell.

Parsons, T. (1949). *The structure of social action: A study in social theory with special reference to a group of recent European writers* (2nd ed.). New York: The Free Press. (Original work published 1937)

Parsons, T. (1951). *The social system*. Glencoe, IL: Free Press.

Parsons, T. (1961). Culture and the social system. In T. Parsons (Ed.), *Theories of society: Foundations of modern sociological theory* (pp. 963–993). New York: The Free Press.

Parsons, T. (1966). *Societies: Evolutionary and comparative perspectives.* Englewood Cliffs, NJ: Prentice Hall.

Patterson, T. E. (2002). *The vanishing voter: Public involvement in an age of uncertainty.* New York: Knopf.

Perinbanayagam, R. S. (2000). *The presence of the self.* Lanham, MD: Rowman & Littlefield.

Perinbanayagam, R. S. (2003). Telic reflections: Interactional processes, as such. *Symbolic Interaction, 26,* 67–83.

Perrow, C. (1999). *Normal accidents: Living with high-risk technologies.* Princeton, NJ: Princeton University Press.

Pianin, E. (2001, July 10). Superfund cleanup effort shows results, study reports. *The Washington Post,* p. A19.

Pitts, V. (2003). *In the flesh: The cultural politics of body modification.* New York: Palgrave.

Plato. (1993). *The last days of Socrates* (H. Tredennick & H. Tarrant, Trans.). London: Penguin.

Plummer, K. (Ed.) (1991). *Symbolic interactionism,* Vols. 1 & 2. Brookfield, VT: E. Elgar.

Plummer, K. (1998). Herbert Blumer. In Rob Stones (Ed.), *Key sociological thinkers.* New York: New York University Press.

Pollner, M. (1991). Left of ethnomethodology: The rise and decline of radical reflexivity. *American Sociological Review, 56,* 370–380.

Popper, K. (1959). *The logic of scientific discovery.* New York: Basic Books.

Porter, R. (2001). *The enlightenment* (2nd ed.). New York: Palgrave.

Rabinow, P. (1984). Introduction. In P. Rabinow (Ed.), *The Foucault reader.* New York: Pantheon.

Rawls, A. (2003). Harold Garfinkel. In G. Ritzer (Ed.), *The Blackwell companion to major contemporary social theorists.* Malden, MA: Blackwell.

Ray, L. (1990). Introduction: The formation of a critical theory of society. In L. Ray (Ed.), *Critical sociology.* Hants, UK: Edward Elgar.

Redford, G., & Kinosian, J. (2008). Your brain on exercise: How breaking a sweat can make you smarter. *AARP: The Magazine, 51*(2A), 26.

Roy, W. G. (2001). *Making societies.* Thousand Oaks, CA: Pine Forge.

Ruzza, C. (2006). Social movements. In J. Scott (Ed.), *Sociology: The key concepts* (pp. 155–157). London: Routledge.

Sacks, H. (1995). *Lectures on conversation.* Malden, MA. Wiley-Blackwell.

Said, E. (1978). *Orientalism.* New York: Vintage Books.

Said, E. (1994). *Culture and imperialism.* New York: Vintage.

Sassen, S. (2007). *A sociology of globalization.* New York: Norton.

Saussure, F. de. (1986). *Course in general linguistics* (C. Bally, A. Sechehaye, & A. Riedlinger, Eds.; R. Harris, Trans.). Chicago: Open Court. (Original work published 1916)

Schutz, A. (1967). *The phenomenology of the social world* (G. Walsh & F. Lehnert, Trans.). Evanston, IL: Northwestern University Press.

Shilling, C. (1993). *The body and social theory.* Newbury Park, CA: Sage.

Simmel, G. (1950). *The sociology of Georg Simmel* (K. H. Wolff, Ed. & Trans.). Glencoe, IL: The Free Press.

Simmel, G. (1971). *Georg Simmel: On individuality and social forms* (D. N. Levine, Ed.). Chicago: University of Chicago Press.

Smith, A. (1937). *An inquiry into the nature and causes of the wealth of nations* (E. Cannan, Ed.). New York: The Modern Library. (Original work published 1776)

Smith, D. E. (1987). *The everyday world as problematic: A feminist sociology.* Boston: Northeastern University Press.

Smith, D. E. (1990). *The conceptual practices of power: A feminist sociology of knowledge.* Boston: Northeastern University Press.

Smith, D. E. (1992). Sociology from women's experience: A reaffirmation. *Sociological Theory, 11,* 1.

Smith, D. E. (2005). *Institutional ethnography: A sociology for people.* Lanham, MD: AltaMira Press.

Snow, D., & Anderson, L. (1993). *Down on their luck: A study of homeless street people.* Berkeley: University of California Press.

Statistical Abstract of the United States. (2002). *The national data book.* Washington, DC: U.S. Department of Commerce.

Stiglitz, J. E. (2003). *Globalization and its discontents.* New York: Norton.

Stryker, S. (2003). *Symbolic interactionism.* Menlo Park, CA: Benjamin/Cummings.

Subject. (n.d.). In *Merriam-Webster's third new international dictionary, unabridged.* Retrieved October 18, 2012, from http://unabridged.merriam-webster.com

Subversion. (n.d.). In *Merriam-Webster's third new international dictionary, unabridged.* Retrieved October 18, 2012, from http://unabridged.merriam-webster.com

Survivor show concept. (n.d.). Retrieved July 27, 2005, from http://www.cbs.com/primetime/survivor/show/concept.shtml

Thompson, K. (1996). Religion, values, and ideology. In Stuart Hall, David Held, Don Hubert, and Kenneth Thompson (Eds.), *Modernity: An introduction to modern societies* (pp. 395–422). Malden, MA: The Open University.

Tilly, C. (2002). *Stories, identities, and political change.* Lanham, MD: Rowman & Littlefield.

Tilly, C. (2007). *Democracy.* Cambridge, UK: Cambridge University Press.

Tocqueville, A. (2002). *Democracy in America* (H. C. Mansfield & D. Winthrop, Trans., Eds.). Chicago: The University of Chicago Press. (Original work published 1835–1840)

Toffler, A. (1991). *Powershift: Knowledge, wealth, and violence at the edge of the 21st Century.* New York: Bantam.

Turner, J. H. (1988). *A theory of social interaction.* Stanford, CA: Stanford University Press.

Turner, J. H. (1991). *The structure of sociological theory* (5th ed.). Belmont, CA: Wadsworth.

Turner, J. H. (1993). *Classical sociological theory: A positivist's perspective.* Chicago: Nelson-Hall.

Turner, J. H. (1998). *The structure of sociological theory* (6th ed.). Belmont, CA: Wadsworth.

Turner, V. W. (1969). *The ritual process: Structure and anti-structure.* Chicago: Aldine.

Ulmer, J. T., & Wilson, M. S. (2003). The potential contributions of quantitative research to symbolic interactionism. *Symbolic Interaction, 26*(4), 531–552.

Urry, J. (2006). Society. In J. Scott (Ed.), *Sociology: The key concepts* (pp. 167–170). London: Routledge.

U.S. Census Bureau. (2012). *Statistical abstracts of the United States.* Retrieved July 23, 2012, from http://www.census.gov/compendia/statab/

U.S. Census Bureau. (n.d.). *Historical income tables—people.* Retrieved June 27, 2005, from http://www.census.gov/hhes/www/income/histinc/incpertoc.html

U.S. Department of Justice. (2008). *Prison statistics.* Retrieved November 12, 2009, from http://www.ojp.usdoj.gov/bjs/prisons.htm

Veblen, T. (1899). *The theory of the leisure class: An economic study of institutions.* New York: Macmillan.

Vitousek, P., Ehrlich, P. R., Ehrlich, A. H., & Matson, P. (1986). Human appropriation of the products of photosynthesis. *BioScience, 34*(6) 368–373.

Wacquant, L. J. D. (1992). Preface. In P. Bourdieu & L. J. D. Wacquant, *An invitation to reflexive sociology.* Chicago: University of Chicago Press.

Walker, R. (2007). Becoming third wave. In E. B. Freedman (Ed.), *The essential feminist reader* (pp. 397–401). New York: The Modern Library.

Wallerstein, I. (1974). *The modern world—system I: Capitalist agriculture and the origins of the European world-economy in the sixteenth century.* New York: Academic Press.

Wallerstein, I. (1980). *The modern world—system II: Mercantilism and the consolidation of the European world-economy, 1600–1750.* New York: Academic Press.

Wallerstein, I. (1989). *The modern world—system III: The second era of great expansion of the capitalist world-economy, 1730–1840.* New York: Academic Press.

Wallerstein, I. (1995). The end of what modernity? *Theory and Society, 24,* 471–488.

Wallerstein, I. (1999). *The end of the world as we know it: Social science for the twenty-first century.* Minneapolis: University of Minnesota Press.

Wallerstein, I. (2000). *The essential Wallerstein.* New York: The New Press.

Wallerstein, I. (2004). *World-systems analysis: An introduction.* Durham, NC: Duke University Press.

Weber, M. (1948). Politics as a vocation. In H. H. Gerth & C. Wright Mills (Trans. & Eds.), *From Max Weber: Essays in sociology.* London: Routledge. (Original work published 1921).

Weber, M. (1949). "Objectivity" in social science and social polity. In E. A. Shils & H. A. Finch (Eds. & Trans.), *The methodology of the social sciences* (pp. 50–112). New York: The Free Press. (Originally published 1904)

Weber, M. (1968). *Economy and society* (G. Roth, Trans., & C. Wittich, Eds.). New York: Bedminster. (Original work published 1922)

Weber, M. (1993). *The sociology of religion* (E. Fischoff, Trans.). Boston: Beacon Press. (Original work published 1922)

Weber, M. (1994). Suffrage and democracy in Germany. In P. Lassman & R. Speirs (Eds.), *Weber: Political writings.* Cambridge, UK: Cambridge University Press. (Original work published 1917)

Weber, M. (2002). *The Protestant ethic and the spirit of capitalism* (S. Kalberg, Trans.). Los Angeles: Roxbury. (Original work published 1904–1905)

Webster's new universal unabridged dictionary (2nd ed.). (1983). New York: Simon & Schuster.

West, C. (1999). The indispensability yet insufficiency of Marxist theory. In Cornel West (Ed.), *The Cornel West reader* (pp. 213–230). New York: Basic Civitas Books.

West, C. (2000). *Cornel West's opening remarks.* Retrieved July 23, 2012, from http://old.essentialschools.org/lpt/ces_docs/87

West, C. (2001). *Race matters.* New York: Vintage. (Original work published 1993)

West, C., & Zimmerman, D. H. (1987). Doing gender. *Gender and Society, 1,* 125–151.

Wiggershaus, R. (1995). *The Frankfurt School: Its history, theories, and political significance* (M. Robertson, Trans.). Cambridge: MIT Press. (Original work published 1986)

Williams, R. (1983). *Keywords: A vocabulary of culture and society* (Rev. ed.). New York: Oxford University Press.

Wilson, W. J. (1980). *The declining significance of race: Blacks and changing American institutions* (2nd ed.). Chicago: University of Chicago Press.

Wilson, W. J. (1996–1997). When work disappears. *Political Science Quarterly, 111*(4), 567–595.

Wilson, W. J. (1997). *When work disappears: The world of the new urban poor.* New York: Vintage.

Wollstonecraft, M. (1993). A vindication of the rights of woman. In J. Todd (Ed.), *A vindication of the rights of woman and a vindication of the rights of men.* Oxford, UK: Oxford University Press. (Original work published 1792).

Wright, E. O. (1978). *Class, crisis and the state.* London: New Left Books.

Wrong, D. H. (1999). *The oversocialized conception of man.* New Brunswick, NJ: Transaction.

Young, R. J. C. (2003). *Postcolonialism: A very short introduction.* Oxford, UK: Oxford University Press.

Zerubavel, E. (1991). *The fine line: Making distinctions in everyday life.* New York: The Free Press.

Index

About the Author

Kenneth Allan received his PhD in sociology from the University of California, Riverside (1995), and is currently Professor of Sociology at the University of North Carolina at Greensboro (UNCG). Before moving to UNCG, he directed the Teaching Assistant Development Program at the University of California, Riverside, and coedited *Training Teaching Assistants,* 2nd edition (1997), published by the American Sociological Association. In addition to teaching classical and contemporary theory at UNCG, Allan also regularly teaches graduate pedagogy courses and oversees the department's online iSchool program, which currently offers university-level courses to over 2,000 high school students per year. Allan's research areas include theory, culture, and the self. He has authored several other works in the area of theory, including *The Meaning of Culture: Moving the Postmodern Critique Forward, Explorations in Classical Sociological Theory, The Social Lens,* and *A Primer in Social and Sociological Theory: Toward a Sociology of Citizenship.* He is currently working on a social history of American individualism.